COMPOSING FEMINIST INTERVENTIONS: ACTIVISM, ENGAGEMENT, PRAXIS

PERSPECTIVES ON WRITING
Series Editors, Susan H. McLeod and Rich Rice

The Perspectives on Writing series addresses writing studies in a broad sense. Consistent with the wide ranging approaches characteristic of teaching and scholarship in writing across the curriculum, the series presents works that take divergent perspectives on working as a writer, teaching writing, administering writing programs, and studying writing in its various forms.

The WAC Clearinghouse, Colorado State University Open Press, and University Press of Colorado are collaborating so that these books will be widely available through free digital distribution and low-cost print editions. The publishers and the Series editors are committed to the principle that knowledge should freely circulate. We see the opportunities that new technologies have for further democratizing knowledge. And we see that to share the power of writing is to share the means for all to articulate their needs, interest, and learning into the great experiment of literacy.

Recent Books in the Series

Mya Poe, Asao B. Inoue, and Norbert Elliot (Eds.), *Writing Assessment, Social Justice, and the Advancement of Opportunity* (2018)

Patricia Portanova, J. Michael Rifenburg, and Duane Roen (Eds.), *Contemporary Perspectives on Cognition and Writing* (2017)

Douglas M. Walls and Stephanie Vie (Eds.), *Social Writing/Social Media: Publics, Presentations, and Pedagogies* (2017)

Laura R. Micciche, *Acknowledging Writing Partners* (2017)

Susan H. McLeod, Dave Stock, and Bradley T. Hughes (Eds.), *Two WPA Pioneers: Ednah Shepherd Thomas and Joyce Steward* (2017)

Seth Kahn, William B. Lalicker, and Amy Lynch-Biniek (Eds.), *Contingency, Exploitation, and Solidarity: Labor and Action in English Composition* (2017)

Barbara J. D'Angelo, Sandra Jamieson, Barry Maid, and Janice R. Walker (Eds.), *Information Literacy: Research and Collaboration across Disciplines* (2017)

Justin Everett and Cristina Hanganu-Bresch (Eds.), *A Minefield of Dreams: Triumphs and Travails of Independent Writing Programs* (2016)

Chris M. Anson and Jessie L. Moore (Eds.), *Critical Transitions: Writing and the Questions of Transfer* (2016)

Joanne Addison and Sharon James McGee, *Writing and School Reform: Writing Instruction in the Age of Common Core and Standardized Testing* (2016)

COMPOSING FEMINIST INTERVENTIONS: ACTIVISM, ENGAGEMENT, PRAXIS

Edited by Kristine L. Blair and Lee Nickoson

The WAC Clearinghouse
wac.colostate.edu
Fort Collins, Colorado

University Press of Colorado
upcolorado.com
Louisville, Colorado

The WAC Clearinghouse, Fort Collins, Colorado 80523–1040

University Press of Colorado, Lousville, Colorado 80027

© 2018 by Kristine L. Blair and Lee Nickoson. This work is licensed under a Creative Commons Attribution-NonCommercial-NoDerivatives 4.0 International.

ISBN 978-1-64215-005-6 (PDF) | 978-1-64215-008-7 (ePub) | 978-1-60732-865-0 (pbk.)

Library of Congress Cataloging-in-Publication Data

Names: Blair, Kristine L., 1963–, editor. | Nickoson, Lee, 1967–, editor.
Title: Composing feminist interventions : activism, engagement, praxis / edited by Kristine L. Blair and Lee Nickoson.
Description: Fort Collins : The WAC Clearinghouse, [2018] | Series: Perspectives on writing | Includes bibliographical references and index. |
Identifiers: LCCN 2018012717 (print) | LCCN 2018061259 (ebook) | ISBN 9781642150186 (pdf) | ISBN 9781642150193 (ePub) | ISBN 9781607328650 (pbk. : alk. paper)
Subjects: LCSH: Feminism—United States. | Feminism and education—United States. | English language—Composition and exercises—Study and teaching—United States. | English language—Rhetoric—Study and teaching (Higher)—United States. | Women—Education—United States—Language arts. | Women in community organization—United States.
Classification: LCC HQ1421 (ebook) | LCC HQ1421 .C66 2018 (print) | DDC 305.420973—dc23
LC record available at https://lccn.loc.gov/2018012717

Copyeditor: Brandy Bippes
Designer: Mike Palmquist
Series Editors: Susan H. McLeod and Rich Rice

The WAC Clearinghouse supports teachers of writing across the disciplines. Hosted by Colorado State University, and supported by the Colorado State University Open Press, it brings together scholarly journals and book series as well as resources for teachers who use writing in their courses. This book is available in digital formats for free download at wac.colostate.edu.

Founded in 1965, the University Press of Colorado is a nonprofit cooperative publishing enterprise supported, in part, by Adams State University, Colorado State University, Fort Lewis College, Metropolitan State University of Denver, Regis University, University of Colorado, University of Northern Colorado, Utah State University, and Western State Colorado University. For more information, visit upcolorado.com. The Press partners with the Clearinghouse to make its books available in print.

ACKNOWLEDGMENTS

We sincerely appreciate the support from the Perspectives on Writing Series editors Sue McLeod and Rich Rice. We know that the many voices that comprise *Composing Feminist Interventions* are stronger based on Sue and Rich's helpful suggestions, as well as on the feedback of our anonymous reviewers. We want to express our appreciation and gratitude to WAC Clearinghouse copy editor Brandy Bippes, whose careful attention to a full manuscript draft brought additional clarity and focus to the conversations shared across chapters. We also are deeply indebted to Mike Palmquist and honored to have *Composing Feminist Interventions* published by the WAC Clearinghouse/University Press of Colorado; we thank Mike for his patience, his time, and his expertise. It has also been an honor to learn with and from the strong feminist teacher-scholars who have shaped the goals of this project. It has been both a privilege and a pleasure to collaborate with the many feminist teacher-scholars who shared a bit of themselves through their discussions of community-based pedagogy and inquiry as forward-thinking activism. Thank you to our many contributors, with a special thanks to Krista Ratcliffe for her insightful, gracious afterword.

Kris: I first want to thank my frequent and fabulous collaborator, Lee Nickoson. *Composing Feminist Interventions* evolved while we were both working at Bowling Green State University, over many coffee conversations that I greatly miss given our distance. I am immensely grateful for such collaborations with Lee and with other colleagues, mentors, and mentees throughout my career, all of whom have helped me foster a recursive relationship between feminism and community activism in my teaching and research. Finally, I want to acknowledge my husband, Kevin Williams, and my mother, Angela Blair, for their constant love and encouragement over the years. Without their support, projects like this would not be possible.

Lee: *Composing Feminist Interventions* provided me the opportunity to learn, question, laugh, and, perhaps most importantly, to imagine possibilities with many feminist colleagues working across subfields of our discipline. My experience co-editing this collection leaves me hopeful that feminist, activist work has meaning for students and our communities well beyond our classrooms. My warmest thanks to the APA wonder team of 215 East Hall: Sara Austin, Lauren Garskie, Kristin LaFollette, and, in particular, Kelly Moreland. And thank you to the always-inspiring Kris Blair. I learned long ago to seize any opportunity to collaborate with Kris as an invitation to observe an embodied example of the feminist, activist spirit of the collection before you.

CONTENTS

Introduction. Researching and Teaching Community as a Feminist Intervention 3
    Kristine L. Blair and Lee Nickoson

PART 1. METHODOLOGY

Chapter 1. Post-Research Engagement: An Argument for Critical Examination of Researcher Roles after Research Ends. 19
    Megan Adams

Chapter 2. Reciprocity as Epicenter: An 'After-Action Review' 35
    Mariana Grohowski

Chapter 3. Methodology & Accountability: Tracking Our Movements as Feminist Pedagogues. 57
    Emily Ronay Johnston

Chapter 4. Listening to Research as a Feminist Ethos of Representation. . . . 75
    Lauren Rosenberg and Emma Howes

Chapter 5. Funding Geography: The Legacy of Female-Run Settlement Culture for Contemporary Feminist Place-Based Pedagogy Initiatives 93
    Liz Rohan

PART 2. PARTNERSHIPS

Chapter 6. Building Engaged Interventions in Graduate Education 115
    Keri E. Mathis and Beth A. Boehm

Chapter 7. Learning Together Through Campus-Community Partnerships 135
    Jenn Brandt and Cara Kozma

Chapter 8. Crafting Partnerships: Exploring Student-Led Feminist Strategies for Community Literacy Projects 155
    Kelly Concannon, Mustari Akhi, Morgan Musgrove, Kim Lopez, and Ashley Nichols

Chapter 9. Ohio Farm Stories: A Feminist Approach to Collaboration, Conversation, and Engagement 173
    Christine Denecker and Sarah Sisser

Chapter 10. Literacy Sponsorship as a Process of Translation: Using Actor-Network Theory to Analyze Power within Emergent Relationships at Family Scholar House............195
   Kathryn Perry

Chapter 11. Knotworking Collaborations: Fostering Community-Engaged Teachers and Scholars............213
   Mary P. Sheridan

Part 3. Activism

Chapter 12. Women-Only Bicycle Rides and Freedom of Movement: How Online Communicative Practices of Local Community Managers Support Feminist Interventions............237
   Angela Crow

Chapter 13. Literacy, Praxis and Participation in Environmental Deliberation............255
   Barbara George

Chapter 14. The Viability of Digital Spaces as Sites for Transnational Feminist Action and Engagement: Why We Need to Look at Digital Circulation............275
   Jessica Ouellette

Chapter 15. Advocating "Active" Intersectionality Through a Comparison of Two Slutwalks............297
   Jacqueline Schiappa

Chapter 16. A Peek Inside the Master's House: The Tale of Feminist Rhetorician as Candidate for U.S. Congress............317
   Angela K. Zimmann

Part 4. Praxis

Chapter 17. Pedagogical Too-Muchness: A Feminist Approach to Community-Based Learning, Multi-Modal Composition, Social Justice Education, and More............335
   Beth Godbee

Chapter 18. Trans/feminist Practice of Collaboration in the Art Activism Classroom............355
   Ames Hawkins and Joan Giroux

Chapter 19. Coming Out as Other in the Graduate Writing Classroom: Feminist Pedagogical Moves for Mentoring Community Activists............373
   Jess Tess, Trixie G. Smith, and Katie Manthey

Chapter 20. *Safely Social:* User-Centered Design and Difference Feminism..391
    Douglas M. Walls, Brandy Dieterle, and Jennifer Roth Miller

Chapter 21. The Unheard Voices of Dissatisfied Clients: Listening to Community Partners as Feminist Praxis.........................409
    Danielle M. Williams

Part 5. Course Designs

Chapter 22. "We Write to Serve": The Intersections of Service Learning, Grant Writing, and the Feminist Rhetorical Agency.................429
    Florence Elizabeth Bacabac

Chapter 23. Making the Political Personal Again: Strategies for Addressing Student Resistance to Feminist Intervention........................445
    Julie Myatt Barger

Chapter 24. "Because your heart breaks and it moves to action": Digital Storytelling Beyond the Gate.............................459
    Stephanie Bower

Chapter 25. Feminist Activism in the Core: Student Activism in Theory and Practice..475
    Katherine Fredlund

Chapter 26. Rhetorical Interventions: A Project Design for Composing and Editing Wikipedia Articles....................................489
    Julie D. Nelson

Afterword...505
    Krista Ratcliffe

Contributors..511

COMPOSING FEMINIST INTERVENTIONS: ACTIVISM, ENGAGEMENT, PRAXIS

INTRODUCTION.
RESEARCHING AND TEACHING COMMUNITY AS A FEMINIST INTERVENTION

Kristine L. Blair
Youngstown State University

Lee Nickoson
Bowling Green State University

It is perhaps no surprise given the title of this collection that we identify as feminists. As such, each of us is committed to continuing the feminist tradition of engaging and disrupting dominant structural systems—to intervening in what *is* and to imagining *what could and ultimately must be*. Lead disciplinary feminist scholars and educators have paved a way for us to engage what is bound to disrupt established notions of writing research and/or writing pedagogy. Over four decades of feminist rhetoric and composition scholarship have devoted attention to disruption. We know disciplinary understandings of research and teaching and the ways in which prevailing philosophies and methods get translated to the work of inquiry and instruction and how those understandings of writing research and teaching translate variously to whom, how, what, and why we understand as the landscape in which we locate ourselves. Feminist disruption intervenes by asking what *if*? What if we approach the questions that guide our work differently? Or what if we ask different questions entirely? What if we study populations and topics beyond those the identified as sites of meaning making? *Composing Feminist Interventions: Activism, Engagement, Praxis* brings together narratives from writing studies scholars whose work represents the many ways we understand and conduct feminist community-based research and teaching from explicitly feminist theoretical positionings. The twenty-six chapter discussions in conversation in this collection articulate a constellation of self-reflexive, critical responses to these *what if* questions.

We are honored to introduce readers to the conversations of intervention assembled here. Thirty-five writing scholars and educators variously situated within rhetoric, composition, and literacy studies offer situated examples of feminist writing research and teaching as explicitly grounded in connections to communities beyond the academy. Each chapter contribution responds to *what if?* . . . by introducing their project as an intervention designed to extended established methods and methodologies for researching or teaching writing as a form of social activism. Because contributors share a commitment to social justice and change, their work illustrates examples of praxis—productively disrupting and evolve possibilities for how we conceptualize research and teaching. What if? What if we understand writing inquiry and pedagogy as deeply collaborative, change-based, inclusive, and reciprocal practice?

Composing Feminist Interventions is at once responsive and forward-thinking, putting examinations of the ways we've come to know and do the work of feminist and community-based writing research and teaching in conversation with the influence of emerging technologies and literacies, the availability of new forms of collaboration, and increasingly fluid notions of writing scholarship (i.e., emerging venues, genres, audiences, and expectations of published accounts of writing research and teaching).

Composing Feminist Interventions also responds to the chorus of disciplinary calls for projects that privilege literate practices within a broader range of cultural and social contexts. As the editors of the collection, we understood our role as bringing together examples of rigorous, dynamic scholarship that is responsive to such calls. The collection is, in part, a response to Jackie Jones Royster and Gesa Kirsch's (2012) challenge for feminist researchers to seek out new landscapes, partnerships, methods, and audiences for change-based inquiry. Contributors worked together with us and each other in order to develop twenty-one chapters and five course designs that provide situation-specific examples of feminist community-based work. We asked that our contributors have in mind as their audience rhetoric, composition, and literacy studies scholars invested in or curious about feminist and community-based teaching and research. We envisioned the audience of invested or curious colleagues to include students enrolled in graduate seminars populated by master's and/or doctoral students and that attend to either feminist or community based. But we also realize there are many colleagues in the field with experience and/or interests similar to ours—scholars interested in continuing their development as researchers, teachers, and activists.

Influences on our own engagement with community-based research and pedagogy are too numerous and many to ever attempt to provide in any comprehensive manner. Within the last decade, there has been similar growth in the areas of community literacy, service learning, and other forms of public, activist rhetorics across the undergraduate and graduate writing curriculum. This has led to a wide range of monographs and collections, such as John Ackerman and David Coogan's (2010) *The Public Work of Rhetoric: Citizen-Scholars and Civic*

Engagement, but none that specifically ground rhetorics of engagement within a feminist framework. However, we shared a common affinity for Linda Flower's (2008) *Community and Community Engagement,* Thomas Deans' *Writing Partnerships: Service-Learning in Composition*, Jeff Grabill's (2007) *Writing Community Change: Designing Technologies for Citizen Action*, and Thomas Deans, Barbara Roswell and Adrian Wurr's (2010) *Writing and Community Engagement: A Critical Sourcebook* all come to mind as foundational texts for each of us. We believe *Composing Feminist Interventions* will add to these conversations and contribute new understandings of and wonderments about the exigencies and implications associated with teaching, researching, and administering writing programs in the early twenty-first century.

As the complement to work on community-based and service learning scholarship and pedagogy, of course, we worked to position the collection as speaking to feminist research methods and methodologies. Historically, collections and anthologies such as Susan Jarratt and Lynn Worsham's (2008) *Feminism and Composition Studies: In Other Words*, and Gesa Kirsch, Faye Spencer Moar, Lance Massey, Lee Nickoson-Massey, and Mary P. Sheridan's (2003) *Feminism And Composition: A Critical Sourcebook*, along with landmark treatments such as Gesa Kirsch and Jacqueline Jones Royster's (2012) *Feminist Rhetorical Practices: New Horizons For Rhetoric, Composition, and Literacy Studies* have come to occupy canonical, yet transformative discussions within our discipline. Recent edited collections with a feminist focus include Michelle Ballif, Diane Davis, and Roxanne Mountford's (2008) *Women's Ways of Making It in Rhetoric and Composition,* Krista Ratcliffe and Rebecca Rickly's *Performing Feminism and Administration* (2010) and Lindal Buchanan and Kathleen Ryan's (2010) *Walking and Talking Feminist Rhetorics*. Also among these influential sources are Eileen Schell and K.J. Rawson's (2012) *Rhetorica in Motion: Feminist Rhetorical Methods & Methodologies,* Patrick Berry, Gail Hawisher, and Cynthia L. Selfe's (2012) *Transnational Literate Lives in Digital Times,* Gesa Kirsch and Liz Rohan's (2008) *Beyond the Archives.*

One of the most recent collections relating to feminism and community action is Susan Van Deventer Iverson and Jennifer Hauver James' 2014 *Feminist Community Engagement: Achieving Praxis*, a compilation of interdisciplinary educational perspectives outside of rhetoric and composition and English studies. As feminist teacher-scholars working in the areas of community literacy, feminist methodology, and service learning, we were delighted by the response both to our collaboration on a 2014 special issue of *Feminist Teacher* on campus-community partnerships—one where the majority of submissions to this multidisciplinary compilation came from rhetoric and composition—and to the response to our call for proposals for *Composing Feminist Interventions*.

Equally important, because each of the feminist texts we mention are print based, we strongly believe there exists a need for contributors conducting community action research in online and multimodal spaces to represent their efforts and potentially those of both students and community partners in the modalities in which they have been produced, distributed, and consumed. For that reason, readers will find that contributors explore the affordances of the aural, the verbal, and the visual. Multiple contributors share their narratives through various new media: images of students, faculty, community partners working in context as well as screenshots of their online work; audio and/or video interviews available via hyperlink with campus and community stakeholders. These multimodal affordances provide readers opportunities to engage the work of the communities represented and experience the communities for themselves through multiple lenses and modalities. Finally, readers will find conversations connected across chapters, with authors and co-authors adding voice to each other's conversations. These connections are purposeful, intended to put into practice careful, critical questioning and response as forms of feminist inquiry, feminist reading, and feminist community-building through research.

Conversations are grouped into five sections: Methodologies, Partnerships, Activism, Praxis, and Course Designs. Our decision to group and organize the sections was perhaps our most difficult editorial challenge, for although there are sections, and though traditional pagination does suggest a linear trajectory, we understand these groups as co-equal points of entry: a reader could easily begin by reading from Partnerships, for example, or reading about partnerships as introduced in classroom instruction (Praxis and Course Design) or as a mode of inquiry of form of activism, as evidenced in Jessica Tess, Katie Manthey, and Trixie Smith's deployment (Chapter 19) of diverse researcher and participant voices to argue for the classroom as a safe, but activist space for coming out narratives. Another example of this productive overlap is Mary P. Sheridan's chronicle (Chapter 11) of the collaborative development and delivery of Louisville's Digital Media Academy, not only a partnership among multiple university departments and the larger community but also a form of feminist activism in its efforts to make technological literacy accessible to adolescent girls from disadvantaged backgrounds and to inevitably equalize the gender, race, and class dynamics surrounding information technology. As a result, we invite our readers to approach each chapter as representing intersectional work: work that is multiply situated and that involves multiple lived experiences. For instance, Christine Denecker and Sarah Sisser's Ohio Farm Stories project (Chapter 9) includes in multimodal form the narratives of participants and thus authenticates rather than co-opts their experiences. Such interventions invite us to engage how feminist scholars and educators can understand, study, value, and represent community in diverse modalities and contexts. The following sections outline the ways all our contributors honor this goal.

METHODOLOGIES

The first four chapters provide extended critical self-reflection of the whys and hows of feminist community-based research, beginning with Megan Adams's exploration of interactive-participatory documentary as a method for capturing community storytellers' efforts and the considerations involved in sustaining the advocacy of such research after the study concludes. For Adams "acknowledging the roles we play in sustaining community projects post-research, when careers, family-life, or other outside influences draw us away from the research site can assist in interrogating the infrastructures we build as well as the roles we play, leaving us better prepared to create rich and lasting impacts in communities."

In "Post-Research Engagement: An Argument for Critical Examination of Researcher Roles After Research Ends," Adams invites readers to consider the ethical complexities involved in feminist commitments to researcher/participant reciprocity and reflexivity. In addition, Mariana Grohowski's "Reciprocity as Epicenter: An 'After-Action Review'" addresses the complexity of reciprocity as an imperative in empirical, community-based writing research. Grohowski details the methods and methodology developed while working with two military veterans to stress the importance of feminist intervention and political activism as driving principles when engaging in research with participants who belong to protected populations. She discusses the process of developing reciprocal relationships with case study co-interpreters through the interrelated methods of listening, understanding, and strategic disclosure and stresses that campus-community partnerships with members of protected populations draw upon innovative approaches and modalities for fostering access and inclusion.

Emily Ronay Johnston then turns our attention to a consideration of boundaries as a form of ethical feminist activism. In "Methodology & Accountability: Tracking Our Movements as Feminist Pedagogues," Johnston narrates her experience as a white, female doctoral candidate at a predominantly white, middle-class university in Central Illinois. She conceptualizes "ethical practice" as methods that challenge students to stretch the limits of their privileged comfort zones—methods that may not be feasible, desirable, appropriate, or indeed "ethical" in other settings where feminist research happens.

Lauren Rosenberg and Emma Howes extend the focus on the ethics involved with community-based inquiry to discussion of research practices and methodological choices as opportunities to embody a feminist ethos of responsible, strategic practice. This inquiry is grounded in each co-author's experience within their chapter "Listening to Research as a Feminist Ethos of Representation." Here, Rosenberg applies Ratcliffe's (2005) concepts of "rhetorical listening" and Royster and Kirsch's (2012) ideas of "strategic contemplation" to a developing study of writing by student-veterans, while Howes explores how archival listening helps researchers reflect on representations of historical literacy sponsorship campaigns in southern mill villages.

In the final section chapter, "Funding Geography: The Legacy of Female-Run Settlement Culture for Contemporary Feminist Place-Based Pedagogy Initiatives," Liz Rohan introduces case study, archival methods to historicize the work of contemporary feminist teachers, researchers, and administrators who develop community engagement and place-based initiatives. Rohan describes historic feminists working and writing in the U.S. progressive era in Chicago and Detroit and historical figures such as Lucy Carner and Borgchild Halvorsen to suggest that community service work among feminist academics has a history linked to the work of progressive era feminists. Rohan historicizes community-based feminist projects as a way to trace contemporary place-based pedagogical movements sponsored by Detroit educators and artists.

PARTNERSHIPS

Keri E. Mathis and Beth A. Boehm provide the first of a series of chapters that provide explicit attention to researcher and community partnerships. In "Building Engaged Interventions in Graduate Education," Mathis and Boehm profile the University of Louisville's efforts at becoming a more engaged university, including receiving the Carnegie Community Engaged University classification and implementing Ideas-to-Action, a quality enhancement plan that holds community engagement as one of its core principles but one that the researchers identify as excluding graduate students. The authors describe their efforts in extending their home institution's programs to focus on engaged scholarship and on developing a year-long academy that will lead to collaborations among graduate students on community projects.

Similar to Mathis and Boehm, Jenn Brandt and Cara Kozma share their experiences developing curricular and co-curricular initiatives at High Point University in "Learning Together Through Campus-Community Partnerships." Brandt and Kozma introduce a series of English Department and Women Studies Program initiatives as a case study and explore the challenges and successes of university and community partnerships that involve multiple stakeholders. In "Crafting Partnerships: Exploring Student-Led Feminist Strategies for Community Literacy Projects," Kelly Concannon and her former students Mustari Akhi, Morgan Musgrove, Kim Lopez, and Ashley Nichols continue attention to community partnerships and argues for a multi-layered partnership as a means of assessing community-based efforts through a focus on mentorship and reflexivity. Concannon shares her experience as a mentor in the Women of Tomorrow Program to illustrate such reflexivity and the value of feminist collaboration. The program links professional woman to a local high school, where they work to empower young, at-risk women. She advocates for such mentoring networks as enabling co-mentors to candidly discuss their attempts to enact feminism/feminist activism.

As we highlighted earlier in this introduction, Christine Denecker and Sarah Sisser's "Ohio Farm Stories: A Feminist Approach to Collaboration, Conversation, and Engagement" reports on a campus-community and grant-funded partnership aimed at showcasing narratives from farmers to provide community members the opportunity to reflect on and discuss local agricultural and economic history. The authors contend that this research partnership with their local community demonstrates how feminist rhetorical practices can foster community engagement beyond academic borders and how their feminist framework allowed them to honor the local stories of Ohio's farming community. Meanwhile, in "Literacy Sponsorship as a Process of Translation: Using Actor-Network Theory to Analyze Power within Emergent Relationships at Family Scholar House," Kathryn Perry brings readers back to Louisville with her study of a local nonprofit, Family Scholar House, which provides a variety of support services to low-income single mothers as they earn college degrees. Perry relies on the Actor-Network Theory (ANT) concept of translation—along with theories of literacy sponsorship—in order to analyze how institutional and material conditions shape literacy practices as well as individual and community definitions of literacy.

Mary P. Sheridan's "Knot-Working Collaborations: Fostering Community-Engaged Teachers and Scholars" closes the section. Sheridan draws on her experience establishing and co-facilitating University of Louisville's Digital Media Academy (DMA) as a site of graduate student professionalization, calling attention to the invisible work of partnership, namely, the upside of following the trial of other do-ers on her campus and also the challenges of sustainability. Examining the academy's design—both in messaging with external, public and funding audiences, and in internal programming with graduate student co-facilitators—Sheridan concludes that such collaborations represent a messy, but significant form of community and intellectual engagement for graduate students.

ACTIVISM

The explicit activist focus of feminist community-based research unites the chapter discussion in the third section. Conversation on the relationship between feminist work and activist aims begins with Angela Crow's "Women-Only Bicycle Rides and Freedom of Movement: How Online Communicative Practices of Local Community Managers Support Feminist Interventions." Crow profiles a group of women bicycle riders, the Staunton, Virginia's Women on Wheels, who wanted to create a safe and welcoming space for women new to cycling. Drawing on contemporary research in mobility studies and material rhetorics, Crow argues that the Staunton group illustrates an historical example of a low-stakes feminist intervention in which women can begin to bicycle within a welcoming community.

In "Literacy, Praxis and Participation in Environmental Deliberation," Barbara George continues a focus on the material, turning readers' attention to energy production policy New York, Pennsylvania and Ohio, and examining the literacies of those navigating institutionalized environmental risk reporting in each state. George documents her participation with environmental activists creating alternative networks of making meaning about their local environments and includes document analysis, interviews, and think-aloud protocols to articulate how these activist literate practices rely upon digital, technical and material networks of environmental justice. Ultimately, George highlights the alternative texts participants create in response to institutional reporting mechanisms in their effort to "rewrite" policy.

Jessica Ouellette also focuses on alternative texts within online activist networks in her chapter "The Viability of Digital Spaces as Sites for Transnational Feminist Action and Engagement: Why We Need to Look at Digital Circulation." Ouellette chronicles how in April 2013, through the use of social media, the global feminist protest group FEMEN staged a "topless jihad" day in support of a Tunisian member, Amina, who was threatened with physical punishment for posting a Facebook picture of her naked breasts, covered in written messages such as, "Fuck your morals" and "My body is mine." Ouellette provides a rhetorical case study of the online FEMEN protest events—specifically the texts that circulated and the political and economic investments undergirding that circulation and argues that in order to foster transnational feminist activism within digital spaces, we need to look at the ways in which texts move and circulate, and how, in and through those movements, textual meanings and rhetorical purposes shift and change. And in her chapter "Advocating 'Active' Intersectionality Through a Comparison of Two Slutwalks," Jacqueline Schiappa reviews the different ways two groups of feminist activists organized "Slutwalk" protest marches in their local communities. Her chapter concludes by advocating for "active" intersectional organizing, as an engaged, intentional process that explicitly foregrounds and values the breadth and depth of perspectives within feminist social groups.

Overall, this section powerfully documents that feminist interventions are not contained to academic or face-to-face spaces, and include a broad range of contexts, including political arenas, as we see in Angela Zimmann's chapter "A Peek Inside the Master's House: The Tale of Feminist Rhetorician as Candidate for U.S. Congress." Zimmann reflects on her recent run for the U.S. House of Representatives, an experience she situates is "steeped in historical precedent." Moreover, she interrogates her experience through a feminist rhetorical framework and considers the material conditions and rhetorical expectations that often limit female rhetors in a variety of settings—politics, business, and the academy.

PRAXIS

Intersectionality runs throughout the pieces organized within our section on Praxis. To begin, in "Pedagogical 'Too-Muchness': A Feminist Approach to Community-Based Learning, Multi-Modal Composition, Social Justice Education, and More," Beth Godbee shares a course titled "Writing for Social Justice," which partnered with the YWCA Southeast Wisconsin's Racial Justice Program. Godbee articulates a pedagogy of "too muchness" and argues for the need to approach feminist interventions as "instead of" rather than "on top of" more traditional approaches. She situates this pedagogical "toomuchness" within and alongside feminist and womanist pedagogies, pedagogy and theatre of the oppressed; and culturally relevant and responsive pedagogy. Godbee stresses that the "toomuchness" of the course and its emphasis on feminist, critical education better positioned students to become agents and actors outside the course and throughout their everyday lives.

In "Trans/feminist Practice of Collaboration in the Art Activism Classroom," Ames Hawkins and Joan Giroux reflect on their experiences collaborating together over many years on a course, *The Cradle Project and One Million Bones*, that brings together writing and art activism, thus casting composition in terms of exhibition. The authors use thick description in order to argue for three principles of effective collaboration: they shared a similar investment in creating change, each understood art as a catalyst for change, and both believed in the power of collaboration in effecting such change, and that such collaboration "needs to be practiced, and that it can be modeled and taught." Jessica Tess, Katie Manthey, Trixie Smith then argue in their chapter "Coming Out as Other in the Graduate Writing Classroom: Feminist Pedagogical Moves for Mentoring Community Activists" that 'coming out' moments of "Otherness" in the graduate writing classroom provides an opportunity to mentor students to foster social change. This commitment to activism can transfer to the many other communities to which students and instructors alike belong. The co-authors each share critically reflective narratives of their own experience "coming out" in graduate school as lived examples from which they build arguments both on the pedagogical moves that support and also those that can prevent such moments of community engagement.

Next, in "Safely Social: User-Centered Design and Difference Feminism," Douglas Walls, Jennifer Miller, and Brandy Dieterle discuss their experience developing and user testing Safely Social, a contextually-designed smartphone application project informed by feminist theory and developed in an effort to "decentralize and redistribute power" by allowing victims of domestic violence the ability to stay in contact with personal and support networks without compromising their safety. Walls, Miller, and Dieterle document how feminist and other social justice theories informed their design methodologies for the smartphone application.

In the final chapter conversation of the Praxis section, "The Unheard Voices of Dissatisfied Clients: Listening to Community Partners as Feminist Praxis," Danielle Williams draws on her recent teaching experience teaching first-year digital writing to examine the benefits of community-based multimodal student projects have for community partners. Examination of their evaluation processes and narratives tell the story of how community partners used the same general understandings to assess student videos: assumptions about the evaluators' own role as mentor for the project, assumptions about the audiences for the project, assumptions about the students' backgrounds and educational experiences, and assumptions about the technical quality of the videos themselves.

COURSE DESIGNS

The final group of conversations turns to pedagogical application of community-based engagement as feminist intervention. Florence Bacabac's "'We Write to Serve': The Intersections of Service Learning, Grant Writing, and the Feminist Rhetorical Agency" features an upper-division course required for English majors emphasizing in Professional and Technical Writing. Intended as an examination of the rhetorical techniques for writing effective grant proposal documents, Bacabac discusses the course as feminist rhetorical praxis. She overviews her experience teaching an undergraduate grant writing service learning course at a regional university, focusing attention in her critical reflection to an examination of the ways in which, by linking students with community partners, the course often forges mutually-beneficial relationships.

In the second course-based project, "Making the Political Personal Again: Strategies for Addressing Student Resistance to Feminist Interventions," Julie Myatt asserts that students often carry misconceptions of feminism and actively resist identifying as feminist even when they agree with the movement's lead tenets. Barger annotates and situates her approach to teaching Feminist Interventions, a class designed to introduce students to the need for feminist interventions through a series of projects in which they encounter a series of situated examples in which women and underrepresented groups are excluded from full participation in the societal power structures that influence their lives. Stephanie Bower presents a reflective narrative of her experience in "Because Your Heart Breaks and It Moves To Action": Digital Storytelling Beyond the Gate." Bower focuses on and upper division course titled "For The Common Good: Writing in The Community and Visual Storytelling," with a focus on social justice and the community. Bower posits digital storytelling in the course as "a vehicle that equalizes the footing between town and gown and shifts cultural and material capital from the university to the community."

In "Feminist Activism in the Core: Student Activism in Theory and Practice," Katherine Fredlund shares her experience teaching a senior-level, writing-intensive general education course. Enrolling 45 students from majors all over campus, Fredlund's students collaborated with our community partner to plan and organize the University's Annual Take Back the Night event. Fredlund argues that instructors must negotiate student resistance to the terms "feminist" and "activist" while asking the same students to participate in explicitly feminist activism. Engaging a community partner, she posits, alleviates some of the tension inherent in requiring feminist activism in general education courses while simultaneously providing instructors an opportunity to teach students about rhetorical effectiveness and civic purposefulness.

Concluding the section is Julie Nelson's "Rhetorical Interventions: A Project Design for Composing and Editing Wikipedia Articles." Nelson shares her experiences delivering Confronting HIStory: Stories of Female Identity and Experience, a sophomore-level special topics general education literature course that introduces students to the diversity of women's lived experiences. Nelson examines the design for, successes, and challenges of asking students in upper-division writing courses to write and edit Wikipedia articles and describes the effort to a digital community in which white male and western histories and epistemologies are privileged. Nelson concludes with a series of suggestions for assignments that encourage students consider how knowledge emerges and is culturally situated in online community spaces.

CONCLUSION: FROM WHAT IF TO WHAT MUST BE

As we put the finishing touches on this introduction and the collection as a whole, we are in the post-election rhetoric of the 2016 U.S. Presidential campaign. These rhetorics continue to divide rather than unite us as nation of diverse individuals who, based on race, class, gender, sexual orientation, religion, ability, and age, experience the presumed freedoms and liberties of our society in differential ways, some empowered, some disenfranchised, some oppressed. The lesson to be learned from this ongoing discursive divide is the critical need to listen: listen to the voices of our students, our community, to those who experience the world differently than ourselves. Such listening manifests itself in the significant amount of self-reflection undertaken by our contributors as they theorize their own experience of their educational, feminist, and activist roles in the academy and beyond. It is no coincidence that numerous chapters in *Composing Feminist Interventions* deploy this concept of listening in the methodologies, the partnerships, the activism, the praxis, and the specific course designs that thematically drive the development and organization of the text itself, and contribute to our triangulated focus on praxis, engagement, and action on the part of teachers, students, and citizens.

A significant touchstone influencing numerous pieces within *Composing Feminist Interventions* is Krista Ratcliffe's 2005 book *Rhetorical Listening: Identification, Gender, and Whiteness*. Ratcliffe defines rhetorical listening as "a stance of openness that a person may choose to assume in cross-cultural exchanges" (p. 1). Ratcliffe's canonical text is primarily focused on the process of her own emerging self-awareness, not to mention the field of rhetoric and composition, of how the framework of gender and race impact the ability to listen in more inclusive ways, acknowledging the need to move beyond monologue, or as Ratcliffe borrows from Jacqueline Jones Royster (1996), to move from listening to language and action. Given this emphasis, we are honored to have Krista Ratcliffe's voice as part of this collection, sharing her thoughts about listening, dialoguing, and acting, and to reflect on the way the contributors respond to her call to listen, and our own call as editors to intervene. Because we have deliberatively defined feminist community engagement broadly across contexts, cultures, and communities, we believe the collection meshes with Ratcliffe's original emphasis on cross-cultural exchange and the importance of developing pedagogies that help students become local and global citizen scholars who "recognize how power dynamics haunt their daily lives and then to discern when and how to perform activism, engagement, and other needed praxes" (Afterword).

We similarly hope that through this rich compilation of successes and challenges to feminist intervention, we have documented the importance of modeling such interventions as not *what if, but what must be*. As our current sociopolitical climate strongly indicates, the conditional term is no longer an option, as initiatives such as the 2017 Women's March on Washington respond to competing discourses surrounding not only women's rights but also our collective civil liberties in a democratic society. Indeed, we cannot presume that these liberties are accessible to all, a presumption our contributors challenge and negotiate on topics that range from environmental activism to political campaigns and within communities as diverse as Appalachia, the armed services, and feminist protest movements online and off. Despite this diversity, the collective emphasis on social justice as the language of action, or *what must be,* drives our contributors to intervene. As co-editors and as feminists, we have learned much from their efforts at listening and calling for future action. We sincerely hope readers of *Composing Feminist Interventions* will as well.

REFERENCES

Ackerman, J. & Coogan, D. (2010). *The public work of rhetoric: Citizen-scholars and civic engagement.* Columbia: University of South Carolina Press.

Ballif, M., Davis, D. & Mountford, R. (2008). *Women's ways of making it in rhetoric and composition.* New York, NY: Routledge.

Berry, P.W., Hawisher, G.E. & Selfe, C.L. (2012). *Transnational literate lives in digital times.* Logan, UT: Computers and Composition Digital Press/Utah State University Press. Retrieved from http://ccdigitalpress.org/transnational.

Buchanon, L. & Ryan, K.J. (2010). *Walking and talking feminist rhetorics: Landmark essays and controversies.* West Lafayette, IN: Parlor Press.

Deans, T. (2000). *Writing partnerships: Service-learning in composition.* Urbana, IL: NCTE.

Deans, T., Roswell, B. & Wurr, A.J. (2010). *Writing and community engagement: A critical sourcebook.* Boston, MA: Bedford/St. Martin's Press.

Flower, L. (2008). *Community literacy and the rhetoric of public engagement.* Carbondale, IL: Southern Illinois University Press.

Grabill, J.T. (2007). *Writing community change: Designing technologies for citizen action.* Cresskill, NJ: Hampton.

Iverson, S.V.D. & Hauver James, J. (2014). *Feminist community engagement: Achieving praxis.* New York, NY: Palgrave Macmillan.

Jarratt, S.C.F. & Worsham, L. (1998). *Feminism and composition studies: In other words.* New York, NY: Modern Language Association of America.

Kirsch, G., Moar, F.S., Massey, L., Nickoson-Massey, L. & Sheridan-Rabideau, M.P. (2003). *Feminism and composition: A critical sourcebook.* Boston, MA: Bedford/St. Martin's.

Kirsch, G. & Rohan, L. (2008). *Beyond the archives: Research as a lived process.* Carbondale, IL: Southern Illinois University Press.

Nickoson, L., Blair, K., Sheridan, M.P. & Jacobi, T. (2014). Special Issue: Feminist campus-community partnerships: Intersections and interruptions. *Feminist Teacher, 24*(2), 49–153.

Ratcliffe, K. (2005). *Rhetorical listening: Identification, gender, whiteness.* Carbondale, IL: Southern Illinois University Press.

Ratcliffe, K. & Rickly, R. (2010). *Performing feminism and administration in rhetoric and composition studies.* Cresskill, NJ: Hampton Press.
Royster, J.J. & Kirsch, G. (2012). *Feminist rhetorical practices: New horizons for rhetoric, composition, and literacy studies.* Carbondale, IL: Southern Illinois University Press.
Royster, J.J. (1996). When the first voice you hear is not your own. *College Composition and Communication, 47*(1), 29–40.
Schell, E.E. & Rawson, K. J. (2010). *Rhetorica in motion: Feminist rhetorical methods & methodologies.* Pittsburgh, PA: University of Pittsburgh Press.

PART 1. METHODOLOGY

CHAPTER 1.
POST-RESEARCH ENGAGEMENT: AN ARGUMENT FOR CRITICAL EXAMINATION OF RESEARCHER ROLES AFTER RESEARCH ENDS

Megan Adams
The University of Findlay

> *Through examination of her own collaborative role in supporting community storytellers engaged with an interactive-participatory documentary, The Hollow Project, Adams foregrounds the issues that arise when researchers and directors leave a community. Specifically, Adams addresses such questions as what can we gain by critically evaluating the ways researcher identities and agency shift throughout the life of a research project and after the project has ended? How can researchers develop and structure community projects that are more self-sustaining? How can digital technologies assist in relationship building and engagement with research projects before, during and after execution? And what can we learn about issues of reciprocity and reflexivity by considering more deeply the life spans of community research projects and our continued involvement with them? Adams ultimately argues that critical reflection and thoughtful consideration of the fluctuating nature of our roles as researchers engaged in feminist community projects provides for more ethical involvement.*

I open this chapter with an audio essay, composed in an effort to make sense of the shift in my identity and agency over the life of a recent research project. I attempt to describe this process at length and in more detail throughout this chapter. To listen to the essay, follow this link: https://soundcloud.com/megadams2/believe-mixdown.

As the introductory audio essay elaborates, as feminist scholars we are often left with a variety of reflections regarding our own identities when community-driven research projects meet their natural ends. The audio clip linked above functions as an attempt at articulation of those emotions through story.

Essentially, it is the product of a process of reflection—completing it alongside this text required me to look inward to make sense of the ways my personal and professional identities shifted and my agency as a rhetor developed over the course of a research project. In other words, this audio work functions as a means to enter into conversations about what happens to our sense of self and engagement with the worlds around us as we engage in research, with particular focus on when we leave a project.

The story shared is a product of the awareness gained from careful reflection of engagement with a community participatory digital storytelling project. In this chapter, I share details of how this feminist intervention allowed me to work with and alongside storytellers to articulate the need for social change in their community. Through the process of composing digital stories and my dissertation with them, we began to trace the ways our identities and senses of rhetorical agency were shifting. This story also provides a picture of the pervasiveness of feminist principles in meaning making and the ways we approach and conduct research. Like other chapters in this collection, the stories shared in this one focus on feminist values of reciprocity, listening, engagement, and collaboration with an emphasis on the ways feminist engagement in community work often leaves imprints on our hearts that we cannot ignore once a project "ends."

Ultimately, this chapter argues that careful reflection on the ways our own identities and agency fluctuate throughout the life of a project can offer insight into the ways perspective shapes research and can serve as moments of personal and professional growth. Therefore, it is important to engage in such processes, despite the fact that they are often complex, messy, emotional, and often difficult, because if we don't, we risk undermining the work we set out to do and may miss the deep understanding that can come as a result.

INTRODUCTION: STARTING AT THE BEGINNING

As feminist scholars, we have long looked at the nature of researcher positionality in the communities we study through debates about how to complicate insider/outsider identities (Naples, 2003; Almjeld & Blair, 2012), articulations of the ways terministic screens affect projects (Kirsch & Ritchie, 2003; Selfe, 2012; Blair, 2012), and discussions of how to honor participants' voices as we work with and alongside them (Chiseri-Strator, 1996; Cushman, 1996; Royster & Kirsch, 2012).

Additionally, we have built substantial partnerships in communities that have maintained these tenets and produced rich, rigorous examinations of how individuals are engaging in literacy practices as a means to better themselves and the spaces they inhabit (Flower, 2008; Grabill, 2007; Heath, 1983). This scholarship makes evident tenets of feminist research in practice: reciprocity, transparency, ethics, reflexivity, and multidimensionality among others.

However, one issue not often reflected in scholarship on feminist community research (understandably so) is what happens after a researcher leaves, or when a project comes to a natural end. Explanations of the impacts on identity, agency and the changing nature of relationships between researchers and participants are relevant; because they affect the ways we understand and frame community projects in current and future research endeavors. For instance, acknowledging the roles we play in sustaining community projects post-research, when careers, family-life, or other outside influences draw us away from the research site can assist in interrogating the infrastructures we build as well as the roles we play, leaving us better prepared to create rich and lasting impacts in communities. Building on this concept in her chapter, Emily Johnston suggests we envision ethical practice in feminist research as a means to hold us accountable for the work we do in communities, "Given our own and our concepts' propensities for movement, becoming conscious of *what we are doing, how we are doing it and how our movements move our research participants*, again and again and again, is ethical, activist practice." In other words, Johnston argues that we reconceive "knowledge-making as one of negotiating what we know, have known, and have yet to know"—a process that begins with our own reflections before, during, and after a research project. Johnston's chapter offers insight on how to accomplish this task in a more pedagogical context; in this chapter I showcase the value of this work in research.

Through examination of my own role along alongside that of the director, Elaine Sheldon's in supporting community storytellers engaged with an interactive-participatory documentary, I examine the issues that arise when researchers and directors leave a community. Specifically, this chapter seeks to answer the following questions:

- What can we gain by critically evaluating the ways researcher identities and agency shift (or not) throughout the life of a research project and after the project has ended?
- What can we learn about issues of reciprocity and reflexivity by considering more deeply the life spans of community research projects and our continued involvement with them?

In fleshing out these questions, this chapter argues that critical reflection and thoughtful consideration of the fluctuating nature of roles as researchers engaged in feminist community projects provides for richer, more ethical involvement in this work and our scholarship.

UNDERSTANDING RESEARCHER ROLE(S)

Delving deeper into the ways researcher identity and agency shifts over the course of a project requires sensitivity to the foundational principles of feminist research which are characterized by the following: a commitment to social justice and the improvement of circumstances for individuals, careful, respectful, critically-reflexive, and dialogic research (Naples, 2003; Harding, 1987; Mortensen & Kirsch, 1996; Kirsch, Maor, Massey, Nickoson-Massey & Sheridan-Rabideau, 2003; McKee & Porter, 2010). Further, as Jacqueline Jones Royster and Gesa Kirsch (2012) point out feminist rhetorical practices are "not only changing research methods but also research methodologies . . . what counts as data, how we gather and interpret data, what role researchers play in relation to participants what ethical stance they assume, and so on" (p. 34). Royster and Kirsch also call for feminists to consider deeply the ethical self in the texts we consume and produce. They claim such a practice provides the opportunity for us to understand, " . . . the interplay of who we personally are as scholars, teachers, and human beings, what our vantage points are, what we see, how we are conditioned to see, how we engage in sense-making processes, and how we turn those sensibilities into actions" (p. 18). As this chapter illustrates, a large portion of this work of understanding the ethical self occurs after our research is completed.

Intersecting with calls made by Royster and Kirsch and other feminist researchers (Blair, 2012; Naples, 2003; Chiseri-Strator, 1996; Heath, 1983) to reveal researcher positionality and potential biases in results, Jeff Grabill has also written about why it is crucial researchers consider and reveal research standpoint or stance. In community-based, participatory, feminist research the practice of developing and articulating a research stance is an integral part of the research process, because such an identity statement "enables a researcher to process methods and make decisions" (Grabill, 2012, p. 215). Similarly, such a reflexive statement and the process of creating it, provides the opportunity for the researcher "to bend back upon herself as well as the other as an object of study" (Chiseri-Strater, 1996, p. 119). According to Grabill articulating a research stance requires reflection on and consideration of the following tenets:

- researcher identity: Who am I personally? as a researcher? in relation to my discipline?
- purposes as a researcher. Why research?
- questions of power and ethics. What are my commitments with respect to research?

These questions serve as a jumping off point to consider the role of the ethical self in the research projects we conduct and represent in scholarly texts.

The reflexive process of looking inward to understand the ways our values and interactions in the world frame what we are able to see and hear and conversely, what remains hidden or unknowable, can best be considered in light of our research projects, or with the perspective we are able to gain after being in the field and completing the process of coding and writing up data. Additionally, consideration and articulation of a research stance helps us to privilege reciprocity and relationships in our methodologies, as Mariana Grohowski points out in "Reciprocity as Epicenter: An After-Action Review."

Nevertheless, engaging in such an analysis can be difficult, but we might start by working to articulate researcher stance at the beginning, throughout, and *at the end* of a research project. These ruminations (which I discuss further in later sections) provide an opportunity to critically reflect on the ways our own identities and agencies fluctuate during the life of a research project as well as impact the course of research and the conclusions we draw as a result. Weaving these stories alongside the voices we share in our published research assists in heeding the calls put forth by feminists for decades, and provides for richer, nuanced, and more rigorous understandings of the ways we acquire and share knowledge in the field of rhetoric and writing. Preserving the voices of our participants with our own provides the opportunity to privilege their voices, a process displayed in Grohowski's chapter as well.

Further, consideration of the ethical self requires an awareness of the ambiguous, shifting notion of identity and how multiplicity affects our relationships with others. In their scholarship, Torre and Ayala (2009) suggest using Gloria Anzaldua's concept of a mestiza consciousness, which recognizes and makes apparent how research is a political activity " . . . and that researchers come from particular communities with their own historically rooted relationships to research and power" (p. 388). Further, a mestiza consciousness acknowledges the "in-between spaces" where relationships are forged and maintained around mutually important issues, and uses conflicts that arise because of social hierarchies as learning points to breakdown and disrupt dualities to inspire change.

Just as we often ask participants to use new media tools and spaces to make sense of their own identities and connections to culture and place (which I explain further in the following section), researchers can also take advantage of digital mediums such as audio and video to tell, complicate and better understand shifting notions of their own identities and agency throughout the course of research projects. According to Sullivan new media technologies provide a "natural fit for blending the personal and political" (as cited in Almjeld & Blair, 2012, p. 102). In commenting on the rhetorically powerful nature of digital literacy narratives Cindy Selfe (2012) has said it is through these accounts:

...which people fashion their lives and make sense of their world, indeed, how they construct the realities in which they live. These narratives are sometimes so richly laden with information that conventional academic tools and ways of discussing their power- to shape identities; to persuade, and reveal, and discover; to create meaning and affiliations at home, in schools, communities, and workplaces—are inadequate to the task. (Narrative Theory and Stories)

Given this acknowledgement, it is not hard to imagine the possibilities of new media tools to more deeply understand and communicate researcher positionality and notions of the ethical self, thus encouraging we stay connected to those we research alongside after a project is completed. As evidenced in the stories shared, this chapter illustrates how entering into research with an awareness and understanding of the roles we inhabit as feminist researchers as well as the fluctuating nature of relationships and responsibilities leads to richer connections, which enable true collaboration to occur in research. This collaboration is often labor-intensive and requires acute sensitivity as we listen to our participants and ourselves. In her chapter in this collection, Grohowski details the ways she applied methods grounded in theories of rhetorical listening to privilege relationships with participants, something outside the scope of this chapter, but central in developing awareness of researcher perspective and influence on a project.

In the following sections, I attempt to articulate how we might go about building and making sense of the ebb and flow of collaborative relationships as I trace the ways my own and the director, Elaine Sheldon's positions and connections to community storytellers shifted and influenced our work through our involvement with *Hollow: An Interactive Documentary* (http://www.hollowdocumentary.com).

For more background and information about the history and current state of the project, visit https://wac.colostate.edu/docs/books/feminist/media/adams2.pdf.

Additionally, more from Hollow's Director, Elaine Sheldon and her role after the project launched can be found at https://wac.colostate.edu/docs/books/feminist/media/adams3.pdf.

RESEARCHER COMMENTARY: TRACING SHIFTS IN IDENTITY AND AGENCY POST-RESEARCH

In 2012, I traveled to McDowell County, West Virginia on a whim. I had read about an interactive documentary project on Twitter (see Figure 1.1) aiming to give voice to residents in the community with the hopes that access to digital tools and spaces would help people envision and enact positive changes in their community. At the time, I was entering into my second year of graduate school, and unsure of my identity as a scholar and an individual. I had just completed a series of interviews with my grandfather, whose health and mind were deteriorating. Our conversations focused on family history and values. After speaking with my grandfather, I was beginning to lay claim to and better understand my Appalachian identity. The chance to travel to the "heart of Appalachia" to assist in filming with a documentary seemed like a chance to explore these issues, and I jumped at the chance to be a part of something that mattered to me.

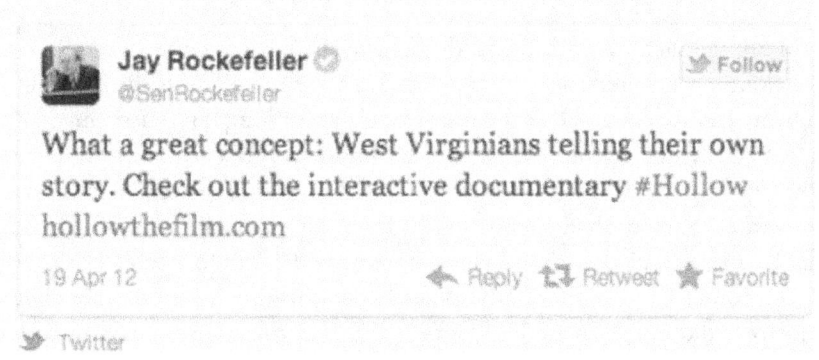

Figure 1.1. Hollow tweet (2011).

Admittedly then, my first ventures in volunteering with the *Hollow* project were selfish—I wanted to do something exciting that would help me make sense of my family's identity—which as I was beginning to understand it was an integral part of my identity. However, the time I spent volunteering with the crewmembers in the community and forming relationships with community storytellers provided the impetus for a tectonic shift to occur in my own personal and professional identity.

Throughout the course of the research, I kept detailed memos that read more like journal entries. Further, data collection occurred over a period of three years from 2012 to 2015, during the phases of pre-production, production, and post-production of the documentary as well as follow-ups a year after it launched. Throughout that time, I gathered mostly qualitative data in the form of interviews, participant observation, and analysis of the media the storytellers chose to share with me. As I was working to keep track of how the identities and agency of the community storytellers involved with *Hollow* were shifting, I found myself articulating connections to their stories—in them I saw my own identity mirrored back. An awareness of this connection and of the ways it affected the interactions and relationships I formed with participants has served as the both the foundation and catalyst to my previous and continued involvement in the community as well as inspired the written and digital research I've completed associated with the project. It is the reason I sought out the work, and the reason I will never let it go.

Sheldon and I have often joked about our first meeting, "I had faith you weren't a weirdo," she has said to me on multiple occasions. On the surface the comment is funny, but it is actually a good indication of the nature of our first meeting which looking back seems serendipitous. I remember keenly pulling into the driveway of an old coal company house on the top of the hill, a small wrought-iron fence lining the property, and being greeted by an overly friendly canine named Keely.

In my interactions with them, the storytellers have often recounted the pull of Sheldon's personality, and I experienced it myself that day as she immediately made me feel welcome. Over the next week, I spent long hours assisting her and the rest of the documentary crew in the community. In each home and at each event, we were greeted with overwhelming hospitality, a pattern I later learned was because Sheldon had spent months building trust with community members. At the end of the trip, Sheldon asked me if I would like to research the project, something her thesis advisor had been pushing her to do, but that she admittedly did not want to do. I agreed, and over the course of completing the research we became fast friends.

As I continue to make sense of my role as a researcher and friend to both Elaine and the McDowell storytellers, I am learning about how to build and sustain collaborative relationships, and how doing so deeply reflects the nature and scope of my work. Through this research experience, I have come to define collaboration as fluid and evolving over the course of and after research; collaboration means truly empathizing with community partners in order to build relationships grounded in care and reciprocity. I have looked to feminists researchers who have taught me why it's important to acknowledge the nuance and vacillating nature of those relationships (Naples, 2003; Sheridan-Rabideau, 2008; Royster & Kirsch, 2012), how to reflect and look inward to understand how relationships affect our terministic screens and future research (Almjeld & Blair, 2012; Blair, 2012) and finally how living and working alongside participants impacts community change (Heath, 1983; Flower, 2008; Grabill, 2007; Rodriquez, 2009). As feminists, we have made strides towards articulating why it's important to engage in research alongside participants and to spend time reflecting on how collaborative research shapes our identities; however, we don't often talk about what happens after a research project meets it natural conclusion, when we leave. As I attempt to articulate it in this section, I have a suspicion that for many of us the relationships we build continue, and the stories we tell stick with us, shaping and influencing our work and ourselves in both minute and broad strokes.

As feminists we value collaboration, and we acknowledge the values and insights of our participants, as we have made calls to treat them as "co-interpreters" in research, a term Thomas Newkirk (1996) described in his research with teachers and students, "When . . . those being studied have access to the researcher's emerging questions and interpretations, there is an opportunity to offer counterinterpretations or provide mitigating information" (p. 13).

I entered into my research with *Hollow* in this mindset. As I worked to build relationships with the documentary crewmembers and community storytellers, I communicated this research stance of openness and collaboration. Additionally, I was aware of issues of reciprocity and worked to be sensitive to the ways I envisioned my research giving back to the community. At the beginning and throughout the course of the research, I felt this professional/academic stance of research begin to fade away. As I became more aware of the spirit of the culture and got closer to the people from whom that spirit emanated, I felt my own identity shift in profound ways. I began to feel a rootedness in my own life (as elaborated in the audio essay), because I experienced the peace that comes from that sense of belonging, belonging to a culture, to a place, to a history, and to a community. In my own longing to discover more about my family ancestry from my grandfather, I was searching for that rootedness, but it wasn't until after the project was completed and the research was finished that I became aware of this transition in myself.

Documentary filmmaker Kaylanee Mam has expressed a similar shift in her own identity as she works with Cambodian people to bring their stories to Western audiences, to introduce and preserve an alternative way of life through film. Her current project focuses on the fight to save the Areng forest in Cambodia and is experienced through the life of a Cambodian woman and her family (to see Mam's work, visit http://www.nytimes.com/video/opinion/100000003025 809/a-threat-to-cambodias-sacred-forests.html). Mam describes the depth and influence of the relationship she has built with this woman in the following statement detailing the ways she envisions collaboration:

> And it's really strange, there are times when I feel like I
> don't even have to express anything to her in words, and she
> understands what I want and how I feel. And I never felt that
> before, you know, especially not with someone in Cambodia.
> So when I started filming her and her husband and her family,
> I felt because I became so connected to her and to them I

> wasn't just filming them, I was actually experiencing this with them. And the story that was being told was not a story that I was telling, but a story that we were telling together. And that is such an incredible feeling when you can get to that place where it's a collaboration between you and your subject and not just you with the objective camera, documenting a story. (Sheldon & Ginsburg, *The camera doesn't even exist*, 2015)

Although Mam's reflection focuses on her work filming this family, the general charge of "telling a story" applies to our research as well. Her acknowledgement that collaborative storytelling exists outside of "having an objective" is a tenet called for amongst many researchers that do community, participatory, feminist research (Torre & Ayala, 2009; Rodriquez, 2009), but rarely do we hear such stories on how these relationships we build affect future research or inform our identities.

As the revelations I shared from my own experiences along with Elaine's reveal, as researchers and filmmakers we are faced with choices: choices about how we interact and build relationships with participants, choices about how we choose to represent them in our work, and choices about how long and how much we stay involved with a community after our work is completed. In line with Mam's observations, I feel it's important to articulate and make known our relationships to hold ourselves accountable for the work we do, but also to avoid superficial relationships. In other words, entering into a community and engaging in truly collaborative work is a difficult, complex, and messy endeavor. It is one that requires much of us personally, but if we are to embody the ideals we say we say we privilege, we must work to achieve this goal. Often, we fall short of our expectations, but we need to think about why that happens and how we can work to do better the next time we embark on a research project. Such reflection makes us more aware, empathetic and better researchers who produce reflexive, dialogic, work.

CONCLUSION

> The process of paying attention, of being mindful, of attending to the subtle, intuitive, not-so-obvious parts of research has the capacity to yield rich rewards. It allows scholars to observe and notice, to listen and hear voices often neglected or silenced, and notice more overtly their own responses to what they are seeing, reading, reflecting on, and encountering during their own research processes.
>
> —Royster & Kirsch, p. 85

In the quote above, Royster and Kirsch explain the importance of instituting what they call "strategic contemplation"—a method scholars can apply to become more attune to the outward and inward journeys we embark on as feminist researchers. They describe the outward journey as the one we take, "in real time and space" (p. 85), the places we visit in fieldwork and the communities we enter into as researchers. However, less often interrogated but certainly not less important is the inward journey we pursue, the one that helps us understand the ways we make sense of our meaning-making processes, or the journey "focused on researchers noticing how they process, imagine, and work with materials; how creativity and imagination come into play; how a vicarious experience that results from critical imagination, meditation, introspection, and/or reflection gets mapped, perhaps simultaneously, as both an analytical one and a visceral one" (p. 85). As this chapter outlines, my own experience engaging with this method of strategic contemplation has meant pausing for critical self-reflection at each part of the research process from the inception of research questions to writing and distribution (Johnston makes a strong case for this type of "discomforting" self-assessment in her chapter as well). Moreover, that reflection has also included the voices of others I've collaborated with, and as we have come through this process together, we have come out with lasting friendships that will extend well beyond the life of a research project. The rich and lasting interactions we've have with the community storytellers continue to influence the life and shape of this project. In their chapter, "Listening to Research as a Feminist Ethos of Representation," Lauren Rosenberg and Emma Howes describe the importance of allowing these relationships to linger and to shape the work we do in influential ways.

Nevertheless, as Gesa Kirsch (2005) has taught us, feminist researchers often interact with participants in ways that reflect "friendliness" and not necessarily "genuine friendship." According to Kirsch, it's important to make the distinction because in doing so we are better equipped to become aware of the nature of our interactions, "recognizing that they are shaped, like all human interactions, by dynamics of power, gender, generation, education, race, class, and many other factors that can contribute to feelings of misunderstanding, disappointment, and broken trust" (p. 2170). Similarly, in her work in indigenous communities, Angela Haas (2005, 2007) notes the importance of considering cultural ways of making meaning and listening to participants as we work with them, so that we might resist the prime narrative that often holds together our beliefs. Additionally, Brenda Brueggeman (1996) reminds us to be conscious and sympathetic to the silence of participants, to respect the distance and withdrawals they may make, and be sensitive to their needs over our own. Each of these women, point to the complexity of collaborative relationships; further, critical reflection and strategic contemplation offer us methods to examine and become more attune to their evolving nature during our research engagement as well as after a project is completed.

As I have written elsewhere (Adams, 2015), through the course of our work in McDowell Sheldon and I have spoken about and interrogated our shortcomings—both in the context of the film itself and the research that developed from it. We talk about what we would do differently "next time," and as the sections above demonstrate we are not afraid to admit or brush over our failures or the constraints of the work. Also, we both continue to be as actively involved with the community as we can—we both stay in touch with community members and assist them however and as much as we can given the scope of our current career paths (I have become an Assistant Professor at a small college in northwest Ohio and Sheldon continues to travel the world on assignment). Our own relationship keeps us close to the community as well as we work to inspire and invigorate each other as new developments occur.

Although Sheldon and I both deal with the constraint of being geographically far away from McDowell, a piece of us will always be there. Social media spaces and new technologies such as Google Hangout provide us with a means to stay relevant in each other's and the storytellers' lives. Because our work is linked in many ways, Sheldon is a media maker and although I also work to make media, my focus is to study it—we stay tied through professional and personal interests. For instance, we recently collaborated on a publication on civic media engagement (http://civicmediaproject.org/works/civic-media-project/hollow), and Sheldon regularly "speaks" with digital media courses I teach via video conferences.

Staying involved with the storytellers is a bit different, since our relationships with them are unique in their nature and capacity. I have come to form those relationships through Elaine, meaning it is because the storytellers trusted her first that they also trusted me. However, over time, through the course of the research and beyond, I have worked to stay involved with their lives, to build and sustain relationships. Important to make relevant is the impetus for those relationships. As I entered into the community, my intentions were framed with the research at forefront. In other words, I was focused on forming collaborative research relationships, engaging my participants in the work, by treating them as co-participants, allowing them to see interviews, coding schemes, and write-ups and prompting them for feedback at each step. But it was during the research that I noticed the nature of our relationships begin to shift from that of co-participants to friends. As a result, my feelings and thoughts about how to create and represent their story collaboratively in research shifted as well.

For instance, as I shared my research with the storytellers, they seemed uninterested in reading it, but when I called them on the phone to check in on their lives and see how they were doing, we often conversed at length about concepts I was articulating in my dissertation. These insights and the comfortable, caring tone of our conversations materialized, because the nature of our relationships had changed—we were friends, and we knew that our friendships would continue past the near future. I provide this example to illustrate the importance of recognizing and articulating a research stance (Grabill, 2012) and also the relevance of understanding the fluctuating nature of a stance given the ways we do or don't engage in relationships through the course of and after our research.

When I think about the ways the storytellers have enriched and added value to my life, I feel immensely grateful for their willingness to engage in this endeavor—to risk (again) the possibility of being misrepresented or being taken advantage of by an outsider. I realize now also that the work I put into building and sustaining these friendships is essential to creating ethical, collaborative work that privileges relationships over stories—over research. When we can see the act of sustaining these friendships not as an obligation, but as an opportunity for growth and reward (for our participants and ourselves), we are able to embody the values we privilege, and our work will serve as a testament to others of the value of research. In writing this chapter, I have reflected on the importance of critically revisiting our understanding of how relationships shift over time, and I am reminded of Ivy Schweitzer's (2006) notion of performing friendship, "Ideally, friends choose each other freely, respect each other's sovereignty, confirm each other's equality, learn together" (p. 290). It is through critical reflection of the nature of relationship building and the evolution of collaboration in feminist community work that we are able to learn from and with each other.

REFERENCES

Almjeld, J. & Blair, K. (2012). Multimodal methods for multimodal literacies: Establishing a technofeminist research identity. In K. Arola & A. Wysocki (Eds.), *Composing(media) = composing(embodiment)* (pp. 97–109). Logan, UT: Utah State University Press.

Billings, D. B., Norman, G. & Ledford, K. (1999). *Confronting Appalachian stereotypes: Back talk from an American region.* Lexington: University Press of Kentucky.

Blair, K. (2012). A complicated geometry: Triangulating feminism, activism, and technological literacy. In L. Nickoson & M. P. Sheridan (Eds.), *Writing studies research in practice: Methods and methodologies* (pp. 63–72). Carbondale, IL: Southern Illinois University Press.

Bradner, A. (2013, January 7). America's favorite joke is anything but funny. *Salon.* Retrieved from http://www.salon.com/2013/01/07/whats_so_funny_about_being_poor/.

Brueggeman, B. J. (1996). Still-life: Representations and silences in the participant-observer role. In Mortensen, P. & Kirsch, G. (Eds.), *Ethics and representation in qualitative studies of literacy* (pp. 17–39). Urbana, IL: NCTE.

Clark, A. M. & Hayward, N. (2013). *Talking Appalachian: Voice, identity, and community*. Lexington, KY: University Press of Kentucky.

Chiseri-Strater, E. (1996). Turning in upon ourselves: Positionality, subjectivity, and reflexivity in case study and ethnographic research. In Mortensen, P. & Kirsch, G. (Eds.), *Ethics and representation in qualitative studies of literacy* (pp. 115–133). Urbana, IL: NCTE.

Cushman, E. (1996). The rhetorician as an agent of social change. *College Composition and Communication, 47*(1), 7–28.

Flower, L. (2008). *Community literacy and the rhetoric of public engagement*. Carbondale, IL: Southern Illinois University Press.

Grabill, J. T. (2007). *Writing community change: Designing technologies for citizen action*. Cresskill, NJ: Hampton Press.

Grabill, J. T. (2012). Community based research and the importance of a research stance. In L. Nickoson & M. P. Sheridan (Eds.), *Writing studies research in practice: Methods and methodologies* (pp. 210–219). Carbondale, IL: Southern Illinois University Press.

Haas, A. (2005). Making online spaces more native to American Indians: A digital diversity recommendation. *Computers and Composition Online*. Retrieved from http://casit.bgsu.edu/cconline/Haas/index.htm.

Haas, A. (2007). Wampum as hypertext: An American Indian intellectual tradition of multimedia theory and practice. *Studies in American Indian Literatures, 19*(4), 77–100.

Harding, S. (1987). *Feminism and methodology*. Bloomington, IN: Indiana University Press.

Heath, S. (1983). *Ways with words: Language, life and work in communities and classrooms*. Cambridge, England: Cambridge University Press.

Kirsch, G., Maor, F. S., Massey, L., Nickoson-Massey, L. & Sheridan-Rabideau, M. P. (Eds.). (2003). *Feminism and composition: A critical sourcebook*. Boston, MA: Bedford/St. Martin's.

Kirsch, G. (2005). Friendship, friendliness, and feminist fieldwork. *Journal of Women and Society in Culture, 30*(4), 2163–2172.

Kirsch, G. & Ritchie, J. (2003). Beyond the personal: Theorizing a politics of location in composition research. In Kirsch, G., Maor, F. S., Massey, L., Nickoson-Massey, L. & Sheridan-Rabideau, M. P. (Eds.), *Feminism and composition: A critical sourcebook* (pp. 140–159). New York, NY: Bedford/St. Martin's.

McKee, H. A. & Porter, J. E. (2010). Rhetorica online: Feminist research in cyberspace. In Schell, E. E. & Rawson, K. (Eds.), *Rhetorica in motion: Feminist rhetorical methods & methodologies* (pp. 152–170). Pittsburgh, PA: University of Pittsburgh Press.

McMillion, E. (2011). *Hollow: An interactive documentary proposal*. Boston, MA: Emerson College.

McMillion, E. (Director). (2013). *Hollow: An interactive documentary* [interactive website]. Retrieved from http://www.hollowdocumentary.com/

Mortenson, P. & Kirsch, G. (1996). *Ethics and representation in qualitative studies of literacy.* Urbana, IL: NCTE.

Naples, N. A. (2003). *Feminism and method: Ethnography, discourse analysis, and activist research.* New York, NY: Routledge.

Newkirk, T. (1996). Seduction and betrayal in qualitative research. In P. Mortensen & G. Kirsch (Eds.), *Ethics and representation in qualitative studies of literacy* (pp. 3–16). Urbana, IL: NCTE.

Rodríguez, C. (2001). *Fissures in the mediascape: An international study of citizens' media.* Cresskill, NJ: Hampton Press.

Royster, J. & Kirsch, G. (2012). *Feminist rhetorical practices: New horizons for rhetoric, composition, and literacy studies.* Carbondale, IL: Southern Illinois University Press.

Schweitzer, I. (2006). For Gloria Anzaldua: Collecting America, performing friendship. *PMLA, 121*(1), 285–291.

Selfe, C. L. (2012). Narrative theory and stories that speak to us. In H. L. Ulman, S. L. DeWitt & C. L. Selfe (Eds.), *Stories that speak to us.* Logan, UT: Computers and Composition Digital Press/Utah State University Press. Retrieved from http://ccdigitalpress.org/stories.

Sheldon, E. & Ginsburg, S. (2015, March 25). Hashtags don't make change. *She does podcast.* Retrieved from http://www.shedoespodcast.com/listen/lina-srivastava.

Sheldon, E. & Ginsburg, S. (2015, Sept. 9). The camera doesn't even exist. *She does podcast* (audio). Retrieved from http://www.shedoespodcast.com/listen/18-the-camera-doesnt-even-exist-kalyanee-mam.

Sheridan-Rabideau, M. P. (2008). *Girls, feminism, and grassroots literacies: Activism in the girlzone.* Albany, NY: State University of New York Press.

Torre, M. & Ayala, J. (2009). Envisioning participatory action research in Entremundos. *Feminism & Psychology, 19*(3), 387–393.

CHAPTER 2.
RECIPROCITY AS EPICENTER: AN 'AFTER-ACTION REVIEW'

Mariana Grohowski
Journal of Veterans Studies

Feminist scholars have critiqued the methods and methodologies of empirical human-subjects research for being hegemonic and exploitative, stressing the imperative for reciprocity in civic engagement and human subject based research in rhetoric and composition. In an effort to "articulate a language that clarifies how civic engagement happens" (Orr, 2011, p. 7), Grohowski details the methods and methodology developed while working with two disabled women veterans to stress the importance of feminist intervention and political activism as driving principles when engaging in research with participants who belong to misrepresented populations. Grohowski discusses the process of developing reciprocal relationships with case study co-interpreters through the interrelated methods of listening, understanding, and strategic disclosure. In addition to outlining a methodology in which reciprocity is epicenter, she stresses that partnerships with minority groups must draw upon innovative approaches and modalities for fostering access and inclusion.

Rhetoric, writing, and literacy studies (RWLS) scholars have shared methods and intentions for developing reciprocal relationships with participants. Some identify their use of reciprocity as experimental (Gorzelsky, 2012); others classify reciprocity as part of an activist agenda (Blythe, 2012; Cushman, 1996, 1999; Goldblatt, 2007). Feminism as a political, ideological, and scholarly perspective has appropriated activism as an essential tenet (Blair, 2012; Blair & Tulley, 2007; Himley, 2004; Jack, 2009; Powell & Takayoshi, 2003; Sheridan-Rabideau, 2009; Royster & Kirsch, 2012). Given the interdisciplinary nature of feminist research, many scholars outside the field of RWLS note the links between feminist research, activism, and reciprocity (Gluck, 1977; Harding, 1987, 1991; Lather, 1988; Naples, 2003; Orr, 2011; Smith, 2012). According to Shulamit Reinharz (1992) specific themes of feminist research make it a form of activism and support the researcher in developing reciprocal relationships with her participants. Feminist research "includes the researcher as person; and attempts to develop special relations with the people studied" (p. 240). Indeed, researchers who conceive of research as relationship building consider reciprocation imperative (Powell & Takayoshi, 2003; Goldblatt, 2007; Cushman, 1996; Gorzelsky, 2012; Selfe & Hawisher, 2012; Berry et al., 2012; Royster, 2000; Grabill, 2012; Adams, this collection). As Mary Sue MacNealy (1999) has explained, when researchers, such as feminists, interrogate "political and cultural issues . . . such research often is, or becomes action research, undertaken with the idea that change will occur in the researcher as well as the research subjects as a result of participation in the research project" (p. 233). The "change" MacNealy speaks of is reciprocally experienced between the researcher and her participants; furthermore, this change is activist-in-nature because it advances the quality of life for those involved (see Berry et al., 2012).

Like Katrina Powell and Pamela Takayoski (2003), I developed reciprocal relationships with co-interpreters amidst conducting research. Like Powell and Takayoshi, my aim is to articulate how and why I negotiate(d)[1] such relationships with co-interpreters. The authors contend: "discussions of reciprocity can take on a mystical aura that avoids engagement with the complicated negotiations of building reciprocity. Without narratives of prior experiences . . . researchers can find themselves unprepared" (p. 401). By detailing the methods and methodologies of case study research conducted with two disabled female U.S. military veterans—Tanya Schardt and BriGette McCoy[2]—I outline a "research stance" (Grabill, 2012) for which reciprocity is epicenter.[3]

According to Jeff Grabill (2012), "A research stance is a set of beliefs and obligations that shape how one acts as a researcher" (p. 211). Heeding Grabill's advice, I explain how my research stance and methodology were developed in the hopes of guiding other researchers to practice reciprocity when working with misrepresented populations. Furthermore, I stress that a methodology for which reciprocity is epicenter is activist, but it must be employed with consideration and care. The interconnected, reciprocal relationship building practices of understanding, listening, and strategic disclosure orient my methodology. I explain each practice to articulate my methodologies, which are a form of feminist intervention. As characteristic of feminist scholarship, exemplified in many of the chapters in this collection, I employ narrative to stress the subjective nature

---

1   While project has ended, our relationships are ongoing.
2   Both women insisted, like Lary in Rosenberg's co-authored chapter with Howe (Chapter 4, this collection), that I use their actual names. Tanya and BriGette's rationale was to ensure that their contributions and sacrifices were written into history.
3   My use of "reciprocity as epicenter" is inspired by Smagorinsky's (2008) article.

of my stance as researcher and friend to co-interpreters Tanya and BriGette. Though feminists have a considerable legacy and expertise on both theorizing and enacting transparency and reflexivity, so does the U.S. military, through the After-Action Review (AAR).

According to the U.S. Army, the After-Action Review (AAR) is "a professional discussion of an event focused on performance standards, that enables soldiers to discover for themselves what happened, why it happened, and how to sustain strengths and improve on weaknesses" (TC 25–20, 1993, p. 1). Drawing on analysis, interpretation, reflection, and collaboration, AARs afford improvement for both "soldiers and leaders" to evaluate and support training operations (p. ii). Furthermore, AARs result from a rhetorical situation and cultural institution that values efficiency and precision. The rhetorical situation of an AAR affords service members clarity surrounding a battle or training exercise, with the intention of fostering a more successful military unit. In principle, the AAR shares with RWLS scholarship—including but not limited to the feminist scholars in this section of this collection—the recommendation to articulate and reflect upon their methods and methodologies (see Williamson & Huot, 2012). I shift now to information about Tanya and BriGette's social locations and the design of our case studies.

ROLL-CALL[4]

Women U.S. military personnel and veterans are misunderstood and misrepresented because their stories and contributions have been marginalized from public accounts (Grohowski, 2014; DAV, 2014; Santovec, 2015). In the paragraphs that follow, I align information about the social locations Tanya and BriGette occupy, alongside national statistics of female U.S. military personnel and veterans; I do so in an effort to foster increased understanding of Tanya and BriGette's positionalities, including the vulnerabilities they face as disabled American women veterans. Information is provided in Table 2.1.

Tanya is a white woman in her late thirties (see Figure 2.1). BriGette is a black woman in her mid-forties (see Figure 2.2). Tanya and BriGette are representative of the two largest demographics of U.S. women military veterans nationally. In fact, the National Center for Veterans Analysis and Statistics (NCVAS) (2016) revealed "White Non-Hispanic" women comprise 67.3 percent of the national population of women veterans, while "Non-White Non-Hispanic" women veterans comprise 24.4 percent (p. 17). These statistics correlate with Pew Research

---

4   In all branches of the U.S. military, roll call is "the act or the time of calling over a list of names of person belonging to an organization, in order to ascertain who are present, or to obtain responses from those present" (Farrow, 1919, p. 519).

findings (see Patten & Parker, 2011), which calculated that white women made up the largest percentage of active duty servicewomen while black women were a close second (p. 5).

Table 2.1. Co-interpreter information

Co-Interpreter	Tanya	BriGette
Race	White	Black
Age	30–40	40–50
# Dependents	0	2
Status	Student & Service-Connected Disabled Veteran; Medically Retired	Service-Connected Disabled Veteran
Military Branch	Army	Army
Military Era	Persian Gulf II	Peace Time / Pre-Persian Gulf I
Military Occupational Specialty	Armament Repaired 45 (Tank Turret Repairer)	Data Telecommunications Specialist
Length of Service (years)	10.5	4
Deployments	3, Iraq	0
Rhetorical practices	Drawing & painting	Television & film public speaking & social media-networking
Noted experiences	Improvised Explosive Device (IED) blast	· Raped twice during service · Homelessness (1+)
+ Traumatic Brain Injury & Post-Traumatic Stress	Yes, both	Yes, both

In the same report by NCVAS, the largest percentages of women veterans served during "Gulf War II or post-9/11 (2001)." Tanya's ten and a half years of service falls into this category. Coming in at a close second is the number of women who served during "'Peacetime only' [from] May 1975 to July 1990," when BriGette served her four-year enlistment (p. 5).

Tanya is a combat veteran, though U.S. military and civilian societies have failed to recognize that women have been serving on the frontlines with men in every conflict since the Revolutionary War (Holm, 1992; Monahan & Neidel-Greenlee, 2010). Moreover, the Defense Business Board (DBB) (2010), using the total number of active duty military in 2010, identified that the majority of personnel, at forty percent, had *never been deployed*, while eleven percent had deployed three or more times (p. 23). In other words, of the less than one percent of the total U.S. population that serves in the post-9/11 military, a smaller segment deploy or see combat during their service (see Pew, 2011).

Figure 2.1. Tanya Schardt photo. Iraq 2003. Image description: Tanya is shown in Iraq in her army fatigues, holding her M16 and wearing a helmet. She is posed in front of a mural on a brick wall of Saddam Hussein with his arm raised. Photo courtesy of Schardt.

Although BriGette, unlike Tanya, was not exposed to combat, she experienced violence and trauma. BriGette was raped on two different occasions during the first year of her service. In 2016, the Department of Defense reported that 6,172 male and female active duty U.S. military personnel reported being sexually assaulted (raped) during the fiscal year—"a 1.5 percent increase from the reports made in fiscal year 2015" (p. 8). Researchers found that a military woman's "race and rank" had significant influence on experiencing sexual harassment (Buchanan et al., 2008, p. 358). Specifically, "black women reported experiencing more severe, less common forms of sexual harassment" than white female counterparts (Buchanan et al., 2008, p. 358). These findings correlate with Tanya's and BriGette's experiences.

Figure 2.2. BriGette McCoy photo. 1989. Photo courtesy of McCoy. Image description: BriGette is shown in Germany wearing her army (dress) uniform and hat.

INFLUENCES OF MILITARY EXPERIENCE

Writing on the over diagnosis of Posttraumatic Stress Disorder (PTSD / PTS[5]), Allan Horwitz and Jerome Wakefield (2012) noted, "twenty percent of returning veterans have PTSD" (p. 186). PTS results from military sexual trauma (MST) (Buchanan et al., 2008, p. 358; Kelly et al., 2008). Military women with PTS from MST have a high probability of homelessness (NCHV, n.d., p. 1). According to the National Coalition of Homeless Veterans (NCHV), the rate of female veteran homelessness has increased and female veterans with MST, "are 6.5 times more likely to experience homelessness" (p. 1). After honorably discharging from the military, BriGette found herself without a place to live while working to support herself and her family. Indeed, these diverse factors of social location influence how Tanya and BriGette experience and make meaning in their lives.

---

5   There's a divide on dropping the word "disorder" from the diagnosis "posttraumatic stress." Whereas Caplan (2011) and Rigg (2013) support the drop to reduce stigma and expose the source of soldiers' stress (e.g., war trauma), the APA support keeping the "D" to ensure veterans receive disability benefits. (See Moore, 2013).

DESIGN AND METHOD

My project, to which Tanya and BriGette contributed as case study co-interpreters, sought to address the rhetorical practices of female U.S. military veterans. Though Tanya and BriGette have unique and distinct multimodal rhetorical practices, both women share the premise that composing is a form of advocacy. Indeed, both women understand their rhetorical practices as forms of activism. Tanya's preferred practice of drawing is a private activity employing tactile composing technologies like pencil, paint, and charcoal; conversely, as a national public figure for women veterans, BriGette engages public technological platforms of video and social media. I conceive of both Tanya and BriGette's rhetorical practices as a form of feminist intervention within and beyond the military veteran community.

Both BriGette and Tanya possess and employ distinct rhetorical practices while negotiating unique barriers in order to compose. Though they share similar barriers in order to compose (e.g., anxiety, exhaustion, headaches, body pain), both enact diverse rhetorical strategies that demonstrate their exigency and agency to compose. Given the barriers they experience, the design and approval of our case studies hinged on reciprocity and collaboration. I had to be inclusive to their needs and preferences and able to accommodate their requests; however, Tanya and BriGette had to inform me of their needs and preferences so that I could oblige. Like Margaret Price (2003), I was approved to design procedures with co-interpreters from inception to account for their access needs. In accordance with the approved methods for our case study, data collection spanned the months of June through September 2013 and accounted for eight meetings. Whereas Tanya and I had face-to-face meetings at her home; BriGette and I held our meetings through telephone or video conferencing, due in part to our geographical distance and at her request—as physical and psychological barriers make electronic communications more accessible. BriGette informed me that when we talked by phone she'd lay in her bed; but when we talked through video conferencing, she sat in her "therapy chair," designed to relieve back pain.

Co-interpreters responded warmly to designing the methods for conducting our interviews and having options for participating. Institutional Review Board (IRB) approval for providing options for interviews was not an issue. Given my desire to foster reciprocity, it was imperative to design and employ accessible data collection methods. Employing accessible data collection methods is a form of political activism; it ensures that individuals whose voices have been historically and systematically marginalized from institutional or research practices can participate, thereby validating their experiences and influencing change (see Berry et al., 2012; Walters, 2010; Price, 2003).

Individual interviews lasted between one and two hours. While the audio of each meeting was recorded, I took handwritten notes to attune myself to listen and retain information. Though I prepared for each interview with a list of topics or questions, I promoted the concept of "co-interpreter" by letting Tanya or BriGette lead. Interviews that generated the most on-point content to my research questions were facilitated through the process of artifact interviews.[6] As Doug Hesse, Nancy Sommers, and Kathleen Blake Yancey (2012) have explained: inquiry upon objects, "provoked observations and feelings, associations and questions we likely would not have produced through other means" (p. 326). Tanya and BriGette exemplified Hesse et al.'s (2012) claim. Because both women suffer from Traumatic Brain Injury (TBI) and Posttraumatic Stress (PTS), as they have explained: psychological and physiological processes influence their memories. However, when our conversations began with their artifacts (e.g., drawings; photographs; videos) both women shared candidly. In order to explain my methodology of reciprocity, I begin with an explanation of how I fostered understanding—a crucial first step in establishing reciprocal relationships and conducting ethical research as a form of feminist intervention.

UNDERSTANDING OR RESEARCH STANCE: EMBRACING THE MARGIN

As a feminist researcher during the ninth and "final" year of the war in Iraq (2011), I found inspiration in Sandra Harding's (1991) call for researchers to "reinvent [them-] selves as other" (p. 268). Lucky for me, I was already ware of my status as "other" to the population and issue I sought to investigate (the rhetorical practices of military women) and as a writing studies researcher. I felt empowered by Harding's call for a "standpoint," or "research stance" (Grabill, 2012) that "exploit[s] the gap . . . [between] margin and center" as a valuable site for meaning making (p. 276). Krista Ratcliffe (2005), Shannon Walters (2010), and Jay Dolmage and Cynthia Lewiecki-Wilson (2010) have identified the advantages of inquiry taken up from the margins. In her work on "cross cultural identification," Ratcliffe (2005) considered "the margin between" identification with others as offering an awareness (p. 73). In their work on feminist disability studies, Dolmage and Lewiecki-Wilson (2010) suggested researchers to "look to the margins to understand the function of the outlier as the ground against which particular forms of knowledge come into view" (p. 32). Though my social location was difficult to accept initially, my ability to move between identification and non-identification with co-interpreters was precisely how I was able to develop reciprocal relationships with Tanya and BriGette.

---

6   The audio and transcript is an example of an artifact interview with Tanya (see p. 48).

My efforts to foster reciprocal relationships with Tanya and BriGette were conceived as a result of understanding my social location or positionality as researcher; reflectively occupying "the margin and the center" (Harding, 1991; Ratcliffe, 2005; Dolmage & Lewiecki-Wilson, 2010) allowed me to sidestep an authoritative "researcher" stance so that I could be open to receive their ideas and expertise. By situating myself "in between" understanding, I became aware of Tanya and BriGette's generosity and of opportunities that I could respond to their offers in kind, thereby fostering reciprocity. Though I primarily use their names, I also use the term "co-interpreter." Articulating my use of the term supports my methodology in which reciprocity is epicenter and the degree to which the reciprocal strategies of understanding, listening, and strategic disclosure facilitated additional opportunities for fostering reciprocal relationships as a form of feminist intervention.

DEFINING TERMINOLOGY: CO-INTERPRETER

My use of the term "co-interpreter" was inspired by Thomas Newkirk (1996), who suggested that researchers invite participants to "respond to interpretations [and] offer counterinterpretations" (p. 13). Newkirk is neither the first nor the only scholar to suggest such collaboration (see Lather, 1986; Kirsch, 1993; Grabill, 2007; Spinuzzi, 2005; Powell and Takayoshi, 2003; Cushman, 1996; Berry et al., 2012; Adams, this collection; Rosenberg & Howes, this collection). Nevertheless, it is from Newkirk that I borrow the term and practice of soliciting counter-interpretations to data, findings, and drafts. At times, I refer to Tanya and BriGette as "co-interpreters." But as Takayoshi (2003) explained in her efforts to foster reciprocity with her research participant Nicky—Tanya and BriGette did not embrace the acts Newkirk and others promote.

Like feminists, disability studies scholars interrogate and subvert issues of hegemony and inequality. A disability perspective challenges "normalcy" and "ability" and substantiates how disability is a critical and generative site for meaning making (Dolmage & Lewiecki-Wilson, 2010, pp. 31–32). Furthermore, as Shannon Walters (2010) has stressed, research methodologies informed by disability are activist in projects that include individuals with disabilities as co-researchers or interpreters (p. 434). Because Tanya and BriGette both identify as disabled American veterans, and because their unique social locations influence their perspectives, I came to rely on Tanya and BriGette as co-interpreters in shaping research findings and outcomes. Integrating Newkirk's concept was one effort I made to foster reciprocal relationships with Tanya and BriGette, an effort facilitated through the process of listening.

LISTENING TO FOSTER UNDERSTANDING

I've been told that I am a "good listener." But after listening to audio-recorded practice interviews, I found I was *not* a good listener. Of course, "good listening" is vital in qualitative human subject-based research and compounded by the fact co-interpreters admitted to feeling unheard in U.S. civilian and military/veteran cultures. A researcher can jeopardize data collection if she does not listen effectively. Listening is challenging and always biased (DeVault & Gross, 2012). Furthermore, to learn to listen one must "unlearn" one's habituated listening practices (Ceraso, 2014; Ratcliffe, 2005).

Determined to listen for understanding and to foster respect for my co-interpreter's unique insights, I followed Margorie DeVault and Glenda Gross's (2012) advice and acknowledged my listening limitations. I made notes and developed codes that accounted for my listening biases, e.g., when I interrupted or spoke over the interviewee and if, when, and how I filled the gaps instead of allowing for silence to bookend the interviewee's response. During a practice interview, I interrupted my interviewee with what I anticipated would be her response. After asking the interviewee a question and before she could answer, I'd offer the guess I'd contrived in my head. I learned that not only were my assumptions always wrong, but by listening to see if my guesses were right, *I wasn't listening*. Indeed, as Ratcliffe (2005) has argued: "listen to discourses not *for* intent but . . . *with* the intent to understand" (p. 28 emphasis original). In other words, to be a good listener I had to stop listening to hear my ideas parroted back.

Though this process was time consuming and humbling, it elicited reflection, questioning, and critical understanding akin to feminist research (See Johnston, this collection; Royster & Kirsch, 2012; Reinharz, 1992). Furthermore, it offered a means of "accountability for checking my practices and approaches" (Johnston, this collection) and the opportunity to unlearn my bad listening habits. Stephanie Ceraso has argued that listening is dependent on making the familiar strange. When I was able to "defamiliarize" the process of listening during practice interviews, I began to grasp Ceraso's suggestion for a heightened approach to listening that is contingent upon occupying a marginal space feminist and disability studies scholars call for to increase understanding (Harding, 1991; Ratcliffe, 2005; Dolmage & Lewiecki-Wilson, 2010).

By listening, I grasped Nancy Naples' (2003) thorough disproving of the "insider / outsider debate," which she identifies as catalyst for neglecting the fluidity of identity and one's social location. However, as Ceraso (2014) and Ratcliffe (2005) attest: listening and as a result, understanding, occurs through multiple modes of communication. Ready to listen to women veterans, I took to social media (i.e., Facebook) where I put in time and effort to listen to women veterans.

Jen Almjeld and Kristine Blair (2012) and Heidi McKee and James Porter (2010) support this approach. While Almjeld and Blair (2012) credit the affordances of the Internet (and social media platforms in particular) for aiding the researcher in establishing and maintaining a transparent identity, McKee and Porter (2010) discuss the considerable labor involved in establishing one's credibility online. By approaching my interactions online from the framework discussed above (offered by Harding, 1991; Ratcliffe, 2005; Dolmage & Lewiecki-Wilson; Naples, 2003), while I clocked many hours listening (or observing) in online communities to female veterans, when I acted, I did so in a reciprocal manner as inspired by Ellen Cushman's (1996) activist efforts—I offered my assistance to women's requests I could provide. I answered one woman's request for help completing a disability claim form. While what I did was according to rhetoric and composition scholars a form of activism (see Blythe, 2012; Cushman 1996, 1999; Gildenspire, 2010; Goldblatt, 2007; Grabill, 2007). I acted with the intention of being reciprocal—to give back for all of the information and insights I received as a member in an online community.

Like Dirk Remley (2012), I was reluctant to use the "activist" label because I tend to think of activism on a grander scale, as being part of a movement. But as a feminist researcher working in an area of disability studies, I am apart of two activist movements. I am by default, performing activist interventions (Dolmage & Lewiecki-Wilson, 2010, pp. 32–33; Walters, 2010, p. 434). The type of activism I am comfortable with is on a personal level—when I am personally equipped to do so. But in re-reading Cushman (1996), I understand that these efforts are activist in nature when, as Blair (2012) has maintained, such actions are "deploy[ed with] an activist politics," or "with the goal of empowerment in mind" (pp. 65–66). These feminist interventions allowed me to interact with women veterans, which compelled women veterans, by their own volition, to "vouch" for me when I posted.[7] Listening with the intent to understand taught me that in the women veteran community, reciprocity and trust are paramount. Thanks to the scholarship of Lauren Rosenberg and Emma Howe, I have come to conceive "*listening [in and of itself as] a feminist intervention*" (this collection, emphasis added).

I was able to initiate the long process of gaining trust and establishing my credibility by practicing transparency and reciprocity on Facebook, which is where I met BriGette. I reached out to her after seeing her in the documentary *Service: When Women Come Marching Home* (2011). Contacting her through

---

7   Requests for participation on electronic surveys for dissertation research.

Facebook was intentional because in the documentary[8] she credits Facebook for helping her meet other women veterans and learn about resources. However, contacting BriGette through Facebook was also my only method. We did not share mutual contacts or a geographic location. Our correspondence was limited to and possible because of social media. I didn't start out by asking her to be my research subject, though I was interested in learning more about her and saw her rhetorical practices as feminist and activist. Instead, I asked if I could do anything for her. Once she learned that I was a student and researcher, she suggested the idea of a case study to me. To listen to that conversation or to read the written transcript of it, visit https://soundcloud.com/mariana-mare-grohowski/clip-of-phone-conversation. I share this short excerpt to exemplify the reciprocal nature of how our conversations occurred. The listener can hear our shared laughter as well as identify how the tones of our voices reflect our feelings and personalities. Though this conversation occurred in 2013, BriGette and I regularly have conversations like the one in the audio clip—full of laughter and dialogic reciprocity.

One of my colleagues, Tanya's former writing teacher, initiated our connection. We met at our campus Starbucks and I offered to buy her chai. She appreciated this small gesture and agreed to meet the following week. It took dozens of cups of chai and conversation for Tanya to trust me to share any of her military experiences. In short, relationships with BriGette and Tanya were established in advance of requests for research studies. Had these relationships not first been established, I would not have sought out the approval to conduct case studies.

I wanted to be as reciprocal as possible for three reasons: (1) Because of the personal relationships I had established with Tanya and BriGette; (2) the generosity of their time, expertise, and support to me as I was undergoing my research; and (3) because I understood that as former members of the military they were trained to serve. In fact, some veterans consider military service as the highest form of civic engagement (Handley, 2016). And recent research indicates that veterans volunteer more than other segments of the U.S. population (Matthieu, 2016). Given Tanya and BriGette's exigency to serve and contribute to my research, I argue that reciprocity as a form of feminist intervention is imperative when working with current, former, and future members of the military.

Over time, it became apparent[9] that both women had their own activist goals in mind. Both women saw the platform of my research as potential to disprove limiting stereotypes about military women and disabled veterans. Indeed, their

---

8   Which she maintains in her Senate testimony. (See H031313, 2013).

9   From the (individual) conversations I had with Tanya and BriGette respectively.

motivation to participate was in part an activist effort to facilitate social change for disabled American women veterans.

STRATEGIC DISCLOSURE AS RECIPROCITY

Whereas reciprocation is defined as an exchange for mutual benefit or as responding to offers in kind; strategic disclosure is defined as an exchange of information. Margaret Gutsell and Kathleen Hulgin (2014) liken strategic disclosure to fostering inclusion through information design. The authors have called for the use of "narratives to construct and promote a common sense . . . [and] provide the opportunity for vicarious experience" between interviewer and interviewee (pp. 91–92). Considered as a practice of active listening, I experimented with strategic disclosure during interviews. Because I wanted to foster understanding and identification with them, at times I disclosed personal information in the hopes of softening feelings of uneasiness when they shared sensitive information.

During interviews, opportunities would arise in their narrative retellings where I related to their expressed emotions or scenarios. For example, as I came to understand the frustration Tanya experienced in her relationships with her sisters, I shared that I too have a complicated relationship with my sister. In short, moments presented themselves where I felt compelled to strategically disclose personal details I would otherwise withhold. DeVault and Gross (2012) classified strategic disclosure as a form of "feminist interviewing" where the interviewer "reveal[s] research interests and political commitments" (p. 215). Keeping with my goals as a feminist researcher to be transparent, reflective, and reciprocal: practicing strategic disclosure was a method not unlike those employed in other areas of my collaborative research i.e., sharing interview codes or emerging findings.

I would employ strategic disclosure when interviewing Tanya and BriGette in order to acknowledge the relevance of their narrative experiences, and to encourage their continued involvement in the project. I practiced brevity and moderation in my efforts, given what I had learned about myself during my practice interviews. I did not want to monopolize the interview, which they could interpret as not listening or invalidating their experiences and perspectives. Acts of information reciprocation (i.e., strategic disclosure) in interviews fostered a conversational approach advocated by Cynthia Selfe and Gail Hawisher (2012), whose work implies the use of strategic disclosure in their interviews with participants; Selfe and Hawisher's work promote the feminist agenda of pushing against "boundaries" of "traditional" research practices by fostering empathy and understanding with co-interpreters, which thereby broadens our understanding of how knowledge is made and shared (Selfe & Hawisher, 2012; Cushman, 1996; Kirsch, 1993). Our interviews were opportunities for collaborative meaning making. For example, the following video clip and written transcript (accessible at https://youtu.be/od8Y5aXWZPQ) showcases Tanya and I discussing her watercolor painting "Chaos."[10]

An additional act of reciprocation initiated through strategic disclosure resulted in a collaborative project between BriGette's nonprofit and my intermediate writing class. During one of our interviews, BriGette expressed her passion for education, digital pedagogy, and a desire to compose and broadcast video interviews with grassroots advocates working on veterans' issues. In the interest of reciprocating her generosity as co-interpreter, I disclosed that I was in the process of designing a service-learning course where my students could treat BriGette as a "community partner" or client to "write for" (Deans, 2000). Students prepared questions and pitched their ideas for executing her plan. Over the course of the semester, students composed a website for her project (see figure 2.3). Each military veteran and advocate has her own individual page with information about her contributions to the veteran social justice community.

Figure 2.3. Screenshot of students' website. Retrieved from https://veteransocialjustice.wordpress.com/

To gather information about their advocate, students had to immerse themselves into the veteran community and become ethical online researchers

---

10   When Tanya speaks I hear strength, certainty, and calm-composure in her voice though she is being vulnerable by sharing the details of her emotional battles. Conversely, in my voice I hear nervousness while trying to convey genuine admiration of her artwork and feelings.

(McKee & Porter, 2010; Almjeld & Blair, 2012). Fostering reciprocity with BriGette while encouraging her expertise and interest was the impetus of the community partnership and students' activist project. BriGette was pleased by this endeavor because she has spoken publically about it.[11] Similar acts of strategic disclosure, reciprocation, and activism happened between Tanya and me. To facilitate Tanya's expressed interest in sharing her military contributions and sacrifices with a broader audience, and in order to change her disparaging experiences as a student veteran on our shared college campus, I introduced Tanya to faculty members and staff who could help her share her story. Tanya has since shared her narrative in multiple class lectures and was spotlighted by her campus and community as a change agent for disabled students and female veterans (see Carle, 2015; Feehan, 2015).

CONCLUSION

A feminist methodology for which reciprocity is epicenter, facilitated through the interrelated practices of understanding, listening, and strategic disclosure has allowed me to develop reciprocal and lasting relationships with co-interpreters, Tanya and BriGette.

Figure 2.4. Mariana & Tanya, 2015. Grohowski photo.

---

11   She shared the partnership in her video interview for Veterans Helping Veterans (see https://www.youtube.com/watch?v=Qqsh8X7Okl4).

Fig 2.5. Mariana & BriGette, 2013. Grohowski photo.

Deploying a methodology that privileges reciprocation and relationship building fostered collaborative, activist efforts within the community of disabled American female veterans and is a form of feminist intervention. While reciprocation is claimed by many scholars to be an "essential" practice for ethical research, it is not a given in all research relationships and should not be treated as such. Indeed, Powell and Takayoshi (2003; 2004) argued that establishing reciprocal relationships with participants is not always in a researcher's best interest, let alone is it always possible. Establishing and maintaining a reciprocal relationship—especially between researcher and a co-interpreter is a member of a vulnerable population—is complicated and labor-intensive work, as articulated by Megan Adams in her chapter in this collection. Like Adams, Eli Goldblatt (2007) has articulated the demands of reciprocal relationship building. In short, Goldblatt, among others link relationship building with research participants and community partners to activism (see Sheridan-Rabideau, 2009; Blair et al., 2011; Blythe, 2012; Cushman, 1996, 1999). Reciprocal relationship building in research with individuals from marginalized populations, such as disabled American female veterans, is considered a form of activism and therefore, feminist intervention because research projects can amplify the voices of individuals who that have been marginalized from traditional research

(Walters, 2010). Working with individuals from marginalized populations and tackling issues of social justice, is and has always been, an essential element of feminist theory building and praxis (see Blair & Tulley, 2007; Blair, 2012; Royster & Kirsch, 2012; Dolmage & Lewiecki-Wilson, 2010; Harding, 2012). As I have articulated, reciprocity and activism can be fostered through many forms. The methodological practices of understanding, listening, and strategic disclosure, though they are fraught with complications and place additional demands on researchers and co-interpreters, offer feminist interventionists a means of fostering

REFERENCES

Almjeld, J. & Blair, K. L. (2012). Multimodal methods for multimodal literacies: Establishing a technofeminist research identity. In K. L. Arola & A. F. Wysocki (Eds.), *Composing (media) = composing (embodiment): Bodies, technologies, writing, and the teaching of writing* (pp. 97–109). Logan, UT: Utah State University Press.

American Psychiatric Association. (2013). Diagnostic and statistical manual of mental disorders. (5th Ed). Arlington, VA: American Psychiatric Publishing.

Blair, K. L. (2012). A complicated geometry: Triangulating feminism, activism, and technological literacy. In L. Nickoson & M. P. Sheridan (Eds.), *Writing studies research in practice: Methods and methodologies* (pp. 63–72). Carbondale, IL: Southern Illinois University Press.

Blair, K. L., Fredlund, K., Hauman, K., Hurford, E., Kastner, S. & Witte, A. (2011). Cyberfeminists at play: Lessons on literacy and activism from a girls' computer camp. *Feminist Teacher, 22*(1), 43–59.

Blair, K. & Tulley, C. (2007). Whose research is it, anyway? The challenge of deploying feminist methodology in technological spaces. In D. DeVoss & H. McKee (Eds.), *Digital writing research* (pp. 303–317). Cresskill, NJ: Hampton Press.

Berry, P. W., Hawisher, G.E. & Selfe, C. L. (2012). *Transnational literate lives in digital times.* Logan, UT: Computers and Composition Digital Press/Utah State University Press. Retrieved from http://ccdigitalpress.org/transnational/.

Blythe, S. (2012). Composing activist research. In K. M. Powell & P. Takayoshi (Eds.), *Practicing research in writing studies: Reflexive and ethically responsible research* (pp. 275–292). New York, NY: Hampton Press

Buchanan, N., Settles, I. & Woods, K. (2008). Comparing sexual harassment subtypes among black and white women by military rank: Double jeopardy, the jezebel, and the cult of true womanhood. *Psychology of Women Quarterly, 32*(4), 347–361.

Carle, J. (2015). Class of 2015 success stories: True grit. Bowling Green State University News. Retrieved from http://bgsu.edu/news/2015/05.html.

Ceraso, S. (2014). (Re)Educating the senses: Multimodal listening, bodily learning, and the composition of sonic experiences. *College English, 77*(2), 102–123.

Chase, S. E. (1995). Ambiguous empowerment: The work of narratives of women school superintendents. Amherst, MA: Massachusetts University Press.

Cushman, E. (1996). The rhetorician as an agent of social change. *College Composition and Communication, 47*(1), 7–28.

———. (1999). The public intellectual, service learning, and activist research. *College English 61*(3): 328–336

Cushman, E., Powell, K. & Takayoshi, P. (2004). Response to 'accepting the roles created for us: The ethics of reciprocity. *College Composition and Communication, 56*(1), 115–156.

Deans, T. (2000). *Writing partnerships: Service-learning in composition.* Urbana, IL: NCTE.

Defense Business Board. (2010). Reducing overhead and improving business operations: Initial observations. Retrieved from http://dbb.defense.gov/Portals/35/Documents/Reports/2010/FY10-10.

Department of Defense. (2017). Annual report on sexual assault in the military fiscal year 2016. Retrieved from http://sapr.mil/public/docs/reports/FY15_Annual/FY15_Annual_Report_on_Sexual_Assault_in_the_Military.pdf.

Department of Labor. (2013). Section 503. Vietnam era veterans' readjustment assistance act of 1973. Retrieved from http://www.dol.gov/ofccp/regs/compliance/vevraa/vevraa_rule_qa_508c.pdf.

Department of the Army. (2003, September). TC 25–20 A leader's guide to after-action reviews. Washington, D.C.: Headquarters Department of the Army. Retrieved from http://www.acq.osd.mil/dpap/ccap/cc/jcchb/Files/Topical/After_Action_Report/resources/tc25-20.pdf.

DeVault, M. L. & Gross, G. (2012). Feminist qualitative interviewing: Experience, talk, and knowledge. In S. N. Hesse-Biber (Ed.), *The handbook of feminist research: Theory and praxis* (2nd ed., pp. 206–236). Los Angeles, CA: Sage.

Disabled American Veterans. (2014). *Women veterans: The long journey home.* Cold Springs, KY: Disabled American Veterans. Retrieved from https://www.dav.org/wp-content/uploads/women-veterans-study.pdf.

Dolmage, J. & Lewiecki-Wilson, C. (2010). Refiguring rhetorica: Linking feminist rhetoric and disability studies. In E. E. Schell & K. J. Rawson (Eds.), *Rhetorica in motion: Feminist methods and methodologies* (pp. 23–38). Pittsburg, PA: University of Pittsburg Press.

Farrow, E. S. (1918). "Roll call." *A dictionary of military terms,* (p. 519). New York, NY: Thomas Crowell Company.

Feehan, J. (2015, May 10). Army vet conquers battle for college degrees at BGSU. *Toledo Blade.* Retrieved from http://www.toledoblade.com/Education/2015/05/10/Army-vet-conquers-battle-for-college-degrees-at-BGSU.html.

Flower, L. (2008). *Community literacy and the rhetoric of public engagement.* Carbondale, IL: Southern Illinois University Press.

Gindlesparger, K. J. (2010). The sadder the story, the bigger the check: Reciprocity as an answer to organizational deficit models. *Community Literacy Journal, 5*(1), 96–106.

Goldblatt, E. (2007). Because we live here: Sponsoring literacy beyond the college curriculum. Cresskill, NJ: Hampton Press.

Gorzelsky, G. (2012). An experimental approach to literacy studies. In K. M. Powell & P. Takayoshi (Eds.), *Practicing research in writing studies: Reflexive and ethically responsible research* (pp. 349–372). New York, NY: Hampton Press.

Grohowski, M. (2014). Moving words, words that move: Language practices plaguing U.S. servicewomen. *Women and Language, 37*(1), 121–130.

Grabill, J. T. (2007). *Writing community change: Designing technologies for citizen action.* Cresskill, NJ: Hampton Press.

———. (2012). Community-based research and the importance of a research stance. In L. Nickoson & M. P. Sheridan (Eds.), *Writing studies research in practice: Methods and methodologies* (pp. 210–219). Carbondale, IL: Southern Illinois University Press.

Gutsell, M. & Hulgin, K. (2014). Superscripts don't fly: Technical communication to support ordinary lives of people with disabilities. In L. Meloncon (Ed.), *Rhetorical accessibility: At the intersection of technical communication and disability studies* (pp. 83–95). Amityville, NY: Baywood Publishing Company.

H031313. (2013). Sexual Assaults in the military: Hearing before the Subcommittee on Personnel, U.S. Senate. [Full transcript]. Retrieved January 24, 2015 from http://www.armed-services.senate.gov/imo/media/doc/13-10-3-13-13.pdf.

Harding, S. (1987). *Feminism and methodology: Social science issues.* Bloomington, IN: Indiana University Press.

Harding, S. (1991). *Whose science? Whose knowledge? Thinking from women's lives.* Ithaca, NY: Cornell University Press.

———. (2012). Feminist standpoints. In S.N. Hesse-Biber (Ed.), *The handbook of feminist research: Theory and praxis* (2nd ed., pp. 46–64). Los Angeles, CA: Sage.

Handley, D. (2016, April). Another mission: Citizenship pedagogy in the first-year writing classroom. Paper presented at the annual Conference on College Composition and Communication. Houston, TX.

Hesse, D., Sommers, N. & Yancey, K. B. (2012). Evocative objects: Reflections on teaching, learning, and living in between. *College English, 74*(4), 324–350.

Himley, M. (2004). Facing (up to) 'the stranger' in community service learning. *College Composition and Communication, 55*(3), 416–438.

Holm, J. M. (1992). *Women in the military: An unfinished revolution* (2nd ed.). Novato, CA: Presidio Press.

Horwitz, A. & Wakefield, J. (2012). *All we have to fear: Psychiatry's transformation of natural anxieties into mental disorders.* Oxford, England: Oxford University Press.

Jack, J. (2009). We have brains: Reciprocity as resistance in a feminist blog community. In K. L. Blair, R. Gajjala & C. Tulley (Eds.), *Webbing cyberfeminist practice: Communities, pedagogies, and social action* (pp. 327–344). Cresskill, NJ: Hampton Press.

Kelly, M., Vogt, D., Scheiderer, E., Ouimette, P., Daley, J. & Wolfe, J. (2008). Effects of military trauma exposure on women veterans' use and perceptions of veterans' health administration care. *Journal of General Internal Medicine, 23*(6), 741–747.

Kirsch, G. E. (1993). *Women writing the academy: Audience, authority, and transformation.* Carbondale, IL: Southern Illinois University Press.

———. (1999). *Ethical dilemmas in feminist research: The politics of location, interpretation, and publication.* Albany, NY: State University of New York Press.

Lather, P. (1986). Research as praxis. *Harvard Educational Review, 56*(3), 257–277.

MacNealy, M. S. (1999). *Strategies for empirical research in writing.* Boston, MA: Allyn & Bacon.

Matthieu, M. (2016). The mission continues: A conceptual framework and selected brief screening measures for evaluating civic service and health outcomes among returning U.S. veterans from Iraq and Afghanistan. *Journal of Veterans Studies, 1*(1).

McKee, H. A. & Porter, J. E. (2010). Rhetorica online: Feminist research practices in cyberspace. In E. E. Schell & K. J. Rawson (Eds.), *Rhetorica in motion: Feminist methods and methodologies* (pp. 152–170). Pittsburg, PA: University of Pittsburg Press.

Monahan, E. M. & Neidel-Greenlee, R. (2010). A few good women: America's military women from World War I to the wars in Iraq and Afghanistan. New York, NY: Anchor.

Moore, B. (2013, April). 'Disorder' is proper label for post-traumatic stress. *Army Times,* 32–33.

Naples, N. A. (2003). Feminism and method: Ethnography, discourse analysis, and activist research. New York, NY: Routledge.

National Center for Veterans Analysis and Statistics. (2016, March). *Profile of women veterans: 2014.* Retrieved from http://www.va.gov/vetdata/docs/SpecialReports/Women_Veterans_2016.pdf.

National Coalition of Homeless Veterans. (n.d.). *Homeless Female Veterans White Paper.* Retrieved from http://www.nchv.org/images/uploads/HFV%20paper.pdf.

Newkirk, T. (1996). Seduction and betrayal in qualitative research. In P. Mortensen & G. E. Kirsch (Eds.), *Ethics & representation in qualitative studies of literacy* (pp. 3–16). Urbana, IL: NCTE.

Orr, C. M. (2011). *Women's studies as civic engagement: Research and recommendations.* National Women's Studies Association and Teagle foundation. Retrieved from http://www.nwsa.org/files/WomensStudiesasCivicEngagement2011Revised_Finalpdf-1.pdf.

Patten, E. & Parker, K. (2011). *Women in the U.S. military: Growing share, distinctive profile. Rep.* Washington DC: Pew Research Center. Retrieved from http://www.pewsocialtrends.org/women.

Pew Research Center Social & Demographic Trends. (2011). *The Military-civilian gap: War and sacrifice in the post-9/11 era.* Retrieved from http://www.pewsocialtrends.org/files/2011/10/veterans-report.pdf.

Powell, K. M. & Takayoshi, P. (2003). Accepting the roles created for us: The ethics of reciprocity. *College Composition and Communication, 54*(3), 394–422.

Price, M. (2003). Mad at school: Rhetorics of mental disability and academic life. Ann Arbor, MI: University of Michigan Press.

Ratcliffe, K. (2005). *Rhetorical listening: Identification, gender, whiteness.* Carbondale, IL: Southern Illinois University Press.

Reinharz, S. (1992). *Feminist methods in social research.* New York, NY: Oxford University Press.

Remley, D. (2012). Re-considering the range of reciprocity in community-based research and service learning: You don't have to be an activist to give back. *Community Literacy Journal, 6*(2), 115–132.

Rigg, J. (2013). Traumatic brain injury and post-traumatic stress: The 'signature wounds' of the Iraq and Afghanistan wars. In R. M. Scurfield & Col K. T. Plantoni (Eds.), *War trauma and its wake: Expanding the circle of healing* (pp. 113–133). New York, NY: Routledge.

Royster, J. J. (2000). Traces of a stream: Literacy and social change among African American women. Pittsburg, PA: University of Pittsburg Press.

Royster, J. J. & Kirsch, G. E. (2012). Feminist rhetorical practices: New horizons for rhetoric, composition, and literacy studies. Carbondale, IL: Southern Illinois University Press.

Santovec, M. L. (2015). Women vets: An underserved population. *Women in Higher Education, 24*(1), 1–2.

Selfe, C. L. & Hawisher, G. E. (2012). Exceeding the bounds of the interview: Feminism, mediation, narrative and conversations about digital literacy. In L. Nickoson & M. P. Sheridan (Eds.), *Writing studies research in practice: Methods and methodologies* (pp. 36–50). Carbondale, IL: Southern Illinois University Press.

Sheridan-Rabideau, M. P. (2009). *Girls, feminism, and grassroots literacies: Activism in the girlzone.* Albany, NY: State University of New York Press.

Smagorinsky, P. (2008). The methods section as conceptual epicenter in constructing social science research reports. *Written Communication, 25*(3), 389–411.

Smith, L. T. (2012). *Decolonizing methodologies: Research and indigenous peoples* (2nd ed.). New York, NY: Zed Books, Ltd.

Spinuzzi, C. (2005). The methodology of participatory design. *Technical Communication, 52*(2), 163–174.

Walters, S. (2010). Toward an accessible pedagogy: Dis/ability, multimodality, and universal design in the technical communication classroom. *Technical Communication Quarterly, 19*(4), 427–454.

Williamson, M. M. & Huot, B. (2012). A modest proposal for common ground and language for research in writing. In K. M. Powell & P. Takayoshi (Eds.), *Practicing research in writing studies: Reflexive and ethically responsible research* (pp. 31–58). New York, NY: Hampton Press.

CHAPTER 3.
METHODOLOGY & ACCOUNTABILITY: TRACKING OUR MOVEMENTS AS FEMINIST PEDAGOGUES

Emily Ronay Johnston
The University of Delaware

Johnston considers negotiating boundaries as a form of feminist activism: a dynamic process of articulating the ethics of our research practices. As a white, female, postdoctoral researcher teaching at a predominantly white, middle- and upper-class university in the Mid-Atlantic, she conceptualizes "ethical practice" as methods that challenge students to stretch the limits of their privileged comfort zones—methods that may not be feasible, desirable, appropriate, or indeed "ethical" in other settings where feminist research happens. To contend with our differing positionalities as feminist researchers, Johnston suggests a conceptualization of "ethical" as "accountable"—one that can travel across the diverse "spaces, conditions, cultures, and migrations" (Kirsch & Royster, 2013) in which we do feminist work; for the borders demarcating those contexts; and for how borders change in relation to our own geographic, positional, ideological movements.

Over the past decade feminist rhetoricians have taken up research methods and methodologies with renewed interest, navigating the vast terrain of how feminist researchers "sustain scholarly work" (Schell & Rawson, 2010, p. 3)—particularly during a cultural moment when feminism has been declared "dead." As our research increasingly permeates the naturalized boundaries between "local" and "global," "private" and "public," "academy" and "community," we risk losing boundaries altogether. Boundaries protect, they help us navigate chaos. Yet if boundaries become rigid, we risk perpetuating the very violence our work resists.

This chapter considers boundary-setting as a feminist intervention: a dynamic process of negotiating the ethics of our research practices in relation to the material, embodied needs and desires of participants in our studies. As a white, female, postdoctoral researcher fresh out of graduate school, teaching at a predominantly white, middle- and upper-class university in the Mid-Atlantic, I conceptualize "ethical" as practices that question the borders of students' privileged comfort zones—practices that may not be feasible, desirable, appropriate, or indeed "ethical" in other settings where feminist research happens. To contend with our differing positionalities as feminist researchers, I suggest a conceptualization of ethical as accountable, a framing of ethics that can travel across contexts, temporalities, and career stages, and that accounts for the diverse "spaces, conditions, cultures, and migrations" (Kirsch & Royster, 2013) in which we do feminist work, as well as how our own geographic, positional, ideological movements (re)shape those materialities.

Accountability signals a need for checking the intentions, desires, assumptions, and beliefs that inform our practices. *Who and what do we deem worthy of research, and why? Where does our research physically happen? In classrooms, online spaces, non-profit organizations, medical labs, courtrooms, movie theaters, archives? At what point in our careers do we take on particular subjects of study? When and why do we postpone others? Do we collect data electronically, manually, aurally, visually, or even spiritually? Who is impacted by our processes of collection, and how?* Asking such questions can help us track where we enter, depart from, or avoid altogether different feminist conversations.

To be sure, feminist scholars have already posed similar questions regarding the ethics of our work (Royster & Kirsch, 2012; Schell & Rawson, 2010; Royster, 2003; Lunsford, 1995; Harding, 1987). For example, Sandra G. Harding (1987) articulates how feminist research raises epistemological questions of "who can be a knower," "what tests beliefs must pass in order to be legitimated as knowledge," and "what should be the purposes of the pursuit of knowledge" (p. 181). These questions are inherent in any research process, regardless of the degrees to which researchers explicitly take them up. Understanding ethical as accountable reveals how ethical practices are measured by how we answer, but more importantly, by having asked such questions in the first place. Questioning our practices is an ongoing setting and resetting of boundaries around what it means to be feminist, what legitimates our contributions to feminist research, what counts as a contribution, and why.

Conceptualizing accountability as an ethics-checker for our practices allows us to consider methodology itself as an accounting system. If we approach methodology etymologically—*method + -ology = the study of our methods*—we can discern how tracking our research methods holds all researchers accountable for how we use, and the effects of, the methods we select—choices that necessarily foreground and exclude particular subjects, locales, evidences, and theories. Approaching methodology as an accounting system allows us to recognize—to become conscious of again—methodological invention as an always-already feature of research. In other words, whether or not we articulate our methodologies, what Harding (1987) describes as our "theory and analysis of *how research does and should proceed*" (p. 3), they already exist, determined by the methods we do and do not employ, as well as by how our positionalities constrain our use of particular methods at any given moment. Constraints are not obstacles to overcome, but limitations to account for as rhetors "always fail" (Crowley & Hawhee, 2004, p. 32) to identify with all readers and listeners; failure "allows knowledge to grow and change" (Crowley & Hawhee, 2004, p. 32). Always partial and imperfect, determined by the methods we select *as well as how we use them*, methodology is the very impetus of scholarly work—a negotiation with ourselves, feminist colleagues and allies, and the communities in which we research.

Conceptualized relationally, methodology and accountability spotlight our own feminist practices as an exigent, ethical domain of inquiry. Moreover, conceptualizing methodology and accountability relationally reveals how all research demands response and reinvention. As Mieke Bal (2002) explains, concepts themselves "travel" (p. 24) across boundaries demarcating disciplines, academic communities, and individual scholars. Concepts' tendency towards "travel" allows us to take notice of what concepts (such as methodology) *do*, how they are *used*, and the *effects* and *risks* of those usages. Characterizing not just our concepts, but also feminist researchers ourselves in strikingly comparable linguistic movements to Bal, the aptly-titled collection, *Rhetorica in Motion: Feminist Rhetorical Methods & Methodologies* (Schell & Rawson, 2010) explicates how motion defines our work. Feminist rhetors inhabit, *Rhetorica in Motion* argues, the in-between. Given our own and our concepts' propensities for movement, becoming more conscious of what we are doing, how we are doing it, and how our doings *move* our research participants, again and again and again, is a feminist intervention. Conceptualizing methodology and accountability in relation to one another can help us approach the complex, often discomforting process of knowledge-making as one of negotiating what we know, have known, and have yet to know.

METHODOLOGY & ACCOUNTABILITY IN A CITIZENSHIP LITERACY CLASSROOM

To exemplify the methodological accountability I propose, I turn to interrogating my own pedagogical practices in teaching what I call *citizenship literacy*: the desire to critically read, listen, speak, and write about—i.e., to rhetorically engage with—our rights and responsibilities, as university members and global citizens, in confronting gendered injustices. In what follows, I examine my methods in a classroom-based study while teaching an undergraduate general education course cross-listed in English and Women's and Gender Studies, "Gender in the Humanities: Gender Violence in Global Contexts," at a Midwestern university (Johnston, 2013) in which I tested and further developed this concept of citizenship literacy. I outline the goals of citizenship literacy, and how I enacted these goals in the course. I reflect on how my intentions, desires, assumptions, and beliefs shaped the course design, as well as how students may or may not have gained from and determined the benefits of citizenship literacy.

Interrogating my pedagogical practices in the citizenship literacy classroom *is* a feminist intervention; it not only enacts the kind of methodological accountability I propose in this chapter, but it also explicitly links our work in the classroom with issues of social (in)justice that often catalyze our work in the first place. Moreover, interrogating my practices exposes the falsity of claims that "feminism is dead." In short, the course in which I did this study, my analysis of it, and the writing of this chapter *are* feminist interventions.

I developed the course as an interdisciplinary exploration of composition and gender through the lens of violence—a writing-intensive inquiry into how gendered norms, roles, and stereotypes can create a culture of violence and moreover, how such violence implicates all genders. The course aimed to help students identify their own rights and responsibilities in responding to issues of gendered violence, and to develop practical courses of action for ending such violence in their own communities. To investigate the relationships between gender and violence, and to develop community-based strategies for intervening in injustices we bore witness to in course content and our daily lives, I assigned a wide range of genres for students to read and produce, facilitated listening-based discussions, and required students to research local programs, groups, and/or other initiatives related to antiviolence.

GENRE DIVERSITY

By assigning readings across print and digital genres, I sought to advance students' engagement in a wide range of literacy learning. Genre diversity in the citizenship literacy course emphasized how "text," broadly understood, can tell us much about the rhetorical functions of a wide range of "material practices" (Royster & Kirsch, 2012, p. 61)—from conventionalized scholarly articles and literary texts that students typically expect in an English classroom, to the Federal Bureau of Investigation's (U.S. Department of Justice, 2014) updated legal definition of rape, which was unfamiliar to the majority of students in the course, and social media coverage of Robin Thicke's and Miley Cyrus's twerking performance of "Blurred Lines" at the 2013 MTV Music Awards (Islandfabrics,

2013). Emphasizing literacy learning as an ongoing dialogic process of crafting a tool that Jacqueline Jones Royster (2000) calls *"critical imagination,"* genre diversity worked to facilitate the course's simultaneous interrogation of "knowledge as truth" and its reimagination of knowledge as an assemblage of *both* what appears on the page, screen, or other medium *and* our speculations about "what is not there" and "what could be there instead" (Royster & Kirsch, 2012, p. 20). In putting different kinds of texts into conversation with one another, with attention to the affordances and limitations of different genres and modes, the course design mirrored how textual meaning is inflected by a writer's and a reader's beliefs and assumptions about the world, which change across time and space. In sum, genre diversity in the citizenship literacy course functioned as a catalyst for critical inquiry into gender.

In addition to advancing students' engagement with a wide range of literacy learning, I also utilized genre diversity to promote literacy learning as a form of civic engagement. Assigning readings across genres worked to trouble the naturalized divide between academic writing and public writing, which normalizes academe's de-authorization of students as knowers. *Color of Violence: The Incite! Anthology* (Incite! Women of Color Against Violence, 2006) inducted students into the intersectionality of violence, and offered writings by scholars, activists, poets, policy makers, and community organizers imagining, "What would it take *to end violence against women of color?*" (p. 4). *Women Write Resistance: Poets Resist Gender Violence* (Wiseman, 2013) modeled writing about embodied experience, in poetic form, of surviving rape, incest, domestic violence, bigotry, colonization, war, and other forms of violence born from misogyny. *Girl with the Dragon Tattoo* (Larsson, 2008; Yellow Bird & Oplev, 2009; Columbia Pictures & Fincher, 2011) opened up discussions of mass media and its ubiquitous representations of rape. By exposing students to these and other critical and creative texts, I intended to provide multiple modal, discursive, representational access points for students to take up course content.

As student responses to our readings revealed, genre diversity elicited an often-painful, yet determined coming-into-consciousness. For example, encountering *Girl with the Dragon Tattoo* in both literary and cinematic modes provoked, for one female student, empathic grief and a burgeoning awareness of how rape systematically traumatizes women. She described the difference between reading and then watching rape scenes in *Dragon Tattoo* as what she called a "brutal" physiological experience: "Although reading about [rape] had made me uncomfortable, actually seeing it brought me many emotions that had given me a scratchy neck . . . I could see [protagonist] Lisbeth crying and how painful she took the rape . . . with any type of gender violence, it destroys who you really are." Another female student's attempt to describe reading and watching

Lisbeth's rape produces a temporary interruption of speech (marked by ellipses), ultimately leading her to articulate her own feminist positionality, as well as a personal resolve to mitigate rape trauma by raising awareness of its misogynist roots: "I can't ignore these [rape] scenes and I need to just . . . try and process what they were for Lisbeth and what it means for women and what it means to me . . . Both incidents are vile displays of control . . . I feel really passionate about it. It's why I see myself as a feminist."

Both student writing samples convey a personal identification with Lisbeth as a female victim of rape, perhaps elicited by the experience of witnessing rape scenes in print as well as on screen. These and other female students in the course enacted a larger-scale feminist identification that went beyond the fictionalized rape victims in *Dragon Tattoo*, deepened their understanding of the long-term trauma of rape, and affirmed (or initiated) their positions as feminists. As these two student-journal excerpts exemplify, genre diversity in the course facilitated my goal of helping students acquire citizenship literacy through a wide range of literacy learning and an emphasis on literacy learning as a form of civic engagement.

Despite the generic diversity of readings, I privileged readings oriented towards feminized, victimized representations of gendered violence. I downplayed readings, discussion topics, writing prompts, and other course activities that explicitly dealt with masculinity or men; with non-cisgender identities such as intersex, bigender, gender fluid, gender non-conforming, genderqueer, and gender variant; and/or with perpetrators or perpetration. These exclusions, in retrospect, stem from what I failed to imagine, to borrow Royster's term—a failure to engage in "making connections and seeing possibility" (Royster & Kirsch, 2012, p. 19). I made a series of assumptions based on the very gendered, racialized paradigms that the course purported to interrogate: *Students need to start with the familiar if I am going to ask them to engage with traumatic material, and "familiar" for students means heterosexual and cisgender. White men are already at the center, so their experiences of victimization are less problematic, less traumatic, less important. Why should we consider perpetrators anyways? They committed crimes; they don't deserve our attention—especially in a feminist course.* While I did not recognize my *failure of imagination* until after the course had ended and I was well into writing this chapter, accounting for assumptions I made, embodiments I overlooked, and prejudices I rationalized as justice becomes a feminist intervention, making explicit my own internalized white misogyny.

LISTENING-BASED DISCUSSIONS

In addition to genre diversity in my selections of course readings, I also enacted course goals by facilitating listening-based discussions centered on Krista

Ratcliffe's (2005) concept of *rhetorical listening*: negotiating our understandings of ourselves in relation to each other, and unpacking the very cultural logics that drive any claim to knowledge (p. 33). Each class began with journaling about three routine questions, in relation to the assigned readings that day, which students then shared in peer groups. *What is this text telling you about gender, violence, and relationships between gender and violence? How does the text align with what you already know, feel, believe, think, sense about gender and/or violence? How does the text extend, challenge, complicate, diverge from what you already know, feel, believe, think, sense about gender and/or violence?* I designed these questions around Ratcliffe's explication of rhetorical listening as a process of identifying "(un)conscious presences, absences, unknowns" (p. 29) that different discourses provoke. In asking students to first engage in "standing under" (p. 28) discourses and reinventing what they read in relation to core concepts in the course, to then put their listenings into dialogue with their peers' listenings, I wanted to cultivate a collective experience of "listening to the texts." I wanted to ingrain this listening practice as a prerequisite to confronting gendered injustices represented in the texts—just as grassroots activist groups listen to the communities they serve to assess the particular needs of the communities, and to allow those needs to drive activist initiatives and strategies.

Listening-based discussions "legitimated as knowledge" (Harding, 1987, p. 181) the experiential knowledges students brought to the table as a result of "standing under" their own and their peers' discourses. Yet as students' contributions in class revealed, these three routine questions may not have actually promoted rhetorical listening as a framework for (or boundary around) class discussions. I assumed students needed no examples of, discussions about, or other forms of explicit guidance in responding to the questions. Distinguishing feeling, believing, sensing, and thinking from one another, I assumed, made sense to students. Further, I denied students the opportunity to examine how these different ways of knowing intersect; thought informs feelings, feelings inform beliefs, beliefs inform worldviews, worldviews inform actions. As juniors and seniors who had already fulfilled core curriculum requirements in composition and communication before taking this course, students, I assumed, already possessed the terminology and broader frameworks essential for transferring (Yancey, Robertson & Taczak, 2014) prior knowledges, feelings, beliefs, thoughts, and sensory experiences into written and spoken language. I overlooked the importance of helping students develop a language for transfer as a basis for rhetorical listening.

Some students readily distinguished thoughts, feelings, and other forms of knowing, transferring them into language with relative ease, such as the students previously discussed who were writing about rape scenes in *Girl with the Dragon*

Tattoo. However, other students failed to transfer their listening into language altogether, as was evident in blank journal pages and "I don't know" or "I have no relevant experience" statements. On the final day of class, one male student said he wished we had read more "light" material. When asked to elaborate, he stated that he left class most days "feeling badly about being a man." The majority of male students in the class expressed agreement, nodding their heads as he spoke. As this student's remark and his peers' agreement exemplify, the listening-based discussions may have marginalized students who did not have a language for, or who resisted, sitting with what they perceived as negative emotions that should not come up in a university classroom—at least not in ours. Rather than approaching resistance as a tool for understanding more about themselves and others, students such as he equated resistance with failure: a failure of the course design to meet their learning needs, and a failure within themselves to recognize points of intersection with course content without becoming overwhelmed by self-loathing. Rather than prompting inquiry into the personal, cultural logics at play in male students "feeling badly," our listening-based discussions triggered a compulsion to fix, change, or reject altogether the perceived source of that feeling (course material and having to respond to it vis-a-vis the three routine questions).

Beyond assuming that students needed no explicit guidance in how to participate in listening-based discussions, I also assumed that they could navigate on their own the tension between *being assessed for a grade* and *becoming vulnerable* in class. At a time when U.S. college campuses are facing increased rates of sexual assault and rape (Gray, 2014), a course on gendered violence can be especially unnerving for students, the majority of whom have likely been witnesses to, survivors, or even perpetrators of sexualized violence themselves. While a classroom setting can provide a safe space for crucial dialogue about rape culture, it can also lead students to censor themselves for fear of how their contributions might impact not only their peers' perceptions of them, but also their grades, GPAs, and career prospects. As became evident in the waning of active participation over the course of the semester, I inadvertently conflated class discussions with everyday conversation, neglecting to recognize how my own positionality as authority figure may have impacted how students engaged in the course.

Students may have also avoided participation as a result of posttraumatic stress disorder (PTSD) or vicarious trauma (Pearlman & Saakvitne, 1995), a form of secondary traumatization that impacts people who come into contact with others' experiences of trauma. The "loss of context" (Rak, 2006, p. 60) or inability to differentiate a narrator's from a reader's experience can silence students with PTSD or vicarious trauma. Traumatic triggers may have been at play. Engaging in the course might have meant confronting personal experiences of violation—something students may not have been ready and/or willing to do, particularly in a setting where their engagement would be assessed for a grade. Fearing student withdrawal or shutdown by my calling attention to trauma, I avoided the subject of PTSD altogether.

Relegating trauma to the margins contradicted what I know about the effects of traumatic experience on the brain's memory functions, on language, and on our ability to express an experience in narrative form, if at all (Caruth, 1995; Herman, 1997; Scarry, 1985; van der Kolk, 2014). Verbal communication may not have been (consistently) possible for students who had encountered rape, sexual assault, sexual harassment, partner abuse, stalking, sex trafficking, pornography, incest, child abuse, and/or other forms of gendered violence in the course material. Nor may verbal communication have been (consistently) possible for students who empathically engaged with course content to such a degree, they temporarily or chronically lost hope, focus, motivation, or interest—like the student who wanted "lighter" material to offset his negative feelings about being a man. The syllabus bore no explicit mention of trauma's tendency to disorient; or how silence could function productively as a form of rhetorical listening (Glenn & Ratcliffe, 2011). Assuming that students could decide for themselves what forms of participation in the course would be most productive and safe for them, I did not adequately prepare students to engage at their own levels of experience, or to recognize any resistance as a productive site of critical inquiry.

While this course was one of several students could choose from to fulfill the University's Language in the Humanities general education requirements, the element of "requirement" may have compounded the frustrating, challenging, or traumatizing aspects of the gendered violence theme. As a graduate student instructor doing a teaching internship (a requirement of my doctoral program), I was eager to finally teach a course in my primary research area. I believed that my enthusiasm would be more than enough for the entire class, and that my enthusiasm would mitigate any trauma responses. I never explicitly acknowledged the tension between "you have to be here" and the mind-body engagement I was asking from students. That is, I failed to acknowledge how the subject matter might interfere with students' abilities to participate in the course. Without explicating how to engage at varying levels of vulnerability, I simply implemented policies I regularly use in first-year writing courses I teach: active participation, regular journal writing, and writing projects that require students to document their learning in relation to any given rhetorical task.

While many students consistently spoke and listened in class discussions, others became virtually (if not completely) silent. While some students demonstrated investment in engaging with texts, others became withdrawn, writing increasingly briefer, more formulaic journal entries. To be sure, multiple factors may have accounted for this dynamic, some of which may have had nothing to do with my failures: exhaustion/lack of sleep, meeting the demands of heavy workloads in other classes, job responsibilities, homesickness, and other common stressors for college students that can affect participation. Some students may have believed that a classroom was not an appropriate or safe space for vulnerability. Silence may not have at all signified what teachers often construe as "fear, boredom, resistance, or ignorance" (Rak, 2006, p. 53), but rather that students were "confronted by material which literally stopped daily life for a time" (Rak, 2006, p. 54). Regardless of why some students' participation waned or never seemed to really "take off" in the first place, my assumption that successful modes of engagement in the course should and would function just as they do in others rendered student-silence an ignored, untapped source of engagement in the course.

On paper, I implied that the course content might interfere with students' abilities and desires to actively participate. The syllabus outlined a basic list of expectations for cultivating classroom community: "Treat our class as a supportive learning community working towards common goals; Speak honestly, openly and respectfully; Listen honestly, openly and respectfully; Be willing to change your mind; Have the courage to hold your ground" (Johnston, 2013). I then followed this list up with a detailed statement about ways to engage in the course: "active participation includes coming thoroughly prepared to every class; consistently earning high scores on reading quizzes; actively listening to one another; contributing relevant and productive questions, ideas, and comments to class discussions; taking copious notes in class; volunteering to take on leadership roles in the classroom, when needed; and offering our talents, ideas, and sustained attention to one another" (Johnston, 2013). Setting expectations is critical for the functionality of any safe, productive community or group endeavor. However, setting expectations is not enough. I needed to also explicitly *model* how to speak about and listen to fear, shame, anger, numbness, and other emotional states that course content evoked. I needed to make space for discussions *about* discussion. While the syllabus identified different options for participating, allowing flexibility for times when students may not have felt comfortable speaking, it did not explicitly acknowledge how course content might affect students' participation from one class session to the next. Put simply, my framing of (the boundaries I set around) the course policies as policies that may have applied to any number of discussion-based classes rendered invisible the very shaming, silencing effects of gendered violence. As feminist rhetoricians, we have a responsibility to model in the classroom the messiness of cross-cultural communication and to offer tools for navigating the mess.

I wanted the course to feel familiar, typical, everyday. I did not want the class to stand out as somehow "special" or "exceptional" *because* it was centered on a controversial theme. Just as gendered violence has become normalized, I wanted to normalize openly speaking, listening, and writing about gendered violence. Thus in addition to outlining course expectations in the syllabus, I also instituted the same participation policy that I use in other composition classes I teach—one that rewards students who consistently and proactively participate:

> I do not designate a particular grade percentage for participation. Rather, a student's final grade will reflect the quality and extent of her/his/their participation throughout the term in the form of an increased, maintained, or decreased final grade. For instance, if a student earning an A on all assignments for the course demonstrates poor or inconsistent participation, the final grade may drop to a B or below. Conversely, if a student earning a B or C on assignments demonstrates strong and consistent participation, the final grade may bump up to an A or B. If a student earning an A on assignments demonstrates strong and consistent participation, the final grade will likely stay at an A. (Johnston, 2013)

This student-centered participation policy has worked well for fostering participation in other courses, encouraging students with writing anxieties that they can still excel by showing up and getting involved. However, in this course, such a policy may not have been appropriate. It may have proved antifeminist, reinforcing the shame and blame that are all too common for victims or bystanders of sexualized violence, who "freeze" or otherwise feel immobilized by violence. It may have also given license to already-dominant voices to take up more space. Just as perpetrators exert power and control over others to instill fear, dominant voices can interrupt, speak louder than, or speak over others. My participation policy may have sent the message to students to keep talking lest their grades would suffer—a highly gendered, male form of listening that relies on challenging, proving, winning—even if they were excelling in other aspects of the course; even if their silence was trauma induced by the course.

REQUIRING COMMUNITY INVOLVEMENT

In addition to assigning readings in different genres and facilitating listening-based discussions, a third way I enacted course goals was requiring students to integrate, in their writing projects, primary research from local organizations and local contacts invested in confronting gendered violence in some way, such as interviewing faculty members doing research on gendered violence, staff members of campus programs providing sexual assault prevention services, and in some cases, students who had witnessed gendered violence themselves. Through these projects I hoped that students would transfer what they were learning in class into on-the-ground strategies for intervening into injustices in their communities. I hoped that making these connections would help students figure out how they might get involved in, or utilize themselves, community antiviolence resources.

Students demonstrated a range of uptakes of the required community involvement, which were highly gendered in and of themselves. Some women in the class wrote about how the plethora of local programs serving victims of gendered violence pointed out women's ongoing status as second-class citizens, despite progress made by feminists. While researching for a project on dating violence, one student emailed me music videos representing women as sexual property, noting parallels with several recent reports of sexual harassment on our University campus. Another emailed me an article about rape myths, expressing her despair in hearing male peers (in and outside of our class) claim that women make false reports of rape, or that women "ask for it" by wearing tight clothing and flirting. Others felt moved to present their research to the class. One presented a blog entitled "The Case Against Female Self-Esteem" (Forney, 2013), in which the blogger describes women's need for self-esteem as "one of the most disastrous social engineering experiments of the modern era;" the student warned the class that "this mentality is '*disastrous*' for women." Another student joined the campus chapter of Bedsider.org, a national nonprofit birth control network advocating safe-sex, while researching preventions for sexualized violence. Urging other students to get involved, she distributed buttons, stickers, and pamphlets about consent.

Many women wrote about personal traumas and what they perceived as their inevitable lot in life to be victimized by men. One woman admitted to deep-seated rage: "when I think about men who are violent in whatever way, I see pigs who have no right to be around." Her anger suggests a feeling of solidarity with other women in what she perceived as a collective experience of being violated by men. Another woman echoed this sense of solidarity, writing, "As a young woman, I have, like all other women, been the victim of sexual harassment. . . . I honestly encounter uncomfortable and unwanted attention pretty often." Yet another student expressed a chronic fear of men, describing how this fear keeps her hypervigilant, at the same time as she second-guesses herself for feeling afraid: "I walk to class every day and to my internship. Every time I walk home, there are cars that stop, honk, wave, and stare. It gets me nervous and sometimes thinking is anyone going to pull over and grab me. I could be overreacting but it's always in the back of my head." As these excerpts from student writing exemplify, the campus involvement requirement in course projects helped many female students connect course material to their daily lives. While they did not always follow those connections up with (explicit commitments to) getting involved on campus or utilizing community resources themselves, they laid the important groundwork of rhetorically listening to our environments as a strategy for assessing and intervening in gendered violence in the community.

Several female students initiated meetings with me outside of class to talk about how our class was "popping up" in other aspects of their lives, leading them to rethink a turbulent relationship or reevaluate an unwanted sexual encounter. They expressed fear that men in the class might perceive them as just another woman "lying about rape" or "seeking attention" to get back at an ex-boyfriend. One felt so enraged by the research she unearthed about sexualized violence on college campuses, she visited my office after the semester was over, asking how she might get involved locally to promote antiviolence. While I also met with male students outside of class, none of them discussed personal matters with me. They simply wanted to go over drafts of their papers to ensure they would earn the highest grades possible. By and large, men expressed agreement that gender inequality continues to pervade society, yet when it came to gendered violence, they tended to assume more distanced standpoints than women.

Male students did not tend to express personal identification (Burke, 1969) with respect to issues of gendered violence on campus, often reiterating versions of rape culture mentality that render sexualized violence interpersonal. For example, one male student argued that acquaintance rape stems not from systems of power and control, as many feminists argue it does, but from a breakdown of communication: "If a person doesn't want to have sex but doesn't say no, how is the other person supposed to know she doesn't want to have sex. . . . If someone doesn't want to have sex then they should just communicate that feeling by saying no." His comment places the onus on the (potential) victim for preventing rape and obscures the paralyzing fear women experience about saying "no" in the face of assault when they experience such assault as a life-threatening act of violence. Moreover, it assumes that simply verbalizing "yes" or "no" is the only form of consent that is necessary or appropriate in sexual encounters.

Related to this perception of acquaintance rape as an interpersonal issue that can be resolved through better communication, the majority of men in the class perceived violence in romantic or sexual relationships as a two-way street. They claimed that men are often stereotyped as perpetrators, while women are never held accountable for violating men's reputations, describing scenarios in which they believed women falsely claimed rape for attention or vengeance. As one male student wrote, "The bottom line is that if a girl is flirty and promiscuous with a guy when they are both drunk . . . chances are something is going to happen. The next morning, a guy would rarely if ever say anything about this decision, even if it was a regret. On the other hand, it is a lot more common for the girl to say that they guy acted with force and that it may have been a situation like a rape or sexual violence." According to this student, acquaintance rape is almost a misnomer, resulting from women denying personal responsibility in sexual encounters. Moreover, his use of "rarely" to describe men's nonchalance about sexualized assault, and "a lot more common" to describe women's alleged overreaction to these encounters, suggests that eradicating rape is a woman's job of changing her perceptions. As these excerpts from male student writings exemplify, the campus involvement requirement in the course shored up men's egos, exposing an underlying fear of or anger about being (perceived as) perpetrators. They did not write about specific strategies for changing such normalized perceptions, beyond reiterating versions of rape myths that women falsely "cry rape," and should just understand that men will inevitably want to have sex with women who pay attention to them.

A CONCLUSION

Writing this chapter, I found myself resisting accountability at every turn. "Standing under" my students' discourses and my own approaches to teaching the citizenship literacy course brought my own experienced *and* perpetrated violations into sharp relief. I have long been engaged in researching violence against women, bearing witness again and again to the utter collapsing of boundaries victimization generates. I have worked in women's shelters, and a women's substance abuse program in which every single client who walked through our doors had not only chemical dependency issues, but also histories of rape, incest, and/ or domestic battery—often, "all of the above." I have my own history of victimization, as well as of retaliation in the face of such victimization. I am a survivor. I have been cracked by rape, emotional abuse, physical violence, stalking, and harassment perpetrated by men. Countless female friends, colleagues, mentors, and family members have also been cracked.

When I "out" myself as a survivor, a necessary move in accounting for my pedagogical practices in this chapter, it threatens to scramble the years of therapy that have brought me back in positive communication with my body. Recognizing my limitations means recognizing that my work, however well-intended, enacts its own forms of violence. Downplaying perpetration overemphasizes victimization as *the* catalyst for inventing antiviolence strategies. Doing so inadvertently perpetuates the belief that victims, not perpetrators, must be the ones to end gendered violence. Embodied knowledge is always partial and evolving, and as a feminist, I have an ethical responsibility to account for what I cannot (yet) perceive, at the same time as I cannot (or will not) perceive it. Accounting for my pedagogical methodology in the citizenship literacy course helps me recognize *that* I fail, *where* I fail, *and to do my work anyway*.

While I have not yet taught this course again, writing this chapter has me *strategically contemplating* (Royster & Kirsch, 2012) the citizenship literacy course design as a collaboration with students. Such contemplation exposes my methodologies, "how [I] process, imagine, and work with materials" (Royster & Kirsch, 2012, p. 85), in relation to my actual experience of teaching the course, the "outward journey in real time and space" (Royster & Kirsch, 2012, p. 85). Put simply, *strategically contemplating* permeates my boundaries. I am letting go of controlling how a course may unfold. During the time when I taught the citizenship literacy course, 2013, I was raped by a white man I knew. My boundaries violated, I became increasingly insistent that students speak up in moments of silence in the classroom—what I perceived as a male unwillingness to engage that spread to female students in the class, causing them to self-censor. The more I called on students at random, the more stilted discussions became.

Rather than becoming vulnerable myself, by way of sharing (in some form) my own experience of assault, I assumed that students needed to push through their anxieties about speaking up by requiring them to do so. While I recognize that a teacher sharing personal stories of victimization with students can be highly problematic, and the possibility that such sharing may not always be appropriate or productive for either teacher or students, I also recognize that by asking students to routinely interrogate their own positionalities in relation to course content, I was asking students to do what I would not or could not do myself.

Teaching the citizenship literacy course was at once empowering and traumatizing. On the one hand, focusing the course on women and victimization, for many female students, worked to denaturalize rape myths that represent women as perpetrators of their own wreckage (e.g., why didn't she just leave?), and represent male perpetrators as victims of traumatic childhoods, violent male role models, and other environmental conditions beyond their control that compel them to perpetrate violence. On the other hand, avoiding men, maleness, masculinity, non-cisgender identities, perpetrators, and perpetration contradicted the larger insight I hoped students would gain: that many of us move in and out of different gender identities; that we may all be victims and perpetrators, at different times or in different spaces; that no one is exempt from responsibility for gendered violence.

I am left with many more questions than I started with: *How can I, having been silenced by violence myself, require students to talk openly about it with relative strangers, and in a setting where they were being assessed for a grade? How can a course promote community, collaboration, and openness at the same time as I, the instructor, single-handedly design it without allowing space for students' needs and interests to shape its contents? Was it the right decision for me not to disclose my own trauma history? Would disclosing have helped? Would it have harmed? What was I afraid of?*

As these questions suggest, accounting for our practices can be a painful process with painful results. Accounting for our practices exposes congruences, but also gaps, between student uptakes and our very best pedagogical intentions. Yet in approaching methodology as an always-already feature of my research, I can refine how I gather and interpret information from my students—movements that impact the effects of their conclusions. It can help me recognize where and how my embodied experiences shape my movements; how my assumptions can silence, shame, or marginalize students, regardless of my good intentions to do ethical, feminist work. It can also help me more appropriately engage student rhetors who may become tomorrow's feminist activists. When we account for our practices, we move our work forward, in closer alignment with the feminist futures we imagine.

NOTES

1. Julie Jung seminar. Many thanks to my mentor, Professor Julie Jung in whose doctoral seminar, *Rhetoric Saves Lives*, I first encountered this way of analyzing concepts in terms of what they do, how they are used, and the risks and effects of their usages.
2. Students of the class (English 128, Fall 2013). The Informed Consent Form for this IRB study can be accessed at https://wac.colostate.edu/docs/books/feminist/media / Johnston_ConsentForm.docx.
3. I'd like to thank my colleagues Lauren Rosenberg and Emma Howes, two other contributors to this edited collection, for their role in shaping this chapter, which originally started as a feminist trilogue collaborative piece about feminist methodologies.

REFERENCES

Bal, M. (2002). *Traveling concepts in the humanities: A rough guide.* Toronto, ON: University of Toronto Press.
Burke, K. (1969). *A rhetoric of motives.* Los Angeles, CA: University of CA Press.
Caruth, C. (Ed.). (1995). *Trauma: Explorations in memory.* Baltimore, MD: Johns Hopkins University Press.
Columbia Pictures (Producer) & Fincher, D. (Director). (2011). *The girl with the dragon tattoo* [Motion Picture]. United States: Sony Pictures Entertainment.
Crowley, S. & Hawhee, D. (2004). *Ancient rhetorics for contemporary students* (3rd ed.). New York, NY: Pearson Longman.

Forney, M. (2013). The case against female self-esteem. *Matt Forney: The man who shouted love at the heart of the world* [Web blog entry].

Glenn, C. & Ratcliffe, K. (2011). *Silence and listening as rhetorical arts*. Carbondale, IL: Southern Illinois University Press.

Gray, E. (2014, May 26). America's campuses are dangerous places. *Time Magazine*, 19–27.

Harding, S. (Ed.). (1987). *Feminism & methodology*. Bloomington, IN: Indiana University Press.

Herman, J. (1997). *Trauma and recovery: The aftermath—from domestic abuse to political terror*. New York, NY: Basic Books.

Hesford, W. (2011). *Spectacular rhetorics: Human rights visions, recognitions, feminisms*. Durham, NC: Duke University Press.

INCITE! Women of Color Against Violence. (Eds.). (2006). *Color of violence: The Incite! anthology*. Cambridge, MA: South End Press.

Islandfabrics. [islandfabrics]. (2013, August 26). *Miley Cyrus and Robin Thicke MTV VMA Awards 2013 performance* [Video file]. Retrieved from https://www.youtube.com/watch?v=YFLv9Ns1EuQ.

Johnston, E. (2013). *Gender in the humanities: Gendered violence in global contexts* [Syllabus]. Normal, IL: English Department, Illinois State University.

Jung, J. (July 2012). *Rhetoric and composition seminar presentation on theory, method and methodology*. Normal, IL: Illinois State University.

Kirsch, G. E. & Rohan, L. (Eds.). (2008). *Beyond the archives: Research as a lived process*. Carbondale, IL: Southern Illinois University Press.

Kirsch, G. E. & Royster, J. J. (2013). Feminist rhetorical practices and the building of global communities. Featured Panel at *Feminisms & rhetorics 2013: Links: Rhetorics, feminisms, global communities*. Stanford, CA: Stanford University.

Larsson, S. (2008). *The girl with the dragon tattoo*. New York, NY: Vintage Crime.

Lunsford, A. A. (Ed.). (1995). *Reclaiming rhetorica: Women in the rhetorical tradition*. Pittsburgh, PA: University of Pittsburgh Press.

O'Toole, L.L., Schiffman, J. R. & Kiter Edwards, M. L. (Eds.). (2007). *Gender violence: Interdisciplinary perspectives* (2nd ed.). New York, NY: New York University Press.

Pearlman, L.A. & Saakvitne, K.W. (1995). *Trauma and the therapist: Countertransference and vicarious traumatization in psychotherapy with incest survivors*. New York, NY: W.W. Norton & Company.

Rak, J. (2003). Do witness: Don't: A woman's word and trauma as pedagogy. *Topia (York University), 10*, 53–71.

Ratcliffe, K. (2005). *Rhetorical listening: Identification, gender, whiteness*. Carbondale, IL: Southern Illinois University Press.

Royster, J.J. & Kirsch, G. E. (2012). *Feminist rhetorical practices: New horizons for rhetoric, composition, and literacy Studies*. Carbondale, IL: Southern Illinois University Press.

Royster, J. J. (2003). Disciplinary landscaping, or contemporary challenges in the history of rhetoric. *Philosophy and Rhetoric, 36*(2), 148–67.

Scarry, E. (1985). *The body in pain: The making and unmaking of the world.* New York, NY: Oxford Univeristy Press.

Schell, E. E. & Rawson, K. J. (2010). *Rhetorica in motion: Feminist rhetorical methods & methodologies.* Pittsburgh, PA: University of Pittsburgh Press.

United States Department of Justice. (2014). *Rape: Definition.* Washington, D.C.: Federal Bureau of Investigation.

van der Kolk, B.A. (2014). *The body keeps the score: Brain, mind, and body in the healing of trauma.* New York, NY: Viking.

Wiseman, L. M. (Ed.). (2013). *Women write resistance: Poets resist gender violence.* Pittsburgh, PA: Hyacinth Girl Press.

Yancey, K., Robertson, L. & Taczak, K. (2014). *Writing across contexts: Transfer, composition, and sites of writing.* Salt Lake City, UT: Utah University Press.

Yellow Bird/Alliance Films (Producer) & Oplev, N.A. (Director). (2009). *The girl with the dragon tattoo* [Motion Picture]. United States: Music Box Films.

CHAPTER 4.
LISTENING TO RESEARCH AS A FEMINIST ETHOS OF REPRESENTATION

Lauren Rosenberg
New Mexico State University

Emma Howes
Coastal Carolina University

In this chapter, we explore how our research practices and methodological choices offer opportunities to embody a feminist ethos of responsible, strategic practice. Our inquiry takes place in two different research sites where we enact ethnographic and archival research methods. Contemplating our research practices, we promote an ethos of valuing multiple perspectives by examining the ideological lenses we use, acknowledging our different, sometimes conflicting, subject positions, and allowing those perspectives to shape our work. We seek to expand traditional conceptions of what counts as knowledge, data, and research as we strive to become more active rhetorical listeners. Our methodologies center on the needs of participants alongside our own, and we are committed to ongoing interrogation of cultural assumptions and biases, including, but not limited to, gender subjugation.

In a 2000 issue of *JAC*, Michelle Ballif, D. Diane Davis, and Roxanne Mountford debated their views of feminism in a trilogue consisting of their alternating voices. Applying Jacques Derrida's term *différance* to their efforts to define feminist intervention, the authors argued that the differences feminists grapple with in unpacking meaning and intention, are sometimes non-negotiable. Yet by acknowledging difference as well as *différance*—a more interrogative, radical commitment to looking at difference—it may become possible to deconstruct and resist binaries, question the privileging of certain positions over others, and open up new spaces of meaning and practice. As Davis (2000) put it in one of her entries, "I would suggest, in fact, that it is *only* in our difference—or, rather, our *différance*—that something like solidarity becomes possible" (p. 584). Ballif (2000) responded with the trilogue's central question: "How do we listen for difference(s)? And how do we listen for *différance*" (p. 586)?

As feminist literacy researchers, we enter the conversation here. We are concerned with ethical practice in our research, our interactions with participants, and with our students. We present Ballif, Davis, and Mountford's (2000) questions with our own spin: How can we responsibly and productively move toward solidarity as feminist researchers, even when differences (difference and *différance*) are not easily reconciled?

The trilogue provided a forum for investigating our research practices as intentional feminist acts in which we consciously choose to collaborate, weaving together our voices and perspectives. In our respective scholarship (Emma's is archival and Lauren's is ethnographic) we defer our own assumptions so that we can listen differently and thus understand the positions of our research participants with greater precision and compassion. In listening, we take interpretive cues from participants. Emma's work on historic southern mill village literacy campaigns employs listening through researcher reflection. She steps back to attend not only to available artifacts but also to the silences that arise from the materials that are not documented in archival collections. Lauren introduces a developing project on military veterans' literacy practices by concentrating on a pilot study of one student-veteran's experiences. In the process of contemplating the data, she and the participant create knowledge together. Our approach echoes Gesa Kirsch's (1999) assertion that "we must develop ethical guidelines to prompt serious and sustained consideration of those whose interests are served in any given research project, and what consequences may follow—especially for research participants—from the influence of those interests" (p. x). Methodological principles thus allow us to acknowledge the economy around the research site and the ways that we benefit from our work; we also hope that participants may draw benefits from their relationships with us. Lauren attempts to show this in her interactions with Lary, former Veterans Center director and student at her previous university; Emma demonstrates it in her explorations of which archival artifacts get saved and which ones do not. Our feminist ethos is informed by our relationships with participants, whether they are people we interact with in the present, or those whose experiences and writing are documented in the archives.

We are both literacy researchers, and as such, we are committed to working with participants to understand their reading and writing practices, and the practices of people in their communities, currently and historically. Throughout this chapter, when we speak of listening to participants or listening in the archives, we refer to our decision to pay precise, ongoing attention to our relationships with participants and the community members we encounter in the research process as a significant feature of our methodology. Our focus on relationship is what Kirsch (1999) and other researchers refer to as a "politics of location" (p. x). This attention and care also impacts the ways in which we encounter our own readings of a situation or artifact, highlighting that our authority as feminist researchers is guided not only by what we see, but what may remain opaque in our work: the documents that may not have been saved for historical prosperity or the stories that require trust to hear. It is this commitment to participants that influences our methodological choices.

Like the trilogue authors and Kirsch, we are committed to "rhetorical listening" (Ratcliffe, 2005) and to understanding how listening can be channeled toward more ethical research practices. We are concerned with our own positions as feminist researchers and with the ways we interact with participants and students; thus, we aim to enact practices that tend to differences among others, while holding ourselves accountable for how our positions orient us as researchers. Although Ballif, Mountford, and Davis (2000) sometimes disagreed with one another about the responsibilities of feminists, they were in agreement that feminism is an "ethical way of being" (p. 611) and a politics. We agree. Feminist research is ethical and political work.

DEFINING A FEMINIST ETHOS OF REPRESENTATION AS RESPONSIBLE STRATEGIC PRACTICE

Along with the researchers before us who were concerned with ethical representation in qualitative studies of writing, and especially with developing a feminist ethics of representation (see Kirsch (1999), *Ethical Dilemmas in Feminist Research,* and Mortensen and Kirsch's (1993/2003) collection, *Ethics and Representation in Qualitative Studies of Literacy*), we define a feminist ethos of representation as a commitment to continually examining the ideological lenses we use, acknowledging our different (sometimes conflicting) subject positions, and allowing our research participants to shape the work itself. For example, Lauren, who has a background in literacy research, entered a world unknown to her when she decided to examine the writing practices of military personnel. The only way she could conduct her study was by deferring to participants' and other informants' expertise. She was, as many ethnographic researchers have described it, approaching the research as an outsider; she had to be led through the study by others' greater knowledge. In letting participants lead, she does reflective work to recognize her own voice as it interacts with the voices of others. We find value in multiple perspectives, acknowledging both difference and *différance* in our interactions with research participants, and in relation to the topics we pursue as our scholarship. One of the most significant turns in feminist methodological intervention has been the recognition of the researcher's influence on her research: the always-already presence of her shadow, which impacts all of the work we do to varying degrees. In different stages of our work, this shadow casts different shapes. But its presence as we collect and understand data, as well as when and how we present findings and contexts, can be telling.

This becomes clear in Emma's reflections on gaps in archival findings and how entering a research setting with certain goals in mind can sometimes make it harder to listen to what we actually find. Formulating research questions around company towns in North and South Carolina at the turn of the century primed Emma to seek working class voices that resisted industrial educational contexts. The available artifacts around this historical moment were limited by the material conditions of the archives where she worked, which consisted of primarily the writings of literacy sponsors, not learners. Her expectations of what she hoped to find made it difficult to maneuver with what she actually found. But by taking a step back and assessing her position in relation to the study, it was possible to reflect and remap. Stepping back and assessing are two strategies that are essential to our feminist ethos. In the space of reflection and pause, we become able to consider our goals and our interactions more mindfully.

We recognize similar goals in the work of our peers in this collection, especially in Megan Adams' (Chapter 1, this collection) reflections on the production of the Hollow documentary, and in Mariana Grohowski's (Chapter 2, this collection) research on the experiences of two women combat veterans. Adams and Grohowksi consider the importance of reciprocity within research relationships as a feminist intervention, a point we highlight as well in our focus on relationship and mutual knowledge-making. We recognize in all of the chapters in this section a common theme of "the role of the ethical self" (Adams) as a feminist researcher. We all are concerned with researcher positionality as we listen intensively to our participants and as we continue to hold ourselves accountable (Johnston, Chapter 3) for our assumptions and the ideologies that "buoy" us (Rohan, Chapter 5).

We turn our attention toward our research methods to concentrate on how our methodological choices offer us opportunities to enact a feminist ethos of responsible, strategic practice. This inquiry takes place in the different research sites in which we enact ethnographic and archival research methods. We find it useful to think about these varied sites of our literacy studies as examples that illustrate the ways feminist methodologies stretch across different material spaces of meaning-making. By gathering varied methods within a common methodological frame, we consider the ways that feminist perspectives concretely impact our work. In particular, we emphasize lingering on relationships with participants and communities, listening, and co-creating knowledge as three principles that guide us as feminist researchers.

LINGERING ON RELATIONSHIPS

To begin conversations about what feminist methodological approaches add to our research, we concentrate on the value of lingering together with participants in ethnography, archival work, and among the communities in which we engage. Feminists have taken on these relationships in Composition and Rhetoric, emphasizing the push to co-create knowledge with those who are the subjects of our work. Cynthia Selfe (2016) argues that as researchers, we can envision ourselves as "partner[s] in knowing and learning" alongside our participants with whom we "enter into a deep collaboration." To do this work together, we need to slow down and pause. The research process becomes one in which we "write or compose *with* and not *about*." When we pause and reflect with participants, we create a different space for invention.

To move through the process of co-creation, we have found it necessary to reflect on our own sense of ethos: as writers, researchers, and agents interacting with communities. If our goal is to temper the sense of expertise that is assumed within the researcher-participant relationship to enact a feminist methodology, where do we locate our authority? Further, how do we honor what specialized knowledge we do have through our interactions? Sophia Villenas (2000) provides insight into these tensions in her article, which examines feminist methodologies in anthropological ethnography. In particular, Villenas (2000), whose project explores her own struggles against the "exotic" in the anthropological gaze, points out that when researchers name "for other women what constitutes oppression and emancipation, there is no room for redefinitions of feminisms and womanisms that do not fit the experience of an almost grand narrative of 'feminist' living" (p. 80). When, as researchers, we enter a context with preconceived definitions of what constitutes resistance, or any other experience, we narrow the scope of what counts in our findings, valuing our own authority over the perceptions of those we study. The focus on some aspects of participant experience at the expense of others reifies the women, men, and children our work seeks to understand, "by privileging some life histories (those that showed resistance) over others" (p. 80–81). While scholars must always make choices as to what data and artifacts are shared in their work, we suggest that these choices are enhanced when we look beyond our own academic training and theoretical lenses to build knowledge from the ground up.

Royster and Kirsch's (2012) *Feminist Rhetorical Practices: New Directions for Rhetoric, Literacy, and Composition Studies* provides analytic tools and methods that further the practice of co-creating knowledge to address cultivating research relationships. This occurs when researchers prioritize "strategic contemplation" and mindfulness as a feminist ethos of practice to formulate research questions, collect data and artifacts, and represent individuals and communities. Royster and Kirsch (2012) coined the term *strategic contemplation* to "reclaim a genre of research and scholarship traditionally associated with processes of meditation, introspection, and reflection . . . Building on critical imagination, this strategy suggests that researchers might *linger* deliberately inside of their research tasks as they investigate their topics and sources . . . ." (p. 84–85, our emphasis). We are mindful that all researchers enter into relationships with the subjects of their work, and we value the time necessary to cultivate such interactions. Ethical practices, then, may be measured by reflecting on these relationships as well as on the methods we employ to address how they may benefit one party at the expense of the other (see Kirsch (1999) *Ethical Dilemmas*). As we articulate an exigence for explicitly *feminist* scholarship, the relationship between the researcher and the researched continues to be a fruitful site for interrogation.

LISTENING

As we linger, we listen. It is the process of listening as a contemplative practice that makes our work feminist. Our focus is on how literacy research, even when not seemingly related to feminist concerns, engages feminist methodologies. For example, Lauren discusses her pilot study with a man who had a career in the military, a subject that may not appear feminist at first. The research subject need not be explicitly about gender or gender issues; the defining of feminist methodologies occurs through larger practices of meaning-making. The practice of feminist methodology is an ontological one; it relates to the ways in which we conceptualize research questions worth exploring and how we assign value to data or artifacts.

Thus, in this chapter, we take up the methodologies we employ and how we approach our research, rather than the gender(s) of the research participant(s) or the topic(s) of the research. We map the landscapes in which we research, evaluating and re-evaluating our positions as we consider our findings. We emphasize the claims of feminist rhetoricians Cheryl Glenn and Jessica Enoch (2010), that amongst historical researchers and other scholars, "the issue is not so much [that] we approach various groups of people or archival collections but why we approach various groups of people or archival collections [and] how we work to understand and honor their perspectives, their experiences" (p. 24). Our work as feminist literacy researchers, therefore, depends upon our willingness to identify and recognize how our motivations for doing feminist work impact the people and archives we study. Our work also depends upon our willingness to continually question our methodologies in relation to our participants and to be open to revising our approaches based on their needs and interests.

CO-CREATING KNOWLEDGE

The primary way in which we address knowledge formation and ethics will likely feel familiar to most researchers who have read or practiced feminist methodologies. We strive to co-create knowledge with our participants, and to practice rhetorical listening (Ratcliffe, 1999; 2005) and strategic contemplation (Royster & Kirsch, 2012), through sharing our writing with the communities we study and in community outreach. These interactions between researcher and participant constitute what Lauren calls *mutual contemplation* (Rosenberg 2015, p. 57), recognizing and encouraging the presence of others in the act of strategic contemplation, as we seek input from knowledge and experience beyond our own in how we work through data. For Lauren's work, this action manifests in direct interactions with participants; for Emma, it is more a matter of reflection and reevaluation as she considers the relationships between literacy sponsors and women workers. Our projects combine to enrich conceptions of what we can achieve when we actively listen.

We turn now to two examples of how we linger, listen, and co-create knowledge. In the following sections, we look at how we are accountable as researchers, first when we engage in rhetorical listening and mutual meaning-making in Lauren's ethnographic literacy research. We continue to trace the methodological principles of our feminist ethos in Emma's work, as we look for new spaces for invention when we encounter *archival silences*. Between these two approaches to studying literacy sponsorship and usage, we hope to illuminate not only what is gained by feminist methodological practices, but also why these tactics are so important.

LAUREN: MUTUAL CONTEMPLATION

As researchers, we have a responsibility, as Royster insists (1996), to foreground our participants' rendering of their experiences over our expectations of them. That same commitment can inform our approach to gathering, interpreting, and reporting on data. In *Rhetorical Listening*, Ratcliffe (2005) develops the concept of listening as deliberate, conscious action. Listening requires that the researcher/teacher/interlocutor pay close attention to the speaker's subjectivity. It also requires that the listener be willing to interrogate her own positions, privileges, and biases. A rhetorical listener attempts to delay interpretation and judgment, choosing instead to stay with the words of others, and to contemplate them without immediate action. In this way, in our overlapping roles of researcher, teacher, and feminist, we can work towards listening to the words of others on their terms, rather than appropriating their narratives to serve our purposes. A component of rhetorical listening, in my view, is mindful awareness, which Royster and Kirsch (2012) attribute to responsible research practice. I believe, however, that contemplative practice necessitates dedicated collaboration between researcher and participants. It is not enough for the researcher to tend to her own ethical concerns; participants also engage in strategic contemplation of their experiences when they join in the research process. Thus, my goal as a researcher is for participants to "linger deliberately" (Royster & Kirsch 2012, 84) along with me during the formal data collection and when we speak informally.

In *The Desire for Literacy: Writing in the Lives of Adult Learners* (Rosenberg 2015), I introduced the concept of mutual contemplation as a co-interpretive act. Mutual contemplation involves researcher and participants joining together, not only to interpret data, but also to reflect on the situation of the study and how it affects participants. Sometimes the process of mutual contemplation requires that one refrain from activity by lingering, listening, and suspending a response. Interactions between researcher and participant, conversations in which the researcher remains open to adjusting the terms of the study and the analysis based on participants' expertise, rely on their perspective and reflecting together as a co-interpretive act. Such collaboration necessitates that the researcher yield the position of expert and allow participants' knowledge to guide the study at times. At other times, it is through prolonged discussion that participant and researcher make decisions in collaboration.

Before heading into a full-scale study of the writing practices of veterans while they are in military service and when they shift into civilian settings such as the university, I conducted a pilot of one student-veteran, Lawrence Schmitz, as a test of my research methods and questions. Lary straddled two roles in the university where I taught and where my study was situated: he was a student-veteran and he directed the Veterans Center. As the Veterans Center Coordinator, he was often in a position of advocating for others and speaking as the front person for his office. Lary was also a writing minor who wanted to use writing to examine his experiences in the Navy. In his various roles in the university, he was a literacy sponsor, as was I. Besides being a student who was sponsored by the United States Department of Veterans Affairs, Lary acted as a sponsor of other veterans like himself. He was simultaneously sponsored by, and a sponsor within, the university (see Brandt, 1998). Our conversations were informed by the multiple ways that we viewed situations from our various perspectives as employees of the university (Lary and me); staff, student, veteran (Lary); faculty, researcher, and military outsider (me). Our mutual contemplation sometimes involved Lary explaining military culture to me, me asking for feedback on my study design, or us looking together at passages in Lary's interview transcript where I noticed intriguing patterns. We lingered together over the data, making meaning through our interaction.

One such example of our collaboration and mutual contemplation is apparent in a conversation we had during an interview in which I asked Lary whether he wanted a pseudonym for my project. Having worked with vulnerable populations of adult learners before, I assumed that Lary would be best protected if he were to disguise himself. He disagreed, insisting that he wanted to use his real name so that he could be a resource for veterans. He was adamant in claiming that he was not vulnerable as an interview subject, and therefore, that he wanted his name to be used. In this way, he illustrated his simultaneous roles as sponsor and sponsored, and he made it clear that he wished for me to understand him differently. Here is how I heard him:

> If somebody reads my name and they know who I am or they hear of me, . . . it might give them the strength to say something down the line that they want to say . . . I want to be able to make sure that veterans feel free to share what their feelings are and that's valid. I don't want veterans to feel like they don't have a story to share. I want to make sure the people—vets—feel like they can speak out and say what they feel, and that it's not marginalized in any way, 'cause that's not fair . . . . And by using your real name, or using my real name, I feel like by doing that I put that out there and give people a kind of, a strength. (L. Schmitz, personal communication, January 24, 2014)

By listening to Lary's comments, I realized why it is more valuable to him to reveal rather than conceal himself. He helped me to see how disclosure helps him claim authority for his own experiences. In doing so, he also used his personal disclosure as a model for other vets, which his comments made apparent. When Lary and I discussed his decisions about self-representation, in and outside of the context of the interview, we considered issues such as naming, representation, and disclosure from various angles. His perspectives influenced mine and vice versa. Together, we engaged in mutual contemplation and co-creation of knowledge.

After I interviewed Lary, we interpreted his responses. My larger study took shape out of this ongoing conversation, a conversation in which Lary was an expert, and I "stood under" him (Ratcliffe, 2005) from my position as a faculty member who had no military experience yet who was rhetorically listening. Lary explained that whatever research I planned on doing with veterans was useful to him too because of his commitment to helping veterans assimilate into civilian life. Working with veterans *is* his life, Lary said emphatically on numerous occasions. If he could help with my work, it also helped with his personal and professional mission. We made plans to work together in creating my larger study, guided by his perspective. We intended to continue to collaborate on its design, selection of participants, and interpretation of data. His knowledge influenced my study design.

In our collaboration, there was always a bit of a power differential, however, and Lary was certainly aware that his participation would advance my research. But he also reminded me that our conversations were significant to our university and his office, to students like him, and ultimately, to how the Veterans' Center could offer greater agency to the students we serve. As a professor in the university where he was a student, and as a researcher who is interested in veterans' writing practices, I was also in a position to turn this conversation to both our advantages as we cultivated our research relationship. Lary was both consultant and collaborator. I assisted Lary by bringing the concerns of student-veterans into more public venues. I used my position as a sponsor of the university to encourage a space for more genres and contexts for writing to become part of the academic conversation. With each meeting to discuss the study, our questions became increasingly complex, and we both became better able to probe them more deeply. This was the mutual contemplation that I sought with Lary, a process in which we were continually questioning and interpreting together. The commitment we made to linger in relationship, listen, and co-create knowledge exemplified the kind of feminist intervention Emma and I advocate.

Lary offered to collaborate with me as a co-investigator, which meant that he would have a designated role in interpreting data. Together we made plans for the upcoming study; we designed a postcard that would be used as a tool for recruiting participants. Lary planned to distribute and collect the cards as incoming student-veterans toured the Veterans Center during their orientation, and he and I would then review the pool of volunteers. And yet, I end this section with a sad sigh. Suddenly and without warning, Lary's life changed course, and I learned that he left the university and relocated to a different part of the country. I was unhappy to lose my collaborator, but curious too because this was a moment when my research changed direction. Such is the case when working with people on issues pertaining to their lives; things happen that are out of our and their control, and their changes steer the research. While I can still rely on the knowledge Lary and I co-created and the contributions he made to the project, I have to sit back and reassess. I let the situation wash over me as I consider what it would mean for this research to go differently. Subsequently, however, other veterans (faculty, retired officers, and students) approached me with their stories of military literacy and their views of writing. Despite my disappointment at losing Lary, their voices took hold of the project and informed what I knew, what we came to know together, as we engaged in new acts of mutual contemplation.

EMMA: ARCHIVAL SILENCE

My research in the archives provided the opportunity to develop my own practices of lingering in relationships, listening, and co-creating knowledge in ways similar to, as well as quite different from, those Lauren has described. While Lauren's work guides us into conversation and mutual meaning-making with participants, my work grapples with the archival silences that studying marginalized populations often produce. Thus, my feminist intervention requires attention to what is said through available artifacts and what is not said; it is a process of accretion in which I use what I know to gesture towards what I don't know. Paying attention to gaps in the archives emphasizes how I understand what I hear, bringing to question how my expectations impact what I find.

In particular, my research addressed mill literacy sponsorship within the historic cotton mill villages of North and South Carolina that targeted women during the early twentieth century. These company towns were often unincorporated spaces, where mills typically owned the land and physical structures on it, providing housing, recreational opportunities, and educational facilities for factory workers and their families. As some companies (though certainly not all) directly invested in the infrastructure making up the daily lives of workers, they set up an exchange from which they expected greater worker efficiency and loyalty (Parker, 1910). Literacy learning was a resource mills offered to draw families into industrial labor and to improve their social and cultural class, without changing their economic class.

I was interested in studying the mill-sanctioned literacies specifically available to adult women and the ways these learners "assimilated to," "appropriated," or "rejected" (Donehower, 2003, p. 349–352) the accompanying relationships. Since my work focused on historical contexts, the necessity of cultivating a feminist ethos that forwarded rhetorical listening and co-creating knowledge was challenging. While accounts of mill workers from 1880–1920 existed within public circulation, there were few, if any, produced by workers themselves. And even fewer stemmed from the direct experiences of women workers in the Southern US. Trying to uncover these absent voices seemed like a perfect formula for an archival project. But seeking artifacts produced by literacy learners during the turn of the century was a job that required more time and resources than were available. Instead of the accounts of learners, the archives I visited surrounded me with documents produced primarily by literacy sponsors within these contexts: mill owners and women and men, called welfare workers, who directed and facilitated literacy distribution. For this reason, the research I hoped might illuminate the experiences of working class women, merely recounted the perceptions of the literacy sponsors who taught them; there was silence where I had hoped to access the voices of women impacted by mill educational campaigns.

My charge was to reimagine the landscape before me. Royster and Kirsch's (2012) concepts of critical imagination and strategic contemplation offer a helpful framework in which researchers "imagin[e] the contexts for practices; speculat[e] about conversations with the people whom they are studying . . . and tak[e] into account the impacts and consequences of these embodiments . . . ." (pgs. 84–85). The limitations of my findings, which only accessed the sponsor side of the equation, left me with the conundrum of how to work with groups "whose values and worldview we may not share" (Royster & Kirsch, 2012, p. 36), at least at first contact. Instead of co-creating knowledge through conversation with worker voices, I had to make meaning using what was available in the archives. While Lauren and Lary could linger in relationship, I lingered in silence.

Encountering silence led me to return to Ratcliffe's (1999) use of listening "as a trope for interpretive invention" (p. 196). Ratcliffe positions listeners as questioning "a system of discourse within which a culture reasons and derives its truths" (p. 204). To perform this act, we must acknowledge the systems at play that influence our own discourses as well as those informing the texts and participants with whom we work. Researchers inhabit spaces where ideologies come together and where they part. As we listen, we take in information and we make meaning while considering the interplay of our own voices, logics, expectations, and hopes in relation with the complex texts we encounter. We pause and listen to hear the harmonies, but we also seek meaning in the hidden and "discordant notes" (Ratcliffe, 1999, p. 203). Lingering allows us to evaluate and re-evaluate, to use strategic contemplation and critical imagination, and to re-map artifacts to consider how and where we are distributing value in the documents available.

It was disheartening and frustrating to encounter archival silence. But the structures of archival projects are notoriously fluid (Hayden, 2016); while we often enter the archives looking for one thing, we might serendipitously find another. At first glance, the texts produced by welfare workers who taught literacy in the mill villages did not provide access to literacy learning as encountered by women living and working there. On the contrary, they seemed to take me further from my starting point. There were no narratives produced by learners that revealed their processes of learning company sponsored literacies, and in fact, the voices of learners were obscured altogether. Many training materials for literacy teachers appeared to simply rewrite the stereotypes of rural and Appalachian women workers circulating during this time period, as the example below illustrates. In addition, the texts only vaguely referenced literacy learning at all, giving me more direct access to cooking and sewing classrooms than ones where reading and writing were centralized.

Grappling with archival silences encouraged me to consider documented artifacts in new ways, striving to understand the "systems of discourse" represented (Ratcliffe, 1999) in order to change how we take meaning from what we find. For example, the bulk of my documents relating to mill literacy campaigns came from the Young Women's Christian Association (YWCA) of the U.S.A.'s Records at Smith College. These records recounted the organization's work during the early twentieth century in mill villages that incorporated the literacy learning campaigns I hoped to study; though as I learned, they were often embedded in classes on other domestic skills (cookery, hygiene, sewing, and so forth). In this way, welfare work economically sponsored by the mill industry was two-pronged: On the one hand, it enacted social conservatism by promoting gendered, raced, and classed identities through women's domestic roles. On the other hand, it embodied progressive social change by expanding the boundaries of women's involvement in early social work as well as the educational opportunities (even if limited) for working-class women. Female welfare workers held complicated social positions; for this reason, I struggled—and still struggle—to understand and to stand under their sponsorship work and navigate the discourses around it.

The literacy events I was able to locate were depicted in occasional photographs of women reading or in the publication of a cookery textbook that circulated in classes taught by the YWCA. Instead of lesson plans for reading classes, I had cookery books that served as primers, prompting me to consider more broadly how I understood literacy in my artifacts. Further, these documents, in conversation with the Association's institutional records, reoriented me in my research questions towards the goals of sponsors, including modernizing the lives of learners. The excerpt that follows illustrates a training document used by sponsoring organizations, which sets the ideological framework to support company welfare practices. "The Work of the YWCA in the Cotton Mill Villages of the South," published in 1909 and archived in the YWCA files at Smith College, describes laborers in Greenville, SC to prepare welfare workers (called "secretaries" within the organization) for the community where they would teach. People living in the mill village are presented as "ante-Revolutionary backwoodsm[e]n" whose "lives were harsh and narrow," full of "superstition, suspicion, and stern religion" ("The Work," 1909, p. 2). The document goes on to claim: "Just as the mountains hold back streams, so for generations they have held back a splendid people from the advantages of civilization. Gross ignorance has intensified suspicion, superstition, and strange ideas about religion" (p. 2). The cultural logics in this text reflect narratives well known and well documented in historical portrayals of the Appalachian region. The trope of the ignorant, yet "splendid" mountaineer highlights difference between mainstream and mill families, and the passage itself marks these differences as reasons why dominant discourses were thought necessary to help workers reclaim the "advantages of civilization."

While working through documents like this one, co-creation of knowledge was difficult to enact because there was no dialogue. Instead, I was left to look at artifacts—archival, primary, and secondary—around the context; I lingered and cultivated a relationship with the archives and the abstract (and sometimes the physical) place and space where my research was rooted. In this way, my research required exploration beyond the physical (and sometimes digital) walls of the archives and my feminist ethos was built on more than just reporting on what I found. My artifacts did not alleviate the silence of mill women; instead they amplified the voices around the gap.

Although I could imagine the conversations between mill women and welfare workers, I knew from informal interviews with women and men still active in mill communities that women's responses were far more complex than anything I could comfortably represent at the time. To listen to—and represent—institutionalized discourses, as well as the silences, I had to be honest about my expectations and my desires as a researcher and to embrace the opportunity to morph my research questions rather than try to force a story. As Lauren's experience with Lary incorporates the need to embrace changes in a study that result from elements beyond our control, my intervention became less about showing women's resistance to mill sponsored literacies (which is what I had expected) and more about using methodological practices like lingering to find meanings embedded in artifacts and the silences around them. These practices opened a space to co-create knowledge as I stepped back from my ideological biases to expand how I understood archival findings.

CONTINUING TO LISTEN

Over time, as we sit with our research, our interpretations deepen and we continue the knowledge-making process. As our studies evolve, conclude, and begin again, we strive to conduct our work in ways that allow us to understand where our biases cast shadows on how we interact with participants and their stories. We counter these tendencies through our ongoing commitment to collaborate with, and be informed by, the voices of those we research. Equally important, as we enact a feminist ethos in our methodologies, we pursue ways to reorient our thinking to cultivate more equitable, mutual, and ethical relationships with the individuals and artifacts with which we engage.

In this chapter, we have articulated a feminist ethos of representation informed by three principles: lingering on relationships with participants, listening, and co-creating knowledge. We have demonstrated the ideals to which we attempt to hold ourselves as we interact with participants and data and as we assess our studies. In conclusion, we consider how the challenges we have faced in these studies have affected us as researchers. We continue to question our positions of authority and how that authority comes into play in our scholarship. Both of us have recounted experiences when the research did not go as expected. In Lauren's case, her main participant who was also a collaborator became unavailable. In Emma's case, the study led toward different artifacts than those she hoped to encounter; her findings steered her towards a population with which she was at odds.

Our examples certainly highlight the disappointment of the researcher. These moments we recount are not ones when the projects failed, but they are situations in which we did not control the study. We were left with surprises that forced us to question our purposes. Could we remain true to the feminist ethical principles with which we identified? For example, how might Emma continue to learn from the artifacts she found in the archives, even when they pointed to the missionary sponsorship she opposed? We ask ourselves how these moments can be productive and how our methodologies can bend to accommodate them.

We have argued for the significance of sitting back and reassessing, of refraining from judgment, of lingering in silence. We have tried to listen carefully to what Ratcliffe (1999) calls the "discordant notes" (p. 203) and not to stubbornly resist them. Our experiences as feminist literacy researchers illustrate that the kind of radical listening and co-creation of knowledge we propose is not easily enacted. Yet we have used this chapter as an opportunity to demonstrate how we have responded to the disappointments and surprises that affect us and our methodologies. As Ballif (2000) asked in our introduction: "How do we listen for difference(s)? And how do we listen for *différance*" (p. 586)? We are reminded that the feminist ethos we work for demands a difficult and ongoing commitment to understanding the discourses and experiences of others, as well as a willingness to interrogate ourselves.

REFERENCES

Adams, M. (2018). Post-research engagement: An argument for critical examination of researcher roles after research ends. In K. L. Blair & L. Nickoson (Eds.), *Composing feminist interventions: Activism, engagement, praxis*. Fort Collins, CO: The WAC Clearinghouse / Louisville, CO: University Press of Colorado. Retrieved from https://wac.colostate.edu/books/perspectives/feminist.

Ballif, M., Davis, D. D. & Mountford, R. (2000). Negotiating the differend: A feminist trilogue. *JAC, 20*(3), 583–625.

Brandt, D. (1998). Sponsors of literacy. *College Composition and Communication, 49*(2), 165–185.

Donehower, K. K. (2003). Literacy choices in an Appalachian community. *Journal of Appalachian Studies, 9*(2), 341–362.

Glenn, C. & Enoch, J. (2010). Invigorating historiographic practices in rhetoric and composition studies. In A. E. Ramsey, W. B. Sharer, B. L.E. & L. S. Mastrangelo (Eds.), Working in the archives: Practical research methods for rhetoric and composition (pp. 11–27). Carbondale, IL: Southern Illinois University Press.

Grohowski, M. (2018). Reciprocity as epicenter: An 'After-Action Review'. In K. L. Blair & L. Nickoson (Eds.), *Composing feminist interventions: Activism, engagement, praxis*. Fort Collins, CO: The WAC Clearinghouse / Louisville, CO: University Press of Colorado. Retrieved from https://wac.colostate.edu/books/perspectives/feminist.

Hayden, W. (2015). "Gifts" of the archives: A pedagogy for undergraduate research. *College Composition and Communication, 66*(3), 402–426.

Johnston, E. R. (2018). Methodology & accountability: Tracking our movements as feminist pedagogues. In K. L. Blair & L. Nickoson (Eds.), *Composing feminist interventions: Activism, engagement, praxis*. Fort Collins, CO: The WAC Clearinghouse / Louisville, CO: University Press of Colorado. Retrieved from https://wac.colostate.edu/books/perspectives/feminist.

Kirsch, G. E. (1999). *Ethical dilemmas in feminist research: The politics of location, interpretation, and publication.* Albany, NY: State University of New York Press.

Mortensen, P. & and Kirsch G.E. (1996). *Ethics and representation in qualitative studies of literacy.* Urbana, IL: NCTE.

Parker, T. (1910). The southern cotton mill village: A manufacturer's view. *South Atlantic Quarterly, 9,* 349–357.

Ratcliffe, K. (1999). Rhetorical listening: A trope for interpretive invention and a "code of cross-cultural conduct." *College Composition and Communication, 51(2),* 195–224.

Ratcliffe, K. (2005). *Rhetorical listening: Identification, gender, whiteness.* Carbondale and Edwardsville, IL: Southern Illinois University Press.

Rohan, E. (2018). Funding geography: The legacy of female-run settlement culture for contemporary feminist place-based. In K. L. Blair & L. Nickoson (Eds.), *Composing feminist interventions: Activism, engagement, praxis*. Fort Collins, CO: The WAC Clearinghouse / Louisville, CO: University Press of Colorado. Retrieved from https://wac.colostate.edu/books/perspectives/feminist.

Rosenberg, L. (2015). *The Desire for literacy: Writing in the lives of adult learners.* Urbana, IL: NCTE /Conference on College Composition and Communication.

Royster, J. J. (1996). When the first voice you hear is not your own. *College Composition and Communication, 47*(1), 29–40.

Royster, J.J. & Kirsch, G.E. (2012). *Feminist rhetorical practices: New horizons for rhetoric, composition, and literacy studies.* Carbondale, IL: Southern Illinois University Press.

Selfe, Cynthia L. (2016). Pushing back, against ourselves: Discipline at the cellular level. Paper presented at the Research Network Forum, Conference on College Composition and Communication, Houston, TX, April 6, 2016.

The work of the YWCA in the cotton mill villages of the south. (1909). (Series IV, box 499, folder 2). Young Women's Christian Association of the U.S.A.'s Records at Smith College, Northampton, MA.

Villenas, S. (2000). The ethnography called my back: Writings of the exotic gaze, "othering" Latina, and recuperating Xicanisma. In E. A. St.Pierre and W. S. Pillow (Eds.), *Working the ruins: Feminist poststructural theory and methods in education* (pp. 74–95). New York, NY: Routledge Press.

CHAPTER 5.
FUNDING GEOGRAPHY: THE LEGACY OF FEMALE-RUN SETTLEMENT CULTURE FOR CONTEMPORARY FEMINIST PLACE-BASED PEDAGOGY INITIATIVES

Liz Rohan
University of Michigan-Dearborn

Rohan's case study deploys archival methods to historicize the work of contemporary feminist teachers, researchers, and administrators who develop community engagement and place-based initiatives. It provides data about historic feminists working and writing in the U.S. progressive era in Chicago and Detroit, with special attention to the history of a Detroit-area settlement house, the Tau Beta Community House, which flourished between 1917 and 1954. Historical figures such as Lucy Carner and Borgchild Halvorsen suggested that community service work among feminist academics has a history that is linked to the work of progressive era feminists, particularly those inspired by Jane Addams, and like minded colleagues running settlements. Thus, this chapter also highlights the dynamics leading to the demise of this feminist-run settlement culture during the politically conservative decades following the Depression. Overall, Rohan historicizes community-based feminist projects as a way to trace contemporary place-based pedagogical movements sponsored by Detroit educators and artists.

This archival study features some historical rhetorical work undertaken by Tau Beta, one of Detroit's upper-middle-class women's clubs, from approximately 1916 to 1958 when Tau Beta members, along with the professional woman they hired, developed and arranged the building of a settlement house in the city of

Hamtramck, Michigan. Hamtramck was first a village, and also an enclave of Polish immigrants that held out from annexation with the city of Detroit when this city multiplied its girth exponentially in the 1920s, in tandem with the expanding U.S. auto industry. Growing separate from the surrounding city of Detroit, the material needs of the village's citizens were nevertheless acknowledged along with those of Detroit's through the city's major philanthropic organizations such as the Detroit Community Union, a major funding source for the Tau Beta Community House (Wood, 1955). Tau Beta settlement work in Hamtramck began in 1916 in a rented a flat before it moved into a neighborhood house that included a library, a nursery, a health clinic, a domestic science room, a boy's club room, showers, and residence for its six workers (Social pioneering, 1926). Eventually the settlement expanded to fill a larger house that was finished in 1928. Some history of Tau Beta showcases historical feminists who built place-based pedagogies through various means of persuasion when relying on nineteenth-century discourse about domestic space, which included espoused cooperation across gender and class lines. The eventual demise of this particular community settlement house project also offers a historical illustration of how the interplay of rhetoric and constructed gender roles can shape community building, and also how a place, in this case Detroit between the world wars, can encourage the invention of specific claims and methods among activists working for change. Featuring the perhaps inevitably temporal circumstances in which individuals wield their power through their rhetoric and related material practices, the study also shows a primary example of the "the social networks in which women connect and interact with each others and use language with intention," which Gesa Kirsch and Jacqueline Jones Royster (2012) name "social circulation" (p. 101).

As Tau Beta leaders gained momentum as feminists in Detroit the influence of U.S. woman's clubs was actually beginning to wane. By the end of the 1920s it was no longer fashionable to make the case for women's work as particularly distinct or women's needs as particularly pressing (Gere, 1997; Ladd-Taylor, 1994), which had been the method of Tau Beta members and their allies during these years in Detroit. But in Detroit, and its micro-community of Hamtramck, the work of women, and the work of Tau Beta particularly, might have been seen differently considering the need for services for and social control of newly arrived African-Americans and immigrants working for the auto industry. As Tau Beta clubwomen began their work, Detroit was being overrun by newcomers responding to Henry Ford's program to pay workers five dollars a day. Confirming the adage that if the country gets a cold, Detroit gets pneumonia, when a short recession hit the US from 1914 to 1915 more than 50 percent of Detroiters were out of work and "an estimated sixty thousand were European immigrants, most of whom could not speak or read English" (Mason, 2008, p. 127). Hamtramck had become one of the most densely populated communities in the country at the time. Just 2.1 miles square miles, the city filled with unskilled immigrants, again, mostly Polish, who were drawn to the Dodge Main plant built in the village (Hyde, 2005; Kowalski, 2006). The perceived need to Americanize new immigrants, as well as these immigrants' real material needs, drew Tau Beta women into Hamtramck where they were particularly encouraged to go (Plumb, 1938; Kowalski, 2010).

A centerpiece of Tau Beta's development work was the aforementioned community building finished in 1928, which also included a big gymnasium, an auditorium, a roof garden, an expanded pottery room, a game room and a "model flat" (Plumb, 1938). The funding for new space was the result of a mass campaign that included cooperative fundraising with other community leaders for a woman's hospital, a YWCA building, and a home for pregnant women. The $4,000,0000 campaign was coined as "building for the womanhood of Detroit" (Social pioneering, 1926). The Tau Beta settlement movement's strengths and weaknesses, including its developmental roots in nativist anxiety, would eventually bring about its demise. After World War II, the rhetoric of the female-run settlement movement was no longer efficacious in Detroit, and elsewhere, because immigration patterns changed, and the field of social reform was professionalized, which marginalized elite female philanthropists and activists. Also in Detroit and elsewhere, when philanthropic organizations such as the United Way grew larger, more bureaucratic, and less interdisciplinary, settlement homes were regarded as costly white elephants. The Tau Beta Community house closed in 1958 just a few years after a male leader took over the work. The large Tudor home that once housed Tau Beta settlement activity was sold to a church and was repurposed as a school (Kowalski, 2006). Three other settlement houses were destroyed altogether for urban renewal projects including the longstandingNeighborhood House whose "neighbors" were forced to relocate (Acomb, 1959; Trolander, 1987).

ABOUT THE TAU BETA COMMUNITY HOUSE: HOMEMAKING AS PLACEMAKING AS PEDAGOGY

Tau Beta began in 1901 as a social club among elite Detroit young women still in high school (Kowalski, 2006). Soon enough the young women were drawn into charity work as the group's methods of community building were developed and its social consciousness was raised. Tau Beta's earliest charity work mimicked the work of another local visiting nurses program. It included preparing and delivering food to Detroit's poor and sick, mostly tuberculosis patients, and when using stoves in the basement of an elite Detroit school. Tau Beta members delivered the food on streetcars, on foot, in their "electrics" and eventually in gasoline cars. To fulfill the stereotype of a Tau Beta member as a rich society woman, one member was occasionally able to use her family's limousine. This work morphed into two other related projects: a diet kitchen, a kind of "meals on wheels," and a tuberculosis clinic, each later taken over by other agencies (Plumb, 1930, pp. 110–111). The women collaborated with established Detroit charities such as Associated Charities as well as the Detroit Community Union, established in 1917 (Mason, 2008). That philanthropic work developed by women was taken over by larger municipalities or organizations would be a trend with Tau Beta's future work and a significant overall result of women's volunteer work in the progressive era. For example, in 1912, U.S. women leaders founded the Children's Bureau, a national agency that provided prenatal and infant care among the underprivileged. The agency had an element of social control typical of elite-founded and run progressive-era civic and philanthropic endeavors at the time (Muncy, 1991). Emma Howes' study of elite women of the Y.M.C.A. working with poor women in Appalachian America described in this collection (Chapter 4, this collection) also draws attention to the social control embedded in benevolent progressive-era projects, which included settlement work.

Tau Beta's Hamtramck settlement work was established late as of 1916 when considering that, as one example, Chicago's well-known Hull House got its start decades earlier in 1889; settlement work began in Detroit as earlier as 1858 when the Neighborhood House settlement was established. But Tau Beta's first philanthropic activities situates the organization's goals in context with similar progressive-era female run endeavors roughly during a time period when settlement houses in the US had proliferated from six to four hundred by 1910 (Jackson, 2001). Tau Beta's settlement work grew along with the previously mentioned Detroit Community Fund, a precursor to United Way Services, as well as with similar settlement initiatives in Detroit, and across the nation. The settlement work that would birth The Tau Beta Community House in its heyday, sprawling into two houses, included sports programming, a music program, an arts program, a health clinic, a laundry, and a "nursery" for working women who needed daycare for their children and a program we might call "latchkey" care today (Tau Beta Community House, 1930). During its formative years Eleanor Clay Ford (wife of Edsel Ford, daughter-in-law of Henry Ford), and her associates, including Eleanor's sister, Josephine Clay Kantzler, were at the helm of the organization and longtime director Borgchild Halvorsen was in charge of running the community house, known as "The House of Hope."

The Tau Beta Community House, like other settlement houses flourishing at the time, extended women's work into the public sphere by grounding this work materially in a particular locality through what I call placemaking via homemaking. When placemaking via homemaking, Tau Beta leaders relied on the same Victorian beliefs that influenced the growth of Hull-House, a settlement that has been heavily studied, and was one model for Tau Beta leaders. As two feminist geographers describe the ideology shaping the growth of Hull-House: the "home was . . . the seat of moral, aesthetic, and cultural stability" and "home decoration was a matter of great consequence" because it expressed "the status, taste and moral character of its inhabitants" (Domosh and Seager, 2001, pp. 7–8). Placemaking through homemaking was a pedagogy in the sense that "creating a good home was seen as integral to creating good moral citizens" and "hence empowered [immigrant women] as important shapers of U.S. democracy" (p. 21). That is, Tau Beta settlers were teachers when modeling and prescribing particular behaviors. Placemaking as homemaking also relied on what historian Molly Ladd-Taylor (1994) calls "maternalism." She explains that "maternalists' genuine concern for the welfare of women and children of other racial and ethnic groups—combined with their culturally specific ideas about proper family life and children's needs—made assimilating immigrants into 'American' culture a vital part of their child welfare work" (p. 5). As one example, one of Tau Beta's first programs in 1917 taught neighborhood women to knit for "their men in the service" (Plumb, 1938, p. 136). Tau Beta leaders working as maternalists capitalized on agreed upon or stereotyped roles for middle-class women when drumming up support for new and expanded physical space and program creation. As Tau Beta historian Mildred Plumb (1938) described the women's initiative, "The village government had little vision of the public's needs. . . . We aimed to undertake what the authorities did not, or could not, provide and demonstrate its value" (p. 133). The women were actually successful in modeling the value of what they considered to be essential services to government agencies when in 1924 the settlement's library became the Hamtramck Library (Plumb, 1938; Kowalski, 2006). The fate of this library parallels another trend characterizing progressive-era clubwomen's work. U.S. clubwomen founded many of the country's first public libraries, to the extent that by 1933 75% of public libraries "owed their origins to women's clubs" (Gere, 1997, p. 122). Tau Beta's founding of Hamtramck's library demonstrates how some progressive-era feminist philanthropy projects were taken up by government agencies and further exemplifies placemaking as homemaking. During the late nineteenth century and early twentieth century, libraries were associated with middle-class homes while library work became associated with women who joined this profession en masse (Jenkins, 1996).

The settlement's "model flat," one result of the 1926 building campaign, further evidences that the Tau Beta Community House promoted domestic space, placemaking as homemaking, as an argument to its clients, and to Hamtramck leaders. Designed as a key teaching tool to be used for bridal showers and also as temporary living quarters for newlyweds post-honeymoon, the model flat was promoted with perhaps some wishful thinking. Ostensibly, when brides and/or the newly married looked at or spent time in the flat, they would be persuaded to set up housekeeping independent from their "in laws," an "all too common practice among this class of people" (Tau Beta Community House, 1930; Tau Beta 23rd annual report, 1928). The new two-storied house was also meticulously decorated, and included Detroit's signature design, Pewabic pottery tile, as well as various decorative gifts including a drinking fountain, a sunlight lamp, and a bronze statue of a "Wild Flower." As at Hull House, the Tau Beta Community house also had rooms set aside for in residence professionals (Plumb, 1938). The model flat and the attention to décor in the new building echoed one means of persuasion via the design for the original Tau Beta settlement space established in 1916; its décor was "finer than the neighbors" when "owing to the standard of taste" (Plumb, 1938, p. 135.).

A leader of the Detroit clubwomen movement who visited the new community house in 1930 relied on maternalism to assess the value of Tau Beta's programming, affirming circulating associations between a beautiful home and moral behavior. The visitor asserted that "by steady growth in influence, community houses like Tau Beta send forth their little beam into a naughty world" (Tau Beta Community House, 1930, p. 21). Placemaking as homemaking was a form of persuasion, a pedagogy, and also inevitably coercive. A historian of Hamtramck, referring to the Tau Beta settlement, put it most astutely in 1955 when he wrote that "the financial support of settlements . . . indicates that the movement did not arise indigenously from a realization of need on the part of the people served" (Wood, 1955, p. 189). The nativist goal of teaching non-assimilated Americans how to live via Victorian-style décor is obviously an outdated pedagogical method. Yet, typical of other settlement projects, including Chicago's Hull House, Tau Beta's settlement also created career opportunities for women. Its "first residents" were "nurses, visiting housekeepers and social workers" who "lived as friendly neighbors" at the flat (Plumb, 1938, p. 139). Perhaps also coercive, but yet progressive from a contemporary perspective, Tau Beta women also taught an American version of feminism in the Hamtramck Polish community, encouraging Polish women to defy their husbands, get out of the house and make time for themselves (Plumb, 1938). The Tau Beta Community House furthermore provided scholarships to Hamtramck community women, one who founded a sorority at Wayne State University that was reportedly open to members of all racial and ethnic groups (Wood, 1955). Encouraging citizenship had real consequence as well when the Polish-American contingent of Hamtramck seized political power of the previously German-American run village and voted to become a city independent from Detroit in 1921 (Kowalski, 2010).

The Tau Beta Community House was at one time regarded one of the best in the nation, and the women leading Tau Beta were among Detroit's most elite citizens. So the Tau Beta Community House could be categorized as a boutique operation, Hamtramck a rich woman's playground. But the relationship between placemaking and cooperation among settlers and those whom they served, was embraced by settlers across the country. In 1945 the well-regarded Chicago area settlement house movement leader Lucy P. Carner emphasized the importance of placemaking among settlers when declaring that "[t]he settlement is <u>rooted in geographical community</u> [sic]. Its purpose is to understand that community, to help develop its potentialities, to provide or aid it in securing needed services." As scholar of Hull House Shannon Jackson (2001) has observed, settlers were "committed to locality" (p. 6). Noting the limits of cooperation between settlers and their clients, Jackson points out furthermore that "settlement reform still meant changing the persons that one encountered" (p. 13). Relying on maternalism, settlers drew "from a discourse of domesticity, a nineteenth century formation that positioned women as sympathetic interpreters of the microperformances of every day life" (p. 6). Roxanne Mountford (2005) relatedly points out the relationship between "rhetorical performance" and "the rituals performed in that space" (p. 37). The expansion of space, creating and maintaining a beautiful home, was the set for to settlers' "performance" to local clients and local stakeholders; a domestic aesthetic embedded in a space also designed like a home tempered an activist agenda. Pretty was power.

Maternalism also softened what could have otherwise seemed too polarizing or too unfeminine. Tau Beta leaders were aware of their privilege and power to create change, and feasibly waves, in the world of Detroit philanthropy, and in the world of competing men of industry such as Henry Ford and the Dodge brothers, Horace and John. Hamtramck's Dodge auto plant was a competitor to the nearby Ford plant. The Dodges had broken business ties with Henry Ford, but these brothers at the same time donated space to Tau Beta for its library, installed shelves for this library and also supplied janitor services for the building (Plumb, 1938). Lore even suggests that the many Polish residents who had flocked to Hamtramck "were promised an 'open' town, free from the Puritanical restrictions of the Ford Motor Company" (Wood, 1955, p. 46). Meanwhile, Eleanor's husband Edsel was a major contributor to the Detroit Community Fund (Contributor's list, 1917) in the same period when the Dodge family donated more than $10,000 to Tau Beta. Kantzler had been a bridesmaid in John Dodge's daughter's wedding (Hyde, 2005), but her husband Ernest, best friend and ally of Edsel, was also a nemesis of Henry (Collier and Horowitz, 1987). Conflict in this small world run by men was just not practical in the so-called domestic sphere of community building via settling. As Tau Beta president Marion Thurber described the value of cooperation in 1909: "Our desire is to work with the other organizations rather than in opposition to them, and we trust that we may some day be of help to them that they have already been to us" (as cited in Plumb, 1938, p. 15). Forty years later in 1949, the longtime director of the Tau Beta Community House, Borgchild Halvorsen, told the *Detroit Free Press* that during her thirty-year career she was most proud of "the fact that Tau Beta staff members, the people served by the center, and the community itself have worked and developed together in 'distinguished cooperation'" (as cited in McIntire, 1949).

Figure 5.1. The new Tau Beta Community House, funded in part by Detroit's "Building For Womanhood," philanthropic campaign. Photo courtesy of Hamtramck Historical Society.

Tau Beta's appeals for a new building as part of the previously mentioned Detroit "Women's Building Campaign," in a 1926 public relations booklet entitled "Social Pioneering," features the inter-relationship between maternalism, nativism, placemaking as homemaking, and pedagogy. The rhetoric used for this campaign furthermore shows how these Detroit women were poised to "perform" so-called women's work, and the rituals enabled by this work, through the expansion of space, as well as by cooperating with community leaders. The stated purpose of the existing house at this time was purportedly to "help in the adjustment of the foreign-born citizen and his [sic] family to American life" (Social pioneering, 1926). Helping immigrants adjust effectively required more space. Quarters for the health clinic that was run in cooperation with the Visiting Nurse Association were cramped. The mortality of infants was at stake as well. Since the Visiting Nurses Association had begun its work in Hamtramck in 1914, infant mortality had decreased by roughly half, an arguable result of the "better babies, better citizens" mantra circulating at the settlement. Space was needed for young women's fine and domestic art instruction and recreation facilities for the boy's youth programming. The opportunities for recreation and amusement in this new space for boys in particular would purportedly cut down on juvenile delinquency. Two hundred and forty-five boys had passed through Hamtramck's Juvenile Court in 1926. The staff had also increased considerably since the settlement's inception. The reported material support in 1926 reflects the method of "cooperation" built into the Tau Beta settlement model: five full-time workers were paid by the City of Hamtramck, seven full-time and 11 part-time workers were paid by the Detroit Community Union, and seven full-time and two part-time workers were paid by the Visiting Nurse Association.

Figure 5.2. Children playing on the Tau Beta Community House playground. Photo courtesy of Hamtramck Historical Society.

Relying on maternalism—babies might die, as well as some arguable nativist anxiety—weak recreation offerings was breeding juvenile delinquency—the argument for more space to support and expand Tau Beta's goals and initiatives through interdisciplinary settlement work is arguably well laid out. Tau Beta's "Social Pioneering" pamphlet, that also represented interests of other Detroit feminist activists, urged philanthropists "to replace . . . inadequate and work out buildings for the womanhood of Detroit" (Social pioneering, 1926). The Tau Beta Community House, it argues, "has grown steadily in usefulness from year to year, and its work has been done so well that the present equipment will no longer accommodate all who seek its advantages." Appeals relying maternalism were still persuasive to Detroit philanthropists in 1926: the building of the new Tau Beta house was financed along with the funding for the new YWCA, and the two women's medical centers (Florence Crittenton, 1930). A 1928 review of the new settlement building in the Detroit Community Fund News shows that the agreed upon value of placemaking as homemaking, and homemaking as a companion to pedagogy, was status quo: "The auditorium, which would be a credit to any community, fulfilled a strong felt need. Here, at last, is a place where the young people as well as their elders may hold their parties, attend lectures, concerts and educational movies" (as cited in Tau Beta 23rd annual report, 1928). Perhaps also convinced of the relationship between beautiful home living and better behavior, Hamtramck's probation officer in the juvenile division was awed by the "cordiality" of the new building's entrance and "all the activities planned to help the individual to enjoy and understand himself through some form of Art" (as cited in Tau Beta 23rd annual report, 1928).

Also in 1928, Kantzler, then chairman of the building committee, reflected on the relationship between Tau Beta community building and the building itself, emphasizing the relationship between the expansion of physical space and the women's proliferating ethos as activists. Assessing the value of the women's investment in space to be $330, 000 (over four and a half million 2017 dollars), and grateful for the funding from the Community Union, Kanztler asserted that "[i]t is a real obligation which we have assumed" (as cited in Tau Beta 23rd annual report, 1928). Growth of the settlement's activities the following year in 1929 was attributed to the expanded space that included multi-uses for the new auditorium. As planned, the new space also allowed for expanded art programs, and more jobs, including the hiring of a pottery teacher, another woman on staff. In her summation of the year's successful endeavors, then Tau Beta president Margaret Watkins emphasized the relationship between new space, and improved services. Watkins also reflected upon the espoused value of cooperation across gender and classes among those engaged in settlement work when declaring, "I think we have become what we always wanted to be, a real community center" (as cited in Tau Beta 24th annual report, 1929). Ironically, the collaboration between Detroit's funding organizations and Tau Beta through the expansion of space that Kantzler remarked upon in 1928, as well as the relationship between space expansion and community building, emphasized by Watkins a year later, would become irrelevant or forgotten just three decades later. Soon enough, and perhaps too soon, settlement houses were regarded as white elephants, costly and irrelevant to community development.

Figure 5.3. The cover for the public relations brochure, Social Pioneering (1926). Photo courtesy of Hamtramck Historical Society.

Figure 5.4. The second but not newest Tau Beta building, built 1919–20, mostly from private donations, at a cost of $54,880.02 (Plumb, 1938), which is 792,000 2018 dollars. Photo courtesy of Hamtramck Historical Society.

While the expanded space of the new Tau Beta Community House provided opportunity for robust programming, the momentum in this space in 1929, the funding of new facilities was also a climax of sorts, the beginning of the end. As the Depression hit, the resources of the settlement were tested. Staff salaries were cut, the nurse was let go, and art programs were slashed, as the house also reached its all time highest attendance (Plumb, 1926). Volunteer work, which included jobs big and small on the part of Tau Beta members, helped to keep the house afloat (Plumb, 1936). Other changes fragmented core leadership at the settlement. In 1935 Olga Wahlburg, a hired settlement activities director, and an immigrant herself, who was reportedly very skilled at negotiating with Hamtramck leaders, left the settlement and by 1937 the members of Tau Beta were more scattered across the Detroit metro area and even the globe (Plumb, 1936). As of 1947 the mission of the settlement was transformed, and excluded reference to Americanizing activities. The settlement's mission at this point was to "supplement the social, education and recreational activities and to initiate new activities to meet new needs" (Tau Beta Community House purpose, 1947). Perhaps acknowledging an increase in African Americans in Hamtramck to 11.7 percent of the population by 1950 (Wood, 1955), the Tau Beta Community House mission statement also claimed that "the facilities of the House are open to children and adults regardless of race or creed" (Tau Beta Community House purpose, 1947). The board running the Tau Beta community house was also transformed to include more community members. Probably the most significant change came about when longtime settlement director Borgchild Halvorsen retired and the settlement was taken over by a male leader, Emeric Kurtagh. A few years later the Tau Beta Settlement House would close.

GEOGRAPHY IS NOT FUNDED: THE END OF THE TAU BETA SETTLEMENT WORK ON LOCATION

The decision to close the Tau Beta Commuity House, along with other settlement houses across the country, was the result of some powerful cultural mandates, an extension of a mass assessment sponsored by United Community Services, the organization into which the Detroit Community Fund had folded. The assessment that likely led to the closing of Tau Beta's settlement house, authored by consultant Lewis Barrett, and referred to at the time as the Barrett report, signified that the rationale for women's placemaking via homemaking was no longer persuasive or relevant because of changing cultural assumptions about the role and administration of community centers. Barrett had already performed similar assessments in New Orleans and Boston (McDowell, 1953). Feminist geographer Doreen Massey (1994) argues that "space, and place, spaces and places, and our senses of them . . . are gendered through and through" (p. 186). The particulars allowing Tau Beta clubwomen to fund a robust community center in a house affirms Massey's argument that space is gendered and culturally constructed. Progressive-era cultural constructions, extending nineteenth-century ideology fusing domesticity and femininity, enabled Tau Beta's work to physically expand when proliferating an ideology, which I also identified as a pedagogy. The efficacy of this ideology had run its course as new brokers like Barrett gained power.

Collectively spelling out the death knell of the settlement culture as birthed by Jane Addams and her ilk dedicated to "locality," and the related practices of placemaking as homemaking, Barrett's incisive tone could shake the boots of any reader whose pet projects have been assessed with the alleged spirit of progress. Barrett's overall task was measuring duplications—that is, ascertaining if private agencies were performing the work that was already being taken care of by public agencies. Barrett first concluded overall that the settlement houses were duplicating services already provided by public schools and tax-supported recreation centers. Mobility via automobiles and public transformation also expanded people's options for education and recreation. Barrett ultimately recommended "a revised pattern of operation for group work and recreational services in Detroit," directed by United Community Services, a pattern that would soon enough frame the funding structure for settlements in the next decades. Along with his many specific recommendations for several Detroit settlement houses, Barrett argued that the Tau Beta Community House, as well as the nearby Highland Park settlement, should create stronger programing for adults "even at the expense of smaller programming for children and youth," and add more men and community members to their boards. Barrett's recommendation that the Neighborhood (settlement) House be closed, because it was now located in an area slated for industry per urban renewal initiatives, was either prescient or successfully prescriptive. As mentioned earlier, this building became a victim of urban renewal and was torn down in 1959 (Acomb 1959).

Kantzler's untimely death when she drowned in a swimming pool in 1954 paralleled the end of the Tau Beta era of settlement work on its grounds when some of the service once sponsored at the house merged with those housed at the eventually torn down Neighborhood House, and also the closed Highland Park settlement. Previously in-house settlement services would become the Neighborhood Service Organization launching its signature program, "Meals on Wheels" (Acomb, 1959). This "reorganization" embraced by 1954 Tau Beta settlement leadership was designed to "shift the emphasis from a building-centered to a problem-centered approach" (Tau Beta Association, 1954). Kurtagh considered the Neighborhood Service Organization a "mutation of the settlement" in "offering a variety of accessible and coordinated social services "(Trolander, 1987, p. 204). In fact, Kurtagh was quoted in the *Detroit Free Press* (Stromberg, c.a. 1959) as claiming, "When we operated in building-centered agencies, we spent 60 percent of our budget for personnel. Now we are able to spend 95 percent on personnel. This means more and better trained workers." For Kurtaugh, houseless mobile social service work was more agile. In 1957 the Tau Beta Community House went up for sale. The Hamtramck Recreation Commission was posed to buy it, but in the end could not afford it (Kowalski, 2006). All services at the house were suspended by January of 1958. Of the closing of the house, the president of Tau Beta, Mrs. George Bushnell, described the event as such, "The community that we entered in 1916 was in sharp contrast to what it is today. Many of our former services are no longer needed, thanks to general community prosperity and maturity" (qtd in Stewart, 1955).

Bushnell's remarks parallel similar rhetoric about female-run settlement work at the end of its heyday and also echo many of the recommendations in the Barrett report, which highlights the interplay between rhetoric, culture and activism as well as the phenomenon of hegemony in shaping major change. As sociologist Leslie Trolander (1987) describes this paradigm shift from local control to agencies using mostly social work personnel: "Gone was the settlement's special identification with a neighborhood" (p. 233). Place-based pedagogy wasn't out of business necessarily, but the value of place itself as a generative tool for social service had been marginalized or was not prioritized in the broader culture of late twentieth-century U.S. settlement work. As one social worker described the dynamic, "Nobody is funding geography" (as cited in Trolander, 1987, p. 230). The new paradigms shaping social service negated the relevance of "locality," and hence the importance of location for activist work. Furthermore, as Kurtaugh's comments suggest, the mobile settlement model relied on social workers rather than volunteers, specialists or trained-on the-job professionals like Tau Beta's Wahlberg and Halvorsen had been. In its flushest years, Tau Beta had its own ceramics teacher and a slew of medical professionals on site. Charlotte Kimerly of Detroit's Sophie Wright Settlement complained in 1952 that the settlement's art program suffered because of the new job classifications, purportedly dictated by United Community Services (later the United Way) that required credentialed social workers. "I, for one, can't figure out how a Master's in Social work qualifies one to teach arts and crafts," Kimerly asserted.

GENDERING SPACE: THE LEGACY OF PROGRESSIVE ERA CULTURE, RHETORIC AND ACTIVISM

When the large homes that had hosted progressive-era female run settlement work were sold, closed or torn down for the sake of agile social services, and also urban renewal programs, elite women activists lost their power that had been conditional. The stellar and otherwise state-of-the-art Tau Beta Community House was also a house of cards. Early twentieth-century-club women succeeded when armed with a certain set of assumptions related to maternalism. Meanwhile, these 'feminine' values became absorbed into dominant (a.k.a. 'male dominated') American culture when government agencies took over some social services when for example, setting up welfare programs for children and also supporting public libraries. The relationship between the home and the actual physical spaces of settlements affirmed 'women's roles' in society as homemakers, which fit the constructed view of a woman's role in society. By the late 1940s, culturally assigned roles for women were particularly in flux as women were encouraged to embody private spaces as homemakers (Enoch, 2012).

To some extent, the mission of Tau Beta's settlement house had already been completed or, was no longer necessary, as Bushnell, the Tau Beta president quoted earlier, suggested. First, libraries were no longer gendered as a particularly female space, at least in Hamtramck. Later, the needs of the poor in Detroit were interpreted and responded to by the Neighborhood Service Association. Moreover, interpreting America to assimilated Americans, or the many African-

Americans who now lived in Detroit neighborhoods once filled with immigrants, put the particular brand of settlement culture espoused by bourgeoisie female settlers in perhaps too radical, too uncomfortable, or too ambitious of a position. As one head worker of the Detroit Sophie Wright Settlement House, Dora Nelson (1952), asserted during the era, "For Sophie Wright Settlement, as for all Settlements working with negroes [sic] there is a particular need to be convincing, courageous, and energetic as the problems of this whole group are more difficult to solve." Nelson argued for the relevance of settlements for activism and problem solving but also hinted at their limitations. The spirit of cooperation embraced by Tau Beta clubwomen early in the century may have required a much different mindset and a more flexible skillset to serve a new generation of neighbors.

Cultural mutations, which erased or made irrelevant maternalism, and the agreed upon associations between homemaking and women's work, in conjunction with the professionalization of social services, were perhaps inevitable. On the other hand, this historical case study suggests that the gendering of space can have real material consequences. This history lesson is therefore potential food for thought among contemporary feminist activists mindful of how culture affects and shapes their work. As Mountford (2005) suggests, "The study of physicality and space, especially in studies of rhetorical performance (formal or informal), is a promising area of research that offers important opportunities for feminists" (p. 152). Historical perspectives can on the other hand illustrate the difficulty of measuring contemporary cultural trends. That is, for historical actors—as well as for us—it has been, and it is nearly impossible to critically interpret and react incisively to the forces that buoy us or bring us down on the spot and in real time. Whether there were mixed feelings on the part of the founders or female leaders of the Tau Beta Community House when it closed is unknown or unavailable. One copy of the Barrett report stamped "Tau Beta," peppered with the annotations of its anonymous reader writing "bunk," does suggest that the ideas and suggestions Barrett espoused were not necessarily agreed upon or mainstream even in their day, or at least by one reader. Even with all of their privileges, Tau Beta leaders weren't impervious to cultural trends that marginalized women's work. Hull House hadn't even made the cut. A highway through a neighborhood served by this settlement house, as well as the building and establishment of the new University of Illinois at Chicago, displaced most if not all of the settlement's nearby residents. The culture of cooperation between settlements, neighborhoods, and the middle-class bourgeoisie, was either forgotten or irrelevant to the writer of an article in the Hull House newsletter who remarked about the planned college campus and asserted that Hull House "would have no place on the campus of a modern university in a metropolitan center" ("Hull House to Continue," c. a. 1963).

This historical case of the growth and demise of the Tau Beta Community House grounded in trends shaping American progressive-era feminist work first highlights the relationship between rhetoric, culture and the gendering of space, and secondly suggests the relevant legacy of the progressive era for those planning thoughtful place-based and civic oriented projects. Studying the "social circulation" of language use and its historical context in this case "can help us see how traditions are carried on, changed, reinvented, and reused when they are passed down from one generation to the next" (Royster & Kirsch, 2012, p. 101). As Emily Ronay Johnston similarly argues (Chapter 3, this collection), knowledge-making includes "negotiating what we know, have known and have yet to know," which should include of the legacy of historical actors. New initiatives in contemporary Detroit designed to meet the educational and material needs of its citizens, such as a new makers space housed in a church (Swan, 2014), furthermore suggests a renewed interest in the progressive-era brand of "locality," when citizens are served on site in neighborhoods and philanthropy fosters neighborhood relations. Detroit activist and writer Yusef Shakur is funding a community house in his boyhood Detroit neighborhood located in one of the poorest zip codes in the US. Committed to "locality," Shakur says he is "bringing the neighbor back to the hood" (Mondry, 2014; DeVito, 2015). Recently deceased philosopher and longtime Detroit activist Grace Lee Boggs (2012), who admired and quoted from the work of progressive giant John Dewey, advocated for place-based learning in a city where neighborhood schools have been shuttered en masse. She imagined a neighborhood school with services akin to historical settlements, shaped by curricula that engages young people, and also an intergenerational citizenship via "a resource center with a community theater, artists' studios and information about the different skills available in the neighborhood" (p. 132). These developments shaping change in Detroit's urban neighborhoods suggest that various aspects of women's historical rhetoric and material practices grounded in place, that too relied on rhetorical work and pedagogical initiatives, should be acknowledged by contemporary activists and feminists. As Enoch (2008) likewise suggests, acknowledging the legacy of historical actors who created, occupied, and shaped space can prohibit presentism about our work's novelty or originality and also encourage awareness that our contemporary work, too, is culturally constructed. Overall, these histories are sources for inspiration and reflection when measuring an inevitably flawed and complicated collective experience among feminists engaged in and affected by place-based pedagogies.

REFERENCES

Acomb, T. W. (1959, Sept. 15). *Letter to Mrs. Radoslav A. Tsanaoff* (Box 73, Folder 27). National Federation of Settlements Collection, University of Minnesota, Minneapolis, MN.

Barrett, L. (1953). *Survey of United Community Services, Inc and its member agencies, Detroit, Michigan* (Box 107, Folder 10). National Federation of Settlements Collection, University of Minnesota, Minneapolis, MN.

Boggs, G. L. & Kurashige, S. (2012). *The next American evolution: Sustainable action for the twenty-first century*. [Kindle version]. Retrieved from http://amazon.com.

Carner, L. P. (1945). *Why new settlements* (Box 43, Folder 13). Northwestern University Settlement Association Records, Northwestern University Archives, Evanston, IL.

Collier, P. & Horowitz, D. (1987). *The Fords: An American epic*. New York, NY: Summit Books.

Contributors list. (1917). (Box 3, Folder 3–1). United Community Services Collection, Walter P. Reuther Library, Wayne State University, Detroit, MI.

DeVito, L. (2015, June 10). The neighborhood evangelist: Yusef Shakur. *Detroit Metro Times*. Retrieved from http://www.metrotimes.com.

Domosh, M. & Joni, S. (2001). *Putting women in place: Feminist geographers make sense of the world*. New York, NY: Guilford Press.

Enoch, J. (2008). A woman's place is in the school: Rhetorics of gendered space in nineteenth-century America. *College English, 70*(3), 275–295.

Enoch, J. (2012). There's no place like the childcare center: A feminist analysis of <home> in the World War II era. *Rhetoric Review, 31*(4), 422–442.

Florence Crittenton Hospital and the Woman's Hospital to be visited this month. (1930). *The Magazine of the Women's City Club*, 15.

Gere, A. (1997). *Intimate practices: Literacy and cultural work in U.S. women's clubs, 1880–1920*. Urbana-Champaign, IL: University of Illinois Press.

Hull house to continue. (c. a. 1962). *Hull House Association News* (Box 1, Folder 499). Hull House Collection, University of Illinois-Chicago, Chicago, IL.

Hyde, C. K. (2005). *The Dodge brothers: The men, the motor cars, and the legacy*. Detroit, MI: Wayne State University Press.

Jackson, S. (2000). *Lines of activity: Performance, historiography, Hull-House domesticity*. Ann Arbor, MI: The University of Michigan Press.

Jenkins, C. (1996). Since so many of today's librarians are women. In S. Hildenbrand (Ed.), *Reclaiming the American library past: Writing the women* (pp. 221–49). Norwood, NJ: Ablex Publishing Company.

Johnston, E. R. (2018). Methodology and accountability: Tracking our movements as feminist pedagogues. In K. Blair & L. Nickoson (Eds.), *Composing feminist interventions: Activism, engagement, praxis*. Fort Collins, CO: The WAC Clearinghouse / Louisville, CO: University Press of Colorado. Retrieved from https://wac.colostate.edu/books/perspectives/feminist/.

Kimerly, C. (1952). *Special committee reports, Charlotte L. Kimerly: 1952 annual report of the president—Elizabeth B. Davis* (Box 73, Folder 19). National Federation of Settlements Collection, University of Minnesota, Minneapolis, MN.

Kowalski, G. (2006). The bunch that helped Detroit. *Michigan History Magazine*, March/April, 8–13.

Kowalski, G. (2010). *Wicked Hamtramck: Lust, liquor and lead*. Mount Pleasant, SC: The History Press.

McDowell, J. (1953, May 1). *Letter to Arthur Chelsea* (Box 74, Folder 5). National Federation of Settlements Collection, University of Minnesota, Minneapolis, MN.

McIntire, E. B. (1949, July 17). Farewell tribute to Miss Halvorsen. *Detroit News*. Borgchild Halvorsen Papers, Edsel and Eleanor Ford House Archives, Grosse Pointe Shores, MI.

Mason, P. (2008). *Tracy. W. McGregor: Humanitarian, philanthropist, and Detroit civic leader*. Detroit, MI: Wayne State University Press.

Massey, D. (1994). *Space, place and gender*. Minneapolis, MN: University of Minnesota Press.

Mondry, A. (2014, June 3). New businesses and new directions for two entrepreneurs in Detroit's Zone 8 neighborhood. *Model D magazine*. Retrieved from http://www.modelmedia.com.

Mountford, R. (2005). *The gendered pulpit: Preaching in American protestant spaces*. Carbondale, IL: Southern University Press.

Muncy, R. (1991). *Creating a female dominion of reform 1890–1935*. New York, NY: Oxford University Press.

Nelson, D. E. (1952). *Supplement of 1952 annual report; Sophie Wright settlement* (Box227, Folder 361). National Federation of Settlements Archives, University of Minnesota, Minneapolis, MN.

Plumb, M. (1936). Adventures in neighborliness. *Hamtramck Today, 29*, 3–8. Tau Beta and Hamtramck Collection, Hamtramck Library Archives, Hamtramck, MI.

Plumb, M. (1938). *History of Tau Beta 1901–1938*. Detroit, MI: Evans-Weber-Hebb.

Rosenberg, L. & Howes, E. (2018). Listening to research as a feminist ethos of representation. In K. Blair & L. Nickoson (Eds.), *Composing feminist interventions: Activism, engagement, praxis*. Fort Collins, CO: The WAC Clearinghouse / Louisville, CO: University Press of Colorado. Retrieved from https://wac.colostate.edu/books/perspectives/feminist/.

Royster, J. J. & Kirsch, G. E. (2012). *Feminist rhetorical practices: New horizons for rhetoric, composition and literacy studies*. Carbondale, IL: Southern Illinois University Press.

Social pioneering. (1926). Borgchild Halvorsen Papers, *Edsel and Eleanor Ford Estate Archives*. Grosse Pointe Shores, MI.

Swan, N. (2014, July 6). The 'maker' movement creates D.I.Y revolution. *Christian Science Monitor*. Retrieved from csmonitor.com.

Stewart, E. S. (1955, Jan. 23). Hamtramck to lose the house of hope. *Detroit Free Press*. Tau Beta Hamtramck, Hamtramck Library Archives, Hamtramck, MI.

Stromberg, W. (c.a. 1959). Social agency steps in saves bully. *Detroit Free Press* (Box 73, Folder 27). National Federation of Settlements Collection, University of Minnesota, Minneapolis, MN.

The Tau Beta Association 23rd annual report. (1928). (Box 228, Folder 365). *National Federation of Settlements Collection*, University of Minnesota, Minneapolis, MN.

The Tau Beta association 24th annual report. (1929). *Tau Beta, Burton Historical Collection*, Detroit Public Library, Detroit, MI.

Tau Beta association. (1954, June 21). *Memo to United Community Services of Metropolitan Detroit* (Box 227, Folder 362). National Federation of Settlements Collection, University of Minnesota, Minneapolis, MN.

Tau Beta Community House. (1930). *Magazine of the Women's City Club, January*, 15–25.

Tau Beta Community House the purpose. (1947). Tau Beta, Hamtramck Library Archives, Hamtramck, MI.

Taylor-Ladd, M. (1994). *Mother-work: Women, child welfare and the state, 1890–1930*. Urbana and Chicago, IL: University of Illinois Press.

Trolander, J. A. (1987). *Professionalism and social change: From the settlement to neighborhood centers, 1886 to the present*. New York, NY: Columbia University Press.

Wood, A. E. (1955). *Hamtramck then and now: A sociological study of a Polish community*. New York, NY: Bookman Associates.

PART 2. PARTNERSHIPS

CHAPTER 6.
BUILDING ENGAGED INTERVENTIONS IN GRADUATE EDUCATION

Keri E. Mathis
University of Louisville

Beth A. Boehm
University of Louisville

Boehm and Mathis profile the University of Louisville's efforts at becoming a more engaged university, including receiving the Carnegie Community Engaged University classification and implementing Ideas-to-Action, a quality enhancement plan that holds community engagement as one of its core principles. Yet these endeavors have focused largely on faculty research and undergraduate education, leaving graduate students out of the mix. Recent scholarship in higher education has documented a similar neglect of graduate student involvement in community engagement projects that challenge conventional types of academic research, teaching, and mentorship. The authors' positions within rhetoric and composition and within the University of Louisville's School of Interdisciplinary and Graduate Studies have afforded them the opportunity to initiate an interdisciplinary graduate community engagement program. Thus, they describe their efforts in extending these programs to focus on engaged scholarship and on developing a year-long academy that will lead to collaborations among graduate students on community projects.

During the last decade, the University of Louisville has made several steps toward becoming a more engaged university, including applying for and receiving the Carnegie Community Engaged University classification and implementing Ideas-to-Action, a quality enhancement plan that holds community engagement as one of its core principles. These endeavors, however, have focused largely on faculty research and undergraduate education, and have left graduate education and graduate students out of the mix. Recent scholarship in higher education pointed out a similar neglect of graduate student involvement in community engagement projects that challenge conventional types of academic research, teaching, and mentorship (e.g., O'Meara, 2008; Gilvin, 2012). The 2014 "Report of the MLA Task Force on Doctoral Study in Modern Language and Literature," in response to both persistent public questioning of the value of doctoral study in the humanities and the changing academic market for language and literature graduates, calls for a robust "public humanities," one in which scholars "combine scholarship, teaching, and creative activity;" such scholars, the report suggests, "are often collaborative, engage with diverse communities, sometimes as cocreators, and consciously articulate their value to their publics" (p. 9). While the MLA report's authors do not go very far to imagine how English scholars might engage in their communities more deeply or what the products of those engagements might be, they do seem to understand that the public humanities might benefit more traditional doctoral programs by explaining the value of the humanities to a skeptical public. Almost a decade earlier, KerryAnn O'Meara and Audrey Jaeger (2006) argued that traditional models of knowledge-making were insufficient and called for a more reciprocal relationship between graduate students (and their faculty mentors) and the public. Such reciprocity suggests that not only will the academy recognize its responsibility to use the knowledge it creates to improve society, but O'Meara and Jaeger argue that doctoral education will improve as a result: "It is imperative that graduate students develop a greater awareness of how their discipline can contribute to solving real-world problems as well as how disciplinary knowledge can be transformed through interaction with real-world settings" (p. 11).

And as the number of academic jobs for those with doctorates declines, particularly for students in the humanities, the professional skills learned by such interactions with "real-world settings" can lead to alternative careers. As Day, et al. (2012) write, "For graduate students, community engagement can provide valuable professional skills and experiences that lead to non-academic careers in business, government (including federal and state agencies), nonprofit organizations, and cultural institutions, and to non-faculty careers on campus in research organizations, outreach, and government relations" (p. 163). Students who seek the connection between their graduate study and the "real world" are not only more likely to find careers outside the academy but to find satisfaction in them. Additionally, if an institution is seeking to be diverse and inclusive, valuing community engagement is one way of attracting underrepresented students, who often "pursue higher education, in part, as a way to gain skills and knowledge that will benefit their communities" (Day et al., 2012, p. 165). Indeed, not valuing community-engaged research or failing to teach students how to do it could make it all that more difficult to recruit, and even more difficult to *retain*, students of color, who might believe the institution values basic research at the expense of the applied or community-based work they hope to do.

In many ways, then, we are seeking an intervention that will address several problems with traditionally conceived doctoral education: 1) we challenge the idea that graduate research takes place only within the academy by encouraging doctoral students to address community problems through their research; 2) we will provide an opportunity for students whose disciplinary mentors are not engaged researchers to learn the principles of engaged scholarship and a venue to apply their skills to address community problems; and 3) we will, thereby, provide a model of mentoring that challenges the traditional "master-apprentice" paradigm by providing students with skills that their mentors don't have, skills that will give them career choices that their mentors could not imagine.

As we construct this intervention, we rely on feminist conversations from rhetoric and composition and women's and gender studies that focus on reciprocal and relational community engagement models that encourage crossing boundaries between the classroom and the community (Iverson & James, 2014). In focusing on core feminist principles such as collaboration and reciprocity, we challenge ways community engagement is often perceived as *service to* the communities on the periphery of the university's campus. Like Concannon, et al. and Brandt, et al. whose essays are included in this section on partnerships, we draw on Royster and Kirsch's *Feminist Rhetorical Practices* (2012) to focus our efforts on helping graduate students learn to *listen* rhetorically in order to both attend to the needs of community partners and to fairly represent them in their research (p. 4). And like Mary P. Sheridan, in her chapter "Knot-Working Collaborations: Fostering Community-Engaged Teachers and Scholars," we explore these tenets of community engagement, rhetoric, and feminist practice to develop a structure that will help graduate students develop professional identities as engaged scholars through threshold experiences and multiple entry points into community-engaged projects. This professional development relies heavily on feminist values and ethics in forming genuine relationships and partnerships with community members to contribute to the community and to enhance the formation of knowledge in the academy. As we build structures for graduate student professionalization at UofL, we have embraced calls from Iverson, James, Royster and Kirsch to re-envision engagement through feminist practice and demonstrate how these core principles influenced our plans and design for our newest interdisciplinary graduate program focused on engaged scholarship.[1]

---

1   Furthermore, as several scholars in rhetoric and composition and in women's and gender studies have noted, these core feminist beliefs intersect directly with scholarship on community engagement. For instance, Leeray Costa and Karen Leong note that " . . . feminist pedagogy val-

Thus, while this work at the intersection of feminism and community engagement has begun, we argue that there remains a need to develop structures for community projects and engaged scholarship from centralized administrative locations to intervene in the traditional model of graduate education, which often reinforces the binary between the institution and its surrounding communities, the boundaries between disciplines within the academy, and the static, hierarchical relationship between mentor and mentee (or between "master" and "apprentice"). Beth, a professor of English, is also the Vice Provost for Graduate Education and Dean of Interdisciplinary and Graduate Studies (SIGS); Keri is a doctoral candidate in Rhetoric and Composition and Beth's research assistant in SIGS, and Beth also serves as a co-director of Keri's dissertation. From the beginning, Beth and Keri have collaborated on designing and implementing the graduate school's newest professional development program focusing on community-engaged scholarship. Our positions within rhetoric and composition and within SIGS, as well as our feminist perspectives, have helped us imagine the program we describe here. The graduate school at UofL currently offers a professional development program called the **PLAN**, which stands for **P**rofessional development, **L**ife skills, **A**cademic development, and **N**etworking. The PLAN program provides professionalization opportunities for graduate students across a wide range of disciplines and at various stages in their programs, including workshops on refining teaching practices, developing resumes and CVs, delivering conference presentations, and publishing research. Furthermore, PLAN also includes several academies, such as the Graduate Teaching Assistant Academy, the Entrepreneurship Academy, and the Grant Writing Academy. In this piece, we describe our efforts in extending these programs to focus on engaged scholarship—in both physical and digital sites—by developing a year-long Community Engagement Academy (CEA), which encourages collaborations among graduate students, faculty, and community leaders on community projects. In doing so, we heed the multiple calls for reciprocity and crossing disciplinary and institutional boundaries to enrich the community and the scholarship being produced in the academy.

In short, we see the need to build a structure that fosters interdisciplinary and reciprocal relationships in the community. Yet we realize the many institutional challenges we will have to overcome—siloed academic disciplines that resist interdisciplinarity, set perceptions of mentorship that privilege the apprenticeship model, budgetary constraints, among others. We recognize these as

---

ues many of the same ideals put forth by scholars of civic engagement, including critical analysis, self-reflexivity, and active participation to accomplish the social good" (p. 172). In developing our program, we used each of these values to inform the steps we took to ensure that participants receive both theoretical foundations for engaged scholarship and necessary practical information to enact this work.

threats to establishing a sustainable program that can ultimately change current understandings of what graduate students should *learn, do,* and *become.* If we wish to see graduate students become stewards of their disciplines and civically-engaged scholars and teachers, we urge the creation of structures and practicable programs from centralized locations that encourage graduate students to cross boundaries between the academy and the public and between disciplines. By describing the development of the University of Louisville's Community Engagement Academy in this chapter, we offer one model for exploring this potential.

PLANNING ARCHITECTURES OF PARTICIPATION

We believe there exists an urgent need in graduate education to be more responsive to both graduate students as future scholars and to the communities that could simultaneously benefit from and enhance these students' research and skills. As Ernest Boyer asserted twenty-five years ago in *Scholarship Reconsidered,* "[F]uture scholars should be asked to think about the usefulness of knowledge, to reflect on the social consequences of their work, and in so doing gain understanding of how their own study relates to the world beyond the campus" (p. 69). At our own university, we recognize that many graduate students who want to be involved in their communities and to extend their learning outside the classroom, lab, or library had no opportunities within their academic programs—or within our own PLAN program—to learn the skills involved in community-engaged research. Thus, heeding Mary P. Sheridan and Jennifer Rowsell's (2010) advice to create "architectures of participation," we have designed our program to reach those students whose academic programs may not encourage or value such research. While Sheridan and Rowsell are primarily focused on digital media literacy practices in their work, we found their theory of creating participation structures useful in considering how "these constructed architectures encourage a variety of participation possibilities for people with diverse motives and abilities" (p. 47). Creating this space for graduate students, we argue, will help them creatively and responsibly explore the potential for engaged scholarship in their academic or non-academic careers after leaving UofL. As Sheridan says (Chapter 11, this collection), "if we believe that doing is central to learning, we need to provide more models of how to enact that doing," and the CEA is one such model.

We draw on many principles that are shared foundational beliefs in feminist research, rhetoric and composition, and community engagement. Some of these core beliefs include *collaboration, reciprocity,* and the discovery of a *common understanding or shared goal* among all involved parties. Royster and Kirsch (2012), for instance, comment on the value of learning to ask questions and to hear a multitude of voices: "[W]e must learn to ask new and different questions and to find more and better ways to listen to the multidimensional voices that are speaking from within and across many of the lines that might divide us as language users . . . " (p. 4). The lines that we are attempting to blur or break down altogether, those between the academy and local community and between disciplinary units, are deeply rooted in long academic traditions and views on what constitutes scholarship; however, by putting Royster and Kirsch's suggestion into practice, we can start to take steps toward these necessary changes and enable the next generation of scholars to see the benefits of rhetorical listening for their own research and for the greater public good.

Furthermore, these values have strongly influenced our discipline's understanding of community-engaged research, creating a rich theoretical landscape on which to create this particular architecture of participation. For instance, Ellen Cushman's (1996) seminal piece "Rhetorician as Agent of Social Change," which marked the turn to public work as a central disciplinary focus, addresses the need "for a deeper consideration of the civic purpose of our positions in the academy, of what we do with our knowledge, for whom, and by what means" (p. 12). Cushman's focus on how this "civic purpose" relates to the production of knowledge with and for communities is central to the tenets of engagement, including *reciprocity*. Cushman offers these principles of engagement as the primary distinctions between "missionary activism" and "scholarly activism," with the former being activism in service *to* rather than *with* communities (p. 13). Scholarly activism, on the other hand, acknowledges the rich resources and information that community partners already possess and that we can help facilitate (and ultimately *benefit from*) in our collaboration with them. It is this type of scholarly activism that we teach and enact in the Community Engagement Academy.

Throughout the process of designing the CEA, then, we have stressed the importance of *collaboration*, a key component of reciprocity, in a number of ways, including internal collaboration within the graduate school and stakeholders throughout the university and external collaboration with community partners. Our understanding of *collaboration* is similar to Sheridan's metaphor of knot-making in that it is, like *reciprocity*, constantly evolving and being shaped by the shifting needs of the stakeholders involved (or being unknotted and re-knotted). Collaboration is thus necessarily flexible—not a rigid, predetermined relationship defined by a single party. Sheridan and Jacobi (2014) similarly define collaboration as "foster[ing] the conditions by which those with less heard voices can be ratified, reciprocal participants of the partnerships" (p. 142). Here, we have focused on three areas of collaboration that are necessarily more fluid than three neatly-confined sites: 1) across disciplines, between the university's graduate students, faculty, and staff; 2) between students, faculty, and staff and the local community partners with whom they work; and 3) between mentor and mentee, as our own research and writing about engaged scholarship and co-development of the CEA show. As we demonstrate in the following discussion on collaboration and reciprocity in relationships, the CEA has become an example of the partnerships we hope that students can establish and facilitate on their own as engaged scholars.

INTERDISCIPLINARY COLLABORATION BETWEEN GRADUATE STUDENTS, FACULTY, AND STAFF

To put our theories into practice, we invited faculty from a variety of disciplines (history, English, social work, public health and education were all well-represented) who are known for their engaged research to a focus group that also included graduate students interested in learning more about engaged scholarship, and staff members who have some responsibility for community engagement or graduate professional development at our institution. We knew that creating the CEA would be messier and more difficult than the other academies because those relied on experts designing workshops to teach content; the CEA would require that students not only learn content, but that they also have the opportunity to put the content into practice—to learn by doing. Additionally, engaged research is time consuming, and unlike the other academies we offer, it does not necessarily have a discrete end point. Since it often takes several years to establish trust with community groups, we knew that we could not just send students out to find their own community partners; faculty experts would have to provide supervision of some projects and perhaps work with graduate students outside their disciplines on projects that they already had developed. Such faculty labor would have to be compensated (and the graduate school's budget is not very large), while students interested in pursuing a project not clearly connected to their work assignment as a teaching or research assistant might have trouble finding the time to work on a community project, or if the student believed she had time, she might have to persuade a skeptical faculty mentor who does not value such research. At the end of the first focus group session, we had more questions than answers, but the group was excited by the prospect of creating opportunities for graduate students to learn the principles of community-engaged scholarship and agreed to continue working on the project. We had also brainstormed a long list of competencies (downloaded from Michigan State University's community engagement certificate program) that we thought an interdisciplinary group of students should have after completing a CEA.[2] We

---

2   See Michigan State's list of core competencies at http://gradcert.outreach.msu.edu/requirements/competencies.aspx

decided to do a pilot of the content in spring of 2016 in the manner of the more traditional academy, and wait until Fall of 2016 to implement the full CEA, with opportunities for students to actually do engaged research throughout the 2016–17 academic year.

During a second meeting of the focus group a month later, we worked through that list of competencies and developed a rough outline of workshops to be offered in 2016. In brainstorming these workshops, we discussed our desire for graduate student participants to consider both the theoretical and practical sides of engaged scholarship. In regard to the theoretical piece, we wanted to respond to Catherine Orr's call in her 2011 NWSA white paper in which she discusses the importance of developing and using shared language to discuss community-engaged work; she writes:

> The work of coming to terms—literally developing a common language to speak about the importance of civic engagement across disciplines, campus, units, and surrounding communities—is urgently required . . . for more meaningful exchanges about the practice of civic engagement at every level of higher education. (p. 5)

In order to develop a common language as Orr suggests and foster meaningful collaborations among the graduate students involved in our academy, we decided the first spring workshop should focus on foundations and definitions of engaged scholarship; then, the students would have some shared vocabulary to discuss engaged scholarship and their specific projects in the subsequent workshops. As a result of these conversations, we decided on the following sessions for the Spring 2016 pilot: "Community-Engaged Scholarship 101," "Making Relationships that Matter: Initiating and Sustaining Community Partnerships," "Navigating the Logistical Landscape of Engaged Scholarship," "Making it Count: Documenting and Communicating Your Engagement Accomplishments," and "Variations in Community-Engaged Scholarship."

We were comfortable designing the pilot, which looked very much like both the Grant Writing and Entrepreneurship Academies: content delivered in workshops by experts. But we made no progress on the goal of providing students with meaningful experiences applying their knowledge to real world problems. For students who worked in disciplines like social work or public health, where such experiences are already part of their training, or for those students who have internships as part of their graduate experience, there was no problem, but for students who were in the liberal arts or sciences, or even some engineering and education disciplines, who were not being mentored by a faculty member who did engaged research, it was hard to imagine how the CEA could provide them with a site and the necessary supervision to use their disciplinary knowledge to contribute to a team of engaged researchers. And the question of compensation for faculty and student time—that was still a major barrier. But again, faculty, staff, and students remained committed to the principles of the CEA, and we agreed to meet again at the beginning of the fall semester, which would give Keri and Beth more time to explore some solutions to these issues.

During the summer of 2015, Keri and Beth continued to refine goals for the academy's pilot. The collaborative teams of graduate student researchers could lead to more collaborative research beyond the one-year duration of the CEA. For instance, specifically in regard to publishing, we saw an opportunity for students to learn from one another's researching and writing skills to gain confidence to publish in academic and non-academic sites. This type of collaboration helps aspiring scholars to break free of institutional academic structures that often lead students to read and write in isolation without seeking the expertise and skills of their peers. Writing with one another is grounded in feminist principles related to listening to and acknowledging multiple voices to create knowledge, and importantly, it provides students the support—both emotionally and professionally—to gain experience in these realms of professionalization that often get ignored in traditional graduate seminars. In "Merge/Emerge: Collaboration in Graduate School," Constance Russell, Rachel Plotkin, and Anne Bell (1998) highlight these alluring aspects of graduate student collaboration on research projects. These authors, who were graduate students at the time of this publication, reinforce the importance of the support they get from one another as friends, claiming that "collaboration with friends and colleagues helps us maintain our strength and has provided us a security we often feel lacking as young female academics" (p. 143).[3]

This type of support and the desire to collaborate with other graduate students was a happy by-product of the pilot; while we cannot promise that these interdisciplinary collaborations among graduate students will continue beyond the work with a community partner during the academy, the program nevertheless encourages graduate students to seek others' expertise, knowledge, and skills in the continuation of their studies at UofL and in their prospective academic or non-academic careers. We selected participants (a total of 17) for the Spring 2016 pilot and had a wide range of disciplinary representation, as Table 6.1 shows.

Since the cohort represented nine disciplines, we hoped that the pilot would foster meaningful interdisciplinary relationships among the participants and with the community partner. Students also included several similar reasons for

---

3   It is also worth noting here that these women come from a variety of disciplinary backgrounds, and two are doctoral students and one is a Master's student.

wanting to participate in the academy in their applications. For example, several applicants indicated wanting to become better "scholar-activists" or continue their social advocacy work. Others indicated a desire to work with students and faculty from other disciplines and to gain skills that would help them navigate logistics in building and sustaining partnerships. Finally, some saw the academy as an opportunity to strengthen research and administrative skills and enhance current partnerships. The final reflections from the academy's participants show that they had some success in reaching their goals. One student, for instance, explained, "I have benefited the most from the collaboration with other doctoral students in various academic programs. I've gained new insight from their perspectives as they are from a variety of disciplines and draw from a multitude of diverse theories and methodologies."

Table 6.1. Participants by discipline

Discipline	Number of CEA Participants
Pan-African Studies	1
Women's and Gender Studies	1
English—Rhetoric and Composition	7
Sociology	1
Urban and Public Affairs	2
Psychology—Clinical	1
Educational Leadership and Organizational Development	1
Education and Human Development	2
Social Work	1

Collaborations among graduate students within community sites can also offer aspiring engaged scholars the opportunity to define for themselves what Jeff Grabill (2012) calls "the research stance." Grabill defines "research stance" as "a position or a set of beliefs and obligations that shape how one acts as a researcher" or "an identity statement that enables a researcher to process methods and make decisions" (pp. 211 and 215). Such a research stance is crucial for engaged scholars, as community sites are particularly messy for even the most experienced researchers. On this point of messiness, Grabill adds that the research methods that students learn within their home disciplines often do not transfer easily to work with communities (p. 210). In planning and implementing the CEA pilot, we acknowledged that, in working with students outside of their disciplines and with community partners, the CEA participants would have the opportunity to develop and identify their research stance to help them address difficult questions, as Grabill notes, about *who* they are as scholars and as people, *why* they research, and for *what* purposes (p. 215). In their final assessment of the CEA, students wrote comments like these: "It made me reflect on what I am coming in with regarding attitudes & identity. Then pushed me to explore what my role in community engagement will be"; "I feel more confident in establishing myself as a CE researcher"; "It has made me more committed to doing community engagement as a part of my work." We believe these quotations show that graduate students will be better prepared to make sound methodological choices in their work with communities and gain a better understanding of why they value this work and how it informs their identities as aspiring engaged scholars.

Reciprocity: Forming Relationships with Community Partners

While we did not have partners in mind at the outset, we always knew we would need either a site that would welcome interdisciplinary teams OR faculty who would welcome students from outside their disciplines onto their already established research teams. We also knew from the beginning that we would draw heavily on the community engagement and feminist principle of *reciprocity* in forming relationships with community partners. In designing our academy, we attempted to theorize *reciprocity*, and we borrowed Ellen Cushman's (1996) definition of the term, which states, "Reciprocity includes an open and conscious negotiation of the power structures reproduced during the give-and-take interactions of the people involved on both sides of the relationship. A theory of reciprocity, then, frames this activist agenda with a self-critical, conscious navigation of this intervention" (p. 16). Relying on Cushman's understanding of reciprocity, we focused on ways that we could introduce this theory of reciprocity in one of our opening workshops on foundations and definitions to help UofL graduate students see the necessity of acknowledging "both sides of the relationship" and understanding the importance of carefully listening to and working *with* and *alongside* community members rather than *for* them.

Furthermore, we knew that we wanted the academy to make the behind-the-scenes work visible for graduate students and the many other parties involved. As Sheridan and Jacobi (2014) suggest, this difficult work that happens in the early stages of forming partnerships with community members often remains unseen or under-valued by the institution. They examine "how feminists continue to engage in this profound negotiation, in part by understanding how feminist community engagement is made not simply visible, but also legible, to a range of stakeholders." (p. 138). As Cushman (1996) suggested when she noted the "give-and-take interactions" between both parties, Sheridan and Jacobi highlight the importance of making community-engaged work both "visible" and "legible" to the many stakeholders involved in such projects, including but not limited to the many members of the community site(s), the faculty and staff, the graduate student researchers, and the administration. Our workshop series identified the key components and competencies of engaged scholarship (described above), including ways to initiate reciprocal relationships with community partners, and through making the beginnings and inner-workings of our collaboration with the Parklands (our eventual partner for the CEA) as visible as possible for all involved parties.

This time, putting our theories into practice required a bit of good fortune. During the summer, Beth was called to a meeting with Ann Larson, Dean of the College of Education and Human Development (CEHD) and Keith Inman, Vice President for Advancement at the University of Louisville to discuss a possible donation that might provide one or two graduate assistantships. A charitable foundation had funded projects in healthcare at the University of Louisville and projects in sustainability at the Parklands, one of the nation's largest donor-supported, non-profit metropolitan parks, with over 4000 acres of protected new parklands in the Floyds Fork watershed; the foundation was now interested in funding a small project that would make partners of the university and the Parklands. Earlier conversations with the foundation, university administration, and the Parklands did not produce a project that the three partners were all interested in pursuing, but they were determined to keep trying. Admittedly, it was serendipitous that Beth was called to this meeting, but the research Keri and Beth had been doing and the work with the focus group allowed Beth to pitch the Community Engagement Academy as a potential partnership project; the Dean of CEHD saw potential for her school and its work with Signature Partnership Schools in STEM education, and the VP for Advancement thought the project might appeal to Dan Jones, the chairman and CEO of the Parklands. A conference call a week later with Dan Jones, Beth, Keith, and Ann began to pave the foundation of the partnership: Dan, who holds a Ph.D. in history but chose to work outside the academy as a business manager, entrepreneur, and social entrepreneur, liked the idea that the academy structure was providing graduate students with opportunities to develop professional skills and to work in the community; the Parklands also has a strong interest in STEM education, sponsoring various field trips and camps for K-12 students and leadership seminars for adults. When he heard that our next academy is likely to be a graduate student leadership academy, he was already volunteering to help in that endeavor as well. So this partnership is truly reciprocal, since the Parklands is not only invested in having some of their needs met by our graduate students, but also in our goal of helping graduate students gain some professional skills.

After another meeting that included a representative with the foundation, Beth asked to begin bringing Keri to the meetings, since we were working together on developing the CEA. The university group (Beth, Ann, Keith, Keri, and Jessica, a grant writer) met with Dan and his associates at Dan's office in preparation for a September 1 meeting of the original focus group, a meeting that several folks from the Parklands would attend, along with the representative from the charitable foundation, and our own development folks. Keri and Beth also invited some additional faculty who we felt would find the partnership with the Parklands a terrific opportunity: faculty from our new sustainability master's degree program (which is an interdisciplinary program housed in SIGS), from history (who have an interest in the history of place, a corresponding interest of the Parklands), and STEM educators from CEHD. All along, we promised (or warned) that the development of the CEA would be a messy project, since we had to collaborate both with faculty within the institution, the dean and faculty of the CEHD, the community partner, now potentially the Parklands, and a group of interdisciplinary master's and doctoral graduate students, whose disciplines we could not comfortably predict. But if we could be transparent in the give-and-take negotiations between these various stakeholders, we felt we could construct a partnership that would benefit both the university's graduate students and the Parklands, and we hoped that our negotiation with the Parklands could serve as a visible example of how to initiate a productive partnership.

During one of these planning meetings, the Parklands group said they were having trouble seeing the intersection of the workshops and what students might do at the Parklands, and Beth drew a picture, with the CEA in the center and various circles with different potential project teams radiating from those workshops. This was, interestingly, an important moment in the negotiations, since it showed that the CEA could accommodate many different types of projects, and that students and faculty could identify their own interests, and that some of the team-based topics would be of greater interest to the Parklands than others. One of the Parklands' team members, for instance, was very interested in park safety and design, and that became one of the pods where we expected that Criminal Justice and Urban Planning students could naturally contribute; their director of education at the parks was very focused, as was Ann, on the K-12 environmental education pod. We asked what other needs they might have, and there was interest in getting a more diverse population of park users, perhaps through UofL's partnership with schools in economically challenged neighborhoods, and with having the parks help improve health in the community, perhaps through work with both CEHD and Public Health. Keri took Beth's crude drawing and made a handout for our September meeting with the focus group, a handout that helped guide our discussions.

Figure 6.1. Potential Research Areas for CEA Participants.

The group that met in September was large (about thirty faculty, staff, and students, plus folks from the Parklands, our advancement office, and the representative from the foundation), messy (as promised) and excited to learn more about the potential partnership. Faculty and graduate students were pleased to learn that there was a site for our engaged research, even if at first they struggled to imagine potential projects that could use their disciplinary expertise, and the Parklands group was excited by the high level of interest and creativity shown by the students and faculty. All of us were encouraged by the possibility of a grant to help fund stipends for graduate students and faculty, and the Parklands folks made it clear that they had much to offer in the way of professional development and much to gain from our expertise. It was a successful meeting, and when we met after the large meeting with just the folks who would be working on the grant, we all agreed that while the conversations had gotten messier, they had also gotten richer, and as both the foundation representative and Dan said, there was nothing that was a deal breaker and that in itself was encouraging. We solicited a subgroup from the focus group which included one Parklands member to work on the workshops, and we have a small group that worked on the grant.

Although we are still in the early stages of our partnership, what has encouraged all of us is that we have been transparent about our expectations and needs, what we can offer the partnership, and what we hope to gain from it. Our open negotiations have been modeled on the idea of reciprocity as used by Sheridan and Jacobi (2014), and we have learned that the values of the Parklands overlap significantly with the values of the University of Louisville. Those shared values include respect for people and the environment, a commitment to access and inclusiveness, and responsible stewardship. During the pilot, we showcased our partnership and its establishment during the session on building partnerships; Keri and Beth worked with Dan and Scott to deliver the session, with Keri and Beth focusing on collaboration, reciprocity and mutuality, and Dan and Scott focusing on the pragmatic aspects of developing partnerships as they built their donor-supported nonprofit park system. Students in the pilot also did a formal needs assessment, and we are using that assessment to select specific projects that will be part of the 2016–17 CEA; we want to make sure that we not only meet our graduate students' needs, but also the Parklands'.

COMPLICATING THE MENTOR/MENTEE RELATIONSHIP: RESEARCHING AND DEVELOPING THE COMMUNITY ENGAGEMENT ACADEMY

The final site of collaboration we wish to address here is our own collaboration in researching and developing this academy. In 2008, when Beth became associate dean of the graduate school, she negotiated with the dean of Arts and Sciences for a graduate research assistant from English who would teach one class per semester to help make up for the loss of Beth's teaching and who would work ten hours a week with Beth to help her continue researching and writing in rhetoric and composition and about graduate education, and to help her develop the PLAN program. The arrangement continued when Beth became Dean, and Keri entered into the SIGS graduate research assistantship in 2014 with an interest in community engagement efforts in graduate education, which corresponded with Beth's desire to develop a future academy on community engagement. While her dissertation research focuses heavily on historical writing processes, Keri wanted to use her position in SIGS to explore how her research interests intersect with broader issues of writing and identity-formation in the community.

We see our relationship and research process as challenging traditional, rigid models of the mentor/mentee relationship in academia, as it relies on a more genuine collaboration between both parties. This collaboration is similar to that of the environmental science graduate students in *Common Ground*, who discuss the desire for breaking down traditional academic relationships: "Collaboration also helps us transgress a variety of boundaries that are often maintained in academia, for example, between doctoral/master's student, teacher/student, academic/school teacher, and expert/activist" (1998, p. 150). In our research and development of the Community Engagement Academy, we have collaborated on every step of the process, challenging the binarized model of mentorship that has been, and often still is, the primary model for relationships between graduate students and faculty members/administrators.

Furthermore, in "Mentoring and Women in Academia: Reevaluating the Traditional Model," Christy Chandler (1996) explores mentoring relationships between women in academia. She asks, "What type of mentoring relationship is supportive and productive for women?" (p. 81). In exploring possible answers to this question, Chandler explains that there are two types of mentoring: *career-enhancing* and *psychosocial*. She then determines that the former type often adheres to the traditional academic model of mentor/protege with strict boundaries between the two individuals involved. The *psychosocial* function of mentoring, however, requires that the mentor take on several roles, including those of "role model, counselor, and friend" (p. 81). Not surprisingly, Chandler concludes that the psychosocial function of mentoring is most beneficial to female graduate students as they develop as academics and professionals. While the career-enhancing function is useful in helping graduate students identify and follow a certain path for a career choice, it is very one-directional and fails to encompass the other important aspects of mentoring that more closely follow feminist models of collaboration.[1]

In short, though there is an obvious difference in rank between us, our goals are unified by our shared desire to build structures for the aspiring engaged scholars across disciplines at UofL. The mentorship and collaboration model that we have adopted challenges the strict, traditional model of mentor and protege often practiced in the academy and is predicated on genuine collaboration and mutual care and respect for one another's goals.

CONCLUSION

Each of these relationships is important for our overall goals for the Community Engagement Academy which includes a genuine and reciprocal relationship between UofL and community partners and a renewed focus on graduate education

---

[1] Other scholarship on feminist mentorship practices that we drew from here includes: Bona, et al. (1995); Jipson, et al. (2000); Mcguire and Reger (2003).

and its benefits to both individuals and to the community at large. Through these sites of collaboration, we are reimagining graduate education as an ideal space for students to grow and develop into community-engaged scholars who not only see the ways communities serve as research sites, but also recognize that they can use the disciplinary skills acquired in graduate school to "establish the common good," as Boyer called for twenty-five years ago. Furthermore, we aim to create a larger structure that fosters graduate education in community engagement and allows for healthy and sustainable collaborations at the multiple levels we describe above. In doing so, we are responding to concerns raised by Brandt, et al. about laying a foundation for learning through community engagement. They write, "When the groundwork is not laid for reciprocal partnerships prior to students' initial service, the placements often put additional stress on community partners or lead to low levels of student learning and engagement" (p. 15). In creating the Community Engagement Academy, we have worked toward establishing this important groundwork so that current and future graduate students at UofL can more easily see and imagine avenues for engaged scholarship that can ultimately contribute to their scholarly identities and their roles as stewards.

While we see these collaborations as promising and necessary in offering graduate students experience in engaged research, we have tried to be transparent about the hurdles that graduate students may face when making engagement a focus of their scholarship. As Catherine Orr (2011) reminds us, when we encourage students to do engaged scholarship, we must also make sure that students acknowledge the larger systems in which they will be doing this work and the institutional challenges they will face. For instance, students should be aware that not all departments and institutions will value engaged scholarship equally and that it could cause some difficulty for them in the tenure and promotion process. Along these same lines, for graduate students hoping to complete engaged dissertations, they should be reminded of the time that it takes to develop genuine relationships with community partners and that the time and resources available to them in graduate school will likely not be sufficient for developing and maintaining these relationships, unless they have already developed these relationships prior to beginning their graduate work or are working with a faculty mentor who has an established community-based research program.

Acknowledging these hurdles is a vital part of training engaged scholars, but at the same time, we believe the skills learned through engaged scholarship lead to promising careers for graduate students. As noted above, work with communities could steer students toward nonacademic or alternative-academic careers, but we also predict that this work will become increasingly valued in academic institutions, as well, because these graduate students will have a deeper understanding of the range of career options available to graduate students. Right now, many faculty members focus primarily on the academic job market when mentoring students because that is all they know, yet there are growing numbers of graduate students who want more information on alternative careers, and we see our role as providing such guidance and helping students develop a language to discuss the transferable skills they have acquired in graduate school. The next generation of scholars who have training in community-based research and who have a knowledge-base and set of unique experiences (experiences that we will offer through the CEA) will be more capable of training future graduate students for multiple career tracks.

We addressed the promises and perils of community-engaged scholarship in the CEA pilot and will continue this conversation with the next academy's cohort. We have tweaked the design of the pilot to add more time and opportunity for research projects at the Parklands in the next iteration of the CEA. Unfortunately, we have also learned that the charitable foundation has put a hold on such grants for the foreseeable future, which obviously threatens the sustainability of the partnership with the Parklands. But these challenges demonstrate the messy, chaotic nature of engaged scholarship, and the Parklands has agreed to partner with us for the year. The university has also carved out some resources to support two summer internships for the Parklands. With so many moving parts in designing an interdisciplinary community engagement program, we have realized that it takes *time*, as community-engaged research does, to develop the long-lasting partnerships with people both inside and outside of the university to make this kind of program a sustainable one, and sustainability is one of the shared goals that all parties involved in this endeavor have identified. With every step in planning we make, though, we learn more from our community partners, as they learn from us, and we are optimistic that making all of the behind-the-scenes work visible will encourage others to create opportunities for engaged research for graduate students.

REFERENCES

Boyer, E. L. (1996). The scholarship of engagement. *Bulletin of the American Academy of Arts and Sciences, 49*(7), 18–33.

Chandler, C. (1996). Mentoring and women in academia: Reevaluating the traditional model. *NWSA Journal, 8*(3), 79–100.

Costa, L. M. & Leong, K. J. (2012). Introduction critical community engagement: Feminist pedagogy meets civic engagement. *Feminist Teacher, 22*(3), 171–180.

Cushman, E. (1996). The rhetorician as an agent of social change. *College Composition and Communication, 47*(1), 7–28.

Day, K., Becerra, V., Ruiz, V. L. & Powe, M. (2012). New ways of learning, knowing, and working: Diversifying graduate student career options through community engagement. In A. Gilvin, G. M. Roberts & C. Martin (Eds.), *Collaborative futures: Critical reflections on publicly active graduate education* (163–182). Syracuse, NY: Syracuse University Press.

Gilvin, A. (2012). *Collaborative futures: Critical reflections on publicly active graduate education.* Syracuse, NY: The Graduate School Press.

Grabill, J. T. (2012). Community-based research and the importance of a research stance. In M. Sheridan & L. Nickoson (Eds.), *Writing studies research in practice: Methods and methodologies* (pp. 210–219). Carbondale, IL: Southern Illinois University Press.

Iverson, S. V. D. & James, J. H. (2014). *Feminist community engagement: Achieving praxis.* New York, NY: Palgrave Macmillan.

MLA Task Force. (2014). *Report of the MLA task force on doctoral study in modern language and literature.* Retrieved from http://www.mla.org/pdf/taskforcedocstudy2014.pdf.

O'Meara, K. & Jaeger, A. J. (2006). Preparing future faculty for community engagement: Barriers, facilitators, models, and recommendations. *Journal of Higher Education Outreach and Engagement, 11*(4), 3–26.

Orr, C. M. (2011). Women's studies as civic engagement: Research and recommendations. The Teagle Working Group on Women's Studies and Civic Engagement and the National Women's Studies Association. Retrieved from http://www.nwsa.org/research.

Royster, J. J. & Kirsch, G. (2012). *Feminist rhetorical practices: New horizons for rhetoric, composition, and literacy studies.* Carbondale, IL: Southern Illinois University Press.

Russell, C., Plotkin, R. & Bell, A. (1998). Merge/emerge: Collaboration in graduate school. In E. G. Peck (Ed.), *Common ground: Feminist collaboration in the academy* (pp. 141–153). Albany, NY: State University of New York Press.

Sheridan, M. P. (2010). *Design literacies: Learning and innovation in the digital age.* London, England: Routledge.

Sheridan, M. P. & Jacobi, T. (2014). Review essay critical feminist practice and campus-community partnerships: A review essay. *Feminist Teacher, 24*(1–2), 138–150.

CHAPTER 7.
LEARNING TOGETHER THROUGH CAMPUS-COMMUNITY PARTNERSHIPS

Jenn Brandt
High Point University

Cara Kozma
High Point University

Guilford Child Development's Learning Together Family Literacy Program provides opportunities for families in Guilford County, North Carolina, to improve family literacy as parents and children learn together under one roof. Most students in the program are women refugees or recent immigrants, and they enroll in ESOL classes while their children participate in early education and homework help programming. In addition to classes twice a week, families are given a book each month to encourage reading in the home, as well as ideas for activities related to literacy and resources in the community. Since 2012, High Point University's English Department, Service Learning Program, and Women's and Gender Studies Program have partnered with Learning Together in developing curricular and co-curricular initiatives that empower students and community members to use literacy studies as a tool for critical reflection and personal agency. This chapter explores the challenges and successes of university and community partnerships that involve multiple stakeholders. Specifically, we argue that the "learning together" approach is a feminist intervention that can serve as a model for campus-community engagement, where diverse pedagogical needs are considered in conjunction with the goals and operation of community partners.

ACTIVISM AND ACADEMIA

As Orr (2011) has noted, "WGS has demurred in defining, delimiting, or in any way offering a sustained interrogation of a term [activism] that is arguably foundational to the discipline's understanding of itself" (p. 90). Quite often there is the assumption of the "academic versus activist" divide, which argues being one precludes being the other, and that current women's and gender studies programs are conservative in their activist leanings (Brown, 2008; Zimmerman, 2002). Or, as it pertains to our composition and rhetoric students, the assumption is that to be an activist, one must be hugging trees, protesting in the streets, and in the case of feminist activists, burning bras. Addressing these conflicting perceptions of activism and their relations to women's and gender studies is a productive entry point in a variety of contexts, but particularly courses where there is a service learning component. Further, in dispelling notions of radical activism as the only method of eliciting change, students not only begin to see ways in which "everyday activism" (Finley & Stringer, 2010) can be integrated into their own lives, but also begin the important work of considering why negative stereotypes exist around certain forms of activism and how these stereotypes relate to some of the larger forms of gendered, racial, and socioeconomic oppressions that will be considered in class. Therefore, for the purposes of our courses and this article's discussion, we use Finley and Stringer's definition of activism, which highlights the stories, activities, and artistic endeavors of "'everyday' people who think, say, and do things that help advance the rights of women and decrease gender inequalities," and note, as Finley and Stringer acknowledge, that this "is not all there is to feminist activism," but is a good place to start with in the classroom (p. viii).

Along with an expanded understanding of everyday activism, the other way in which the learning together model positions itself as an activist strategy for campus-community partnership is through the methodology of standpoint theory. Like activism, the effectiveness and positioning of standpoint theory has been debated (Harding, 2004); however, as a "feminist critical theory about relations between the production of knowledge and practices of power" that empowers oppressed groups and values their experiences, it has been a useful method in approaching our campus-community partnership in a way that allows both parties to be heard and have their needs met (Harding, 2004, p. 1). While larger debates as to whether "women as culturally diverse collectivities" can produce knowledge that answers questions about social relations are outside the scope of this chapter, the learning together model we propose takes up Harding's (2004) assertion that "standpoint projects must 'study up'; they must be part of critical theory, revealing the ideological strategies used to design and justify the sex-gender system and its intersections with other systems of oppression, in the case of feminist projects" (pp. 4–6). In this way, we argue that the learning together model employs the methodologies of standpoint theory to expose the activist potential of literacy as a tool by which students and the women of Learning Together can examine a host of other economic, political, and material oppressions that refugee and immigrant women face in contemporary U.S. society.

With respect to composition and rhetorical studies, our approach echoes Royster and Kirsch's (2012) argument that,

> The idea in developing a feminist-informed operational framework is not simply to make a clearer, more coherent place for feminist work in rhetorical studies but also to bring a better balancing for how qualities of excellence are negotiated and constituted in the field generally, given the values added by feminist methodologies. We begin the process, therefore, with a basic principle: We accept the notion that there is indeed value to be recognized and appreciated in the lives, words, participation, leadership, and legacies of women. (p. 18)

The "learning together" model we propose is rooted in literacy and uses rhetoric and composition studies in its practice, but has wider applications outside of these fields. The feminist and cooperative ethos of "learning together" is one that encourages multiple perspectives and voices, with active participation from all parties—student, faculty, and community partners. Further, as our discussion will detail, the stories and experiences of women often become the driving force of classroom activities and projects. With these theoretical and methodological concerns in mind, then, this chapter models the learning together approach and is organized around the experiences of the Director of Women's and Gender Studies (Jenn) and Assistant Director of Service Learning (Cara) at High Point University, and it draws on interviews with Molly Betton, former Program Coordinator at Guilford Child Development, and Lexi Koperna, a student in WGS 2274 who also completed an independent study project with Learning Together. After discussing these individual experiences, we conclude with a section devoted to how we have employed the learning together model at other service sites and how others might use this model to enhance partnerships between institutions and community agencies.

LEARNING TOGETHER: A WGS DIRECTOR'S EXPERIENCES WITH FEMINIST ACTIVISM AND SERVICE LEARNING (JENN)

As debated in a number of disciplinary discussions (Bickford & Reynolds, 2002; Dugger, 2008; Orr, 2011; Berger, 2013), a tension surrounds the rhetoric of "service," "civic engagement," "volunteerism," and "activism" as they relate to women's and gender studies and service learning. When housed under the language of "service" or "volunteerism," there is the risk that these programs ultimately highlight the differences between campus and community, furthering a divide of "us versus them" and reinforcing preexisting stereotypes on the part of both students and community members. "Activism," on the other hand, "argues for relationships based on connection" (Bickford & Reynolds, 2002, p. 237). Activism, which is most closely aligned with women's and gender studies, is the term least often used in contemporary academic discourse on the subject, raising the suspicion of many women's and gender studies faculty with respect to service learning and civic engagement initiatives. Further, given the rich and foundational history of activism and community engagement implicit with women's and gender studies, for many WGS affiliates there is unease around the commodification of "institutionally sanctioned versions" of work that has been considered "unique to the discipline" (Orr, 2011, p. 21). That is, as service learning programs and civic engagement initiatives become mainstream in the academy, the rich history of women's and gender studies and its work in this area is frequently overlooked and WGS faculty are often left out of these conversations. The learning together model we discuss, then, applies as much to institutional discussions between departments and programs as it does to campus-community relations.

Upon my hire, I was awarded a grant through HPU's Service Learning Program to develop a service learning (SL) course in women's and gender studies. The grant stipulates that awardees attend three professional development workshops, which introduce them to the theories of service learning, as well as provide networking opportunities with a number of partner agencies and organizations in the city of High Point. This training aligns well with the first recommendation of the NWSA's 2011 White Paper "Women's Studies as Civic Engagement: Research and Recommendations," which stresses the importance of faculty support, noting, "Faculty require skill and training to prepare students for engagement beyond the classroom. The time and skill required to develop effective university-community partnerships as well as the on-going assessment of the efficacy in local communities must be recognized as the real work of the institution" (Orr, 2011, p. 24). Since its inception, HPU's SL Program has worked hard at creating sustained relationships with the city of High Point, recognizing that effective SL programs meet the needs of both the university and the community. HPU's SL Program also stresses the importance of training and continued faculty support in order to facilitate educational experiences that benefit all involved parties. While HPU's SL Program does not explicitly label itself "feminist" or have official ties to the Women's and Gender Studies Program, it does embody many of the tenets laid out in the NWSA White Paper.

It was through one of the workshops that I was first introduced to Learning Together. New to both the city and the university, it was important to me that I develop my own understanding of the High Point community and its needs before developing a service learning course or bringing my students into partnerships with various organizations. I spent a year volunteering with a number of local agencies, including Learning Together, before teaching my first SL course. I had previous experience as a literacy volunteer, and, as an English professor, I advocate the significance of literacy, personal narrative, and literature in empowering individuals, understanding the particular importance of this to those for whom English is not their first language. These prior experiences led to my initial work with Learning Together in the fall of 2012. I began working weekly with the program, offering a women's conversation hour focused on increasing the students' agency through literacy and language skills. In addition to the conversation circle, it became clear that my training and job as an English faculty member could be helpful in the classroom. I began to develop weekly grammar lessons, as well as lessons in practical writing skills, that could be useful for the women on job applications, corresponding with their children's teachers, and navigating other daily tasks that required a grasp of the written form of the English language. While these practical skills are certainly beneficial in helping to empower these women to lead more independent and full lives here in High Point, Learning Together also provides a strong sense of community that is particularly important to the women and not necessarily seen in typical ESOL classes.

In an interview[1] for this collection, we asked Molly Betton, former Program Coordinator at Guilford Child Development, about why the program attracts almost exclusively women. She explained that:

> Although Learning Together does not exclude men/fathers from participation, our program attracts over 99% female participation, and so we frequently frame our approach as working with "women" and "mothers." Most of the women in our program come from cultural backgrounds that value the woman as the matron of the household and the primary caregiver in the family. Because they carry more responsibility for raising the children, the women in our program have a higher

---

1   Keeping with the learning together model, we asked Molly Betton, former Learning Together Program Coordinator for Guilford Child Development, to contribute her thoughts about the HPU-Learning Together partnership. After discussing our aims and hopes for this chapter, we gave Molly the option of being interviewed in-person or via email. Molly chose to respond to our questions via email and gave her written permission to include her responses in this chapter and collection.

interest in seeking the kinds of parenting and child supports that we offer (versus just the ESOL or the GED).

Molly also discussed the "social role" that the program fills for its female participants, saying, "Many immigrant women end up living in a state of isolation. For some women in the program, Learning Together is their only social outlet, their only time without young children, when they can focus on themselves. Many of the men in their lives already have opportunities to socialize with other adults, usually though work." In Learning Together's ESOL class, family hardships, life changes, as well as happy occasions, are discussed and celebrated, strengthening the bond between participants. As a new member to the city of High Point myself, I also found this sense of community beneficial, developing friendships with the women through these experiences.

After my first semester volunteering, it became clear that the women had a particular interest in wellness, as many of them found the American diet much different from that with which they were accustomed. Also, many of them were intrigued by our culture's preoccupation with exercise and wanted to learn more about how to keep themselves and their families healthy and fit. Therefore, in the spring, as a group we decided to structure our grammar and vocabulary around fitness and nutrition and incorporated exercise such as Zumba, yoga, and strength training with household objects into our conversation sessions. This plan came directly from the Learning Together students and is one way in which the community need dictated the curriculum, as opposed to the other way around. It was during this semester that one of Cara's students completed her service learning hours in the adult classroom with me. An exercise science major, she was tasked with developing lessons on fitness and nutrition and was asked to design accompanying worksheets that would be appropriate for English language learners.

While ultimately this was a positive experience, it did require a great deal of negotiation in terms of my role as both an advocate for the women of Learning Together and as a professor. As the organizer of these weekly sessions, I was serving as a community volunteer at Learning Together, not as a university professor, and I became the SL student's primary community partner. I helped her develop materials and advised her on the type of information the women wanted and what was appropriate for their language level. Although the student and I enjoyed a positive working relationship, there was also some tension, as we had to navigate our roles in the Learning Together classroom. While both she and I recognized each other as student and professor, in the space of Learning Together we did not function in these capacities. Drawing on models of community and feminist activism, I saw her as an equal partner in designing an effective and empowering experience for the students at Learning Together. I was not her professor in the service learning course, and did not see it as my role to interact with her in this way. The student, however, did not enter the relationship with the same expectations, and in hindsight, I realize it was my fault that I did not more clearly articulate my goal for the program or her role in it. Also, in assuming that she was prepared for the work (she had chosen this assignment for her service hours and final project), I failed to consult with her on which tasks, exactly, she was willing and able to perform. As a sophomore, she did not have as extensive a background in her major as I had assumed, nor was she particularly comfortable leading exercise demonstrations or explaining wellness terms to a group of adult women who were non-native English language speakers. While the HPU student and the Learning Together students got along well with each other and genuinely enjoyed each other's company, they saw me primarily as the instructor, even though I was not functioning in my role as professor. This often happens at the service site, where, whenever there is a question regarding one of the HPU students, it is directed toward me, even when I am not the instructor of the service learning course.

In this case, not only did the student have difficulty at times differentiating my role as community member versus professor, but I did as well. While I wanted to see her as my equal in the classroom, I could not ignore the fact that outside of this context I was aware of what was expected of her in Cara's course. I grew frustrated when I felt she was not completing tasks that were in the purview of her assignment, and I was conflicted as how to proceed in these situations. If I did not pick up the slack, then the students in the Learning Together classroom would suffer, but at the same time, I knew that I should not be doing the work that was part of her service learning requirements. In speaking with Cara about this situation, I became aware that the student in question felt that I was placing too great of a responsibility on her in comparison to what was expected in the course and what was being expected of her classmates, and that she did not feel prepared for the work nor confident in her skills in completing all the tasks I had assigned. These conversations helped Cara and me become more personally aware of the fact that transparency and open dialogue are crucial in creating effective partnerships for all parties involved, which includes students. Working with Cara's student in my capacity as a community member afforded me insight into the responsibilities of the student and community partner that I may not otherwise have had as a service learning professor. In this capacity I was better able to negotiate the needs of both the community partner and the service learning course. This experience was also invaluable to me as I began to prepare my own service learning courses, as I had a more complete picture of the needs and expectations of the various participants.

Although I taught a SL course ("Feminist Theory and Praxis") in the academic year following this experience, it was another full academic year before I partnered with Learning Together for a service learning section of the course "Women, Gender, and Culture." As explained in my course description for students, a primary goal of the course was to examine the lives of women across cultures through the lens of service learning, with particular attention paid to the role of globalization in the lives of women in the United States and abroad. In partnering with three community programs that empower and address the needs of women in our city of High Point—the YWCA of High Point, West End Ministries/Leslie's House (which provides transitional housing for women ages 18 and older without dependents), and Learning Together—students were to consider the effects of globalization here in High Point, while thinking more broadly about the material reality of women's lives globally. Although not explicitly stated on the syllabus, a guiding theme of the course was interrogating the activist potential of service learning as it relates to women's and gender studies. The readings assigned on the first day of class were John Eby's "Why Service Learning Is Bad" and *Ms.*'s Fall 2011 section of articles on women's and gender studies programs, which includes the pieces "So You Want to Change the World?," "Women's Studies Brings Global Change," and "Taking Women's Studies Into the Streets." These articles and the surrounding debate of the activist potential of both service learning and women's and gender studies set the tone of the course and were frequently referenced by students in class and in their writing throughout the semester. Assigning these texts at the outset was a strategic move on my part for a number of reasons. First, I wanted to stress to students the responsibility associated with service learning, and I made sure that they were aware of my previous experiences with our partner agencies and my personal commitment to these organizations. In doing this, I attempted to establish myself as not only their teacher in the classroom, but as an activist in our community. In addition to working with virtually all of the students on their service at least once during the semester, I routinely referenced our partner agencies and community members when appropriate during class lectures. This was important not only to establish my credibility, but to ensure that my students were making connections between the work we were doing in the community with the work we did in the classroom.

My second reason for assigning the first set of readings was not only to acknowledge women's and gender studies' history with activism and service learning, but also to help students see women's and gender studies as a dynamic academic discipline that operates with its own pedagogy and demands students take equal responsibility in all aspects of the learning process. Thus, in a way, I was extending the learning together model to engage students in their own learning process through feminist, team-based, and service learning pedagogies. While I was continually impressed by the work that students were doing in the classroom and in the community, at times they expressed their frustrations at what they considered were "failures": low quiz scores, initial difficulty interacting with community members, and navigating complicated assignments as the semester progressed. Despite overwhelmingly remarking that the course was more "challenging" than they were expecting or prepared for, their own assessment of their quality of *learning* at the end of the semester was a 4.79/5. Further, as the semester progressed and the students adjusted to the expectations of the course, the quality of their work and their grades improved. Once students realized that the expectations of their work placed on them by both me and their community partner were not going to be lowered, their assumption of responsibility increased, the level of confidence grew, and standards of performance improved.

While it would be an exaggeration and overestimation to say that all of the students' lives were dramatically transformed through activism and SL, the learning together model and their service learning work brought a greater awareness to their own personal responsibility as it relates to both their learning and their place within local and global communities. Further, as a result of the course, one student in the class, Lexi, elected to undertake an independent study project building upon her work with Learning Together, and another student applied for and was chosen to be an AmeriCorps VISTA in the city of High Point upon her graduation.

LEARNING TOGETHER: A COMPOSITIONIST'S EXPERIENCES PROMOTING ACTIVIST-ORIENTED SERVICE LEARNING (CARA)

I came to High Point in 2010 as an Assistant Professor of Rhetoric and Composition with the desire to develop sustainable community partnerships that would support and enhance students' and community members' multiple literacies.[2] Prior to being appointed Assistant Director of HPU's Service Learning Program, I began the process of developing a service learning (SL) course by applying for and being awarded a course development grant. Through my research on service learning within composition studies and my prior experiences teaching SL as a graduate student, I was keenly aware of scholarly critiques suggesting that problematic SL models can privilege ideologies of service or volunteerism over critical reflection (Butin, 2010; Eby, 1998; Herzberg, 1994; Howard, 2001;

---

2   Cope and Kalantzis (2000) describe multiliteracy as the notion that literacy is not fixed and that there is no single way to teach literacy because language is acquired and interpreted in multiple ways and through multiple contexts.

Flower, 2008); value university knowledge over community knowledge (Flower, 2008; Stoecker, Tryon & Hilgendorf, 2009; Tryon et al., 2008); lack authentic collaboration between students and partners (Flower, 2008; Schutz & Gere, 1998); perpetuate stereotypes of others (Eby, 1998; Himley, 2004; Schutz & Gere, 1998); and support "drop-in" service experiences rather than sustainable partnerships (Cushman, 2002; Stoecker, Tryon & Hilgendorf, 2009; Tryon et al., 2008). Therefore, I approached the task of choosing a partner for my course with the aim of developing a long-term, reciprocal relationship with a local literacy organization.

I heard about the Learning Together program and reached out to staff members to determine if it might be a good partner for my class. I first met with Molly at a local coffee shop near campus for an informal conversation about Learning Together's goals and needs and the content and learning objectives of the course I was developing. I hoped that meeting in a casual off-campus environment would offer a space where we could talk honestly about whether the potential partnership could be mutually beneficial. While the idea that "those being served control the service" has been a widely accepted principle of good practice within SL for decades (Sigmon, 1979), partnerships that prioritize community (versus academic) needs and make community partners active participants in designing service projects have proved difficult for many programs and practitioners to enact. When the groundwork is not laid for reciprocal partnerships prior to students' initial service, the placements often put additional stress on community partners or lead to low levels of student learning and engagement. Howard (2001) suggests that faculty should be highly selective and intentional about students' service learning placements in order to ensure that partnerships will allow students to understand the relevance of their service in relation to course content and meet defined learning objectives. Therefore, the first step in developing service learning partnerships is often for faculty and community members to make time for conversations to understand each other's goals and needs. Community partners may feel reluctant to turn away potential university partnerships even if they are not well-equipped to train or accommodate students, so faculty members often assume the responsibility of having to decline organizations that do not seem like the right match for their courses.

Molly describes Learning Together as a family literacy program for low-income immigrant, refugee, and minority parents and their preschool-age children that engages participants through a four-part approach: 1. To empower mothers to set and reach personal, educational, and vocational goals. 2. To connect families to other resources and to their greater community. 3. To support parents as their child's first educator and advocate. And 4. To give the children skills they will need to be successful in school. Although not explicitly a feminist organization, like the Family Scholar House program discussed by Kathryn Perry (Chapter 10, this collection), given its approach, Learning Together can be interpreted as a feminist intervention. Given Learning Together's diverse participant demographic and literacy-oriented goals, Molly and I felt there was enough cohesion between organizational needs and course objectives to move forward with the partnership. I volunteered at the organization on several occasions, and I shared drafts of my syllabus and relevant assignments with Molly to solicit feedback. When the class began, she and the homework help program coordinator came to campus to speak to students about Learning Together's mission and participants, and they also held an on-site orientation and training for students.

The first service learning course that I collaborated with went through several versions with significant modifications to course content and student service requirements. These revisions were based on observations made at the site and conversations between Learning Together staff and myself. During the first version of the course, HPU students were placed in either the child-care room for babies and preschoolers or the homework help room for K-8 students. Following that semester, however, we placed all SL students with the homework help program—the college students seemed be babysitting the younger children rather than learning with or from them. I also changed my grading criteria for students' final projects to include community partner response/feedback as a component of the grading rubric, because we noticed that students were seeking input for the design of their projects primarily from me rather than from the community partners for whom their projects were intended.

Despite the effort Molly and I put into our initial planning of the SL component, the first version of the course encountered many problems typical of SL partnerships, and the course evaluation data suggested that the experience did not particularly enhance student learning.³ However, because we were committed to maintaining an open dialogue and making changes as needed, subsequent courses partnered with the program have run more smoothly, and student evaluation data have shown significant gains in student learning and overall satisfaction with the SL component. Through our experiences partnering with Learning Together and other local organizations, Jenn and I have found that even when intense energy is given toward working collaboratively within

---

3   Other institutional factors may have also contributed to the evaluation data in addition to the "kinks" with the SL component and logistics. In 2012, HPU's SL program had just implemented a new course designation system that was unfamiliar to many students and academic advisors. Therefore, many students in the course had unintentionally enrolled in SL, and in the written portion of the evaluations, some respondents expressed frustration about being required to fulfill SL hours in addition to traditional class time and coursework. Since that semester, the course designation system has become more familiar to the campus community, which has led to higher percentages of students who enroll in SL by choice.

university-community partnerships, it takes time to enact genuine collaboration, and efforts toward this goal must be sustained on both ends.

As the learning together model implies, each course or project in which we have participated has led to a diverse range of issues that must be negotiated through a learning process involving campus and community stakeholders. It was in the second version of the course that Jenn became the community partner for a young woman in my class who had chosen to complete her service by implementing wellness activities with the women and developing materials related to fitness and nutrition. As Jenn described, despite her intention to partner with the student as a community volunteer, her professional position at the university created unanticipated tensions. Because the final project rubric included a community partner feedback component (my tweak to the grading criteria in response to issues from the previous semester), the student was concerned that she was being evaluated more critically by Jenn than other students in the course who were partnering with Learning Together staff and volunteers unaffiliated with the university. Jenn had also spoken with me about her anxiety that the student might not be capable of completing a quality project that would benefit the women in the program, and she expressed concern that she might be taking on too many of the student's responsibilities in order to fulfill her own duties as a community volunteer. These conversations raised interesting ethical questions for me as an SL instructor, and I recognized the validity of the student's and Jenn's anxieties that their roles within the partnership were functioning differently than other partnerships in the class. Through a series of conversations, the wellness project and culminating "Learning Together Olympics" were ultimately successful and well-received by all stakeholders. However, the situation raised questions about whether faculty members can ever genuinely detach themselves from their associations with institutions when doing activist work in the community. While I still think that faculty members can absolutely partner with students in non-faculty community volunteer roles, I now avoid giving faculty any evaluative role when working with students in this capacity.

Despite the speed bumps encountered by having to renegotiate students' roles, assignments, grading criteria, and faculty and community partner expectations (bumps which I think are typical of and perhaps even necessary to enacting the learning together model), even early stages of our partnership with Learning Together were effective in achieving some feminist activist goals. When asked what she considers the best experience with respect to the partnership, Molly says that it has been the expanded services that the organization has been able to provide to participants: "With the help and support of HPU, we are able to offer tutoring to 25 school-aged children whose parents and younger siblings attend the program; to provide one-on-one or small group computer classes; and to provide more individualized English-language-instruction to our adult learners." While these expanded services have helped Learning Together work toward feminist goals of improving women's lives through enhanced access to literacy and community support, I think where the first courses I taught fell short was that the college students didn't perceive their work as the type of everyday feminist activism that Finley and Stringer describe. The process of partnering with Learning Together for multiple courses and projects has allowed me opportunities to develop and implement an activist-oriented SL model that more explicitly addresses feminist aims and demonstrates to students and community members our deep commitment to the Learning Together program.

To discuss this progression toward a feminist activist approach, for the remainder of this section I focus on an upper-division course I taught for writing majors, "Community Writing." In the class, students collaborated with some of Learning Together's immigrant and refugee women to develop a community publication—a printed book collection of literacy narratives,[4] *Women's Stories of Literacy*, which was distributed within the community and now serves as a course text for other SL courses that partner with the organization. To develop a foundation in literacy studies, students read seminal works such as Mike Rose's *Lives on the Boundary*, Richard Rodriguez's *The Hunger of Memory*, Deborah Brandt's *Literacy in American Lives*, and Ellen Cushman's *The Struggle and the Tools*, as well as excerpts from well-known literacy narratives by Frederick Douglass, Malcolm X, Helen Keller, and David Sedaris, among others. The students enrolled in the course, who happened to all be women,[5] were each paired with a Learning Together participant. Over the semester, the students conducted multiple oral history interviews with their partners, and they adapted these interviews into literacy narratives written from the first-person perspective. Similar to the method that Concannon et al. discuss in their chapter in this collection, the students composed multiple drafts of the narratives, which were presented to their partners for feedback and revisions. In addition to these stories, each student composed her own literacy narrative as well as a critical analysis of her community partner's narrative. Each chapter in the book, with the exception of one that I discuss in more detail, includes the community partner's literacy narrative, the HPU student's literacy narrative, and the student's critical analyses of her partner's narrative.

---

4   A literacy narrative is a genre in which the author offers a narrative, typically from the first-person perspective, about the processes of reading, writing, or teaching or learning to read or write. These narratives take many forms, including print, oral, visual, digital, etc.

5   The fact that the class was composed of all female students is not surprising. Studies have found women are more likely to volunteer in college than men, and SL classes at HPU tend to be majority women (A.W. Astin & Sax, 1998; Cruce & Moore, 2007; Marks & Jones, 2004).

The project received IRB approval—all participants consented to participate and the women made decisions about whether to use their names or to include pictures with their stories, and they worked through multiple drafts with the students to prepare for publication. Most of the community partners chose to use pseudonyms, while all of the HPU students opted to use their real names. While the composing process in itself encouraged deep listening between students and partners, an ethical dilemma arose that amplified the experience. Several Muslim women decided to withdraw their stories from the collection, although they had initially asked to participate in the project and signed consent forms. Their narratives discussed gender and political violence, and they became afraid of retaliation. The students faced the difficult task of moving forward with the project in a way that would be responsive to these women's fears while also honoring their commitment to other women involved with the project who wanted their stories published.

Initially, the community members' fears about publishing their stories in the collection did not sit well with students in the class, who expressed concern that the women's reluctance stemmed from gender oppression within Muslim communities that would be perpetuated by the removal of their stories. Through conversations in class and with the Learning Together women, however, the students developed the understanding that the women were asserting authorial agency by deciding, and voicing their views about, the conditions on which their stories, names, and pictures could be shared. All of the Learning Together women, for instance, chose to share their stories orally in a final culminating event at the community center where the program meets. One participant, Mays, an Iraqi Muslim woman who opted to use her name and picture in the book, visited Jenn's class "Women Writing Worldwide" as a guest speaker and shared her story with other HPU students. Ultimately all but one woman, who asked to be referred to as Toma, decided to have their stories included in the collection. Toma requested that she be provided with three printed copies of the story that she could share with her young children when they got older, and she allowed her partner, Sally's, critical analysis essay to be included in the collection. The process that the women and the students went through to share and document their literacy narratives and to produce a final collection agreeable to all stakeholders in the project was a true example of the learning together model in action. The students in the class perceived their work on the book as a type of feminist activism, even when, as in the case of Toma, that activism chafed against their own views of Western feminism.

Community publishing projects such as this one are part of a growing subfield within rhetoric and composition. There have been a number of books and edited collections that address the value of community publishing projects (Parks, 2010; Goldblatt, 2007; Mathieu, 2005; Mathieu, Parks and Rousculp, 2014), and scholars propose the integration of community publishing into writing programs as a method of expanding the focus on what Mathieu, Parks, and Rouscamp (2014) have termed the "community writer." Bickford and Reynolds (2002) argue that although the field of composition has a long history of research on service learning, many scholars "share a discomfort with *activism*, a term far more likely to be used in women's studies" (p. 230). They suggest that even well-known scholarship that refers specifically to activism, such as Cushman's (1999) and Schutz and Gere's (1998) frequently cited work, tends to conflate the term activism with the notion of service (p. 230). Parks (2014) points to the decline in activist work within composition, and he suggests that the discipline's emphasis on rhetorical agency and critique have compromised its political agenda. Which is why, according to Parks, "we tend to conclude with *discussion* instead of moving on to *collective action*" (p. 511). He points to community publishing as "a modern manifestation of early disciplinary attempts to foster activist connections between the literacies of our students and literacies in the neighborhoods that surround our campuses" (p. 485), an idea that has been highly influential to my own pedagogical progression from using more traditional SL models to the activist-oriented learning together model we propose.

Since the book project, I have continued using the learning together model in my administrative work with the SL Program, particularly in how I offer training and faculty development across the disciplines. Community publishing has become a key component of how I implement the learning together model as an activist-oriented approach, and it is an approach that faculty have used in other SL classes related to narrative medicine, poetry, business ethics, and health and nutrition. As students and community members collaborate to create published texts, the negotiation and production processes help to encourage students and community members to be active participants within the partnership.

CONCLUSION

In 2012, the White House released *A Crucible Moment: College Learning and Democracy's Future*, a report by the National Task Force on Civic Learning and Democratic Engagement commissioned by the Department of Education. The report, referred to as a call for action, comes in response to a "civic recession" (p. 7), a term used to describe a massive deficit in civic knowledge and public engagement in the democratic process. While acknowledging the immense value of the civic work already being done at colleges and universities, the report suggests that these endeavors have laid a partial foundation for civic learning but have not been enough to foster a culture of engagement within higher education. The authors assert that in order to create a pervasive culture of engagement within higher education, civic learning must become a central part of *every* college student's education.

While our courses were not necessarily framed in terms of civic engagement, this notion of service learning as "civic involvement and public engagement" naturally "clicked" for many of our students. One student, Lexi, who undertook an independent study project with Learning Together following Jenn's class, said that her "best experience" with service learning was "the moment it made me question the construct of 'citizenship.'" Interviewed for this piece, she elaborated,

> It [service learning] made me re-evaluate everything I thought I knew and felt comfortable with regarding my identity. One of the biggest challenges that I faced during my Learning Together experience was trying to explain aspects of my own culture. It was not a challenge I originally predicted prior to my initial experience with service learning in general because I realized I did not always have a concrete answer.

The question of "citizenship" came up during one of the lessons in the adult classroom at Learning Together, but its association with identity more broadly speaks to the feminist intervention potential of personal narrative as a strategy in the composition classroom. The experiences of Lexi and her classmates, as well as those documented in *Women's Stories of Literacy: A Writing Project Featuring Refugee and Immigrant Woman and High Point University Students*, demonstrate Royster and Kirsch's (2012) suggestion that:

> One strategy might be to use our classrooms as innovative experimental sites in recognizing that while we are tacking out into the world, the imperative may be simultaneously to tack in as we consider the presence of the world at home. We look toward the world, but simultaneously we have the opportunity to look at the world in us—within our nation, in our communities, in our classrooms. (p. 127)

What may at first glance appear to be a very simple concept—citizenship—is revealed to be far more nuanced for both our students and the students in the Learning Together classroom as they reflect on their own identities, stories, and the individual journeys that brought them to this shared space. Attempting to define the term "citizenship" became much more than a simple exercise in vocabulary building. Reflecting on what it means to be a "citizen" and the social constructs related to our identities created a situation where students could think more deeply about "civic awareness" and the need to advocate for change in their own communities.

When students become aware of their roles as advocates for social change, it then becomes possible to move past general conceptions of service in relation to civic engagement and citizenship, toward a more defined sense of activism. This collection's aim of aligning feminist and rhetoric and composition specialists to initiate or build activism through campus-community partnerships is something that we have found incredibly valuable in our work with Learning Together and other community organizations. The institutional partnerships between the English department and the service learning and women's and gender studies programs have allowed us to build more deeply sustained community partnerships. Parks (2014) argues that composition, as a field, has turned away from political activism and "settled for a soft vision of progressive change, a vision that at best produces a hesitant and halting trek across a neoliberal landscape eager to validate our students and our own 'protestations' as a sign of rich democratic debate" (p. 506). While we do not dispute Parks's claim that rhetorical agency has become a prevalent stand-in for genuine advocacy and action, the chapters in this collection offer examples of how the activist ethos deeply ingrained within women's studies and feminist composition theory can help reinvigorate the political aims of community partnerships and community literacy projects within writing studies. Moreover, the learning together approach we describe serves as a potential model that we hope will help others work toward social justice goals through sustained campus-community partnerships.

REFERENCES

Astin, A. W. & Sax, L. J. (1998). How undergraduates are affected by service participation. *Journal of College Student Development, 39*(3), 251–263.

Astin, A. W., Sax, L. J. & Avalos, J. (1999). Long-term effects of volunteerism during the undergraduate years. *Review of Higher Education, 22*(2), 187–202.

Berger, M. T. (2013). Learning from women's studies. *Contexts, 12*(2), 76–79.

Bickford, D. M & Reynolds, N. (2002). Activism and service-learning: Reframing volunteerism as acts of dissent. *Pedagogy, 2*(2), 229–252.

Brown, W. (2008). The impossibility of women's studies. In J. W. Scott (Ed.), *Women's Studies on the Edge* (pp. 17–38). Durham, NC: Duke University Press.

Butin, D. W. (2010). *Service-learning in theory and practice: The future of community engagement in higher education*. New York, NY: Palgrave Macmillan.

Cope, B., Kalantzis, M. & New London Group. (2000). *Multiliteracies: Literacy learning and the design of social futures*. London, England: Routledge.

Cruce, T. M. & Moore, J. V. (2007, November 1). First-year students' plans to volunteer: An examination of the predictors of community service participation. *Journal of College Student Development, 48*(6), 655–673.

Cushman, E. (2002). Sustainable service learning programs. *College Composition and Communication, 54*(1), 40–65.

Cushman, E. (1999). The public intellectual, service learning, and activist research. *College English, 61*(3), 328–36.

Dugger, K. (2008). *Handbook on service learning in women's studies and the disciplines.* Towson, Md: Institute for Teaching and Research on Women.

Eby, J. (1998). Why service-learning is bad. Retrieved from http://www.messiah.edu/documents/Agape/wrongsvc.pdf.

Evans, S. & Kozma, C. (2015). *Women's stories of literacy: A writing project featuring refugee and immigrant women and High Point University students.* High Point, N.C: High Point University.

Finley, L. & Stringer, E.R. (2010). *Beyond bra burning: Feminist activism for everyone.* Denver, CO: Praeger.

Flower, L. (2008). *Community literacy and the rhetoric of public engagement.* Carbondale, IL: Southern Illinois University Press.

Goldblatt, E. (2007). *Because we live here: Sponsoring literacy beyond the college curriculum.* Cresskill, N.J: Hampton Press.

Harding, S. (2004). *The feminist standpoint theory reader: Intellectual and political controversies.* New York, NY: Routledge.

Herzberg, B. (1994). Community service and critical teaching. *College Composition and Communication, 45*(3), 307–19.

Himley, M. (2004). Facing (up to) "the stranger" in community service learning. *College Composition and Communication, 55*(3), 416–438.

Howard, J. (2001). *Service-learning course design workbook.* Ann Arbor, MI: OCSL Press.

Marks, H. & Jones, S. (2004). Community service in the transition: Shifts and continuities in participation from high school to college. *The Journal of Higher Education, 75*, 307–339.

Mathieu, P. (2005). *Tactics of hope: The public turn in English composition.* Portsmouth, NH: Boynton/Cook.

Mathieu, P., Parks, S. & Rousculp, T. (2012). *Circulating communities: The tactics and strategies of community publishing.* Lanham: Lexington Books.

National Task Force on Civic Learning and Democratic Engagement. (2012). *A crucible moment: College learning and democracy's future.* Washington, DC: Association of American College's and Universities.

Orr, C. M. (2011). Women's studies as civic engagement: Research and recommendations. *The Teagle Working Group on Women's Studies and Civic Engagement and the National Women's Studies Association.*

Parks, S. (2010). *Gravyland: Writing beyond the curriculum in the City of Brotherly Love.* Syracuse, N.Y: Syracuse University Press.

Parks, S. (2014). Sinners welcome: The limits of rhetorical agency. *College English, 76*(6), 506–524.

Royster, J. J. & Kirsch, G. E. (2012). *Feminist rhetorical practices: New horizons for rhetoric, composition, and literacy studies.* Carbondale, IL: Southern Illinois University Press.

Schutz, A. & Gere, A. R. (1998). Service learning and English studies: Rethinking "public service." *College English, 60*(2), 129–49.

Sigmon, R. L. (1979). Service-learning: Three principles. Synergist. National Center for Service-Learning, *ACTION, 8*(1), 9–11.

Stoecker, R., Tryon, E. A. & Hilgendorf, A. (2009). *The unheard voices: Community organizations and service learning.* Philadelphia: Temple University Press.

Tryon E., Stoecker, R., Martin, A., Seblonka, K., Hilgendorf, A. & Nellis, M. (2008). The challenge of short-term service-learning. *Michigan Journal Of Community Service Learning, 14*(2), 16–26.

Zimmerman, B. (2002). Women's studies, NWSA, and the future of the (inter)discipline. *NWSA Journal, 14*(1), viii–xviii.

CHAPTER 8.
CRAFTING PARTNERSHIPS: EXPLORING STUDENT-LED FEMINIST STRATEGIES FOR COMMUNITY LITERACY PROJECTS

Kelly Concannon
Nova Southeastern University

Mustari Akhi
Florida Atlantic University

Morgan Musgrove
Nova Southeastern University

Kim Lopez
Nova Southeastern University

Ashley Nichols
Nova Southeastern University

Relationships have served as a cornerstone to feminist research in community-based research and service learning sites, as feminist scholars have argued for co-constructing knowledges in these sites, while being attentive to the reciprocal nature of these relationships within any context of and for learning (Bayer, Grossman & Dubois, 2015; Parks & Goldblatt, 2000; Novek, 1999). These relationships are especially crucial when feminists attempt to create real and sustained partnerships through mentoring in their community-based literacy site (DuBois & Karcher, 2005). We stress the value of cultivating sustained relationships, as oftentimes discourses surrounding service learning exhibit a level of engagement that is not sustained and/or does not adequately expose the workings of power and privilege in a

> *systematic way (Deans, 2002). In light of our feminist motivations, we need to continuously create spaces to foreground the value of experience and take seriously the process of cultivating relationships with students in ways that are both ethical and accountable.*

Feminist pedagogues in composition and rhetoric have long illustrated that the role of pedagogy is to create conditions to transform social relationships (Ritchie, 1990; Bishop, 1990). To this end, feminist pedagogies reveal a strong commitment to examining how power and privilege factor into multiple elements of writing instruction—from the stances pedagogues assume—to the types of writing assignments and discussions that are implemented and assessed: "Feminist pedagogies connect local, personal experience to larger context of world making . . . within writing studies, activist pedagogical functions are linked to writing and literacy practices broadly conceived, making clear that there is no bracketing the world or politics from the classroom" (Micciche, 2014, p. 129). Our feminist pedagogies and practices in composition and rhetoric continue to evolve, as we find creative ways to move between the local and the global; the theoretical and the practical, all while revealing a relentless commitment to creating spaces with students, as we explore how political motivations materialize both within and beyond the classroom. Various authors in this collection highlight the role of reflection and collaboration in creating sustained partnerships, which closely involve students (See Mathis and Boehm, Chapter 6, for example). The overall impetus is to revise the discourse and to account for the absence of students' voices, while revising the *processes* through which collaboration happens both inside and outside of the classroom.

Students should always "trouble" our theories about the most effective methods through which to create change, because it is *their* stories that point to gaps, disconnects, and/or limitations (Kumashiro, 2002) in how we conceptualize the most effective ways to cultivate partnerships and relationships to community members within our service learning and/or community-based research sites. Continuing to create spaces where students are active agents in the construction, implementation, and reflection on feminist-based community literacy projects afford us with insight that can greatly enhance the types of relationships that we make in literacy-based sites. "When participants become full collaborators, co-authors, and co researchers, their roles are transformed: they cease to be the 'subjects' or participants in our research" (Kirsch, 1999, p. 64). Creating alternative opportunities to co-construct knowledges that emerge from students' lived experiences privileges student identities and experiences in the construction of knowledge about how to create conditions of and for social change, as we continue our commitments to feminist pedagogues and practices. To this end, our work calls for a similar initiative as the "learning together," model, which is explored by Brandt and Kozma in this collection (Chapter 7). This model allows for multiple narratives to equally come together and create a more kaleidoscopic view of how feminist interventions happen.

Our feminist pedagogical intervention draws from our collective experiences in a community-based feminist partnership. Throughout this piece, we argue that as feminists, we must engage in the process of reflection—as a political feminist intervention strategy—to make meaning about our lived-experiences in community-based research sites, as community-based pedagogies stress the value of experiential learning as a tool through which to make meaning (Goldblatt, Livingston & Julier, 2014, p. 56–57). This process allows us to re-evaluate the role of identity and experience in constructing knowledges, thereby-prioritizing the value of experience-based knowledge claims to ". . . democratize the classroom by drawing on a full range of student and faculty subject positions in the production of knowledge" (Sanchez-Casal and Macdonald, 2002, p.2). This process creates spaces where feminist students feel authorized to use their experiences in these sites, given the complexities involved in the use of narrative to disrupt discourses (Allen and Faigley 1995).

This chapter illustrates how a multi-layered approach to partnerships can help feminists assess community-based efforts through a focus on feminist mentorship and reflexivity. Our chapter foregrounds the voices of four feminist undergraduate students at Nova Southeastern University, as we draw from our work as co-mentors through the Women of Tomorrow Program. The WOT program links professional woman to a local high school, where are afforded the opportunities to create conditions through which young, at-risk high school women feel empowered. The motivation behind this organization is to "change the world, one woman at a time," and it is "designed to inspire, motivate and empower at-risk young women to live up to their full potential through a unique mentoring program" (https://womenoftomorrow.org/about/).

Reflections on our community-engaged partnership created conditions where students' writing emerged from a unique rhetorical context. The work that feminist students did within our site, and the reflection of that work, stemmed from their commitments to providing feminist interventions into the lives of young women through a pre-existing partnership. I used both my position as a Women of Tomorrow mentor and my role as a university professor to informally mentor a small group of college women to create initiatives intended for empowerment. Thus, it was our hope to recognize the value of bringing together action and reflection in order to make sense of these types of experiences outside of a traditional classroom (Goldblatt, Livingston, and Julier, 2014, p. 58–59; Spigelman, 2004).

All of the students who chose to participate in this project made critical decisions about how they wanted to represent themselves in the research, and all of the students self-selected the types of narratives that they wanted to present. Significantly, the position that students were placed in authorize them to become experts and join an academic conversation (Bacon 2000). In this way, we believe that this chapter calls for a more active and deliberate account of our feminist students and creates alternative discourses about how community-based partnerships happen. Students' representations of their own experiences serve as a point of social action and intervention. Thus, in this chapter we will argue that how we represent the work we do as feminists within community-based research sites should be approached as a methodology that involves inquiry. In *Traces of a Stream* Jackie Jones Royster (1994) argues for the use of "critical imagination," as a new methodology where we engage in inquiry as we use what we know and then stretch and expand our perspectives. She argues that from inquiry, we can continue to expand how we come to know, and speculate on what may, in fact, be possible" ("Critical Imagination," p. 71). Critical imagination thus becomes a significant tool through which we can look more carefully at the gaps, possibilities, and potentials in how we choose to actively represent our work, and students actively speak up and speak back through their epistemological stances. While their representations are in no way intended to be definitive, we suggest that students' accounts of themselves serve as an analytic for engaging in feminist activism.

PROJECT DESCRIPTION

The Women of Tomorrow Mentor and Scholarship Program pairs "at risk" high school girls with local mentors in the community. The intention is to create positive and lasting relationships; to inspire women to re-create their futures. According to the organization, it functions to "expose at risk girls to opportunities otherwise unavailable to them; teaches vital personal and professional skills necessary for life success; helps set and achieve goals; increases their self-esteem; and helps to reduce and prevent engaging in risky behaviors" (Womenoftomorrow.org). The program partners with local public schools. Young women are selected to be in the group based on need and the organization notes that its definition of "at-risk" includes: "low income, abuse, disability, likelihood of dropping out of high school, becoming involved in gangs, drugs, criminal activity, getting pregnant or academic, social, behavioral, medical or other risk factors" ("What we Do," *Mentoring Handbook*, p. 3). The organization is especially aligned with feminist goals and outcomes, as it operates under the assumption that it is powerful for women to be helping women reach their full potential. The program suggests that mentors address issues related to a wide-range of topics. These range from academic achievement, which highlights study skills and the significance of pursuing an education beyond high school, professional/personal successes including how to carry yourself while giving a speech and how to maintain proper hygiene/health and safety. At the core of the monthly sessions is an insistence to engage in critical thinking, interpersonal communication, and skills for academic and personal success. Our position to the local high school afforded us with the opportunity to build a unique partnership because we were not confined by the institutional constraints of a classroom environment. Unlike service-learning courses where university students' work with community members and are guided by course-work and motivated by a final grade, we were working as a collective with common goals and purposes.

RE-PRESENTING STUDENT VOICES

I served as the faculty member who selected former undergraduate feminist students who I felt would enrich our approach to the WOT program. Feminist undergraduate students at Nova Southeastern University were asked to participate in the process of reflexivity about their relationships to our feminist project. I attempted to address these power differences head on by asking feminist students to self-select how they wanted to engage in the process of research and representation; in the process, we foregrounded the role of reflexivity in the research process. Reflexivity has taken on a variety of forms in service-learning and community-based research and serves as a social justice tool because it allows researchers to actively and carefully explore knowledge construction (Dewey, 2012). To that end, reflexivity is a key component to producing ethical and responsible research (Royster and Kirsch, 2012). I decided against using interviews as a method through which to gauge students' understandings of their role in bringing about change within our site. I felt that the interviews may function to overly formalize and structure some of their responses in ways that may stifle how they have been thinking about their agency in the research process. Also, I felt as if being the interviewer may work to reinforce, or make hyper visible, our varying roles (and the power dynamics that accompanied those roles) in the research process.

Feminist students identified what they saw as key themes that emerged in the construction, implementation, planning, and engagement of this partnership with the local high school. In the following section, I have included student accounts of how they see particular themes reflected throughout their work. All students represented below included their personal, un-edited reflective narratives. This was to maintain the integrity of *student* representation. The themes students discuss overlap in significant ways and raise serious questions about the role of different themes in feminist activism work.

STUDENT NARRATIVES

Kim—Theme #1: Getting the Most of Mentoring by Establishing Relationships

When one wants to introduce themselves as a mentor to an individual's life, it is important to take note that he/she enters in an unknown territory, and that it could be difficult to explore or make a clear path if he/she is not seen as welcoming. As a person participating in the WOT program, I believe that establishing genuine relationships with high school students could provide greater success within their lives. My purpose in the WOT program is to be able to educate the young ladies in the best possible manner allowing them to think about the type of life they want to engage in and the possible decisions they are entitled to. With this in mind it is important for the students to make choices for themselves instead of what others may think, including me, since in the end it is wanted for them to feel a sense of control in their lives.

Even if a mentor may have good intentions, sometimes it is not easy to become vulnerable to a person with unknown intentions. As a person who once needed guidance, I could empathize with those who may have reluctance of expressing certain discomforts of their lives which may have left vast feelings such as disappoint, fear, anger, regret or hate. Feeling exposed is a difficult matter especially if it is in front of a person who may judge or could care less of the individual. Which is why it is important when one is trying to help an individual, to establish a relationship where the person can have the sense of security that he/she is being helped to make decisions of his/her life that is beneficial.

From what I have experienced throughout my life and the WOT program I could understand how establishing relationships as a mentor is important in the outcome of an individual. As a young child, I always thought of how I was perceived in this world and what I perceived myself as. I lived a content life, however, there were aspects of it that bothered me such as developing negative body image which almost resulted to an eating disorder, certain types of harassment, discrimination and prejudice, especially from those who were supposed to be close to me. Although I am very close to my parents and always spoke to them with no discomfort, I seldom spoke about the problems that personally hurt me as I didn't want them to feel that they did not do a great job as parents. The only one I shared my bottled feelings at that time was my younger sister, however, I tried not to as there was no need to drag her into my problems.

When I was in high school reaching towards senior year, I had a self-awareness of the expectations many had, and questioned who exactly was living my life. I knew that I wanted to attend college, yet as a first-generation student I did not know what steps to take at all. I wasn't sure what college or university I wanted to attend and started to doubt in my intelligence and decisions. Confused, I turned to my former Spanish AP teacher whom I trusted. Her advice was important to me since I knew she really cared about my well-being and was always willing to listen with genuine interest. She was able to see my vulnerability without force and managed to compliment me as a person. At that time, all I needed was some guidance from someone who saw great potential within me, someone who knew that I had worth within me. I was compliant with her advice and up to this day I attend a university which I love and also got to meet amazing people throughout who also saw the same potential within me.

I barely thought of other people like me who also sought aid from others like my former Spanish AP teacher, however, when I went for the first time to the WOT meeting I envisioned myself, except they were multiple strong energetic young girls with minds of their own. I didn't know from what backgrounds each may have come from, but I knew each were there for personal reasons. Unfortunately, at the beginning it was hard to gain their attention, which didn't surprise me as it was my first time there and knew it would take time, yet as I observed, I got the sense that all of them wanted a better future for themselves such as attending college. Throughout the event I wanted the high school students to know that they are worthy individuals, that they can seek the change they want if they saw value within themselves. As I shared my personal struggles I wanted them to understand that change is gradual and must be persistent; that being imperfect is alright, but also not to let those imperfections be the reason one cannot seek improvement. As other mentors from the WOT program spoke about their struggles and improvements I could see the interests forming from the young ladies. They saw people they could relate to and trust, which was important as it allowed them to actually reflect upon their situations and the possible choices they have to approach them. When I saw their willingness to be compliant as we tried to provide them with guidance, I realized the importance of forming relationships as a mentor and that how this should be implemented within all mentorship or other aiding program.

As the WOT program progresses, hopefully I will have some success in empowering some, if not, most of the young girls as they reevaluate their lives. Although I wish to form connection with them, I do hope I do it is in a manner that they are comfortable with. It is not my intentions to make them feel forced to become beings that they don't want to be or make them feel insignificant. Yet I believe through experience, that establishing genuine relationships between the mentor and student can lead into a positive outcome for the students.

Ashley—Theme #2: Feminism in Mentorship

I have played sports all my life. I have been an athlete from dancing, to lifting weights, to playing football. Throughout these vast sporting experiences, I never failed to hear "you throw like a girl," "you run like a girl," or even "this is a boy sport." Some young people may have been discouraged by statements as stupid as this. I treated these "insults" as compliments and fueled myself to be the best me that I could be. I always knew that no matter what I was doing, I was going to give it everything I had and make it something I could be proud of. Entering college was the means of a new beginning for myself and many others. I set out to explore who I am as a both as a student and as an individual. I finally discovered who I had been all along, a feminist. Unearthing the true name to my personal beliefs left me searching for more definite foundations of this cause. Luckily, I was able to explore feminism further through one of my college courses. After countless hours delving into to countless articles, studies, and passages and conducting a couple surveys, and a few interviews I was able to produce not one but three different term papers on the subject. After conducting educational and personal research I was then confident that I was indeed a feminist. Sadly, when I mention feminism I usually get scoffed at . . . even by women. This saddens me the most because if women don't even believe in feminism, how will we ever get the world to believe. I believe that the reason for this is that no one ever taught these women what feminism really stands for: what feminism really is. Feminism is not just a bunch of women advocating for female supremacism. Feminism is a fight to make right everything that is so, so, wrong in this world. Feminism is fighting for expression, fighting for equality, fighting for every person who has ever been told that his or her voice doesn't matter. Feminism is for men and women, people of all measures of the gender scale, people of all ages, people of all races, and people of all religions. Feminism is so much more than I will ever be and feminism is bigger than most people can fathom. Being in a college atmosphere that fosters personal growth, I found feminism. I don't know how I went so long without knowing about feminism and this knowledge has changed my life. Feminism has proved to me that I can be more than just a girl from a small town that no one can find on a map. This is why I think it is very important to work with young girls in the name of feminism.

Working with Women of Tomorrow gives me the opportunity to spread feminism on a level that may be more important than any other. I rejoice in the opportunity to get to know the students of this program, to see a little bit of myself in their eyes, and maybe help them to understand that they aren't limited to the perceptions of others. The young girls who are involved in this program are going to be a huge part of the future of the world. We have already seen big steps in creating equal rights for the gay community, the black community, and yes even the female community. We have been fortunate enough to witness so much change, but there is still so much to do. These women could be part of the generation that finally breaks through the glass ceiling. They could be a part of the generation with the first female president. They could be responsible for making giant leaps in creating true equality. I feel that it is my social responsibility to form genuine relationships with the girls I mentor; it is important to instill in them the ideas of true feminism. With these relationships comes support, encouragement, and trust. These elements are the basis of a strong foundation to personal growth. It is of the utmost importance that these young women see the potential that exists in each and every one of them. The potential to make a difference for the generations that are to follow them. Women fought so long and so hard in the women's suffrage movement and still, so many women don't exercise their right to vote. Giving these girls the opportunity to have access to a feminist influence also gives them an environment that fosters self-exploration. Much like the environment that initiated my own self-actualization. This kind of mentoring gives me to opportunity to teach the feminist principles I have come to know and create a group of colleagues to stand up for what is right.

I hope I never see a world without feminism. This make my mission as a mentor even more important. It is imperative that the young women involved in Women of Tomorrow mentoring program learn and understand how much of a difference they can make. It is essential that they exercise their right to vote, their right to live as productive and self-aware members of their communities and all of the communities that they will come to be a part of.

Mustari—Theme #3: Providing Access: Blazing a Path for Others through Mentorship

"Access" and "excess" are two things that, despite their phonetic similarities, are conceptually different. Notwithstanding, both things can also be intertwined, and I believe both play a distinct role in mentorship. One can argue that a mentor is the most successful and efficient in being able to guide and nurture the growth of another individual when the mentor him or herself has access to knowledge or opportunities that can be then passed down to his or her mentee. Other times, when an individual has an excess of something in his or life, that surplus can also be shared with others who lack it. Both themes of access and excess have played a critical role in my motivations and commitment to become a mentor for the Women of Tomorrow (WOT) program. Interestingly, it was actually my own initial *lack* of access and the *lack* of excess in my life that cemented my drive to mentor others in the future.

As immigrants, my family moved to America with little to flourish on. Both my parents, who both were unable to pursue a college education in our home country due to the lack of financial access, instilled the importance of education in all of my siblings and I. We were told that in order to get access to the rest of the world and its many untouched opportunities, we had to excel in scholarship and service. However, the problem was, we didn't know *how*. We lived in a socioeconomically disadvantaged neighborhood and attended underprivileged schools. Our neighborhood and schools lacked sufficient access to federal assistance programs that were critically necessary to help nurture the academic and personal growth of its residents and its students, respectively. At my home, my family struggled on multiple fronts; there was a lack of access to financial stability, for the time for recreational activities, and for simple necessities and desires. While I don't believe an excess is necessary to leave a sustainable life, it did make me wonder what life was like for those who *did* have the freedom to access the opportunities the world had for them, and for those who *did* have an excess to be able to live somewhat in comfort or afford luxuries. At the same time, I wanted someone to connect with on an emotional level, someone who could share my personal struggles with or someone who encouraged me to strive for my happiness and success further down the road. It was then when I began to seek advice from those who *did* have the access and the knowledge to share with me their wisdom on how I could find my own window for success and growth.

I was drawn to the WOT for this very reason. Many of the public-school girls who participate in the WOT program in order to seek scholarship and mentorship come from difficult backgrounds or underprivileged that have resulted in them being at-risk for academic failure, future pregnancies, low self-esteem, or future unemployment. Another factor that they all share in common is the lack of access to a program or mentors who could otherwise show them their potential for success and growth. Learning about these girls made me immediately reflect on my own childhood and my own desperation for 'access,' for 'excess,' and for a mentor. It made me realize that I was finally in a position in life where I could become the very person I once needed for myself as a child. As a college student, I finally had access to a plethora of opportunities, had an 'excess' of knowledge to share, and had the personal experience to potentially mentor another. Most of all, I wanted the WOT girls to know that their current position in life was not permanent like I once thought it was for myself, but they had untapped potentials that was waiting to be ignited so they too could go on to become successful.

That's exactly the mindset I walked into my first WOT meeting with, and the reception was outstanding. The room was full of high school girls who were bustling with energy and radiating with potential. Many of them seem enthusiastic and engaged and willing to ask questions. I, in addition to my other peer mentors, indulged in the girl's curiosities, aspirations, and unique personalities in order to create an atmosphere where we could learn to comfortably trust each other and form a friendship that went beyond just mentor and mentee. Through each session both the mentors and mentee empowered each other to not only embrace our flaws and learn to love who we are, but to also work towards eliminating insecurities, negative influences, and personal restraints that were keeping us back to becoming who or where we wanted to be. I wanted to focus on making them comfortable with themselves first and showing them that you don't need to completely change who you are or disregard your past in order to change, but that change must first come from accepting who you currently are. I also wanted to show them that change cannot be forced but it is something that need to come from within, and that if they personally wanted to work towards improving themselves for the better, that I and the other WOT mentors were here to help them along each step of the way.

The girls seemed extremely receptive to learn about and from our personal hardships and experiences with body positivity, relationships, and healthy lifestyles. Most importantly, they seem especially keen about learning how to pursue a post-secondary education or successful careers, but didn't know where to begin or where to go in order to find information, similar to I once had. As a first-generation college student, I shared my experience with breaking out of my shell and overcoming socioeconomic hardships in order to try to reach for my own goals. Using me as role model, many of them turned to me for advice for not only applications for schools and scholarships, but also about their own insecurities of succeeding in the world. Overall, it was a two-way street, and I had just as much to learn from and about the girls and my fellow mentors as they did from me.

However, I soon learned that being a mentor requires more patience, diligence, and dedication that I had previously assumed. Although the beginning of the school year started off with a lot of promise, much of that energy depleted, and the number of girls who participated in our program painfully dwindled with each consecutive meeting for reasons that were unknown to us. Sometimes it was difficult to maintain the relationships we had formed with the girls, to keep them engaged, or to get them to trust us with their personal thoughts. Other times, it was tough to make them look past their own insecurities and socioeconomic restraints to show them their untapped potentials. I began to see that mentorship and change is also a slow process with many challenges along the way. Nevertheless, the experience of being able to help another, while also personally growing as an individual due to what you have learned from others, is the most rewarding experience. My journey as both a mentor and a mentee is one that is still ongoing, and is one where I am still learning from every day.

While I once lacked the access to many opportunities as a child, I am finally in a position where I am able to share my 'excess' of experiences and opportunities with others, and I am able to provide others with the chance to 'access' these opportunities for themselves. I also understand now that there are both ups and downs of becoming a mentor or being a mentee, and that patience and commitment is needed on both ends for positive change to happen. As I continue my involvement WOT, I hope that somewhere down the line my experiences will be able to help another person find their own personal success and happiness and that they too will go onto continuing the cycle of empowerment. I have always told myself to "be who you needed when you were younger," and while I'm still trying to grow into that kind of a person for myself today, I hope that through WOT that I can also become that person for someone else.

Morgan—Theme #4: The Divide of Access and Power: a fight for balance in mentorship

Working with the WOT program, I have found that these opportunities, academic and nonacademic, are greatly valued by mentees purely because this information would not have been available to them without it. This complicates how we look at our resources and how we divide limited access between those who really need it and those who could benefit from it. While all students might benefit from preventative programs, the major goal is to provide such programs to individuals who have no other means of accessing this information. Taking this into consideration, WOT provided a great place for me to develop more community outreach and involvement. This especially affected how I view the things that I do as a student. I am extremely privileged with access to benefiting factors of education, like professors and free educational workshops, that these students do not have as high schoolers and I did not have as a high schooler. The experience of limited access made me realize how difficult it is to develop as a student and pushed to be involved in the WOT program.

This same objective of limited access can be applied to finding the mentors for preventative programs. Many students and community members have the ability to share knowledge with mentees; however, such members do not have access to the correct programs to provide these services. Outlets, such as WOT, require an individual to have the correct resources to find their way into the system. Programs that require a certain extent of knowledge are often thought of as off limits for students, those of which who might not feel confident being deemed a mentor when they are still learning themselves.

Access and goals of inspiration where my major motivators when asked to be involved with the WOT program. Being an individual who did not have access to the aspects that the WOT program provides, I know first-hand how this can complicate a student's capacity for success. Success being defined as achieving the goals said students have set for themselves, be it a degree or to practice sex safely. To have the capability to give this knowledge, it would be an injustice not to give the access to students in a similar situation.

When working first-hand with the students in the WOT program, my critical role as a peer becomes more clear. As students are faced daily with the constraints placed on them when working with individuals in a power position, to be introduced to knowledge with a peer figure makes the students feel more comfortable. As power can create fear, relatability can make a safe space for questions and further explanation. This places a huge amount of importance on the fact the academic dynamic of school is challenged during WOT meetings. Students are welcomed to ask questions that a teacher might deem inappropriate for school, such as questions about their bodies or questions about the complexities of relationships. Mentorship is not only engaging students in academic based learning, but also applying life experience to allow for growth from personal sources.

Access is a defining factor in the mentoring process. As a student, mentee, it limits your chances of gaining knowledge important to your goals. As a mentor, it defines your credibility and chances of providing knowledge. Acknowledgement of these factors can be an exceptional motivator for both mentors and mentees to take advantage of these limited opportunities. The question then arises, how do we then create access for all parties?

CONCLUSION

This chapter intends to allow feminist-students agency over the representation of their narratives as they enrich discourses surrounding the most effective methods to create feminist partnerships. All feminist co-mentors noted the significance of drawing from their personal experiences as a way to connect to individual students and/or to connect to the overall expectations of the program. Similarly, all students discussed the role of emotions in creating multiple relationships to the high school girls and illustrated just how powerful it is to be mindful of their relationships to power and privilege in the mentoring process.

Students are represented throughout discourses that highlight the effects of our feminist collaborations within community-based research sites. In these spaces, students are provided with the opportunity to reflect on their experiences of what it was like to engage in the community. (See *Michigan Journal of Com-*

munity Service; Undergraduate Journal of Service Learning and Community-Based Research.) These processes of self-representation disrupt more traditional, and linear accounts of how students experience service-learning, and positions community literacy as "a search for alternative discourse" (Higgins et.al). As a result, these discourses become less monolithic, and provide spaces where students can negotiate multiple identities. "Thus, participants' identity is formed through their narratives, and can be considered a gradual formation of 'becoming'" (Gomez, Allen & Black, 2007).

Conflicts arise when we attempt to make meaning from the types of representations that are created about collaborative partnerships in any stage of the research process: "The question, then, becomes, how to interpret the experiences of research participants when their analytical framework, their values, and their view of the world differ sharply from ours" (Kirsch, 1999, p. 48). Not only do institutional contexts affect students' abilities to perform in ways that are meaningful and grounded in their individual experiences, but the discourses that always already define students constrain their representations and add another layer to how students choose to represent themselves. Identities are never static and always shift based on the demands of the rhetorical contexts that produce these identities (Harding, 2004; Hallman, 2013). Further, these constraints factor into the overall process of interpretation. Even as we attempt to assuage the multiple risks of misrepresenting others (Alcoff, 1991), thereby reifying how different institutional structures and academic discourses position the student-teacher relationships, we still have a long way to go. In other words, when our goals, and outcomes are at odds with students, as a result of the politics of representation, we may lose valuable insight. Our research is always already implicated (Reynolds, 1993). Creating spaces *with* co-mentors must, then, be a continuous process that feminist scholars are committed to as we form new relationships to our research and our communities: "Representation, of ourselves as well as [others] can never be innocent—whether that representation involves writing an essay . . . or teaching a class. Nevertheless, without representation we cannot engage in discourse, nor can we create spaces that, potentially at least, enable others—as well as ourselves—to speak" (Ede and Lunsford p. 176.).

Significantly, students noted that it was a struggle to create their narratives. They indicated that they were unsure how to effectively address the themes, and weren't certain how to incorporate their personal experiences alongside of the particular themes. Even as students identified what they saw as key themes in the work that should be done within feminist-based activist sites, the constraints of the discourse factored into their overall processes. Morgan, in particular, discussed the nature of the writing process and the difficulties that she experienced as a result of the constraints of the real (or imagined) genre. Through informal conversations and writings, the majority of students expressed their uncertainty in presenting an argumentative piece for a scholarly audience and creating a more personal account of their understandings of what constitutes an effective partnership. This ambiguity was reflected through their formal discussion of what they completed, or the uncertainty they expressed when submitting their work. Regardless, co-mentors felt authorized to discuss what they saw as significant themes yet had some difficulty in actually re-presenting those themes for the chapter. These conflicts point to larger issues to consider: who is and who is not authorized to participate within academic discourses? Further, to what extent are these narratives shaped by the audiences that read them? And, how do their narratives resist and/or replicate larger patterns regarding young women's roles in community-based partnerships? (Andrews, Squire & Tamboukou, 2013). In her project, *Ethical Dilemmas in Feminist Research*, (1999) Gesa Kirsch exposes the effects of misrepresenting others and asks, "whose words, whose reality—am I representing in my work?" (p. xi). Kirsch reminds us of the power of subjectivity within the re-construction of *our* (mis)representations, illustrating just how important it is to make visible how subjectivity affects the work that we do. She argues that our goals should be tied to making explicit how *our* political and personal commitments shape how we make meaning. "The goal of situating ourselves in our work and acknowledging out limited perspectives is not to overcome these limits—an impossible task—but to reveal to readers how our research agenda, political commitments, and personal motivations shape our observations in the field, the conclusions we draw, and the research reports we write" (p. 14).

We are interested in exposing how the work we have undergone, and the work that we hope to accomplish has emerged as a reciprocal process, whereas feminist theory and activism, personal and political motivations, and reflection have served as an overarching motivation for us to continue to sustain our work. In their article "Community Literacy: A Rhetorical Model for Personal and Public Inquiry" Higgins et al. indicate that "community literacy was . . . *a search for alternative discourse*,' a way for people to acknowledge each other's multiple forms of expertise through talk and text and to draw on their differences as a resources for addressing shared problems" (Peck, Flower & Higgins, qtd. p. *205 emphasis is ours*). Throughout their narratives, co-mentors offered ways to continue to engage in feminist research and in ways to cultivate partnerships. It is our hope that this piece captures the energy of student-led initiatives beyond the classroom that reveal the value of community-action and reflection, as we work to create new theories of forming partnerships that take seriously the role of our feminist student leaders.

REFERENCES

Allen, J. & Faigley, L. (1995). Discursive strategies for social change: An alternative rhetoric of argument. *Rhetoric Review 14*(1), 142–172.
Alcoff, L. (1991). The problem of speaking for others. *Cultural Critique, 20*, 5–32.
Andrews, M. & Squire, C. & Tamboukou, M. (2013). *Doing narrative research.* New York, NY: Sage.
Bacon, N. (2000). Building a swan's nest for instruction in rhetoric. *College Composition and Communication, 51*(4), 589–609.
Bayer, A. & Baldwin Grossman, J. & DuBois, D.L. (2015). Using volunteer mentors to improve the academic outcomes of underserved students: The role of relationships. *Journal of Community Psychology, 43*(4), 408–429.
Bishop, W. (1990). Learning our own way to situate composition and feminist studies in the English Department." (1990). *Journal of Advanced Composition 10*, 339–55.
Casal-Sanchez, S. & Macdonald, A. (2002). Feminist reflections on the pedagogical relevance of identity." In A. Macdonald and Susan Sanchez Casal (Eds.), *Twenty-first-century feminist classrooms: Pedagogies of identity and difference.* Palgrave, New York, 2002. 1–28.
Deans, T. (2000). *Writing partnerships.* Urbana, IL: NCTE.
Dewey, J. (2012). *Democracy and education.* New York, NY: Simon & Brown.
DuBois, D. L & Karcher, M. J. (Eds.). (2005). *Handbook of youth mentoring.* Thousand Oaks, CA: SAGE.
Ede, L. & Lunsford, A. (1990). *Singular texts/ plural authors: Perspectives on collaborative writing.* Carbondale, IL: Southern Illinois University Press.
Ellsworth, E. (1992). Why doesn't this feel empowering? Working through the repressive myths of critical pedagogy. In C. Luke & J. Gore (Eds.), *Feminism and critical pedagogy* (pp. 90–199). New York, NY: Routledge.
Gomez, M. L., Black, R. W. & Allen, A. (2007). "Becoming" a teacher. *Teachers College Record, 109*(9), 2107–2135.
Hallman, H. (2013). Victims of free agents? Constructing the ethical representations of "at risk" youth. In C. S. Rhodes & K. J. Weiss (Eds.), *Ethical Issues in Literacy Research* (pp. 21–30). New York, NY: Routledge.
Haraway, D. (1988). Situated knowledges: The science question in feminism and the privilege of partial perspective. *Feminist Studies 14*, 575–99.
Harding, S. (2004) A socially relevant philosophy of science? Resources from standpoint theory's controversy. *Hypatia, 19*, 17–25.
Journet, D. (2012). Narrative Turns in writing studies research. In L. Nickoson and M. Sheridan (Eds.), *Writing studies research in practice: Methods and methodologies.* Carbondale, IL: Southern Illinois UP.
Julier, L., Linvingston, K. & Goldblatt, E. (2014). Community-engaged pedagogies. In G. Tate, A. Rupiper Taggart & H. Hessler (Eds.), *A guide to composition pedagogies.* New York, NY: Oxford University Press.
Himley, M. (2004). Facing (up to) "the stranger" in community service learning. *College Composition and Communication, 55*(3), 416–37.

Kirsch, G. E. & Ritchie, J. (1995). Beyond the personal: Theorizing a politics of location in composition research. *College Composition and Communication, 46*, 7–29.

Kirsch, G. (1999). *Ethical dilemmas in feminist research.* Albany, NY: State University of New York Press.

Micciche, L. (2014). Feminist. In G. Tate, A. Rupiper Taggart & H. Hessler (Eds.), *A guide to composition pedagogies.* New York, NY: Oxford University Press.

Novek, E. M. (1999). Service-learning is a feminist issue: Transforming communication pedagogy. *Women's Studies in Communication, 22*(2), 230–40.

Parks, S. & Goldblatt, E. (2000). Writing beyond the curriculum: Fostering new collaborations in literacy. *College English, 62*(5), 584–606.

Powell, K. M. & Takayoshi, P. (2003). Accepting roles created for us: The ethics of reciprocity. *College Composition and Communication, 54*(3), 394–422.

Rhoads, R. (1997). *Community Service and Higher Learning: Explorations of the Caring Self.* Albany, NY: State University of New York Press.

Reynolds, N. (1993). Ethos as location: New sites for understanding discursive authority. *Rhetoric Review, 11*, 325–38.

Ritchie, Joy. S. (1990). Confronting the "essential" problem: Reconnecting feminist theory and pedagogy. *Journal of Advanced Composition, 10*, 249–73.

Royster, J. J. (2000). *Traces of a stream.* Pittsburgh, PA: University of Pittsburgh Press.

Royster, J. J. & Kirsch, G. (2012). *Feminist rhetorical practices.* Carbondale, IL: Southern Illinois University Press.

Spigelman, C. (2004). *Personally speaking: Experience as evidence in academic discourse.* Carbondale, IL: Southern Illinois University Press.

Webb, P. & Cole, K. & Skeen, T. (2007). Feminist social projects: Building bridges between communities and universities. *College English, 69*(3), 238–59.

CHAPTER 9.

OHIO FARM STORIES: A FEMINIST APPROACH TO COLLABORATION, CONVERSATION, AND ENGAGEMENT

Christine Denecker
The University of Findlay

Sarah Sisser
Hancock Historical Museum

The Ohio Farm Stories project began with a grant from the Ohio Humanities Council and a goal of collecting and showcasing narratives that focus on family farm life and the ways in which agriculture has and continues to shape lives and local Ohio communities. Integral to these narratives are emergent themes of how farming practices and values have evolved to meet societal demands in the past century. This chapter situates the farm stories research within Royster and Kirsch's three-step inquiry framework layered with notions of narrative and place. The result is a series of Ohio Farm Stories montages that provide both fixed and open interpretations. Portions of this chapter allow readers the opportunity to "listen deeply and respectfully" to the words and images of the project. The chapter closes with insight into the trajectory of the project and the project's "public life"—specifically the complexity of interpretation when narrative becomes a collective, collaborative endeavor among the researchers, the participants, and the community.

In *Feminist Rhetorical Practices*, Jacqueline Royster and Gesa Kirsch (2012) argue that current feminist rhetorical scholarship is pushing beyond its former goals of "rescuing, recovering and (re)inscribing women rhetors" (p. 25) to more general methodologies that position researchers to "discover new genres, voices, and ways of reasoning that have been cast in shadow for many decades if not centuries" (p. 150). Furthermore, these methodologies apply to subjects beyond the female, and provide "mechanisms by which listening deeply, reflexively, and multisensibly become standard practice not only in feminist rhetorical scholarship but also in rhetorical studies writ large" (Royster & Kirsch, 2012, p. 20). Such feminist rhetorical methodologies undergird on-going collaborative research between The University of Findlay and The Hancock Historical Museum, research that serves to preserve and reflect upon the agricultural history of Ohio.

This campus-community collaboration, entitled *Ohio Farm Stories*[1], began with a grant from the Ohio Humanities Council and a goal of collecting narratives from six Hancock County farmers in order to provide community members with the opportunity to trace the ways agriculture has and continues to shape the cultural landscape in northwestern Ohio. Integral to these narratives are emergent themes of how farming practices and values have evolved to meet societal demands in the past century.

Specifically, this campus-community partnership demonstrates an application of feminist rhetorical practices used to foster community engagement beyond academic borders. As feminist scholars, we have been challenged to answer Royster and Kirsch's call to study non-traditional texts and local sites with the goal of "look[ing] beyond typically anointed assumptions in the field in anticipation of the possibility of seeing something not previously noticed or considered" (p. 72). Likewise, in this research, we have employed feminist thinking and practice in order to collect and then rightfully honor the stories of our local farming community and, in doing so, move these stories "from the 'margins to the center'" by "eliminating boundaries that privilege dominant forms of knowledge building, boundaries that mark who can be a knower and what can be known" (Hesse-Biber, 2012, p. 3). As such, we consider our work a form of feminist intervention derived from and infused with "an ethos of humility, respect, and care" (Royster & Kirsch, 2012, p. 21) meant to put forth and nurture conversations about the history of Ohio agriculture.

In this chapter, we reflect upon the ways in which feminist rhetorical methodologies afforded us the means to honor the farmers' stories in ways fitting with how they view their experiences. We begin with an explanation of the project's roots and then situate our research within Royster and Kirsch's three-step inquiry framework layered with notions of narrative and place. The multiple layers of this framework create a methodological structure that allows for the farmers' voices, their homes, their barns, and their farms to co-mingle with the emotive experiences of all those involved in the research process. The result is a series of *Ohio Farm Stories* montages that foster both fixed and open interpretations. To

---

1   Originally, the project was entitled, *Ohio Farm Histories*. We chose to change the title after the initial work, as we believe the word "Stories" more accurately reflects the narrative function of the project, whereas "Histories" has a different connotation not as closely in keeping with the intent of the project.

increase the probability of open interpretations, portions of this chapter are constructed as to allow readers the opportunity to "listen deeply and respectfully" to the words and images of this project, just as we have strived to do. Finally, we conclude this chapter by reflecting on the trajectory of the project and the public life of the project—specifically the complexity of interpretation when narrative becomes a collective, collaborative endeavor among the researchers, the participants, and the community.

PROJECT ROOTS

> "It all starts on a farm, somewhere, somehow"
>
> —Farmer Gary Wilson

The *Ohio Farm Stories* project has its roots in two distinct places. First[2] is the successful Historic Barn Tour hosted by the Hancock Historical Museum in September 2013.

The self-guided tour, enjoyed by over 700 individuals, included stops at six century-old barns along with the opportunity to experience the sights, tastes, and sounds of the County's heritage. Owners of three of these properties along with owners of three other County properties[3] were eventually invited to participate in the *Ohio Farm Stories* project.

A short digression puts this tour and the subsequent *Ohio Farm Stories* project into context. In 1900, Hancock County had 3,263 farms; as of 2015, 831 farms encompassing 230,261 acres blanket the County. Of the 531.4 square miles of the County, 80% is used for agricultural production (G. Wilson, personal communication, September 1, 2015). In the late nineteenth and early twentieth centuries, Hancock County farmers were diversified, raising livestock and various crops. However, as agriculture became more commercialized, farmers found that diversified farms yielded small monetary returns (G. Wilson, personal communication, September 1, 2015). As a result, many were forced, in the words of farmer Miles Von Stein, "to get big or get out." Specific to the dairy industry, in 1920, the County boasted over 10,000 head of dairy cattle. By the year 2000, that number had dwindled to fewer than 1,200 head, and today there are just four dairy farms in Hancock County[4] (G. Wilson, personal

---

2   Subsequent successful barn tours were held in 2014 and 2015 (up to the time of this chapter's publication).

3   The farmers were chosen specifically by Sarah who had already developed working relationships with them via other projects through the Hancock Historical Museum.

4   See the final video montage segment in *Function of the Farm* for Gary Wilson and David Spahr's discussion on the number of dairy farms in Hancock County, 2015.

communication, September 1, 2015). In brief, while Hancock County remains a predominantly agricultural region, the nature and scale of farming has changed in the area over the past century. Thus, while not the intent of the 2013 Historic Barn Tour, this event served as a means for resurrecting, remembering, and celebrating the County's agricultural past. It also helped sow the seeds of the *Ohio Farm Stories* project.

Figure 9.1. Barn Tour Announcement.

Along with the Barn Tour, the project's roots can also be traced to ideas birthed from work with the Digital Archive of Literacy Narratives (DALN). This public archive "provide[s] a historical record of the literacy practices and values of contributors, as those practices and values change" (DALN home). As a result, when we—a faculty member at The University of Findlay (who had participated in collecting DALN contributions) and the director of the Hancock Historical Museum (who had organized the Historic Barn Tour)—were asked to brainstorm project ideas in response to a potential Ohio Humanities Grant, the notion of digitally collecting and archiving the stories of Hancock County farmers emerged.

Upon securing the grant, we considered, to borrow the words of Royster and Kirsch, how best to "honor their [the farmers'] traditions" (p. 20) in our gathering of their stories. We also grappled with other questions posed by Royster and Kirsch's framework, such as " . . . how do we render their [the farmers'] work and lives meaningfully?"; "How do *they* frame (rather than *we* frame) the questions by which they navigated their own lives?"; "How do we transport ourselves back to the time and context in which they lived knowing full well that it is not possible to see things from their vantage point?" (p. 20).

Our commitment to answer these questions and to "listen carefully and caringly" (Royster & Kirsch, 2012, p. 147) led us to conduct pre-narrative-collection conversations with each farmer. In March 2014, we traveled to each farmer's home to build relational bonds; that way, when it came time to record their stories, the experience would be more of a conversation than a potentially stiff exchange between researchers and research participants. Torrill Moen (2006) underscores the "necessity of time and space to develop a caring situation in which both the researcher and the research subjects feel comfortable" (pp. 61–62). Likewise, to borrow from Kris Blair, et al. (2009), our pre-interview discussions helped negate researcher-research subject hierarchies, and instead, cultivated a "non-hierarchical, co-equal model among colleagues" (p. 17). This approach also met the goal of feminist rhetorical practices in that it opened a space "for a more dialectical and reciprocal intellectual engagement" (Royster & Kirsch, 2012, p. 14) among us and the farmers, not unlike the "learning together" model described by Jenn Brandt, et al. (Chapter 7, this collection), which "encourages multiple perspectives and voices with active participation from all parties" (this collection). Thus, we came to view the farmers in the study as co-researchers and co-learners rather than subjects or participants.

These co-researchers consisted of five men and one woman[5]. It may be of interest to note that, according to the 2012 Census of Agriculture, 784 of the

---

5   These co-researchers included Mark Metzger, David Spahr, Wayne Marquart, Jacki Johnson, Gary Wilson, and three generations of the Von Stein family: Harold, Dennis, and Miles.

farm operators in Hancock County were men, and 47 were women. As such, women's voices, at least those at the helm of farm operation, are an anomaly in Hancock County. With that said, farming in the County is historically a generational, familial enterprise; therefore, the initial pre-interview discussions (and the subsequent interviews, themselves) included family members other than just the farmers, themselves[6]. This was not by design. Instead, as these conversations unfolded across kitchen tables, other family members joined in to add to each narrative. Specifically, in four discussions, the farmers' wives played significant roles in shaping the narratives shared, and in one of those cases, three generations of family members simultaneously contributed to the storytelling.

At play here were notions of place and belonging in our choice, as researchers, to literally meet the farmers where they lived. Roxanne Mountford (2001) suggests the importance of material space and its effect on a "communicative event" when she states, "The material [space] . . . often has unforeseen influence over a communicative event" and "rhetorical spaces carry the residue of history within them" (p. 17). Consequently, feminist theories of space/place impacted our decision to conduct all narrative collection work within what bell hooks might call the farmers' "culture of belonging." This phrase denotes the place in which one's "sense of identity was shaped" (2009, p. 7); a place where "ways of belonging were taught" and where "cultural legac[ies] [were] handed down" (p. 13). For us, it was not enough to meet farmers within the culture of Hancock County; instead, we found it pertinent to meet the farmers in their homes, walk with them through their fields, and stand inside their barns since these places were important in the shaping of each farmer's identity. In doing so, we followed Royster and Kirsch's call to be "mindful of the locations we visit . . . and to our own embodied experiences, the responses invoked in us by visiting historical sites and handling cultural artifacts" (2012, p. 22).

The Spring 2014 pre-narrative-collection interview sessions were followed with non-scripted video recordings of each farmer at his or her farm. Equipped with a borrowed video camera, microphone, and minimal videography experience, we set out to record the stories, knowing that those stories (and not the quality of the video) were what mattered. We arrived at each farm with questions to use as prompting; however, we quickly found it best to let the farmers "frame the questions" as they shared how they had "navigated their own lives" (Royster & Kirsch, 2012, p. 20). Most began their stories with a history of the farm. For our part, we simply listened, absorbed into this, our shared culture of belonging. In the end, we walked away with hours of raw footage and a sense that our journey was far from complete. Indeed, our County's agricultural past was within

---

6   Often, as in the case of the Metzgers, Spahrs, and VonSteins, these additional family members were off camera; however, their voices can sometimes be heard as part of the recordings.

Ohio Farm Stories

reach: it lie curled up in the shadows of century-old barns; it peered at us from around the corners of abandoned migrant buildings; it waited patiently in cellars and silent milk houses. These recorded conversations were our first glimpses into what would become *Ohio Farm Stories*.

In amassing the stories of the six farmers, we logged over twelve hours of videotape relating how our County and its agricultural heritage had evolved over the past century. These partially edited videos ran on a continual loop as part of an exhibit at the 2014 Hancock County Fair and were accompanied by professionally designed posters depicting each farm(er) featured in the project.

Figure 9.2. Mark Metzger Ohio Farm Stories Poster.

In Summer 2014, we analyzed the hours of video in preparation for a September presentation at The University of Findlay, entitled "Life on the Farm." The fair exhibit and lecture arguably became sites of feminist intervention in that both provided spaces for university and community members to experience the farmers' stories and for us to move what might be considered a rhetorically "marginalized group" to "the center of social inquiry" (Hesse-Biber, 2012, p. 3).

THEORY MEETS THE FARM

"Farming's in your blood. The smell of fresh dirt plowed over. There's really just no other smell like that."

—Farmer Dennis Von Stein

Feminist rhetorical principles, and the extent to which these principles are interwoven with concepts of material place and narrative, provide insight into the ways in which the *Ohio Farm Stories* project tells us "something about ourselves, our community, the nature of storytelling, and the role of the academy in creating and sustaining community activism" (Blair & Nickoson, 2016, this collection). In particular, Royster and Kirsch's (2012) inquiry framework consisting of critical imagination, strategic contemplation, and social circulation informed our scholarly practices and helped make meaning of the stories we collected on a number of levels—from the personal to the communal. The fact that our study focused on mostly white, male farmers may seem methodologically mismatched or in contradiction to Royster and Kirsch's support of breaking "through habitual expectations for rhetorical studies to be overwhelmingly about men and male-dominated arenas" (p. 17). Still, the authors suggest that their three-part inquiry framework has the propensity "to propel general knowledge-making processes in the field at large . . . to another, better-informed, more inclusive conceptual space" (Royster & Kirsch, 2012, p. 18). Therefore, while on the surface the *Ohio Farm Stories* project may appear to re-inscribe traditional patterns of rhetorical scholarship, a deeper look reveals how feminist rhetorical principles legitimized our intervention on behalf "of those whose voices have rarely been heard or studied by rhetoricians" (Royster & Kirsch, 2012, p. 20).

In particular, the first part of Royster and Kirsch's framework, "critical imagination," helped us shape an open, participant-driven research approach that resulted (for the most part[7]) organically in the stories our co-researchers wanted to tell. We approached this work not unlike Kathryn Perry (Chapter 10, this collection), who sought to empower the single mothers in her study "to tell their stories as uniquely as they could" (this collection). Equipped with a healthy understanding that narratives are "shaped by the audiences to whom they are delivered" (Andrews, et al., 2013, p. 6), we consciously worked to craft a space in which the farmers could "frame . . . the questions [and thus, the stories] by which they navigated *their* own lives" (Royster & Kirsch, 2012, p. 20; italics, ours).

Next, in culling through the unedited videotape, the second element of Royster and Kirsch's schema, "strategic contemplation," allowed us to achieve interpretations that honored the complexity of the narratives in ways that transcriptions of the stories alone could not. To explain, according to Molly Andrews, et al. (2013), when it comes to narratives, "Sometimes you don't get the 'whole story'; and all stories are incomplete, since experience and subjectivity cannot fully make their way into language" (p. 10). Furthermore, criticisms of

---

7   In our final interview session, we used more prompting questions than in the other sessions. Therefore, this session seemed less organic than the others. See the Conclusion section of this chapter for a more thorough explanation of this point.

narrative argue that its privileging of "transcripts—mostly speech" overlook the contributions of "paralinguistic material, other media, interpersonal interactions or other social context" (Andrews, et al., 2013, p. 9). Through strategic contemplation, though, research becomes a "lived process" where attention can be given to physical interaction with objects and to the emotions derived from a particular moment and/or place. In other words, significance is attached to "the materiality of archival work—visiting places, handling artifacts, following unexpected leads, standing in silence, and allowing for chance discoveries and serendipity" (Royster & Kirsch, 2012, p. 89).

Our presence, then, was necessary at each place of inquiry in order to "get the 'whole story,'" and to better realize the contention that opens this section—that "farming's in your blood." Consequently, we found it imperative to walk alongside the farmers through the barns and pastures, sit with them in breezy gazebos, gingerly handle their Civil War letters and heirloom quilts, crank ancient corn shellers, and stoop to avoid the careening paths of noisy barn swallows in an abandoned milk shed. Simply put, each material space (and our physical and emotive reactions to those spaces) contributed to each story told. Mountford (2001) argues that material spaces—and we extend that to objects here—carry a "physical representation of relationships and ideas" (p. 17). Thus, our embodied reactions to *these places, these objects*, and *these stories* enabled us to better analyze and "to consider with critical intensity what may be more in shadow, muted, and not immediately obvious" (Royster & Kirsch, 2012, p. 76) in the narratives each farmer chose to share.

That is not to say that we, as researchers, do not acknowledge the subjectivity of such endeavors. As life-long inhabitants of Hancock County, we are "members of [this] culture and can scarcely remain unaffected by the narrative forms that are already imbedded therein" (Gergen & Gergen, 1988, p. 261). Kelly Concannon, et al., in their study of community literacy partners (Chapter 8, this collection), also grapple with divorcing the researcher's context from interpretation and ask, "To what extent are these narratives shaped by the audiences (professors/feminists) that read them?" (this collection). Undoubtedly, our personal imbedded narrative forms had an impact on our analysis of the stories and our eventual decision to organize the patterns of discussion (that were apparent to us) into five themes: 1) the *Barn*—its function and purpose; 2) the *Role of the Farmer*—and how it has evolved; 3) the *Evolution of the Farm* itself; 4) the *Economics* of farming in Hancock County; and 5) the *Disconnect* between rural and urban life. Hunter McEwan (1997) suggests that a feminist approach to narrative research "conveys a sense of the author as engaged in a gender related enterprise—weaving together the world we experience with its various peoples and events so that it becomes a believable whole" (p. 89). While we might take issue with the notion of *Ohio Farm Stories* as a "gender related enterprise"—we see it as a decidedly *human* enterprise—merit resides in McEwan's notion that our attempts at organizing the stories thematically is, in fact, a "weaving together" of the "world we experience(d)" through strategic contemplation of our physical presence in the place where the narratives occurred both literally and through reminiscence.

This space, then, opened by Royster and Kirsch's framework, allowed us to consider both embodied and disembodied elements in our analysis. It also afforded us the opportunity to move fluidly and nimbly across the past, the present, and the future of the farmers' narratives and, as a result, provided us with deeper, richer insight into how *Ohio Farm Stories* are nested among the (presumably many) agricultural narratives of the County. Narrative researchers such as Andrews, et al. (2013) argue that "a focus on the chronological or experienced 'time' may close off information about unconscious realities and material causalities"; in contrast, feminist approaches to narrative research recognize "the co-presence of futurity and past in the present, the reconstruction of the past by new 'presents,' and the projection of the present into future imaginings. . . ." (p. 12). Thus, the interplay across past, present, and future impacted our interpretations of the narratives. Likewise, this melding of experiences across time undergirds the third element of Royster and Kirsch's framework: social circulation, a notion that serves to "flesh out the contours of social spaces" in order to "make more visible the social circles within which they [women] have functioned and continue to function as rhetorical agents" (2012, p. 24).

When applied to the *Ohio Farm Stories* narratives, social circulation points to the significance of co-mingling the farmers' words with their work on the farm and in other locations.[8] Similarly, their tools, equipment, and barns, as well as their familial ties (and the importance of those ties to their work) "take on different meanings in different contexts across time and space" (Royster & Kirsch, 2012, p. 156). Likewise, their land; the use of migrant labor; their participation in organizations such as 4-H and FFA[9]; and myriad other factors, including, but not limited to shared cultural, social, and rhetorical tropes such as "it was all work back then—hard work"[10] all contribute insight into the complexity,

---

8   Many of the farmers shared stories of having to obtain employment off the farm to supplement their farming income.

9   4-H is a national youth mentoring organization which includes a focus on agriculture. In Hancock County, 4-H members regularly participate and demonstrate their leadership, citizenship, and agricultural skills at the annual County Fair. FFA stands for Future Farmers of America. Similar to 4-H, the goals of this organization are to "strengthen the future" by "growing leaders and building communities."

10 These words were stated by Farmer David Spahr in his interview. See his video in the section entitled *Role of the Farmer*.

the deepness, the vastness of the farmers' stories. But not *just* their stories; social circulation pushes researchers to contemplate the significance of lives and lived experiences as "evolutionary" as well as "dynamic" "creating knowledge and legacies of action and performance" (Royster & Kirsch, 2012, p. 23, p. 25).

QUILT-WORK OF NARRATIVES

> "Isn't that something how life kind of turned on me from farming to this?"
>
> —Farmer Mark Metzger

This co-mingling of elements across time enabled us, as researchers to better "see, hear and understand more ecologically" the public and private "contours" and "challenges" (Royster & Kirsch, 2012, p. 24) of the farmers' lives and histories. In particular, through this approach, we could acknowledge and honor the "hard work" trope and others like it without simplifying the stories. In addition, our capturing of the narratives through video also allowed us to go beyond simplistic analyses or limited representations indicative of traditional print research described by Elizabeth Daley (2003) as "technological bias." She states, "Print supports linear argument, but it does not value aspects of experience that cannot be contained in books. Print deals inadequately with nonverbal modes of thought and nonlinear construction" (p. 34). Case in point, the comment that opens this section (made by Mark Metzger) would read differently in print than in its verbal rendering: "Isn't that something how life kind of turned on me from farming to this?"[11] At first glance, the print reading limits the interpretation and would call for additional clarification, since the phrase "turned on me" carries negative connotations. However, the actual verbal rendering remit with tone, gestures, and facial expressions conveys a much different message—one which displays Mark's delight in how his barn has now become a place of "play" when it was once all about work. Furthermore, when Mark's message is positioned at the end of a montage of the farmers' memories about barns, the result is a quilt-work of narratives "that could never exist in the physical world but are thematically and conceptually related" (Daley, 2003, p. 35).

Montage allows feminist narrative researchers to consider critically the process of how they might "become 'witness' to another's life" (Royster & Kirsch, 2012, p. 23), while pushing back against simplistic interpretations. In discussing film and media literacy, Daley (2003) argues, "If one wants to go beyond the predictable and formulaic, there needs to be room for serendipity during the production or creation of a film or multimedia document" (p. 36). This process, known as "'the collision of intelligences' . . . produces something unforeseen by the creative

---

11 This quote can be heard in the sixth video of the *Barn* montage.

team" (Daley, 2003, p. 36). As researchers, we had (and continue to have) no way of knowing exactly how viewers might react to the *Barn* montage and its stories of building barns by hand in World War II juxtaposed with Gary Wilson's memories of his children "growing up in the barn" while their mother bottle-fed lambs. What we *did* know is that we had reacted viscerally to these stories (and those found in the subsequent montages[12]) at the moments of their telling.

Video 1. Barn Montage. https://youtu.be/WtK5phUoGyA

In the words of Daley (2003), "Montage permits an interaction between the creator and the receiver, as well as among the elements of the creation. It not only allows but encourages the recombination of elements to create new meanings" (p. 35). Said another way, the quilt-work of narratives that we created might have one meaning to us as researchers, but it would likely create messages and meanings for our audience(s) that we could not anticipate. Moen's argument, similar to that of Daley, suggests that the fixed (or what he might deem "final") interpreted narrative is open to multiple, cascading interpretations (p. 62). Thus, we knew that audience members at our *Ohio Farm Stories* lecture would layer their own memories, experiences, and biases into that story-sharing space. Ultimately, then, the audience would contribute to both the public and the private messages of each montage, resulting in the—"something unforeseen"—of interpretation.

Selecting the video clips for each montage was difficult, though, and unsettling, because, as Moen (2006) argues, "interpretation starts immediately when

---

[12] Five montages in all were created for the September 2015 lecture at The University of Findlay.

one story is selected out of any number of other possible stories, and it continues during the entire research process" (p. 62). Therefore, the very act of beginning the interpretative process meant that particular footage would be privileged, and other pieces of footage would be left out. So as patterns of *Barn, Role of the Farmer, Function of the Farm, Economics,* and *Disconnect* emerged, other clips—no less important—fell away: clips of Mark Metzger scurrying squirrel-like up a ladder to the apex of his barn and clips of Jacki Johnson pulling Civil War letters out of Zip-loc bags. Still, what remained gave us pause in its power, and as Daley (2003) suggests, the act of choosing and quilting the footage into "thematically and conceptually related" sequences "allow[ed] for and respect[ed]" our use of intuition (p. 36). And intuition told us immediately that a poignant clip of Mark Metzger discussing the sale of his dairy cattle and the transition of his farm from livestock to crop production had to lead off the montage entitled *Function of the Farm*:

Video 2. Function of The Farm Montage. https://youtu.be/qzu0mMTxaio

We would like to think that the vulnerability Mark displayed in the story of his farm's (and his own) evolution, demonstrates the best of feminist rhetorical principles with regard to collaborative research. As Freema Elbaz-Luwisch (1997) argues, "stories are most instructive and revealing when they are most personal, and often when the owners of the stories are most vulnerable. As researchers, we cannot easily protect them [owners of stories]: In fact, it is precisely in wishing to treat them as equals that we expose them to risk" (p. 82). We trace our instincts to "protect" Mark's story to the culture of belonging we shared with him—a culture that suggests (if not dictates) that men do not demonstrate emotional vulnerability. However, we also saw in Mark's narrative, the ways in which "An ethics of caring, connectedness, and collaboration" (McEwan, 1997, p. 85) can lead to a powerful moment of story-telling. His narrative also stands as evidence of the co-mingling of public and private that often occurred in these story-telling exchanges.

Public and private were similarly intertwined during one of our conversations with Jacki Johnson. In her pre-interview, Jacki spoke with pride about her family—from her parents to her children to her grandchildren. Later, in her subsequent recorded interview, she haltingly revealed that her teenage granddaughter had passed away unexpectedly just days prior. As researchers, we struggled to compose ourselves upon hearing this news put forth in such a raw, unsolicited manner. Unexpectedly, we found that our feminist inquiry had positioned us in a moment where our "hearts were on our sleeves" (Sullivan, 1992, p. 57). The recorded discussion changed directions briefly as Jacki proceeded to share photographs of her granddaughter and the details of her death. In that moment, we were simply three mothers sharing the burden of unexpected loss.

Here, Lisa Ede's (1992) words seem fitting: "I increasingly find myself looking for ways to connect, rather than to separate, what I experience as my 'personal' self with my scholarly and pedagogical work" (p. 328). Our personal "selves" connected to Jacki's grief and prohibited us from including this exchange within any of the montages prepared for the public lecture. Here, we made a conscious choice as researchers to protect Jacki's vulnerability. As Sullivan (1992) suggests, "The researcher's own race, class, culture, and gender assumptions are not neutral positions from which he or she observes the world but lenses that determine *how and what the researcher sees*" (p. 56, italics ours). We would add: *and what that researcher shares in public venues.*[13]

Our protective impulses toward Mark and Jacki demonstrate that strong push-pull of public/private that continued to problematize our efforts "to align feminism with community engagement beyond academic borders" (Blair & Nickoson, this collection). Still, it was through the private that we and (we believe) our co-researchers experienced a growing sense of hooks' "culture of belonging" in a more public sense. Here a juxtaposition of Gergen and Gergen's notions on "nested narratives" (1988) with Royster and Kirsch's ideas on social circulation helps explicate this phenomenon. Both sets of academics theorize about evolutionary social relationships; Gergen and Gergen within the context of narrative and Royster and Kirsch within the context of feminist inquiry. According to Gergen and Gergen, "Not only do people enter social relationships with a variety of narratives at their disposal, but, in principle, there are no tem-

---

13 Obviously, we have chosen to share a textual recounting of Jacki's story in this particular public forum; however, we demonstrated our commitment to protecting the integrity and vulnerability of the video-taped version of the moment by not including it in any of the montages.

poral parameters within which events must be related through narratives" (1988, p. 263). Likewise, Royster and Kirsch's (2012) social circulation "involves connections among past, present, and future . . . " (p. 23). In terms of the *Ohio Farm Stories* project, the farmers shared narratives in non-linear ways and criss-crossed generations, time, and social spaces in doing so. The result of shedding temporal parameters, says Gergen and Gergen, is "nested narratives, or narratives within narratives"; likewise, the storytellers "may come to see themselves as part of a long cultural history" (1988, p. 263).

The point then is that the farmers' individual, private narratives are nested within a larger, over-arching public narrative of Hancock County that could be equated with a "long cultural history" as spoken of by Gergen and Gergen and even hooks. We also argue that just below that over-arching history reside many other intact as well as nebulous sub-narratives specific to the farmers. These narratives have public as well as private elements and are evidenced in the montages. Below *these* narratives lie nested the private narratives that weave across time, such as those of Jacki and the loss of her granddaughter: thus, nests reside within and among nests, which reside within and among nests, and so on. Elements of community can be derived from or read into any of these layers.

Furthermore, a drill down into these "community nests" reveals a number of binaries, such as Hancock County resident v. non-Hancock County resident, country v. city, past v. present. While not all neat or exact, these binaries emerge more clearly in the *Disconnect* montage:

Video 3. Disconnect Montage. https://youtu.be/5QAPQgldMrk

Images of distancing criss-cross the community binaries in this montage: Gary Wilson's observation, "The farther away you get [from the farm], the less connected you become" is echoed in Jacki Johnson's lament that current society is "too many generations away from the farm." David Spahr uses the phrases "far away" and "several generations away from the farm" in his comments, and Miles Von Stein points out the distance between farmer and non-farmer by stating, "We're going to have to teach the people who don't know [about agriculture]." In *The Responsibilities of Rhetoric* (2010), David Zarefsky notes: "Rhetoric brings a public or community into being. It accomplishes this task by enabling people to recognize common bonds, to see their interests, experiences, and aspirations as consubstantial" (p. 16).

In the case of the *Disconnect* narratives, bonds among farmers and the binary of country versus city constitute the farmers' sense of community and create as well as define what it means to be "of the same substance or essence." That shared substance includes tropes of hard work, shared labor and responsibility among family members, and the push-pull of shepherding a farm toward future sustainability while at the same time maintaining century-deep roots. And while we, as researchers, recognized the commonalities among these notions about community even before the transcription phase, we also acknowledge that, in positioning the disconnect comments within the same montage, we have privileged and increased the volume of the binary. Still, that binary reflects, what Zarefsky might call, one of the "larger values," shared within the farming community that serves to contribute to a "sense of who we are" (p. 17). And ironically, *that* binary serves to blur other binaries: public v. private, academic v. community.

REAPING WHAT'S BEEN SOWN

> "We're getting so far away from the land in our thinking and our living . . . the rest of the world is several generations away from the farm"
> —Farmer David Spahr

Without exception, the farmers in this project shared a fierce pride in their heritage and a common view that parts of that heritage were slipping away, as is evidenced in the quote above by David Spahr. Likewise, the artifacts they shared were illustrative of a language of agriculture and of manual labor that has been all but lost save for those few "native speakers" who recall how the implements were used, whether from their observations as youngsters or from the demonstrations of their ancestors. Many of the objects the farmers shared embodied pride in their family heritage, from a worn ledger illustrating the economic efficiency of an ancestor, to a draw-knife used by an industrious forefather to craft shake shingles for an early homestead. When the farmers shared these objects, our honest, visceral reactions seemed to serve as validation of the significance of these honored symbols.

Only once did we stray from the feminist methodologies that had fostered mutual respect and had led to open vulnerable discourse. This occurred in July during our final interview with the three-generations of VonSteins. Nearly two months had passed since we had completed the other five interviews, and it had been four months since we had originally visited the VonStein farm. The delay in the recorded interview precipitated several outcomes not in keeping with our feminist methodologies. First, it created a space of time which eroded the previous social relationship we had cultivated with the VonSteins during our pre-interview conversation. In that discussion, three generations gathered around the kitchen table to share photos of the devastation caused to the farm during the 1965 Palm Sunday tornado outbreak[1]. The conversation that ensued was not confined in any temporal or generational manner—the discussion layered past and present and moved fluidly among grandfather, father, mother, and granddaughter. However, when we returned to the farm in late July, a spot was set up in the barn for the discussion. Gone was the familial feel of the kitchen table; gone was the non-hierarchical dialogic mode of collaboration; both were replaced by a "setting" for an interview.

The time gap and change in setting resulted in a strained discourse, despite the fact that we were in the VonStein's barn. Quiet ensued when videotaping began, so we reverted to asking pointed questions and prompting discourse related to the themes we had already isolated for the montages rather than letting the VonSteins tell *their* story. To borrow David Spahr's words from the beginning of this section—we were "getting too far away" from our feminist methodologies in how we were thinking about and living our research. And when we veered from those methodologies, there were fewer authentic moments, less vulnerability, and less potential for the research to be a *"lived process"*[2] (Royster & Kirsch, 2012, p. 87). In the case of the final interview, we neglected to create space where we could "see and hold contradictions without rushing to immediate closure, to neat resolutions, or to cozy hierarchies and binaries" (Royster & Kirsch, 2012, p. 21–22), even though we had fostered such a connection in our pre-interview-conversation. In retrospect, we should have stopped the interview and encouraged discussion that flowed more naturally by walking with the

---

1   On April 11–12, 1965, the Midwest experienced the second biggest tornado outbreak (to that date) of all time. Tornado damage was widespread throughout Hancock County, Ohio.

2   Kirsch and Royster (2012) describe a researcher's *"lived process"* as the ways in which a researcher "moved back and forth between past and present, between visiting historical sites and bringing them into the present, between searching archives and walking the land" (87).

VonSteins through their greenhouses or around their vast gardens of sunflowers. In this mistake, we learned intimately what Kirsch and Royster (2010) are getting at when they state, "Experience, in fact, has taught us that it takes patience, humility, and honesty to develop well-grounded principles for engagement and excellence" (p. 664). Said another way, "You reap what you sow."

CULTIVATING THE ENDEAVOR

> "That's what this country was started on, God and farming. You get away from that, and there's not much else."
>
> —Farmer Jacki Johnson

Video 4. Final Thoughts Montage. https://youtu.be/jZNnwFSz9bg

As this chapter suggests, utilizing feminist rhetorical principles in gathering and then analyzing the farmers' stories was at once liberating and confounding. Yes, we had agency to consider *all* elements of the storytelling experience in making meaning for ourselves, the farmers, and our community. The rub was that the complexity and tangled interplay of these elements resisted any simplicity in our attempts to corral them into a neat, cohesive whole. Declarations such as Jacki Johnson's that "God and farming" undergird America have a surface simplicity, but it is the teasing out of the layers of stories, and time, and tradition beneath her comment that feminist researchers seek to reveal. Luckily, place and materiality give feminist researchers space to do that. Still, the auto-ethnographic elements that seeped into our work—while legitimized by Royster and Kirsch's framework—also positioned us as "both product and producer of a given cultural phenomenon" (Wood &

Fassett, 2003, p. 288), and at times, we were not entirely comfortable negotiating those roles. But isn't that the point, after all? To engage in this "back and forth movement" of analytical *and* embodied research and ground that research "in the communities from which it emanates" (Kirsch & Roster, 2012, p. 86)? In the end, we embraced the intertextuality of the entire enterprise as the farmers' voices co-mingled with our emotive experiences as well as the material spaces in which we interacted to create the polyphony of *a community* and of many subcommunities. Ultimately, we learned "to attend to our own levels of comfort and discomfort, to withhold quick judgment, to read and reread" (Royster & Kirsch, 2012, p. 76) the texts and experiences our co-researchers afforded us in order to honor the stories shared with us—tangles and all.

Like Moen (2006), "We would like the stories to be thinking tools for our research colleagues, as new inquiry questions might arise from the narratives" (p. 65). Said another way, we see *Ohio Farm Stories* as a type of scholarly activism, not unlike that advocated by Keri Mathis and Beth Boehm in their chapter, "Build Engaged Interventions in Graduate Education." Similarly, we recognize "the rich resources and information that community partners already possess and that we can help facilitate (and ultimately *benefit* from) in our collaboration with them" (Mathis & Boehm, Chapter 6, this collection). Thus, the interpretation and meaning-making does not end with us, since our plan to make the raw footage of the narratives accessible in archive form open to the public allows for an infinite number of future interpretations, connections, reminisces, and community-building experiences. Much like the potential outgrowth of the community engagement "knot-work" described by Mary Sheridan (Chapter 11, this collection), we envision others cultivating the narratives into projects and endeavors we have not imagined. With that happy thought, we will continue to do the good work of feminist intervention, adding to the archive in order to move the voices of agriculture inward from the margins of rhetorical research. Feminist rhetorical principles make that movement possible, just as those principles make possible the complexity of interpretation when narrative becomes a collective, collaborative endeavor among the researchers, the participants, and the community.

REFERENCES

Andrews, M., Squire, C. & Tamboukou, M. (2013). *Doing narrative research*. Los Angeles, CA: Sage.

Blair, K., Gajjala, R. & Tulley, C., Eds. (2009). *Webbing cyberfeminist practice: Communities, pedagogies, and social action*. New York, NY: Hampton Press.

Blair, K. L. & Nickoson, L. (2018). Introduction. Researching and teaching community as a feminist intervention. In K. L. Blair & L. Nickoson (Eds.), *Composing feminist interventions: Activism, engagement, praxis.* Fort Collins, CO: The WAC Clearinghouse / Louisville, CO: University Press of Colorado. Retrieved from https://wac.colostate.edu/books/perspectives/feminist.

Brandt, J., et al. (2018). Learning together through campus-community partnerships. In K. L. Blair & L. Nickoson, L. (Eds.), *Composing feminist interventions: Activism, engagement, praxis.* Fort Collins, CO: The WAC Clearinghouse / Louisville, CO: University Press of Colorado. Retrieved from https://wac.colostate.edu/books/perspectives/feminist/.

Concannon, K., et al. (2018). Crafting partnerships: Exploring feminist strategies for Community literacy projects. In K. L. Blair & L. Nickoson, L. (Eds.), *Composing feminist interventions: Activism, engagement, praxis.* Fort Collins, CO: The WAC Clearinghouse / Louisville, CO: University Press of Colorado. Retrieved from https://wac.colostate.edu/books/perspectives/feminist/.

Daley, E. (2003). Expanding the concept of literacy. *EDUCAUSE, March/April,* 33–40.

Digital Archive of Literacy Narratives. (2015). The Ohio State University. Retrieved from http://daln.osu.edu

Denecker, C. & Valasek, T. (2013). The University of Findlay—Ohio Humanities Mini-Grant.

Ede, L. (1992). Methods, methodologies, and the politics of knowledge: Reflections and Speculations. In Kirsch, G. & Sullivan, P.A. (Eds.), *Methods and Methodology in Composition Research* (pp. 314–329). Carbondale, IL: Southern Illinois Press.

Elbaz-Luwisch, F. (1997). Narrative research: Political issues and implications. *Teaching and Teacher Education, 13*(1), 75–83.

Gergen, K. J. & Gergen, M. M. (1988). Narratives and the self. In Berkowitz, L. (Ed.), *Advances in Experimental Social Psychology: Social Psychological Studies of the Self.* (pp. 17–63). San Diego: Academic Press.

hooks, b. (2009). Kentucky is my fate. *Belonging: A Culture of Place* (pp. 6–24). New York, NY: Routledge,

Kirsch, G. E. & Royster, J. J. (2010). Feminist rhetorical practices: In search of excellence. *College Composition and Communication, 61*(4), 640–672.

Hesse-Biber, S. N. (Ed.), (2010). *The handbook of feminist research: Theory and practice.* Los Angeles, CA: Sage.

Mathis, K. E. & Boehm, B. A. (2018). Building engaged interactions in graduate education. In K. L. Blair & L. Nickoson, L. (Eds.), *Composing feminist interventions: Activism, engagement, praxis.* Fort Collins, CO: The WAC Clearinghouse / Louisville, CO: University Press of Colorado. Retrieved from https://wac.colostate.edu/books/perspectives/feminist/.

Mountford, R. (2001). On gender and rhetorical space. *Rhetoric Society Quarterly, 31*(1), pp. 41–71.

McEwan, H. (1997). The functions of narrative and research on teaching. *Teaching and Teacher Education, 13*(1), 85–92.

Moen, T. (2006). Reflections on the narrative research approach. *International Journal of Qualitative Methods, 5*(4), 56–69.

National 4-H Organization Home. (2015). Retrieved from http://www.4-h.org.

National FFA Organization Home. (2015). Retrieved from http://www.ffa.org/home.

Ohio Bicentennial and Century Farms (2015). Ohio Department of Agriculture, Office of Communication.

Perry, K. (2018). Literacy sponsorship as a process of translation: Using Actor-Network theory to analyze power within emergent relationships at Family Scholar House. In K. L. Blair & L. Nickoson, L. (Eds.), *Composing feminist interventions: Activism, engagement, praxis*. Fort Collins, CO: The WAC Clearinghouse / Louisville, CO: University Press of Colorado. Retrieved from https://wac.colostate.edu/books/perspectives/feminist/.

Royster, J. J. & Kirsch, G. E. (2012). *Feminist rhetorical practices: New horizons for rhetoric, composition, and literacy studies*. Carbondale, IL: Southern Illinois University Press.

Sheridan, M. (2018). Knot-working collaborations: Fostering community engaged teachers and scholars. In K. L. Blair & L. Nickoson, L. (Eds.), *Composing feminist interventions: Activism, engagement, praxis*. Fort Collins, CO: The WAC Clearinghouse / Louisville, CO: University Press of Colorado. Retrieved from https://wac.colostate.edu/books/perspectives/feminist/.

Smith, M. & Warnick, B. (2010). *The responsibilities of rhetoric*. Long Grove, IL: Waveland Press.

Sullivan, P. A. (1992). Feminism and methodology in composition studies. In G. Kirsch & P. A. Sullivan (Eds.), *Methods and Methodology in Composition Research*. (pp. 37–61). Carbondale, IL: Southern Illinois Press.

Wood, A. F. & Fassett, D. L. (2003). Remote control: Identity, power, and technology in the communication classroom, *Communication Education, 52*(3/4), 286–296.

Zarefsky, D. (2010). Plenary address: Reclaiming rhetoric's responsibilities. In M. Smith & B. Warnick (Eds.), *The Responsibilities of Rhetoric* (pp. 13–21). Long Grove, IL: Waveland Press.

CHAPTER 10.
LITERACY SPONSORSHIP AS A PROCESS OF TRANSLATION: USING ACTOR-NETWORK THEORY TO ANALYZE POWER WITHIN EMERGENT RELATIONSHIPS AT FAMILY SCHOLAR HOUSE

Kathryn Perry
California State University, Los Angeles

This chapter examines a moment of literacy at an educational nonprofit called Family Scholar House (FSH) to understand the multiple dimensions underlying literacy practices, including material conditions, social relationships, and institutional ideologies. Based on interviews with both low-income single mothers who are full-time college students as well as FSH staff, this chapter analyzes an application for government assistance using Actor-Network Theory. By examining this literacy moment as a process of translation in which diverse elements interact with the goal of achieving a successful application, this study shows how this population of college students are made (in)visible in specific ways by the negotiated power dynamics of the application itself, the individual applying, and her social support relationships.

"I guess one thing I want to do, I want to be able to make it, you know? I would like, you know I feel like depending on these services are good, but they help, it's easy to get comfortable, and you know to be stuck . . . Being assisted, like I get assistance and stuff, and it's easy to get stuck there. But I want to be able to make my own money, you know, and be able to provide for my kids without any help and assistance from nobody."

—ChaRay, personal interview

"You have to really be organized with your time . . . to get everything accomplished. I would say, it's not so much school but it is the demands of everything, everybody ... You know ... that everybody has expectations of what they, whether it's the government, you know ... Because I get government assistance ... They have requirements ... And so it's just, trying to juggle everything, I would say time ... I always, I always say ... I wish I had more time. So that would be the biggest challenge."

—Sofia, personal interview

On a typical weekday during the semester, Sofia is up early to take her kids to school, after which she comes home and is able to enjoy a quiet cup of coffee and start on her homework. She says this is her favorite time of day—the time when she can focus on school and get to work accomplishing the many goals she has set for herself and her family. The rest of the day is a constant stream of activity, between attending her classes, squeezing in homework when she can, picking up the kids from school and helping them with their homework, playtime, dinner, and bed. Sofia doesn't have a job, and she relies on government assistance to support her family while she finishes her Bachelor's degree. They live in the subsidized apartments of one of Family Scholar Houses's (FSH) four campuses in Louisville, Kentucky.

Sofia's narrative is an increasingly familiar, yet still elided by many, story of a low-income single parent attempting to earn a college degree and improve the life of her family. Though higher education has seen, over the past 45 years, an increasingly diversified student body with the accompanying awareness of the diverse experiences and expectations that students bring with them into our classrooms, our field still searches for ways to understand students' lives and incorporate our understanding into our teaching and research. I begin with the above anecdote in order to illustrate one way into students' lives and literacies. A key point to observe about Sofia's day is the abundance of people, places, objects, institutions, and relationships making up the networks she moves through throughout the day. And, although literacy is one of these elements, her literacy practices are also a prism that catch and reflect the fluctuating elements that contribute to those literacy practices (from her cup of coffee to the expectations of the professor whose assignment she is working on to her own childhood literacy experiences). Taking on literacy from a more complex angle is not a new task, as demonstrated by the work of Brian Street (1984), David Barton and Mary Hamilton (1998), and others. The scholarship of New Literacy Studies approaches literacy from the social perspective, analyzing the ideological and contextual forces that influence the various shapes that literacy practices can take. In this chapter I offer an alternative to this social emphasis in literacy studies, along the lines of Deborah Brandt and Katie Clinton's (2002) call for a need to recognize the "legibility and durability of literacy: its material forms, its technological apparatus, its objectivity; that is, its (some)thing-ness" (p. 344), and Steve Parks' (2013) argument that "our pedagogical goal within community partnerships should be to understand how any one 'literate' moment is a resting point within a dynamic relationship between a series of diffuse literacy practices. The point is to study the process by which such resting places occur" (p. 43).

This chapter is a glimpse of the many, real life constraints of low-income single mothers living at FSH via analysis of their literacy practices to understand the variety of actors and actants that shape these practices. In Chapter 9, Denecker and Sisser describe how their "embodied reactions" to both the physical spaces and objects of the farms and the farmers' narratives reveal less obvious meanings arising from these interactions. Similarly, I recognize the significance of material and social elements in my analysis of literacy moments at FSH. To do so, I will draw on Actor-Network Theory (ANT), a complex socio-material approach arising from Bruno Latour's (2005) work in science and technology studies. ANT allows us to extend the scholarship on literacy and literacy sponsorship so that, rather than examining a broad swath of sponsorship over generations (Brandt, 2001), and rather than examining specific literacy sponsors in depth (Grabill, 2001), ANT demands that a rich array of diverse elements be included in the analysis of any given literate moment. In other words, we reconceive our goal as researchers to describe the literacy *relationships* as opposed to specific "*agents*." In the words of W. Michele Simmons, Kristen Moore, and Patricia Sullivan (2015) as they describe how they use ANT to approach a civic engagement project, they follow "the actors and their relationships to one another . . . As we write up the research, we don't choose which of the many groups involved in civic engagement we will study, rather, we watch actors assembling and disassembling at any given time and find data in the traces of those assemblings and disassemblings" (pp. 284–285). My theoretical approach acts as a feminist intervention because I follow the "traces" of literacy sponsorship that are manifested through the shifting *relationships* surrounding a particular moment of translation.

I use the ANT concept of translation in order to a) reveal the mechanisms behind a specific literate moment, and b) analyze how these mechanisms make these students visible in specific ways and invisible in others. I'm analyzing the pieces of the network surrounding the literate moment of translation that is an application for government assistance so that we can stop seeing these women as only "students" or only "single parents" but also in terms of their relationships and their individual perspectives. Kirsch argues that the core principle of feminist research methodology is that research needs to be *for* women, not just *about* women ("Ethical Dilemmas" 2–3). FSH is an organization run almost entirely by women, serving a majority female population. My feminist intervention in doing research at FSH is one that recognizes the significance of gender but opens up the analysis to other factors that shape participants' lives. I perform a feminist intervention by acknowledging that gender is not the only or most important aspect of these students' experiences and by analyzing the factors surrounding literacy that seem significant to the participants themselves. Given the intense feminization of poverty, I examine an application for federal assistance and take into account the variety of material circumstances, social relationships, and individual perspectives that are at work within this sort of literate moment but that we might not normally see given how the application tends to construct women in a particular, one-sided way, and this is my way of enacting a feminist approach to literacy studies research at the intersection of university and community agendas. I undertake this ANT analysis keeping in mind the concerns of scholars such as Gesa Kirsch (1997), Jacqueline Rosyter & Gesa Kirsch (2012), Ellen Cushman (1998), and others regarding the need for more reflexive, collaborative, and experimental research partnerships. By paying close attention to tensions that arise between the actors and actants within this specific network, my work answers the call for community engagement research that acknowledges the complexities and divides within any given community context while resisting the tendency to reduce the community angle to a singular, rosy hue (Harris, 1989).

The unique space of Family Scholar House reaches beyond but also straddles the university and community dimensions. Looking at students' literacy practices at this organization opens up the feminist agenda by expanding traditional notions of literacy, particularly by focusing on the relationships and relationship work supporting an application for government assistance. This is one of many rich literacy moments occurring at FSH; others include the collaborative writing of a financial aid appeal letter by students and academic advisors, as well as FSH's annual fundraising luncheon at which students present essays they have written to win college scholarships. I have chosen to narrow my analysis in this chapter to the Kentucky Transitional Assistance Program application (or KTAP) because this moment has such far-reaching consequences upon the actors and actants involved, including effects on a student's finances and family relationships as well as effects on the relationship between the student and her FSH social worker.

Beginning as Project Women in 1995, Family Scholar House was created in 2008. Family Scholar House is a non-profit organization in Louisville, KY whose "mission is to end the cycle of poverty and transform our community by empowering families and youth to succeed in education and achieve life-long self-sufficiency" (Family Scholar House). (To get an idea of what FSH does, explore their website (http://familyscholarhouse.org), and watch the video at http://www.youtube.com/watch?v=eyodchYl7pQ&feature=share&list=UUZSKXdktekR1subN7Xqfe0w.) With four active campuses and more in the pipeline, FSH provides subsidized housing for its residential members and support services such as academic advising, financial aid advising, mentoring, life skills training, group workshops, tutoring, and more for both residential and non-residential members. All FSH participants are low-income, the majority of them are female, and many have experienced domestic violence. FSH, as an organization, is a feminist intervention: it is run by women almost exclusively, serves a majority female population, and works to promote social justice for a historically underserved student population specifically by building relationships and community ties.

I developed a relationship with FSH while doing dissertation research there, a feminist intervention of the kind Sheridan recognizes as a "threshold experience": "a learning-by-doing opportunity that changes many participants' views of themselves and of their research, teaching, and community-engaged work in and beyond graduate school" (p. 223). For the study this chapter is drawn from, I conducted eleven interviews: six with FSH students, three with FSH staff, and two with local university writing program administrators. I identified the six students with help from Will, the academic services coordinator and my main contact at the organization (as well as one of my staff interviews). Both before and while I collected data, I volunteered at FSH in various capacities, from filing documents to assessing students' computer needs. I tried to maintain as reciprocal a relationship as possible between myself as researcher and the organization and its participants. As Mathis and Boehm point out in Chapter 6, collaboration and reciprocity are "necessarily flexible—not a rigid, predetermined relationship defined by a single party" (p 120). Thus, when one interviewee mentioned needing evening writing help, I made myself available at FSH one evening a week as a writing tutor. While my research was not collaborative in the sense that many feminist scholars call for—the multivocality, co-authorship, and participatory action angle to research—I tried to design my interview questions in ways that would allow the women to tell their stories as uniquely as they could. As Brandt et al. emphasize, these everyday stories can become crucial touchstones in activist collaborations surrounding literacy. During the interviews themselves, I kept a semi-structured approach and tried to follow the narrative arc of each interviewee as she told her stories.

ACTOR-NETWORK THEORY, TRANSLATION, AND POWER

For this project, the relevant aspects of networks as Latour and those following Actor-Network Theory theorize them concern the work being done in the formation of networks and the significant uncertainty involved in that work. Latour (2005) critiques the term "network" and its overemphasis when it comes to deciding how to use ANT, arguing that in addition to the importance of "being connected," networks should draw attention to the actual work taking place: "Really, we should say 'worknet' instead of 'network.' It's the work, and the movement, and the flow, and the changes that should be stressed" (p. 143). In other words, my analysis focuses on the relationships and the work that flows between actors and actants making up those relationships. Specifically, as I describe the different people involved in the completion of an application for government assistance, I emphasize how key relationships impact the application, and vice versa, how the document itself influences its networked relationships.

Just as Harris (1989) critiques the field's tendency to reify the notion of "community," scholars using ANT also point out that networks exist around a particular function and often hide the many people and activities that went into creating that function, using the example of "a textbook or an educational article" which "each bring together, frame, select and freeze in one form a whole series of meetings, voices, explorations, conflicts and possibilities explored and discarded" (Fenwick & Edwards, 2012, p. xiii). The authors emphasize the fact that "these inscriptions appear seamless and given, concealing the many negotiations of the network that produced it" (p. xiii–xiv). In order for my analysis to get under the "seamless and given" appearance of networks surrounding literacy practices, I focus on the translation occurring during this particular literate moment of completing an application for government assistance. In ANT, translation occurs when actors/actants are enrolled into a network in order to accomplish a specific purpose. As Latour (2005) writes, translation is "a connection that transports, so to speak, transformations . . . the word 'translation' now takes on a somewhat specialized meaning: a relation that does not transport causality but induces two mediators into coexisting" (p. 108). In other words, Latour understands translation as the connection between actors in a network, and it is this connection that is responsible for bringing multiple actors together which results in a network (that then gets traced by the researcher). Because translation is the "connection that transports . . . transformations," this makes translations especially rich things to study.

It's the instability of these moments of translation that make them appealing for literacy research as feminist intervention that seeks to recognize the diverse and shifting factors involved in any given literacy moment—factors that we might not be able to see otherwise. As Simmons et al. (2015) point out, "In its reliance on uncertainties as a heuristic, Latour's ANT insists researchers resist and refuse the assumed, the foundational, and the stable in systematic and rigorous ways. Because stability is exclusionary, Latour-like unstable portraits likely reveal connections otherwise obscured . . . " (p. 278). Not only does an ANT analysis reveal the hidden connections and relationships that create a moment of translation, it can take on the visibility trap of Foucault's panopticon by pointing to specific ways in which those with less power—the women applying for assistance—are forced into visibility, while also revealing the less visible ways in which these women are interacting with this literacy moment and how that influences their lives and relationships.

Translation is essentially another way of making networked actors/actants and their relationships visible. This is important work considering that what we usually see as literacy researchers tends to be, despite our best efforts, bounded by the constraints of the literacy expectations in any given context. As Mary Hamilton (2012) points out, looking at translations allows us to see beneath the seemingly ordered reality: "ANT has been called a 'sociology of translations' and the key process I will focus on is that of 'translation' whereby the messy complexities of everyday life are ordered and simplified for the purposes of the project at hand" (p. 44). By identifying literate moments that seem to represent a unified coherence of purpose, we can tease out the underlying tensions and differences. Hamilton draws on Sakari's articulation of translation to point out the repercussions of power dynamics within translation:

> Translation, as Sakari (2006) argues, is not a simple process of making equivalent two different but predetermined entities. It is, rather, a process of articulation—"a poietic social practice that institutes a relation at the site of incommensurability [. . .] a process of creating continuity in discontinuity" (p. 75). The result is productively emergent, the smoothing of differences, the alignment and sequencing of a number of sub-projects, a set of differences held—precariously—in tension because, as Sakari again points out, 'translation is always complicit with the building, transforming or disrupting of power relations' (p. 72). (p. 44)

Translation is about relationship-making between distinct actors, and about providing the opportunity for connection between various actors/actants that, by coming into contact with each other, change in all sorts of ways. In this chapter, I'm identifying the KTAP application as a particular moment of translation in which a variety of actors/actants seem to be working together towards a common purpose (a purpose provided by the moment of translation as it creates opportunities for relationships), and in which there is an element of literacy at work. I analyze the relationship work happening within this KTAP moment in order to start on the micro-level and to avoid lumping particular motivations for these moments together and attributing them solely to macro social forces.

As Sarah Read (2015) points out, " . . . for Latour the tracing of associations, or the 'peculiar *movement* of re-association and reassembling' (RS; emphasis added), is an explanatory activity that describes the translations that induce two actors, two intermediaries, into coexisting (RS 108) . . . " (p. 256). In other words, the key to translation is in tracing the movement—or work—that creates relationships between actors/actants as they're enrolled into a specific network with a shared purpose. One way that translation takes power into account is by recognizing the fluidity of the negotiations between actors/actants and the mutability of agency in these relationships. In addition to recognizing the fluctuations of power dynamics, I consider how examining a moment of translation can help us to see *how* actors are made visible or identified as they interact with other actors and actants within the network. Analyzing the KTAP moment of translation allows us to see the mechanisms and consequences of Foucault's panopticon as they play out here, and also to work on identifying how the important and complex ways in which these students are interacting with the KTAP application tend to get subsumed and hidden by the application itself as a powerful institutional document.

KTAP ANALYSIS

The Kentucky Transitional Assistance Program (KTAP), nested within several state departments, provides monthly financial assistance as part of the Temporary Assistance for Needy Families (TANF) cash benefit program to families with children, for a maximum of five years. Most parents at FSH receive KTAP benefits and must complete the application every month. In what follows, I analyze the KTAP application as a literacy moment of translation, which means I focus on how relationships are created, with whom, to accomplish what purpose, and amidst which tensions.

The KTAP application represents a kind of continuity of purpose and process that comes from its power as an established institutional document and procedure, but this continuity hides the tensions, differences, and fractures that arise when FSH students apply for government assistance. Just as Mathis and Boehm delve into their specific preparations and "behind-the-scenes work" of the Community Engagement Academy in order to reveal how significant collaborative relationships are being built, my analysis of KTAP reveals "behind-the-scenes" tensions underlying this document: the tension between needing assistance and being stuck on it, the tension in family relations, the tension between the KTAP applicant and her sponsor signing off on it, and the tension arising from the material circumstances and time constraints surrounding the application. These tensions get hidden by the one-dimensional way in which the powerful KTAP application constructs the less powerful applicants. Thus, also important here are the points of connection for relationship-making that KTAP provides opportunities for. This relationship work is a form of feminist intervention that can help to make students visible in different, complex ways.

During my interview with Rose, the Family Services Coordinator at FSH, the KTAP application first came up when I asked her what kinds of writing she actually did with participants, such as filling out forms. Because all FSH participants are low-income single parents, KTAP applications are a common literacy event as participants need financial assistance. KTAP came up again when I asked Rose about the common struggles and obstacles that participants dealt with. Her answer initially had to do with the financial difficulties participants are dealing with, and then she moved on to address other, related challenges that arise through the KTAP application and the process it entails. It became clear that the KTAP application is a very powerful document representing the state government, and it requires interventions and relationships in order for participants to successfully negotiate it on many levels.

Part of the KTAP application's power comes not only from a very firm deadline that, if missed, means no assistance that month, but also from the fact that the KTAP document requires acknowledging existence of the child's father, which then results in the state demanding that he pay child support, which then has all sorts of consequences on relationships (between the mother and father, between the father and child, etc.). As Rose explains,

> Because it is government assistance, the government's going to say "Well where is Dad? What is he doing? How is he involved?" . . . So that will push a person into child support . . . And so we have hesitation for people to get KTAP because they, because a lot of times what they think or feel is "Oh, by putting my child's father on child support he's getting, I'm getting him in trouble." And that's a feeling from both sides, mom's side and dad's side . . . And he might say, which is, these are statements that have been shared with us, like "Ok well then I'm not going to see my child anymore," or "I want visitation," or somebody gets physically assaulted because of this. (Rose, personal communication, December 14, 2014)

Submitting a KTAP application therefore has very real and potentially negative consequences on the family relationships. This highlights further tension in this translation moment, because FSH students may rely on KTAP assistance to support their families while they're in school, but at the risk of damaging relationships between the mother and father and between the father and the kids. I don't necessarily want to argue that FSH students see this decision in this way—as choosing between earning a degree and maintaining positive relationships—but I do want to emphasize the potential for tension crystallized in this KTAP moment. What happens with this tension depends on the individual circumstances of each FSH student.

Dorothy Smith (2006) argues that analyzing how texts are used by different people in a sequence of activities reveals the disjunctures between different realities, individuals' perspectives, and institutional purposes that we wouldn't otherwise be able to see based on analyzing texts alone. Drawing on Smith, even though we aren't able to know how a KTAP form gets read and interpreted down the road by a government employee, what we can see is Rose's interpretation of the consequences of varying interpretations of the KTAP form upon FSH students and their families. For example, Rose indicates that the father's different interpretation of KTAP's request for child support—that he's now in trouble with the state—can result in a change in his relationship with the mother and the kids. The power here fluctuates, with another potential scenario being that applying for KTAP could mean that the father does end up paying child support, which then helps the mother support her family and continue her education. I want to point out the variability of different versions of the KTAP moment of translation in order to emphasize the tenuous, continually negotiated nature of power here. KTAP provides the points of connection "that transport transformation," and the shape this transformation takes varies. It's also significant that the KTAP application makes both the applicant and the child's father visible: it identifies the applicant as in need of financial assistance, and then identifies the father as someone who is then required by the state to help provide some of this assistance in the form of child support payments (even if he cannot make them). Identifying the mother and father in this way, as a one-dimensional focus on the material circumstances and needs of their lives, ignores other complex dimensions such as, as Rose points out, the nature of the pair's relationship.

Just as the KTAP application has potential consequences on family relationships, this tension creates the opportunity for a relationship between the student and Rose, as she points out: "And so I can help them, let me help you navigate this system and that you understand it well enough to take away some of the stressors that you could potentially experience. And if there is a relationship issue with dad, let me help you have a better conversation with dad so he can understand . . . That it benefits him too" (Rose, personal communication, December 14, 2014). The relationship work here between Rose and the participant becomes a feminist intervention, but not intervention in order to halt or prevent action—rather, intervention in the literal sense of the word. Their relationship "comes between" the actors and actants (the people involved and the KTAP application itself), acknowledging the necessity of KTAP and easing its repercussions. Mary Hamilton (2012) points out that "ANT asserts that the effects of power can be traced through assemblies, or mixtures, of objects, animals, people, machines, discourses and so on to which agency is delegated" (pp. 41–42). It is only through looking at the *relationships* connecting these various actors that we are able to understand how power works within the translation process. As Sarah Read (2015) points out in her Latourian analysis of a child care program, the agency of these child care workers to implement material change based on state mandates "is coextensive with these powerful structures. Their agency is an effect of their association with the whole assemblage and their work to enact, maintain, and extend it" (p. 270). Thus, ANT allows us to describe how the relationships between actors being translated into a network shape the ebb and flow of power within that network. We can see the interdependencies of power dynamics that develop out of relationships within the KTAP moment of translation in how Rose describes her relationships with participants as well as how she develops her coaching approach to these relationships.

Rose describes the way she approaches her role with students as "encouragement coaching," and we can see how her specific angle creates perspectives on her students' lives that the KTAP application ignores.

> And I really take the approach . . . of coaching with our families . . . Seeing that our families are the experts, or the parent is the expert in their life . . . That I'm not here to tell them what to do . . . So I think that approach is really helpful for rapport-building . . . and again giving that person the tools and feeling that "Hey I can take care of this situation." (Rose, personal communication, December 14, 2014)

In voicing her coaching approach, Rose identifies the FSH families as "the experts" and the parent as "the expert in their life." This particular tact demonstrates a significantly different way of "seeing" or constructing these women from how the KTAP application sees them: as dependent, as needing the supervision of a sponsor. So, in this moment of translation, the relationship work between Rose and the women involves a shift in the perspective on the women, or on how they are "seen." By recognizing that the women are the experts in their own lives, Rose brings a more complex dimension to a literacy moment that typically reduces individuals to one-dimensional types. She thus counters the visibility trap of the KTAP application by refusing to see the women only as the document portrays them, but rather seeing their complexity. This shift in "seeing" extends the relationship work here as a kind of feminist intervention with deeper consequences, because in seeing the women as experts of their own lives, Rose helps them to see themselves this way.

The tension arising from relationships surrounding the KTAP application includes possible discomfort between the applicant and the sponsor she must get to sign off on her application. Rose points out that people applying for KTAP must find someone to sign off on their application, such as an employer or professor if they don't have access to FSH staff:

> So if you're a person who, let's say you didn't have FSH to sign off . . . I have a relationship with the folks to sign off, no big deal . . . But if a person maybe has to ask a professor or maybe has to ask an employer to sign this, well that could be embarrassing to them because Oh, here I am wanting you to sign my form . . . And you're going to ask me, and now you're going to know that I receive government assistance. (Rose, personal communication, December 14, 2014)

The potential embarrassment arising from applicants having to divulge private information about their lives and financial situation to relative strangers becomes an obstacle. And perhaps this remains an obstacle for FSH students, too, who may not all have strong relationships with FSH staff and who might not be comfortable sharing that information. Here, the points of connection that KTAP, as a moment of translation, allows for between the applicant and her sponsor can lead to unpredictable kinds of relationships and consequences. Just because translations are a "connection that transports transformation" doesn't mean that this transformation is necessarily positive. In this scenario, where KTAP applicants must find a person to sign off or may still feel uncomfortable with the FSH staff, the consequences involve a shift in social capital where applicants may lose power specifically in the form of social capital because of the negative associations that accompany government assistance. The sponsor signing gains a degree of power because he knows more about the applicant's life than he did before, and perhaps at least partially against her will. The document shapes the relationship between the sponsor and the applicant by mediating this relationship along the roles of supervisor/supervised, have/have not.

I attempted to locate a copy of the KTAP application itself but was told I could only obtain one with an in-person interview with a city social worker. Rose gave me a copy of the Verification of Kentucky Works Participation, or PA-33 which, while not the exact same thing as the KTAP application, does give an idea of the kind of supervision required from a sponsor (such as an employer or teacher). This is the form that documents the work/educational activities of applicants every month and is signed by the "provider."

Based on this form, we can see that the provider must document the exact hours an applicant works each day, including absences and holidays, and the provider must also "enter comments for any excused absences." Just like a teacher tracking a student's attendance in order to help determine her grade in the course, this level of supervision is close, precise, and shapes the financial situation of the applicant each month (the PA-33 must be completed each month). In other words, this document makes an applicant's labor visible, but in strictly prescribed

Literacy Sponsorship as a Process of Translation

ways, namely, in terms of hours. The only potential for more detail comes from the requirement to "Enter comments for any excused absences," or, in other words, explanations for an applicant's lack of visible labor. The form itself emphasizes the significance of the monthly deadline: "If this form is not correctly completed and returned by **October 5, 2014**, we cannot give you credit for your participation, pay for transportation for **November 2014**, or help with other items you may need" (original emphasis). Not only does the PA-33 emphasize time in terms of an applicant's hours of work, it also constrains/defines the temporal aspect in which applicants interact with the document with the strict monthly deadline.

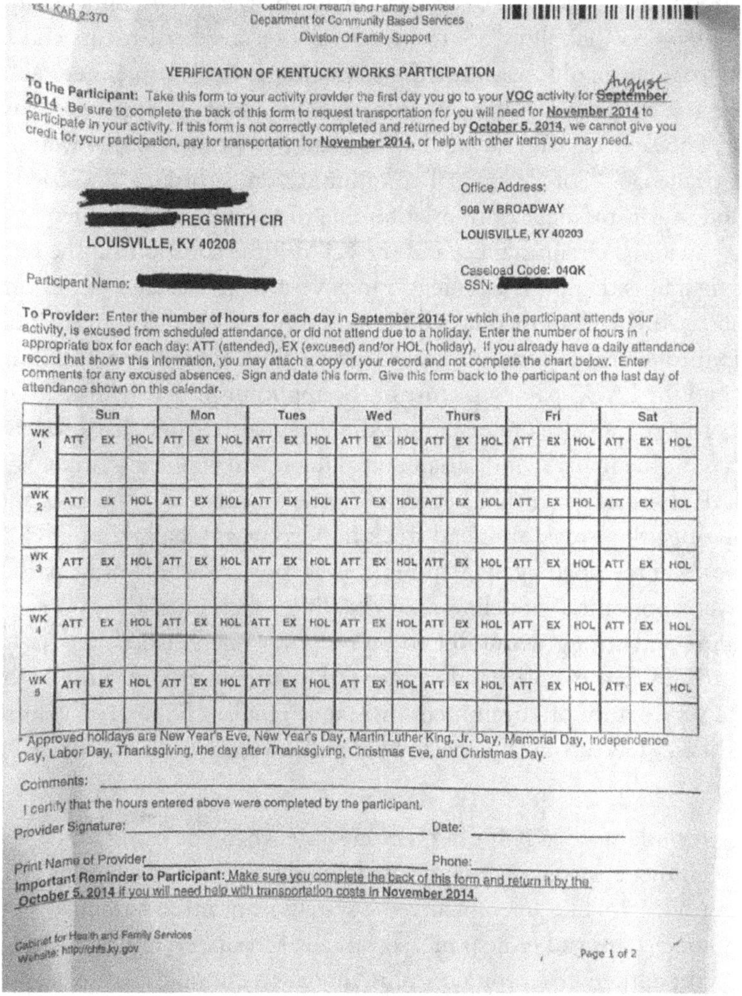

Figure 10.1. Verification of Kentucky Works Participation, PA-33. Photo taken by the author during data collection.

207

The KTAP application deadline imposes time-sensitive constraints upon the individual completing the application, and Rose points to the potential difficulties this might create for applicants who are juggling many variables when she says, "If you don't turn in that paperwork on time your benefits get cut off," which then means that person has to go to an appointment to reapply; "You also have situations where, and you may see this both for KTAP and Section 8, where they say, they send the letter and say 'Hey, you have an appointment on Dec 4th at 11:00.' Well that just so happens to be my math class" (Rose, personal communication, December 14, 2014). In this example, the high-stakes constraints placed upon this participant by her school and by the state require her to juggle her time in ways that allow her to successfully receive her benefits and to successfully pass her math class. As Sofia points out in this chapter's epitaph, time is her biggest challenge: "And so it's just, trying to juggle everything, I would say time . . . I always, I always say . . . I wish I had more time. So that would be the biggest challenge" (Sofia, personal communication, February 20, 2015). There is tension in this moment of translation due to the potential conflict between a student's material circumstances and the KTAP time constraints. The same material constraints that push a student into government assistance—full-time college coursework, lack of income, children to support—can also make it difficult to jump through the necessary hoops to receive the assistance. And, although the KTAP and the PA-33 paint a picture of the applicant primarily in terms of time (hours of labor), this maintains a one-dimensional portrait that does not take into account the many living variables making up an applicant's time.

KTAP also creates tension between a student's need to be on assistance and the trap of getting stuck on it and stuck in poverty, as ChaRay, an FSH participant, notes in the opening epigraph to this chapter. Not only must participants follow the application guidelines and deadlines, they must do so despite their discomfort and strong desire not to be on government assistance. As LeeAnn (another FSH staff member and former FSH participant) and Rose both point out, the very nature of government assistance requires FSH participants to remain in a very low income bracket to be eligible to receive this assistance. LeeAnn articulates this best:

> I think there's a point in everyone's life when you're on government assistance and you are low-income, that you sort of realize, it's like an epiphany, the system is meant to suppress me . . . Instead of help me, sort of . . . I mean, even if that's not entirely true, you do realize that at one point . . . I have to stay low-income in order to receive these benefits . . . you know you're broke, you know you're low-income, you're very

> aware of all this stuff while you're here . . . But if you try to do anything to better yourself right now, it's going to hurt you more than help you. (LeeAnn, personal communication, December 10, 2014)

In this scenario, the KTAP document seems to take power away from participants by limiting their opportunities for employment. Simultaneously, however, the government assistance provides opportunities by giving recipients income. This very real and embodied contradiction demonstrates the inability of a document like the KTAP application to fully portray applicants as they work, study, and live amidst a tremendous variety of elements making up their networks. And I'm not arguing that it should, or even that it could, given how institutional documents like the KTAP application have to function. But it is important to understand exactly how the KTAP application translates the students into needs and numbers, ignoring their complexities out of necessity, and thereby creating opportunities for feminist interventions in the form of the relationship work between Rose and the participants.

In fact, it is this contradictory and imbalanced power of the KTAP document that necessitates Rose's intervention to help students navigate the system:

> . . . there are so many different barriers that come into play in helping a person get out of poverty . . . And, it's just helping our folks be strategic about that . . . And that's where I hope that I can help them . . . KTAP is only a 5 year program . . . And it's ideal right now because you're in college, and you're only going to be in college for, hopefully about 5 years . . . And so I can help them, let me help you navigate this system and that you understand it well enough to take away some of the stressors that you could potentially experience. And if there is a relationship issue with dad, let me help you have a better conversation with dad so he can understand . . . That it benefits him too . . . And ultimately it's your decision, you know, because I have people who get KTAP, it doesn't work for them, and they would rather work, and that's fine . . . So it's really case by case. (Rose, personal communication, December 4, 2014)

We can see here that the KTAP moment of translation provides the opportunity for a relationship between the FSH student and Rose, and it is this relationship specifically that helps the student to successfully navigate the KTAP application in ways that reduce the negative consequences (on her family relationships, for example).

CONCLUSION

It is the uncertainty and tension represented in the KTAP document (the tension between needing assistance and that same assistance requiring applicants to stay poor, tension between needing assistance and needing strong family relationships, etc.) that necessitates these working relationships—these feminist interventions—between FSH students and FSH staff. So, another way to look at the KTAP moment in terms of translation, in light of the notion of translation as "a process of creating continuity in discontinuity," is to recognize the seeming continuity and strength of these relationships and then to look at what lies beneath those relationships, namely, the reasons that those relationships exist. If translation is a "connection that transports . . . transformations" (Latour, 2005, p. 108), then the KTAP application as a moment of translation is a point of connection between all of the involved actors/actants that supports potential transformations of those actors/actants via the relationships created by this point of connection. As Latour argues, "So, the word 'translation' now takes on a somewhat specialized meaning: a relation that does not transport causality but induces two mediators into coexisting" (p. 108). In other words, KTAP does not cause transformation; rather, the KTAP application induces the relevant actors/actants into coexisting, and it is the relationships arising from this coexistence that have the potential to transform those involved. In this way, we can conceive of feminist interventions as necessary parts of a complex system of sponsorship surrounding literacy practices. These feminist interventions enact relationship work that balances the reductive lens of institutional documents and processes. As Sheridan argues in Chapter 11, "Knot-working collaborations emerge out of what I consider a threshold concept within our field: doing is a leading edge of learning. Unfortunately, our desire to provide opportunities for this learning-by-doing faces institutional and individual obstacles that hinder feminist community engagement" (p. 214). Knot-working is an example of this feminist intervention of relationships that develop through "doing"; identifying moments of translation can allow us to recognize what the "doing" of this relationship work looks like in the practice of community engagement and research.

The most significant negotiations of power in this moment of translation seem to lie in the relationships among the people involved. It initially seems as though the KTAP document itself has the most power, because the students and staff are working to navigate the document successfully and there are material consequences on students' lives. Perhaps another way of looking at power is to argue that the KTAP document has the present power—in the present conditions of students' lives as they're on assistance—but it's the students who have the power over their potential futures because they are using the KTAP assistance in order to work towards the kind of futures they want (futures in which they are not on assistance).

Literacy Sponsorship as a Process of Translation

In other words, power shifts over time and between actors/actants within a given translation. In this sense, it's important to analyze the relationship work and the ways in which students are being made visible/invisible in this KTAP moment of translation because by seeing the complexity here, we can also begin to see how this literacy moment could influence students' potential futures.

In using the ANT concept of translation to examine the network of literacy sponsorship surrounding the KTAP application, I have been able to trace the relationship work taking place between human actors as well as nonhuman actants. This relationship work between Rose and the participants allows FSH participants to change how they perceive their own lives and how they imagine their futures. Literacy sponsorship at FSH becomes not only about the literacy practices themselves (practices which, as demonstrated here, are not exclusively 'academic' or 'extracurricular' but are multifaceted, pragmatic, and significantly related to finances), or even about the goal of "life-long self-sufficiency" that these practices help achieve, but about the relationships and negotiations unfolding around even the smallest literacy event, where those relationships and power dynamics come from, and how they then keep on playing out within these actors' lives and networks. By making visible the mechanisms underlying this specific moment of translation and revealing the ways in which applicants are made visible (as poor, as single parents, in stark terms of work hours) and the complexities that are hidden (tensions in family relationships, the material conditions of their lives), I hope to emphasize the significance of the relationship work happening here. This relationship work not only provides opportunities for students to navigate the system and to see themselves differently (as Rose helps them to navigate KTAP and to see themselves as "the experts" on their lives), it also demonstrates the kind of deeply layered, prismatic work going on at places like Family Scholar House. This work is not worthy of attention simply because it exists in the "community" versus the "university" (because actually, I'd argue FSH exists in both at once), or because of its devotion to literacy and education. Rather, the relationship work happening in this moment of translation is valuable because it mirrors the kind of complex, deeply felt but rarely understood relationship work surrounding literacy in classrooms, living rooms, community centers, and workplaces everywhere. In identifying this relationship work as a kind of feminist intervention, the next question becomes, "How do we build heuristics and scaffolding to support and sustain the relationship work of feminist interventions in ways that don't squash the serendipitous, unpredictable, and joyful nature of these encounters?"[1]

---

1   I model this question after a similar one asked by Paul Feigenbaum at the inaugural Conference on Community Writing about the nature of community-university partnerships: "What would it mean to build engaged infrastructure that cultivates a flow milieu even while connected to institutions that tend to disrupt it?"

REFERENCES

Barton, D. & Hamilton, M. (1998). *Local literacies: Reading and writing in one community.* London, England: Routledge.

Brandt, D. (2001). *Literacy in American lives.* Cambridge, England: Cambridge University Press.

Brandt, D. & Clinton, K. (2002). Limits of the local: Expanding perspectives on literacy as social practice. *Journal of Literacy Research, 34*(3), 337–356.

Cushman, E. (1998). *The struggle and the tools: Oral and literate strategies in an inner city community.* Albany, NY: State University of New York Press.

Family Scholar House. Retrieved from http://familyscholarhouse.org/.

Feigenbaum, Paul. The community writing believing game: Discovering and dreaming about flow. *Conference on Community Writing.* University of Colorado, Boulder. Boulder, Colorado. 15 October 2015. Keynote Address.

Fenwick, T. J. & Edwards, R. (2012). *Researching education through actor-network theory.* Malden, MA: John Wiley & Sons.

Grabill, J. (2001). *Community literacy programs and the politics of social change.* Albany, NY: State University of New York Press.

Hamilton, M. (2012). Unruly practices: What a sociology of translations can offer to educational policy analysis. In T. J. Fenwick & R. Edwards (Eds.), *Researching education through actor-network theory* (pp. 40–59). Malden, MA: John Wiley & Sons.

Harris, J. (1989). The idea of community in the study of writing. *College Composition and Communication, 40*(1), 11–22.

Kirsch, G. (1997). Multi-vocal texts and interpretive responsibility. *College English, 59,* 191–202.

Latour, B. (2005). *Reassembling the social: An introduction to actor-network theory.* Oxford, England: Oxford University Press.

Parks, S. (2013). Beginnings of a polemic: Shaking the borders of a literate education. *Literacy in Composition Studies, 1*(1), 42–44.

Read, S. (2015). Making a thing of quality child care: Latourian rhetoric doing things. In P. Lynch & N. Rivers (Eds.), *Thinking with Bruno Latour in rhetoric and composition* (pp. 256–274). Carbondale, IL: Southern Illinois University Press.

Royster, J. J. & Kirsch, G. (2012). *Feminist rhetorical practices: New horizons for rhetoric, composition, and literacy studies.* Carbondale, IL: Southern Illinois University Press.

Simmons, W. M., Moore, K. & Sullivan, P. (2015). Tracing uncertainties: Methodologies of a door closer. In P. Lynch & N. Rivers (Eds.), *Thinking with Bruno Latour in rhetoric and composition* (pp. 275–293). Carbondale, IL: Southern Illinois University Press.

Smith, D. E. (2006). *Institutional ethnography as practice.* Lanham, MD: Rowman & Littlefield.

Street, B. V. (1984). *Literacy in theory and practice.* Cambridgeshire: Cambridge University Press.

CHAPTER 11.
KNOTWORKING COLLABORATIONS: FOSTERING COMMUNITY-ENGAGED TEACHERS AND SCHOLARS

Mary P. Sheridan
University of Louisville

Sheridan draws on her experience founding and co-teaching the Digital Media Academy (DMA) to propose knotworking collaboration as a central practice for alternative forms of graduate education and professionalization. Examining the academy's design—both in messaging with external, public and funding audiences, and in internal programming with graduate student co-facilitators—Sheridan concludes that such collaborations represent a messy, but significant form of community and intellectual engagement for graduate students.

For a variety of reasons, academics have been trying to explain what we do to those inside and outside the academy. One current strategy is to articulate *threshold concepts* (Meyer & Land, 2003), the ways disciplinary insiders make meaning (e.g., the epistemologies and practices that mark certain disciplines). Not surprisingly, newcomers often struggle to learn these insider threshold concepts, but this theory holds that once students grasp these disciplinary ideas and practices, the learning is irreversible.[1] Scholars investigating how to foster students' understandings of such concepts have forwarded the idea of *threshold experiences,*

---

1 The richness (and critique) of this idea has found traction in many disciplines, including our own where threshold concepts have been taken up, perhaps most overtly in Linda Adler-Kassner and Elizabeth Wardle's *Naming What We Know: Threshold Concepts of Writing Studies* (2015), a book that forwards our own field's threshold concepts (surrounding the metaconcept that writing is an activity and an area of study), as well as the possibilities and difficulties of fostering the learning environments for people to engage and adopt such threshold concepts. A quick Google search illustrates how threshold concepts are playing out in many disciplines; readers of this collection may be interested in the Launius and Hassel's *Threshold Concepts in Women's and Gender Studies: Ways of Seeing, Thinking and Knowing* (2015).

what community-engaged scholars Barbara Harrison, Patti H. Clayton, and Gresilda A. Tilley-Lubbs (2014) define as "reflective encounters with dissonance that give rise to deeper understandings and sometimes internalization of threshold concepts" (p. 5). For Harrison et al., threshold experiences combine the experiences and the reflections on those experiences that can lead to the deep learning, the irreversible changes described in threshold concepts. Yet not every experience qualifies as a threshold experience; threshold experiences require full engagement with the complexities and contradictions that dismantle pat understandings and move us toward a deep learning. As teachers, researchers, community partners, and mentors, we are called to create the conditions for people to learn these threshold concepts, in part by constructing opportunities for threshold experiences.

Taking up that challenge in regards to this collection's focus on how feminist community engagement can be fostered in higher education, I forward one threshold experience: knotworking collaborations. Knotworking collaborations emerge out of what I consider a threshold concept within our field: doing is a leading edge of learning. Unfortunately, our desire to provide opportunities for this learning-by-doing faces institutional and individual obstacles that hinder feminist community engagement. The obstacles have been well articulated, from the mismatch of academic and project timelines (Lindquist, 2012), to struggles with community partners (Mathieu, 2013), to changes in our professional or personal lives (Deans, 2013). The dilemmas are real. And yet, if we believe that doing is central to learning, we need to provide more models of how to enact that doing.

The threshold experiences provided through knotworking collaborations, I argue, construct such opportunities. Essential to this deep learning is the feminist practice of destabilizing unhelpful hierarchies found within traditional academic partnerships, both those inside and outside the university. Knotworking collaborations do that destabilizing by helping participants interrogate issues of power, knowledge making, and relationship building within their collaborative partnerships.

In this chapter, I explore how knotworking collaborations can provide threshold experiences for graduate students interested in community engagement. After discussing ways to rethink how graduate education can build threshold experiences in community engagement, I detail how knotworking collaborations can enhance these efforts. I then offer an example of such a project: the Digital Media Academy (DMA), a free, two-week summer camp for rising 6th grade girls taught by University of Louisville graduate students and faculty. I conclude with a call for us, feminist community-engaged scholars, to find ways to foster such threshold experiences in our own settings.

RETHINKING GRADUATE EDUCATION IN COMMUNITY ENGAGEMENT THROUGH FEMINIST, WRITING STUDIES AND HIGHER EDUCATION LENSES

As external pressures push higher education to re-examine both what it does and how it engages with diverse stakeholders,[2] universities have found great interest in engaging with the community—a point made plain in the fact that hundreds of academic institutions applied for the most recent Carnegie Foundation designation of a "Community Engagement University," with 240 U.S. colleges and universities earning that designation in 2015 (Carnegie Classification), and that even more universities are building the infrastructures for such designations.[3] What this engagement looks like in practice varies but, generally, projects align with the oft-cited Carnegie Foundation's definition of community engagement, which focuses on "the mutually beneficial exchange of knowledge and resources in a context of partnership and reciprocity" between institutions of higher education and people in "the public and private sectors" in order "to enrich scholarship, research, and creative activity; enhance curriculum, teaching and learning; prepare educated, engaged citizens; strengthen democratic values and civic responsibility; address critical societal issues; and contribute to the public good" (New England Resource Center for Higher Education, 2015). Enacting this definition requires an attention to both philosophical orientations and pedagogical practices (Butin, 2014), if, as the name indicates, academics are to truly engage with a community. It is here that feminist and Writing Studies traditions have much to offer as universities reimagine graduate education to include the doing of community engagement.

---

2   As has been well documented (e.g., Center on Budget and Policy Priorities, 2014), the government is withdrawing significant support from higher education, prompting institutions to raise tuition to cover the shortfall. Moreover, as the numbers of grants decrease and the amount of student debt increases, the public understandably asks if higher education is worth the price. As I have argued elsewhere (Sheridan, 2014), this questioning can be dangerous when those of us in higher education, including those in writing studies, struggle to explain our value to those beyond our classrooms (cf Duffy, 2012).

3   The Carnegie Foundation designation is but one measure. According to the Campus Compact's 2013 annual membership survey, support for community engagement is growing, as evident in rising levels of support for faculty (via faculty development workshops; sample syllabi and assessment materials; tenure and review rewards) (p. 3); for students (via service considered in admissions criteria; graduation requirements; student awards) (p. 4); and for alumni (via service opportunities; public recognitions; university awards) (p. 4). Similarly, budgets for campus engagement centers are rising (p. 8), and center staff are increasingly credentialized. Collectively, these efforts show that universities are not only valuing community engagement, they're devoting more material resources to foster such engagement. And though such work may be, in part, to redress the current public relations crisis that questions higher education's price tag and relevance, higher education has an opportunity to demonstrate its value in part through developing meaningful community engagement.

Since the earliest days of Women (and Gender) Studies Departments, feminist scholars have advocated for community engagement as fundamental to the university's mission, as Adrienne Rich outlined in a "Woman-Centered University:"

> "Ideally, I imagine a very indistinct line between 'university' and 'community' instead of the familiar city-on-a-hill frowning down on its neighbors, or the wrought-iron gates by which town and gown have traditionally defined their relationship" (1979, p. 152).

While some have asked what makes *feminist* community-engaged scholarship distinct (cf Iverson & James, 2014), in general, it's that scholars in are asking questions similar to ones feminists have been asking for years: Who gets to decide on the project, and how? Whose voices are heard? Who benefits? How do we foster genuine, reciprocal relationships?[4]

Such feminist questions highlight the importance of examining power, knowledge making, and genuine partnership—topics the university would be wise to address in its deep dive into community engagement (cf Orr, 2011).[5] Yet while such questions prompt us to think about relations *between* university members and community partners,[6] they are also relevant for relations *within* university groups, such as within faculty and graduate community-engaged collaborations. This is certainly the case for feminist community-engaged scholars committed to designing threshold experiences for graduate students, both for their current education and for opening possibilities for similar work in their future.[7]

Writing Studies also has a long history with community engagement, from democratic impulses that call for class mobility or critical consciousness to scholars promoting reciprocal relationships between academic and community partners, as the chapters in this collection demonstrate. Writing Studies scholars have built on these histories to the point that community engagement is prev-

---

4   In the same ways that feminists focus on power and the consequences of that power, feminist community engagement scholars also examine power and privilege in their work, as evident in the types of questions they ask: How can we change the fact that the voices least heard in community-engaged research, according to Stoecker and Tryon (2009), are community partners—those with the least power to shape the scholarly write-up and discussions about such partnership work? Or, how is it that community engagement is defined in a way that, as Mena and Vaccaro (2015) argue, frequently occludes engagement by women of color, precisely because their work often focuses on everyday community survival for those without much privilege?

5   For a history of divergent trends of current feminist community engagement scholarship, see Costa and Leong (2013), especially their distinctions between more individually-focused entrepreneurial models and the more structural, social justice models of community engagement.

6   See Stoecker and Tryon (2009) about the need for more attention to community partners.

7   For discussions in this collection, see Mathis & Boehm about graduate student experiences and see Brandt et al. as well as Concannon et al. about undergraduate student experiences.

alent. Individual papers and panels focusing on community engagement are becoming more prominent at our local, national, and international conferences; engaged scholarship is not only being accepted into flagship journals, but also becoming the focus of special issues, monographs, edited collections, and books; MLA Job List postings are calling for community-engaged specializations in their announcements; and graduate programs are adding course offerings in community literacies (Fero et al., 2008), civic responsibility (Bowen et al., 2014), or service learning within feminist activist frames (Webb et al., 2007).

The calls to develop models for community-engaged, graduate education within Writing Studies parallel those circulating elsewhere in higher education. For example, Professor of Higher Education Kerry Ann O'Meara (2008) argued that graduate students should have multiple, repeated opportunities for community engagement—from coursework to a practicum to extended projects that may lead to dissertation work. MIT Urban and Environmental Policy and Planning professor Lorlene Hoyt (2010) similarly proposed an expansion of the sites for community engagement both within higher education (e.g., in individual assignments, within individual courses, across multiple courses, and in thesis and dissertations) and within the community (e.g., working on city boards; including graduate student salaries as a budget line in community grant applications). These and other opportunities to engage with communities beyond our classrooms could change the way knowledge is created and shared, a goal for graduate education. This potential may be pursued by focusing on what Hoyt called "reciprocal" knowledge making: "For higher education, [this reciprocal knowledge making] means conceiving of knowledge differently, rethinking how professionals are prepared in

> **[Doing DMA, I learned] that I really LOVE community engagement like I thought I would. . . . It has [also] been a crash course in logistics management. There are so many things to juggle that I never would have thought of if I hadn't experienced it. It has also been a crash course in responsivity (my favorite word). We obviously had really detailed plans on our way into camp but also adjusted them a lot to what was actually happening, and not just what we thought was happening. I also got to see the way [my research on] trauma impacts community work in some incredibly interesting ways that I'm still processing but can't wait to write about.**
>
> – Michelle, 2015 Camp Blog, https://dma2015research.wordpress.com/2015/06/25/day-nine/

> I think it would be almost more appropriate to think of this experience [in DMA] as equivalent to a course for me. . . . . It was like a practicum in doing place-based, you know, person-based research. I think it was really cool that we got to plan it from the very earliest stages, everything from who do we involve, how do we involve them, and what age, and do we do just girls, you know, do we do all one grade, do we do this a couple times over the summer or do we only do it once? And then, obviously, day to day, a lot of planning, too: purchasing tools and technology, and software, and so on. So we were heavily—we were given basically sole control over the project. Mary P was very hands-off and that was really cool from a learning perspective. I feel like I did learn a lot about planning this sort of camp and, you know, teaching in general [and] research in general.
>
> – Elizabeth, interview

the academy and how knowledge generated by citizens is valued in the university; it also means adopting broader and more humanistic modes of scholarship evolving into more nimble and responsive civic institutions" (2010, p. 86).

Such efforts in feminist studies, Writing Studies, and community-engaged scholarship provide expertise the university could tap as it investigates how to infuse community engagement in graduate education while minimizing the "push and pull" graduate students may face when attempting to do community-engaged work (Feigenbaum, 2008). As Paul Feigenbaum explained, despite good intentions and genuine desire from many quarters on campus, students wanting to do such work in graduate school need more "systematic means" to meet the challenges and opportunities of both participating in genuine community engagement and graduating within the given timeframe (2008).

Providing knotworking collaborations within graduate education could be one such systematic means.

WHY KNOTWORKING COLLABORATIONS IN GRADUATE EDUCATION

From the outset, let me say I struggle with how to name this project; I'm working with the provisional title of knot-working collaborations with the hopes that others can build on this project to find alternative naming options. I want these collaborative opportunities to be part of an institutional structure, but I'm aware of the tactical suppleness central to community-engaged projects—projects that arise and fade based on myriad factors that are often at odds with academic, institutional structures. *Knotworking* attempts to get at this. Although I appreciate concepts like *community, community of practice, or discourse communities*,[8] these terms also evoke more homogenized, almost utopic spaces that simplify the complex multiplicity happening in these temporary groups that are coming together in a shared project that is shot through with diverse, even conflicting histories and goals (see Prior, 2015). In contrast, knotworking, according to Engeström, Engeström, and Vähäaho's model (1999), refers to braided activities when people collaborate on an issue or project, bringing together their own (often disparate) agendas, histories, tools, and goals, to form a stabilized-for-now group. Work is distributed, often unevenly, and, upon completion, participants go their separate ways. This uneven work distribution in stabilized-for-now groups better captures what I am looking for.

Similarly, while *collaboration* may have halcyon associations that are important to interrogate, I prefer this to other common terms like *apprenticeship* and even *mentoring* given that these latter terms often focus on one-to-one as opposed to group relations, and often emerge out of hierarchical models (Rickly & Harrington, 2002) that feminists generally work against. Fully recognizing the default power relations in student-faculty community-engaged projects, I am nonetheless persuaded by Sosnowski and Burmeister (2006) that collaboration, perhaps especially in graduate studies, provides a viable way to overtly address this concern. Such a premise is part of Dana Bisignani's (2014) feminist model, with its goal of creating structures that give newcomers legitimate ways to contribute to a project. Through what she has described as "collective responsibility and problem-solving" (96), Bisignani seeks to defamiliarize students of their traditional roles and routine, thereby creating what I call threshold experiences that can help graduate students develop new projective identities (Gee, 2003). By changing the traditional, hierarchical relationships through new participation possibilities, those within such projects enact a feminist goal of creating the conditions for, as Bisignani has described it, "students [to] actively engage in critical problem-solving and participate in *constructing* their knowledge rather than simply *receiving* it" (p. 96).

In my proposal of knotworking collaborations, graduate students and faculty come together on a shared project, during which they jointly engage in deep

---

8   Writing studies has long interrogated the idea of community, whether in reference to language communities (Prior, 1998) or communities of practice (Lave & Wenger, 1991; Wenger, 1998). Prior's (2015) "Community" essay in *Keywords in Writing Studies* provides a nice overview of this critique.

learning (in this case developing the dispositions and skills that mark community engagement threshold experiences), and after which they take what they have learned to form new collaborations in future projects. As is typical of community engagement projects, the specifics of what knotworking collaborations may look like in practice will vary depending on the local resources and conditions, but what distinguishes knotworking collaborations are the participation roles that exceed those typical of many community-engaged projects. To learn the expectations of such roles, students new to a group need multiple, low-barrier entry points with helpful guides along the way (cf Jenkins, 2009) and intense commitments of time, responsibility, and guided opportunity so that students develop the skills and dispositions to take on leadership roles whereby they are poised to rework power dynamics that permeate typical master-apprenticeship models.

Figure 11.1. 2014 DMA teachers—faculty and graduate students alike—collaborate in low-barrier activities as they prepare for that day's storyboarding workshop.

By providing graduate students with experiences in which they are challenged and supported to become meaning makers who co-construct knowledge helpful to the group, knotworking collaborations provide threshold experiences that can help students reorient their understandings of themselves, in this instance about what it means to be a community-engaged scholar-teacher. This was the case at DMA.

DIGITAL MEDIA ACADEMY (DMA): KNOTWORKING COLLABORATION AS A FEMINIST THRESHOLD EXPERIENCE

DMA illustrates how knotworking collaborations can function as a feminist-informed threshold experience by providing deep learning opportunities to do community engagement. To achieve that goal, DMA seeks to destabilize power hierarchies that prove unproductive to graduate education and, instead, provide both opportunities for collaborative knowledge making on complex issues and opportunities for participants to redefine themselves and their roles in this knowledge-making process.

Within this framework, DMA, like all community engagement projects, emerged within specific conditions, some that may be familiar and some that may be distinct. The University of Louisville is like so many others in its ramping up of attention given to community engagement. On the one hand, the university has initiated projects designed to integrate community engagement across campus. For example, in AY 2013–2014, DMA's inaugural year, the university was completing what would become its successful application for re-accreditation as a Carnegie Foundation Elective Community Engagement Classification university; the Delphi Center for Teaching and Learning hosted a year-long, interdisciplinary Faculty Learning Community on Community Engagement; there were on-going campus presentations on successful university-community partner projects; and, the Provost appointed a faculty member to conduct a year-long study of UofL and comparator schools with the goal of figuring out how to facilitate community engagement throughout the university. On the other hand, in many parts of the university, community engagement remained largely ad hoc, and often absent. This was the case in the English department, though the department was open to more structured initiatives, if someone would take the lead.

In 2013, a year after arriving at Louisville, I offered a graduate seminar in Community Literacy where students read community engagement scholarship and participated in a semester-long project. About 3/5 of the class worked with community partners of their choosing, spending regular hours in those sites, and composing documents that these community organizations desired; the other 2/5 worked with two Jefferson County Public Schools on an on-going digital storytelling project I coordinated before the semester, a project led by teachers in the College of Education. During this graduate seminar, we all composed documents that "did work in the world" (i.e., documents negotiated with community partners for their use) with the goal of understanding the systemic forces shaping these sites (for an example of this understanding, see Perry, Chapter 10, this collection). Several of us wrote grant proposals, and three community partners received grant funding, as did I for the Digital Media Academy.

DMA first ran in June 2014, when five University of Louisville doctoral students and I inaugurated this two-week digital media camp for rising sixth-grade girls from two Jefferson County Public Schools in Louisville. Connecting with two public elementary schools, one of which scored in the bottom 3 percent of Kentucky public schools, we developed shared goals. Initially, we sought to address the "summer slide," when children (particularly lower-income children) tend to lose academic skills—especially in reading and writing—during the school-free summer months (National Summer Learning Association, 2009; Borman, 2000). This goal was gradually superseded by a second goal: slightly modifying Stuart Selber (2004), we sought to help girls develop the technological, critical, and design literacies they needed to create digital messages of their choosing, thus encouraging girls to be critical producers, not just consumers, of digital media. Building on literature that showed how STEM fields had high income possibilities but few females (U.S. Department of Commerce, 2011), DMA sought to provide role models and hands-on experiences that might encourage girls to persevere in their academic and personal interests, perhaps even pursuing STEM opportunities. In addition to exposing the systematic economic roadblocks girls face, DMA worked to help girls recognize and redesign the pervasive sexualized and commercialized images of what it means to be a girl today (for a fuller description, see Chamberlain, Gramer & Hartline, 2015; Sheridan, 2015).

In addition to the girls and their communities, DMA targeted a second group of participants: graduate students. Balancing teaching, research, administration, and community engagement is messy work (see also Mathis & Boehm, Chapter 6, this collection), and my goals for DMA included creating structured opportunities for participants to reflect upon and engage in that mess of creating curriculum, conducting individually defined research based on that curriculum, and being a community-engaged teacher-scholar

> I also learned a lot about graduate education. I mean, just the fact that, I just think that teaching, and research, and the sort of crazy on-the go stuff that you end up having to do in administrative work—they were all working together. They were all happening at the same time, in ways that they will all be happening at the same time when we're all eventually faculty members somewhere. So it sort of gave us all a chance to experience that, that I think was really good, and valuable.
>
> – Megan, interview

through that curriculum. Such structured opportunities are often underdeveloped in graduate education (cf Miller et al., 1997), and this absence makes it a struggle for graduate students' transition to faculty ways of doing (Moore & Miller, 2006). In contrast, DMA requires this doing and reflecting, and partially through this process becomes a site of deep learning, a possible threshold experience that exposes graduate students to the complexity they may face in their careers.

It is this part of DMA—the feminist practices seeking to intervene in current graduate education in community engagement that I am calling knotworking collaborations—that I want to explore here.

Across its institutional lifespan and in myriad ways, DMA and ongoing reflection on this project function as a threshold experience, providing participants a learning-by-doing opportunity that changes many participants' views of themselves and of their research, teaching, and community-engaged work in and beyond graduate school (for examples of the complications of this work see Brandt et al. and Concannon et al., this collection). As detailed above, for such work to be successful, students must be active participants in a shared experience that shifts authority and expertise from a centralized knower to a group of knowers with authority and expertise distributed across the group.

Figure 11.2. I provide logistical support during a workshop led by graduate student Michelle Day, DMA's specialist in trauma-informed pedagogy.

In the first year of DMA, that transition of knowledge-making authority happened over several months, with reflection spreading out for over a year. Living out such a shift in power and subsequent knowledge making, I argue, is part of a threshold experience.

Before the camp, I held much of the power: since I imagined and founded DMA—designed the project, wrote the grants for funding, selected the graduate students, developed the community partnerships, secured the speakers, and so forth—I clearly shaped the structures of DMA.[9] And yet, once we started our six months of weekly meetings before the camp, we began to forge a more collaborative path for enacting a particular instance of DMA within those structures. Along the way, I structured opportunities for graduate students to take up new responsibilities for knowledge making through activities such as choosing readings, creating curriculum, designing assessments, and teaching newly learned digital media programs and platforms (e.g., Gimp, iMovie, WordPress, Instagram).

During DMA, the transition continued as lessons learned from camp shaped all of our research, teaching, and community engagement. As Keri wrote in our daily de-brief blog entry during camp, "I feel like I've learned so much about how to be flexible and respond to a wide range of situations, whether those were technical issues or responding to emotional or behavioral issues. I have also never worked this closely with a team of teachers, and I appreciated learning from all the other fabulous teachers at camp this year. I learned different pedagogical techniques that I am certain I will take into my college classrooms (like Sara's excellent discussion of how to talk to be a culturally sensitive educator)."

After camp, we drew upon our individual histories and anticipated futures to pursue our distinct DMA-inspired projects. These research projects addressed a range of topics, such as professionalizing new teachers in alternative ways, exploring digital humanities projects in our field, and identifying structures to foster community engagement in higher education. We also used this camp as a research site for publications (Chamberlain, Gramer & Hartline, 2015; Sheridan, 2015), conference presentations (Gramer, 2015; Hartline, March 2015; Hartline, October 2015; Sheridan, March 2015; Sheridan, April 2015), grant proposals (Sheridan, Gramer & Hartline, 2014–15; Sheridan, 2015), dissertation projects, and even awards.[10] DMA likewise shaped the graduate students' teaching trajectories: one

---

9 In this way, DMA started as what Engeström, Engeström, and Vähäaho (1999) call individually-focused knotworking as opposed to collectively-focused knotworking. As I argue, this focus shifted during DMA both in a given year as teachers took on more responsibility and over several years as Dr. Andrea Olinger takes over as point faculty person for DMA in 2016.

10 Elizabeth Chamberlin, Rachel Gramer, and Megan Hartline won the Carolyn Krause Maddox Prize in Women's & Gender Studies, University of Louisville. I won

person chose to teach a digitally mediated class, others included community-engaged projects in her undergraduate teaching, and another continued her interest in teacher training as an assistant director in the writing program. Finally, graduate students pursued their community-engaged work in future projects in ways they had not before (e.g., a community-engaged Art as Memory collective project that three DMA teachers participated in).

These possibilities demonstrate a *knotworking* collaboration in that participants brought their own histories and agendas to a common project and applied what they learned on subsequent individual and collaborative projects, unbraiding and, at times, re-braiding with other DMA participants (and others) in new ways. As DMA teacher Rachel Gramer (2015) noted, there seems "a 'need' for present and current professionalization, to come together and disband across time, space, contexts (and not just with ideas, but also with knowledge of tools and administrative systems for getting

> In terms of community engagement work, I think that DMA has really ignited a spark in me to continue this work. I would appreciate the opportunity to replicate this project at another institution when I graduate from UofL. That said, I feel like I have a lot still to learn about this kind of work. For instance, because the tasks were divided up so much from the outset and because Mary P already had such good relationships established with the schools, I still have a lot to learn about the "behind-the-scenes" work or how to get a project like this one started. I would like to continue having conversations with Mary P and other faculty who have started and sustained community engagement projects to learn more about these aspects of community engagement. I feel like DMA has been an excellent experience in getting to carry out a community engagement project, though, and I have appreciated the chance to design and teach this program and hope to have an opportunity to do a similar project in the future.
>
> – Keri, 2015 Camp Blog, https://dma2015research.wordpress.com/2015/06/25/day-nine/

work done in institutions—no easy feat)." Gramer continued, "For me, the notion of groups coming together and dispersing as needed is something that happened

---

the University of Louisville's Gender Equity Award, the Dr. Mary K. Bonsteel Tachau Award in 2015 largely based on my work with DMA.

with DMA as a whole, and then again in our smaller groups (pedagogy, tech). And then these experiences spread into other projects with other folks in different configurations," which included curricular, extra-curricular, and community-engaged projects. As Gramer pointed out, the "doing" that happened in DMA facilitated other kinds of "doing" (e.g., teaching, researching); having developed skills and dispositions central to community-engaged scholar-teachers, these graduate students sought out additional opportunities for deep learning (possibly threshold experiences), often in community-engaged projects.

This knotworking happened on timescales beyond any one iteration of DMA. During the second annual DMA, one graduate student returned, and four graduate students and one faculty member joined as new DMA teachers. I continued as an initial leader, especially with ongoing structural aspects (e.g., securing funding; selecting teachers and community partners; negotiating for space and resources; liaising with community partners and outside publicity). Meanwhile, the returning teacher, Megan Hartline, took on many leadership roles related to the everyday, informal mentoring of new DMA teachers.

As the camp approached, power again shifted away from the more seasoned participants and became better distributed across all DMA teachers, who again chaired the various subcommittees needed to ensure DMA's success. The following year, this knotworking reconfigured yet again as participants and participation roles continue to change. Dr. Andrea Olinger was the primary faculty member; one teacher, Michelle Day, returned, and four were new; and, our DMA knotworked group again braided together, pursuing goals determined by new participants with new priorities, new histories, and new projected futures. What remains constant is the opportunity for deep learning, both with hands-on experiences to renegotiate power relations, thereby allowing participants interested in community engagement to wrestle with the complexities of such labor, and with opportunities for reflection, thereby helping participants articulate the dissonances and possibilities such profound and uncommon opportunities for feminist-infused knowledge making can provide.

CONCLUSION

If we in Writing Studies share the threshold concept that doing is the leading edge of learning, the question for our field is how do we foster the type of doing/learning that can change the way people orient their thinking and themselves. Threshold experiences are designed to do just that, and these experiences may be particularly beneficial when we encourage students to wrestle with threshold concepts seldom modeled in traditional education structures, such as concepts surrounding community engagement. Yet to provide graduate students with these experiences that generally exceed the course of a semester, we need new models of graduate education. Knotworking collaborations within feminist community-engaged frameworks—particularly with attention to power dynamics, participation roles, and knowledge creation—provides one model of such a threshold experience, as DMA illustrates.

As a feminist community-engaged project, DMA not surprisingly follows Rich's exhortation that a research institution "should organize its resources around problems specific to its community" (1979, p. 152). For example, DMA attempts to loosen the barriers between the University of Louisville and the surrounding community by inviting local girls who may never have been on a college campus to a free, two-week camp, where they are provided with meals, technology when they leave (e.g., an iPod touch), hands-on opportunities to learn about and play with top-of-the-line equipment, and conversations about possible local resources and structural obstacles girls face in their education and in their communities. We teachers are provided with opportunities to develop long-term partnerships with local schools so that we can better learn with and from this

> I'm really glad I got to experience DMA for a second time. Much of the project was the same, but it was also very different. And I liked getting to work on assessment and technology after doing logistics and pedagogy last year. I'm really grateful for the experience to do this type of engaged work—as service, as pedagogy, and as research. I realized over the course of the year that these types of experiences are not universal for graduate students, and I think it's really helpful for those of us who want to do this type of scholarship. And it's a great opportunity to do research, think about pedagogy in a different way, and take on the logistical challenges of administrative work.
>
> – 2015 Camp, https://dma 2015research.wordpress .com/2015/06/25/day-nine/

community about what resources they find available and what is needed for girls and ourselves, individually and collectively, to become genuine problem-solvers. Together, we explore how shared experiences with digital composing can help create structures that call for and temporarily create more interesting, equitable, and engaging worlds for all of us.

It is the *process* of pursuing that goal that marks DMA as a knotworking collaboration focused on the messy efforts inherent in being a feminist community-engaged faculty. Much of this collaboration is premised on creating opportunities to develop new roles and new ways of doing that can lead to new skills and new dispositions.

Figure 11.3. "J" and "L'N" share with Keri Mathis their ideas for the final showcase video. After working at DMA, Keri worked for Dean Beth Boehm to collaboratively run the Community Engagement Academy (Chapter 6, this collection), a project that supports graduates students from across the university for community-engaged projects of their own.

And it is through opportunities to engage in and reflect upon these experiences that we help graduate students learn what it means to be a feminist community-engaged scholar.

This work is not easy. For example, one obstacle we face is addressing hierarchical structures that make it difficult for graduate students to take up new knowledge-making roles. This is he case at DMA. In the first two cohorts, all teachers took classes I taught during the year they taught at DMA; I serve on 9 of the 10 teachers' dissertation committees and was chair of the 10th teacher's culminating MA project. Power is present. Although we overtly created opportunities to negotiate this during DMA, the ground work for redressing traditional power dynamics was ongoing.[11] For instance, prior to DMA, we incrementally reworked traditional graduate student-faculty roles (e.g., we collaborated on campus workshops and national conference presentations with each of us focusing on our own areas of ex-

---

11   Graduate school often provides thick networks of varied interactions (classes, community projects, shared learning opportunities, social occasions) across extended periods of time, which can facilitate such renegotiations. These varied and extended opportunities are less common for undergraduates. In this collection, see Mathis and Boehm as well as Brandt et al. for examples.

pertise; I asked graduate students to lead campus workshops on topics where they had more digital expertise than I; graduate students took primary responsibility for segments of a national conference I ran, such as creating a digital archive or co-editing print publications emerging from the conference). At DMA, graduate students took the lead in making a particular iteration of the camp, whether in teaching their specializations to all of us (e.g., Michelle Day's workshop on trauma informed training; Sara Alvarez's workshop on culturally sustaining pedagogy) or perhaps just to me (e.g., Elizabeth's Chamberlain's digital tutorials; Rachel Gramer's refresher course on teacher training). After DMA, they accepted my push for research and teaching projects to come out of DMA, but tweaked my suggestions to demystify available power structures for women and girls' participation in digital media (Blair & Tulley, 2007; Jaschik, 2013; Juhasz & Balsamo, 2012) to pursue projects *they* cared about; building on their understandings of themselves as problem-posers, they asserted their knowledge creation. Throughout this process, these students enacted feminist epistemologies and methodologies within *and beyond* the extended moment of doing DMA. Such threshold experiences, I believe, were facilitated by the conscious attention to modulating power dynamics—a practice that had the added benefit of encouraging buy-in, often a concern if a project feels foisted upon graduate students (Rickly & Harrington, 2002).

Figure 11.4. Elizabeth Chamberlain helps "M" realize her goals for creating her "I Am" project. After reflecting on such DMA experiences, Elizabeth altered how she positioned herself on the job market the following year. (Photo Credit: Stone, 2014)

As DMA illustrates, knotworking collaborations are messy and complex, requiring flexibility and time that exceed more traditional academic experiences. Nonetheless, by providing such alternative models of graduate education, such collaborations encourage graduate students to tactically join together to *do* (rather than solely imagine or read about others doing), which can help graduate students understand themselves and their disciplinary projects in new ways.

Moreover, the collaborative braiding and rebraiding of these deep-learning projects help all of us investigate our future identities as faculty, as we come together in joint activity, then go our own ways, possibly changed for having taken part in the process. Such time-intensive threshold experiences provide an alternative model of graduate education that can pave the way for training future cohorts of feminist community-engaged teacher-scholars.

REFERENCES

Adler-Kassner, L. & Wardle, E. A. (2015). *Naming what we know: Threshold concepts of writing studies.* Logan, UT: Utah State University Press.

Bisignani, D. (2014). Transgressing intellectual boundaries begins with transgressing physical ones: Feminist community engagement as activist-apprentice pedagogy. In S. V. D. Iverson & J. H. James (Eds.), *Feminist community engagement: Achieving praxis* (pp. 93–111). New York, NY: Palgrave.

Blair, K. L. & Tulley, C. (2007). Whose research is it anyway? The challenge of deploying feminist methodology in technological spaces. In H. A. McKee & D. N. DeVoss (Eds.), *Digital writing research: Technologies, methodologies, and ethical issues* (pp. 303–317). Cresskill: Hampton Press.

Blair, K. L., Fredlund, K., Hauman, K., Hurford, E., Kastner, S. & Witte, A. (2011). Cyberfeminists at play: Lessons on literacy and activism from a girls' computer camp. *Feminist Teacher, 22*(1), 43–59.

Borman, G. D. (2000). The effects of summer school: Questions answered, questions raised. *Monographs of the Society for Research in Child Development 65*(1), 119–27.

Bowen, L. M., Arko, K., Beatty, J., Delaney, C., Dorpenyo, I., Moeller, L., Robers, E. & Velat, J. (2014). Community engagement in a graduate-level community literacy course. *Community Literacy Journal, 9*(1), 18–38.

Brandt, J. & Kozma, C. (2018). Learning together through campus-community partnerships. In K. L. Blair & L. Nickoson (Eds.), *Composing feminist interventions: Activism, engagement, praxis.* Fort Collins, CO: The WAC Clearinghouse / Louisville, CO: University Press of Colorado. Retrieved from https://wac.colostate.edu/books/perspectives/feminist.

Butin, D. (2014). Preface. In S. V. D. Iverson & J. H. James (Eds.), *Feminist community engagement: Achieving praxis* (pp. vii–x). New York, NY: Palgrave.

Campus Compact. (2013). *Creating a culture of assessment, 2012 annual member survey.* Retrieved from http://www.compact.org/wp-content/uploads/2013/04/Campus-Compact-2012-Statistics.pdf.

Carnegie Classification of Institutions of Higher Education. Retrieved from http://carnegieclassifications.iu.edu/.

Center for Budget and Policy Priorities. (2014, May 1). State funding for higher education remains far below pre-recession levels in most states: changes in state spending per student, inflation adjusted, FY08-FY14. *Center for Budget and Policy Priorities*. Retrieved from http://www.cbpp.org/research/states-are-still-funding-higher-education-below-pre-recession-levels.

Chamberlain, E., Gramer, R. & Faver Hartline, M. (2015). Mess not mastery: Encouraging digital design dispositions in girls. *Computers and Composition Online*. Retrieved from http://cconlinejournal.org/fall15/dma/.

Concannon, K., et al. (2018). Crafting partnerships: Exploring student-led feminist strategies for community literacy projects. In K. L. Blair & L. Nickoson (Eds.), *Composing feminist interventions: Activism, engagement, praxis*. Fort Collins, CO: The WAC Clearinghouse / Louisville, CO: University Press of Colorado. Retrieved from https://wac.colostate.edu/books/perspectives/feminist.

Costa, L. & Leong, K. (2013). Critical and feminist civic engagements: A review. *Feminist Teacher, 22*(3), 266–276.

Deans, T. (2013). Sustainability deferred: the conflicting logics of career advancement and community engagement. In J. Restaino & L. J. C. Cella (Eds.), *Unsustainable: re-imagining community literacy, public writing, service learning, and the university* (pp. 101–11). Lanham: Lexington Books.

Duffy. J. (2012, March 16). Virtuous arguments. *Inside Higher Ed*. Retrieved from https://www.insidehighered.com/.

Engeström, Y., Engeström, R. & Vähäaho, T. (1999). When the center does not hold: The importance of knotworking. In S. Chaiklin, M. Hedegaard & U. J. Jensun (Eds.), *Activity theory and social practice: Cultural-historical approaches* (pp. 345–74). Oxford, England: Aarhus University Press.

Feigenbaum, P. (2008). The push and pull of being publicly active in graduate school. *Reflections, 7*(3). Retrieved from http://reflectionsjournal.net.

Fero, M., Ridolpho, J., Chrobak, J. M., Can Duinen, D. C., Wirtz, J., Cushman, E. & Grabill, J. T. (2008). A reflection on teaching and learning in a community literacies graduate course. *Community Literacy Journal, 1*(2), 81–93.

Flower, L. (2008). *Community literacy and the rhetoric of public engagement*. Carbondale, IL: Southern Illinois University Press.

Gee, J. P. (2003). *What video games have to teach us about learning and literacy*. New York, NY: Palgrave Macmillan.

Gramer, R. (2015, March). Designing a new camp curriculum of digital collaboration: What the teachers learned. Presentation at the Conference on College Composition and Communication, Tampa, FL.

Gramer, R. (2015, September 27). Personal communication.

Harrison, B., Clayton, P. H. & Tilley-Lubbs, G.A. (2014). Troublesome knowledge, troubling experience: an inquiry into faculty learning in service-learning. *Michigan Journal of Community Service Learning, 20*(2), 5–18.

Hartline, M. F. (2015, March). What counts as success? Examining the digital literacy practices of middle-school girls. Presentation at the Conference on College Composition and Communication, Tampa, FL.

Hartline, M. F. (2015, October). Engaged scholars in the making: Designing, teaching, and researching the Digital Media Academy. Presentation at the Conference on Community Writing, Boulder, CO.

Hoyt, L. (2010). A city-campus engagement theory from, and for, practice. *Michigan Journal of Community Service Learning, 17*(1), 75–88.

Iverson, S. V. D. & James, J. H. (2014). *Feminist community engagement: Achieving praxis.* New York, NY: Palgrave Macmillan.

Jaschik, S. (2013, August 19). Feminist anti-mooc. *Inside Higher Ed.* Retrieved from https://www.insidehighered.com/.

Jenkins, H. (2009). *Confronting the challenges of participatory culture: Media education for the 21st century.* Cambridge, England: MIT Press.

Juhasz, A. & Balsamo, A. (2012). An idea whose time is here: FemTechNet—an online distributed online collaborative course (DOCC). *ADA: A Journal of Feminism, Science, Technology & Media 1*(1). Retrieved from http://adanewmedia.org/2012/11/issue1-juhasz/.

Launius, C. & Hassel, H. (2015). *Threshold concepts in women's and gender studies: Ways of seeing, thinking and knowing.* Routledge. Taylor and Francis Group, New York. Retrieved from http://samples.sainsburysebooks.co.uk/9781317656449_sample_867920.pdf.

Lave, J. & Wenger, E. (1991). *Situated learning: Legitimate peripheral participation.* Cambridge, England: Cambridge University Press.

Lindquist, J. (2012). A time to grow them: practicing slow research in a fast field. *JAC: A Journal of Rhetoric, Culture & Politics, 32*(3–4), 645–666.

Mathieu, P. (2013) After tactics, what comes next? In J. Restaino & L. J. C. Cella (Eds.), *Unsustainable: re-imagining community literacy, public writing, service learning, and the university* (pp. 17–31). Lanham: Lexington Books.

Mathis, K. E. & Boehm, B. A. (2018). Building engaged interventions in graduate education. In K. L. Blair & L. Nickoson (Eds.), *Composing feminist interventions: Activism, engagement, praxis.* Fort Collins, CO: The WAC Clearinghouse / Louisville, CO: University Press of Colorado. Retrieved from https://wac.colostate.edu/books/perspectives/feminist.

Mena, J. & Vaccaro, A. Role modeling community engagement for college students: narratives from women faculty and staff of color. In S. V. D. Iverson & J. H. James (Eds.), *Feminist community engagement: achieving praxis* (pp. 53–74). New York, NY: Palgrave.

Meyer, J. H. F. & Land, R. (2003). Threshold concepts and troublesome knowledge: Linkages to ways of thinking and practicing. In C. Rust (Ed.), *Improving student learning—theory and practice ten years on* (pp. 412–424). Oxford, England: Oxford Centre for Staff and Learning Development.

Miller, S. L., Brueggemann, B. J., Blue, B. & Shepherd, D. M. (1997). Present perfect and future imperfect: Results of a national survey of graduate students in rhetoric and composition programs. *CCC, 48*(3), 392–409.

Moore, C. & Miller, H. (2006). *A guide to professional development for graduate students in English*. Urbana, IL: NCTE.

National Summer Learning Association. (2009). Know the facts. *National Summer Learning Association*. Retrieved from http://www.summerlearning.org/?page=know_the_facts.

New England Resource Center for Higher Education. Carnegie community engagement classification. *New England Resource Center for Higher Education*. Retrieved from http://nerche.org/index.php?option=com_content&view=article&id=341&Itemid=92#CE%20def.

O'Meara, K. A. (2008). Graduate education and community engagement. *New Directions for Teaching and Learning, 113*, 27–42.

Orr, C. (2011). Women's studies as civic engagement: research and recommendations. A Teagle Foundation White Paper prepared on behalf of The Teagle Working Group on Women's Studies and Civic Engagement and the National Women's Studies Association.

Perry, K. (2018). Literacy sponsorship as a process of translation: Using actor-network theory to analyze power within emergent relationships at Family Scholar House. In K. L. Blair & L. Nickoson (Eds.), *Composing feminist interventions: Activism, engagement, praxis*. Fort Collins, CO: The WAC Clearinghouse / Louisville, CO: University Press of Colorado. Retrieved from https://wac.colostate.edu/books/perspectives/feminist.

Prior, P. (1998). *Writing/disciplinarity: A sociohistoric account of literate activity in the academy*. Mahwah, NJ: Lawrence Erlbaum Associates.

Prior, P. (2015). Community. In P. Heilker & P. Vandenberg (Eds.), *Keywords in writing studies* (pp. 26–31). Logan, UT: Utah State University Press.

Rich, A. (1979). Towards a woman-centered university. In *On lies, secrets, and silence: Selected prose, 1966–1978* (pp. 125–155). New York, NY: Norton.

Rickly, R. J. & Harrington, S. (2002). Feminist approaches to mentoring teaching assistants: Conflict, power, and collaboration. In B. P. Pytlik & S. Liggett (Eds.), *Preparing college teachers of writing: Histories, theories, programs, practices* (pp. 108–120). New York, NY: Oxford University Press.

Selber, S. (2004). *Multiliteracies for a digital age*. Urbana, IL: Conference on College Composition and Communication, NCTE.

Sheridan, M. P. (2014). Responsivity: Defining, cultivating, enacting. *JAC, 34*(1–2), 11–24.

Sheridan, M. P., Gramer, R. & Hartline, M. (2014–15). Digital Media Academy: Designing responsive structures of graduate student professionalization. CCCC Research Initiative Grant, Conference on College Composition and Communication.

Sheridan, M. P. (2015). Extending Scholarship in Composition's responsive reach. *CCC, 66*(4), 689–693.

Sheridan, M. P. (2015, March). The promise and pitfalls of feminist frameworks as responsive practice: Conversations on risk and reward. Presentation at the Conference on College Composition and Communication, Tampa, FL.

Sheridan, M. P. (2015, April). Graduate student mentoring through community engagement. Talk presented for panel, Leveraging your digital scholarship for community engagement. Engaged Scholarship in Action Series, University of Louisville.

Sheridan, M.P. (2015, June). *Coding and Community at the Digital Media Academy*, The Verizon Foundation.

Sheridan, M. P. (2015, October). Paving the way: Efforts to promote community engagement in graduate student programs at the University of Louisville. Presentation at the Conference on Community Writing, Boulder, CO.

Sosnoski, J. & Burmester, B. (2006). New scripts for rhetorical education: Alternative learning environments and the master/apprentice model. In V. Anderson & S. Romano (Eds.), *Culture shock and the practice of profession: Training the next wave in rhetoric and composition* (pp. 325–46). Cresskill, NJ: Hampton Press.

Stoecker, R. & Tryon, E. (2009). *Unheard voices: Community organizations and service learning*. Philadelphia: Temple University Press.

Stone, M. (Photographer). (23 June 2014). In D. Carter (Reporter), U of L academy teaches girls to make eye-opening videos. *The Courier Journal*. Retrieved from https://www.courier-journal.com/story/life/2014/06/23/middle-school-girls-learning-master-technology/11270629 .

U.S. Department of Commerce Economics and Statistics Administration. (2011, August). Women in STEM: A gender gap to innovation. *U.S. Department of Commerce Economics and Statistics Administration*. Retrieved from http://www.esa.doc.gov/sites/default/files/reports/documents/womeninstemagaptoinnovation8311.pdf.

Webb, P., Cole, K. & Skeen, T. (2007). Feminist social projects: building bridges between communities and universities. *College English 69*(3), 238–259.

Wenger, E. (1998). *Communities of practice: Learning, meaning, and identity*. Cambridge, England: Cambridge University Press.

PART 3. ACTIVISM

CHAPTER 12.

WOMEN-ONLY BICYCLE RIDES AND FREEDOM OF MOVEMENT: HOW ONLINE COMMUNICATIVE PRACTICES OF LOCAL COMMUNITY MANAGERS SUPPORT FEMINIST INTERVENTIONS

Angela Crow
James Madison University

This chapter examines the rhetorical practices of a group of women bicycle riders, Staunton, Virginia's Women on Wheels, who wanted to create a safe and welcoming space for women new to cycling. At first glance, a "women's only" cycling night, a separate "Women's cycling group" Facebook page (with male members) and a website wouldn't necessarily represent activism, but as Rachel Aldred, et al.'s (2015) statistics suggest, "in low-cycling countries, cycling is not evenly distributed across genders and age groups" (p. 1). For Crow, the Staunton group creates a low stakes environment in which women can begin to bicycle within a community of welcoming cyclists. Drawing on contemporary research in mobility studies, particularly focused on women cyclists and discipline-specific discussions about online activist strategies in social media venues such as Facebook and Twitter, along with relevant conversations in material rhetorics, this chapter documents one community's take on contemporary community literacy practices.

Whether in Britain or the United States, contemporary reports on bicycling and women studies indicate that women ride bicycles at lower rates than men. The League of American Bicyclists marks the number at 24% of all cyclists (Jones, 2015) based on the 2009 National Household Travel Survey (Milne, 2014), numbers similar to those in Britain (Lacker; Aldred, 2012), but in England, columnists are quick to point out that just across the way, Denmark and the Netherlands boast gender equity in bicycle usage. They use those percentages to argue for safer infrastructures in England (Lacker; Haddad, 2010; Aldred, 2015). In the States, some research suggests that women would cycle more if issues of convenience, infrastructure, and bike friendly places were addressed (What would cause you, 2011). Of those three, infrastructure is often cited as the leading reason that women don't cycle (Broache, 2012; Chalabi, 2014). However, Liz Cornish Jones (2015) reminds readers that the solutions require more than an improved infrastructure for bicyclists. As she notes, women's reasons for not cycling also are dependent on "complex equation of interlocking variables" (p. 6). In addition to risk concerns, women are "more likely to travel with passengers, often small children" (p. 5), more likely "to commute to work or run errands than men" (p. 5; Akar, et al., 2013, p. 349), and Jones encourages readers to consider the importance of understanding how "sexism, racism, homophobia, ableism, classism" (p. 5) participate in women's choices. These factors affect a woman's decisions regarding transportation and influence her freedom of movement.

While some of the disparity in numbers may rest with children and errand obligations, in the Netherlands, women still participate at the same rate as men, while still attending to family needs. Companies and institutions, aware of the health costs associated with immobility, understand the importance of creating bike friendly and walkable cities, accessible to all members of a community (Step it Up, 2016; Florida, 2012; 2014). In the States, in locations in which the infrastructure has been radically improved, but women aren't yet participating in numbers comparable to the men, companies like Citi-bike in NYC, explore different methods to raise women's rentals of their bicycles from the current 21% (Fitzsimmons, 2015). Specifically, they have explored the possibility that women might consider participating if they could try out bicycling in a low stakes, low speed environment, surrounded only by other women.

Women, these articles argue, might well take to the streets even in locations with a paucity of adequate infrastructure if only the right kind of encouraging community existed. While most of the attention is focused, in national articles, on large city streets, similar arguments would hold for small towns like mine. In the midst of two new county bike and pedestrian plans that are helping to raise awareness and shape policy, a local women's bicycling group has explored a range of strategies for encouraging women and in 2015 moved to "women-only" rides, a decision that reflects a larger trend whether in the states or in England where similar groups are flourishing. In fact, Citi Bike has chosen to collaborate with local women cycling groups (Fitzsimmons, 2015) as one approach to their marketing agenda. Whether in rural or urban spaces, women who already have the habit of bicycling may be puzzled by these groups and wonder about their necessity (Haddad, 2010), but women only bicycling communities seem to be beneficial because women find these venues more conducive to building "confidence" and because women may want "to ask gender-specific questions, from tips on what to do when skirts get caught in back brakes, to the more intimate issues regarding saddles and underwear" (Diane Foster, interviewed in Haddad, 2010).

Women also may want to ride with women for an increased sense of safety in numbers, a worry about being dropped on a ride, and a concern with cycling compatibility. Dawn Foster argues that "cycling alone on roads, especially in cities, can be unnerving and whenever I've ridden with male friends I always worry I won't be able to keep up" (Cited in Haddad's blog, 2015). This desire for a women's only space has seen the growth of funded projects like the women only "Breeze" rides in Britain (Lacker) and Cycletta, a group focused on women only event rides in England (Haddad, 2015). The approach is similar perhaps to a range of organizations formal and informal in the States that include "women on wheels" groups, and racing support sites like Girl Bike Love and Cyclofemme (supported by the League of American Bicyclists). While these groups and their rides predominantly are focused on pleasure and exercise, they may eventually lead women to try commuting or to participate in local infrastructure improvement initiatives. In the nineties, texts like *Meeting at the Crossroads* (1992) and *Women's Ways of Knowing* (1986) proved helpful for understanding how a range of women internalized messages regarding appropriate risk-taking for women, and these texts continue to seem relevant in trying to understand the strategy of women-centric events like the Disney marathons and this local group's experience.

At first glance, bicycling may not seem like an obvious venue for feminist rhetorical interventions in the United States; however, social and physical mobilities intersect with material and cultural capital (Zayas & Stanley, 2015; Urry, 2012; Aldred, 2015), shaping the options for how women literally move from place to place. As feminist scholars we participate in a very different "moving whole" (Bennett 2010), a very different relation to mobility depending on region, and whether we inhabit sub/urban or rural environments, depending as well on a range of identity markers that may or may not allow us easy passage. We also witness others' freedom of movement and know implicitly who can move where, who can literally travel easily across the country in an automobile without much fear of being pulled over by the police, who can afford the financial costs of evacuating a city during a hurricane, who is welcome on sidewalks or on bicycles in various neighborhoods within a range of towns and cities. Literal physical freedom of movement plays a part in an individual's shaping of her imaginary regarding social mobility, and factors into an individual's relationship to health and happiness (Florida). In many ways, studying women's choices for transportation, I'm reminded of Linda Brodkey's text, *Writing Permitted in Designated Areas Only* (1996). Women, choosing alternative forms of transportation, raise, through their placement of themselves in the roads differently, questions about the kinds of stories that are appropriate regarding mobility and freedom of movement. Some would argue that when we accept and defend car-centric framings for transportation policy, we stack the deck against the possibility of increasing social interactions (Aldred, "Disappearing Traffic" (2015); Appleyard's traffic map in Britton (2011), and limit a person's literal possibilities for moving. Street design is intertwined with social mobility whether in cities or small towns and in both venues, sidewalks, separated bike lanes/roads, and public transportation exist intermittently, affecting the possibility of safe transit for those not able to afford access to their own or others' motorized vehicles.

In addition, in the States, motor vehicle crashes remain one of the leading causes of death with 33,000 deaths in 2013 alone (Key Injury, 2015), a risk that a recent study suggests, disproportionately affect the poor and uneducated for a number of potential reasons, not the least of which is limited access to newer cars with better safety features (Badger & Ingraham, 2015), but instead of an impatience with these mortalities that one can find in the Netherlands' responses in the seventies (Powers, 2013; Van der Zee, 2015; Jordan 2013), in the States, we seem to take these risks as necessary for our economic stability. What would it mean for us as a nation to respond to these deaths and to global warming concerns with goals that move us "Beyond Traffic" (Jaffe, 2015). The last Department of Transportation budget proposal submitted by President Obama to congress shifted "away from car reliance toward the type of mobility system better suited to cities" (Jaffe, 2016). If one expands this emphasis to rural spaces as well, significant transformation of streets could mirror changes in street design in New York City (Sadik-Khan, 2016).

As it stands now, whether in cities or rural venues, if we suggest that more people might consider bicycling as a viable means of commuting to work, we may hear people say that traveling by bike is too risky because of distracted motorists (Sadik-Khan, 2016), and instead of creating reasonable changes to existing infrastructure that would improve safety (see, for example, Macon's pop up bike lanes (Rogers, 2016) or Sadik-Khan's description of NYC in her Ted talk 2013), contemporary news coverage often report bicycle / motorist crashes with strategies that implicitly and explicitly suggest that the bicyclist shouldn't have taken the risk in the first place. In the coverage of crashes, in other words, often the onus for safety rests with the cyclist (Weiss, 2015). Were her clothing choices bright enough? Was she visible? Instead of asking local transportation authorities to make relatively inexpensive changes that would radically improve safety for all users on roads, the inclination has been to see bicyclists as taking unnecessary risks, simply by choosing to be on these roads that car-centric perspectives would see as exclusively devoted to motorized travel. Given what we also know about how women and men are trained to take up and engage with risk differently, we can anticipate that women may hear these risk messages differently than men and might be more inclined to limit their activities accordingly (Slovic, 1999; Harris, Jenkins & Glazer, 2006).

BICYCLE ADVOCACY, FREEDOM OF MOVEMENT, AND FEMINIST RHETORICS

> Let me tell you what I think of bicycling. I think it has done more to emancipate women than anything else in the world. It gives women a feeling of freedom and self-reliance. I stand and rejoice every time I see a woman ride by on a wheel . . . the picture of free, untrammeled womanhood. —Susan B. Anthony (qtd in Women's Rights Movement, 2013)

Throughout my career, I have been interested in adult literacy centers, and the politics of defining and teaching functional literacy. This interest has morphed as different technologies have intersected with literacy instruction. Wanting to explore embodied literacies, I chose to become certified to teach people how to bicycle more safely on roads. As Royster and Kirsch (2012) suggest, my interest reflected a trend in field—"scholars are much more willing to . . . "identify material practices that may not include written words (though perhaps stitched words), and expand the genres we consider worthy of study" (Kindle 897–900). Like all of my other experiences volunteering in literacy centers, this experience has been a humbling one, as I discover just how complicated a functional literacy can be. I have struggled to explain to new riders how to use their bodies to speak a particular message when cycling on roads. I try to speak to the set of possible moves that might help a person to join the flow of that traffic, try to talk about how one reads and assesses others' messages as one travels, try to show, with demonstrations, how to move one's body as if one were a large sign, indicating one's intentions.

Riding a bike requires an embodied way of knowing. Not only must one learn to balance and propel the bike forward, but cycling requires repetitive scanning, in order to adapt to a constant set of changing environmental factors. It requires understanding the ability to read "text" as including a range of alphabetic signs, images, lines on the road, and movement created by other participants, or in Kristie Fleckenstein's framework from *Embodied Literacies* (2003), it requires the ability to enact an image that produces the desired relationships.

Her idea of the play between imagetext and relationships seems an apt description of what happens on roads in the complex ecology of imagetexts articulated there, for all motorists, cyclists, and pedestrians. A female bicyclist may not feel comfortable taking up the smaller space offered by a bicycle when negotiating with large motorized vehicles. However, women who take up bicycling in women only group spaces may find that they more easily learn to embody a message that informs other motorists and bicyclists of intentions through the set of the shoulders, through the maintenance of a clear line, the wheel a consistent distance from the curb. If a woman joins a group of five women cycling, and all five women signal to cars behind them their intent to make a left turn, she can feel more secure with the safety in numbers, and can, over time, accumulate the knowledge to create a larger presence when out on the roads alone.

At first glance, this essay's focus seems nothing like the courage needed to enter a race for a national office as Angela Zimmann describes (Chapter 16, this collection), or the kind of the courage Jessica Ouellette's study (Chapter 14, this collection) examines. Compared to the complexity of interactions in social media, given the challenge of negotiating highly charged political statements in transnational spaces, a bike ride seems tame in comparison. However, the very act of getting on a bicycle, of taking to the streets and suggesting an alternate form of mobility in a country that remains steadfastly car-centric requires a certain courage. When these women take a weekly ride, hoping to negotiate with people driving machines that could easily kill or harm the riders, that very act is one that could have radical future implications. These small recreational trainings in alternative forms of transportation might help local women to then turn to local advocacy, altering the strategies that have enabled mobility almost exclusively for those rich enough to afford automobiles.

In what follows, I focus on my local women's cycling group who frequently ride out together on the town's streets and rural roads. I suggest that in the small acts of facilitating group rides, in these simple practices, one community is in the process of shaping the possibility for much more (echoing here the hope of "tacking in" from Royster and Kirsch's text). I also hope to suggest the importance of understanding subtle and not so subtle nuances in seemingly monolithic audiences when considering online community management strategies. While companies like Citi Bike might want to collaborate on women's cycling face-to-face events, it matters to also study how local women's groups promote bicycling through their communicative practices. In other words, if we want to understand how women come to adopt these embodied literacies necessary to move on bicycles within existing transportation infrastructures, it's not enough to pay attention to the very literate demands necessary to create the embodied text (Fleckenstein, 2003; Marvyn, 1994) on the road. To see how these women learn the genres of the road, we need to pay attention to how local women leaders in these groups become social media community "managers" (Swarts, 2015; Blythe, Lauer and Curran, 2014) creating the online communicative practices that facilitate local action.

MOVING LOCALLY

In deciding on an organization for this essay, I chose to begin with a broader overview of bicycling and women's participation there, in part because cycling isn't a typical topic in our field, and while a woman's right to move freely about the country both literally and in terms of social mobility matters to women rhetoricians, I hoped that "tacking out" might provide a context, a "broader view," in which to situate a "tacking in" that "simulate[s] an interactive encounter with women who are not us, that is, the women whom we study" (Royster and Kirsch). While at first glance I might seem to fit the population of women I studied, one of the interesting outcomes from this research was a growing realization that part of these women's success came from the ways they understood the nuanced challenges of women who are not like me, who have chosen other life frames, different from my own, ones that affect their ability to pull out their bicycles and ride.

AN OVERVIEW OF THE GROUP

In 2012, a local woman, new to bicycling as an adult, created a Facebook group for women cyclists in our town. At the time, the other Facebook group, the general Staunton Cycling group was dormant, though with the rise of the posts on the women's group, the other site began to have more general posts. The women's group quickly began to have members, and they used a range of strategies to announce themselves. I found out about the group at the winter holidays, walking around the downtown park because the women cyclists had contributed a decorated bicycle and information about the group. I joined the group and occasionally participated in rides, following the calls for rides and seeing the pictures of riders out on the road. My research interest emerged because the third year's season was far more successful than the earlier two years' organized rides, and I wanted to understand what had happened. In the third year, the leaders changed their approach. Instead of calling many rides which included at least one beginner ride and one more advanced ride on different days each week (which meant they committed to attending those rides as well), they consolidated to one night, offering two rides—a short one and a long one, both leaving from the same location which allowed the leaders to commit to leading fewer rides. They moved the

243

starting point to the same location for every ride—a brewery that was opened before and after the ride, facilitating any needs to use restrooms and encouraging a social opportunity after the ride. These changes of strategy consolidated and simplified the message. They might change up the routes, but the group's venue, time, and type of rides wouldn't. In terms of online messaging, they notified the entire group on Facebook that these rides would be women only. They also started a listserv for women who weren't members of the Facebook group, or who weren't seeing the group's announcements in their Facebook Feeds.

In order to understand why these changes might have made a difference, I began this study by first logging every post, every like, every reply from July 2012 until August 2015. In the first year, three women, initial leaders of the group, posted most frequently and they reflected the identity markers of the community's membership: these three were married to men, were in their thirties and early forties, and had children still under their care. Most of the women in this group were predominantly heterosexual; most were married or divorced, between the ages twenty and sixty with the lion's share in their thirties and forties; many had children living at home; most were juggling a career, husbands, and children's activities. This group was predominantly white, predominantly marked as what counts as the middle class. The vast majority of the members, if not all, drove automobiles, and most lived within the town or nearby.

This women's group, located in the Shenandoah Valley, formed in 2012, at a point where women from these age groups and class locations were increasingly present on Facebook, and could quickly and easily track messages and posts through their cell phones (Duggan & Rainie, 2012; Duggan & Brenner, 2012). According to information on the Facebook page, the group aimed "to connect women cyclists within and around [the town] to ride with." In explaining the group on the external website created by one of the three women who started the group, the leaders summarized the online community further: "By empowering women with this connection to one another, women in the group noted that they were riding more frequently both within the group and on their own." In July 2012, several joined by way of invitation and word of mouth, and by the following year, the group counted over a hundred members.

While it may be feasible for a local women's group to maintain a vibrant organization without social media, any attempt to understand this local group requires a focus on the digital venue. For the leaders studied, they demonstrated an awareness not only of the targeted audience but a growing understanding (over the three years studied) of the possibilities and limitations of organizing rides and building community through social media. As several studies of social media have suggested, local groups often draw on social media in order to facilitate local face-to-face interactions and not as a means of connecting to strangers

(Hinton & Hjorth, 2013, p. 3). For these leaders, the more familiar they became with the venue selected, the more they played to its strengths and developed other resources for its weaknesses, demonstrating their increasingly sophisticated ability to act as social media managers (Blythe, Lauer & Curran, 2014) or community managers (Swarts, 2015; Frith, 2014) skilled at moderation. I discovered, by reviewing and categorizing all of the interactions, that these leaders tried in multiple ways, in multiple configurations, to reach out and draw in riders. The success in year three could be attributed to these women who never seemed to tire of trying different strategies in the first two years, building off of small successes, figuring out what worked. While they changed many different face-to-face variables—location, time, course, frequency—their communicative strategies stayed steadily focused on their group's goal. In other words, their styles for interaction didn't shift.

For the purposes of this venue, I want to focus on only a few issues, ones that suggest viable communicative strategies for local feminist interventions, and ones that highlight, in that tacking in, the differences between my ways of communicating and these women's ways, women who face different negotiation challenges than I do. I've been most interested in the ways this local group shapes its discourse in the midst of a predominantly heterosexual audience, living on the edges of what most would see as the South, a group of people with advanced degrees in a range of white collar professions. At a logistics level, I could have predicted some of the patterns and strategies for the group, but at the level of basic interactions amongst women and between men and women, I live in different social circles and communicate differently enough that I fear I might have alienated people, were I managing such a group without first understanding some of the community norms. As an academic from the Midwest, and as a queer woman, as someone who has chosen not to have children, I think I entered differently. In addition, bicycling has always been an activity I've enjoyed from early childhood until now. Mostly, I have chosen a bicycle as a form of recreation, though at times when I was in college and extremely poor, as transportation, and as a result, I am accustomed to riding out alone. Many of these women started cycling again only recently, in their thirties and forties. Because of my experience difference, I often forget the work involved in reaching a level of comfort about cycling on city streets, but the facilitators of this group were keenly aware of how it feels to start riding on city and rural streets as adults.

WHAT WORKED, GENERAL STATEMENTS

This group has obvious successful strategies. The three group leaders communicated a very specific goal—to offer more opportunities for women to ride out with other women. They were savvy about the medium, posting frequently (but not too frequently), calling predictable rides, encouraging others to call rides, and they each chose a role that increased the chances that the group's posts would make it into individual group members' feeds, according to the strategies available through Facebook in those years. Not only were they good at articulating the goal, and developing a method for calling rides, but each of the women took a role—one in community advocacy for improved infrastructure, one in announcing formal riding events in the region, and one for taking the time to encourage participation by responding to almost every post offered in the group, whether by "liking" the post or by commenting.

They decided on their goals, and their roles, and they decided, as well, on their tone. *This was a site that would encourage riders.* They decided to offer two rides a week, one challenging ride to reach a population of more experienced riders, and one beginning ride. People would indicate, in the first two years, whether they would attend so that the leaders would know whether to wait for riders, and in those first two years, people who indicated that they would attend, might also frequently post to the group, indicating a last-minute challenge and the need to drop out for that day. These leaders had a clear agenda: *no shaming* anyone for changing their mind about their availability for participating at any point in the process. In all the posts, over the first two years, with numerous people indicating that they would attend a ride and then dropping out, the tone of the responses to those cancelations is positive, a message of "next time," implicit or explicit in every response. *They maintained an encouraging and supportive tone for women* who were often juggling far too many responsibilities and who couldn't predict how others' changes in schedule would affect their own. *They requested informal feedback, often on the rides.* The leaders checked in frequently with riders, trying to assess what might create a better bicycling environment, and in their attempts to address concerns, they tried a host of different meeting points, times, and types of rides. They kept tinkering with rides that weren't working, and kept approaches that worked. *They also offered formal assessment* through an online survey after the season's end and made changes based on findings. For example, after the second year, when they realized that the algorithms weren't functioning for some of their members, they added an old-fashioned listserv, and started duplicating calls for ride in both venues.

COMMUNICATIVE CHALLENGES—GENDER

For a host of reasons, the leaders chose to move from rides attended predominantly by women to an announcement of Women Only rides at the beginning of the third season. Anyone could call a ride on any day at any location and include men in the call, but on Wednesday nights, only women were welcomed. The combination of a women's only ride that began and ended at a brewery, together with the decision to hold the harder, longer ride on the same night as the shorter, beginner's ride, and to announce those rides in two venues, seemed to work. Numbers jumped from 3–5 regular riders to between 15 and 30 riders. We might conclude that *face-to-face meeting points matter, that habits are formed by keeping many variables constant, that people want to be able to select a hard or easy ride at the time of the ride,* depending on how they felt after a long day. But what role did the gender only rule play?

The question of gender was one of the first challenges faced by the organizers. On the first day of the Facebook group's, one of the first posts came from a man I'll call Scott who wrote: "By its very title, it would seem that my genitalia disqualifies me from the group/rides. [frown emoticon] Boohoo." The leader (who I'll call Nadia) responded with the following encouraging comment: "Perhaps we should change the name to ladies and gentleman [sic] riders who are kind enough to ride at our meager paces." When I think about this response, I consider what I might say, in the same situation. While I would have responded politely, I fear that I wouldn't have been so welcoming and might have alienated a fair number of women who wouldn't have felt comfortable participating because their husbands were also reading interactions online, and it mattered to be welcoming to these men. To contrast, the leader's response conveyed a welcoming gesture that afforded this man and many others to join and follow along with the ride information posted to the group. Men felt comfortable calling rides and joining in on rides. It reminded me that in discussions of women's ways of communicating, even with a seemingly uniform population of people—predominantly white women of similar age groups with advanced degrees and living versions of a middle-class reality, we can miss the nuances of "woman." We aren't all the same, and I wasn't quite sure whether some of my ways of speaking were because of a queer framing, because I don't think about a male husband as weighing in on my bicycling activities, because I'm not really from the south (this region), or because of my academic enculturations.

While the group remained welcoming, after two years, leaders decided to experiment with this question of women only rides. On February 19, 2015 as the leaders turned towards the start of the next season for riding, the leader Nadia made the following initial announcement:

> Calling all Women Cyclists Join Us March 18th at 5:30 for some shop talk at [the local bike shop]. Come learn how to change a tire and hear about safe road cycling in groups in anticipation of our new Group ride. Women On Wheels A

new Wednesday evening women only group ride! Rides begin March 25th Drinks afterwards at [the local brewery]

On March 12, 2015, Nadia sent out a reminder about the shop talk, and then added this sentence: "If you want to receive emails about the route we will be doing each week please email groupemail@gmail.com and we will add you to the group ride list." One man liked the post, and Nadia sent out a friendly note: "Sorry, [Name of rider] we dearly love you but you are not invited. Muah," and he responded with: "Ha ha, I wasn't coming, I am just glad you all are doing this type of stuff!!!! You all have a bunch of fun!!"

In February, another of the leaders posted an announcement about the formation of an email listserv and asked for women's interests when they signed up for the listserv, emphasizing that there would be two venues—Facebook for general calls and the listserv for the women's only ride. One of the husbands responded with: Count me in!!!, and Nadia responds with: "These rides will be for ladies only. We love our men and are happy to have them join in afterwards for a drink but Wednesday rides will be women only!!! Yes, we are being exclusionary." The husband responded with "OK, let me know if I can help out in any way," and another husband also echoed that sentiment: "Interested in helping."

When announcing the listserv after two years of exclusive reliance on Facebook, they addressed a challenge they were experiencing with Facebook's algorithm—not all the people in the group were seeing the posts. And not all the women interested in the group wanted to be in the Facebook Group or they weren't on Facebook. But it became an opportunity for them to also emphasize the shifting nature of the rides, and by this time, the men who were responding knew that they were welcome to participate in the group—just not ride out on Wednesdays. They understood the group's agenda, looked forward to the beers afterwards, and were able to accept the terms.

Gender, it seemed mattered. Some women were only willing to consider participating once they knew that their enthusiastic husbands were not allowed to participate. In my informal conversations with the leaders about whether they would continue the women-only rides, they indicated that people who filled out the year end survey felt very strongly about keeping the women only rides. They wanted a place to ride and a time to ride with other women, at paces they enjoyed, without feeling like they were slowing down their husbands. Were I announcing the shift to a women only ride, I suspect that my language would match that offered by group leaders, but in the exchange with the individual men, I think I would have failed to include enough endearing terms—"we dearly love you;" "we love our men." These words would not come to mind, but clearly the men felt seen and wanted to offer support.

Were I group manager, I fear that I would have failed not only with the men but also with the women. When I discuss this research with friends, and I say this statement, sometimes I'll get a puzzled look from someone, and I'll offer a small example—I realized, in studying this group, that I try never to use the word "ladies," but these women often leaned on this word. While posts referred to women several times, but predominantly when linking to an article about women. To contrast, ladies was used in a range of situations, mostly as an introductory address but also some of the following kinds of instances:

> What time were you *ladies* thinking? Have fun ladies! You *ladies* have fun this afternoon; No centuries, *ladies; Ladies* (& Gents)—I'm new to biking again (what fun!). I nominate the fast *ladies* do a race in Waynesboro!; all pretty darn fast *ladies* are the folks I have heard from so far; We have a bunch *ladies* racing in Page County Saturday! Fourteen *fabulous ladies rocked it!* (etc).

While people also relied on the word "guys" (and with more frequency), which I might use, the words "darn fast ladies" would never be something I would write. I never would think to use the combination of "fabulous ladies" and rocking. Were I to take up a role of social media manager for this kind of group, having chosen to study the language choices carefully, I realize that one could learn the codes. I learned, from this study, that a new social media manager might benefit from studying the habits of posters—what words they use to address one another, how they welcome members or inform members that they're not welcome at some events.

In this group's case, the specific strategies for addressing the secondary audience draws on face saving gestures that afford men the ability to remain supportive. For the primary audience of new women riders, the leaders and participants are far more nurturing than I would expect. For example, every year, at least once or twice, new women riders post a query, asking about distance and speed. Sometimes when they ask, it's clear that they have no idea how quickly they ride; they have no speedometers. When the answer includes mph, the thought of a short ride—typically 10 miles—may intimidate but the rider also has no sense of distance. Once on the bike, 10 miles can pass very quickly. This group has had to hone its message on this repeated query. While the group routinely calls out rides, they try to encourage new riders who often join with very limited experience riding bicycles as adults. For example, in 2013, The following post and replies offer a typical example of this kind of exchange:

> **Jessica:** What exactly is a "beginner ride"? I am hoping not to bite off more than I can chew?

Hailey: 10 miles ish. You never know until you try [smile emoticon]. All bikes, hybrid, mountain, road welcome.

Nadia: We'll get you through; it's a hand-holding ride!

Jessica: I might need a pre-beginner ride [smile emoticon]. Perhaps I can work up to beginner by the time it gets warmish.

Melissa: Hi Jessica- I will ride with you and turn back with you whenever you want. I plan on riding the beginner ride tomorrow morning.

Nadia: And I'm doing today's (Wed) 5:30 ride from Valley Dance Theatre, and I can turn around, or stop and rest, whenever too.

Jessica: You guys are very kind and welcoming. I may attempt it next week.

New riders may in fact be intimidated by the thought of Hailey's casual statement of 10 miles, and often, with new riders, a sense of mileage and speed fail to help assess preparedness. Trying to reassure new riders is difficult because the new riders don't want to be a burden to the more experienced riders. However, the group members are sincere in their desire to help new riders. Melissa in the above example offers to ride with Jessica and turn back at any time; Most of the women in the group rode when they were young, until early teens, and many took up bicycling again when they joined this group, so they're not too far away from their own memories of starting to bicycle again. Nonetheless, this encouragement exchange is a challenging one, perhaps the most challenging of the types of communications for the group because it requires an embodied experience to assess preparedness. Because this exchange occurs yearly, by 2015, the message is shaped more clearly:

Ann asks: On average, how fast do the weekly rides go in mph?

Nadia responds with a message that's a little more developed than the answer in 2013: "We are not about speed. Our motto is no one is left behind. If I had to guess the 11-mile route averages 11mph and 20 mile Route averages 13mph. But again, speed is not the goal, getting out and riding safely on the road with women is the goal.

Hailey echoes Nadia's encouragement: "Come join us! Come out and ride! We'll let you ride any speed you want."

If a person then said that she couldn't meet at the time the group is riding, invariably someone will post a message asking for potential times the individual could ride. Consistently, this group indicates a desire to welcome new riders. For a community, trying to be welcoming, this response fits with the group leaders' approach to communication. This group responds, across the board, with encouragement, an approach established in the first interactions amongst the small group of initial leaders and continues in the three years of posts studied.

Community managers of this online social media group offer an example of a consistent message for the audience, a willingness to revise and rework their approaches for encouragement, and an ability to revise and rework venues and ride formats based on assessment suggest viable strategies for others engaged in community management online.

Their commitment to bicycle advocacy may not, at first glance, seem like a social justice movement, a feminist intervention, but in a climate in which women opt out of sustainable transportation not for a lack of interest but for a range of other concerns, this set of small moves matter. They open the space for women to have more freedom of movement. In addition, this group has led to women participating in local infrastructure interventions. Several of the leaders have volunteered with the city's advisory committee on bicycling and pedestrian concerns; others have signed up to learn how to teach bicyclists how to ride on roads.

When a woman decides that she can expand her mobility options to include bicycling, when she begins riding, worrying over speed and distance, and then gains the confidence to develop into someone who leads bicycling rides, that labor is an example of embodied literacies reshaping local possibilities not only for herself but for the larger community as well. This brief look at a local group suggests that freedom of movement might begin because of the safety of a welcoming women's only community.

REFERENCES

Akar, G., Fischer, N. & Namgung, M. (2013). Bicycling choice and gender case study: The Ohio State University. *International Journal of Sustainable Transportation, 7*(5), 347–365.

Aldred, R. (2015). Disappearing traffic? Retrieved from http://rachelaldred.org/writing/thoughts/disappearing-traffic/.

Aldred, R. (2012). The new mobilities paradigm and sustainable transport: Finding synergies and creating new methods. Retrieved from http://rachelaldred.org/wp-content/uploads/2012/10/Sustainable-Mobilities-8_edited-aldred-2.pdf.

Badger, Emily and Christopher Ingraham. (2015) The hidden inequality of who dies in car crashes. Retrieved from https://www.washingtonpost.com/news/wonk/wp/2015/10/01/the-hidden-inequality-of-who-dies-in-car-crashes/.

Bennett, J. (2010). *Vibrant matters: A political ecology of things*. Durham, NC: Duke University Press.

Belenky, M.F. (1986). *Women's ways of knowing: The development of self, voice, and mind*. New York, NY: Basic Books.

Beyond traffic 2045: Trends and choices draft. (2015) Report report prepared by the Department of Transportation, and presented by Anthony Foxx, Secretary of Transportation. Retrieved from https://www.transportation.gov/sites/dot.gov/files/docs/Draft_Beyond_Traffic_Framework.pdf.

Blythe, S., Lauer, C. & Curran, P.G. (2014). Professional and technical communication in a Web 2.0 world/ *Technical Communication Quarterly, 23*(4), 265–287.

Britton, E. (2011). Defining principles: Remembering Donald Appleyard. Retrieved from https://safestreetstrategies.wordpress.com/2011/12/20/defining-principles-remebering-donald-appleyard/.

Broache, A. (2012). *Perspectives on Seattle women's decisions to bike for transportation*. Master's thesis. University of Washington.

Brodkey, L. (1996). *Writing permitted in designated areas only*. Minneapolis, MN: University of Minnesota Press.

Brown, L.M & Gilligan, C. (1992). *Meeting at the crossroads: Women's psychology and girls' development*. Boston, MA: Harvard University Press.

Chalabi, M. (2014). Why women don't cycle. *Five Thirty Eight*. Retrieved from http://fivethirtyeight.com/datalab/why-women-dont-cycle/.

Duggan, M. & Brenner, J. (2012). The demographics of social media users—2012. *Pew Charitable Trust Report*. Retrieved from http://www.pewinternet.org/files/old-media//Files/Reports/2013/PIP_SocialMediaUsers.pdf.

Duggan, M. & Rainie, L. (2012). Cell phone activities: 2012. *Pew Charitable Trust Report*. Retrieved from http://www.pewinternet.org/files/old media//Files/Reports/2012/ PIP_CellActivities_11.25.pdf.

Fitzsimmons, E. G. (July 7, 2015). A mission for Citi Bike: Recruiting more female cyclists. *New York Times*.

Fleckenstein, K. (2003). *Embodied literacies: ImageWord and a poetics of teaching*. Normal, IL: Southern Illinois University Press.

Florida, R. (June 22, 2012). America's top cities for bike commuting: Happier, too. *The Atlantic: Citylab*.

Florida, R. (Dec 11, 2014). Walkability is good for you. *The Atlantic: CityLab*.

Frith, J. (2014). Forum moderation as technical communication: The social web and employment opportunities for technical communicators. *Technical Communication, 61*(3), 173–184.

Haddad, S. (May 24, 2010). Are women-only cycling events a good idea? *The Guardian*.

Harris, C.R., Jenkins, M. & Glaser, D. (2006). Gender differences in risk assessment: Why do women take fewer risks than men? *Judgment and Decision Making, 1*(1), 48–63.

Hinton, S. & Hjorth, L. (2013). *Understanding social media*. Los Angeles, CA: Sage.

Jaffe, E. (Feb 3, 2015). A 30-year plan for U.S. transportation summed up by one word: Choice. *The Atlantic-City Lab*. Retrieved from http://www.citylab.com

/commute/2015/02/a-30-year-plan-for-us-transportation-summed-up-by-one-word-choice/385111/.

Jaffe, E. (Feb 10, 2016). A bold transportation plan for urban America—Dead on arrival." *The Atlantic-City Lab*. Retrieved from http://www.citylab.com/cityfixer/2016/02/obama-budget-dot-transportation-2016/462021/.

Jones, L.C. (2015). Engaging more women in bicycling. *League of American Bicyclists*. Retrieved from http://issuu.com/bikeleague/docs/womens_outreach_report_waba_web?e=1335002/11573001

Jordan, P. (2013). *In the city of bikes: The story of the Amsterdam cyclist*. New York, NY: Harper.

Haddad, S. (May 24, 2011). Are women-only cycling events a good idea? *The Guardian*.

Key Injury and Violence Data. (Sept 30, 2015) *Within injury prevention & control: Data and statistics*. Retrieved from http://www.cdc.gov/injury/wisqars/overview/key_data.html.

Lacker, L. (n.d). Alpha males take a hike, women-only cycle rides are popping up all over the UK" *Bike Hub*. Retrieved from http://www.bikehub.co.uk/featured-articles/womenonlycycling/.

Marvin, C. (1994). The body of the text: Literacy's corporeal constant. *Quarterly Journal of Speech, 80*(2), 129–149.

Milne, A. (Sept 23, 2014). Who bikes and walks in the United States (and why). *Alliance for biking and walking*. Retrieved from http://www.bikewalkalliance.org/blog/401-who-bikes-and-walks-in-the-united-states-and-why-.

Murthy, V. (Sept. 2015). Step it up! The Surgeon General's call to action to promote walking and walkable communities. Retrieved from http://www.surgeongeneral.gov/ library/ calls/walking-and-walkable-communities/trials_102670.

Ouellette, J. (2018). The viability of digital spaces as sites for transnational feminist action and engagement: Why we need to look at digital circulation. In K. L. Blair & L. Nickoson (Eds.), *Composing feminist interventions: Activism, engagement, praxis*. Fort Collins, CO: The WAC Clearinghouse / Louisville, CO: University Press of Colorado. Retrieved from https://wac.colostate.edu/books/perspectives/feminist.

Powers, M. (Sept. 22, 2013). After every crash in Netherlands, intense scrutiny. *The Boston Globe*. Retrieved from https://www.bostonglobe.com/metro/2013/09/21/wake-bike-fatalities-government-response-demonstrates-support-for-cyclists/WGxTPDNw1pBm5ZUAP4IP9K/story.html.

Rogers, J. (Sept. 2016). Macon, GA to coordinate largest ever pop-up bike network. Retrieved from http://georgiabikes.org/blog/482-macon-ga-to-coordinate-largest-ever-pop-up-bike-network.

Royster, J.J. & Kirsch, G.E. (2012). *Feminist rhetorical practices: New horizons for rhetoric, composition, and literacy studies*. Carbondale, IL: Southern Illinois University Press, Kindle Edition.

Sadik-Khan, J. (2013). New York streets? Not so mean anymore. Retrieved from https://www.ted.com/talks/janette_sadik_khan_new_york_s_streets_not_so_mean_any_more?language=en.

Sadik-Khan, J. & Solomanow, S. (2015). *Streetfights: Handbook for an urban revolution.* New York, NY: Viking.

Slovic, P. (1999). Trust, emotion, sex, politics, and science: Surveying the risk-assessment battlefield. *Risk Analysis, 19*(4), 689–700.

Step It Up! (2016). The Surgeon General's call to action to promote walking and walkable communities. U.S. Department of Health and Human Services. Retrieved from http://www.surgeongeneral.gov/library/calls/walking-and-walkable-communities/.

Swarts, J. (2015). Help is in the helping: An evaluation of help documentation in a networked age. *Technical Communication Quarterly, 24*(2), 164–187.

Urry, J. (2012). Social networks, mobile lives and social inequalities. *Journal of Transport Geography, 21,* 24–30.

Van Der Zee, R. (May 5, 2015). How Amsterdam became the bicycling capital of the world. *The Guardian.* Retrieved from http://www.theguardian.com/cities/2015/may/05/amsterdam-bicycle-capital-world-transport-cycling-kindermoord.

Weiss, E. (April 15, 2015). Don't make bicyclists more visible. Make drivers stop hitting them. Mandatory helmet laws and glow-in-the-dark spray paint just show who really owns the roads. *The Washington Post.* Retrieved from https://www.washingtonpost.com/post everything/wp/2015/04/15/dont-make-bicyclists-more-visible-make-cars-stop-running-them-over/.

What would cause you to start or increase your cycling? (2011). *Women Cycling Project.* Retrieved from http://womencyclingproject.info/wp-content/uploads/2015/01/Causes_Q27_sm.pdf.

Women Cycling Project. (2017). Retrieved from http://womencyclingproject.info/women-cycling-survey/.

Women's Rights Movement of the Late Nineteenth Century. (n.d.) Cornwall Historical Society. Retrieved from http://cornwallhistoricalsociety.org/exhibits/women/late19th.html.

Zayas, A. & Stanley, K. (April 17, 2015). How riding your bike can land you in trouble with the cops—if you're black. Retrieved from http://www.tampabay.com/news/publicsafety/how-riding-your-bike-can-land-you-in-trouble-with-the-cops---if-youre-black/2225966.

Zimmann, A. (2018). A peek inside the master's house: The tale of feminist rhetorician as candidate for U.S. congress. In K. L. Blair & L. Nickoson (Eds.), *Composing feminist interventions: Activism, engagement, praxis.* Fort Collins, CO: The WAC Clearinghouse / Louisville, CO: University Press of Colorado. Retrieved from https://wac.colostate.edu/books/perspectives/feminist.

CHAPTER 13.
LITERACY, PRAXIS AND PARTICIPATION IN ENVIRONMENTAL DELIBERATION

Barbara George
Kent State University

This chapter considers the ways in which public participants deliberate about environmental risk in regards to high volume hydraulic fracturing for natural gas in their communities. I employ a feminist lens to examine literacies surrounding environmental risk representation. This research compares social constructs of official environmental risk reporting processes in three different states, then explores the ways in which activists counter these literacies through feminist interventionist technical networks that attend to notions of environmental justice and precaution through praxis. This investigation suggests that feminist and praxis-oriented turns within Writing Studies contributes to the complexities and uncertainties inherent in environmental deliberation.

Recent writing studies scholarship considers ways in which researchers can more fully engage with community activism to generate social change. Jeffrey Grabill (2007) argues for the importance of rhetorical invention through "information infrastructures that allow people that make things that matter to them," offering a praxis-oriented opportunity for scholarship within Writing Studies (p. 3). This attention to praxis intersects with feminist scholarship within writing studies to highlight the ways in which technological spaces might transform from top down prescriptive approaches to more clearly "foster identity construction" of those who might be engaging in these spaces (Blair, 2012, p. 63). This meeting point of praxis, technology and feminism informs my own research: What happens when public participants, particularly those who must navigate complex scientific and technical spaces, are able to more fully co-create knowledge about complex environmental risks in their communities? Might such literacies consider a more feminist, contextualized approach to knowledge making about environmental issues?

This chapter focuses on the literacy practices citizens engage in when making meaning about their material environments. Here, literacy practices are understood in terms of a social theory of literacy; they are "cultural ways of utilizing written language in which people draw upon in their lives" (Barton & Hamilton, 2000, p.7). By extension, my research explores community literacy practices, which, according to Elenore Long, investigates the rhetorical implications of "discursive sites where ordinary people go public" (2009, p. 15). My research includes document analysis, interviews and think aloud protocols in three adjacent states impacted by hydraulic fracturing: Ohio, Pennsylvania, and New York, each having varied state institutionalized responses to emerging industry.

In this chapter, I first make explicit the theories that intersect feminism and environmental deliberation. My work then interrogates the ways in which public participants attempt to engage in literacies surrounding public environmental risk deliberation as related to the increased practice of high volume hydraulic fracturing (HVHF) technologies and its attendant infrastructure[1]. While participants largely rejected risk participation mechanisms and representation through state and federal mechanisms, it is important to understand public participants' articulations as to *why* they did so, and how these critiques informed counter-literacies. Many participants felt that both materials and online processes, which included broad definitions of "risk" and "regulation" as defined by state and federal agencies routinely oriented users towards what participants noted was a "status quo" approach to industry and environmental risk that ignored local concerns.

In response to exclusions many public participants attempt to navigate, this chapter explores alternative, more inclusive ways by which public participants might deliberate complex environmental risks. Beverly Sauer (2003) suggests that communication scholars might look more deeply at ways varied participants might communicate about risk to "make visible those marginalized forms of representations" (p. 6). I explore how community participants, impacted or potentially impacted by the hydraulic fracturing industry, challenge traditional notions of authority and agency within environmental policy deliberation. Long's (2009) work with community action within rhetorics of environmentalism, community action literacies, and public engagement reveals situated, or contextualized local knowledges, which are uniquely positioned to "invent" ways of making meaning about the environment that is often lost in traditional risk reporting mechanisms sponsored by state and federal institutions. I look at patterns of public participants engaging in counter-literacies, found in material and digital networks, that reimagine knowledge making about environmental policy as informed by feminist interventions that might interrupt dominant policy and practices of environmental risk representation. Counter-literacies in my

---

1 The U.S. Geological Survey defines HVHF as a quickly emerging energy source in the United States.

study are based in the notion of counter-public discourse—one that offers the opportunity for marginalized voices to offer expertise in public discourse. Localized and contextualized representations of environmental risks are increasingly shared through digital networks among activists, and show broader stakeholder concerns of environmental risk that include environmental justice and precaution ideologies.

THEORETICAL CONSIDERATIONS: WHO CAN ENGAGE AND HOW CAN THEY ENGAGE?

To foreground my study, some definitions and theoretical grounding are necessary to outline concerns about who can (or cannot) engage in public deliberations about environmental risk, and how feminist frameworks within writing studies contribute to this conversation. According to Beverly Sauer (2003), "A feminist analysis reveals both the hidden power structure that governs the construction of a text and the silent and salient privileging of one voice over another" (p. 64), suggesting a critical inspection might be made of what, exactly, is lost by such silencing. The terms *stakeholders, public participants,* and *citizens* are often used interchangeably in research about environmental communication; definitions generally point to the notion that actors should be able to understand or engage in some decision-making processes regarding their material environments (Cox, 2006; Rowe & Frewer, 2004). For the purposes of my study, I define stakeholders, public participants and citizens as actors who deliberate in any way about environmental issues that might impact them. I will use the term *public participants* through this portion of the chapter.

Similarly, it is important to detail the activity of environmental risk deliberation. In this study, public participation and deliberation about environmental risk can happen in many ways, from little or partial public involvement (typical), to full public participation (rare) (Simmons, 2007, p. 38–39). Environmental risk participatory mechanisms, as defined by Rowe and Frewer (2004), are "processes, techniques, instruments" that enable citizens to participate in environmental risk deliberation (p. 252). These deliberations might include public hearings, public surveys, or public written comment processes (Fiorino, 1990).[2] These mechanisms may be spoken, print, or digital; they might require public participants to attend policy meetings in a particular place and time (public hearing), or ask that participants engage in comment via writing (print or digital public comment). Increasingly, these mechanisms fall under scrutiny; Rowe and Frewer (2004) call for more scholarship to attend to imprecise definitions of

2   It is important to note that many of these have moved online in the last decade, which causes both affordances and constraints for public participants.

these mechanisms, uncertainties in execution of mechanisms, and lack of evaluation of these mechanisms.

Environmental deliberation considerations can be informed by feminist approaches from writing studies. Patricia Sullivan's (2012) discussion of "reinterpretation" of composition scholarship involves a "metarhetorical" stance allowing for feminist critique of "methodological assumptions" within composition (p. 127). I extend such a critique to assumptions of literacies that public participants must navigate when attempting to voice an environmental concern. While environmental laws ensure a citizens' legal right to know, right to comment, and right of standing (legal status) about an environmental risk issue that might impact them (Cox, 2006), there are questions about how public participants read and write to navigate these processes and documents, particularly those that employ highly technical and scientific literacies. More importantly, in the case of new industries, such as HVHF, publics also attempt to represent risks within emerging industry; various federal environmental laws do not extend to perceived risk of HVHF due to the Energy Policy Act of 2005. In HVHF deliberation, public participants must navigate and represent complex scientific and technical knowledge to prove "extraordinary circumstances" should participants suspect environmental risk. As such, participants face an often unspoken assumption of having to find and represent "proof" of such loosely defined terms as "significant environmental effect" (Brady, 2011).

Both risk and feminist scholars discuss how public participation is explicitly and implicitly stymied during environmental risk communication; these exclusions are tied to notions of risk representations that are socially situated and socially contested (Beck, 1987; Sauer, 2003). Environmental risk assessment[3] is often linked to certain notions of science; scientific rhetoric reveals nuances of authority, ethos, and the way certain notions of "science" result in prescriptive, top-down approaches to environmental policy. However, several scholars suggest that good policy does not depend on traditional linear models of science expertise; instead, attention is paid to social constructs of science and environmental risk. Feminist science scholars, such as those in Keller and Longino's (1996) edited collection, *Feminism and Science*, have called for more situated studies of science and more complicated notions of "objectivity" and "reflexivity" in science (Haraway, 1996; Harding, 1996). Karen Warren's work (2000), *Ecofeminist Philosophy*, explores conceptual intersections between feminism, science and nature. Beverly Sauer's scholarship of risk rhetorics investigates rhetorical and feminist theory in an effort to understand, more deeply, those who participate in science and technology deliberations (2003). Similarly, several sustainability

---

3   Bäckstrand notes "Risk assessment is still regarded as the exclusive domain for science experts" (2003, p. 34).

communications scholars call for a more complex notion of post-positive science that includes the use of extended peer communities to address complex, costly and potentially lethal uncertainties (Funtowicz & Ravetz, 1993; Goggin, 2009; McGreavy, Silka & Hart 2012; Wells, 2013; Herndl & Cutlip 2013).

In application to my own study, Royster and Kirsch's (2012) notion of strategic contemplation became salient in seeking patterns noted above within participant literacies. Strategic contemplation is "a space where we can see and hold contradictions without rushing to immediate closure, to neat resolutions, or to cozy hierarchies and binaries. The intent of such strategic contemplation is to render meaningfully, respectfully, honorably the words and works of those whom we study . . ." (p. 21–22). For example, to understand experiences of participants attempting to make meaning about risk in their environments, I took pointers from Selfe and Hawisher (2012) to contextualize the participant's literacy experiences by asking for "elaboration, encouraging them to reflection stories they tell, and, occasionally, telling stories of (our) own when we find points in common" (42). This contextualization yielded unexpected moments of insight into literacy practices participants were navigating. Similarly, as it was important for me to acknowledge the "contextual" and "situated" spaces where and why interventions were being composed, particularly in terms of online spaces, I attend to Haas, Takayoshi and Carr's (2012) suggestion that a researcher "employ the technology under study" to more clearly challenge my own assumptions about online literacy tools and processes used by participants . . . both tools that might alienate and empower them (p. 56). As a concerned citizen myself, I quickly learned that attempting to make meaning through various technological literacies might offer varying levels of affordances and constraints.

ARTICULATING CRITIQUE: INSTITUTIONAL ENVIRONMENTAL RISK PARTICIPATORY MECHANISMS

I begin an analysis of my data with an investigation of how participants in each state interacted with institutional participatory risk mechanisms. Through my research, participants felt that uncertainties about risk within the HVHF industrial activity was positioned as an issue that is managed by experts for profit; Dryzek (2005) refers to this orientation as administrative and economic rationalism. More specifically, while Ohio and Pennsylvania participants noted there has been more representation of "regulation" about hydraulic fracturing on the institutional website pages or in public meetings, participants revealed that it is "regulation" as defined by expert authorities. Participants in my study were concerned that they had never had a space within public policy deliberation to approach precaution, or to question whether the industrial industry should occur at all. Instead, agencies repeatedly offered "expert" stance on the ability to regulate activities, according to participants, felt had uncertain outcomes in the communities in which they were living. Participants felt that "disclosure" of risks, such as well locators, spill locators, and chemical disclosure such as those found on FracFocus (an online chemical disclosure tool used in each of these states' institutional sites) were intentionally difficult to navigate, even for those who had extensive online technological expertise, did not account for the cumulative effects of chemicals, and had been added after the HVHF industry was widespread versus any deliberation about a precautionary approach to risks of hydraulic fracturing.

When precaution was at times considered, participants often reported that public comment about precaution deliberation was in name only—public participants repeatedly found they often had no agency, even though, at times, there was an opportunity within institutionalized environmental risk participatory mechanisms, to submit a comment. Many times, participants reported meetings for public comment were deliberately designed so that it was difficult for them to attend: meetings were held on short notice with little advertising to local communities, public officials purposefully left little time for public comment, meetings were held during working hours, or required public participants to walk through police barracks to find a meeting room. Even if public comment might be collected, public participants widely noted that such comment was not used in any significant way in expert deliberations. It is at this point that I consciously shift to from referring to actors as "public participants" to "activists" in this chapter. Activists moved to "counter-literacies" because existing institutionalized literacies marginalized their experiences, moving participants to self-identified as "activists."

With the exception of some deliberations of some processes of the HVHF industry in New York, activists felt that institutionalized environmental risk participatory mechanisms did not offer deliberation about the lack of long-term situated studies of the uncertainties of the entire process: drilling, storage, disposal of waste, and transportation before or when widespread hydraulic fracturing practices commenced. Activists, who became so because they not only witnessed, but felt spills, air quality issues, and earthquakes, were frustrated by the minimization of unforeseen issues that could not be regulated (despite assurances). Activists pointed out that the few industry studies that had been completed before the industry commenced were often short term; they did not account for cumulative and long-term exposure to varied industrial contaminants, or emerging concerns about the effects of this industry on global climate change. Similarly, regulations to known risks applied to short-term industrial activities. Activists had an ethos of belonging to "place" and time that often did not line up with what they saw represented on expert institutional sites or during public meetings. Local inhabitants would live with the disposal of short-term industrial process for a much longer time frame but living with the residual effects of this industry was routinely not acknowledged in HVHF deliberation.

Also, activists found a lack of discussion of cumulative effects of the industrial practices within institutionalized environmental risk participatory mechanisms; scientific air, water, soil studies might be conducted separately (and, again, after the industry has already begun), avoiding a broader tale of what might happen to those living near industrial sites. The practice of hydraulic fracturing, activists pointed out, was deemed "safe" through decontextualized and divided studies of extraction or disposal practices that did not take into account compounded risks to air, water and soil over time. And activists were frustrated by a lack of social inquiry into regulatory guidelines; what happens when industries do not follow recommended regulations which is the case documented in several locations across the three states? While absent corporations might pay a fine for a lapse in regulation, it would be the local people who live for years with the results.

ACTIVIST TECHNICAL NETWORKS: INVENTION AND ENVIRONMENTAL PRAXIS

As a response to the marginalization felt by participants, I explore texts and procedures that participants[4] create in their effort to "rewrite" institutional literate practice. I suggest that such texts and processes are rich places to explore in an effort to provide more inclusive processes for public participation about environmental risks, and suggest that such a feminist approach offers insights into possibilities of praxis as related to environmental risk deliberation.

Simmons and Grabill (2007) note the opportunity for a more inclusive position of citizens in a rhetorical situation, one that is capable of creating knowledge that offers alternatives to dominant environmental risk discourses. This possibility occurs through invention in which "citizens as themselves producers—of knowledge, of values, of communities" (p. 437). This public participant knowledge might inform institutional knowledge making "by creating the institutional space within which risk can be collectively constructed and more effectively communicated" (p. 437). As such, my research extends to some public participants whose situated literacies *include* complex networked technologies. One important strand of this discussion is the way in which "technology" and "expertise" need not be separated from public participants. With this said, access to technology is always a concern, so there should be no essentialist assump-

---

4 I make the point of referring to participants as activists to highlight the performative praxis of counter-literacies.

tions that all participants can and want to access complex technologies, though some do. Judy Wajcman's work articulating the concept of technofeminism is important in my study as it explores the social constructions questioning who might feel comfortable (or not) navigating various technical spaces, and considers a feminist approach to reconsidering those spaces: "Feminist research has been at the forefront of moves to deconstruct the designer/user divide, and that between production and consumption, emphasizing the connectedness of all phases of technological development (Cockburn & Ormrod, 1993)" (as cited in Wajcman, 2007 p. 293). The literacies used by public participants navigating environmental risk are increasingly digital, technical and networked; Herndl and Cutlip (2013) and Grabill (2007) point specifically to environmental activist engagement through technology that situates scientific rhetorical studies towards praxis.

In my data, activists engaged in clear patterns of networks and activities to "counter" the marginalization they feel when working with institutionalized participatory mechanisms. The activist activity often occurs in what Simmons and Grabill (2007) refer to as "distributive activities" (p. 436). Here, individuals within groups represent complex technical information to networked community groups that are "connected to larger rhetorical situations and communication practices" (p. 437).

Research about literate practices of environmental risk reveals publics as active participants in building technological networks accessing and responding to highly technical knowledge vs. passive recipients of technical knowledge from experts. Most activists in my study attended various local, and sometimes state, national and international events as concerned citizens, but reported a fair bit of networking occurred online to inform what was verbalized in a public setting or a publically shared text. In this collection, Ouellette discusses possibilities of digital circulation, invention, and social action: "Moving beyond the notion that rhetorics are individual speech acts, or occasion-bound events, I consider rhetoric as a larger, circulating, affective network of arguments, and thus propose that we rethink our understanding of social action on the web, and see it in terms of circulation" (2018, this collection). Similarly, Royster and Kirsch (2012) refer to the concept of "social circulation" to situate circulation more firmly within a social context: "we wanted a useful metaphor for re-anchoring in a more generative way the convergence of both the values added by the use of feminist ideologies in rhetoric and analyses and the use of rhetorical theories and criticism in feminist analyses, all well considered within a thickly rendered social, political economic, cultural context" (p. 23). Social circulation, then, attends to the many complexities of socially-situated environmental risk representation. Additionally, Royster and Kirsch (2012) note the need for contextualizing com-

Literacy, Praxis and Participation

plexities of such circulating rhetorical practices: "Noticing . . . rather than ignoring—ecological conditions, or the ethical, political, cultural dimensions of rhetorical enterprises, or the materiality of ideas, arguments, sites, and situations, we come to *rhetoric* as an embodied polylogical social practice that needs to be understood symphonically and in high definition" (p. 94). Understanding the ways in which alternatives to institutional risk circulate within social constructs becomes important in terms of how activists engage in counter literacies to enact praxis within their communities.

SOCIAL MEDIA AND TECHNICAL NETWORKS

Social media sites like Facebook were cited by many activists as a gateway for networks for other, more technical investigations. As a community member in an area impacted by hydraulic fracturing I turned to area activist group sites on Facebook after a seismic event to attempt to find groups that might share information that was not available on Ohio state institutional sites, including local meetings not published on state environmental sites. I also found groups who organized initiatives to invite publics to write letters to pressure the state to disclose earthquake data, which led to my discovering other groups pressuring the state to force companies to disclose chemical make up of HVHF. Many other activists sought social media to seek individuals or groups who were sympathetic to similar environmental risk marginalization experiences.

Others found that social media was an important space to direct activists to forums to share technical risk information not yet represented on institutional sites, and to find activists that might question, or conduct citizen's audits, critiquing the risk information that was on the sites. While there is no way to measure specific levels of "agency" through social media sites like Facebook and activist blogs or websites, these activists began to engage in groups who regularly posted updates about local, state and federal laws, ways to gather information or critique what was represented on institutionalized sites, to find sites and processes that might represent environmental risk in more complexity than on institutionalized sites, to find emerging scientific studies about risks about the production of, storage, and transport of hydraulic fracturing materials, to understand emerging public health studies about varied risks, to find and engage in citizen science opportunities, and to find and engage with professionals (toxicologists, radiation specialists, health experts, etc.) not represented on institutionalized sites who were willing to work with activists about localized issues related to the hydraulic fracturing industry. Social media oriented activists towards spaces where activists might engage in critical discussion, at with local higher education institutions, to question academic alignment of pro-industry research agendas, to allow activists to about how academic institutions might engage communities in critical conversations about the uncertainties of the complex hydraulic fracturing industry, and to suggest and even demand that universities might invest in research exploring alternative energy technologies and divest from fossil fuel investments. Social media allowed activists to learn about and participate in activist events, including coordinating public comment sponsored by local, state and federal institutions, and, events opposing the limitations of such institutions.

As such, activists began to form identities bolstered by these findings. Again, in this collection, Ouellette points to the following in terms of social circulation: " . . . the emotional reactions and the circulation that results from those reactions determines, in large part, which amplified messages gain velocity and the kinds of social relations that emerge. Such affective circulation further determines what messages/rhetorics endure" (2018). In the case of my study, activists routinely cited that social media was often the "entry" into other, networked sites and activities that allowed for the formation of "counter" representation of risk with varying agency in each state. Activists noted the extensive time spent understanding complexity of risk inherent in hydraulic fracturing by exploring legal documents, mapping (paper and digital), local, state and federal environmental policy, impacts of chemicals in a variety of contextualized scenarios, air quality, and hazardous waste through all parts of production, including transportation and disposal.

Narrative and Multi-Modal Representations of Environmental Risk

Activist interviews revealed patterns of narratives that became socially circulated. Narratives offer important spaces for environmental risk deliberation scholarship, and composition studies are helpful to understand both the limitations, and agency narratives might provide. As writing studies scholar Debra Journet notes, "narratives are still being written against the grain of academic discourse." Journet asks us to consider personal narrative, but to also consider, more clearly, "genred narratives" and how historically, the validity of narratives that "correspond to the reality of the phenomena under discussion" (2012, p.19). At issue with hydraulic fracturing are the competing narratives of risk, and how agency is given to particular narratives. While public comment (if offered) might allow activists to discuss personal, anecdotal experiences in a public setting, scholarship suggests these narratives, even if revealing localized phenomena of risk, often do not have much agency in the traditional top-down approach to environmental risk decision making.

However, among activists, narratives propel new ways of considering environmental risk, challenging the positioning of "regulation" of an industry by experts without widespread scientific studies. Journet challenges writing studies scholars to think more critically about *how* personal narratives might or might not be privileged in a particular situation. In my study, narratives allowed activists to share personal experiences about HVHF risk among themselves that were not being represented by regulatory institutions. Shared narratives such as those in *Shalefield Stories: A Project of Friends of the Harmed* allowed activists to respond with support, in immediate ways, to those who could not afford, in terms of money and time, for the institutional regulatory to make reparations about possible material environmental damage—to the living organisms in ecological systems which activists contend were affected by HVHF. Narratives allowed activists to contextualize highly technical risk information, such as the information represented on the *FracTracker Alliance* site, which combines data from institutional sites with narrative within multimodal digital storytelling formats.

Similarly, counter-literacy narratives allowed for multi-modal, sophisticated representations of risk shared on community-based risk reporting sites such as the *FracTracker Alliance* site, which re-represents data from state institutional sites, but also sites like Google mapping, to reveal disclosures of wells sites, accidents, spills and proposed pipelines that is not found on easily on state and federal institutional sites. Interfaces on *FracTracker* maps consider feminist geographies[5] to provide risk exploration beyond "permitting" and "regulation" and to more critically interrogate how geographic spacialities of risk are being represented. Activists found that the crowd-sourced images and video clips of all parts of the industry process shared online tell a more contextualized tale of risk, again, a narrative of the industry that institutional sites did not share. The *FracTracker Alliance* site organizes and categorizes risks beyond what institutional sites represented as risks at all, for example, the inclusion of an "environmental justice" tool as a mapping layer allows users to investigate hydraulic fracking more critically.

Also, multi-modality allows for the representation of what material feminist and ecofeminist scholars recognize as the relationship of the flux between the human body and material surroundings; Stacy Alaimo (2007) refers to "trans-corporeal feminism," which suggests that bodies in space become marginalized through toxins created from socio-cultural constructions. "As a particularly vivid example of trans-corporeal space, toxic bodies insist that environmentalism, human health and social justice cannot be severed. They encourage us to imagine ourselves in constant interchange with the 'environment'" (262). Alaimo points to varied, but connected, inquires into the sources and consequences of such tox-

---

5   Feminist geography, according to Moss and Falconer Al-Hindi (2000) attends to issues of authority (both claiming and contesting authority) and power in terms of representing spatial phenomena.

icity: "the traffic in toxins reveals interconnections between various movements, such as those of environmental health, occupational health, labor movements, environmental justice, environmentalism, ecological medicine, disability rights, green living, anti-globalization, consumer rights, and child welfare" (260).

Material feminist theory underscores how, in my study, activists found ways to represent complex fracking industry results on and within organisms: land, and human bodies and the human social systems that promote such industrial activities. Often, these photos or videos of material risks were shared between activists in cyberspace, but through images, notions of powerful material risk circulated. The results of earthquakes on properties (cracked foundations) was shared among activists long before the Department of Natural Resources in Ohio formally made a formal and official link between injection wells (that store hydraulic fracturing waster) and earthquakes. Maps of trains carrying hazardous materials through densely populated neighborhoods and schools shifted conversations about what officials claimed was the "safe" transport and disposal of fracking waste. Images of children with nosebleeds by those living near hydraulic fracturing compressor stations in several states were widely shared to advance networks of inquiry into possible connections between public health and hydraulic fracturing.

Post-positivist Notions of Science: Environmental Justice and Precaution—Representing Public Health

Several of the activists I have met in my study are involved in persuasive performances in highly technically complex rhetorical spaces; for example, some shared highly technical information about solar or wind technologies that might act as alternative infrastructures for communities. Other stakeholders involved in "citizen science" initiatives are taking active roles in complex, technical, but often localized, scientific studies (Conrad and Hilchey, 2011) to study air or water. But what was noteworthy was the way in which networks of agency invoked when activists investigated issues of public health. These notions of localized sciences within shared networks created knowledge in proactive ways. As noted earlier in this chapter, post-normal notions of science expand notions of uncertainty and risk. Within these systems, powerful new ideologies can be brought to light, with which activists engaged: in this case, environmental justice and decisions based on the precautionary principle are feminist in terms of a call for ecological democracy, situated in a critique of cultural constructs that lead to marginalization of ecologies and organisms, including people, in them (Dryzek, 2005). Frameworks of environmental justice explore discursive possibilities attending to expanded notions of citizen risk reporting in space and time

(Holifield, Porter & Walker, 2010). Environmental justice attends to resituating discourse about environmental risks due to "the legacy of a disproportionate burden imposed on poor and minority communities by environmental harmful conditions, [and calls for] more inclusive opportunities for those who are most affected to be heard in the decisions made by public agencies" (p. 290, 2006, Cox). Environmental justice frameworks seek more complex ideas about how places are labeled for industrial practices, and how those living in geographically stigmatized spaces, as defined by dominant discourses, might find agency in re-defining place, and, by extension, personal identity. In this collection, Schiappa discusses "intersectionality" as a more complex representation of oppressions: "the fact that many social groups experience oppression along *multiple* planes, and second, that those planes are conceptually and materially *inseparable*" (2018, this collection). This acknowledgement of layers of oppression through time and space is crucial to understand in terms of the silencing of activists through largely ineffective institutional public comment that does not consider the complex marginalization activists feel: there are cumulative issues of air quality, water quality, soil quality, seismic issues, long term economic quality that are not often included in deliberations. Added to this, these fracking activities often occur near locations of economic poverty from past industrial cycles, often in communities that do not have resources or agency to represent these varied risks.

Ideologies of precautionary politics suggest that in complex and uncertain environmental issues, where scientific consensus cannot or has not been reached, the public should not bear the burden of "proving" risks as is currently the case; publics, instead, should be protected if a reasonable risk has been found (Whiteside, 2006). By adopting environmental justice and precautionary ideologies, both feminist in nature, activists were able challenge normate views of the environment as a "resource" to be "managed" or "regulated" that fulfills a dominant economic narrative, and to call of more rigorous and expanded scientific studies.

Environmental justice and precautionary frames are useful for spurring new knowledge making, which was widely represented and shared in the technical reading and writing practices of activists. Activists networked outside of localities to represent risks not sanctioned by institutional environmental in their own states. In Pennsylvania and Ohio, activists were frustrated that there are no statewide spaces to explore issues of human health effects as a result of the hydraulic fracturing industry. Neither Pennsylvania nor Ohio Departments of Health listed any part of the hydraulic fracturing industry (extraction, storage, or transport) exposure as a concern on their state environmental health data systems. Also, there were no institutionally state-sponsored base-line studies about health and fracking. However, activists pointed to community groups, like the Center for Coalfield Justice, that linked risk of known risks (the coal industry), with other extractive practices which was helpful in networking, particularly along environmental justice argument in Appalachia in both Pennsylvania and Ohio, for positioning legislation for laws to protect ecosystems and people in them. It should be noted that such an approach, though compelling, often not successful as laws regulating hydraulic fracturing simply have yet to be written, and further studies about various impacts of hydraulic fracturing have yet to be funded and executed.

However, in each state, expert/activists in the medical field worked to provide such information to the public, and these works were widely shared among activists. For example, in Pennsylvania, the Southwest Pennsylvania Environmental Health Project provides online resources and health services and monitoring of human bodies and equipment to monitor air quality to those living near gas wells. In Ohio, the Center for Health, Environment and Justice, again, not affiliated with a state agency provides a "Prevent Fracking Harms" page with links to resources about health effects, including a database about emerging health studies, grounded in a recognition of possible embodied risks of this industry, and contextualizing risk in local environments and in local bodies.

Interventions: Counter-Literacies Leading to a New York Ban on HVHF

Simmons and Grabill's (2007) research on communities accessing technology to "invent" and "perform persuasively" valued knowledge given a complex rhetorical situation related to environmental deliberation dovetails nicely with the New York activists I encountered in my study (2007, p. 422). Interestingly, one resource included on the Ohio site Center for Health, Environment and Justice page links to several of New York's deliberations about the decisions to ban fracking in New York State, highlighting the networking that occurs among activists that I observed during my interviews and think aloud protocols across states. The New York State ban on high volume hydraulic fracturing acts as a literate artifact; in many ways is the end result of interactions between grassroots activists and experts in many states sharing and compiling information challenging an industrial "norm" of hydraulic fracturing.

Many activists in my study contributed to knowledge building that resulted in a state-wide ban: sharing studies about emerging health issues in places like Pennsylvania and Ohio and building political and legal cases for bans in various communities, then networking successes to statewide discussions of the practice. It is important to note that prior to the ban that activists were assured by officials from the New York Department of Conservation that the fracking industry could be regulated and that spills and accidents were extremely rare. However, activists in New York traveled to neighboring states of Ohio and Pennsylvania and witnessed results of explosions, water contamination, and methane leaks. Their "felt" sense of risk, and conversations with their neighbors' perceptions of risk did not match up to the "institutionalized" representations of risk. The Dimock, PA water case (easily accessible to New York), in which industry denied that fracking caused widespread water contamination in the Dimock area, generated investigations by activists into both "knowledge making" about HVHF risk and bans.

Across the state of New York, anti-fracking activists attended public meetings, and flooded local and state public comment. The New York activists I spoke to discussed networks of knowledge that supported this grassroots movement: how to write letters to local, state and federal representatives, how to navigate legal issues to impose industry bans in local areas, (culminating in a "home-rule" orientation which allowed local governments, not the state, to control how drilling might occur, if it occurred at all), and how to read and represent highly technical information from emerging scholarly studies about environmental and public health risks.

In response to the perceived lack of true deliberation about potential risks, many New York activists turned to the "body" as a form of speech. Their "bodies" spoke through marches, blockades and arrests, and these experiences and rationales for them were widely shared online. Several activists I interviewed shared information about how to commit acts of civil disobedience, using literate networks to plan who and how to be arrested; groups also coordinated fundraising to pay fines and legal representation for arrested activists. While activists in Ohio and Pennsylvania employed similar tactics, it was the reaction in New York to what had happened in the nearby states that created a large community-based outcry against what activists felt were very real risks in the fracking industry.

The ban on the extractive practice of hydraulic fracking occurred in December of 2014. In June of 2015, the New York Department of Environmental Conservation (DEC) announced the following: "The SEQR Findings Statement for high-volume hydraulic fracturing (HVHF) was issued on June 29, 2015. This concluded DEC's comprehensive, seven-year review and officially prohibits HVHF in New York." This page, as earlier noted, is situated within the DEC site, and takes some navigating to find, but does offer acknowledgment of the public comments that helped to shape the way risks were investigated, including a prioritization on public health not represented in the Ohio or Pennsylvania institutional sites, where HVHF is still legal. While the New York Department of Environmental Conservation puts some authority for this decision in the hands of the New York State Department of Health, a longer statement refers to a rare meaningful interaction between the public and a state agency to create knowledge about risk. It is clear here that questions of contestation of the "value" of HVHF have been represented, at the insistence of citizens, beyond the expertise of regulation of an industry. Expertise in public health is represented in this decision. While activists in New York were pleased with these successes, they noted the opposition they faced in attempting to articulate this aspect of risk. The entire deliberation centered on citizens and experts proving that there was enough risk to warrant the state-wide ban. The activists still currently face deliberations about transport and storage of gas, which are still hotly contested throughout the state as transportation infrastructure for HVHF continues in light of gas exports.

IMPLICATIONS FOR FURTHER STUDY

While the New York ban is important to explore, it is also important to understand that public participants who are not part of regulatory institutions may not have agency to offer technical knowledge if state or local laws do not "value" that kind of knowledge. Indeed, in Pennsylvania and Ohio, health officials have not been able to make a case to restrict fracking activity based on health concerns. Even highly technically-literate public stakeholders might find that certain "sciences," "technologies" or types of expertise are not valued or even represented in risk reporting documents or processes (indeed, as energy risk assessment currently varies by state, state policies vary widely). Simmons critiques the lack of reflection of what it means to fail to acknowledge socially constructed nature of risk communication and public participation, "This failure to see risk and environmental policy as socially constructed leads to unethical and oppressive risk communication practices because the public is denied democratic participation in the decision-making process" (2007, p. 2).

Here I turn again to Royster and Kirsch's (2012) concept of strategic contemplation, this time, to encourage research that attends more to complexities of environmental deliberation: "this process of paying attention, of being mindful, of attending to the subtle, intuitive, not-so-obvious parts of research has the capacity to yield rich rewards. It allows scholars to observe and notice, to listen and hear voices often neglected and silenced, and to notice more overtly their own responses to what they are seeing, reading, reflecting on, and encountering during their research process" (p. 85). In this sense, I found compelling patterns by which activists make meaning of their physical surroundings, finding that activist-driven representations of risk invented *outside* of institutional reporting that have shown some success in advancing agency to influence some environmental risk assessment policy). My research, which is informed by feminist approaches, points to moments where participants invent beyond top-down "objective" models to consider ways in which a larger deliberation about environmental risk might occur, and how to communicate and create praxis about these concerns. I find this to be increasingly compelling as it is acknowledged that local inventions and interventions have environmental impacts on a global scale.

REFERENCES

Alaimo, S. (2008). Trans-corporeal feminisms and the ethical space of nature. In S. Alaimo & S. Heckman (Eds.), *Material Feminisms* (pp. 237–264). Bloomington: Indiana University Press.

Bäckstrand, K. (2003). Civic science for sustainability: Reframing the role of experts, policy-makers and citizens in environmental governance. *Global Environmental Ethics, 3*(4), 24–3.

Barton, D. & Hamilton, M. (2000). Literacy practices. In D. Barton, M. Hamilton & R. Ivanic (Eds.), *Situated literacies: Reading and writing in context* (pp. 7–15). London, England: Routledge.

Beck, U. (1996): Risk society and the provident state. In S. Lash, B. Szerszynski & B. Wynne (Eds.), *Risk, environment & modernity: Towards a new ecology* (pp. 27–43). London, England: Sage.

Blair, K. (2012). A complicated geometry: Triangulating feminism, activism, and Technological literacy. In L. Nickoson & M. Sheridan (Eds.), *Writing Studies Research in Practice: Methods and Methodologies* (pp. 63–72). Carbondale, IL: Southern Illinois University Press.

Brady, W. (2011). Hydraulic fracturing regulation in the United States: The laissez-faire approach of the federal government and varying state regulations. University of Denver, Sterm College of Law.

Center for Health, Environment and Justice. (2015). *The Prevent Harms Campaign; Resources.* Retrieved from https://web.archive.org/web/20150809143707/http://chej.org/campaigns/nofracking/.

Coalfield Justice. (2015). *Issues: Fracking.* Retrieved from https://www.coalfieldjustice.org/issues/.

Conrad, C. C. & Hilchey, K. G. (2011). A review of citizen science and community-based environmental monitoring: issues and opportunities. *Environmental Monitoring and Assessment, 176*(1–4), 273–291.

Cox, J. R. (2006). *Environmental communication and the public sphere.* Thousand Oaks, CA: Sage.

Dryzek, J. S. (2005) *The politics of the earth: Environmental discourses.* Oxford, England: Oxford University Press.

Fiorino, D. J. (1990). Citizen participation and environmental risk: A survey of institutional mechanisms. *Science, Technology & Human Values, 15*(2), 226–243.

FracTracker Alliance. (2015). *Fractracker oil and gas photos.* Retrieved from https://www.fractracker.org/resources/photos/.

Funtowicz, S. O. & Ravetz, J. R. (1993). Science for the post-normal age. *Futures, 25*(7), 739–755.

Grabill, J. (2007). *Writing community change: Designing technologies for citizen action.* New York, NY: Hampton Press.

Goggin, P. (2009). *Rhetorics, literacies, and narratives of sustainability.* New York, NY: Routledge.

Haas, C., Takayoshi, P. & Carr, B. (2012). Analytic strategies, competent inquiries, and methodological tensions in the study of writing. In L. Nickoson & M. Sheridan (Eds.), *Writing Studies Research in Practice: Methods and Methodologies* (pp. 51–62). Carbondale, IL: Southern Illinois University Press.

Haraway, D. (1996). Situated knowledges: The science question in feminism and the privilege of a partial perspective. In E. Fox Keller & H. Longino (Eds.), *Feminism and Science* (pp. 249–263). New York, NY: Oxford.

Harding, S. (1996). Rethinking standpoint epistemology: What is "strong objectivity"? In E. Fox Keller & H. Longino (Eds.), *Feminism and Science* (pp. 239–248). New York, NY: Oxford.

Herndl, C. & Cutlip, L. (2013). "How can we act?" A praxiographical program for the rhetoric of technology, science, and medicine. *Poroi, 9*(1), 1–13.

Holifield, M., Porter, R. & Walker, G. (2010). *Spaces of Environmental Justice.* Malden, MA: Wiley-Blackwell.

Journet, D. (2012). Narrative turns in writing studies research. In L. Nickoson & M. P. Sheridan. (Eds.), *Writing Studies Research in Practice: Methods and Methodologies* (pp. 13–24). Carbondale, IL: Southern Illinois University Press.

Long, E. (2009) Rhetorical techne, local knowledge, and challenges in contemporary activism. In P. Goggin (Ed.), *Rhetorics, Literacies, and Narratives of Sustainability* (pp. 11–38). New York, NY: Routledge.

McGreavy, D., Silka, B. & Hart, D. (2012). Creating a place for environmental communication research in sustainability science. *Environmental Communication, 6*(1), 23–43.

Moss, P. & Falconer Al-Hindi, K. (2008). An introduction: Feminisms, geographies, knowledges. In P. Moss & K. Falconer Al-Hindi (Eds.), *Feminisms in Geography: Rethinking Place and Knowledges* (pp. 1–29). Lanham, MD: Rowman & Littlefield Publishers.

New York State Department of Health. (2015). *High-volume hydraulic fracturing in New York state.* Retrieved from https://www.dec.ny.gov/energy/75370.html.

Ouellette, J. (2018). The viability of digital spaces as sites for transnational feminist action and engagement: Why we need to look at digital dirculation. In K. L. Blair & L. Nickoson (Eds.), *Composing feminist interventions: Activism, engagement, praxis.* Fort Collins, CO: The WAC Clearinghouse / Louisville, CO: University Press of Colorado. Retrieved from https://wac.colostate.edu/books/perspectives/feminist/.

Rowe, G. & Frewer, L.J. (2004). Evaluating public-participation exercises: a research agenda. *Science, Technology & Human Values, 29*(4), 512–556.

Royster, J. & Kirsch, G. (2012). *Feminist rhetorical practices: New horizons for rhetoric, composition, and literacy studies.* Carbondale, IL: Southern Illinois University Press.

Sauer, B. (2003). *The rhetoric of risk: technical documentation in hazardous environments.* Mahwah, NJ: Erlbaum.

Schiappa, J. (2018). Advocating "active" intersectionality through a comparison of two Slutwalks. In K. L. Blair & L. Nickoson (Eds.), *Composing feminist interventions: Activism, engagement, praxis.* Fort Collins, CO: The WAC Clearinghouse / Louisville, CO: University Press of Colorado. Retrieved from https://wac.colostate.edu/books/perspectives/feminist/.

Selfe, C. & Hawisher, G.(2012). Exceeding the bounds of the interview: Feminism, mediation, narrative, and conversations about digital literacy. In L. Nickoson & M. Sheridan (Eds.), *Writing Studies Research in Practice: Methods and Methodologies* (pp. 36–50). Carbondale, IL: Southern Illinois University Press.

Simmons, W. M. (2007). *Participation and power: Civic discourse in environmental policy decisions.* Albany, NY: SUNY Press.

Simmons, W. M. & Grabill, J. T. (2007). Towards a civic rhetoric for technologically and scientifically complex places: Invention, performance and participation. *College Composition and Communication, 58*(3), 419–448.

Shalefield Stories: A project of Friends of the Harmed. (2014). *Shalefield Stories vol. 1.* Retrieved from http://www.shalefieldstories.org/.

Southwest Pennsylvania Environmental Health Project. (2015). Residential environmental screening tool. Retrieved from https://web.archive.org/web/20150914112529/http://www.environmentalhealthproject.org/wp-content/uploads/2014/05/EHP-Residential-Environmental-Screening-Tool-May-14.pdf.

Sullivan, P. (2003). Feminism and methodology in composition studies. In G. Kirsch, F. Spencer Maor, L. Massey, L. Nickoson-Massey & M. Sheridan-Rabideau (Eds.), *Feminism and Composition: A Critical Sourcebook* (pp. 124–139). Urbana, IL: Bedford/St. Martin's.

Wajcman, J. (2007). From women and technology to gendered technoscience. *Information, Communication & Society, 10*(3), 287–298.

Warren, K. (2000). *Ecofeminist philosophy: A Western perspective on what it is and why it matters.* United States: Rowman and Littelfield.

Wells, J. (2014). *Complexity and sustainability.* Cambridge, MA: Routledge.

Whiteside, K. (2006). *Precautionary politics.* Cambridge, MA: Routledge.

CHAPTER 14.

THE VIABILITY OF DIGITAL SPACES AS SITES FOR TRANSNATIONAL FEMINIST ACTION AND ENGAGEMENT: WHY WE NEED TO LOOK AT DIGITAL CIRCULATION

Jessica Ouellette
University of Southern Maine

In the early spring of 2013, through the use of social media, the global feminist protest group FEMEN staged a "topless jihad" day in support of Tunisian member, Amina Tyler, who was threatened with physical punishment for posting to Facebook and Twitter images of her naked body, covered in written messages such as "Fuck your morals" and "My body is mine." Because new media systems have vastly changed communication and information-sharing processes, they have also altered the ways we engage rhetorically in feminist activism. Ouellette argues that in order to engage effectively in feminist activism and foster transnational connections within digital spaces, we need to look at the ways in which texts move and circulate, and how, in and through those movements, textual meanings and rhetorical purposes shift and change. To achieve such goals, Ouellette provides a case study of the events and protests surrounding Tyler and FEMEN's protests—specifically the texts that circulated, and the political and economic investments undergirding that circulation.

In early March 2013, the circulation of two particular images sparked a series of debates, deliberations, and discussions in the digital sphere. Images of a topless woman, Amina Tyler, holding a cigarette in one hand, and a book in the other, moved throughout social media sites at rapid speed. Across Tyler's chest were messages written in English and Arabic, messages that read, "Fuck your morals" and "My body is mine, not somebody else's honor."

Figure 14.1. Amina Tyler, Arabic.

Tyler, a citizen of Tunisia and an outspoken member of FEMEN, a Ukrainian-born international feminist group, decided to post these images on her Facebook as a response to her nation's policies regarding women's rights. At the time of her posting, the government of Tunisia was in the process of drafting a new constitution, one that would allegedly alter, and perhaps take away, some of the rights already in place for Tunisian women. Following Tyler's response to this specific political moment, and following the rapid circulation of her images by Tyler's Facebook and Twitter friends (and thus other friends of friends), Tyler was threatened with physical punishment and death threats from national officials of Tunisia for posting "nude portraits." As a result of these threats, Tyler deleted her social media accounts and fled Tunisia. Despite her withdrawal, her texts took on lives of their own, becoming the subjects of many news articles, blog posts, and social media posts across the globe. As Tyler's images circulated, they encountered various kinds of rhetorics involving feminism, human rights, and nationalism. These instances of rhetorical contact led to changes and shifts in meaning, prompting the circulation of new texts and thus new kinds of arguments that, oftentimes, conflicted with the original rhetorical purpose of Tyler's texts.

Figure 14. 2. Amina Tyler, English.

For rhetoricians, this event is particularly compelling. Not only does it highlight a moment in which feminist action and intervention prompts transnational conversations, it illustrates the scope and global reach afforded by digital circulation, and further illuminates the often unexpected consequences of such circulation. Tyler's case is not unique, however. Over the last decade, protests involving women's rights have been very much present in the media. Since 9/11, we have seen a wave of feminist movements addressing various political issues—reproductive rights, acts of violence, the need for economic support, wage inequities, and rights regarding women's bodies, among others. These various global upheavals have not surfaced without external influences. The "war on terror," the perceived increased need for national security alongside the push for open trade markets, and the continuous move from national governance to supranational governance have caused many disjunctures between the state and peoples' actual needs. Because of these pressures and their effects on lived experiences, social activist groups from all around the world have looked to the digital web as a productive place for protest and a powerful site for demanding change.

For these reasons, this piece, which is part of a larger research project, emerges out of an interest in and exploration of the possible efficacy of digital spaces as sites for transnational feminist engagement and intervention. These questions, for me, are inextricably linked to my interests in the intersections between writing, gender, and technology. Although the digital is the site of my inquiry, at its core is a concern for transnational feminist discourse and activism: the digital came into the project as one of the most viable places for such action to occur. The crux of this research, then, is an effort to understand both the possibilities and limitations of transnational feminist engagement within digital spaces. As a result, I examine and expose how the circulations of discourses on women's issues oftentimes serve as exigencies for national and global agendas within these spaces. In doing so, I argue for a new theory of rhetorical production—a theory that acknowledges the ways in which circulation operates as an affective movement and co-constitutive process that necessarily structures and shapes public life. Looking at digital circulation, I believe, can help us identify how the practices of writing and rhetoric within a transnational context reproduce and resist current ideologies so that we might write for social change more effectively in these spaces.

In recent years, scholars such as Rebecca Dingo and Wendy Hesford, among others, have begun attending to the transnational, looking at how rhetorics are inextricably linked to processes of globalization and the transnational flows of people, ideas, technology, and communication across national boundaries (Hesford, 2005, 2006, 2008; Hesford & Schell, 2008; Dingo, 2012; Queen, 2008). In her essay entitled, "Global Turns and Cautions in Rhetoric and Composition Studies" (2006), Wendy Hesford calls on the field of rhetoric and composition to turn its focus to global matters—matters that necessitate "a reexamination of existing protocols and divisions, and the formation of new critical frameworks in light of a changing world" (p. 796). While Hesford's article was published over a decade ago, much of it still remains relevant for our field today. Hesford's deliberate reference to a "changing world" speaks to the ways in which the intersections between culture, power, politics, and economics have been changing significantly due to the uneven processes of globalization. The increased production and advancement of information and media systems, and the ways in which these systems have vastly changed the processes of communication and information sharing, has undoubtedly altered the ways we engage in writing and rhetorical practices. And yet, rhetorical scholars have rarely examined digital writing's role in transnational exchange and processes of globalization with the exception of a few (Queen, 2008; Blair, Tulley & Gajjala, 2009; Royster & Kirsch, 2012).[1] Scholarship on the "digital" has, for the most part, been focused on the implications for digital literacies within transnational contexts (Berry, Hawisher & Selfe, 2012; Warriner, 2007; Lam, 2004) and questions related to web genres and digital writing (Miller & Shepherd, 2009; McKee & DeVoss, 2007; Porter, 2009; Giltrow & Stein, 2009).

Because Web 2.0 is a site of user-generated content, the "writeable" phase of the web, it not only facilitates and encourages participation, collaboration, and information sharing, it is driven and run by such content. This phase of the web has demanded new ways of thinking about rhetorical strategies. One of the most important concepts for understanding rhetorical action on the web may be "rhetorical velocity," a term coined by Jim Ridolfo and Danielle DeVoss (2009) to talk about rhetorical delivery within the context of user-generated content. Rhetorical velocity, they argue, is both a "strategic approach to composing for rhetorical delivery" and a term that describes "the understanding and rapidity at which information is crafted, delivered, distributed, recomposed, redelivered, redistributed, etc., across physical and virtual networks and spaces" (p. 1). The speed of information, the nature of remixing and citation, and the ability to instantaneously respond, modify, and copy are just a few of the changes intrinsic to the reimagining of rhetorical action within Web 2.0. Given these changes, the potential effects of circulation within a digital space are not just between a writer and a reader; rather those effects are caught up in larger networks of interaction or, to use Jenny Edbauer-Rice's term, "rhetorical ecologies" of meaning that are quite different from print or Web 1.0 (Edbauer, 2005). The time-space compression of digital communication is, in fact, one reason why we might view the web as a space where our everyday interactions and conversations happen transnationally and where those interactions and conversations, as they circulate, have transnational effects.

---

1 See Mary Queen, "Transnational Feminist Rhetorics in a Digital World" (2008); see Kristine Blair, Christine Tulley, and Radhika Gajjala's edited collection, *Webbing Cyberfeminist Practice: Communities, Pedagogies, and Social Action* (2009); and see Jacqueline Jones Royster and Gesa Kirsch's *Feminist Rhetorical Practices* (2012).

This study, then, speaks to the digital more broadly, emphasizing rhetorical analyses of digital circulation in order to understand how to productively and affectively engage in these digital mediums. While many scholars in rhetoric and composition have theorized digital circulation as part of an intentional mode of rhetorical delivery, and thus rhetorical deliberation (Porter, 2009; Warnick & Heineman, 2012; Ridolfo & DeVoss, 2009), I argue that circulation is a process through which various, and oftentimes conflicting, intentions and goals come into contact with each other, creating new meanings and new kinds of knowledge. Moving beyond the notion that rhetorics are individual speech acts, or occasion-bound events, I consider rhetoric as a larger, circulating, affective network of arguments, and thus propose that we rethink our understanding of social action on the web, and see it in terms of circulation and affect. Royster and Kirsch's definition of "social circulation," one of the four terms of engagement they put forth as part of their theoretical paradigm for feminists interested in engaging in rhetorical work, is helpful for thinking about the productive lens circulation can provide digital feminist activists. Social circulation, they argue, centers on "connections among past, present, and futures in the sense that the overlapping social circles in which women travel, live, and work are carried on or modified [generationally] and can lead to changed rhetorical practices" (Royster and Kirsch, 2012, p. 23). This piece attempts to hone in on such "overlapping circles"—the various connections made (or forestalled)—by looking at the process of digital circulation and the web's ability to provide texts with heightened amplification and velocity such that certain rhetorics become privileged over others. In other words, deliberation is not always the end goal, or the end result. Circulation does not work only (or even primarily) in favor of discursive interactions with others; it is as often prompted by emotions, feelings, and lived experiences.

In looking at the case of Tyler, I use transnational feminist scholar Inderpal Grewal's method of interarticulation (2005), which describes the ways in which discourses permeate rhetorics and change their meaning. Methodologically, this research project involves an examination of over 300 texts within three different timeframes: (1) the initial two weeks surrounding Tyler's post; (2) two months following Tyler's post; and (3) two years after Tyler's post. In focusing on four themes that emerged from the data (two of which I examine in this particular piece), all in relation to the rhetorical trope of the body—body as protest, body as object, body as madness, and body as nation—I show how texts, in their digital movements, become the basis for further representations, and how events and arguments get coopted and repurposed. In analyzing this data, I developed a three-part concept of circulation involving the following components: amplification, velocity, and endurance.

The Viability of Digital Spaces

To be more specific, I define amplification as the process through which a certain aspect of a text gets highlighted over the rest of the text. A specific ideology embedded in a text, for example, becomes magnified in such a way that it becomes detached from its original purpose, context, and history, thus changing its meaning and overall message. In other words, the volume is figuratively 'amplified' as some messages get louder and others move to the background. Velocity follows amplification, referring to the speed and scale of circulation a text can achieve and the various social alliances that form as a result.[2] Endurance corresponds to the ways in which certain texts retain such high levels of circulation over time that they become normalized, connecting and revising other ideologies, such that they stick and re-solidify as "reality."

Figure 14.3. FEMEN Topless Jihad.

---

2   While Ridolfo and DeVoss (2009) argue that rhetorical velocity involves a "rhetorical concern for distance, travel, speed, and time," particularly in relation to the ways in which writers "strategically" compose texts for third parties, this definition implies that the writer has a certain level of agency over the recomposition and appropriation of their text by third parties: and this is where my use of velocity differs. Instead of focusing on the writer, I examine velocity with an attention to the circulation process.

Emotion and the need to identify and align one's self with others plays a large role in determining the movement of texts—how they get picked up and amplified, where they go, what gains velocity and visibility and what doesn't, which voices are heard and taken seriously, and which ones are silenced. In other words, the emotional reactions and the circulation that results from those reactions determines, in large part, which amplified messages gain velocity and the kinds of social relations that emerge. Such *affective circulation* further determines what messages/rhetorics endure.

In this chapter, I illustrate the concept of affective circulation as it relates to my data, particularly the themes of body as protest and body as object. I begin with amplification: the figurative act of turning up the volume on a specific aspect of a text and thus, moving the rest of it to the background. In FEMEN's instance of circulation (the group of which Tyler was a part), the theme of the body as protest becomes foregrounded and amplified as the main message of Tyler's text. This happens in two ways. First, FEMEN uses Tyler's text as a catalyst for organizing a "topless jihad day." In social media posts, as well as an open letter published on *The Huffington Post*, FEMEN calls on women across the globe to support Tyler's cause by using their bodies "as poster[s] for the slogans of freedom," by "baring their breasts against Islam" and circulating the hashtag "#freeamina" (FEMEN Homepage, 2013).

Figure 14.4. FEMEN Protest.

The Viability of Digital Spaces

Figure 14.5. Amina Tyler on FEMEN's Facebook Page.

On FEMEN's Facebook page, we see Tyler's image against a backdrop of her supporters with the following statements written on their bodies: "Our tits are deadlier than your stones" (FEMEN Facebook, 2013). In these messages, what gets amplified is the call for a topless protest, and for two reasons: to oppose the religion of Islam and to help liberate a woman from an Arab nation. It is in these changing meanings that I locate the social action of circulation.

Inna Shevchenko, leader of FEMEN, in an article published by *The Guardian*, explains why she believes naked protest is necessary. She claims, "A woman's naked body has always been the instrument of the patriarchy . . . They use it in the sex industry, the fashion industry, advertising, always in men's hands. We realized the key was to give the naked body back to its rightful owner, to women, and give a new interpretation of nudity . . . I'm proud of the fact that today naked women are not just posing on the cover of Playboy, but it can be an action, angry, and can irritate people" (Shevchenko as cited in Cochrane, 2013). Once again, Shevchenko's references to the naked body as an "instrument" and as a kind of "action"—an action that gets people angry and irritated—speaks to the ways in which affect is always already caught up in the act of amplification, that the move to amplify something is indeed emotionally driven. Such references also call to mind what Zimmann (Chapter 16, this collection) argues in her piece, "A Peek Inside the Master's House": the belief that feminist rhetorical action and intervention always already brings with it an inherent link between the personal and political—in this case, the body as a personal representation of one's self becomes a political platform for feminist work (Zimmann, 2018).

In continuing with the amplification of the body as a kind of protest, other web users responded similarly, calling on others to join in the "fight for Amina."

283

One blogger, in particular, posed the following question: "You joining in this fight for women's rights or are you staying covered up? I'm currently writing this with no top on, just to do my part . . . . Every little bit helps!" (Byrne, n.d.). Again, we can see how quickly Tyler's text becomes re-positioned as a global symbol of bodily protest regarding women's rights and the rights to owning their bodies. Amplified in these moments of circulation is the belief that *the act of naked protest is analogous to the "fight for women's rights,"* the belief that the physical female body should be used as a canvas for protest and a tool to unite women on a global scale, to create solidarity—a "body" of feminists. Byrne's reference to "doing one's part" points to the way in which amplification functions as a kind of world-making, to use queer theorist Michael Warner's term (2002)—the ways in which texts become the basis for further representations, creating and foreclosing certain subject positions in order to create a world in which one wants to live.[3] On the one hand, we can see how the rhetoric of FEMEN and FEMEN supporters is being used as a means to propose and put forth solutions to shared matters of concern—gender inequities, for example. Many of these activists and feminists participate in amplifying Tyler's text because they feel they are furthering the cause for women's rights. On the other hand, amplifying the body as protest also moves Tyler's goal to the background, making the local case of Tunisia only a side note. Allying with Tyler, then, becomes a way of allying with her means of protest rather than with its goal (or more accurately, allying with Tyler, and by extension FEMEN, makes the means more important than the cause for which she is protesting).

As feminists and other activists, including FEMEN, circulate Tyler's text as an amplified narrative about the body and women's rights, they reposition Tyler as a silent victim in need of saving. This kind of western feminist ideology not only elides the local and specific context from which Tyler's text emerged, it also perpetuates a problematic perspective of Muslim women as an essentialized group of oppressed women, thus perpetuating certain essentializing beliefs about Islam and the Middle East.

While the body as protest theme continues to be amplified in multiple venues, other writers/responders also focus on the body, but amplify its rhetorical functions quite differently. In the mainstream media's portrayal of Tyler's story and the #freeamina campaign, certain news outlets focus solely on the "entertainment" factor of Tyler's and FEMEN's nudity. As journalist Matt Gurney of the *National Post* claims, nudity always garners attention: "When presented with nude protesters, enjoy the show, and say so," he wrote (Gurney, 2013). What we can take away from this statement is the belief that women's naked bodies alone, regardless of the images' purposes or contexts, will inevitably lead to more

---

3   See Michael Warner's *Publics and Counterpublics (2002).*

readers, and thus generate more capital. This demeaning sentiment becomes amplified as other social media users and bloggers post similar statements. For example, one blogger writes, "My opinion of feminists has gone right up . . . this is a jihad I could live with. Titslamism, is the future" (Kafir Crusaders, n.d.). Other statements include, "Feminist babes getting their boobs out against militant Islam" and "Not a body hair in sight on these sexy feminist nude protesters breaking the mental image of your excessively hairy razor-shy traditional feminist" (Kafir Crusaders, n.d.).

In these moments of amplification, we can see how the original message and rhetorical purpose of Tyler's text becomes completely erased. The amplification of both Tyler's and FEMEN's texts as objectifications of the female body illustrate the ways in which one component of a text—the naked body itself, pulled from its relationship to protest, to politics, to the messages literally written on those bodies—can be reconstructed as its own narrative, producing new, and oftentimes conflicting meanings. Amplified in these moments is the problematic correlation between feminism and what the body of a feminist should look like. And once again, amplified in these texts is also a western ideology of the liberated naked body versus the presumed conservative practices of Islam.

The variety of amplifications that emerged, particularly the two examples that I have described thus far, when traced to the next level of circulation in this study, highlight how such amplified meanings become the basis for further circulation, interanimating ideologies far from the original post. As the first layer of texts continued to circulate, certain texts gained a higher level of velocity due to the affective charges underlying the ideologies amplified in their circulation. Thus, the narratives around the body as a form of protest and the body as object took on lives of their own. The velocity of these particular texts not only sped up the circulation of certain messages, ensuring they continue to be heard, but that velocity also performed a kind of rhetorical action, creating alliances and oppositions and establishing and structuring certain social relations in sometimes surprising ways.

The mainstream media's focus on objectifying women's naked bodies, for example, prompted various reactions to and disagreements with FEMEN and Tyler's mode of protest. In an ironic move, Tyler and FEMEN are criticized for not being feminist enough because their mode of protest—the body—can only be understood as an object. As a result, "feminists" who might have aligned with FEMEN come to distance themselves from the protest. As writer for *The Daily Beast* Janine Giovanni states, "Any protester knows that the only way activism works is to get the people on your side. Femen is not exactly endearing themselves to anyone, except perhaps to hormonal teenage boys" (Giovanni, 2013). She ends the article with the following quote: "Amina's heart might be in the right place, but I wish she would cover it up with a T-shirt and protest quietly, but effectively, rather than getting her kit off." The reference here to "getting people on your side" depicts a clear understanding of how users reacted to these texts, and how the velocity of texts can enact a kind of allying mechanism, initiating and changing social relations.

Both the use of body as protest *and* the body as object also beg a question not amplified at all in the initial response, but rather one that emerges in the texts' increased circulation and velocity: that is, whose body? As protest becomes connected to (and almost collapsed into) the body as object theme, another group that might have allied with the national context of Tyler's protest comes to *protest her* based on the previously amplified messages of the body, specifically a raced body that purportedly speaks for all women.

The Facebook group, Muslim Women Against FEMEN, for example (a group that formed in response to FEMEN's call for a topless jihad day), points out in an open letter to FEMEN (published on their Facebook wall) that the "bodies" protesting are not the bodies of brown women, nor the bodies of Muslim women.

Figure 14.6. MWAF Facebook Page.

Because of this, they resist FEMEN's idea of a "global sisterhood" and critique FEMEN's attempt to operate as a "collective mouth piece." Through the mediums of Twitter and Facebook, MWAF re-appropriates FEMEN's protest with a "counterprotest" and FEMEN's "topless jihad day" with a "Muslimah Pride Day," reshaping and recontextualizing the discourse of the body as protest within a more localized, context-specific framework. In other words, what gets highlighted here is the way in which solidarity needs to be and must be tied to issues of race and religion, not *only* gender. This same message becomes more apparent in the embodied texts produced by MWAF. As another form of "counterprotest," Muslim and non-Muslim women circulated photos of themselves to Facebook and Twitter as a response to FEMEN's topless images. Some women took photos of themselves wearing hijabs, others with signs reading: "Nudity does not liberate me and I do not need saving," "Do I look oppressed to you?!," "Shame on you FEMEN. Hijab is my right!," and "I am a Muslim and a Feminist." In a similar way, we can think of this kind of activism alongside Barbara George's (this collection) analysis of counter-literacies, as MWAF's acts serve as a kind of feminist intervention that "challenge[s] traditional notions of agency" and "interrupt[s] dominant policy and practices" (George, 2017, p. 2)

Figure 14.7. MWAF (1).

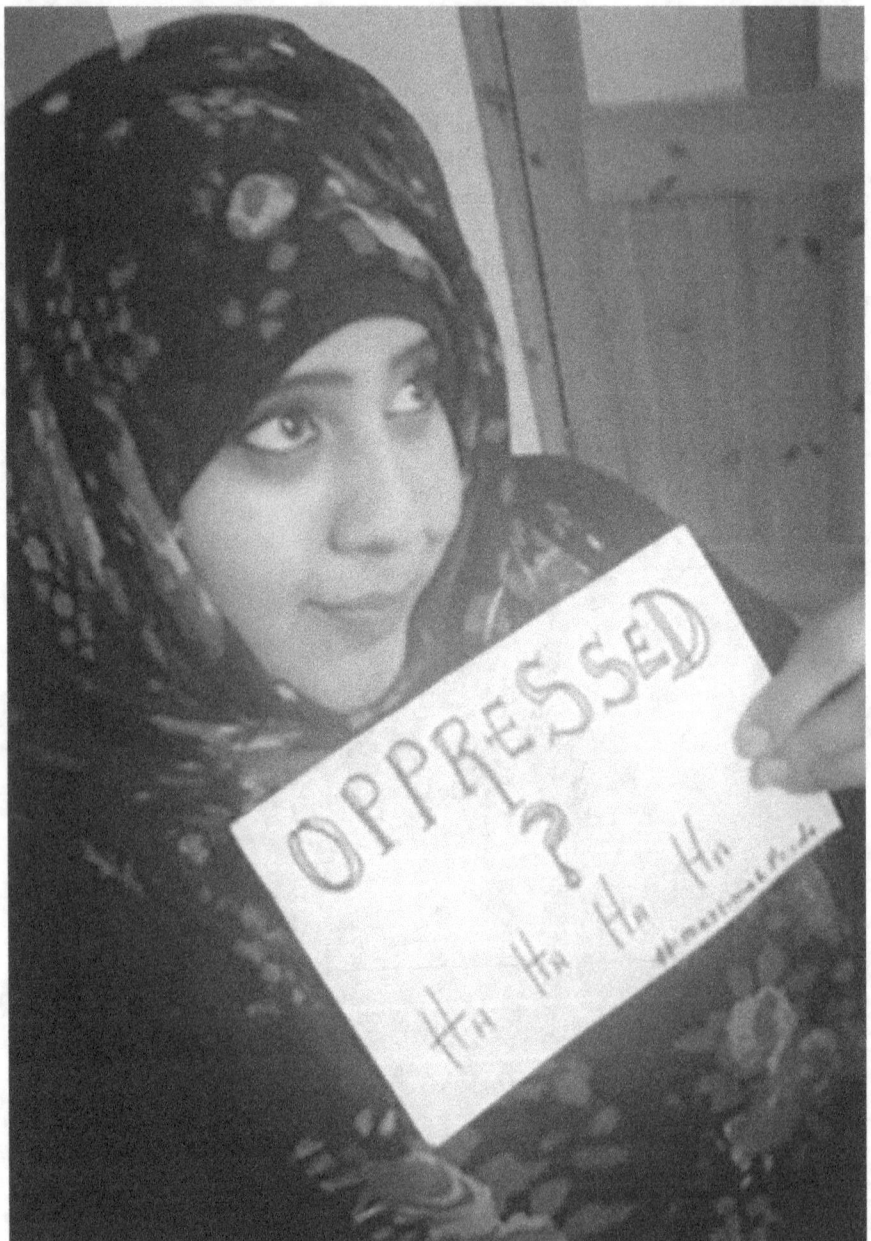

Figure 14.8. MWAF (2).

The re-appropriation of FEMEN's rhetorical mediums (the open letter and the use of images and bodily messages on Twitter and Facebook), as well as the re-appropriation of the language and words used by FEMEN (words such as "feminist," "liberation," and "oppression") increases the velocity of these texts. But this velocity is not merely an act of resistance; this circulation is also an act of feminist intervention and revision, an act that challenges, changes, and destabilizes previous rhetorical meanings. Rather than "universal solidarity" among all women, MWAF implores FEMEN and the larger public to acknowledge difference, to take on a critical consciousness by recognizing that the universalizing rhetorics of Western feminism do not speak to/for *all* women. Furthermore, MWAF's redistribution and revision of FEMEN's rhetoric operates as a mode of resistance to the dominant discourses of globalization interarticulated in FEMEN's rhetoric. In re-characterizing FEMEN's essentializing rhetoric—FEMEN's idealistic notion of a "global sisterhood"—MWAF, in their open letter to FEMEN, take on FEMEN's constant use of the third person plural to signify a different "we," alluding to a solidarity among "Muslim women and women of colour from the Global South" (Open Letter to FEMEN, 2013). In other words, the "we" for MWAF encompasses not just gender, but also race, religion, geographic location, and class. This kind of affective circulation showcases both FEMEN and MWAF's efforts to redistribute *and* revise ideologies related to "liberation," "freedom," and "oppression." These ideologies are premised on emotional and personal attachments, attachments that then help to construct connections and disconnections—"awayness" and "towardness"—between FEMEN, MWAF, and others. As was the case with FEMEN's reaction to and circulation of Tyler's image, MWAF's circulation of their counter-texts demonstrates an affect with roots in different material and historical contexts and differing evaluations of collectivity and solidarity. In other words, MWAF's moments of affective circulation—the fomenting anger regarding FEMEN's silencing, universalizing moves—represent instances of critical confrontation regarding women's lived experiences and differences. As Jacqueline Schiappa (Chapter 15, this collection) reminds us in her piece on intersectional activism, "Difference itself has become one of the most valuable truth-tools feminism has skilled . . . Pursuing freedom from oppression involves recognizing the ways in which systematized exclusions are distinctive and yet also emerge and are sustained by intersecting dominant cultural logics" (p. 299). In considering these texts, we can see how contesting and restructuring meaning facilitates the creation of alliances and social relations in these instances of circulation.

In these same moments, though, MWAF is responding to the "body as protest" and "body as object" themes as more generalizable to women across the globe than to the specificity of the Tunisian context of Tyler's original post. Although I cannot know for sure, MWAF's posts suggest that they may be in line with Tyler's goals if not the means by which she executed her protest. But due to the velocity of the amplified themes I discussed earlier, this original context gets lost and instead becomes re-contextualized by MWAF as a response to white, Western feminism.

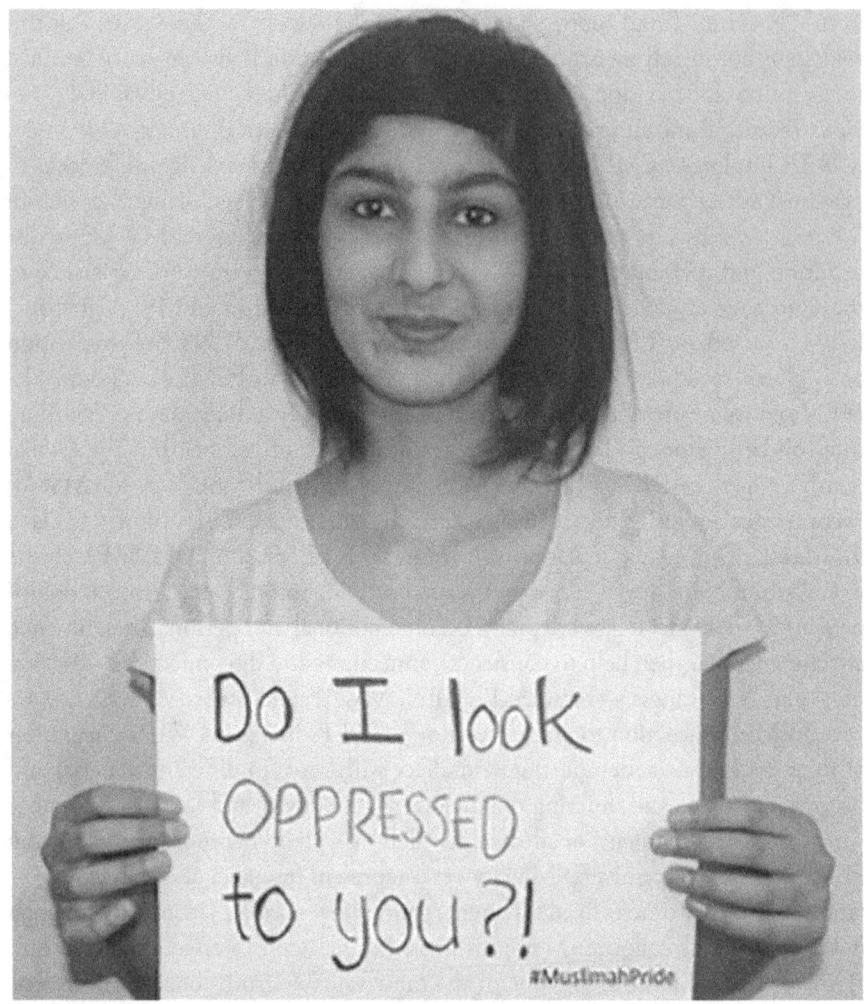

Figure 14.9. MWAF (3).

To further highlight how velocity, undergirded by affective charges, works to construct social relations, let us return to FEMEN. FEMEN ultimately accepts MWAF's reframing of the conversation, altering the social relations among feminists to form groups "for" and "against" that did not exist in the first layer of circulation. For example, in an open letter to MWAF (published by the *Huffington Post UK*, 2013), Shevchenko writes, "So sisters . . . You say to us that you are against FEMEN, but we are here for you and for all of us, as women are the modern slaves and it's never a question of skin color" (Shevchenko as cited in Nelson, 2013). It is important to note how the sentiment and meaning of solidarity differs here. Whereas in MWAF's texts, they attempt to point out the intersections between race and gender (among other markers of identity), FEMEN employs a rhetoric that distinguishes gender and race as separate experiences. In other words, FEMEN suggests that gender can and should be conceived of universally, regardless of other differences. Further down in the letter, Shevchenko attempts to characterize this idealistic, universal world, writing:

> And do you know what I see? I see a world without Serbs, Croats and Muslims being massacred, without 9/11, without witch-hunts, a world without suicide bombers and without the Taliban, without Israeli-Palestinian wars, without persecution of Jews as 'Christ-killers,' without Northern Ireland troubles, without Crusades, a world where there are no, "public beheadings and no flogging of female skin for the crime of showing an inch of it. See you on the battle lines!" (Shevchenko qtd. in Nelson, 2013).

In this excerpt, several moves take place. First, we can argue that this letter represents an attempt to affectively circulate and characterize a rhetorical imaginary—a "world" in which people are no longer subjected to violence. And yet in this projection, we see slippages between rhetorics of solidarity and rhetorics of geopolitics, particularly in Schevchenko's own rhetorical incitement of violence (e.g., her references to war and "battles" in describing FEMEN and their activist pursuits). Within her assertions about violence, other rhetorics emerge that produce other kinds of affect, and thus other kinds of knowledge. By resituating, and in many ways dismissing, MWAF's rhetoric around race and difference, Shevchenko's response uses the concept of a unified collectivity to suggest that the focus on difference comes from the problematic responses of those in power (men, religion, nationhood). This affective collision becomes one that suggests geopolitical solutions, something the mass media then runs with as their circulation of this particular text morphs into fear-mongering rhetorics around terrorism and 9/11.

Through amplification, then, we see the swift circulation and conflation of body as object and protest that allows the body to become a symbol, undifferentiated in how both MWAF and FEMEN see it. It is this meaning that gains significant velocity as we see in the back and forth between the two groups as well as multiple posts commenting on the two groups. But what also happens as a result of such emotionally motivated velocity is the conflation of women's bodies with questions of the nation due to how race and religion are positioned by FEMEN. This meaning is the one that, unfortunately, endures past this second layer of response.

We can see its beginning in mass media responses within the same time period as the MWAF/FEMEN debate. *A New Yorker* headline (Greenhouse, 2013), for example, reads: "How to Provoke National Unrest with a Facebook Photo."

APRIL 8, 2013

HOW TO PROVOKE NATIONAL UNREST WITH A FACEBOOK PHOTO

BY EMILY GREENHOUSE

In the middle of March, a nineteen-year-old Tunisian woman named Amina Tyler posted two topless photos of herself on Facebook. In one, she looks straight at the camera, her middle fingers up, with the words "Fuck Your Morals" painted across her bare chest, the black "O" of "morals" not quite closing over her navel. In the other, she is wearing eyeliner, or maybe kohl, and bright lipstick, her mouth compressed into a tight frown. Between a book in her right hand and a cigarette in her

Figure 14.10. The New Yorker Article.

In the article, writer Emily Greenhouse not only positions the nation of Tunisia as "ill-equipped to deal with the possibilities of public broadcasting afforded by the World Wide Web," she goes on to strategically argue that Tunisia is no longer a "progressive Arab country that respects women's rights." The article then ends with a citation and re-characterization of FEMEN's call for a topless jihad day (and I should note that there is no mention of MWAF's counterprotest in the article). Greenhouse writes, "Femen has issued a call for a new Arab Spring in a strongly worded statement against the 'lethal hatred of Islamists, for whom killing a woman is more natural than recognizing her right to do as she pleases with her own body.' It pleads, 'Long live the topless jihad!'"

Here, we can see how the media's use of FEMEN's texts—particularly FEMEN's affect of righteous anger in favor of women's rights—serves as an incentive to construct an "us-them" relationship in which the powerhouses of the west (the US and the UK) are seen in opposition to the Middle East. This change in meaning—the move from an effort to invoke a narrative on universal freedoms and rights (FEMEN) to a fear-mongering narrative about 9/11, terrorism, and national progression (mainstream media) can be located in the disjuncture between textual content and emotion. FEMEN's affective use of warfare language to talk about the need for universal women's rights actually undermines FEMEN's call for universal rights, thus enabling the media to discount that call as well. What gets re-circulated by the media, then, is the affect—the fear and "ethical" kind of anger that undergirds the content of FEMEN's message. That affect alongside the content of the media's messages—discussions about terrorism and national backwardness/progression—produces a fear-mongering narrative of blame, purporting, further, racial anxieties about Muslims and Islam.

Such fear-mongering becomes what endures out of the "body" rhetorics; we can trace meanings from the body as protest and object, to the body as anti-protest and raced, to the body as nation-state, indicating the insurmountable differences of the West and the Middle East, resulting finally in Islamophobic rhetoric. What begins as a feminist protest ends up solidifying and reinforcing a firmly held ideology of fear directly at odds with the original protest.

This kind of rhetorical endurance indeed poses many more questions and concerns regarding the nature of the digital as a site for feminist activism. However, we would be remiss to not acknowledge the kind of feminist interventionist work at play here. As Angela Crow points out in her piece on embodied literacies and activism, such activist "labor," regardless of the outcome—and I am referring to both FEMEN and MWAF's protests—are "example[s] of embodied literacies reshaping local possibilities not only for themselves but in their work to address infrastructure, the build for the larger community as well" (Crow, 2018, p. 49). These cycles of amplification, velocity, and endurance point to a new form of rhetorical action in digital spaces that allows for the reshaping of possibility: circulation powered by affect. For those of us interested in the transnational effects of rhetoric, it behooves us to pay attention to digital circulation in order to understand how rhetorics and the affect undergirding their movements lead to co-options of meaning and thus the production of knowledge and social relations. It is this movement that I term affective circulation. For the web, affective circulation speaks to an unstable process where words and images (memes, tweets, citations, for example) operate as metonymic moments, bringing about certain associations and disassociations, forming social alliances while also producing exclusions by "othering" certain bodies. A text detached from its original history and context via the speed of circulation *and* the emotional weight of repetition allows the political weight of a message to both be obfuscated and coopted. And it also allows the message to become an agent for mobilization. As Sarah Ahmed (2014) suggests, "Emotions are relational: they involve (re)actions or relations of 'towardness' or 'awayness'" (p. 8). These kinds of movements—the changing and shifting of rhetorics depending on the contexts of their encounters—allows us to see how circulation represents a co-constitutive process, an assemblage of events and knowledges that necessarily affect the "lived encounters of public life" (Edbauer, 2005, p. 21). The kind of rhetorical repurposing that takes place within digital spaces is unique in that those processes are always already immediate, rapid, pervasive, and widespread.

What we can take away from looking at this kind of circulation is the way in which rhetorics necessarily become tied to discourses of globalization for various purposes. Tyler's image, once taken up by sponsors with vastly different economic and political goals, became the basis for purporting neoliberal logics about women's rights and propagating Islamophobic claims and beliefs. In many ways, the mainstream media's circulation of these particular events allows us to see how women's bodies get defined and repurposed for national and supranational projects. As rhetorical scholar Catherine Chaput (2010) reminds us, theorizing circulation within spaces dominated by neoliberalism "demands a structural reorganization in the way we think about political-economic and cultural practices within capitalism from situation to transsituation" and it demands "a new understanding of rhetoric as continuously moving through and connecting different instantiations within this complex structure" (p. 6). In addition, viewing circulation as an affective process—and even more so, as a rhetorical tool for feminist intervention—can help us understand circulation not only as an intricate process within the digital, but also an intricate and vastly material process within a global information economy. Thus, in using a transnational feminist lens for looking at circulation, we can question the ways in which texts engage in and/or dispute discourses of globalization so that we might better understand the limitations of and possibilities for feminist rhetorical action to occur on the web. More importantly, though, attending to circulation in this way can also help us think more critically about how we as rhetoricians and feminist activists can intervene and leverage affective circulation towards a more productive kind of social change and rhetorical efficacy.

REFERENCES

Ahmed, S. (2014). *The cultural politics of emotion*. Edinburgh: Edinburgh University Press.
An Open Letter to FEMEN. (2013). Retrieved on April 12, 2013 from http://www.facebook.com.
Annas, P. J. (1985). Style as politics: A feminist approach to the teaching of writing. *College English, 47*(4), 360–71.
Bacchetta, P., Campt, T., Grewal, I., Kaplan, C., Moallem, M. & Terry, J. (2002). *Transnational feminist practices against war. Meridians, 2*(2), 302–308.
Berry, P. W., Hawisher, G. E. & Selfe, C. L. (2012). *Transnational literate lives in digital times*. Logan, Utah: Utah State University Press.
Blair, K., Gajjala, R. & Tulley, C. (2009). *Webbing cyberfeminist practice: Communities, pedagogies, and social action*. Cresskill, N.J: Hampton Press.
Byrne, N. & Taylor, A. Retrieved November 21, 2014 from http://www.NoelByrne.ie.
Chaput, C. (2010). Rhetorical circulation in late capitalism: Neoliberalism and the overdetermination of affective energy. *Philosophy and Rhetoric, 43*(1), 1–25.
Cochrane, K. (2013). *Rise of the naked female warriors. The Guardian*. Retrieved from http://www.theguardian.com.
Cooper, M. M. (2011). Rhetorical agency as emergent and enacted. *College Composition and Communication, 62*(3), 420–449.

Crow, A. (2018). Women-only bicycle rides and freedom of movement: How online communicative practices of local community managers support feminist interventions In K. L. Blair & L. Nickoson (Eds.), *Composing feminist interventions: Activism, engagement, praxis*. Fort Collins, CO: The WAC Clearinghouse / Louisville, CO: University Press of Colorado. Retrieved from https://wac.colostate.edu/books/perspectives/feminist.

Dean, J. (2010). *Blog theory: Feedback and capture in the circuits of drive*. Cambridge, UK: Polity.

Dean, J. (2002). *Publicity's secret: How technocultural capitalized on democracy*. Ithaca, NY: Cornell University Press.

Dingo, R. A. (2012). *Networking arguments: Rhetoric, transnational feminism, and public policy writing*. Pittsburgh, PA: University of Pittsburgh Press.

Edbauer, J. (2005). Unframing models of public distribution. *Rhetoric Society Quarterly, 35*(4), 5–24.

Fairclough, N. (1992). *Discourse and social change*. Cambridge, UK: Polity Press.

FEMEN Facebook. (2013). Retrieved April 5, 2013 from http://www.facebook.com.

FEMEN Home Page. (2013). Retrieved April 5, 2013 from http://www.FEMEN.org.

George, B. (2018). Literacy, praxix, and participation in environmental deliberation. In K. L. Blair & L. Nickoson (Eds.), *Composing feminist interventions: Activism, engagement, praxis*. Fort Collins, CO: The WAC Clearinghouse / Louisville, CO: University Press of Colorado. Retrieved from https://wac.colostate.edu/books/perspectives/feminist.

Giltrow, J. & Stein, D. (2009). *Genres in the Internet: Issues in the theory of genre*. Amsterdam, The Netherlands: John Benjamins.

Giovanni, J. D. (2013). Can bare breasts save Tunisia? *The Daily Beast*. Retrieved on April 10, 2013 from http://www.thedailybeast.com.

Greenhouse, E. (2013). How to provoke national unrest with a Facebook photo." *The New Yorker*. Retrieved from http://www.thenewyorker.com.

Grewal, I. (2005). *Transnational America: Feminisms, diasporas, neoliberalisms*. Durham: Duke University Press.

Grewal, I. & Kaplan, C. (1994). *Scattered hegemonies: Postmodernity and transnational feminist practices*. Minneapolis, MN: University of Minnesota Press.

Gries, L. (2013). Iconographic tracking: A digital research method for visual rhetorics and circulation studies. *Computers and Composition, 30*(4), 332–348.

Hennessy, R. (1993). *Materialist feminism and the politics of discourse*. New York, NY: Routledge.

Hennessy, R. (2000). *Profit and pleasure: Sexual identities in late capitalism*. New York, NY: Routledge.

Hesford, W. S. (2006). Global turns and cautions in rhetoric and composition Studies. *PMLA, 121*(3), 787–801.

Hesford, W. S. & Kozol, W. (2005). *Just advocacy?: Women's human rights, transnational feminisms, and the politics of representation*. New Brunswick, N.J: Rutgers University Press.

Hesford, W. S. & Schell, E. E. (2008). Introduction: Configurations of transnationality: Locating feminist Rhetorics. *College English, 70*(5), 461–470.

Kafir Crusaders. (n.d.). Retrieved November 15, 2014, from http://www.kafircrusafers.com.

Lam, W. S. E. (2004). Second language socialization in a bilingual chat room: Global and local considerations. *Language Learning & Technology,* 8(3), 44–65.

McKee, H. A. & DeVoss, D. N. (2007). *Digital writing research: Technologies, methodologies, and ethical issues.* Cresskill, N.J: Hampton Press.

Miller, C. & Shepherd, D. (2009). Questions for genre theory from the blogosphere. In J. Giltrow & D. Stein (Eds.), *Genres in the Internet.* Amsterdam: John Benjamins Publishing Company.

#MuslimahPrideDay. (2013). Retrieved on April 4, 2013 from http://www.twitter.com

Muslim Women Against FEMEN. (2013). Retrieved April 5, 2013, from http://www.facebook.com.

Nelson, S. (2013). Inna Shevchenko responds to Muslim women against Femen's open letter in wake of Amina Tyler topless jihad. *The Huffington Post UK.* Retrieved April 10, 2013, from http://huffingtonpostuk.com .

Porter, J. E. (2009). Recovering delivery for digital rhetoric. *Computers and Composition,* 26(4), 207–224.

Queen, M. (2008). Transnational feminist rhetorics in a digital world. *College English,* 70(5), 471–489.

Ridolfo, J. & DeVoss, D. N. (2009). Composing for recomposition: Rhetorical velocity and delivery. *Kairos: A Journal of Rhetoric, Technology, and Pedagogy,* 13(2).

Royster, J. J. & Kirsch, G. (2012). *Feminist rhetorical practices.* Carbondale, IL: Southern Illinois University Press.

Schiappa, J. (2018). Advocating "active" intersectionality through a comparison of two Slutwalks. In K. L. Blair & L. Nickoson (Eds.), *Composing feminist interventions: Activism, engagement, praxis.* Fort Collins, CO: The WAC Clearinghouse / Louisville, CO: University Press of Colorado. Retrieved from https://wac.colostate.edu/books/perspectives/feminist.

Sullivan, L. L. (1997). Cyberbabes: (self-) Representations of women and the virtual (male) gaze. *Computers and Composition,* 14(2), 189–204.

Trimbur, J. (2000). Composition and the circulation of writing. *College Composition and Communication,* 52(2), 188–219.

Trimbur, J. (2004). Delivering the message: Typography and the materiality of writing. In. C. Handa (Ed.), *Visual Rhetoric in a Digital World* (pp. 260–271). Boston, MA: Bedford/St. Martin's.

Warner, M. (2005). *Publics and counterpublics.* New York, NY: Zone Books.

Warnick, B. & Heineman, D. (2012). *Rhetoric online: The politics of new media.* New York, NY: Peter Lang.

Warriner, D. S. (2007). Transnational literacies: Immigration, language learning, and identity. *Linguistics & Education,* 18, 201–214.

Zimmann, A. (2018). A peek inside the master's house: The tale of feminist rhetorician as candidate for U.S. congress. In K. L. Blair & L. Nickoson (Eds.), *Composing feminist interventions: Activism, engagement, praxis.* Fort Collins, CO: The WAC Clearinghouse / Louisville, CO: University Press of Colorado. Retrieved from https://wac.colostate.edu/books/perspectives/feminist.

CHAPTER 15.

ADVOCATING "ACTIVE" INTERSECTIONALITY THROUGH A COMPARISON OF TWO SLUTWALKS

Jacqueline Schiappa
Macalester College

A central contribution of Women's and Feminist Studies is the concept of intersectionality: the notion that many social groups experience oppression along multiple systems, and that those systems are conceptually and materially inseparable. Examining how community organizers actually do and do not employ intersectionality in their activism advances civic engagement scholarship seeking to improve emancipatory activist practices. This chapter briefly reviews intersectionality as a concept, and then reviews the different ways two groups of feminist activists organized "Slutwalk" protest marches in their local communities. While one group, Slutwalk Toronto, demonstrates an effectively intersectional civic action, the other, Slutwalk Minneapolis, shows how a passive approach to intersectionality fosters community exclusion. The chapter concludes by suggesting that "active" intersectional organizing, as evidenced by Slutwalk Toronto, is an engaged, intentional process that explicitly foregrounds and values the breadths and depths of perspectives within feminist social groups. Furthermore, Slutwalk Toronto willingly held identity differences in productive tension with one another at multiple levels throughout the organizing process.

In the 2011 National Women's Studies Association White Paper, "Women's Studies as Civic Engagement: Research and Recommendations," contributors conclude with a final recommendation on civic engagement in higher education: to "come to *terms*," by developing "common language to speak about the importance of civic engagement across disciplines, units, and surrounding communities" (Orr, 2011, p. 24). They argue that doing so is "urgently required, not just to make Women's Studies contributions intelligible beyond its disciplinary borders but to allow for more meaningful exchanges about the practice of civic engagement at every level" (p. 24). If part of improving civic engagement scholarship depends on better utilizing insights from Women's Studies and establishing common language, then the term and value that is *intersectionality* must be included, because as McCall (2005) writes, intersectionality may well be "the most important theoretical contribution that women's studies, in conjunction with related fields, has made so far" (p. 1771).

Since many disciplines take up civic engagement in their work, intersectionality offers a significant opportunity for the unique disciplinary contributions of Women's Studies to be recognized as integral to related civic scholarship. This chapter aims to help develop common language and understanding about what intersectional activism is in civic engagement. I begin by reviewing what intersectionality means, followed by a comparative evaluation of two seemingly similar feminist protest events through an intersectional lens, and conclude with a discussion of how an expectation of *active* intersectionality (rather than *passive*) may help scholars evaluate intersectionality in activism. Moreover, the concept of active intersectionality can help feminist teachers interrogate their roles in, and the material conditions of, developing ethical feminist community engagement.

UNDERSTANDING INTERSECTIONALITY

The concept of intersectionality is owed to non-white feminists and is frequently cited as the signature of "third-wave"[1] feminist theory and praxis. Asian American feminist activist Kristina Wong summarizes a basic definition nicely: "Third wave feminism was a response by women of color and others who felt homogenized by a movement defined by the goals of middle-class, white women" (2003, p. 295). Feminist writers Baumgardner and Richards extend this idea further, suggesting, "it is exactly that multiplicity—of individuals and of expertise, among other qualities—that we believe defines third wave leadership" (2003, pp. 159–160). Diversifying narratives, challenging interpretive frameworks that emerge from particular standpoints, geopolitical locations (white, hetero), is therefore a signature of third wave thought.

Discourses of *difference itself* have become one of the most valuable lenses of truth feminism has skilled. Rather than divide feminist agendas along lines of difference, third wave theorists suggest that difference be recognized, named, respected and empowered as a mechanism of camaraderie. Pursuing freedom

---

[1] Much has been published about how the wave metaphor in feminist history is problematic and Zarnow suggests that the feminist wave metaphor is not only artificial, but detrimentally "compresses the highly nuanced reworking of feminist thought and practice," (2010, p. 274). See also: Fernandes, 2010; Sandavol, 2000; Schiappa, 2015; Thompson, 2010, to name a few.

from oppression involves recognizing the ways in which systematized exclusions are distinctive *and yet also* emerge and are sustained by intersecting dominant cultural logics. For example, both patriarchal and white supremacist ideologies position women and people of color as dehumanized objects. Thus, many feminists agree that the third wave feminism must be particularly alert to issues of intersectionality, multiculturalism and identity politics (Fernandes, 2010, p.99). Emphasizing how various forms of institutionalized inequity, such as racism and classism, are not only necessarily *relevant* to feminist interventions but are *inherently* intersecting processes and must be discussed together. Despite intersectionality being a trademark of third wave feminism, mainstream feminists relentlessly prioritize white, hetero, middle-class experiences.

As women of color continued to reject, overcome, and negotiate their marginalization by mainstream feminism's exclusivity (namely along lines of race but also in its homophobia and classism), several key transformative works emerged. With the publication of Demita Frazier, Beverly Smith, and Barbara Smith's *Combahee River Collective Statement* (1977), Cherríe Moraga and Gloria Anzaldúa's *This Bridge Called My Back* (1981), Barbara Smith's *Home Girls: A Black Feminist Anthology* (1983), Audre Lorde's *I Am Your Sister: Black Women Organizing Across Sexualities* (1986), among many others, the key voices of influence in western feminism shifted. The ideas and experiences at the heart of these works were not new then and are not very different now, but the publication and amplification of such voices impacted mainstream feminism forever. The aggregate result of the increased visibility of women of color in mainstream feminism is the moral and material necessity of intersectionality in organizing feminist interventions, and community engagement initiatives. No longer can mainstream feminism deny its long-overdue obligation to a more inclusive social project that actively foregrounds issues of race, class, ability, and sexual orientation. Intersectionality must inform any feminist pedagogical or activist project seeking social, political and moral viability.

Despite its nearly ubiquitous reference in contemporary feminist discourse, few writers thoroughly define what it means for an idea or practice to *actually* be intersectional, especially in relation to civic engagement and feminist rhetorical pedagogies. I submit a brief summary of the concept here in an effort to clarify what intersectionality itself means and the common language that surrounds it. This summary serves as a way to ground a comparative analysis of two feminist interventions by the same name, Slutwalk, and the organizing activities shaping each. Both Slutwalks seemingly emerge from the same feminist ethos, but ultimately differ in the ways they do, and do not, demonstrate intersectional praxis.

Most broadly, intersectionality represents feminism that explicitly connects women's issues to issues of race, class, sexuality, and ability (Third Wave

History). Further, intersectionality is a value and term underscoring two coexisting truths: first, the fact that many social groups experience oppression along *multiple* planes, and second, that those planes are conceptually and materially *inseparable*. For example, consider Audre Lorde's (1986) essay describing her experiences as Black lesbian in the feminist community, in which she articulates her own necessarily intersectional identity:

> When I say I am a Black feminist, I mean I recognize that my power as well as my primary oppressions come as a result of my Blackness as well as my womanness, and therefore my struggles on both these fronts are inseparable. (Lorde, 1986, p. 4)

The term 'intersectionality' itself was first introduced by Kimberle Crenshaw in 1989 and 1991. In 1992, Rebecca Walker authored a brief *Ms.* magazine article titled "Becoming the Third Wave" signaling a call for a collective shift in feminist consciousness that explicitly includes civically engaged activism (Third Wave History). Walker wrote, "My involvement must reach beyond my own voice in discussion, beyond voting, beyond reading feminist theory. My anger and awareness must translate into tangible action" (1992, p. 40). Thus, as feminists of color were working diligently to mobilize, protect, and uplift their communities they were also animating contemporary examples of actively intersectional feminist praxis.

Perhaps the most famous iteration of intersectionality is found in bell hooks' influential phrase "imperialist-white-supremacist-capitalist-patriarchy" (Media Education Foundation, 2006). Other iterations of these connections are found across social justice scholarship. Iris Marion Young's (2011) excellent work differentiating "five faces" of oppression suggests that most social groups experience oppression in the form of marginalization, violence, cultural imperialism, exploitation, and/or powerlessness. Most feminists are personally familiar with at least one of these faces, but many know them all. Mexican American women experience not only cultural imperialism in a nation that devalues and appropriates Mexican culture, but also exploitation and marginalization in the form of unequal power, labor and commodity distributions between men and women. It is with such an identity experience in mind that intersectionality goes further, past differentiating faces of oppression, to insisting that exploitation not be theorized without marginalization, because they function cooperatively. An intersectional critique of exploitative working conditions must necessarily examine factors constraining workers' abilities to influence those conditions, such as disenfranchisement through powerlessness.

Therefore, a fundamental piece of intersectional work is the prioritization of liberating those social groups who experience several faces of oppression simultaneously throughout their lives. Finally, intersectional theory asserts that the moments or places oppressive systems intersect are *knowable and therefore changeable*, making intersectionality a useful, relevant practice in feminist interventions and pedagogies. To better illustrate how intersectionality can be assessed and practiced in real ways, I compare two activist events, each organized separately but both part of the same broader feminist movement against sexual violence and rape culture. Organized by women in their local communities, each activist process culminates in an annual protest march called *Slutwalk*.

SLUTWALK

> "You know, I think we're beating around the bush here. I've been told I'm not supposed to say this—however, women should avoid dressing like sluts in order not to be victimized."

The inexcusable words of Toronto police officer Constable Michael Sanguinetti have been etched in my mind since I first encountered them in April of 2011, only weeks after he'd uttered them at a poorly attended safety discussion at York University. I often wonder what Sanguinetti might say now of his comments, knowing they'd serve as the fertilizer for sowing one of the most controversial public feminist interventions in decades. His 32 careless words spurred a small group of young women, mostly students, to organize a march that would eventually inspire tens of thousands of women and men to protest rape culture and sexual violence in hundreds of cities across over sixty countries.

The first Slutwalk, Slutwalk Toronto, took place on April 3, 2011. An estimated 3,000+ community participants marched from a local park to a city police station with signs and chants denouncing rape culture, victim blaming, slut shaming, and inadequate police training on sexual violence. The walk's name, aesthetic and message garnered substantial media attention and quickly circulated the feminist blogosphere, receiving hefty support and criticism. Subsequently, other Slutwalks popped up across North American cities, some in communication with Toronto's original organizers, and others wholly autonomously. Every Slutwalk is initiated, organized, and funded independently. Most walks include a mission statement denouncing rape culture and working to challenge mindsets and stereotypes of victim blaming and slut-shaming around sexual violence. Walks also tend to include community-specific outcomes.

Despite many characterizations of Slutwalk as a headquartered movement with a consistent mission, the differences between Slutwalks are as varied as feminists and communities themselves. When I compare Slutwalk Toronto with Slutwalk Minneapolis, I am comparing two versions of the same feminist interventionist ethos, but also the earnestly different ways in which each group of feminist community activists organized their local protests. I contacted the lead Slutwalk Minneapolis organizer, Kim directly and obtained permission to closely observe Slutwalk Minneapolis's organizing process over the next year,[2] culminating in Slutwalk Minneapolis 2012.

SLUTWALK MINNEAPOLIS

Throughout the summer there were sporadic meetings organized via unidirectional emails to existing organizers for Slutwalk Minneapolis, who often proclaimed intersectional values. On average, seven to nine people attended, sitting in the back community room at a local coffee and gelato shop that seemed familiar to those there. With no spare seating, I sat on the floor and mapped the room, noting that it could not have easily accommodated individuals with limited physical mobility. Aside from myself, no one took notes, and discussion was driven by a sparse agenda provided by Kim. In contrast to Slutwalk Toronto's all-female organizers, Slutwalk Minneapolis's meetings featured three men, one of whom was the head organizer's close friend. My records consistently remark upon the heavy-handedness of Kim and her friend Nick's influence on the meeting's topics, organization, scheduling, and decision-making.

The more I observed, the clearer it became that the foremost priority for that year's walk was increasing the number of attendees and finding ways to generate income. Organizers worried that the attendance from the year prior, approximately 500 people, would not be matched, as they anticipated 200 participants. Beyond growing attendance to increase the walk's visibility, organizers sought to recruit "membership" subscriptions requiring membership fees and increasing sales of merchandise to produce income.

When discussing building stronger relationships with potential allies in the community, several participants suggested reaching out to a particularly reputable local nonprofit focused on counseling and advocating for survivors of sexual violence and abuse. I observed the following conversation regarding involving that organization:

> **Participant:** "I can try to meet them on [these] days?"
>
> **Kim:** "I can't meet then."
>
> **Nick:** "Fuck them."

---

2   Regarding IRB, I met with faculty and exchanged emails with an IRB contact and found the research work to be exempt if I worked within the territory of *Public* events and personas, and did not ask participants any questions regarding their personal experiences (especially avoiding potentially triggering subject matter), instead focusing on organizing strategies and public discourses.

That was the entirety of the exchange, the collective suggestion not only rejected, but also flippantly disregarded. During a later organizing meeting the lead organizers feigned interest in "trying to build stronger allies within the community, but it probably won't happen until after the walk." Currently Slutwalk Minneapolis' webpage lists one local shelter as a local resource for survivors and victims of domestic abuse and sexual violence (Slutwalk Minneapolis).

Most ideas presented by other volunteers were dismissed or scorned outright. This began with suggestions to better employ social media to reach the community more broadly. Whenever the subject of social media arose it'd quickly be characterized as "a distraction" or "an electronic thing that's getting harder and harder," or, anecdotally, a thing "I fucking hate right now." When one volunteer suggested not underestimating social media tools, and several individuals in attendance nodded in passionate agreement, Nick groaned, "we've mined out the social media angle," and my notes concluded: "the idea didn't grow." Toward the end of one meeting Kim openly asked the group, "Anything else?" Gently, a young transgender woman named Andrea, a particularly active volunteer, shared that she'd felt excluded in the decision-making process:

> **Andrea**: "I don't always know how to fit this in, but, we didn't reach out enough to male victims. I don't know where to fit this in but I really wanted to bring it up tonight."
>
> **Kim**: "*Survivors.*"
>
> **Andrea**: "We need to make it more open for people to participate."
>
> **Participant**: "Maybe a more inclusive message for all people. . . ."
>
> **Kim**: "We do stress to not focus on female victims like other Slutwalks."
>
> **Andrea**: "But we stress "my dress isn't a yes" and what does that mean for men? Let's make them know they're welcome too. I have a lot of ideas."
>
> **Kim**: "Let's table it until after the walk."

This exchange was rare, in that Kim was not often challenged at all. The room felt uneasy, and Kim's tone defensive. Andrea walked outside and did not return to the meeting that evening. I later noticed her smoking a cigarette nearby and approached to ask how she felt about what had just occurred. Her voice hesitant and eyes tearful, she expressed frustration with the process and feeling silenced. Subsequently I frequently noted Andrea's distance from Kim and the organizing group; she was energetic with other volunteers and led many chants during the walk, but did not make any other suggestions during meetings.

Figure 15.1. Andrea, preparing to lead chants at the 2012 Slutwalk, photo taken by author.

During a final meeting a different volunteer stepped outside of 'business as usual' and broached the importance of race, commenting that "given that Slutwalk has had to deal with racial issues—" she was immediately cut off by Kim, who objected, "We want to try to totally avoid that." Another participant added, "we did have those issues last year but it's glossed over quickly," while another rebutted, "but that makes it look like a white woman's walk," followed by silence. Later, in a follow-up interview, I asked Kim if she had ever intentionally reached out to community groups focused on racial justice. Her response took only two lines in my notebook: "I tried once, they were very critical, they can come to us if they want to, it's up to them." Her tone was worse than indifferent, it was annoyed and hostile. What I did not know then was that Kim had published two posts on the official Slutwalk Minneapolis blog on the subject of White Supremacy issues in the Slutwalk movement about a year prior, which I find quite revealing. The first, "White Supremacy and the Walk . . . " wonders:

> Where is that White Supremacy? Would it have made it any better if it were a group of black/hispanic/asian women who banded together and started the SlutWalk? And how so? Would these people who have written about White Supremacy

have raised a ruckus if the SlutWalk were for people of colour only? Or would they have been upset if someone pointed out that it was reverse discrimination? *Sherva, May 18, 2011*

These comments are a clear expression of closedness to critique, an absence of awareness about how local racial justice projects are actually working diligently across the Twin Cities and addressing every single one of the issues she names, and an ironic call for increased intersectional work whilst indicting local people of color for not being "fun" to organize with. This is passive intersectionality, this is what happens when feminist interventions and activities do not explicitly vertically integrate diversity in their work; it is exclusive feminism in action. Slutwalk Minneapolis was organized by a handful of nonstudent activists who pursued a much narrower agenda grounded in their personal experiences, rather than an intentionally intersectional feminist approach committed to community listening and collaboration.

Ultimately Slutwalk Minneapolis did not sincerely attempt an intersectional feminist intervention by refusing to engage local communities of color, or impoverished neighborhoods, or existing community organizations and resources. In my observation of the walk itself, attended by just over two hundred people, I counted two Black women, amounting to 1% in a community where 19% of residents are Black (State and County, 2014). The failure on Slutwalk Minneapolis' part is not just in the unequal power balances or exclusion of more diverse and intersectional persons, but in the absence of an intentioned, committed, reflexive process.

The consequences of Slutwalk Minneapolis's failure as an intersectional interventionist project include further marginalizing the Twin Cities' women of color, further entrenching religious, racial, ethnic, and cultural minority groups' distrust of purportedly feminist projects that end up functionally excluding intersectional identities, and literally having no meaningful local material impact. There were no demands made of local universities to better support survivors of sexual assault, there were no demands of increased police accountability, or policy reform, or improved criminal justice processes, no direct messaging or engagement with local media outlets, and no efforts made to advance community outreach and educational programming. There was no sincere effort made to include diverse participants representative of the community other than those on the LGBT*QIA spectrum. In all of these ways, Slutwalk Minneapolis was inadequately intersectional and therefore inadequately feminist.

My experiences with Slutwalk Minneapolis stirred a curiosity in me about Slutwalk Toronto's founders and how they approached organizing within their community. I'd read plenty of criticisms of Slutwalk as a bourgeoisie white feminist movement and sought to personally meet the women who started the first march, to discover firsthand their intentions and thoughts about intersectional interventions.

SLUTWALK TORONTO

After securing enough funding to pay for airfare and lodging for three days, I traveled to Toronto to interview as many of the Slutwalk Toronto organizers as I could. When emailing didn't work, I reached out on Twitter to the names I knew. In the end, Twitter helped me coordinate just as many interviews as emailing. Since there weren't organizing meetings during my trip and I was less familiar with the local community, I focused my questions on how past Slutwalk Toronto marches had been developed, what changes had occurred if any to those processes, reactions to criticism, and how organizers had or had not involved other community groups.

What I learned first was that despite considerable criticism that presumes otherwise, the first Slutwalk in Toronto, Canada was not organized by only bourgeois straight white women, or even feminist-identified persons. In fact, the original Slutwalk founders (of which there are five) included two women of color, at least two queer-identified women, and who earned annual incomes placing them below the poverty line. Uniquely, lead organizer Heather Jarvis resists classification as a feminist because she is uncomfortable aligning herself with a movement that empowers primarily white, westernized ideologies about women.

Another founding organizer, Alyssa Teekah, identifies as a "queer, brown (mixed South Asian roots), fat woman with middle-class privilege" (Teekah, 2015, p.33). When I asked about the composition of participants, Jarvis responded with an enthusiasm that suggested she'd been hoping I'd ask:

> There were men, there were women, there were people whose gender I'm not going to try to assign, there were people who were outwardly identifying as trans, as sex workers, and people of color, and indigenous groups, and mothers groups and I mean it was everybody you could imagine. (personal communication)

Mischaracterizing Slutwalk Toronto's original organizers and the demographics across participants is not the only common misconception influencing feminist debates on Slutwalk. As the creators of Slutwalk, the original organizers fell under a heavy and constant barrage of criticism, much of which rested on mistaken assumptions. Another erroneous assumption about Slutwalk Toronto is that organizers did not attempt to coordinate with existing community resources focused on sexual violence. Slutwalk Toronto worked with the White Ribbon Campaign, a local program focused on teaching men and boys about fighting violence against women, as well as the Toronto Rape Crisis Center, also known as the Multicultural Women Against Rape (Jarvis, 2013, personal communciation). Reaching out to local groups and individuals whose diversities reflect the community alone is not intersectional activism. The next step is to *empower* and *integrate* those groups and individuals in the organizing process early on and being responsive to critical feedback.

Figure 15.2: Heather Jarvis, Slutwalk Toronto Organizer, leading the first Toronto march in 2011, unknown photographer.

Slutwalk Toronto's intersectionality is reflected not only in its mission statement but its organizers' willingness to renegotiate that mission statement's application based on community feedback. When participants voiced concerns, in meetings and social media spaces, about including Toronto police reform or training in the march's goals, the organizers listened. In subsequent Slutwalk Toronto marches the walk's destination changed from the Toronto police headquarters to walks that traverse the community in different ways. Slutwalk Toronto also took greater efforts to build allies in the community, especially with existing resources. Jarvis explained:

> The one thing that we did do was work towards ally-ships through, in our own ways we all had our own connections, some more strong in Toronto in certain rounds (more student associated or not), I knew a lot of places like Womens Resource Centers, Women in Trans Centers, um, non-profits, people that we thought. we did a lot of outreach saying, "This

is who we are, we're inviting you to come, if you'd like to stand with us as an ally just let us know" that happened a lot. We contacted a lot of people, some of whom got back enthusiastically some of whom didn't, some of whom we've built relationships with since. (personal communication)

Furthermore, Slutwalk Toronto's event speakers have recently included Monica Forrester, "a 2-spirit, black, queer, Trans-femme, radical, sexworker, and activist," Blu Waters, a grandmother and member of the Metis nation of Ontario of the Cree/Métis/Micmac-Wolf Clan, Jeff Perera of the White Ribbon Campaign, known for "men working towards re-imagining masculinity and inspiring men, young men, boys and male-identified people to help end gender-based violence," Akio Maroon, who identifies as "Black, queer, mother, activist, and sex positive educator," and Kira Andry, a "agender, queer, mixed, activist and student," among several others (#SWTO2014). An assemblage of such diverse identities speaking about their communities' experiences is sufficiently representational intersectional community engagement. The point is not that diverse identities were merely physically present (although there is significance in that presence), but that they *informed* the organizing process itself and were empowered to shape the walk's goals, dialoguing language choices with organizers, and revising the outcome-goals of the walk to better address Toronto's patriarchal policing of sexual violence and treatment of victims.

After reflecting on the divisiveness of Slutwalk's naming and reassessing community goals, principle organizer Heather Jarvis left the organization and focused on founding the first International Day Against Victim Blaming only one year later, on April 3rd 2012, the anniversary of the first Slutwalk. Slutwalk Toronto's organizers, however problematic, have consistently practiced reflexivity, transparency, listening, and adjustment. Indeed, these practices may be required for effective, just intersectional feminist interventions. In addition to recognizing, valuing, involving, and empowering intersectional voices, intersectional intervention depends on commitment to a kind of changeability. The values motivating individual organizers and promoting solidarity must be versatile if they are to psychologically and materially enable transformation. Slutwalk Toronto can serve as a good example of intersectional activism, primarily in their organizing approach, openness to critique, and revision of the movement's 'mission' to better practice intersectionality and acknowledge the unique ways women of color experience sexual violence. Finally, the sheer volume of conversation, increased awareness, and viral growth of the Slutwalk movement is deserving of some honor as a feminist intervention. Because of the young feminists who organized the first ever Slutwalk, there have been over two hundred cities where other activists organized Slutwalks to address sexual violence in their own communities and cultures, including cities across North America, Europe, Latin America, and Asia, with particularly vibrant walks in Colombia, Brazil, and India.

ACTIVE INTERSECTIONALITY

Moving forward, scholarship on feminist and intersectional community-engaged projects, and related pedagogies, may benefit from differentiating between *passive* and *active* intersectionality. Next, I review one argumentative or discursive habit I observed in feminist critiques of Slutwalk's intersectionality that permeates much of contemporary, usually white, feminist organizing and related discussion. This habit is one of *passive* intersectionality. In the first (and currently only) academic anthology on Slutwalk, *'This is what a Feminist Slut looks like': Perspectives on the Slutwalk Movement* (2015), more than half of the scholarly chapters cite and discuss an open letter to Slutwalk from a collective called Black Women's Blueprint (BWB). With great care, BWB critique Slutwalk and its organizers for choosing a name with the term 'slut' in it, a term that is experienced differently by women of color historically and currently. The letter is leveraged, often somewhat ignorantly, as an encompassing example of Black feminists' take on Slutwalk, freeing an author from needing to engage Slutwalk's racism more deeply or complexly. Across academic and popular feminist conversations, the letter is repeatedly positioned and utilized as the foremost substantive critique of Slutwalk as a white feminist project.

The problems with this pattern are at least threefold. First, non-Black feminists tend to begin and end their interrogation of whiteness in Slutwalk with the letter. That tendency implies haphazard anti-racist praxis, but also results in perpetuating the next two issues. Second, the letter is used to paint Black feminist criticism with one broad brushstroke, dissolving the many differing interpretations within that critical frame. That brushstroke is, in turn, often used to taper Black feminisms from many to one, and portray other racial identities' (such as Native American women who experience tremendously disproportionate sexual violence) exclusion from Slutwalk without much nuance. That being said, I have not encountered any discourse from women of color that fully rejects the racialization of the word *Slut*. Instead, I have found much disagreement on what to do about that racialization in organizing and conversation. Although BWB does not find reclaiming *Slut* useful, other women of color do; it is either ignorant or dishonest to describe the myriad meanings women of color have ascribed to Slutwalk as singular (Schiappa, 2015). For example, a group of queer identified Black women in Toronto thought that Slutwalk should rename the walk "Take Back the

Slut," pulling on a Toronto-based protest that had happened a couple of years earlier. Upon listening to and later speaking with BWB, Heather Jarvis commented:

> Having a certain kind of privilege to access certain language and be under certain labels without the same consequences, that's a very, very important criticism. However, many people, many women of color in Toronto had already identified as sluts. It's really difficult to say we can't just take your advice, and say we're going to do exactly what you people from New York telling us in Canada, Toronto—no, we're going to root in our cities and communities. (personal communication)

Unfortunately, the habit of employing a popular "intersectional" critique as definitive, collapses diverse opinions within feminist social groups and excuses oneself from deeper interrogation, traverses many subjects. It is a habit of purportedly intersectional praxis that Slutwalk Toronto organizer Alyssa Teekah describes as "ironic—so static that we can fail to see fluidity and diversity," where only the "most bombastic critique is king" (2015, p.32). It is to interpret only one intersection in a singular, reductive way.

Third, the persistent patterned uses of the letter have resulted in arguments about Slutwalk's intersectionality that work from an "all or nothing" place. In her essay *Feminism Forged through Trauma: Call-Out Culture and Slutwalk,* Teekah (2015) writes about her experience with "call-out culture" as a Slutwalk Toronto organizer, or with "the way current, heavily Internet-based feminism can turn into a process of publicly shaming people for not enacting the most "foolproof" politics" (p.31). Teekah goes further to describe her experience with hypercriticism as "an unwanted child of intersectionality theory" (p. 32). Here a helpful delineation is made: intersectional community engagement is not foolproof by virtue of naming itself such. It's somewhat fair to measure the intersectional character of a movement or civic activity by the presence and involvement of diversely identified persons. That, however, is clearly not a sufficient metric alone and is too often a mechanism of dismissal. Perhaps a better measure is to assess whether or not a civic project is *actively* intersectional.

Intersectional activism should demand recognition and prioritization of race, class, sexual orientation, age, and ability, in addition to gender. *Active* intersectionality is an engaged, intentioned process that foregrounds the breadths and depths of perspectives within feminist interventions and willingly holds them in a productive tension at multiple levels. I submit that at a minimum, these levels include the imagination/creation and actual material organization processes.

An actively intersectional project would make sustained efforts to understand the implications of its work in relation to diverse identities and multiplied oppressions; it would be intersectional at the level of imagination. If feminist participants do not already represent the diversity of their community, intersectional imagination will almost always consist of reaching out to existing local resources and organizations run by and for women of color, people in poverty, and groups of diverse abilities and ages. Such efforts must include sufficient outreach and listening before and while material organizing occurs so that the process is intersectional from the moment of inception. If Slutwalk Toronto's organizers had first prioritized listening to local groups about what they thought of the march's name, they may have gained invaluable insights about the ways in which the word Slut is racialized; thus changing the name, or adding statements clarifying their choice. If most conversations ended in hearing support of the name Slutwalk, if most outreach concluded that the name reflected the community's intentions and anger too, then that'd have been a reasonable rebuttal to the criticism that later invalidated their good work for many potential allies.

Where the first level of active intersectionality consists of outreach and listening, the second requires including and empowering community members who are also interested and invested in the work of intervention. Actively intersectional community engagement is intersectional at the level of organizing, production, and practice. Slutwalk Toronto failed on the first level but attended to the second, coordinating the walk alongside existing community resources and adding organizers with diverse social locations. Slutwalk Minneapolis' head organizers may have begun with representationally intersectional leadership, but they did not actually empower others to influence the process in any meaningful sense. Organizers shut down a student's concerns about a lack of focus on campus rape, for example, by simply not recognizing the concern as valid. The student's presence in the organizing meetings had no effect whatsoever on the process itself. Inclusion must occur in earnest at the level of imagination and the level of membership agency.

This is not to suggest that *all* feminist interventions need equally accommodate one another, because they already do not and frequently cannot when it comes to actually planning protest or community engagement events. In practice, intersectional interventions present endless challenges, as they likely should to fodder listening and growth. Feminist organizers and teachers in a community with an active trans* population, for instance, should not necessarily headline or even officially recognize, a trans-exclusive radical feminist (TERF[3]) ideology

---

3 TERF is an acronym used to name and describe (often against but not within) Trans-Exclusionary Radical Feminism, or a branch of radical feminism claiming that trans* people, especially women, are not "real" women who rightly be included in feminism. TERF arguments frequently rely on biological determinism and reflect transphobia. A related radical feminist subgroup is Sex Worker Exclusionary Radical Feminism, or SWERF.

as legitimate for the intervention at hand. They might, however, set aside time and space for participants or students to dialogue and construct boundaries regarding the presence of TERFs in their activist community, for instance.

CONCLUSION

Looking back while moving forward, I want to emphasize why active intersectionality matters and how I came to understand its necessity. In their book *Feminist Rhetorical Practices: New Horizons for Rhetoric, Composition, and Literacy Studies* (2012) Royster and Kirsch describe a concept and research tool that reflects a significant part of my research process: strategic contemplation. They write,

> Ultimately, with the term strategic contemplation, we want to reclaim a genre of research and scholarship traditionally associated with processes of meditation, introspection, and reflection. We suggest that using a meditative/contemplative approach allows researchers to access another, often underutilized dimension of the research process. . . . [T]his strategy suggests that researchers might linger deliberately inside of their research tasks as they investigate their topics and sources—imagining the contexts for practices; speculating about conversations with the people whom they are studying. . . . paying close attention to the spaces and places both they and the rhetorical subjects occupy in the scholarly dynamic; and taking into account the impacts and consequences of these embodiments. (pp.84–85)

Royster and Kirsch go on to suggest, "A sense of place—the physical, embodied experience of visiting places—can become a powerful research tool and an important dimension of strategic contemplation" (p.92). In the case of researching activism, where protest marches and other physical and material elements shape the actual work at hand, strategic contemplation, along with listening, is even more relevant and valuable. Strategic contemplation is a means for understanding how our sense of self and embodied experiences in physical places with people (such as attending organizing meetings in a coffee shop in Minneapolis, or in discussion with colleagues about learning objectives), impact scholarly discoveries. In other words, the physical, psychological, and emotional experiences I have encountered through my research on Slutwalk warrant critical reflection as a part of research and pedagogical development processes. For example, when I attended Slutwalk Minneapolis organizing sessions, much of what my notes reflect are the expressions on participants' faces, whether or not an idea was supported in nonverbal ways (head nodding or shaking), the shifting mood of the space as conversations unfolded, and how the visibility of my note-taking influenced the formality of discussion. This evidences why these practices should, as Royster and Kirsch recommend, "be brought out of the shadows and highlighted as important and empowering aspects of research and teaching processes (p.86)."

When I came across a participant, Andrea, crying outside after a meeting, I had to balance professional distance with a naturally empathic urge to support her, a woman who had been hurt and diminished in a space that ought have been securing for her. That experience revealed to me, as a researcher and feminist teacher, how important it truly is to practice active intersectionality in relevant contexts. When organizers performed passive intersectionality, when they invited diverse bodies but did not sincerely value or listen to what those bodies had to say, they effectively marginalized people. If a feminist intervention such as Slutwalk, through poor feminist praxis on the part of leaders, actually serves to further marginalize groups or individuals who are already oppressed, then it is a moral failure. I come to such understandings in part through strategic contemplation and listening, because such "incidents, actions, circumstances, conditions, and experiences endow our sense of being, inform the ways in which we see and interpret events" (Royster & Kirsch, 2012, p. 94).

My observations, interviews, and participation in the Slutwalk marches eventually drew my attention more toward the attendees and how feminist engagement strategies impacted their experiences. I gained clarity about what active intersectionality can or should look like and why it matters as a practice in feminist interventions of community and pedagogical engagement. Moving forward, effective feminist interventions, ones that sincerely engage, value, respond, and empower intersectional identities throughout the stages of imagination, organizing, will improve communities and depths of learning. Interventions or teachings that do not practice active intersectionality will continue to marginalize and disempower historically underrepresented groups, the very same groups third wave feminism professedly seeks to uplift. And these are not trivial matters, for women are still disproportionately victims of violence and silencing, especially sexual violence, and are then rendered virtually helpless by patriarchal social, criminal, and educational systems.

In making Women's and Feminist Studies' contributions more intelligible to other disciplines, especially those invested in good community and educational work, I suggest increasing attention to the practice of intersectional process. Actively intersectional activism is grounded in communities and students, listening, and material outcomes for those who are intersectionally oppressed and in immediate need of increased agency and transformation. Slutwalk is a movement focused on rejecting rape culture and sexual violence, on empowering survivors and displacing victim-blaming narratives, issues that impact women of color, poor women, and disabled women at disproportionate rates, necessitating an intersectional approach. Feminist interventionist activities will be enriched through dedication to intersectionality, and this requires involving diversity in imagining a work and executing that engagement, with an earnest willingness to empower participants and adapt over time. From Slutwalk Minneapolis we might gain insight into the limitations of not doing so, where the result is an exclusive, distant expression of a few; whereas Slutwalk Toronto offers an example of how including the voices of the many sustain a movement's visibility, impact, and intersectionality.

REFERENCES

#SWTO2014 (Sat. July 12) Speakers announced! *Slutwalk Toronto*. Retrieved from http://www.slutwalktoronto.com/swto2014-sat-july-12-speakers-announced.

Alan. (Photographer). (2012). *SlutWalk Minneapolis_0010*. Retrieved from https://www.flickr.com/photos/hot_ion_foundry/8065539196.

An Open Letter from Black Women to the SlutWalk. (2011, September). *Black Women's Blueprint*. Retrieved from http://www.blackwomensblueprint.org/2011/09/23/anopen-letter-from-black-women-to-the-slutwalk/.

Barnett, Sonya. (2011, February). Because we've had enough. *Slutwalk Toronto*. Retrieved from http://www.slutwalktoronto.com/welcome.

Baumgardner, J. & Richards, A. (2003). Who's the next Gloria? The quest for the third wave superleader. In R. Dicker & A. Piepmeier (Eds.), *Catching a Wave: Reclaiming Feminism for the 21st Century* (pp. 159–170). Boston, MA: Northeastern University Press.

Choo, H. Y. & Ferree, M. M. (2010). Practicing intersectionality in sociological research: A critical analysis of inclusions, interactions, and institutions in the study of inequalities. *Sociological Theory, 28*(2), 129–149.

Crenshaw, K. (1989). Demarginalizing the intersection of race and sex: A black feminist critique of antidiscrimination doctrine, feminist theory, and antiracist politics. *University of Chicago Legal Forum 1989*, 139–67.

Crenshaw, K. (1991). Mapping the margins: Intersectionality, identity politics, and violence against women of color. *Stanford Law Review, 43*(6), 1241–79.

Cullman, S., St. John, C. & Jarecki, E. (Director). (2012). *The House I Live In* [Motion Picture]. United States: Virgil Films and Entertainment.

Fernandes, L. (2010). Unsettling "Third wave feminism": Feminist waves, intersectionality, and identity politics in retrospect. In N. Hewitt (Ed.), *No permanent waves: Recasting histories of U.S. feminism* (pp. 98–118). New Jersey: Rutgers.

International Day Against Victim Blaming. (2015). *National Sexual Violence Resource Center*. Retrieved from http://www.nsvrc.org/calendar/22554.

Janzen, J. (2012, February). So long and thanks for all the fish. *Slutwalk Toronto*. Retrieved from http://www.slutwalktoronto.com/so-long-and-thanks-for-all-the-fish.

Lorde, A. (1986). *I am your sister: Black women organizing across sexualities*. New York, NY: Kitchen Table: Women of Color Press.

McCall, L. (2005). The complex of intersectionality. *Signs: Journal of Women in Culture and Society, 30*(3), 1771–1800.

Media Education Foundation. (2006, October 3). *bell hooks: Cultural criticism & transformation*. Retrieved from https://www.youtube.com/watch?v=zQUuHFKP-9s.

Moraga, C. & Anzaldúa, G. (1981). *This bridge called my back*. New York, NY: Kitchen Table: Women of Color Press.

Royster, J. J. & Kirsch, G. E. (2012). *Feminist rhetorical practices: New horizons for rhetoric, composition, and literacy studies*. Carbondale, IL: Southern Illinois University Press.

Sandoval, Chela. (2000). *Methodology of the oppressed*. Minneapolis, MN: University of Minnesota Press.

Schiappa, J. (2015). Practicing intersectional critiques: Re-examining "Third-Wave" perspectives on exclusion and white supremacy in SlutWalk. In A. O'Reilly & M. Friedman (Eds.), *'This is what a Feminist Slut looks like': Perspectives on the Slutwalk Movement* (pp. 63–77). Ontario, Canada: Demeter Press.

Schiappa, J. (Photographer). (2012). *Andrea* [Photograph].

Sherva, K. (2011, May 18). White supremacy and the walk. *Slutwalk Minneapolis Tumblr Blog*. Retrieved from http://slutwalkminneapolis.tumblr.com/post/5627688718/white-supremacy-and-the-walk.

Slutwalk Minneapolis. (n.d.). *Slutwalk Minneapolis Webpage*. Retrieved from http://www.slutwalkminneapolis.org.

Smith, B. (1983). *Home girls: A black feminist anthology*. New Brunswick, NJ: Rutgers University Press.

State and County Quickfacts. (2014). Retrieved from http://quickfacts.census.gov/qfd/states/27/2743000.html.

Teekah, A. (2015). Feminism forged through trauma: Call-Out culture and Slutwalk. In A. O'Reilly & M. Friedman (Eds.), *'This is what a Feminist Slut looks like': Perspectives on the Slutwalk Movement*, 31–45. Ontario: Demeter Press.

Third Wave History. *Third Wave Fund*. Retrieved from http://thirdwavefund.org/history.html.

Thompson, B. (2010). Multiracial feminism: Recasting the chronology of second wave feminism. In N. Hewitt (Ed.), *No permanent waves: Recasting histories of U.S. feminism* (pp. 39–60). New Brunswick, NJ: Rutgers University Press.

Untitled photograph of Slutwalk organizer Heather Jarvis. (2011). Retrieved from http://lubbockonline.com/local-news/2011-09-26/slutwalk-making-way-lubbock.

Walker, R. (January, 1992). Becoming the third wave. *Ms., 11*(2), 39–41.

Wong, K. S. (2003). Pranks and fake porn: Doing feminism my way. In R. Dicker & A. Piepmeier (Eds.), *Catching a wave: Reclaiming feminism for the 21st century* (pp. 294–307). Boston, MA: Northeastern University Press.

Young, I. M. (2011). *Justice and the politics of difference.* New Jersey: Princeton University Press.

Zarnow, L. (2010). From sisterhood to girlie culture: Closing the great divide between second and third wave cultural agendas. In N. Hewitt (Ed.), *No permanent waves: Recasting histories of U.S. feminism* (pp. 273–302). New Brunswick, NJ: Rutgers University Press.

CHAPTER 16.

A PEEK INSIDE THE MASTER'S HOUSE: THE TALE OF FEMINIST RHETORICIAN AS CANDIDATE FOR U.S. CONGRESS

Angela K. Zimmann
United Lutheran Seminary

In 2006, at the Conference on College Composition and Communication, Geneva Smitherman proclaimed "the master's tools can be used to bring truth to the master's house," a twist on Audre Lorde's statement that "the master's tools will never dismantle the master's house." In 2012, I made the decision to "peek inside the master's house," as a candidate in U.S. electoral politics. I ran for a seat in the U.S. Congress (Ohio-5), cognizant that both my opponent, a three-term incumbent with a radically conservative agenda, and my district, a traditionalist fourteen-county area which had never elected a woman, would provide fertile ground for delving into auto-ethnographic research. Although my opponent engaged in rhetorical techniques such as silencing (refusing to debate in a public forum), there were equally powerful rhetorical approaches that could be creatively employed to circumvent the double-bind. This is the narrative of that experience interwoven with feminist rhetorical theory.

"The notion that women were uniquely fashioned for the private realm is at least as old as Aristotle," writes Amanda Vickery (Morgan, 2006, p. 75). Women were to operate in the "oikos," the domestic realm, while men functioned primarily in the "polis," as citizens. "Within this system, the minds and words of women are considered complementary, and inferior, to those of men; masculine intellect is seen as transcending the feminine character, which is biologically driven and firmly bound to the body and the home," continues Cheris Kramarae (Foss, Foss and Griffin, 2004, p. 43). The voices of women were (and are) constrained, and yet, our creative foremothers found ways, within and through these limitations, to make their voices heard. Much of the scholarship in the area of women's rhetoric(s) has been done in an earnest effort to faithfully rescue, recover and re-inscribe that which has been lacking in the traditional rhetorical canon, including the voices of women. Now, however, even as the aforementioned work must continue, scholars such as Jacqueline Jones Royster and Gesa E. Kirsch have issued a clarion call to expand the scope of study, including a broader range of voices. Patricia Bizzell writes, in the forward to Royster and Kirsch's 2012 work *Feminist Rhetorical Practices: New Horizons for Rhetoric, Composition and Literacy Studies*, that "scholars soon realized that research on women and rhetoric needed to go beyond traditional scholarly methods" (p. x). Indeed, traditional scholarly methods can have the unfortunate result of marginalizing the very subjects with whom the scholarly content seeks to engage. Furthermore, continue Royster and Kirsch, as they reflect upon scholarship methods and practices, "We must pay attention also to *living* [emphasis in original] women . . . " (p. 38).

Recent writing studies scholarship considers ways in which researchers can more fully engage with community activism to engender social change (George, 2018, this collection): In this chapter, I offer my lived experience as an activist scholar in my community, as a subject of rhetorical interest, responding to Royster and Kirsch's invitation. My voice is an intersectionality, the voice of a feminist, an activist academic and a politician: as Kramarae notes, "The distinction between rhetors within and outside of academia is not always clear: These 'states are not mutually exclusive . . . sometimes the academic woman *is* also the activist in the community,'" (Foss, Foss and Griffin, 1999, p. 54). To wit, Royster, a leading scholar in the arena of rhetoric(s) and feminism(s) defines herself as precisely one who straddles the boundaries, "an academic activist," (Royster and Kirsch, 2012, p. 8). And yet, as Jacqueline Schiappa (2018, this collection) reminds us in "Two Slutwalks," the intersectionality of which I speak and the positionality from which I write as a white heterosexual middle-class female is clearly quite different from that of many of my feminist sisters, and I want to be clear in claiming only where I stand. I do not seek to over-generalize my experience.

To ground the situation in context, I was teaching full-time in the General Studies Writing Department at Bowling Green State University when I mounted a serious campaign for a seat in the United State House of Representatives, OH-5. I had served on the county school governing board (Lucas County Educational Services Center, now the Educational Services Center for Lake Erie West) for more than four years, having recognized my desire to dissolve the dichotomy between the academy and the mainstream world. This next, more extensive move into the national political arena resulted in an opportunity to reflect from a unique positionality. At the same time, I was well aware that "any considerations of deliberately taking time away from the relentless march of making progress in the completion of a scholarly project . . . have not been viewed as strength moves for serious scholars," (Royster and Kirsch, p. 86). I hope these musings will encourage others to be brave enough, when the time seems right, to disavow the traditional white, male, elite forced and false binary of academy/mainstream world with as much rigor as we seek to escape the idea of the separate spheres of "oikos" and "polis." *In the current political milieu, as in the academy, greater mindfulness and reflective practice is sorely needed, and this is the first reason for which I write*: the second is elucidated below.

Entering into the realm of public political life, I was grateful to those who had gone before me. Wendy K. Kolmar and Frances Bartkowski (2005) address the continuing issue of disempowerment of women, but also enthusiastically discuss the work that has been done in recent history: "Like their nineteenth-century sisters, twentieth-century liberal feminists attempted to address the unequal distribution of power through reform of public legal and political institutions. On the other hand, second wave radical feminists made central the theoretical insight that the 'personal is political,' that power relations operate in personal as well as in public life," (p. 52). The work that was done on both of these fronts enabled me to make the decision to become a candidate for U.S. Congress; I was legally granted the right to fulfill certain obligations (gathering signatures, paying a small fee), and have my name placed on the ballot. But this technical "equality" to my male opponent, while a pivotal first step, could threaten to diminish or overshadow the material *inequality* in access to power and privilege between the two of us. Therein lies the second purpose for this writing: not simply to encourage others to take up the mantle and become involved, but to *shine the light on the reality of the experience of congressional candidacy for one woman—me—in a specific context. I understand that my experience is not in any way universal, but there are parts and pieces which may serve to illuminate the path for those who follow.*

bell hooks wrote over twenty-five years ago, "there remain many unexplored areas of female experience that need to be fully examined, thereby widening the scope of our understanding of what it is to be female in this society . . . . We might better understand our collective reluctance to commit ourselves to feminist struggle, to revolutionary politics or we might also chart those experiences that prepare and enable us to make such commitments," (Foss, Foss and Griffin, p. 61). Regrettably, not enough has changed in the past quarter-century: Chantal Maille, professor of Women's Studies at Concordia University in Montreal, names one of these sparsely inhabited and under-explored public spaces in her 2015 article "Feminist Interventions in Political Representation in the United States and Canada: Training Programs and Legal Quotas," explaining that "The alarming reality is that American women are still vastly underrepresented in elected office all across the nation, and are losing ground when compared to other nations," (p. 2). Indeed, not only are women underrepresented in political campaigns and elected office, but *reflections on the experience* from the perspective of a feminist "insider" are woefully absent. What a timely coincidence that in the very year I launched the congressional campaign, Royster and Kirsch foregrounded the idea that it is "not enough to focus mainly on the fact of women's existence in rhetorical history," arguing instead for an understanding of rhetoric as a "lived and thereby embodied experience," (p. 132, p. 42). This chapter is both the story of a feminist rhetorical intervention as lived, embodied experience—and, in the recounting, the story *itself* becomes intervention.

For all intents and purposes, this story began when, in the 2009 book *Turning the Noose that Binds into a Rope to Climb: A Textual Search for Rhetorical and Linguistic Gender-Markings in Speech Samples of Three Contemporary Female Orators*, I posed the question: "If a woman remains and works within the system, is she necessarily a fool, catering to a cruel patriarchal regime?" (Zimmann, p. 175). In that study, I found that "there will be moments when perhaps they [women] must 'play the game'—and there will be other moments when the words these women speak and the actions they choose can work to undermine the very system that has placed them in positions of power," (p. 175). I wanted to live into that research for myself, mindfully exploring those moments which might possess the potential for feminist intervention. At my dissertation defense, Dr. Sue Carter Wood, a member of the panel, offered these closing words: "Don't sit on this important work. Keep going."

For me, this challenge was taken up by stepping into public political service. Yet, as Audre Lorde notes, "white women face the pitfall of being seduced into joining the oppressor under the pretense of sharing power . . . for white women [as opposed to their Black sisters] there is a wider range of pretended choices and rewards for identifying with patriarchal power and its tools," (cited in Kolmar and Bartkowski, 2005, p. 340). The lure of the system is strong, and the incentive to embrace the privilege proffered to those who are willing to turn their backs on the oppressed and maintain the status quo is not insubstantial. I was afraid, fearful that, perhaps, I would be absorbed into the very machine I had set out to battle. "Pursuing freedom from oppression involves recognizing the ways in which systematized exclusions are distinctive *and yet also* emerge and are sustained by intersecting dominant cultural logics," writes Schiappa. Indeed, I had been both an object of exclusionary cultural logic, *and yet also* not wholly oppressed, and not identically oppressed. It is into this subjective, intimate and paradoxical space that I step, offering the beginnings of a rhetorical analysis of my 2012 run for a seat in the United States House of Representatives in Ohio's 5th Congressional District, and how feminist intervention happened (and didn't) along the way.

For the purpose of this chapter, I will focus on *three specific methods of feminist rhetorical intervention* (again, these methods could be modified and emulated in a variety of settings). The first is the *appropriation of technology*, specifically YouTube and Facebook, to garner national support and increase public awareness of the campaign. The second and third interventions were of a much more personal nature, and centered on *private conversations*: in the case of the second intervention, tens of thousands of private conversations to secure funding for taking the campaign to a television audience. In the case of the third intervention, there was one conversation, resulting in the endorsement of a major regional newspaper. There were necessarily dozens of other feminist rhetorical interventions that occurred throughout the course of the campaign, many of which were illuminating in myriad ways, but for the purpose of this writing, the focus will be on the three feminist rhetorical interventions delineated above.

This chapter focuses upon my experience as a candidate for the United States House of Representatives (OH-5), explores and illuminates the laborious and often intensely solitary and lonely feminist rhetorical interventions which were foundational to the campaign. The subsequent feminist rhetorical interventions, aiming to give voice to the thousands of women experiencing political marginalization at the hands of an ultra-conservative legislator, were entirely dependent upon the preliminary intimate and private conversations which took place throughout the earlier stages of the campaign: my public presence was limited by the typical Western, male, elite patriarchal privilege of my opponent.

While this chapter is case-specific, the concepts have substantial implications far beyond the traditional political realm. This chapter seeks to galvanize feminists working in all spheres with the understanding that rhetorical interventions are often not the grand-scale public work of known rhetors, but can happen in any space or time: the momentary, whispered exchange on a parade route may, in fact, be the most life altering intervention imaginable. In this way, whether functioning in the "oikos" or the "polis," the academy or the mainstream world, (or, more probably, some combination of the two), feminist rhetors are poised to stage effective interventions for the betterment of society.

THE FIRST INTERVENTION: ENTERING THE MILIEU

The assumption that feminist rhetorical interventions are primarily the province of the rhetor with access to a traditional public arena for communication has been challenged through the advent of advancing technology. Where at one time only those holding positions with considerable public resonance were able to communicate with a wide audience, the genesis of YouTube, Twitter, Facebook, and a host of other social media sites now enable participation by a much wider constituency. Royster and Kirsch note that, "as technology changes rapidly, so do different sites of rhetorical agency. Scholars have only begun to study small fragments of the vast array of new rhetorical activities unfolding via the Internet . . . " (p. 66).

The first intervention took place on December 15th, 2011, when a friend with a video camera met up with my husband and my nominally-paid local campaign manager at an area park, and we shot an unrehearsed, forty-two-second video parodying Texas Governor Rick Perry's "Strong" commercial: Strong. Then, they posted the video to the internet. "Rhetors who do not conform to normalizing processes are ultimately forced to occupy and to function in whatever spaces are left"—and in this case, "the space left" was the internet (Royster and Kirsch, 2012, p. 103). Unheralded by traditional media sources, our campaign took to the web.

The next day, we received a phone call from Max Rosenthal at *The Huffington Post*. HuffPo had picked up the video, and ran it here: Strong Parody on Huffington Post.

Within less than twenty-four hours, the video had thirty-six thousand views. Suddenly, our homespun campaign was on the radar of a few more people—still a very small number in an e-world where millions of views mark the beginning of renown, but we were nearly a year out from election day and instead of the few dozen friends who were initial supporters, we had a wider base: and a well-known progressive web publication that was interested in us.

While we continued to shoot videos (all at no cost, as friends made in-kind donations of their time), none were ever quite so widely circulated as the "Rick Perry Parody." However, it was quickly becoming clear to us that the internet could provide a low-cost and possibly effective channel for quickly spreading the word about the campaign.

The next opportunity arose when, purely by chance, I stumbled across Democracy for America's website for "Grassroots All-Stars." The website invited progressive congressional candidates to post a simple picture and biography, and invite people to vote for them. The ten top vote-getters were then asked to submit a video so the public could vote again, and the top five would receive the DFA endorsement, which carried both cash funding for the campaign and the promise recognition that would result in a wider network of support.

Initially, I was not excited but horrified to see that this site existed and *I had no knowledge of it*. I quickly entered our information and formulated a plan: we needed to drive friends and supporters to the website to vote. There were dozens of candidates, and I was nearly dead last.

The internet race was on. Emails worked, some. This was prior to the popularity of Twitter, but Facebook was a possibility. About a year before Amina Tyler employed Facebook to declare her frustration with the Tunisian government (Ouellette, Chapter 14, this collection), our campaign turned to Facebook to seek a pathway into the governmental structure. We began to message people, then recruit the campaign team to message people in real-time, when they were clearly online, and ask for a vote. We created a standard message which could then be personalized as hour after hour we worked.

Days passed, and we moved up in the rankings, within striking distance of the top ten. The decision was made to visit local coffee shops, the student union at a university where I was employed, and other public areas, with the DFA website pulled up on our laptops, asking for votes. As the voting closed, we were in the top ten. Now, it was time for another video.

Again, with no funds to pay for professional videographers, and with me out of town for a school board meeting, friends and family came together to produce this video: Chelsea Says Vote for Angela! There was a special power in having a little girl ask for the voter to support her mother. In my dissertation, I had identified the linguistic tendency for women to publicly identify powerful men in order to win public support; instead, I looked to the authority of a female child, thereby empowering her and inviting others, typically disempowered, to understand that in this campaign, all people mattered (*Turning the Noose that Binds into a Rope to Climb*).

Huffington Post ran an article on the Grassroots All-Stars including this quote: "Another relatively unknown 'All-Star,' Angela Zimmann, has grabbed attention with her homemade campaign videos. Zimmann, running in Ohio's 5th District against incumbent Bob Latta, submitted a video starring her young daughter as part of her push to win Democracy for America's approval." (http://www.huffingtonpost.com/2012/02/16/howard-dean-democracy-for-america-_n_1283117.html).

And we won—we finished in the top five.

We were lucky, we worked hard, and we believed that if people saw what we could do, we had a chance. Greater accessibility via the internet demonstrates, in this case, the potential of new technology to undermine the pervasive, disingenuous and often disempowering notion that feminist rhetorical interventions, particularly of a political nature, must begin in the traditional public sphere, and are only possible for those with significant capital and powerful connections. Yet, as Jessica Ouellette powerfully demonstrates, one cannot control the amplification of a message on the internet, and the directions in which it travels: my opponent appropriated a piece of one of my videos and used it to his own advantage: to be fair, my campaign manager also took footage of my opponent, and clipped it to our advantage. At any rate, We certainly could have and would have performed differently with increased resources, and these additional resources became increasingly necessary in order to be granted credibility within the system, as will be discussed below—but at this point, following in the footsteps of our courageous feminist forebears, we refused to be thwarted by our lack.

THE SECOND INTERVENTION: RAISING THE MONEY

On the Democracy for America Grassroots All-Stars page in February of 2012, I enthusiastically reported that the campaign had over one hundred and fifty financial supporters. That number would grow, by the end of the race, to over two thousand individual donors, including individuals from every state in the US. But in February and March of 2012, I had not yet grasped the significance of fundraising and financial resources in the current political climate of the United States. We had made our videos on a shoestring budget—could we not do the entire campaign using the same methodology? Couldn't we show constituents a dedicated, compassionate, energetic, intellectually engaged candidate for whom they would be inspired to vote without spending a fortune? The answer I was given was a resounding "No."

Let me set the scene:

"A hundred thousand dollars of your own money, minimum," the dark-haired young political operative, easily fifteen years my junior, says to me, without so much as glancing at the carefully prepared professional CV I hand to him.

We sit in a small conference room at the headquarters of the Democratic Congressional Campaign Committee offices on 430 S. Capital Street in the heart of Washington, DC. I am dressed for the occasion, as instructed, with minimalist jewelry, bedecked in the signature red blazer purchased at Savers, the local thrift shop back in Northwest Ohio. My mind is spinning, and my faith in the party I have loved all of my life is withering.

Blinking, and sitting up straight, I remind myself that I am an elected official already, entering my second term on the local Educational Services Center Board, where my colleagues appointed me president. Could my bona fides truly not matter? I have three degrees—a bachelor's in Engineering, a Master's in Divinity, a Ph.D. in Rhetoric. I am a wife, a mother, a foster parent, an ordained pastor. My children are the fifth generation to on the same small patch of farmland which is now a part of Ohio's Congressional District #5. My background check dating to my teen years is clear: one marriage, no police record, no drugs, no underage drinking in college. No late credit card bills, or late bills of any kind. A credit rating over 740. A few speeding tickets. Ran a stop sign once. This is the type of squeaky-clean that is almost annoying.

But there is no wealthy relative in my back pocket; no "Daddy Warbucks" to come in and save the day. Raised in a lower-middle-class family, I was once again bumping up against the hard edges of the patriarchal preference for the elite. A hundred thousand dollars is a second mortgage on the house where our family lives. I don't have it, can't give it, and so the man nearly young enough to be my son dismisses me, barely disguising his disgust at having to bother with this burdensome conversation.

Pushing myself to my feet, I leave the building with a gracious smile and a shattered heart. There will be no help here, no assistance from the political party which I have enthusiastically supported since casting a ballot for William Jefferson Clinton in 1992. Born on the wrong side of the socioeconomic divide, no amount of merit or virtue will close the gap in this case.

There is a decision to be made.

In order to run this race with any degree of impact, to have my voice heard, to intervene in a way that might have measurability, to avoid being dismissed immediately, I realize that I must pose a legitimate threat to the re-election of my ultra-conservative opponent, a three-time incumbent and the son of a popular former Congressman. While I can shake hands and knock on doors day after day, the size of the district (fourteen counties, mostly rural), prohibits grassroots campaigning from having a powerful effect. I must use media to deliver the message, and the most efficient and effective media, still, is the traditional television. And television advertising is prohibitively expensive. A hundred thousand does not begin to cover the costs.

Either I raise the money, and go on television, or I go away: back to the classroom, back to the pulpit, out of the public eye.

Thus began an immersive experiment, a feminist intervention into the potential for rhetorical training to impact authentic experience in the contemporary political realm through that bane of all political activities: fundraising.

Political fundraising is, in itself, an arduous process, universally loathed by politicos of all stripes. For a challenger from a congressional district that has not elected a Democrat since the time of Roosevelt, it often felt like a gut-wrenching and debasing exercise in futility.

For upwards of eight hours a day (sometimes longer, because I could call people on the West Coast until about 11 PM EST), I sat in a tiny room with no windows, with huge signs and goals taped to the walls, and I talked. The hundreds of thousands of phone calls were generally to strangers, although occasionally I would recognize a name: George Soros, for instance. (While I am certain that George would have appreciated my campaign, I never was able to penetrate the barricade of administrative assistants who answered his phones—although I tried about a dozen times.)

I smiled when I talked, as women are often told to do. It made my voice sound better.

I was polite, but firm. My general message was tailored to the audience, but the theme was generally the same: you don't know me, but I have been endorsed by Democracy for America and I am running for U.S. Congress in Ohio. My opponent is an ultra-right-wing conservative, and we have a chance to win—but I cannot win without the help of people like you. Here, you can check out my website, or this video that was picked up by *The Huffington Post*. I can send you a pledge letter, or would you like to speak to my assistant and donate online right now?

More than once, I had a surprised Californian or shocked New Yorker exclaim, "*Are you the actual candidate?* I'm going to donate just because it is *you* making these calls, and not some other staffer." Women, traditionally, have not had the legions of secretaries at their beck and call—we do it ourselves, and so I did. Yes, certainly, it was me making the call.

It was in this rhetorical space that I learned the power, without knowing the term, of what Royster and Kirsch label "tacking in" and "tacking out" (p. 87). "Tacking in can be described as an inward journey, focusing on researchers noticing how they process, imagine and work with materials; how creativity and imagination come into play . . . ," while "tacking out" is "more in line with traditional notions of fieldwork," according to Royster and Kirsch (p. 85), and this tension between the two poles is illustrated by Kathleen Wider, who writes: "I had to go out into the world and deep within myself" (p. 69). Indeed, that is what I had to do: even as I called donors from every state in the union, I had to reach deep within myself. As I listened closely to my conversation partners, I listened too to "the visceral changes in mind, heart, backbone and stomach that the discovery proves occasions" (Royster & Kirsch, p.87).

It would be more glamourous, certainly more stunning and memorable, to recount that I delivered a speech, participated in a debate, conducted a town hall meeting, dazzling the listeners with compassion, brilliance and policy initiatives guaranteeing revitalization of our ailing corner of the Midwest. But the truth is, my opponent refused to debate, the few town halls I did conduct by myself early in the campaign were sparsely attended, and speeches were often largely ignored by the traditional media outlets.

Another truth: Going away was not an option. I was going on television. And in order to make that happen, the political would become deeply personal as I doggedly staged feminist rhetorical interventions in a small, windowless room at the rear of the campaign office in a rented strip mall in Perrysburg, Ohio: I would make telephone calls and fundraise. Forty hours each week, for nine months, I would sit in the tiny windowless blue room (or stand, when the sitting became unbearable), across from a paid operative who would hand me sheets with names and numbers. I would dial and dial and dial for dollars, using feminist rhetorical interventions in the most intimate and private of spaces, talking and listening my way into the hearts, minds, and financial contributions of over two thousand individuals, encompassing all fifty states, and raising just under half-a-million dollars. Eventually, I talked my way to television.

THE THIRD INTERVENTION: LEGITIMIZATION

The final feminist rhetorical intervention began before the other two, but did not bear fruit until nearly a year later.

On a cold December afternoon in 2011, I traveled from Toledo, Ohio, to Pittsburgh, Pennsylvania: the Boulevard of the Allies office of the editor/publisher of *The Pittsburgh Post-Gazette,* John Robinson Block. Block Communications, Inc., also owns *The Toledo Blade* newspaper, the largest daily publication within the congressional district. In the 2010 election cycle, *The Blade* had offered their endorsement to my incumbent opponent, Robert Latta. While I understood that statistically, the likelihood of victory was quite small, I had full confidence in my ability to serve the constituents with a compassionate heart and a critical mind, and regardless of what happened on Election Day, I was certain that I would be the better-qualified representative for the people of Northwest Ohio. Although it sounds like hubris to female ears well-trained in the practice of self-effacement, I saw no reason to hesitate in seeking the endorsement of the publisher of *The Toledo Blade* (or anyone else, for that matter).

My campaign manager had arranged for the meeting, and when we arrived at the *Gazette,* we had no idea what to expect. Anecdotally, we had heard that Block was a bit of an eccentric who valued independent thought, and he was also quite politically savvy. The campaign manager was not invited to accompany me on the elevator to the publisher's office; instead, he waited downstairs in the lobby. Alone, I entered the large and ornate office of the publisher of *The Pittsburgh Post-Gazette,* and took a seat on the sofa. He sat across from me, and the questions began, ranging from foreign policy to domestic funding for education, renewable energy to labor negotiations. On and on we talked, for three hours. The sun set over Pittsburgh, and outside the windows the day was shifting into evening. The executive assistant gathered her personal belongings and left.

Throughout that long afternoon, although I had neither a bathroom break nor a glass of water, I did have support from a most unusual and unexpected source: the beautiful basset hound, Clementine, John Robinson Block's beloved canine companion, who saw fit to lay on the couch next to me, her head in my lap, while I responded to the seemingly endless volley of questions. Clementine, as it turned out, was quite ill and died on March 14th. Because of her presence with me during that challenging interview, I felt a kinship to Clementine: when she died, I sent a note and flowers to John Robinson Block. He responded, thanking me. Although it was no intentional feminist rhetorical intervention, I suppose that this "ethic of rhetorical care," (about which Mary Anne Taylor writes in her 2014 dissertation *She the People: Personal Politics and Feminist Advocacy as the Democratic Ideal*) may indeed have been the follow-up to the initial meeting wherein I was able to illustrate my compassion for the suffering of others in real-time, with no audience.

At any rate, as I headed toward the elevators on that cold December evening, hoping that my campaign manager had not left the building nor the city, John Block walked out with me.

"You realize," he stated, "that your chances of winning are one in a hundred? Maybe?"

I shrugged. "I'm not afraid to work. I'm a fighter."

The elevator door closed, and he was gone.

On October 2, 2012, I received the official endorsement of the Toledo Blade: "Ohio's redrawn 5th U.S. House District favors the re-election of incumbent Republican Bob Latta. But Democratic challenger ANGELA ZIMMANN offers ideas, energy, and a commitment to overcoming the stalemate in Congress that make her a better choice for the district" (http://www.toledoblade.com/Editorials/2012/10/02/Zimmann-for-U-S-House.html).

The endorsement legitimized the campaign, and indeed, we won Lucas County, which included part of Toledo, with 49,575 votes (http://www.co.lucas.oh.us/DocumentCenter/View/55188)

The rhetorical intervention was personal, authentic and unmediated, and it required boundary-breaking and courage. There was no invitation to sit for a formal endorsement interview; there was no protocol to follow. Instead, like the feminist rhetors in whose footsteps I humbly follow, I was playing by my own rules, bending, breaking, re-inventing, and pushing through the extant conventions to make a place for myself and the men and women I hoped to represent.

CONCLUSION: WE MAKE A WAY

I lost the race with just under forty percent of the vote.

Yet, it is time to "renegotiate traditional notions of success," Royster and Kirsch proclaim (p. 139). Citing Katrina M. Powell's extensive work on the writing of Virginia mountain women who challenged the federal government, Royster and Kirsch call for a definition of success that includes rhetorical moves representing agency and the finding of a voice, as well as demanding accountability and establishing "dignity, moral values and rights as citizens" (*The Anguish of Displacement, Feminist Rhetorical Practices, p. 139).*

Although I lost by the numbers, the campaign was celebrated (by most of those involved) as a success. I went on television, and I forced my opponent to engage in the race, buying his own television advertisements (unprecedented!), sending mailings, and, finally, depleting his cash reserve of nearly two million down to that magic number which the DCCC had insisted I have on hand—a hundred thousand dollars.

The immediate question in the days following the election was "When will you run again? Will you run next time?" The answer was no, although I appreciate the supportive response, and authored the following article for The Toledo Blade as a means of encouraging those who might feel compelled to enter the fray: I Can't Run, But Rep. Latta Needs a Challenge.

Will I run again?

I entered into this writing endeavor with the full knowledge that self-disclosure and critical rumination on the patriarchal capitalist-political system and the military-industrial complex that supports it will likely render me unelectable in the future—at least at the federal level. In essence, I find myself faced with a classic double-bind: if I speak (or write), my electoral voice will be silenced, and yet if I do not speak, *I am silenced already.* For me, the choice is clear and the price is worth paying, although I fully sympathize with and encourage my sisters (and feminist brothers) who opt, instead, to toil forth in silence, hoping to make a sliver of difference through election to office. This writing represents a lifting of the veil, a peek into the master's house; since I could not dismantle it with his tools, at least I can open the door and reveal a fresh, first-hand perspective. *Turning the Noose that Binds Into a Rope to Climb* details how three women rhetors have successfully negotiated the double-bind of being a woman and a powerful rhetor: however, that body of work could not go deeply enough. By looking only at the finished productions of white women already occupying positions of power, I failed to see beneath—what preceded and precipitated their rise to public prominence. Through my own lived experience, I offer one account of that which "comes before"—the journey through the campaign and a select few of the rhetorical interventions employed.

I posit that, bearing in mind the twinned mantras that the "personal is political" and "all politics is local," it is a logical assertion that feminist rhetorical interventions in politics may conclude, but seldom begin, in public spaces. Very little, in fact, of what we consider to be "politics" actually happens in the eye of the larger community. Similar to the interventions staged in our campaign (and I use the word "our" with purpose, since it truly was a group and not an individual undertaking), much of the work of the politician happens behind closed doors, in small groups, or one-on-one. Happily, due to the very nature of feminist philosophy, which is built upon the ideals of community, reciprocity and mutual respect, rhetorical interventions are most likely to emerge in relationship: healthy relationships form through personal communication. There it is, the gift(!) of the oppressors to the oppressed: because of the very constraints placed upon women, they are perfectly situated to slip the double-bind and use these avenues of interpersonal communications for rhetorical interventions that are powerful and politically effective.

It would be remiss not to mention that such an assertion has significant implications across genres. In a variety of settings, including the academy, what is spoken, written, and otherwise communicated within the context of a one-on-one interaction can be a feminist rhetorical intervention of stunning magnitude, particularly when coupled later with communication in the public sphere. Consider the teacher who spends hours with an individual student, and then stands in front of the classroom lecturing—the words spoken in the public space resonate much more clearly when they are heard within the context of a relationship built in the private sphere, for good or ill. Likewise, the administrator, the pastor or preacher—any public figure who also spends a significant amount of time in private, "oikos"-type conversations—when she speaks in the public sphere, the "polis" (boardroom, pulpit, faculty meeting), the groundwork for successful interventions has been laid.

I began this chapter by providing two reasons for my writing and your reading: one, to encourage others to participate in the broader life of politics and society, and secondly, to illuminate how far we have yet to go by telling my story. I echo feminist scholar Jen Almjeld (2014), as she introduces her ethnographic research on computer-mediated dating—a dissimilar topic with analogous implications: "Like other feminist scholars, I continue to believe that the personal is truly political and that our lived experiences shape who we are and the questions we ask in our research. Feminist theory is often rooted in individual experience, and one way to explore texts and spaces is to speak from within them," (p. 72). While I composed from within this space, rooted in my own subjective experience, I experienced a third reason for writing: not merely to share a tale, but to hear the story myself again for the first time. Paulo Freire writes, in *The Pedagogy of the Oppressed*, "I am more and more convinced that true revolutionaries must perceive the revolution, because of its creative and liberating nature, as an act of love," (cited in Kolmar and Bartkowski, 2006, p. 469). In writing the story, re-living the experiences, I was powerfully taught that, (while I am no revolutionary) the most successful feminist interventions are grounded in love and seeking after dignity: for our sisters, our brothers, those who came before us and those who will follow. When I acted out of love, out of a rhetoric of care, whether it was compassion for the people of U.S. Congressional District OH-5, care for Clementine the beloved basset hound, or even benevolence toward my difficult opponent, interventions spun themselves inexorably and joyfully forth, unbidden and unstoppable.

Finally, I turn to my current milieu, and the material impact that living into the positionality of subject-researcher has had upon the quotidian reality of my life. I serve as the Vice-President for Advancement at United Lutheran Seminary. In this role, I recognize and consciously, regularly practice the feminist interventions noted above: I fundraise, collaboratively and in community, by listening and talking, discovering shared values and highlighting the importance of putting our tangible resources into the place where our ideologies lie. The rhetoric of care permeates my work as a feminist-scholar-servant-leader. I anticipate further reflection on this next phase of the journey.

REFERENCES

Almjeld, J. M. (2014). A rhetorician's guide to love: Online dating profiles as remediated commonplace books. *Computers and Composition, 32,* 71–83.

Editorial Board. (2012, October 2). Zimmann for U.S. House. *The Toledo Blade.* Retrieved from http://www.toledoblade.com/Editorials/2012/10/02/Zimmann-for-U-S-House.html.

Foss, K. A., Foss, S. K. & Griffin, C. L. (1999). *Feminist rhetorical theories.* Thousand Oaks, CA.: Sage.

Foss, K. A., Foss, S. K. & Griffin, C. L. (2004). *Readings in feminist rhetorical theory.* Thousand Oaks, CA: Sage.

Kolmar, W. K. & Bartkowski, F. (2005). *Feminist theory: A reader* (2nd ed.). Boston, MA: McGraw-Hill Higher Education.

Lucas County Board of Elections. (2012). Lucas county board of elections: Election results 2010 to present. 21. Retrieved from http://www.co.lucas.oh.us/DocumentCenter/View/55188.

Maille, C. (2015). Feminist interventions in political representation in the United States and Canada: Training programs and legal quotas. *European journal of American studies, 10*(1), 1–15.

Morgan, S. (Ed.). (2006). *The feminist history reader.* London, England: Routledge.

Ouellette, J. (2018). The viability of digital spaces as sites for transnational feminist action and engagement: Why we need to look at digital circulation. In K. L. Blair & L. Nickoson (Eds.), *Composing feminist interventions: Activism, engagement, praxis.* Fort Collins, CO: The WAC Clearinghouse / Louisville, CO: University Press of Colorado. Retrieved from https://wac.colostate.edu/books/perspectives/feminist.

Perry, R. [RickPerry]. (2011, December 6). *Strong.* [Video file]. Retrieved from https://www.YouTube.com/watch?v=0PAJNntoRgA.

Powell, K. M. (2007). *The anguish of displacement: The politics of literacy in the letters of mountain families in Shenandoah National Park.* Charlottesville, VA: University of Virginia P, 2007.

Reilly, M. (2012, February 16). Democracy for America names top ten progressive candidates for 2012. *The Huffington Post*. Retrieved from http://www.huffington post.com/2012/02/16/howard-dean-democracy-for-america-_n_1283117.html.

Rosenthal, M. (2011, December 16). Rick Perry ad spoofed by Ohio congressional candidate. *The Huffington Post*. Retrieved from http://www.huffingtonpost.com/2011/12/16/rick-perry-gay-ad-spoofed_n_1154109.html.

Royster, J. J. & Kirsch, G. E. (2012). *Feminist rhetorical practices: New horizons for rhetoric, composition and literacy studies*. Carbondale, IL: Southern Illinois University Press.

Schiappa, J. (2018). Advocating "active" intersectionality through a comparison of two Slutwalks. In K. L. Blair & L. Nickoson (Eds.), *Composing feminist interventions: Activism, engagement, praxis*. Fort Collins, CO: The WAC Clearinghouse / Louisville, CO: University Press of Colorado. Retrieved from https://wac.colostate.edu/books/perspectives/feminist.

Taylor, M. A. (2014). *She the people: Personal politics and feminist advocacy as the democratic ideal*. (Unpublished doctoral dissertation). University of Texas, Austin.

Wider, Kathleen. In a treeless landscape: A research narrative. Kirsch and Rohan 66–72.

Zimmann, A. (2009). *Turning the noose that binds into a rope to climb: A textual search for rhetorical and linguistic gender-markings in speech samples of three contemporary female orators*. Saarbrücken, Germany: VDM Verlag Dr. Müller.

PART 4. PRAXIS

CHAPTER 17.

PEDAGOGICAL TOO-MUCHNESS: A FEMINIST APPROACH TO COMMUNITY-BASED LEARNING, MULTI-MODAL COMPOSITION, SOCIAL JUSTICE EDUCATION, AND MORE

Beth Godbee
Marquette University

Godbee shares a course titled "Writing for Social Justice," which partners with the YWCA's Racial Justice Program. The course simultaneously integrates community-based learning, multi-modal composition, undergraduate research, contract grading, co-authoring, and attention to racial and social justice—with feminist interventions as the underlying and ultimate goal. Based on these connections, Godbee articulates a pedagogy of "too-muchness" and argues for the need to approach feminist interventions as "instead of" rather than "on top of" more traditional approaches. She situates this pedagogical "too-muchness" within and alongside feminist and womanist pedagogies; pedagogy and theatre of the oppressed; and culturally relevant and responsive pedagogy. In addition to articulating how the YWCA represents an ideal partner for feminist community-based work, Godbee stresses that the "too-muchness" of the course and its emphasis on feminist, critical education better positioned students to become agents and actors outside the course and throughout their everyday lives.

Anyone who has done social justice education knows that it is more than an intellectual activity. Of course, we need to expose people to new perspectives, facts, theories, and analyses. Students need to acquire more accurate and complex information about issues which the mainstream media often ignore, simplify or distort. Yet, even when enlightening

> facts and theories are provided, people may still be unmoved and remain uninvolved.
>
> —Diane J. Goodman (2011, p. 33)

I often hear educators (typically ones from privileged groups) express concerns about the difficulty of a feminist, critical, or otherwise justice-oriented approach: the work involved in social justice education[1] is perceived, even criticized, as "too much." It's perceived as "too much" on top of other labor-intensive demands of an academic career, "too much" on top of other educational demands of a college course, or "too much" on top of other pedagogical apparatus already in place. This sense of too-muchness may arise from the need for critical emotional literacy (Winans, 2012); likely discomfort (Banks, 2003; Tatum, 1992); and the inherently embodied nature of the work, as "[m]any educators are more comfortable staying at an intellectual level" (Goodman, 2011, p. 34). Whatever the origin, this sense of "too-muchness" allows social justice education to be written off as an addition rather than the core of what we do.

Shifting this language of "too-muchness" involves, I argue, approaching feminist interventions as "instead of" rather than "on top of" more traditional approaches. Typically, education prioritizes the curriculum or content, keeping histories of colonization, inequity, and injustice firmly rooted (e.g., Paulo Freire's critique of the banking model of education [1970] or bell hooks's discussion of feminist pedagogy as a "decolonizing political process" [1994, p. 47]). As educators, when we feel responsible to a shared syllabus, program of study, or other external criteria, we may inadvertently prioritize content and imagine feminist interventions as "on top of" these implicit priorities. By naming social justice education as "instead of" rather than "on top of," I maintain that the curriculum and course structure need to be rethought from the bottom to the top, from the details to the whole. Rather than tweaking an existing syllabus to add components that critique injustice, we need to ask fundamental questions about the values, purposes, and intended outcomes of education. That is, in the words of feminist scholar bell hooks (1994), we need to "imagine ways that teaching and the learning experience could be different" (p. 5) and to "celebrate teaching that enables transgressions" (p. 12). This rethinking can lead us in directions that look and feel very different from our conditioned expectations of schooling. And, yet, the very different—perhaps "too much" different—nature

---

1   I equate feminism with social justice education, as both seek to counter injustice and enact a more equitable and just world. In *Feminism Is for Everybody* (2000), bell hooks maintains that feminism must engage colonialism, class struggle, race/ism, and other intersectional issues. Valuing intersectionality (Crenshaw, 1991), feminist education must address sexism in relation to other -isms and as part of justice-oriented movements, which the YWCA articulates in its mission.

of these changes can help us shake up and shake off normalized actions, dominant beliefs, and damaging discourses.

The need to shake up/off typical schooling and to replace it with something truly transformative links social justice education with feminist interventions. Both social justice education and feminist interventions require commitment, ongoing education, and openness to revision. These commitment-driven, reflective, and revisionary values align with the what Jacqueline Jones Royster and Gesa Kirsch (2012) describe as four "critical terms of engagement" for feminist rhetorical practices: "*critical imagination, strategic contemplation, social circulation,* and *globalization*" (p. 19). As an educator committed to equity and justice, I strive to teach—to *critically engage* myself and students—in ways that challenge and change our everyday ways of being, doing, and relating in the world. As I've written with colleagues, this pedagogical stance has multiple dimensions, as it is (1) *processual and reiterative*, (2) *reflective and attentive*, and (3) *embodied and engaged* (Diab, Ferrel, Godbee & Simpkins, 2012). It involves centering the body to interrogate systemic power and to "move-think in ways that disrupt habitual acts and dominant narratives" (Godbee, Ozias & Tang, 2015, p. 99). And it has the potential for transformation, especially when we come to see ourselves in relation with others across asymmetrical power (Godbee, 2011). This understanding of social justice education draws on and aligns with feminist and womanist pedagogies (e.g., Royster & Kirsch, 2012; hooks, 1994; Lorde, 1984); pedagogy and theatre of the oppressed (e.g., Horton & Freire, 1990; Boal, 1973; Freire, 1970); and culturally relevant (Ladson-Billings, 1994, 2001), responsive (Gay, 2000), and contested (Li, 2005) pedagogies.

Though differently positioned to intervene into systemic inequities, these scholar-educators teach us that *power* underlies all relations; that systemic (and political) matters are also embodied (and personal); and that work that supports gender justice intersects with and must enact related forms of justice: racial justice, decolonization, Indigenous rights, and others. In Goodman's (2011) words above, social justice education—and I'd add feminist interventions—must be "more than an intellectual activity" (p. 33). From this scholarship, a few key principles or definitional qualities emerge, indicating that feminist interventions:

1. engage our *full selves*—not only our minds, but also our bodies, emotions, and spirits;
2. prioritize *relations*, or put the time and effort into building and sustaining meaningful (and often cross-status) connections among people and organizations;
3. understand *power* as related to (in)justice so that efforts against sexism and for gender-and-sexuality-justice are linked with other justice-oriented

work, since identities and issues are intersectional and injustice anywhere is injustice everywhere;

4. cultivate *agency* so that students and other actors see themselves as having the responsibility to act, as well as the questions and insights to ask *who* is responsible to act, when, where, why, and how (troubling savior and victim narratives);

5. seek *interconnectedness* among ways of seeing, thinking, doing, and being in the world so that we work toward coherence across spheres of activity and recognize that our work occurs within complex socio-cultural, historical, and rhetorical systems.

Certainly, other principles emerge, and our different positions within systems of power and privilege make some principles more salient than others. I share these five, however, in an attempt to define how I see feminist interventions aligning with social justice education and underlying a feminist pedagogy, one that can be characterized by "too-muchness."

To be clear, pedagogical too-muchness describes two sides of the same coin. The first refers to educators' perception of feminist or justice-oriented education as an addition or extra (i.e., "on top of"). The second refers to an intentional layering, texturing, or piecing together of multiple critical pedagogical approaches (i.e., "instead of"). Each of these critical approaches—from community-based learning to multi-modal composing—can be perceived as "too much," especially when looking from the first side of the coin. Yet, each helps achieve the purposes of disrupting the status quo, overcoming resistance, fostering commitments to justice, and building agency beyond the classroom. Each enacts the five key principles, moving us closer to critical imagination (Royster & Kirsch, 2012; Royster, 2000) and transgression (hooks, 1994). As such, the second side of the coin helps us see the layering of critical approaches not as haphazard or "too much" in the sense of energies going everywhere and nowhere. Rather, this pedagogical too-muchness provides a rich texture to a learning experience, helping us design courses that are complex, critical, and potentially transformative.

In what follows, I demonstrate why pedagogical too-muchness is crucial to social justice education (generally) and to the teaching of one course, "Writing for Social Justice" (specifically). In doing so, I make reference to the syllabus, assignments, and videos that students created, which appear at http://epublications.marquette.edu/english_4210/. I share these documents to illustrate the argument I make in this chapter: that feminist interventions prioritize interconnectedness not only among course content, assignments, and assessment, but also among ways of seeing, thinking, doing, and being in the world. This interconnectedness (like the other principles of engaging our full selves, prioritizing relations, understanding power, and cultivating agency) necessitates layering, texturing, or piecing together of critical approaches. That is, the feminist principle of interconnectedness necessitates pedagogical too-muchness.

CO-CONSTRUCTING A SHARED LEARNING EXPERIENCE

This chapter relates one attempt at feminist interventions, as I describe the community-based learning course "Writing for Social Justice" that emerged in partnership with the YWCA Southeast Wisconsin's Racial Justice Program and with Marquette University's Digital Media Studio (DMS). Like other courses in this "Praxis" section, students engaged in project-based learning. In other chapters, Ames Hawkins and Joan Giroux (Chapter 18, this collection) describe art activism; Douglas Walls, Jennifer Miller, and Brandy Dieterle (Chapter 20, this collection) explain development of a smartphone app; and Danielle Williams (Chapter 21, this collection) shares a public video project. Here I describe how undergraduates created short educational and promotional videos for Everytown Wisconsin, a week-long camp intended to help teens develop leadership skills, challenge stereotypes, and build self-confidence—all while having fun. The videos highlight participants' experiences with the camp, showcase what participants have learned, and promote the camp to various stakeholders.

When developing the course, I repeatedly heard concerns about "doing it all at once"—meaning that it seemed too much to integrate video composition and multi-modal projects with community-based learning, explicit attention to race/racism/antiracism, undergraduate research and collaborative authorship, frequent one-with-one conferences, and even grading contracts and portfolios that center student agency—and all within a feminist framework. This sense of "doing too much" stemmed largely, I believe, from ideas about how far the course deviates from what's typical at my institution (and from many colleges and universities). Yet, as I argue in this chapter and as I found to be true, the course needed all of these pieces because one without the others would not have allowed us to do the type of feminist education I hoped the course could achieve. It would not have allowed us to produce videos that could be of use to our community partner. It would not have positioned students to become agents and actors outside the course and throughout their everyday lives. It would not have given us the critical insights into power relations that are needed for making change. Yet, change is greatly needed—in and out of school—and many students recognize and seek this more-than-intellectual engagement.

"Writing for Social Justice" attracted students who were seeking such engagement. Offered as an upper-division special topics course for writing-intensive English majors, the course was small with fourteen students. Like my colleagues, students expressed concerns early on that the course was "too much"—too demanding, requiring too many hours/week, asking for too much reflective self-work, etc. When processing at midterms and finals, many students shared stories of being initially "scared" or "overwhelmed by" the course, but so glad they stayed—with the ultimate payoff worth the effort. The high demands kept the class size small, and the small size, in turn, allowed us to build the intimate and challenging community that is needed for social justice education. Happily, I found that students opened to each other and to me (a white woman): I witnessed the eleven white students listen more carefully, learn about whiteness, and articulate commitments to racial justice—with and alongside three students of color who shared their experiences with differential risk, tightrope positioning, and asymmetrical power in ways that helped us all with self-reflexivity. Through ongoing, self-reflexive dialogue, we all learned about and contested the inhospitable conditions in higher education that lead to many marginalized peoples, especially women of color, being "presumed incompetent" (Gutiérrez y Muhs, Niemann, González & Harris, 2012). Such reflexivity and contestation constitute a feminist project on their own.

In framing the course, it was important to me that we explicitly link ways of seeing, thinking, being, and doing (seeking interconnectedness). Therefore, I framed our partnership with the YWCA, the role of community-based learning, and the culminating video project as necessary components so that we would not only explore but also practice and engage in the action of "writing for social justice." I asked us to answer in creative, inquiry-based, and reflective ways the following questions:

- How is writing involved in social justice work? What genres of writing are associated with movements for and thinking about social and racial justice?
- How do we understand central concepts of (in)equity, (in)justice, power, and rights?
- How might we, as communicators, use writing to intervene into injustice and to bring about a more socially just world?

These questions align with learning objectives and competences, which helped to structure the course and named types of conceptual, rhetorical, technical, affective/emotional, and other knowledge. They ranged from broadening our understanding of "writing" to include visual, oral, and multi-modal composition to pairing critique *against* injustice with the critique *for* justice.

Starting the course (and course materials) with articulations of questions, objectives, and competences proved important for thinking about why our semester's work mattered beyond the course, semester, or site. Because students wrote their own learning objectives, they adopted the language of "goals" and "objectives" in ways I have not observed in other courses. From processing shared learning objectives to setting personalized ones, students assumed agency in the first days of the semester—a time that is too-often spent with teacher-directed instructions. Moreover, collaborative goal-setting communicated the principles of feminist interventions from the start, engaging students in active and personal work as well as explicitly linking what we learn with how we see, what we do, and where we relate in the world.

ENACTING TOO-MUCHNESS THROUGH SEQUENCED AND SCAFFOLDED ASSIGNMENTS

From collaborative goal-setting (articulating *the why* of the course), we moved into the layered, textured, or pieced together too-muchness (achieving *the how* of feminist interventions). A view into the course (and I hope you'll take a look at the syllabus online) reveals scaffolded assignments; in-class workshops; out-of-class conferences; instruction from our DMS partners; consultation with our YWCA partners; and significant attention to the process, revision, and rethinking. Much of this work was collaborative in nature, involving co-authoring, collaborative learning, and undergraduate research. Much of it also involved ongoing reflection through in-class processing, freewriting, movement-based exercises, and contemplative practices. This active hands-on work was guided by scholarly readings—from foundational pieces like Iris Young's "Five Faces of Oppression" (1990) and Beverly Tatum's "Talking about Race, Learning about Racism" (1992) to excerpts of in-field texts like Paula Mathieu's *Tactics of Hope* (2005) and Tiffany Rousculp's *Rhetoric of Respect* (2014). Additional multimodal materials included music; blogs, comics, and webtexts; short videos; and materials provided to us by the YWCA, such as the grant application for Every town Wisconsin. We also *all* read excerpts from three books with each person choosing to read and report on one in full: Gloria Anzladúa's *Borderlands/La Frontera* (1987), Myles Horton and Paulo Freire's *We Make the Road by Walking* (1990), and Elaine Richardson's *PHD (Po H# on Dope) to Ph.D.* (2013).

Already the sense of pedagogical too-muchness emerges here in the course overview. To make sense of this range of activities, the course needed to scaffold students through manageable, sequenced assignments—with later projects building on earlier ones:

1. *Introductory Letter Forecasting the Semester*, an informal letter due in week #2 relating anticipations, expectations, and goals for the course.

2. *Statement on Writing for Social Justice,* a large-scale, semester-long effort to articulate a vision of "writing for social justice." As a culminating statement, this creative piece synthesized course readings, discussions, community-based learning, and insights gained through assignments. The statement included an annotated bibliography kept throughout the semester to document and engage the sources that shape one's vision.

3. *Critical Importance Video,* a short video (just 1 to 1½ minutes) to teach others about one of our shared books—taking up a line of inquiry, a passage of the text, a story reported, or something else that others will benefit from learning. This was not simply a summary or synopsis of the book, but a presentation to relate what is of "critical importance."

4. *Community-Based, Collaborative Video Project,* short (2–5 minute) educational and promotional videos to promote Everytown Wisconsin, made in partnership with and for use by our community partner, YWCA Southeast Wisconsin's Racial Justice Program.

Of these four assignments, the two video projects directly involved the DMS and YWCA. The other two—the introductory letter and statement on writing for social justice—focused on reflection: students set and tracked progress toward learning objectives, personalized knowledge and language of the course, and articulated a vision to carry forward. These reflective writing assignments aimed at *critical imagination and strategic contemplation,* to use Royster and Kirsch's (2012) terms, as they served as inquiry tools for "seeing the noticed and the unnoticed" (p. 20) and created "space for rigorous contemplation" (p. 21). They helped students understand and transfer the five key principles of feminist interventions that we practiced through community-based learning and video production.

The video assignments, in turn, allowed us to build and rehearse the key principles of feminist interventions, as we worked in relationship and cultivated agency, while also building understandings about power, (in)justice, and other matters. As part of prioritizing relations, I consulted colleagues in the Center for Teaching and Learning, Service Learning Program, and Digital Media Studio (DMS) before and throughout the course. These campus partners provided financial and curricular support. As an example, a grant through the Serving Learning Program allowed the DMS to pilot a course tutoring program—having an undergraduate tutor (in addition to the director) work closely with students during both in-class workshops and out-of-class conferences. The DMS Director, Elizabeth Andrejasich Gibes, co-taught multiple classes to help students build technical, collaborative, and research skills—skills that were not isolated from the critical and feminist approach to the course, but instead made possible our feminist interventions. We also co-created the critical importance video assignment as a video (investing in collaboration and strengthening our relationship) and used this assignment for students to build conceptual knowledge from readings, while developing technical know-how.

What I'd like to underline is that the complexity, range, and depth of this wide-ranging work allowed us to seek interconnectedness—to recognize connections among systemic inequities and movements for social justice. For instance, along with the readings, in-class activities, and four primary assignments, collaboration with the YWCA allowed us to focus on one type of social justice: that is, racial justice. Throughout the semester, we explored race/ism and racial justice alongside intersectional identities, asymmetrical power, prejudice, and privilege. Seeking interconnectedness meant that we took seriously the YWCA's mission of "eliminating racism, empowering women"—identifying relationships among forms of (in)justice (e.g., linking racism and sexism). Seeking such interconnectedness is necessary for feminism to be more than white women centering whiteness, as hooks (2000) and Lorde (1984) remind us. Also, seeking interconnectedness meant gaining conceptual knowledge (beyond technical skills) that would aid in creating informed and quality videos for the YWCA. Danielle Williams (2018, this collection) identifies the need for such conceptual knowledge when sharing how students reproduced stereotypes: without investigating their own biases, students wrote prejudice into the GED videos they created. Hence, I highlight the value of interconnectedness, as it is essential for enacting other principles of feminist interventions: engaging our full selves, prioritizing relations, understanding power, and cultivating agency.

As further illustration, I'd like to highlight a moment in which the planning and activities of the course created the conditions for feminist interventions, but truly the students had to act, as agents, with openness and courage. When discussing the importance of developing "bias literacy," we noted the need to personalize and internalize (not just intellectually rehearse understanding of) this concept. We asked questions like: When do we recognize privilege in the body? When do guilt, hurt, or other emotions get in the way of authentic relationship? When are biases unintentionally creeping into thoughts and actions? Students evidenced their embodied learning in subsequent interactions. On the day we discussed microaggressions (Sue, 2010), students responded through a "popcorn share": each person shared a response or example from the reading before naming a colleague, who would next respond. As I watched students pass the speaking turn, I noticed that a white student volunteered to begin and that white students were naming other white students. The three students of color were the last to speak and were left naming each other, before naming me (returning the speaking turn to the teacher). We needed to address what happened, and this could be the moment for folks to embrace racial justice work or to resist.

Gently, I asked: "We're talking about microaggressions, and we just enacted one. What happened?" A long silence. No one spoke. I interjected, "Does anyone know what I'm talking about?" Several people began nodding, and then one of the students of color described what happened, noting that this happens "all the time" in her classes. Luckily, the white students *got it*: they made connections with the readings; noted how their actions had been unintentional but consequential manifestations of bias; and said they could see why microaggressions are so significant, insidious, and unseen by people with privilege. Rather than resistance, strategic contemplation emerged. Students used the language of the readings, and they made connections to their lives, later tracking microaggressions they witnessed or participated in outside of class. Moments of self-critique like this one were essential. They not only embodied and personalized learning (engaging our full selves), but they also prepared us for working with the YWCA and facing a number of similar, potentially transformative moments throughout the semester.

BUILDING RELATIONS THROUGH COMMUNITY-BASED LEARNING

The course's central project—the collaborative video—involved students in working closely with each other and with the YWCA to promote Everytown Wisconsin. These collaborative videos involved co-authoring and editing in small groups; conducting and filming interviews with camp participants; making use of already-recorded video footage and images; revising based on feedback; and producing a video that met the YWCA's vision and intended audiences. To accomplish this ambitious project, we worked closely with the DMS staff, who joined weekly in-class workshops and frequent out-of-class conferences. And students took active leadership roles, serving as co-authors, project managers, editors, photographers, designers, outreach coordinators, and record-keepers.

Though we used a timeline to help structure this semester-long project, we also adapted in response to the needs and feedback of our community partner. The YWCA helped us to learn about the work of nonprofit organizations, including their publicity and communication needs. To understand and create videos about Everytown Wisconsin, we learned about the needs of distinct audiences: (1) teens (or potential delegates to the camp); (2) their parents, teachers, or other adults involved in their lives; and (3) the public, including funding organizations and citizen donors. In response, we created three different videos targeting these different audiences. (These videos can also be viewed through the course URL.)

This course was the first time I worked closely with the YWCA and with Martha Barry, Director of the Racial Justice Program. Much of the semester involved building a relationship that we could sustain and grow beyond this course, which we now are continuing to do. In many ways, though we all wanted the final videos to be of real use to the YWCA, the video project was less important than the relational and processual work of community-based learning. Throughout the semester, the students and I read together work problematizing altruistic "service" or "service-learning" and arguing instead for more robust, reciprocal, and relational models of community engagement (e.g., Rousculp, 2014; Mathieu, 2005; Cushman, 1999; Peck, Flower & Higgins, 1995). Readings and discussions led students to reflect more critically on previous service-learning experiences and to consider what community engagement would look like beyond this course.

Many "service" experiences not only at my institution (Marquette University, an urban Jesuit university) but also at institutions across the United States invoke troubling notions of altruistic "helping" (e.g., Rousculp, 2014; Cushman, 1999) or reinscribe whiteness (e.g., Seider & Hillman, 2011; Green, 2003). Given the problematic ways that service-learning can be enacted, my hope was that our relational, project-oriented approach would help us to disrupt the status quo, rethink past experiences, and imagine new relations. DiAngelo & Sensoy (2012), for instance, find that white students often "complain they are (or fear being) 'attacked'" in cross-racial discussions and, therefore, depict race discussions as "unsafe spaces, as arenas of violence" (p. 1). By enlisting white students to work for racial justice (and not just to sit back and talk), community-based learning can help circumvent resistance and communicate the responsibility to act. Taking action, in turn, teaches what Horton & Freire (1990) have expressed: "without practice, there is no knowledge" (p. 97), and to act, one must "start doing it and learn from it" (p. 40). These are arguments for the value not only of community-based learning, but also for writing, research, and multimodal projects that engage students in action, hence why I argue for pedagogical too-muchness and the layering, texturing, or piecing together of multiple, critical practices. Each of these puzzle pieces gets us closer to seeing the picture, but we need them all to complete the puzzle. In other words, we need the many pieces for an intervention that is truly feminist, that is both aligned with and working to enact social justice education.

To explain further, I think of Paula Mathieu's (2005) argument for why community writing needs a tactical orientation that resists "charity" and is based in both projects and partnerships. Our video project was "tactical" in that it was limited to a specific term and project and, therefore, small-scale in the face of the YWCA's larger mission. Tactical in nature, the video project (1) addressed a specific issue (Everytown Wisconsin); (2) had a long-term vision (aimed at enacting racial justice and practicing "writing for social justice"); and (3) took a project, rather than problem, orientation. A problem orientation "operates from a negative space," has a "transactional quality to it," and "runs the risk of leaving participants overwhelmed, cynical, and feeling weak" (p. 50). In contrast, a project orientation "privileges creation and design," particularly within set "length, scope, and parameters" (p. 50). By contrasting problems with projects, Mathieu offers language and a framework for understanding why a tactical orientation is so crucial to community writing.

Similarly, I'd argue, feminist interventions necessitate a tactical orientation that emphasizes projects and partnerships—cultivating agency and prioritizing relations—rather than trying to fix problems. While the relational work of partnerships involves ongoing and sustained investment, the project itself can be immediate and fixed-term (i.e., semester-long). Such projects need not be multi-modal, and, in fact, Mathieu cites other examples of multi-genre research papers (Mack, 2002), oral history projects (Cassell, 2000), and service learning with a Boston-area street paper (Mathieu, 2005). We find still other examples in this collection, such as collaborative art activism for The Cradle Project (Hawkins & Giroux, Chapter 18, this collection), digital storytelling to produce local documentaries (Bower, Chapter 24, this collection), and the collection and retelling of farm histories (Denecker & Sisser, Chapter 9, this collection). Whatever the project's nature, such work means, in Mathieu's words, "doing many things at once" (2000, p. 53), as is the nature of public writing and much of our everyday lives. Rather than seeing these "many things" as a problem or as "too much" in the negative sense, it is possible to embrace pedagogical too-muchness. It's possible to appreciate a project's and partnership's ability to influence students' views of, responsibilities to, and roles within social justice work. It's possible, too, to see community-based learning, like other critical pedagogical approaches, as central to feminist interventions aimed at more equitable relations.

To see this, I'd like to share another powerful moment—one that emerged from a day of reviewing videos with the YWCA staff. During this workshop day, we noticed and discussed how one co-authoring group started their video with four white speakers back-to-back, putting the voices and experiences of white people first *before* those of people of color. Two YWCA staff members began their feedback by asking about this sequence and the messages it would send. The class took time to identify the problem—engaging in the critique *against*—and then proposed solutions—providing the critique *for* (a framework we used throughout the semester). Building on this familiar framework and earlier moments like our discussion on microaggressions and bias literacy, the co-authoring group received the feedback well; showed a willingness to revise; and recognized their implicit, yet consequential, bias.

During end-of-the-semester processing, a member of this co-authoring group said they continued to think about this feedback and would invest in further developing bias literacy. These moments indicated to me that students were truly personalizing their learning, making it more than intellectual and part of their full selves. I greatly appreciated our community partners' willingness to give this and other *real* feedback—feedback addressing the logic/narratives of the videos and not only its design or genre conventions. In contrast to a vision of community members as "clients," to pick up on Danielle Williams's language in her chapter (this collection), our partners at the YWCA truly served as "mentors." They helped students see, investigate, and revise biased perspectives. The end result not only made the final video products useable, but also made the process deeply learning-full for all involved. Because feedback spoke to conceptual knowledge we worked to build through readings and other course materials, it helped us synthesize ways of knowing with ways of doing (toward interconnectedness). Through pedagogical too-muchness, we learned that "writing for social justice" was not rote practice or technical know-how. It was instead about recognizing and rewriting damaged discourses (like those around race/ism and sex/ism), aiming toward equity and justice.

CULTIVATING AGENCY IN ASSESSMENT

In my mind, as important as "the work" of the course (e.g., the readings, projects, and community-based learning) are the self-reflexive stances students develop and the commitments they tap into, deepen, and hopefully take beyond the semester. To help students cultivate agency and the habits of mind needed for self-reflexivity and self-directed learning, I approached assessment as an ongoing, negotiated, and active process. In other words, assessment came *not* in hindsight or separate from but instead as part of "the work" itself. Because grades matter and are so central to schooling, the means of assessment need also to challenge "business as usual": we cannot ask students to take significant responsibility without demonstrating how this responsibility manifests in grades. Further, because students typically care about grades, rethinking assessment helps in shaking up/off assumed ways of being and operating in school. All of these goals underlie feminist interventions, which seek to disrupt inequities. Disruption must engage matters of power, agency, rights, and responsibilities.

Pedagogical too-muchness, therefore, involves alternative means of assessment. For me, these alternatives include portfolios and contract grading, both of which present opportunities for students to shape the reception of their work and to see themselves as actors with insights. In "Writing for Social Justice," students engaged, for instance, in a wide range of self-reflection, relationship-building, reading, writing, and digital production. To frame and interpret this work, students set their own learning objectives; wrote and revised grading contracts;

compiled work into midterm and final portfolios; and composed carefully crafted cover letters, reflecting on their agency and growth throughout the course. Midterms and finals served as reflective moments for looking backward and forward. Explaining this process began in the syllabus and continued in one-with-one conferences, through assignment sheets, and by sharing samples of past students' portfolios and cover letters.

In composition and rhetoric, many of us are accustomed to the use of portfolios and cover letters, even if our timing, construction, or expectations of these documents differ (e.g., Reynolds & Davis, 2014). What is less frequently used is contract grading (e.g., Inoue, 2015, 2012), which can go a far way toward demystifying the grading process, involving students in self-assessment, and fostering students' ownership of learning. Similarly, conferences are important for instructors to listen and mentor—toward cultivating a relational pedagogy, which underlines the deep valuing of relations and agency. Together, conferencing/mentoring with alternative assessment (portfolios and grading contracts) give instructors deep insights into students' experiences and students deep insights into their legacies of schooling.

What I found in this course was that assessment especially helped us think about privilege, power, and inequities. Assessment exposed lower expectations or deficit thinking facing *some* students and higher expectations or excess thinking for *others*. To tell this story, I must explain that this course was *most* students' first experience creating their own learning objectives, and it was *all* students' first experience with grading contracts. During conferences, I found that some students needed to talk through conflicting responsibilities, others needed reassurance that they could succeed, and still others needed direct permission to claim academic success. What struck me was that two of the three women of color planned to contract for lower grades than most white students. In talking with them, I learned that they had come to accept that they should aim for "good" (i.e., not great) grades—likely a sign of the larger legacy of being "presumed incompetent" in schools (Gutiérrez y Muhs, Niemann, González & Harris, 2012). After talking through their personal learning objectives (some of the most ambitious in the course), I asked, "why not try for the higher grade?" This question opened reflection on years of schooling, which led to narratives of teachers seeing and grading them differently and worries about being "not enough." When these students chose to abandon the narrative of "not enough" (a choice that realized their agency), they were also able to let go negative expectations, countering internalized oppression.

In contrast, three white students (two of them men) initially contracted for high grades despite their relative inattention to the first assignment and grading contract. With these students, talking about the contracts allowed me to clarify expectations for successful completion of the course. Throughout the semester, we talked frequently about their contracts, using learning objectives as a guide. At different points (midterms, post-midterms, and finals), these three students re-contracted for lower grades. Their decisions seemed to be made with ease and without anger, along with an increasing recognition that they expected from years of schooling to "get by" with minimal engagement. Guided by ongoing and clear communication, these three students re-contracted without a sense of letting themselves, me, or their colleagues down and with, I hope, questions lingering about how privilege allowed them to be perceived as "doing well" without doing much. Here again, students assumed agency in their assessment and in ways that called them to consider their relative rights and responsibilities. It also opened reflection on past experiences, and one student commented that they had never truly been challenged because they had always been seen as already "doing enough." These contrasting ideas of *enough* ("not enough" versus "already enough") lead me to argue that we, as educators, must reconsider the inequitable messages that grades send, stripping students of their agency to succeed and to grow.

As a teacher, I especially appreciated the re-contracting process, as it gave me insights into students' expectations, while lessening the stress of grading. I put attention toward responding and mentoring instead of sorting and ranking, and students reported feeling secure about their grades and, therefore, open to taking risks. With other causes for stress (e.g., ongoing talk about race/ism, responsibilities to our community partner, and frustration with video editing), it was a relief not to put too much emotional energy into assessment. Further, I believe that, at its best, education gives students the sense that they have responsibility (response + ability) to act in the world. Hopefully, students will transfer the self-determination they practiced in the course outward into their writing, organizing, and other feminist interventions.

EMBRACING PEDAGOGICAL TOO-MUCHNESS

The methodological layering of pedagogical too-muchness is something I've come to over years of observation, experimentation, and reading-reflecting-thinking with others. My first classroom teaching experience gave me insight into the need to change not just components of a course or curriculum, but essentially the whole of the educational endeavor. When I began teaching high school social studies, I was not only unprepared to consider the interactional dynamics in a learning environment for 30+ individuals, but I was also trying to do things too differently from what students had come to expect. I realized that students needed help transitioning into the experience I was attempting to create with them. And I learned that this "help in transitioning" required not just changes to course content or a single assignment. Rather, we needed to question—and largely to change—inherited ways of operating in a classroom. This meant rethinking roles, the use of time, the sequence of assignments, the outcomes of the course—and all starting with guiding questions, learning objectives, and competences. In other words, to embrace hooks's (1994) call for feminist educators to "teach to transgress," we must rethink the whole (all components) of education.

Despite having heard grumblings over the years that social justice education is "just too much," it is only recently that I've thought to embrace the language of "too-muchness." I now believe that pedagogical too-muchness describes the great extent to which we need to change for our teaching to be critical, feminist, and transformative. In Mathieu's words, community writing involves "doing many things at once" (2005, p. 53). If my lived experience is any indicator, much of living, working, organizing, and acting in the world similarly involves "many things at once."

Many changes at once can be overwhelming, and to be clear, I am not indicating that we overwhelm ourselves, students, or anyone else. On the contrary, I believe pedagogical too-muchness aligns with the move to connect contemplative pedagogy with anti-oppression education. More mindful, engaged education aligns with the goals of more just, reflexive communities. This too-muchness simply means that we let go of past, often-unspoken priorities to instead piece together the complex puzzle—assembling a new set of critical practices. Such practices, in turn, allow us to enact key principles of feminist interventions, including the five I have addressed throughout this chapter: (1) engaging our full selves, (2) prioritizing relations, (3) understanding power, (4) cultivating agency, and (5) seeking interconnectedness.

As a final story, I will share that "Writing for Social Justice" is my first course in which students have asked at midterms for *more* work. Specifically, they asked for each other (their colleagues) to share popular news stories and examples that would help make sense of the scholarly readings and to take greater leadership roles in class discussions. They also suggested doing more out-of-class freewriting to create space for more in-class processing. Then, post-midterm, students acted on these requests—signing up to lead class sessions, assigning each other freewriting prompts, sharing protest music at the start of class, and emailing webtexts through the course listserv. Something happened by changing the regular classroom script: as I co-created with students, they began investing *more* in their own learning.

Having witnessed and participated in this experience, I will continue to embrace pedagogical too-muchness. In doing so, I hope to create more meaningful, learning-full experiences. The more we strive for equity in education, the more we can work toward social justice in the world around us. Therefore, I call for us to keep rethinking education, asking: *How might we intervene into and rewrite the scripts of schooling? How might we approach our roles differently? Who might we partner with in this endeavor? What will we need to learn along the way?*

REFERENCES

Anzladúa, G. (1987). *Borderlands/la frontera: The new mestiza*. San Francisco, CA: Aunt Lute Books.

Banks, W. P. (2003). Written through the body: Disruptions and "personal" writing. *College English, 66*(1), 21–40.

Boal, A. (1973). *Theatre of the oppressed*. New York, NY: Routledge.

Cassell, S. L. (2000). Hunger for memory: Oral history recovery in community service learning. *Reflections, 1*(2), 12–17. Retrieved from http://reflectionsjournal.net/purchase-articles/vols-1-3/.

Crenshaw, K. (1991). Mapping the margins: Intersectionality, identity politics, and violence against women of color. *Stanford Law Review, 43*(6), 1241–1299.

Cushman, E. (1996). The rhetorician as an agent of social change. *College Composition and Communication, 47*(1), 7–28.

Diab, R., Ferrel, T., Godbee, B. & Simpkins, N. (2012). A multi-dimensional pedagogy for racial justice in writing centers. *Praxis: A Writing Center Journal, 10*(1). Retrieved from http://www.praxisuwc.com/diab-godbee-ferrell-simpkins-101.

DiAngelo, R. & Sensoy, Ö. (2012). Getting slammed: White depictions of race discussions as arenas of violence. *Race Ethnicity and Education, 17*(1), 1–26. Retrieved from http://www.tandfonline.com/doi/abs/10.1080/13613324.2012.674023#.VgQJ23vgw7w.

Freire, P. (1970/2006). *Pedagogy of the oppressed*. New York, NY: Continuum.

Gay, G. (2000). *Culturally responsive teaching: Theory, research, and practice*. New York, NY: Teachers College Press.

Godbee, B. (2012). Toward explaining the transformative power of talk about, around, and for writing. *Research in the Teaching of English, 47*(2), 171–197.

Godbee, B., Ozias, M. & Tang, J. K. (2015). Body + power + justice: Movement-based workshops for critical tutor education. *Writing Center Journal, 34*(2), 61–112.

Goodman, D. J. (2011). *Promoting diversity and social justice: Educating people from privileged groups* (2nd ed.). New York, NY: Routledge.

Green, A. E. (2003). Difficult stories: Service-learning, race, class, and whiteness. *College Composition and Communication, 55*(2), 276–301.

Gutiérrez y Muhs, G., Niemann, Y. F., González, C. G. & Harris, A. P. (Eds.). (2012). *Presumed incompetent: The intersections of race and class for women in academia*. Logan, UT: Utah State University Press.

Hawkins, A. & Giroux, J. (2018). Trans/feminist practice of collaboration in the art activism classroom. In K. L. Blair & L. Nickoson (Eds.), *Composing feminist interventions: Activism, engagement, praxis*. Fort Collins, CO: The WAC Clearinghouse /

Louisville, CO: University Press of Colorado. Retrieved from https://wac.colostate.edu/books/perspectives/feminist.

hooks, b. (2000). *Feminism is for everybody: Passionate politics*. Cambridge, MA: South End Press.

hooks, b. (1994). *Teaching to transgress: Education as the practice of freedom*. New York, NY: Routledge.

Horton, M. & Freire, Paulo. (1990). *We make the road by walking: Conversations on education and social change*. B. Bell, J. Gaventa & J. Peters (Eds.). Philadelphia, PA: Temple University Press.

Inoue, A. B. (2015). *Antiracist writing assessment ecologies: Teaching and assessing writing for a socially just future*. Fort Collins, CO: The WAC Clearinghouse / Anderson, SC: Parlor Press. Retrieved from http://wac.colostate.edu/books/inoue/ .

Inoue, A. B. (2012). Grading contracts: Assessing their effectiveness on different racial formations. In A. B. Inoue & M. Poe (Eds.), *Race and Writing Assessment*. New York, NY: Peter Lang.

Ladson-Billings, G. (2001). *Crossing over to Canaan: The journey of new teachers in diverse classrooms*. San Francisco, CA: Jossey-Bass.

Ladson-Billings, G. (1994). *The dreamkeepers: Successful teachers of African American children*. San Francisco, CA: Jossey-Bass.

Li, G. (2005). *Culturally contested pedagogy: Battles of literacy and schooling between mainstream teachers and Asian immigrant parents*. Albany, NY: State University of New York Press.

Lorde, A. (1984). *Sister outsider: Essays and speeches*. Freedom, CA: Crossing Press.

Mack, N. (2002). The ins, outs, and in-betweens of multigenre writing. *English Journal, 92*(2), 91–98.

Mathieu, P. (2005). *Tactics of hope: The public turn in English composition*. Portsmouth, NH: Boynton/Cook.

Peck, W. C., Flower, L. & Higgins, L. (1995). Community literacy. *College Composition and Communication, 46*(2), 199–222.

Reynolds, N. & Davis, E. (2014). *Portfolio teaching: A guide for instructors* (3rd ed.). New York, NY: Bedford/St. Martin's.

Richardson, E. (2013). *PHD (Po H# on Dope) to Ph.D.: How education saved my life*. West Lafayette, IN: New Community Press and Parlor Press.

Rousculp, T. (2014). *Rhetoric of respect: Recognizing change at a community writing center*. Urbana, IL: NCTE.

Royster, J. J. (2000). *Traces of a stream: Literacy and social change among African American women*. Pittsburgh, PA: University of Pittsburgh Press.

Royster, J. J. & Kirsch, G. (2012). *Feminist rhetorical practices: New horizons for rhetoric, composition, and literacy studies*. Carbondale, IL: Southern Illinois University Press.

Seider, S. C. & Hillman, A. (2011). Challenging privileged college students' othering language in community service learning. *Journal of College & Character, 12*(3), 1–7.

Sue, D. W. (2010). *Microaggressions in everyday life: Race, gender, and sexual orientation*. Hoboken, NJ: Wiley.

Tatum, B. D. (1992). Talking about race, learning about racism: The application of racial identity development theory in the classroom. *Harvard Educational Review, 61*(1), 1–24.

Walls, D., Dieterle, B. & Miller, J. R. (2018). Safely social: User-centered design and difference feminism. In K. L. Blair & L. Nickoson (Eds.), *Composing feminist interventions: Activism, engagement, praxis.* Fort Collins, CO: The WAC Clearinghouse / Louisville, CO: University Press of Colorado. Retrieved from https://wac.colostate.edu/books/perspectives/feminist.

Williams, D. M. (2018). The unheard voices of dissatisfied clients: Listening to community partners as feminist praxis. In K. L. Blair & L. Nickoson (Eds.), *Composing feminist interventions: Activism, engagement, praxis.* Fort Collins, CO: The WAC Clearinghouse / Louisville, CO: University Press of Colorado. Retrieved from https://wac.colostate.edu/books/perspectives/feminist.

Winans, A. E. (2012). Cultivating critical emotional literacy: Cognitive and contemplative approaches to engaging difference. *College English, 75*(2), 150–170.

Young, I. M. (1990/2010). Five faces of oppression. In M. Adams, W. J. Blumenfeld, C. Castañeda, H. W. Hackman, M. L. Peters & X. Zúñiga (Eds.), *Readings for diversity and social justice* (2nd ed.) (pp. 35–45). New York, NY: Routledge.

YWCA Southeast Wisconsin. (2015). Racial justice. Retrieved from http://www.ywcasew.org/site/c.7oJELQPwFhJWG/b.8083605/k.9A7C/Racial_Justice.htm.

CHAPTER 18.
TRANS/FEMINIST PRACTICE OF COLLABORATION IN THE ART ACTIVISM CLASSROOM

Ames Hawkins
Columbia College Chicago

Joan Giroux
Columbia College Chicago

In 2007, the authors of this article were inspired by an object—a "Call to Artists" postcard for The Cradle Project—to write a description for a class in art activism that eventually manifested as two cross-listed courses in Cultural Studies and Art+Design that we taught together in January 2008, and again in 2012. This chapter begins with conscious consideration of the object of inspiration in order to establish the disciplinary positions from which we eventually move as we engage in a trans/feminist practice of collaboration. We explore how teaching this co-created and co-taught course led to shifts in modes of practice and the redefinition of disciplinary positions. We conclude with a recognition of how this trans/feminist practice invited students to shift with us—and to shift us—performing activism and collaboration vis-à-vis social practice.

This essay has been collaboratively written, but our story here is not necessarily about the writing of this essay, even though it's never not about the writing of this essay.

Our story begins with an object, a postcard Joan Giroux handed to Ames Hawkins at a meeting in Fall 2006. On the front appears a photo of the interior of a large abandoned warehouse. Set in American Typewriter-like font, roughly 36 point, tracked out to occupy more horizontal space, the text "Call To Artists" is superimposed on the image. In smaller font below: "In Spring of 2008 one thousand cradles and cribs made by artists from around the world, will form an installation in Albuquerque, New Mexico. We call this vision The Cradle Project."

This postcard was the catalyst for a nearly seven-year arts activist pedagogical collaboration, one that began with more than eight months of conversation that both prompted and compelled us to create the cross-listed courses *22-3254J Special Topics in Studio Art: Art and Activism Studio Project and 46-2505J Art and Activism Studio Project*. Nearly eighteen months after Joan handed Ames the postcard, we co-taught this course in January 2008, during which, all told, 22 students collaboratively made eight cradles. With support of a Faculty Development Grant, Ames drove these eight cradles, and another seven made by faculty, staff, and community members, to Albuquerque, New Mexico. Eventually displayed in The Banque Building in downtown Albuquerque, during June 2008, over 6000 people came to see the exhibition of 555 cradles. Each cradle was sponsored for $100 and eventually auctioned off, raising $79,000. Another $20,000 was raised through *The Cradle Project* book featuring a number of cradles and artist statements.

We taught the course together again in January 2012, this time inspired by Naomi Natale's second project, One Million Bones. As stated on the website, "One Million Bones is a large-scale social arts practice, which means we use education and hands-on art making to raise awareness of genocides and atrocities going on around the world, this very day." This time we also collaborated with the Arts, Entertainment, and Media Management Department to present One Million Bones as part of an exhibition, working with faculty member Bob Blandford and students in the *Decision Making: Visual Arts Management class to create Crafting Hope: An Arts Activism Project,* an interactive installation featuring art activism and One Million Bones in a student-run gallery, The Hokin Project, in April 2012. During the nine-day immersive course experience, students made 5500 bones, a portion of the almost 50,000 bones made and collected throughout Chicagoland and the Great Lakes area. Collaborators included student organizations, academic departments, faculty groups and student support services at our campus. In the community we worked with refugee groups, regional primary and secondary schools, a girl scout troop, crafts centers, and other universities.

Between 2009 and 2013, we were involved in hundreds of interactions with volunteers, were a part of a number of smaller bone installations and public performances in a variety of setting and public spaces, and found ourselves, in the final six months before the installation, working an average of ten hours a week on this project. As Ames wrote in an article for *@LAS*, the magazine of the School of Liberal Arts and Sciences at Columbia College Chicago:

> Together, Joan and I made bones, moved bones, counted bones, boxed bones, stacked bones, and engaged in all man-

ner of work—intellectual, emotional, pedagogical, physical—to support the larger vision of Naomi Natale, Founder and Director of One Million Bones. Joan and I created curricula, schlepped clay, talked to media, made college visits, negotiated with administration, encouraged students, and provided support to community groups. (p. 9)

Our work culminated in May 2013 when the bones we worked to make and collect were loaded onto a UPS truck bound for Washington, D.C., where we and more than twenty individuals comprising Team Great Lakes joined a thousand others laying out more than one million bones on the National Mall, June 8–10, 2013.

Even now, seeing in print all we accomplished astounds us. We are excited to list out the numbers: of bones, of community collaborators, of students we worked with, and so on. However, we are aware that when we focus on what happened in terms of data, we risk glossing over the complicated, relational, interdisciplinary nature of the work and boiling it all down to quantitative ways to evidence success. From the outset, we embraced and retained the complexity of this work—the ambiguity—of our collaboration through recognition of it as socially engaged practice. In an educational primer on the subject, Pablo Helguera (2011), asserts that:

> Socially engaged art functions by attaching itself to subjects and problems that normally belong to other disciplines, moving them temporarily into a space of ambiguity. It is this temporary snatching away of subjects into the realm of art-making that brings new insights to a particular problem or condition and in turn makes it visible to other disciplines. (p. 5)

It is this space of ambiguity, a discursive realm within which we become less, rather than more, able to see our work as bound to any particular discipline. It is this space of ambiguity, a kind of betwixt and between wherein change can occur, that we believe to be one of the more powerful aspects of socially engaged practice. Socially engaged practice guides our teaching. It has allowed each of us to exist within this space of ambiguity, to see our way to different ways of making, writing, teaching, moving, living, breathing, experimenting.

The Cradle Project postcard was the catalyst for a nearly seven-year arts activist pedagogical collaboration. But it also marks the beginning of a deep friendship, one that moved from co-teaching to co-authoring, from a collaboration focused on making art and an incredible learning experience for students, to the making of knowledge through the writing of this and other essays (Giroux & Hawkins, 2012). We know that we fall into a tradition of feminist research and writing partnerships collaborations that cite characteristics and qualities such as friendship (Kaplan & Rose, 1993), intimacy (Alm, 1998), support (Russell, Plotkin & Bell, 1998), pleasure (Leonardi & Pope, 1994; Estes & Lant, 1998), and an alliance against academic anxiety (Singley & Sweeny, 1998), as locations of the feminist power of this sort of work. It is, perhaps, because of our move from the classroom to the page, from the space of co-teaching to co-authoring, that we have come to see the relevance of our work not just in terms of its connection to socially engaged practice, service learning, or art activism, but to the ways our collaboration is itself a form of activism. We want you to know: *This essay has been collaboratively written, but our story here is not necessarily about the writing of this essay, even though it's never not about the writing of this essay.*

In this essay, we argue that our collaboration prompted each of us to do more than share our perspectives and expertise for the good of the project. By engaging in our work as trans/feminist practice, we each moved across the space between our disciplines, translated our work and desires not only for each other, but also for ourselves. Through our collaboration on our co-developed class, our work on The Cradle Project and on One Million Bones, Ames became able to see herself as a maker as well as a writer, and Joan found new ways to reimagine the relevance of writing in the making classroom. In the end, we each literally moved our own classroom and scholarly practices into new, unknown-to-us disciplinary and practical realms. In doing so, each of us transformed.

This essay has been collaboratively written, but our story here is not necessarily about the writing of this essay, even though it's never not about the writing of this essay. In a first section, we return to the postcard, using it as a way to illustrate how we initially positioned ourselves within the academic fields of composition and rhetoric and art respectively, as a writer and a maker working toward the creation of one collaboratively created and co-taught course. We explain how, though an object-oriented approach to collaboration is useful, a trans/feminist understanding of our disciplinary positions allow for recognition of relationality and movement as the location of activism.

In a second section, we note that relevance of trans/feminist practice has less to do with the co-creation of the syllabus than it does with the teaching of the class. Or rather, that while we can argue that both co-creation of the syllabus and teaching of the class are dialogic collaborations, it's in the seams and gaps noted while teaching the course that inspired us to move from our clear disciplinary positions. It isn't simply that we can call our *work* interdisciplinary. Through conscious practice and trans/feminist collaboration, we have become interdisciplinary artists and scholars.

Finally, in the last section, we discuss what happened when we co-taught the course in 2012, a full six years after the postcard moment. Confronted by unanticipated student complaints, we found that in order to address their resistance, we would have to move from our positions not only for each other and because of our own desires, but also in a larger context. In order to practice ethical trans/feminist collaboration, we would have to do so and thus recognize our students as collaborators, not only in the art activist projects, but in the making of our co-taught and co-developed class.

POSITIONING PERSPECTIVES: AS WRITER, AS MAKER, AS TRANS/FEMINIST COLLABORATORS

Joan and Ames often talk about our collaboration. Can say, are proud to say: We collaborated. And yet, the work of the collaboration, discussion of how collaboration works, seems less accessible, more difficult to articulate in any clear way. One possibility for our inability to talk about collaboration has to do with the ways that collaboration itself has been inextricably linked from what William Duffy notes as the conversational imperative. In "Collaboration (in) Theory: Reworking the Social Turn's Conversational Imperative," Duffy (2014) notes that that while he's to be credited for establishing the relevance of collaboration in the field of composition and rhetoric, Kenneth Bruffee inadvertently set up *conversation* as the "default metaphor scholars invoke to explain the nature of collaboration itself" (p. 417). Duffy asserts that the problem with such a metaphor is that we are led to assume that collaboration exists in any situation in which we note conversation—any exchange between two people. We're left to recognize, and argue that any and all conversation indicates the presence of collaboration. He further argues that in the larger field of composition and rhetoric, we then extend this idea to mean that all collaboration is writing, from which follows the logical assumption that all writing is collaboration. Through this tautology, we construct a closed system of simplistic inevitable logic. Without any space for complexity and growth, we inadvertently render *collaboration* powerless as a scholarly term.

As a way of complicating our understanding of collaboration as connected to conversation, Duffy (2014) offers an object-oriented approach, one that is informed by Davidson's notion of *triangulation*. The idea is that in order engage in conversation, collaborators enter into a relationship, one identified through a shared desire to speak together about something—an object, an idea, a problem. The triangle here is formed by two collaborators and the reason for the relationship in the first place: the object/topic/issue concern, about which they talk, research, and write. Duffy (2014) explains the advantages of triangulation:

> When we approach it from an object-oriented perspective, what collaboration makes possible is the ability to draw upon one another's positioning to recognize new connections between and among the various objects relevant to the work at hand. In short, collaboration has the potential to widen the scope of available discourse for its participants. (p. 425)

It is this idea of positioning that we believe becomes critical to investigations of collaboration. As anyone who has ever collaborated knows, each individual in the project will likely need—because of a perception of resistance, made manifest in the form of conflict—and have to work with and through their own desires, hopes and perspectives in order to keep the project moving. Understanding and reflecting upon one's position is, then, a first step in being able to trace the continually iterative, recursive process of collaboration.

An object enables positioning. Ames always thought about the postcard as an effective rhetorical composition, a multimodal text combining both image and print copy with particular affordances regarding circulation and design, recognizing in the postcard a Barthesian seam of pleasure created by juxtaposition of post-apocalyptic images, and the hope of activism, contextualized through imperfect images of modernity. She always saw in the image her connection with and to the city of Detroit and her emergence as an activist in her job as a soup kitchen manager. From the outset, Joan made concrete visual leaps to art works she knew: from studio and art history classes, exhibitions she had seen in the last twenty plus years, works she had become familiar with during artists' talks at residencies, or through contemporary art blogs and videos. In her own thinking about the construction of real objects as purveyors of meaning, she considered the power of the many as what would ultimately resonate in that empty warehouse.

This essay has been collaboratively written, but our story here is not necessarily about the writing of this essay, even though it's never not about the writing of this essay.

In "Screaming Divas: Collaboration as Feminist Practice," Susan J. Leonardi and Rebecca A. Pope (1994) are "trying to formulate an alternative to the mode of scholarly production that the dissertation epitomizes" (p. 259). They do so through an essay that is as much form as it is about content, as much about process as product. Written as a dialogue, the piece explores the possibility inherent in understanding collaboration via metaphors of desire and sexuality, most specifically through an exploration of the metaphor of the NAMES Project, the AIDS quilt. Leonardi and Pope ultimately decide the quilt metaphor isn't completely useful because it "doesn't capture the changes that occur in the pieces we bring to the project as we talk and work things out" (p. 269). Though as art activists we fully appreciate the connection between the NAMES Project, desire and collaboration, we aren't here to pick up the thread of this argument whole cloth. Rather, we are interested in their observation that the quilt calls attention to seams, visibility of gaps (p. 264).

If focused only on the results and goals of the collaboration, an object-oriented approach can be problematic since it tends to flatten the plane of relations, even dismissing relationality. For us—Ames and Joan—the activism in our collaboration isn't simply a result of the content of the course and our shared desire to use art to make change in the world. It isn't just about us establishing expertise, in articulating what it was we achieved. Our activism also resides in the the recognition of gaps—between ideas, need, power dynamics—and a shared desire to constantly be ready and willing to move across and perhaps beyond them, to bridge, to translate, to transform.

Our collaboration is a trans/feminist practice; the site of our activism. Trans/feminism is a term we borrow from Marjory Pryse's 2000 *National Women's Studies Association Journal* article, "Trans/Feminist Methodology: Bridges to Interdisciplinary Thinking." Nearly a decade before the explosion of literature focusing on issues of performance and materiality with respect to transsexuality and transgender identity, Pryse makes a connection between the relevance of this queer subject position and the groundbreaking project by Gloria Anzaldúa and Cherrie Moraga, *This Bridge Called My Back* (1983). Perhaps one of the most influential volumes with respect to the intersection of feminism and race, *Bridge* brings together indigenous, black, Asian and Latina voices, writing in a wide array of genres and forms. Pryse (2000) notes that *trans*, as is explored by Anzaldúa, Moraga and contributors, is connected to translation, to borderlands, to "a bridge, a span across a chasm or otherwise untraversable terrain" (p. 105). In doing so, Pryse offers *trans* not only as a metaphor, but as a theoretical and methodological "place from which we may embark, a site of trans/port and of trans/formation" (p. 105).

Pryse's piece may not even be the very first academic essay to do this work, but it is the first that we can find that emphasizes *trans* as connected to a scholarly practice, not simply scholarly content or subject position. Pryse (2000) argues, and we agree: "'Trans perspectives offer new ways to think about interdisciplinarity" (p. 105). Or rather, in thinking about what it means to (be) trans—what it means to be engage in feminist practices as a bridge, as moving across a bridge, in motion spanning a space between—we may find ourselves with a better understanding of collaboration as a feminist practice. We do so thinking less about how it is we need and desire positioning ourselves in relationship to or with any specific field, and more so with an eye toward how this work has invited us to move beyond and across discourse borders, to transform, translate, transcend disciplinary boundaries. We do so in order to better illustrate the power in this ambiguity.

To further explore this idea, we return to Marjorie Pryse and her observations about trans/feminist methodology. While Duffy's description pays close attention to the object and the position, Pryse offers for consideration the subsequent movement. Pryse (2000) explains:

> A transversal interdisciplinarity requires feminist scholars to learn to "shift" and "pivot" as an ongoing aspect of our own methodological practice. It does not require us to become experts in all research methodologies and the creative arts, but rather to focus on the ways in which "rooting" makes "shifting" possible; and it is the "shifting" that is the "trans" in the movement in feminist thinking. It is learning to "shift" and "pivot" while remaining grounded in a lattice work of identities and research methodologies that I am proposing as the design for a transversal, trans/feminist methodology. (p. 110)

It is this ability to *both* root *and* position, to be *both* aware of an original identity/story/disciplinary expertise, *and* willing/able—desirous—of the work involved in making a shift, a pivot, in movement elsewhere that is relevant in our areas of focus of community-based research and art activism. A trans/feminist practice of collaboration involves moving from one position toward another perspective, across whatever it is that may be understood as the gap, the fissure, a divide. Here, we also note a clear connection with and to what Jaqueline Jones Royster and Gesa Kirsch (2012) refer to in their collaborative project *Feminist Rhetorical Practices: New Horizons for Rhetoric, Composition and Literacy Study* as the critical imagination, a method of inquiry that exposes the gaps left by white male-dominated research in rhetoric. Royster and Kirsch bring attention to the presence of the gap. Trans/feminist practices of collaboration provide a way of thinking about what it means not only to move across and bridge them, but to shift in ways that reposition and remake the work and space of the gap altogether.

This movement isn't necessarily linear; it isn't premeditated or predetermined. These moves are iterative and recursive, not in terms of content (i.e., how I changed my mind about something) but in terms of form: the movement itself is indicative of personal, pedagogical, professional and political evolution. One needs not know where they will move, only to understand that if the interaction is trans/feminist collaboration, they will be moving. And it is the movement, as much as the eventual repositioning, that matters. The movement that may not be mediated by, but occurs because of, an object. The object—in this case the postcard—allowed us to locate ourselves in an area of expertise, to ready ourselves just before the music begins and we agree to dance.

It's about this dance. And as much as it may be a dance between two people, choreographed in terms of partnered dancing in which sometimes you lead, and sometimes I lead, sometimes the partners are of different genders/sexes and sometimes the same (Estes & Lant, 1998). Most often, we might assert, no one is leading. Sometimes this dance is less one imaged in terms of Western cultural formats of couples, and more closely connected to dance forms with any number of dancers moving in a space together, in rhythmic relationship with their bodies, shared energy, the space and the earth. Sometimes the dance begins with two, and more people join. Sometimes the music changes, and we drop the beat. Sometimes I write a paragraph and you write one. Sometimes you design the assignment, while I evaluate; sometimes it's the other way around. Sometimes I am the one who delivers the lectures, sometimes it's you. We move and/into position, and then reposition ourselves. In this movement, we transform ourselves as teachers, as makers, as artists, scholars and thinkers, exactly as who we are, finding it's possible to be more than we ever imagined we could become.

TRANSLATING THE INTERDISCIPLINARY PROJECT INTO A PROFESSIONAL IDENTITY

In co-designing *22-3254J Special Topics in Studio Art: Art and Activism Studio Project and 46-2505J Art and Activism Studio Project*, we experienced the kind of synergistic excitement that often accompanies collaborative work. We shared ideas, documents, and assignments, riffing off one another to design a course that sought to bring into conversation the history and theory of art activism with the social focus and practice of art making. Guided by a desire to provide a strong liberal arts foundation for their object making, students were required to read a wide range of articles, from the history of art activism to postcolonial theory, from first-person narrative to current events in, and the politics of, Africa.

Because of her experience in the writing classroom, Ames was largely responsible for the daily reflection essays that required students to analyze and synthesize the content of and connections between nightly readings, lectures, and class discussions. Joan took the lead in designing assignments that would scaffold toward the construction of cradles. What's most important to know is that though these were two courses offered in two different programs, we decided that *all* students would complete *all* the assignments. All students, regardless of major, would engage with the course as one single curricular experience even though we had to design it as two courses in order to get departmental and school approval.

In their groundbreaking study on collaborative writing processes, *Singular Texts/Plural Authors: Perspectives on Collaborative Writing*, Ede and Lunsford (1990) articulate two principal types of collaborations: hierarchical and dialogic. If we were to analyze our practices with respect to syllabus creation, we could most certainly characterize the process in terms of what Lisa Ede and Andrea Lunsford (1990) identified as a dialogic collaboration:

> This dialogic mode is loosely structured and the roles enacted within it are fluid: one person may occupy multiple and shifting roles as the project progresses. In this mode, the process of articulating goals is often as important as the goals themselves and sometimes even more important. Furthermore, those participating in dialogic collaboration generally value creative tension inherent in multivoiced and multivalent ventures. What those involved in hierarchical collaboration see as a problem to be solved, these individuals view as a strength to capitalize on and to emphasize. In dialogic collaboration, this group effort is seen as an essential part of the production—rather than the recovery—of knowledge and as a means of individual satisfaction within the group. (p.133)

As far as making a syllabus goes, we occupied shifting roles between and among the duties of course design. We discussed all of the choices we made in terms of topics to cover, readings, writing prompts, organization of time, working to articulate rationales for our perspectives. We continually revisited the goals of the course—landing finally with a decision to have the larger question on the table be: Can art save lives? We each offered differing ideas, and negotiated through tensions that were often created because of our own disciplinary experiences, knowledge and perspectives. There were only two of us directly involved in the collaboration, but we often had to also think through how to achieve our goal when the larger institutional systems made such a collaboration appear to be impossible. To be sure, we were incredibly satisfied with the syllabus we produced.

The question then becomes, if we can identify our work as trans/feminist collaboration, as well as dialogic collaboration, is all dialogic collaboration trans/feminist? Or, was this dialogic collaboration also trans/feminist, and if so, why introduce the new term at all?

The issue here isn't one of inclusion, or exclusion, but of shifting focus from the quality of the collaboration to the reasons why a collaborator might engage in such work in the first place. Even when there's a focus on process over product, and discussion regarding the means by which the collaboration occurs, most commentary is framed in terms of successes achieved rather than unforeseeable growth, to disciplinary knowledge-making as a gain for a singular field, rather than knowledge-making as an interdisciplinary venture. Trans/feminist practice has to do with moving from one perspective, one way of seeing, to *end up by project's end in a different place entirely*. In other words, the individual will, through this interaction—this dance—have transitioned. The transition isn't simply actions intended to change the world, or society. Trans/feminist practice means that the practitioner moves in order to change themselves, not just because they want to succeed, but because there's an awareness that the shift itself will, by virtue of an expansion in the way they understand their own abilities and efficacy, enable them to effect greater change.

In our first teaching of the course in 2008, we began the course clearly situated in our own disciplinary realms, interacting with students from comfortable positions of expertise. Each morning, for three weeks, we gathered in a classroom where Joan and Ames would alternate presenting lectures and providing students with different information for inquiry and discussion. In the afternoons, Joan took the lead in the studio, while Ames met with students independently to discuss response essays and writing. In many ways, one might have been able to recognize cooperative, rather than collaborative elements of classroom management and curriculum delivery.

But then, something interesting began to happen. As we worked with the students, encouraging them to push themselves, each recognized a desire to move from their positions of expertise to try something new, to shift into the unfamiliar territory of the other, to risk exposure of what each did not know, rather than remaining in the safer territory of disciplinary expertise. Inspired by watching Joan talk to the students about the nesting projects, Ames decided she would make her own cradle. Though she did not at the time consider herself to be an artist, Ames decided to repurpose some four inch vinyl squares left over from a reiterative art activist project paying homage to the AIDS quilt. Each afternoon, when she wasn't working with students on their writing, she was hunched over the squares, popping small holes around the perimeter using a hand-punch awl so that she could sew the squares together using "thread" made from plastic grocery bags. As she made this cradle, she saw her writing in direct relationship to making; she realized that if she could say "I am a multimodal composer," then she realized she could claim and begin to explore the subject-position of the artist as well.

Since seeing her piece in The Banque Building in Albuquerque on June 8, 2007, as a part of The Cradle Project exhibition, Ames has continued to explore an understanding of self as an artist. She has engaged in performance, created visual/print text installations, published video essays, and is currently co-hosted of a scholarly podcast focusing on alt-alphabetic texts and creative-critical scholarship. This is not to say that she claims the same kind of expertise that Joan might, but that she has become better able to both understand and include art and making-practices in her classroom, and consider the disciplinary perspectives of artists in her teaching and creative-critical scholarly work.

While Ames—the writer—ultimately responded to the postcard, the project's call to construct a cradle and to being physically present in the making studio, Joan—the maker of objects—ultimately did not construct a cradle during that first class. She pivoted off Ames's writing prompts in that class to consider models of how to engage as a teacher-reader in the studio making classroom. Asking students to address particular and specific, yet highly open-ended prompts delving into theoretical aspects of readings and class discussions presented an approach she would adopt in a semester long section of Art and Activism Studio Project with a focus on the environment and ecological art. As a teacher-reader she reflected on methods of eliciting critical thought and analysis, and the development of each student's individual voice in textual image alongside concrete objects. Subsequently, as co-author with Ames, Joan moved into making and shaping through language and writing in academic texts such as this, and other essays.

We entered a collaboration with each other and developed as interdisciplinary scholars because of our own desire to move between gaps between our own disciplinary positions. Our trans/feminist collaboration invited us to not only rely upon each other to lead in their areas of expertise, but to both recognize and attempt to bridge the gaps we saw in the ways we did not know. We each made space for the other, honored and delighted in the risk-taking, the uneasy experience of moving into uncharted territory, into a different disciplinary space. Because of this move, we recognize an increase in our willingness to listen to others, to engage in dialogic collaboration because of the ways trans/feminist practice has transformed our lives. And as much as we acknowledge each other as crucial to this process, to our own transformation, we are also clear about the ways that our students have assisted us in articulating an ethics of trans/feminist collaboration as well.

TRANSFORMING STUDENT DISSENT THROUGH TRANS/FEMINIST MOVES

The second time we taught the course, in January 2012, we required students to read and engage with Terry Tempest Williams' 2004 commencement speech at The University of Utah, a post-9/11 call to "protect and preserve" the integrity and possibility what she identifies as "the open space of democracy":

> In the open space of democracy there is room for dissent.
>
> In the open space of democracy there is room for differences.
>
> In the open space of democracy, the health of the environment is seen as the wealth of our communities. We remember that our character has been shaped by the diversity of America's landscapes and it is precisely that character that will protect it. Cooperation is valued more than competition; prosperity becomes the caretaker of poverty. The humanities are not peripheral, but the very art of what it means to be human. In the open space of democracy, beauty is not optional, but essential to our survival as a species. And technology is not rendered at the expense of life, but developed out of a reverence for life. (pp. 9–10)

Williams' text reveals both her facility with language—her identity as an artist/writer—and her conviction as an art activist. Joan and Ames offered the text as a way for students to consider whether the installation of One Million Bones on the National Mall could create this open space. We talked about their collaborative groups as these open spaces, sites where every day for nine days they would come together to work on behalf of an art activist project and speak freely with one another about issues surrounding genocide. We discussed the importance of beauty to this open space, the relevance of art to our lives and how they, as emerging artists already understood the resistance to the arts that exists in American culture. We believed, as we provide an opportunity for students to reflect, to agree, and even to dissent, that we offered our class as an open space of democracy.

We have no way of knowing whether these discussions are what empowered a few students to speak up and relay their displeasure with the course, but the fact is that near the end of the first week a few people were incredibly upset because they felt and expressed that they had somehow been tricked, duped into working on something in which they had no interest. They expected to be able to work on their own art, not, as one person said during class, "be slaves to Joan and Ames's project." A similar percentage and disenchantment was voiced in 2008, but it was muted, we now believe, by the fact that students were, even if they were in small groups, at least working on *their own* cradles. They may not have wanted to work together, but they could at least hold onto the idea that the art was, as they saw it, theirs. Bone making, a few had decided, had nothing to do with their art, their vision, and their ideas. They had no interest in being a part of our collaboration.

Given their reasoning, it seems to us that the student resistance is in large part a result of their understanding of our requirements as what Beth Godbee

(Chapter 17, this collection), identifies as the "too-muchness" of our course. In the same way an educator might challenge or reject an arts activist, social justice, socially engaged practice curriculum on the basis of it being, "on top of other educational demands," so might a student reject course work they identify as requiring more of them. In the case of our students, we also noted that their resistance was coming from a place of privilege. They believed that being "slaves to Ames and Joan's project" ought not have been required of them. They were artists wanting to make their art, unwilling to move from their own disciplinary notions of the *auteur*, and engage in socially engaged practice.

Initially, we wanted to ignore the dissenters, focus upon students who were telling us things like, "this is the best class I ever had at Columbia," and, "I wish every class could be like this one." But if this were to truly be an open space of democracy, we needed to quit trying to explain to the dissenters why they should make bones, or convince them they would and could get something valuable out of the experience if they'd simply open themselves to it. We weren't going to be able to, nor would it be ethical to, shove our students from their positions and make them move. In order to continue collaboration as trans/feminist practice, we would have to move from ours. We had to see the *class*—not simply the project—as the site of collaboration. We'd need to hear and honor the student positions and create an opportunity that would enable all of us to move together.

Toward that end, we revised the prompt for one of the response essays to offer students an opportunity to write about a project they may have wanted to work on, to imagine a social arts practice that speaks about and for an issue of their own choosing. We repositioned One Million Bones more *as one particular example of* social arts practice so as to open a space for their political concerns. We emphasized that Naomi had only been twenty-six when she founded The Cradle Project and that there was no reason they couldn't begin a project if they wanted. We asserted that a first step would have to be presentation of their idea in writing—alphabetic text. In this way, they had to practice what many artists, designers, filmmakers, and other creative producers practice on a regular basis in seeking support for their work: they had to craft a verbal pitch, not unlike what grant applications, or other applications for support, would require of them in the future.

Unless students are invited to reimagine and recreate the artistic vision of a particular art activist project from their own perspective, or be guided in socially engaged practice of their own choosing, they are not actually *collaborating* with us on the art activist project at hand. They are not being asked to move from their own personal positions, but are *being positioned by us* in order to experience and take part in a particular kind of art from a hands-on perspective, whether they like it or not. In short, they are serving the project because we are requiring it of them. We have heard the critique that it's wrong to require students to make bones, to work on a project if they don't agree. Again, we believe these critiques to be emanating from a general distaste for the "too-muchness" of our course and agree with Godbee that such changes to a curriculum "can help us shake up and shake off normalized actions, dominant beliefs, and damaging discourses."

When we taught these courses, we had not yet developed an understanding of collaboration as a trans/feminist practice. We didn't specifically invite students to articulate their initial positions, or examine how and where they subsequently moved. Even so, in the final paragraphs of the final essays written by two different students from two different J-Session classes, one focused on The Cradle Project, the other on One Million Bones, we see clear evidence that the course transmogrified their perspectives and practices. As a recursive move that both brings you back to the beginning and the creation of a class, we choose to end with these two short passages of student writing about their experiences of making.

This essay has been collaboratively written, but our story here is not necessarily about the writing of this essay, even though it's never not about the writing of this essay.

In the spirit of collaboration, let them, by name, be the ones to help you better understand the ways they also appear to have shifted their perspectives, moved and bridged gaps they seemed to notice for themselves. Let them show you what we recognize as the beauty of this work:

> As there are six billion other people in the world, conflict is inevitable, as is collaboration. All we can do is try to make the most of our circumstances and maybe learn something about ourselves. Over the past three weeks I have learned that I am still a control freak. I have also learned that it is hard to change other people. It is best to accept them as they are and lead by example. I still prefer to work individually, but I know that there is no way I could have created and completed the same cradle by myself. Incompatible as we were, I needed my group to be successful. I could not have done it alone.
>
> —Jaime Rovenstine, reflecting on her work with
> The Cradle Project, January 22, 2008.

> Personally, I am very thankful I was able to be involved in this project. Not only did I work with my peers to reach a common goal, I learned valuable information on how to design an exhibit. Before this, I would have never know how much time it takes to plan an exhibition, let alone the materials and directions required to create it. The information I learned is invaluable. The skepticism I started this class with has been completely erased, and replaced with hope. Hope that our vision for

the One Million Bones Project is carried out, and that it makes a true difference. I'm now a part of the voice that OMB has created, and I hope that my voice, as well as everyone else's in my group, and this class, is able to be heard.

—Matt Schieren, reflecting on his work with One Million Bones, January 12, 2012.

REFERENCES

Alm, M. (1998). The role of talk in the writing process of intimate collaboration. In E. G. Peck & J. S. Mink (Eds.), *Common ground: Feminist collaboration in the academy* (pp. 123–140). Albany, NY: State University of New York Press.

Anzaldúa, G. & Moraga, C. (Eds.). (1981). *This bridge called my back: Writings by radical women of color*. New York, NY: Kitchen Table: Women of Color Press.

Duffy, W. (2014, May). Collaboration (in) theory: Reworking the social turn's conversational imperative. *College English, 76*(5), 416–435.

Ede, L. & Lundsford, A. (1990). *Singular texts/plural authors: Perspectives on collaborative writing*. Carbondale, IL: Southern Illinois University Press.

Estes, A. & Lant, K. M. (1998). Lesbian collaboration and the choreography of desire. In E. G. Peck & J. S. Mink (Eds.), *Common ground: Feminist collaboration in the academy* (pp. 155–171). Albany, NY: State University of New York Press.

Giroux, J. & Hawkins, A. (2012). Art activism in the classroom: One imagined future for service-learning. *Interdisciplinary Humanities, 29*(3), 88–101.

Godbee, B. Pedagogical "too-muchness": A feminist approach to community-based learning, multi-modal composition, social justice education, and more.

Hawkins, A. (2014, Spring). One million bones: Collaboration, interdisciplinarity, and art activism. *@LAS Magazine*. Retrieved from http://www.colum.edu/atlas/volumes/fall2013-spring2014/stories/one-million-bones-.php.

Helguera, P. (2011). *Education for socially engaged art: A materials and techniques handbook*. New York, NY: Jorge Pinto Books.

Kaplan, C. & Rose, E. C. (1993, Spring). Strange bedfellows: Feminist collaboration. *Signs, 18*(3), 547–561.

Leonardi, S. J. & Pope, R. A. (1994, Autumn). Screaming divas: Collaboration as feminist practice. *Studies in Women's Literature, 13*(2), 259–270.

Peck, E. G. & Mink, J. S. (Eds.). (1998). *Common ground: Feminist collaboration in the academy*. Albany, NY: State University of New York Press.

Pryse, M. (2000, Summer). Trans/feminist methodology: Bridges to interdisciplinary thinking. *National Women's Studies Association Journal, 12*(2), 105–118.

Reagan, S. B., Fox, T. & Bleich, D. (Eds.). (1994). *Writing with: new directions in collaborative teaching, learning and research*. Albany, NY: State University of New York Press.

Rovenstine, J. (2008, January 22). Collaboration response (Unpublished essay).

Royster, J. J. & Kersch, G. (2012). *Feminist rhetorical practices: New horizons for rhetoric, composition and literacy study*. Carbondale, IL: Southern Illinois University Press.

Russell, C. L., Plotkin, R. & Bell, A. C. (1998). Merge/emerge: Collaboration in graduate school. In E. G. Peck & J. S. Mink (Eds.), *Common ground: Feminist collaboration in the academy* (pp. 141–154). Albany, NY: State University of New York Press.

Singley, C. J. & Sweeny, S. E. (1998). In league with each other: The theory and practice of feminist collaboration. In E. G. Peck & J. S. Mink (Eds.), *Common ground: Feminist collaboration in the academy* (pp. 63–79). Albany, NY: State University of New York Press.

Schieren, M. (2012, May 31). Personal reflection (Unpublished essay).

Williams, T. T. (2004). *The open space of democracy.* Barrington, MA: The Orion Society.

CHAPTER 19.

COMING OUT AS OTHER IN THE GRADUATE WRITING CLASSROOM: FEMINIST PEDAGOGICAL MOVES FOR MENTORING COMMUNITY ACTIVISTS

Jess Tess
Oakland University

Trixie G. Smith
Michigan State University

Katie Manthey
Salem College

We argue that facilitation of coming out moments of otherness in the graduate writing classroom is a way to mentor students to foster social change. In order to study the pedagogical moves made by instructors that facilitate (or not) moments where graduate students come out as other, we conducted surveys and interviews with students and instructors in order to elicit stories about their coming out moments in classroom settings. We examine writing as a social-justice practice that can be important for coming out, itself a feminist rhetorical act. Then we consider how seemingly micro moments can become macro moments to the students involved. Likewise, we look at how instructor reactions to coming out moments model behaviors for other students in the class, arguing for feminist pedagogies that can guide or support transformations into activist stances in classes and in students' lives.

INTRODUCTION: RECONSTRUCTING OURSELVES AND OUR STORIES

[I[1] was sitting in my office a few hours before class started during the second week of fall semester. It wasn't my office hours, but I have an open-door policy and it's not uncommon for people to come in. This morning, I was running behind on a project and was, admittedly, a little annoyed when a student in one of my writing classes came into my office and said, "I need to talk to you. Can I talk to 'Katie' right now instead of 'Dr. Manthey'?" I smiled warmly at her and offered her a chair. She sat down, looking very distraught, and told me, "I'm a terrible writer. I just can't do it."

She explained to me that when she came to campus this morning she had planned to drop out of school. She was a perfectionist and a "casual" 200-word blog entry about goals for the semester took her four hours and left her in tears. She felt that her inability to write the way she thought, and the way she talked, was a personal flaw and beyond repair. She told me that she didn't have any confidence in herself—or her writing.

So I asked her: "Who are you? How did you get here? What happened that has led you to believe this about yourself?"

This surprised her. She sat back and looked at me for a minute. Then, she leaned forward, smiled at me for the first time that day, and told me about herself.

She had been a professional model, and had been in a car accident and had to have her entire face reconstructed. She was now a motivational speaker because of her experiences with bouncing back from her surgery. She had always been terrified of writing and had found other ways to communicate her complex, engaging emotions to others: through visual art, poetry, and theater. For her, speaking extemporaneously was significantly easier than writing an outline. And she was damn good at it. The story that she told me about herself sounded like a motivational speech—and it was all off the cuff.

When she finished I smiled at her and told her that she was a writer. I suggested she audio-record herself talking through her writing assignments and transcribe herself. She couldn't believe that that wasn't considered cheating. This felt safer to her

---

1   You will see three different fonts used throughout this essay. This font for the argument of the essay. **This second font for our stories.** *This third font for participants' stories.*

because she was confident in her ability to convey a message through speech.]

We start our chapter with this story because we see story as the theoretical foundation for our work and an important strategy for feminist interventions. Thomas King (2003), native novelist and scholar, tells us that "The truth about stories is that that's all we are" (p. 2). He also tells us (warns us?) that they are wondrous and dangerous. Our stories illustrate what we believe, how we act, and how we envision and experience the world. From King's theorizing and our own experiences with stories/theories, we have come to the conclusion that storytelling as embodied knowledge production is an important methodological practice for making, theorizing, and sustaining feminist projects such as ours.

Furthermore, we start our chapter with this story because it highlights a coming out moment, a feminist student-to-teacher moment that was made possible by Katie's willingness to listen and to ask why—to issue an invitation for more. These moments also happen in classes, student-to-student, or student-to-class. In *Techne: Queer Meditations on Writing the Self*, Jackie Rhodes claims that it is "an ethical, feminist move to come out" (2015, p. 6A). She stresses that it's important because "We pay for (in)visibility when we seek to contain or erase our multiple spaces, identities, affiliations" (p. 6A). Furthermore, the ways we as instructors react to students in these moments set the tone for how others will react (see Godbee, Chapter 17, in this collection for more on cultivating agency and interrelatedness for/with our students); we become the model for the rest of our students and perhaps other instructors as well. How then should we react as feminists interested in mentoring our students and in modeling activist stances and behaviors?

Our own experiences as students coming out to professors or classes, as well as our experiences as instructors who have had students come out in our classes,[2] led us to question this phenomenon and to ask in what ways we facilitate and/or hinder growth in these pivotal moments as students take the risk of coming out. But what exactly do we mean by the phrase coming out? Coming out is a shortened term for the phrase "coming out of the closet." In *Another Mother Tongue: Gay Words, Gay Worlds*, Judy Grahn (1984) explains that the "term 'closet' implies a scandalous personal secret, or skeleton, in the family closet." More specifically for many gay persons it refers "to *being* the skeleton in the family's closet," where the reality of being gay, or gayness itself, becomes the skeleton (p. 23). People remain in the closet to maintain the illusion of the expected—heterosexuality, which as Michael Warner (1993) explains is the default for sexuality and what is always assumed unless one indicates something different, an idea he calls "heteronorma-

---

2   Which you can listen to on Soundcloud and read in Google Docs at https://drive.google.com/open?id=0B2Vu6VfSpS_rOHppMVpIMlIzbVk

tivity" (p. xxi). According to Warner, every ideological, political, and economic structure in mainstream society is built around or upon a heterosexual norm or model (as well as a white, middle to upper class model), which is, as are most forms of oppression, "pervasive, persistent, and severe" in nature (Weber, 2009, p. 23).

People come out of the closet to contradict this assumption and to break the illusion of heterosexuality. Coming out is a rite of passage into a gay or lesbian identity, according to Gilbert Herdt (1992). In *Inside/Out* Diane Fuss (1991) explains that, when one comes out, one comes into a new identity and into a new community. The act of coming out and the narrative about it, the coming-out story, permeates gay culture. The telling of these stories helps constitute membership in the community and lets other members know where someone stands. Naturally, these stories differ from person to person. Even one person's story can change as she moves from one context to another.

Many theorists, however, have expanded the idea of coming out and what one might come out about; the term has come to be used in contexts other than sexuality, which we in this paper call coming out as Other. That is, people come out about many other identifications and identity categories that can be anything other than what Audre Lorde (2009) calls the mythic norm: white, male, thin, middle to upper class, heterosexual. It is this expansive form of coming out, personal moments of vulnerability, that we reference throughout this essay and that we label a feminist act.

We start with our own varied coming out stories, pieces of our identities, and how they led us into research and collaboration. We then move to some stories generously shared with us by participants also interested in this work. We discuss the patterns we see emerging from the data of these collective stories and what they tell us about mentoring students into and through coming out, particularly through writing. We consider all coming out moments as a feminist rhetorical practice because it is a moment of making the personal political and of taking a stance that often sets oneself up as other. Therefore, it is important to consider how seemingly micro moments often are and/or can become macro moments to the students involved. Likewise, we look at how instructor reactions to coming out moments model behaviors for other students in the class; feminist pedagogical responses require rhetorical listening and self reflexivity as instructor, perpetual student, and cognizant citizen (see Royster and Kirsch (2012) for more on this concept). It is only through such feminist responses to students that we can possibly guide or support their transformations into activist stances in their classes and their lives. For other examples of feminist response in practice, refer to Walls et al. (Chapter 20, this collection), who employ feminist theories of listening in their design of a smartphone app and Williams' discussion of listening to community partners as feminist praxis.

METHODS: ORAL HISTORY OF DISCOMFORT

We begin our methods section by linking to our own stories about coming out as other in our graduate writing classrooms. Since this study emerged from those stories, we present them reflexively as the foundation for our research questions and design and will refer to them again in our discussion section. These were the stories that we told (and retold) each other when we met early last year to talk about a common issue: feeling out of place in graduate school. As women who identified as straight, white, able-bodied, and cisgendered at the time, Jess and Katie felt conflicted about their feelings of discomfort in the graduate writing classroom. Coming from places of privilege, coming out and feeling like an other seemed like something that they couldn't claim as their own embodied experiences. So Jess and Katie met with Trixie, an out queer woman, and together the three of us discussed the validity of our feelings, and the commonality of these moments for the three of us. We wondered if other people had experienced these feelings, both within and beyond coming out in relation to sexuality, in the context of the graduate[3] writing classroom.

In order to study the pedagogical moves made by writing instructors that facilitate moments where graduate students come out as other in graduate writing classrooms, we conducted surveys and interviews using oral history methods[4] with graduate students and instructors. We wanted to elicit their stories/theories about their coming out moments in these classroom settings, similar to those we have given above. Through various listserves, we distributed surveys and solicited interviews from both students and faculty because we expected to see differences between these perspectives that relate to authority and wanted to investigate those divisions.

We collected five participant stories through these various methods. Interestingly, all participants turned out to be students; no professors responded, or at least no one responded from a professorial point of view. We present these stories, these theories, in the form of short vignettes in our results section, followed by very brief points of discussion. We performed our analysis of the stories by looking for emerging patterns in the data. To frame our analysis we specifically asked 1) What stood out or came up repeatedly? and 2) What connections can

---

3   We have chosen to only look at graduate classes at this time as a way to narrow our focus, but we all believe what we've experienced and learned is also applicable in the undergraduate classroom.

4   "Oral history interviews seek an in-depth account of personal experience and reflections, with sufficient time allowed for the narrators to give their story the fullness they desire. The content of oral history interviews is grounded in reflections on the past as opposed to commentary on purely contemporary events." Oral History Association. "Principles and Best Practices." 2009. http://www.oralhistory.org/about/principles-and-practices/

be made across these stories? This analysis is presented in the discussion section following our results. We conclude with our list of feminist interventions for instructors teaching in graduate writing classrooms who have and do grapple with these coming out moments.

RESULTS: OUR EXTREMELY VULNERABLE POSITIONS

A's Story

> [An asexual, white, female grad student explained that, "in my very first course as an English graduate student, I took a literary theory class. Eventually, we were asked to contribute a short essay on Queer Theory in literary criticism. We were then asked to share a summary of our paper with the class. I felt that I was in a safe, judgment-free environment that called upon me to be honest. I didn't feel as though I could fake my way through the assignment, so I chose to reveal why. I wrote about my confusing experience as an asexual, and how I identify with the community; specifically, I wrote that my disinterest in and inexperience with sexuality left me at a bit of a loss at understanding works of literature through a sexual perspective."
>
> She explained that most of her classmates seemed to accept what she was saying, but some seemed confused. She stated that, "one particular student (on older, 50s-something woman) told me openly that she didn't think asexuality was an orientation." While the instructor of the class didn't intervene at that moment, she later "called me 'brave' when I received feedback on my paper."
>
> Looking back on the experience, she reflected that coming out to the class "definitely made me a bit defensive with that particular student. But overall, I felt relieved to have come out at all. Being open about my asexuality allows me to accept it as a real orientation that others share. Before, it just seemed like a quirk that was wrong and shameful. I never thought anyone would understand the fact that I don't feel sexual feelings for anyone of any gender."]

A's story brings up important pedagogical opportunities for instructors wishing to model feminist/activist stances: instructors should thank students for sharing (at the very least); instructors should invite further discussion in these moments or on these topics—inspiring confidence, especially in vulnerable moments/situations; instructors should be prepared for private discussions of these public moments.

They's Story

[A self-identified white, working class, nonbinary/trans/genderqueer, first generation, queer grad student explained that, "our instructor had everyone teach something to the class—spending 2-5 minutes on it per person. I chose to teach about using gender neutral pronouns and why it's a good idea. In the process I mentioned that I am nonbinary and use 'they' pronouns."

There was no immediate reaction from the class, and this ended up being the trend for the entire semester: both the students and the instructor "ignored [the information] and continued using the wrong pronouns." The instructor even kept using the wrong pronouns through email. They explained that, "I stayed in the class, but stopped trying to be social/interact with my classmates. I stopped sharing personal information with instructor and classmates even when relevant and even when it might have helped. Because neither students nor instructor 'heard' me, I knew they wouldn't hear me about anything else. So I stopped trying. My final paper for the course included personal information by nature of the method I was using. Because of the way that my instructor responded to me in class, I heavily edited out the information I included in the essay."

They stated that this coming out experience, for them, ultimately hindered their personal and professional growth, "I withdrew into my shell that I had just started getting rid of."]

Again, a feminist pedagogical intervention would be to listen to every student, every time—true listening that results in engagement with what is being said or asked. More importantly, an appropriate feminist response would be to honor the student's request and practice/model the appropriate use of pronouns and encourage others in the class to do so as well.

R's Story

[R, a 28-year-old heterosexual white male "from an affluent family in an affluent town," began responding to our main prompt about experiencing any coming out moments of otherness in any of his graduate writing classes. R explained that he didn't experience a peak moment but rather underwent an ongoing process of realization around his identity in regard to privilege. R then explained that he began experiencing distress at the contrast between the outlooks

> *of his grad school colleagues, who were aware of privilege, and his friends and family back home in an affluent town, who were not.*
>
> *He used the example of the protests over the death of Michael Brown to illustrate his point. R and his grad school classmates and some instructors attended a rally to join in protesting the issue of systemic violence in the African American community as exemplified by the shooting of Michael Brown. Soon after, R also went to visit his hometown where he heard his privileged friends and family criticize the protesting as barbaric and inappropriate. R felt paralyzed and painfully torn between these two communities.*
>
> *When asked if he ever shared his feelings of distress over his new-found views of identity and privilege with his classmates he reflected, "Oh yes. During most of my classes last year I would preface something by 'I'm coming to terms with the evil and imperialism of the white male (apparently I read different history books?), so please forgive my ignorance. I am desperately trying to learn' And that led to rewarding conversations outside of class as well. My classmates would explain things in more detail and talk me through power structures in ways I'd never thought of. I'd never HAD to think of." When probed for further detail about the typical responses both his instructors and classmates would give R in response to his questions he said, "They've almost always been friendly. My instructors were always women, always a double minority (Eastern European, Black) and were perhaps more eager to help guide a student to realization. My classmates never derided me. They saw the struggle in me. They saw the hurt and sadness." He concluded that these conversations in his graduate writing classrooms affected him by completely changing his views and his research interests.]*

The feminist pedagogical practices modeled for R included inviting him into the conversation, both in class and outside of class, and providing space for him to come out and ask questions or reveal his struggle without derision or ridicule.

M's Story

> *["I have come to know how important my body is to all the ways that I come to academia. Knowing that my body matters in terms of what and how I interact with students, colleagues, research subjects and communities is an extremely vulnerable position to embody. I must account for the privileges that I have as well as the ways in which I choose to mark my body. The notion of studying my own*

body, my own story as part of my research has been difficult to navigate. "Coming out" time and again to talk about infertility in an academic setting can be emotionally grueling. I recognize that not everyone understands why I study infertility and why I account for my own identification with it. But it is this continued pressure to silence myself and my infertile body to others that serves as a reminder of exactly why I should be talking about it and studying it. This felt desire to keep quiet is exactly the type of power systems that must be better understood so as to explain how such systems marginalize and silence so many "othered" bodies. This capturing of my body, my body's relationship to other infertile wo/men's bodies, and the stories that our bodies carry are all traces of a cultural rhetoricians orientation to research."]

A feminist intervention means that we need to remember that coming out is a recursive process that happens over time to varying degrees. It can be a transformative moment, for you and/or your audience, but it doesn't (always) have to be. Also, keep in mind that coming out is a choice; we encourage you to measure how safe you feel in the particular moment, program, class, assignment, etc.

J's Story

["In the classroom in 2014, I was in a class called Literary Methods and Practice, which was an Intro to English Studies kind of course for grad students, both Lit and Comp, and we had a guest lecturer talking about the place of story sharing in English Studies. She was a Comp professor. She asked people, if they were comfortable, to tell a story of sharing something important and getting an unexpected reaction. So I briefly recalled the story of my coming out at college, disclosing that I'm gay, and repeating my cousin's comment about "butt lovers," which I think made people uncomfortable (I don't blame them, as it had made me uncomfortable years before). That said, I think people were pretty accepting."

When asked how he felt about this experience, J responded, "Maybe like I'd had a load off my back, but it wasn't anything huge. There was another lit/philosophy class in my grad program called Re-Thinking Race & Gender that was a bit more difficult for me to come out in. It was a 10-day intensive seminar over 3 weeks with a lot of difficult reading, with some history I was familiar with, but because I did know some about African American Studies (I took some classes in it in undergrad), I took a conscious step back so that

> *I wouldn't take over the classroom by talking a lot. I believe it was around the second week, where we were reading about transsexual and transgender issues as well as gay and lesbian history, and at the very end of the day, as like the last comment (if I remember right), I raised my hand and said that I was gay. I had my eyes closed because I was really nervous, which is not always the case when I come out, and I think I sounded kind of shaky (another person said I seemed nervous or scared), and I think part of it was that I wasn't sure how much bigotry or negative reaction there might be. I talked about internalized self-hate that one of the authors had talked about and how that's very real for a lot of LGBT people, including me, so that felt a lot more vulnerable."*

> "*The reactions that I got after were positive. I go to a pretty working-class institution with some progressive English faculty (like really into Marxism or Feminism or any number of other schools of thought that are conscious of justice), so that may explain why it was safe. The next week there was a presentation by a guest faculty about homophobia in popular culture, and I also shared that I have Asperger's syndrome when we were asked about messages we got about gay people growing up: my anti-social behavior was called "gay" as an insult, and later I realized I was actually gay."]*

J's story illustrates how important it is for feminist instructors to monitor their own affect, while paying attention to that of the students in the class. Paying attention to both the words and body language of those in class, will clue you in to how they are feeling and what types of responses they are looking for.

DISCUSSION: MAKING COMING OUT MOMENTS TRANSFORMATIONAL

These diverse stories offer a lot to think about in terms of writing pedagogy, coming out as feminist practice, and responses to coming out that embody feminist practice. We will discuss some of these themes in this section and will end the essay with a call for more stories, more research.

WHY WRITING?

We have chosen to situate our study in writing classrooms partially because it is a convenience sample for us and partially because of how we understand the nature of writing and its potential as a social justice, and hence feminist, practice (in this collection, see Sheridan, Chapter 9, as well as Mathis and Boehm,

Chapter 6, for more on writing and community engagement). If we accept that the personal is political and vice versa (see Myatt in this collection for more on this personal/political connection) and that the goal of a social justice-informed pedagogy is to help students become better/more informed, more critical, citizens/consumers, then we must help them learn to begin by being reflexive about their identities and positions. It means helping them write from what Harriet Malinowitz (1995) calls "their most secure rhetorical footing" (p. 37), the place(s) and/or experiences they truly know and feel confident in. Consequently, this reflexivity often expresses itself in moments of coming out—to oneself, in one's writing, and potentially to others, as our stories show.

These stories indicate that writing, and prepared presentations that also require moments of planning and composing, affords the writer some measure of control over the coming out moment that may be lacking in other rhetorical situations. Trixie and Katie, as well as A, all used specific assignments to reveal things about themselves and their lives and how these experiences affected their academic work. Using assignments like this allowed time for planning, thinking, and revising to occur. Similarly, this time allowed They to remove these personal moments from their final paper since their initial coming out met with resistance and outright denial. Jess's spontaneous classroom moment was also met with resistance, but perhaps it would have been different if she'd had more time to express herself in writing, allowing for more precision and thought behind her words. Writing happens in various modes, for varying audiences, and for varying weight or credit, especially within the context of the classroom, all of which allow for control over what is revealed or not. We should also note here, however, that this control can also be a burden as people struggle over what to say and as they have to make continual, repeated choices about coming out. As M reveals, "'Coming out' time and again . . . in an academic setting can be emotionally grueling."

We believe it can often be grueling because writing is an embodied meaning making practice that is also part of a composing or making process (for more on this topic see Kristin L. Arola and Anne Frances Wysocki's excellent collection (2012) *composing(media) = composing(embodiment): bodies, technologies, writing, the teaching of writing*). For example, in A's story, they found that coming out as asexual made their orientation seem more real: "Being open about my asexuality allows me to accept it as a real orientation that others share. Before, it just seemed like a quirk that was wrong and shameful." Coming out in their writing (and in the writing classroom) made it more real, concrete, and able to be shared. Likewise, coming out as fat in her queer rhetorics course was a career-changing moment for Katie, concretely pushing her into fat studies and activism around body positivity. The same transformational moment happened for Trixie as the first coming out in writing led to coming out moments in class discussions, which led to study and research in gender/queer studies and scholarship and activism focused on creating "safe enough" space for diverse students. We use the term "safe enough" as a way to acknowledge that safe space is a mythical ideal that can never truly be achieved. The very circumstances that make a space safe for one person can make it threatening for another. We also acknowledge that writers often take risks even though they don't feel completely safe, just safe enough. Through these various risk-taking moments, one can see the process of becoming more and more out, more and more public, more and more vocal and potentially activist, marking both the story and the body in ever-increasing ways.

Micro Moments Are Macro Moments

One commonality among these stories of coming out is that they can seem like micro-moments to the instructor/classmates, but in reality they feel like huge moments to the student. One place we saw this was in Trixie's story, as she came out about her sexuality when talking about communicating with her same-sex partner. While this was reportedly her first coming out moment in the classroom, and thus felt extremely risky, she received no response from the instructor. This caused her disappointment but also led to questioning: "How could he know the pain I had suffered writing this simple report?" On the other hand, R reported that he usually received friendly and receptive feedback from his classmates/instructors when he asked questions related to his ignorance about privilege; as a result, R ended up changing his research interests and entire life outlook.

In both of these examples, the micro moments are actually macro moments because they are recursive in nature. In order for these recursive moments to become transformative and lead to growth, it is the job of the instructor to catch them and give them proper attention. Otherwise, the rejection or ignoring of these moments may lead students to shut down or remain stagnant in their learning and personal/professional growth. Jess, for example, was derailed in her academic pursuits when she came out about her lack of knowledge and met with resistance. They also shut down and withdrew when their efforts to educate the class on pronoun usage were met with denial. R, as mentioned above, continued to come out and to become more and more vocal as his initial coming out moments were not just acknowledged but embraced by instructors and classmates. As we see in these stories, when the response from the instructor takes the form of acknowledgement, receptivity, and/or requests for extrapolation, students will be encouraged to engage in what we call "recursive risk." This is the idea that students (when they are not shut down or ignored) will come out continuously over time and reveal a little bit more each time as long as they continue to feel heard (see also Hawkins and Giroux in this collection for a related discussion on the iterative process of collaboration which also leads to growth and evolution).

Take J for example. He tells a story of coming out as gay in a variety of university or classroom settings, all of which carried what seemed like different levels of risk for him. In a class about stories, it made perfect sense to tell his own story about coming out, which then served as another coming out moment. Later, in a class focused on race and gender, telling his story was more difficult but his previously positive experiences helped him push through, even if he did close his eyes to the class as he announced, *"I'm gay."* As he states,

> It did help my personal growth in that class. I felt a lot freer afterwards, like there was less of a load on my shoulders. At that point, I think it helped my academic performance—not like a better grade because of it, but because I was able to be more open in my final portfolio describing [my] relationship to race and gender privilege.

In addition, these coming out moments led to his coming out as a person with Asperger's:

> The next week there was a presentation by a guest faculty about homophobia in popular culture, and I also shared that I have Asperger's syndrome when we were asked about messages we got about gay people growing up: my anti-social behavior was called "gay" as an insult; later I realized I was actually gay.

We see this practice of recursive risk as similar to Ahmed's idea of re-orienting. In *Queer Phenomenology* (2006), Ahmed describes orientation as the way an ideology gets perpetuated until it seems "normal" or "the way things have always been" by discussing the phrase "a path well trodden." On page 16 she explains that

> A path is made by the repetition of the event of the ground 'being trodden' upon. We can see the path as a trace of past journeys. The path is made out of footprints—traces of feet that 'tread' and that in 'treading' create a line on the ground. When people stop treading the path may disappear. And when we see the line of the path before us, we tend to walk upon it, as a path 'clears' the way. So we walk on the path as it is before us, but it is only before us as an effect of being walked upon . . . Lines are both created by being followed and are followed by being created.

Ahmed goes on to discuss how stepping off of a well-worn path onto another less worn path can be "disorienting" and potentially dangerous for an individual. We believe that coming out is an example of choosing an unfamiliar path. Under the right circumstances, walking along this path and being supported can lead to what we call "coming to." Fuss, as mentioned previously, says that coming out leads to coming into community; this is true, but there is more, a coming to that is about self realization, the personal understanding that often leads to activism. J for example comes to a realization about how coming out as gay has helped him come out as a person with Asperger's. R's coming out as a privileged white male trying to understand colonialism and oppression has led to moments of stress and depression but also an activist determination to make a change in the world.

MODELING FEMINIST RESPONSES

We mentioned above that it is the job of the instructor to catch and nurture moments of vulnerability. We believe that this action is a way to practice feminist mentoring and pedagogy; as Sheridan notes elsewhere, "doing is central to learning," so we must "enact that doing" (Chapter 11, this collection). To underscore the power implicit in this practice, some of our examples show what can happen when an instructor doesn't do this. For example, in the story of They's coming out as genderqueer, the instructor's inattention to their request for certain pronouns (and the instructor's continuous use of the wrong pronouns) led the student to shut down. Due to this response, this student also "heavily edited out the [personal] information" about themselves from the final paper and felt like their learning and growth in the class was noticeably hindered.

In terms of coming out moments from students, we argue that being publicly vulnerable asks for an equally public response of some kind from instructors, every time. In the example of coming out as asexual, the instructor made no comment neither directly to the student's vulnerable revelation, nor when the student received an unaccepting response from a fellow student. Instead, the instructor later chose to privately tell the student that she was brave in the form of written feedback on the assignment. While in this case the student continued to only feel defensive with the one fellow student, it was also possible for students in this situation to interpret the lack of public comment from the instructor as lack of support for the student who came out or as agreement with the fellow student who argued back that asexuality wasn't real. Such unresponsiveness from the instructor can cause students to shut down more generally. It is important to explicitly note here that we are arguing that non-reaction is still a reaction, especially in front of a classroom. We acknowledge that silence can be used to empower voices when performed in the act of truly listening and understanding (see Ratcliff's (2005) work on rhetorical listening, for example). However, while it may not be true in all situations, especially in the context of Western cultural conventions, lack of response is often interpreted negatively or as rejection in itself. Thus, in the context of public response, we should not view a lack of response as somehow neutral. Likewise, when preparing to respond verbally, instructors should also monitor their nonverbal responses, which can just as easily communicate feelings like acceptance, indifference, or even hostility. In Jess's case, while none of her fellow students said anything positive or negative, their nonverbal cues such as avoiding eye contact, resulted in feelings of rejection.

Feminist pedagogy should also include reflection or examination of things that don't allow for full participation from all students. In A's story, for example, she chooses to come out about her asexuality because she finds the prompts they have been given too limited. She says that her "disinterest in and inexperience with sexuality left [her] at a bit of a loss at understanding works of literature through a sexual perspective." This is a learning moment for the whole class to think about making inclusive, open-ended prompts and assignments that allow room for everyone's story and point of view. We don't have this part of the story, but hope that the students in the next iteration of this class found more inclusive assignments.

In general, the behavior instructors model for their students, especially in the complex moments of revealing vulnerability and coming out, is critically important because it serves as an example to other students for how they should respond. In this manner, instructors can model behavior that helps students grow in their reflexive vulnerability personally to eventually becoming reflexive activists publicly (for a great example of this, see Godbee's example (Chapter 17, this collection) of dealing with microaggressions enacted in her class, Writing for Social Justice). We will discuss specific examples of what instructors can do to nurture these moments in the conclusion.

Finally, while we emphasize the importance of appropriate public response from instructors to coming out moments made by students, we would like to also note that students come out in classroom settings in different ways, not all of them public. Students may choose to come out privately to the instructor during a one-on-one session, like in the example of Katie's student who discussed her lack of confidence with writing during office hours. Likewise, students may take the opportunity to privately come out to the instructor in online discussion forums or classroom assignments not shared as a class. Similar to the manner in which we often have pedagogical discussions about how instructors should allow for different ways of student participation, not just public class discussions, especially in the case of introverted students, we argue that instructors should also allow and prepare for nonpublic coming out moments by their students. We would also like to suggest that modeling open accepting responses allows room for positive coming out experiences through other classroom spaces and activities, where the instructor might not be found such as discussion groups, collaborative project groups, or even just one-on-one sharing or peer review. We offer suggestions for both public and nonpublic coming out moments in the conclusion.

CONCLUSION: PAYING ATTENTION

Negotiating moments of coming out in graduate writing classrooms opens room for feminist conversations and interventions about the role of writing and identity in spaces that are both public and private, personal and political, concurrently. Such negotiations can ultimately lead to deeper discussions of how we foster the development of activist student citizens who are reflexive in words and actions.

Based on our findings in these particular stories, here are some things for instructors interested in enacting feminist pedagogies to keep in mind when students come out in their classrooms:

- Thank students for sharing (at the very least)
- Say "tell me more about that." Comments like this allow the instructor to situate the student's moment in the larger context of the class and goals of the day.
- Listen to every student, every time.
- Recognize and honor what your students tell you about themselves.
- Monitor your affect!
- Invite private discussion and confidence, one-one-one, e.g., private forum messages, individual reading responses, email correspondence.
- Remember ways of coming out are varied and different—and are not always public.
- Similarly, based on the findings from these particular stories, we advise students interested in feminist and/or activist stances to keep these ideas in mind:
- Be open. There are many reasons why other people might not recognize a coming out moment when it happens. Something big to you might seem small to others—this is not a measure of the value of your embodied experience.
- Pay attention to your classmates, both their words and their body language; these will clue you into how they are feeling and what types of responses they are looking for.

- Remember that coming out is a recursive process that happens over time to varying degrees. It can be a transformative moment, for you and/or your audience, but it doesn't (always) have to be.
- Keep in mind that coming out is a choice; we encourage you to measure how safe you feel in the particular moment, program, class, assignment, etc.

These two categories of bullet points highlight the multitude of ways that coming out as other can 1) be a feminist rhetorical practice as well as an activist performance itself, and 2) provide space for modeling feminist pedagogical practice. We know this is not an exhaustive list and invite more ideas and continued conversations about feminist pedagogies and the role of coming out in the writing classroom.

NOTE

1. All appendices referenced in the text, including the authors' own coming out stories as both sound and text files, are located online at https://drive.google.com/drive/folders/0B2Vu6VfSpS_rOHppMVpIMlIzbVk.

REFERENCES

Ahmed, S. (2006). *Queer phenomenology: Orientations, objects, others.* Durham, NC: Duke UP.

Arola, K. L. & Wysocki, A. F. (Eds.). (2012). *Composing(media) = composing (embodiment): Bodies, technologies, writing, the teaching of writing.* Logan, UT: Utah State University Press.

Fuss, D. (1991). *Inside/out: Lesbian theories, gay theories.* New York, NY: Routledge.

Godbee, B. (2018). Pedagogical too-muchness: A feminist approach to community-based learning, multi-modal composition, social justice education, and more. In K. L. Blair & L. Nickoson (Eds.), *Composing feminist interventions: Activism, engagement, praxis.* Fort Collins, CO: The WAC Clearinghouse / Louisville, CO: University Press of Colorado. Retrieved from https://wac.colostate.edu/books/perspectives/feminist.

Grahn, J. (1984). *Another mother tongue: Gay words, gay worlds.* Boston, MA: Beacon.

Hawkins, A. & Giroux, J. (2018). Trans/feminist practice of collaboration in the art activism classroom. In K. L. Blair & L. Nickoson (Eds.), *Composing feminist interventions: Activism, engagement, praxis.* Fort Collins, CO: The WAC Clearinghouse / Louisville, CO: University Press of Colorado. Retrieved from https://wac.colostate.edu/books/perspectives/feminist.

Herdt, G. (1992). *Gay culture in America: Essays from the field.* Boston, MA: Beacon.

King, T. (2003). *The truth about stories: A native narrative.* Minneapolis, MN: University of Minnesota Press.

Lorde, A. (2009). Age, race, class, and sex: Women redefining difference. In M. Marable & L. Mullings (Eds.), *Let nobody turn us around: An African American anthology* (pp. 515–522). Lanham, MD: Rowman & Littlefield Publishers.

Malinowitz, H. (1995). *Textual orientations: Lesbian and gay students and the making of discourse communities*. Portsmouth, NH: Boynton/Cook Publishers.

Mathis, K. E. & Boehm, B. A. (2018). Building engaged interventions in graduate education. In K. L. Blair & L. Nickoson (Eds.), *Composing feminist interventions: Activism, engagement, praxis*. Fort Collins, CO: The WAC Clearinghouse / Louisville, CO: University Press of Colorado. Retrieved from https://wac.colostate.edu/books/perspectives/feminist.

Myatt, J. (2018). Making the political personal again: strategies for addressing student resistance to feminist intervention. In K. L. Blair & L. Nickoson (Eds.), *Composing feminist interventions: Activism, engagement, praxis*. Fort Collins, CO: The WAC Clearinghouse / Louisville, CO: University Press of Colorado. Retrieved from https://wac.colostate.edu/books/perspectives/feminist.

Oral History Association. (2009). Principles and best practices. Retrieved from http://www.oralhistory.org/about/principles-and-practices/ .

Ratcliffe, K. (2005). *Rhetorical listening: Identification, gender, whiteness*. Carbondale, IL: Southern Illinois University Press.

Rhoads, R. A. (1994). *Coming out in college: The struggle for a queer identity*. Westport, CN: Bergin & Garvey.

Rhodes, J. & Alexander, J. (2015). *Techne: Queer meditations on writing the self*. Computers and Composition Digital Press. Logan, UT: Utah State University Press.

Royster, J. & Kirsch, G. (2012). *Feminist rhetorical practices: New horizons for rhetoric, composition, and literacy studies*. Carbondale, IL: Southern Illinois University Press.

Sheridan, M. (2018). Knotworking collaborations: Fostering community engaged teachers and scholars. In K. L. Blair & L. Nickoson (Eds.), *Composing feminist interventions: Activism, engagement, praxis*. Fort Collins, CO: The WAC Clearinghouse / Louisville, CO: University Press of Colorado. Retrieved from https://wac.colostate.edu/books/perspectives/feminist.

Smith, T. (2002). *Identifying space for GLBT writers: A phenomenological investigation of teachers' and students' perceptions of the composition classroom* (Unpublished doctoral dissertation). University of South Carolina, Columbia, SC.

Warner, M. (1993). Introduction. In M. Warner (Ed.), *Fear of a queer planet: Queer politics and social theory* (pp.vii–xxxi). Minneapolis, MN: University of Minnesota Press.

Weber, L. (2009). *Understanding race, class, gender, and sexuality: A conceptual framework*, (2nd ed.). New York, NY: Oxford University Press.

CHAPTER 20.
SAFELY SOCIAL: USER-CENTERED DESIGN AND DIFFERENCE FEMINISM

Douglas M. Walls
North Carolina State University

Brandy Dieterle
University of Central Florida

Jennifer Roth Miller
University of Central Florida

Feminist concerns about decentralizing and redistributing power are rarely met in information design and environments. Social media conglomerates are gathering, compiling, and profiting from location information obtained from geolocation enabled smartphones. Participants exchange small amounts of privacy at a time for minimal return, sometimes unknowingly. Top down design decisions are especially problematic in the context of domestic violence where abusers can use geolocation technologies to target, control, and intimidate survivors through the monitoring of social media technologies. In this chapter, we describe the development of Safely Social. Safely Social is a contextually-designed smartphone application, currently in development by the authors, that seeks to ease location-based services' adverse effect on domestic violence survivors by disrupting abusers' power who can utilize location-based services as a means for tracking survivors' social and geospatial activity. We further discuss the theoretical and methodological implications of interventionist feminist projects like Safely Social.

Domestic violence impacts more than the two partners in a relationship; it engages multiple discourses: family life, support communities, social groups, and the legal system. We begin our chapter with a disturbing example of the multiple discourses and lives affected by domestic violence. In 2012, a man entered a Casselberry, Florida, hair salon where his ex-girlfriend, Alice,[1] worked as a stylist. This man had a history of appearing at the salon unannounced and unwelcomed, and his family encouraged his ex-girlfriend to get a restraining order because they believed he was mentally unstable. His ex-girlfriend filed a temporary court-ordered separation injunction to remain more than 500 feet away from one another less than two weeks prior to her murder, and at that time she explained he had made threats to kill her.

The man proceeded to murder her, another stylist, another customer, and later the same day committed suicide. The murders took place just hours before the two were to appear before a judge to make the injunction permanent. A single instance of domestic violence impacts the family members of those involved, such as the family members who encouraged a restraining order, as well as the victims not directly tied to the conflict between the ex-girlfriend and her murderer. Social groups are also impacted as the co-worker and customer of the salon lost their lives too. The terrible tragedy we describe above has multiple causal factors, but for those interested in information design the most appalling is that several people's lives were impacted because of the assailant having easy access to information regarding his ex-girlfriend. This chapter discusses one approach for disrupting this flow of information through the use of a smartphone application that facilitates domestic violence survivors' ability to manage geolocation settings.

Feminist concerns about decentralizing and redistributing power are rarely met in design and environments. These top-down design decisions are especially problematic in context of domestic violence where abusers can use geolocation technologies to target, control, and intimidate survivors. When seeking assistance through community shelters, oftentimes survivors are asked to give up smartphones to further protect their privacy, but by doing so the abuser still retains power over the survivor. By making smartphones and social media places of danger, abusers continue to isolate and control survivors' social worlds.

Our project, *Safely Social*, is a contextually-designed smartphone application design project informed by feminist theories of listening, activity theory, and user-centered design to provide contextual understanding of domestic violence survivors' perspectives (see Anderson, 2012; Bowie, 2009; Kaptelinin & Nardi, 2006). Specifically, *Safely Social* seeks to ease location-based services' adverse effect on survivors by disrupting abusers' power gained by utilizing location-based services to track survivors. The feminist research process involved organizing and collaborating with a participatory design community comprised of repre-

---

[1] Alice, is a pseudonym as are all the names of individuals used in this piece.

sentatives from local domestic violence organizations, shelters, police, and the legal system. Drawing on user-design, the committee worked through three iterations of user interfaces in an effort to authenticate contextually relevant and user-centered features for survivors to maintain important social relationships without compromising safety. In other words, our community partners played significant roles in every step of the project as we built in multiple instances of feedback and assessment from the community partners, much like what Danielle Williams called for in this collection (Chapter 21).

This chapter documents the research process behind *Safely Social* as well as how feminist listening, activity theory, and user-centered design impacted our design considerations. While these three lenses are aimed at accounting for different voices and experiences, using all three of these theories together enabled us to keep in mind the needs and experiences of domestic violence survivors. We think that the development process of *Safely Social*, as well as the pre-production app itself, point to new kinds of feminist materialist interventions for the field. The theoretical and methodological design deliverable that emerged from a research project on domestic violence survivors' safety engages in feminist methodology by supporting a marginalized populations' control over their privacy in social media spaces as well as providing an example of applied feminist theory in information design contexts.

LISTENING FOR DIFFERENCE FEMINISM

Researchers cannot hope to implement effective change without knowing the subjectivities involved. As Patricia Sullivan and James Porter (1997) reminded us, "the rhetorical situatedness of participants," (p. 15) is especially important when working with marginalized populations like domestic violence survivors. In particular, the work of many feminist scholars like Malea Powell (2002), Krista Ratcliffe (2005), Terese Guinsatao Monberg (2008), and Jacqueline Jones Royster and Gesa E. Kirsch (2012) have focused on rhetorical listening as a research methodology itself. Rhetorical listening provides an avenue for hearing other narratives that tend to go untold or are told by those in power. In the context of feminist fieldwork, to attend to the needs of unheard groups, researchers must listen for the alternative discourse since it is the dominant discourse(s) at the root of marginalization and oppression. Monberg (2008) advocated an approach discussed by Jacqueline Jones Royster who "listens for the 'traces' that are visible in order to reveal the larger 'stream' of women in that tradition" (p. 87). In this way, researchers are able to give voice to marginalized and oppressed populations, thus providing opportunity to challenge essentialist perceptions. Furthermore, by listening and seeking the 'traces' and 'streams' Powell (2002),

Monberg (2008), and others speak of, researchers provide insight into "the rhetorical situatedness of participants" (Sullivan & Porter, 1997, p. 15). These positions take populations being studied in the field as subjects who are "actively negotiating, shaping, and building spaces, institutions, and histories of rhetoric" (Monberg, 2008, p. 91). In our work with *Safely Social*, this move towards rhetorical listening for other subjectivities became a key component for paying attention to the right kinds of activity streams of survivors. However, it is noteworthy that practicing rhetorical listening with marginalized populations, like domestic violence survivors, is not an easy feat. To simultaneously collect the traces and streams of survivors' lives without potentially causing harm by diverting survivors' attention from learning to live their lives without abusers, the research team practiced Royster and Kirsch's (2012) strategic contemplation and social circulation. Through strategic contemplation and social circulation, we used public stories and experiences told by advocates as a tool for mapping the overlapping and complex relationships involved in escaping an abuser, and then we contemplated and imagined the stories still untold and, ultimately, how we could make an effort to reach survivors with varying experiences. These stories and experiences are what Jess Tess, Trixie G. Smith, and Katie Manthey refer to (Chapter 19, this collection) as "coming out as other" and "personal moments of vulnerability," and sharing these moments were crucial for our project.

Turning to designing technologies and usability, subjectivities play an important role as researchers decentralize the dominant narratives in place to better serve marginalized populations. As advocate designers, two key theories that assist researchers in the field when conducting this work are activity theory (Kaptelinin & Nardi, 2006) and the universe of users (Bowie, 2009). Activity theory is focused on a more holistic picture or stream of an activity by documenting actions of multiple subjectivities involved in seeing a goal accomplished (Kaptelinin & Nardi, 2006). To fully understand a single activity, researchers need to be in the field observing and interacting with those involved with that activity. Likewise, collaboration, as Ames Hawkins and Joan Giroux discussed (Chapter 18, this collection), played a crucial role in our research and design process.

INFORMATION AND OPPRESSION

Applying feminist rhetorical listening to activity theory was helpful in understanding the issue of domestic violence survival as an activity. Drawing on social circulation (Royster & Kirsch, 2012), the design team worked with survivors, domestic violence organizations, police, and the legal system to develop our map of the complex actions involved with domestic violence. These persons, groups, and institutions work to achieve and maintain privacy in an effort to ensure safety, the desired outcome. Further, they employ artifacts such as cell phones and applications to control privacy and maintain safety. The division of labor involves controlling phone, social media, and geolocation settings from multiple subjectivities but rarely does that control lay at the feet of survivors. Our approach was shaped specifically on identifying different activity streams of participants. For example, drawing on Powell's (2002) encouragement of researchers to reimagine by identifying the differences, we were able to use activity theory to create a complex narrative by listening to the traces and streams from individuals who are survivors and those who advocate for survivors, as Monberg (2008) recommended. To that end, survivors' lives are completely reorganized when leaving a violent situation, leaving no time or energy for technology training to serve as an intervention in the safety and privacy concerns associated with geolocation technologies. Due to survivors' vast array of experiences and backgrounds, a user-design theory (Bowie, 2009) is needed to account for as many of those experiences and backgrounds as possible.

While activity theory was fruitful for a complex understanding of survivors' lives, using activity theory with social justice work poses challenges. Due to the nature of domestic violence, as researchers our access to survivors was limited and we elected to rely on information that would be openly given to the public in an effort to protect survivors' privacy. This meant relying heavily on domestic violence organizations and representatives to give voice to survivors. Protecting survivors is of the utmost priority for the organizations and institutions involved, and as researchers we can adopt reflexive practices so that a research project can overcome such obstacles (Sullivan & Porter, 1997). To this end, activity theory can remain a fruitful approach, but as Victor Kaptelinin and Bonnie Nardi (2006) emphasized, the theory may need to be reshaped to better fit particular projects like ours. In our case, this meant relying on secondary source material—those who give voice to the survivors' stories publicly—to provide key insight into the activity system.

The concept of the universe of users is grounded in the idea that there is no single user that is representative of the entire user population due to differences in gender, race, and socioeconomic status (Bowie, 2009). Focusing on the universal user results in other groups not being considered in the design and then being forced to interact with tools not designed with their use in mind. Jennifer Bowie's (2009) universe of users, though, enables researchers and designers to consider a whole network of potential users as a part of the design process so that various users with differing backgrounds are considered. With social justice projects, the universe of users approach facilitates feminist listening for developing a rhetorically-situated project. The more users who can be involved, the more voices can be accounted for to avoid essentializing the user population.

Our desire to create an inclusive view of activity, one that contained multiple perspectives and subjectivities traditionally marginalized, encouraged us to look beyond a universal user.

LISTENING IN THE FIELD

Our team engaged in the feminist and rhetorical listening principles and theories described in earlier sections, particularly Royster and Kirsch's (2012) strategic contemplation and social circulation resulting in Sullivan and Porter's (1997) notion of critical praxis. By employing qualitative research methods to observe, experience, and understand the work of domestic violence survivors and organizations, our team engaged the researched and their advocates as co-researchers and co-developers of knowledge and interventions. Employing activity theory, feminist listening, and ethnography, research findings were gathered, organized, visualized, and shared with a participatory design community by mapping inferred relationships and charting activity streams. Involving and meeting with a participatory design community provided a forum of strategic contemplation aimed at social circulation (Royster & Kirsch, 2012) through feedback, listening, and revision. Ultimately, design choices for the final iteration of the *Safely Social* app interface directly reflected research findings and input from the design community obtained through feminist and rhetorical listening, ethnography and discourse, mapping, participatory user experience design, and praxis.

The full thrust of research involved becoming immersed in the domestic violence survivor culture and activity streams to prepare for contextual and participatory design. Team members engaged in extensive ethnographic activities to better understand the context and framework in which domestic violence survivors work to control their privacy to ensure safety. At the time of our research, it happened to be domestic violence awareness month. Domestic violence organizations hosted many events in our local area seeking to raise awareness, support, and funds for the issue. The domestic violence events and activities we dwelled in ranged from university to community to nationally sponsored initiatives. Additionally, we dwelled at our county courthouse to observe how survivors navigate injunctions and separation logistics. Team members attended several of these events and activities, which provided worthwhile opportunities for feminist listening and inference, particularly what Royster and Kirsch (2012) define as critical imagination, to understand the discourse, language, activities, and stories of the people affected by domestic violence as well as chances to make connections with the local domestic violence organizations. Ultimately, this research, paired with analyzing the issue in terms of activity theory, allowed our team to map complexities and design new technology for this vulnerable population.

National initiatives discussions: Domestic violence is a broad issue that is approached from various angles and collectively is eased at the national, government, private, community, and grassroots levels. The National Domestic Violence Hotline offers phone-based advocates that are available to provide survivors assistance in planning a safe escape ultimately by connecting them to local resources. The United States government assists by providing funding for programs like the National Domestic Violence Hotline and other projects such as some of the apps we discovered in our research. Local non-profit organizations, such Harbor House in our area, lead critical efforts in the form of managing shelters, raising awareness, organizing fundraising efforts, relocation services, court advocates, and local hotlines connecting survivors to resources. Private donors and foundations also assist in funding both national and localized efforts, projects, and services. On a grassroots level, individuals are recruited as volunteers and fundraisers for service activities. Additionally, family members, friends, and other caregivers such as doctors and nurses are educated about the signs of domestic violence through events and projects of the local organizations and are encouraged to refer women in need to resources. Finally, community pillars and organizations such as university victim services departments, county governments, and police also serve to ease the issue of domestic violence in local communities through education and events that raise awareness, funding, and connections to resources.

University of Central Florida (UCF) Light Up the Night, an event honoring survivors of domestic violence and remembering those who did not survive, was especially helpful in our research process. Attending the UCF Light Up the Night event allowed the team to engage various positions and listen to different "streams" (Monberg, 2008) from survivors willing to speak publicly about their experiences. We sat and listened to many survivors share their experiences and perspectives, what Monberg (2008) described as oral histories. Accounts of domestic violence from many survivors of all ages and backgrounds were shared, yet the "traces" (Monberg, 2008) that emerged echoed each other.

One local domestic violence shelter, Harbor House of Central Florida, hosts a fundraising and awareness event each year called the Purple Door Luncheon. There, we learned about Harbor House's app, R3, which encourages families, friends, and doctors to recognize abuse and refer survivors to resources for help. By learning about this app, doctors, families, and friends were added to the landscape of activity in helping report abuse and obtaining help for the survivor. We also learned about other apps such as Circle of 6, which promotes dating safety. A different view of the issue is considered for dating populations, and this perspective was added to the mapping of activities. The keynote speaker, Martha, spoke of her daughter Lexi's murder by an ex-boyfriend just months before her college graduation. The ex-boyfriend had discovered Lexi's location and set out to harm her. We learned the term domestic violence is typically associated with marriage, but college-aged and young people also experience dating violence. This discovery prompted further discussions with UCF Victim Services and UCF Police that provided perspectives of young people, as well as information and apps for dating safety. We researched a variety of other pre-existing domestic violence related apps and determined the functionality of those apps. Then, we worked to critically imagine (Royster & Kirsch, 2012) and uncover gaps that our app could fill.

Listening to the range of speakers at the events and activities attended and mapping in terms of activity theory (Kaptelinin & Nardi, 2006), we began to understand the roles of collaborators and discourses involved in such a high impact issue like domestic violence. Using a feminist centered activity theory approach, we began to understand smartphones' and social media's role in eroding privacy and safety for survivors, specifically by paying attention and listening for various subjectivities and relationships to information. The interplay of various subjectivities (users, survivors, advocates, perpetrators, corporations, app designers, etc.) each have a different relationship to information. Smartphone, geolocation, and social media technology are not innately created for alternate subjectivities. As a tool or artifact in activity theory terms, it is a hindrance rather than an aid for survivors, leaving them open to potential control and violence. Additionally, considering Sullivan and Porter's (1997) reflexive and critical practices, we began to consider the "rhetorical situatedness" of the technology. The technologies are rhetorical in how their use is intended. We began to see how the intent of the technology doesn't work for survivors. Users not in healthy relationships jeopardize their safety if they participate in the mainstream fashion. Further, the smartphone is a tool that is detrimental during an escape and starting a new life because survivors don't have the domain knowledge to control geolocation settings. The smartphone is designed for a universal user, rather than a "universe of users," as Bowie (2009) advocated.

After observing and dwelling in the lives of actual survivors and listening to firsthand experiences as well as listening to their advocates, we were able to further map out the complex network of relations, activities, knowledge, and tools involved when survivors begin to engage the process of asking for help. Observing survivors navigating the system and administration of the courts was critical in understanding how they start a new life with relocation assistance, injunctions, preservation of new addresses and phone numbers, etc. all while allowing fathers to still have relationships with their children.

We followed up with the connections made at public events and activities, like Light Up the Night, Purple Door Luncheon, and injunction court, through telephone conversations and email messages with survivors and survivor advocates. Through these conversations, we collected additional data regarding the culture of survivors and organizations, their activity streams, and how the app could help most, again drawing on Royster and Kirsch's (2012) social circulation. We learned that survivors vacillate between staying and leaving; it takes eight attempts to leave. In fact, another telling story from a survivor, Becky, at Light Up the Night illustrated this well. Becky shared a detailed account of how escaping involved creating a new life: moving, changing phone numbers, email addresses, and creating new social media accounts. She described how any unguarded trace of her new life or location would be discovered by her ex and she had to try several times to ensure her privacy. Maintaining her privacy is a key concern and effort to this day.

Through our labored process of critical imagination and strategic contemplation (Royster & Kirsch, 2012), it became clear smartphone, geolocation, and social media technology is designed for people in healthy relationships, not for alternate subjectivities. In conversations with survivors and organizations, technologies were discussed as hindrances to remaining safe after leaving an abusive relationship. In fact, we learned from Harbor House that survivors are given old cell phones without geolocation when entering the shelters because they often don't know how to control the related settings. We added all of these complexities learned directly from survivors and their representatives to our visual mapping of the issue of domestic violence.

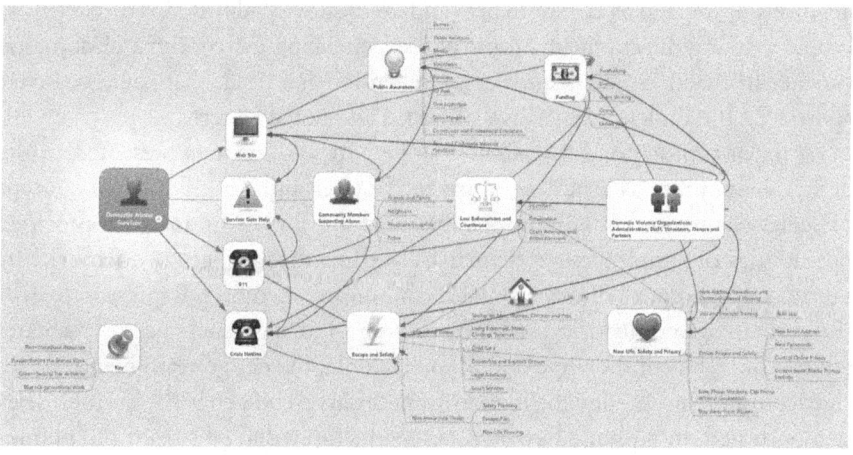

Figure 20.1. The team mapped the issue of domestic violence to visualize relationships.

We experienced difficulties in gaining direct access to the survivor population due to the sensitivity of the issue, however, we found solutions. In traditional application development, user stories are difficult to capture but are not, typically, loaded with threats of violence or emotional harm. In our context, data collection was a much trickier designer/research problem. The design team delicately approached the survivor stories by listening to personal accounts of domestic violence shared by survivors publicly at events, obtaining perspectives of representatives from domestic violence organizations, and observing survivors at injunction court. Written success stories from the organizations were also collected and reviewed. Paying attention and listening to various subjectivities as a design choice meant we needed a different kind of design community, one that respected differences in position and did not privilege one kind of context and did not position us as designers as understanding the entirety of the user/survivor perspective.

The team strived to establish a design community to accomplish a participatory and contextual design process adapted from Karen Holtzblatt and Hugh Beyer (1993). The resulting design team included representatives from several local domestic violence organizations, UCF Victim Services, an injunction court judge, two police officers, a courthouse representative, an app designer, representatives from a domestic violence foundation created by Alice's family and friends, and three doctoral students. Drawing on the need for inclusion and listening to subjectivities, this participatory design community was intentionally representative of the collaborators uncovered during our initial phases of research. The design community actively participated in the design process and collaborative knowledge creation by discussing and offering recommendations for revisions of subsequent iterations of the app as co-researchers and co-creators (Sullivan & Porter, 1997). People working directly in the cause and experiencing the concerns of domestic violence firsthand expressed areas of apprehension and needs that could be better addressed. The student team actively listened and noted patterns.

A paper prototype of a possible mobile app solution was presented to the design community as a starting point for Royster and Kirsch's (2012) concept of social circulation, offering a possible medium for disruption. We provided possibilities of simple design elements based on meeting needs uncovered by our research and prior discussions with community members. Representatives of the design community critiqued the prototype and suggested changes to better address the needs of the population. For example, the design team helped us see shortcomings in our design, like an unnecessary "contact 911" button. They demonstrated on a phone how it is faster to simply dial 911 from the phone's main screen than to enter an app to make the call. In an emergency situation, a survivor only has moments to call 911 before a potentially deadly incident escalates. Through employing feminist listening (Powell, 2002; Monberg, 2008) and user-centered design principles (Holtzblatt & Beyer, 1993) at this stage of the project, our team received very specific feedback about what the technology needed to do for survivors. At this point in the design process, the app was being designed for and by survivors and their advocates to better support Bowie's (2009) "universe of users" concept through incorporation of those users subjectivities.

A theme that emerged during prior conversations was that the greatest need for an app would be to help survivors control their privacy. The organizations expressed that survivors are in great need of an app that, with a push of a button, could indicate which applications are monitoring them and turn them off. According to the organizations, many survivors need maximum privacy to guard their safety. This greatly influenced design choices. *Safely Social* features an opportunity to restrict all applications' ability to access geolocation services on the device.

The initial stage of the design team's research involved online research of statistics, identifying cases linking geolocation to crime and polling via social media. Geolocation technology purposes are designed to positively connect people with location-based information. Conversely, companies and criminals are utilizing it for other reasons—to target specific markets for products or, alternatively, to monitor, track, and harm others. Even while some use this technology for harm, products continue to see geolocation technologies embedded within them—social networking sites and exercise and fitness technologies, for example.

Social media and online conglomerates receive monetary benefit by integrating geolocation services. As statistical data being sold to marketing and advertising agencies, participants become invisible and marginalized. Furthermore, it becomes difficult for users to maintain privacy due to constantly changing policies, and such technology marginalizes users experiencing domestic violence by not addressing their needs and considering that, sometimes, it is best to keep one's location private. Aside from the changing policies, conglomerates exert social pressure to engage in social media. If a person is not participating, one may begin feeling left out. Yet, participating in location sharing practices can expose survivors to further harm as abusers could gain access to this information made public.

We wish to pause here and state that we never would have reached this conclusion without careful feminist rhetorical listening, activity stream mapping, and our universe of users approach. Survivors experience isolation from the world of social media, doubling the amount of impact that abusers have on survivors by cutting them off from one of the ways people maintain social relationships. When survivors give up the entirety of their phone, many also give up the ease in which they maintain contact with their most important emotional support networks. Losing ease of access to these supportive networks, especially when the survivor needs that support the most, is especially hurtful. Like the abuser tactic of separating survivors from friends and family socially, removing social networks that phones provide unintentionally further isolates survivors. When geolocation technology is abused and used against survivors, it can result in violence as abusers can use that information to intimidate, manipulate, harass, degrade, and physically harm survivors. How then can survivors maintain connections to supportive networks while remaining safe? The *Safely Social* app provides a tool for social circulation disruption (Royster & Kirsch, 2012) that domestic violence survivors can use to safeguard location information and safety while they participate in social environments via their smartphone.

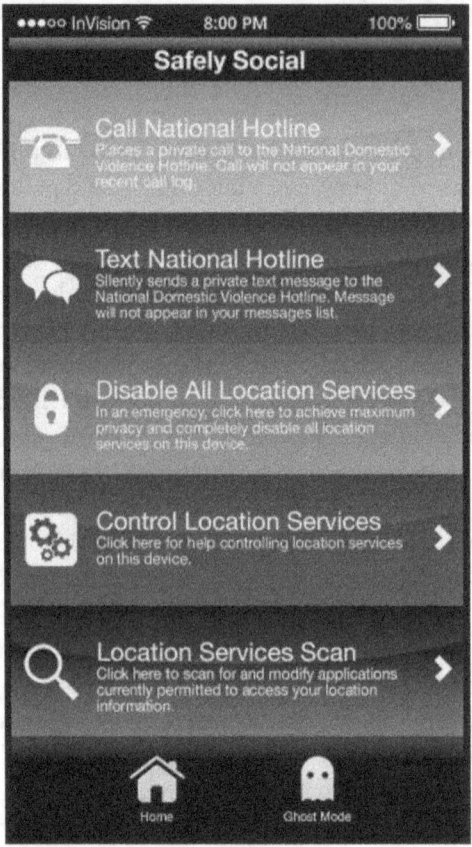

Figure 20.2. From Safely Social's home screen, survivors of domestic violence can control privacy to help maintain safety. A dynamic, clickable version of this image is available at http://invis.io/2BKEXP95

For survivors with a less immediate need, *Safely Social* offers abilities to help control geolocation services through push notifications as applications attempt to access location services, as well as live scans. The design community also expressed desire for the app to provide basic education to survivors about risk levels. In response, notifications will include educational aspects in the form of brief risk level assessments.

Another important, and perhaps the most interesting, thread focused on the fact that survivors are under constant monitoring by abusers. After presenting a paper prototype, the design community said there was a need for the app to be hidden on the phone. Advocates described how abusers monitor every aspect of a survivor's life, including survivors' phones and computers. Another obstacle is that abusers and survivors usually share cell phone and app store accounts. In an effort to address monitoring concerns, the development team chose to design a "camouflage" or a "cloak" for the app. The cloak is simply a login screen that appears to be a game. Once logged in, the actual home screen appears. *Safely Social* also features a "stealth" mode. With a quick click, the app reverts back to the "cloak" screen. This allows the survivor to toggle between the "cloak" or game and the real functionalities of the app.

Figure 20.3. "Cloaking" feature of Safely Social. A dynamic, clickable version of this image is available at http://invis.io/2BKEXP95

Survivors at Light Up the Night, such as Becky, reported feeling isolated and unable to make the calls necessary to get help because of fear of a violent incident if caught obtaining help. In John's case, a male survivor story shared at Light Up the Night, the relationship was even more violent because the taboo of hurting a woman did not exist. In same sex relationships between two men like John's, violence is often heightened because a man is assumed to be able to defend himself. John shared his story illustrating how some men are victims of domestic violence as well but harder to see as a result of societal gender and heteronormative behaviors. The design team learned there is always the factor of dominance in relationships exhibiting domestic violence. The most important way dominance is established and maintained is through monitoring and isolation.

The advocacy groups contacted and community partners indicated *Safely Social* could serve as a powerful tool, what we ultimately imagined as a tool for social circulation (Royster & Kirsch, 2012), in helping survivors plan escape if it could call and text silently for help and not leave any trace of communication planning escape. The final iteration of *Safely Social* features integrated the ability to call and text resources without leaving traces of conversations in call or text logs. The ability to silently communicate or text resources such as the National Domestic Violence Hotline are a result of meeting with the design community.

Safely Social is a culmination of feminist and rhetorical listening, ethnography and discourse, mapping, and user design in practice and ultimately praxis (Sullivan & Porter, 1997). *Safely Social's* ultimate design choices are in direct response to research and feedback from the participatory design community that uncovered cultural and activity contexts in which the app must operate to be useful. Survivors of domestic violence can utilize this artifact for social circulation (Royster & Kirsch, 2012) controlling integration of geolocation services in social networking to manage privacy and maintain safety. *Safely Social* is an intervention that redistributes power to ease the social injustice presented by geolocation technology for this vulnerable population. Ultimately, *Safely Social* allowed for the specific design of an artifact centralizing tools for a more diverse universe of users, enhancing smartphone capabilities to accommodate multiple subjectivities and offering a more complete view of activity.

DISCUSSION AND CONCLUSIONS

We think that *Safely Social* as an interventionist feminist project provides two large deliverables for scholars and activists. First, we think that theoretical implications of the project are strong in terms of applied feminist theory. Those engaged in interventionist projects must always concern themselves with the material conditions that theorists write about. Projects like *Safely Social* engage critical practices in rich ways, which help to build out and test theories in material and lived existences of students, designers, and research participants. Rhetorical listening allows designers and researchers to engage their theories with others in a tight loop of theorizing and reflection which makes for more robust theories. In other words, it is one thing to be in a classroom and talk of the violence of patriarchy and another to encounter it sitting across from somebody speaking of their experiences and having to design an intervention. We feel that for many, these have seemed separate activities but each, in close loops of reflection, build on one another making our critical theories more useful both in terms of explanatory power and material impact. Stories like those of Alice, Becky, and John that the research the team engaged in to dwell in the multiple discourses that constitute domestic violence (policy, familiar, gendered, legal, advocate) demand researchers ground their theories in the material conditions of people's lives. Such work grounds the stakes and contributions of feminism in real material designs. Simultaneously, when feminist theories like rhetorical listening are applied, activity theory and the development user-centered design become much more robust, capturing subjectivities that might otherwise be lost or not considered in typical design situations. Recognizing and paying attention to multiple rhetorical subjectivities supports a more accurate universe for a universe of users (Bowie, 2009) while grounding feminist theory as an important material perspective. As such, feminist theories become important ways to see and understand the problem of theoretically integrating the multiple discoursal formations that feminist theoretical research demands of us. Such moves guide theorists away from essentialism about theory and experience by encouraging us to encounter and listen to others in important and serious ways if only because participants, in our case survivors and their advocates, are able to correct essentialist views and discourses.

Second, we think that the methodological deliverables of applied feminist theory and application development have considerable implications for the field. As outlined and as the theme of this collection, feminism must engage in interventionist practices to have impacts on the lived experiences of people. User centered design, when done well, must engage these same feminist principles such as listening for subjectivities that are not accounted for in design work. Rhetorical theories of listening allow for more robust interventions because the experiences of users are better understood. Much interventionist work focuses on the work done by researchers to help, aid, and assist marginalized populations. However, what *Safely Social* points to is the idea that researchers can design with community partners in careful ways to design technological artifacts as a product of research methodologies. Design work with communities, and even with marginalized populations is nothing new. However, changing research methodologies to create real and lasting deliverables for the participants may be. While in our case the design of interventionist, helpful, feminist influenced technology was the goal, the methodologies involved in dwelling in research sites, listening for subjectivities, and user testing may have useful implications away from application development itself and contribute to how we think about the impact of feminist research methods.

Additionally, such research helps theorists ground their own assumptions about lived experience and subjectivity while, at the same time, flattering power relationships between designers, technologies, and users. In the work we speak of here, materially designing and receiving feedback from advocates and survivors themselves allowed for stronger contextual design features. However, our designs to map and dwell in multiple discourses were only attempted after significant time in the field as well as several iterations and understanding of the problem was tested and shown to the user base. In cases where user populations are at risk, feminist theory allows designers new methodologies to understand user experience in radically different ways from industry standards. Alice, Becky, and John are not "typical" users. When violence is a real possibility of not being able to accomplish a task, getting design language correct has more at stake. While not generalizable, we think that the design process behind *Safely Social* points to complicated forms of digital development that could, in short, save people's lives.

Feminism has a long history of both materialist interventions, making a difference in people's lives. So does design. Smartphones and their applications influence and mediate elements of social lives including safety. Top down design decisions can be problematic in terms of unrecognized or marginalized populations. We think that *Safely Social* can, in part, push feminist theory into materialist and interventionist efforts to decentralize and redistribute power. *Safely Social*, both as an application and as an application design/research process proves that feminist theory can be used along with user-centered design and activity theory to make real impacts in women's lives by paying attention to differences of subjectivities' relationships to information and activity.

The feminist work of decentralization and redistribution of power circulates through design of information systems, devices, and interfaces. Not only the design of applications and information, as we have shown here, but also in the design of process. Like other interventionist projects in this collection, our hope is that *Safely Social* inspires others to engage in other projects of applied feminist theory in information design contexts.

REFERENCES

Anderson, E. (2012). Feminist epistemology and philosophy of science. In E. N Zalta (Ed.), *The Stanford Encyclopedia of Philosophy*. Stanford, CA: The Metaphysics Research Lab, Center for the Study of Language and Information, Stanford University.

Bowie, J. L. (2009). Beyond the universal: The universe of users approach to user-centered design. In S. K. Miller-Cochran & R. L. Rodrigo (Eds.), *Rhetorically rethinking usability* (pp. 135–163). Cresskill, NJ: Hampton Press.

Hawkins, A. & Giroux, J. (2018). Trans/feminist practice of collaboration in the art activism classroom. In K. L. Blair & L. Nickoson (Eds.), *Composing feminist interventions: Activism, engagement, praxis*. Fort Collins, CO: The WAC Clearinghouse / Louisville, CO: University Press of Colorado. Retrieved from https://wac.colostate.edu/books/perspectives/feminist.

Holtzblatt, K. & Beyer, H. (1993). Making customer-centered design work for teams. *Communications of the ACM, 36*(10), 93–103.

Kaptelinin, V. & Nardi, B. A. (2006). *Acting with technology*. Cambridge, MA: MIT Press.

Monberg, T. G. (2008). Listening for legacies. In L. Mao & M. Young (Eds.), *Representations: Doing Asian American rhetoric* (pp. 83–105). Logan, UT: Utah State University Press.

Powell, M. (2002). Listening to ghosts: An alternative (non) argument. In P. Bizzell, C. Schroeder & H. Fox (Eds.), *ALT DIS: Alternative discourses and the academy* (pp. 11–22). Portsmouth, NH: Heinemann-Boynton/Cook.

Ratcliffe, K. (2005). *Rhetorical listening: Identification, gender, whiteness*. Carbondale, IL: Southern Illinois University Press.

Royster, J. J. & Kirsch, G. E. (2012). *Feminist rhetorical practices: New horizons for rhetoric, composition, and literacy studies*. Carbondale, IL: Southern Illinois University Press.

Sullivan, P. & Porter, J. (1997). *Opening spaces: Writing technologies and critical research practices*. Westport, CT: Ablex Publishing.

Tess, J., Smith, T. G., and Manthey, K. (2018). Trans/feminist practice of collaboration in the art activism classroom. In K. L. Blair & L. Nickoson (Eds.), *Composing feminist interventions: Activism, engagement, praxis*. Fort Collins, CO: The WAC Clearinghouse / Louisville, CO: University Press of Colorado. Retrieved from https://wac.colostate.edu/books/perspectives/feminist.

Williams, D. M. (2018). The unheard voices of dissatisfied clients: Listening to community partners as feminist praxis. In K. L. Blair & L. Nickoson (Eds.), *Composing feminist interventions: Activism, engagement, praxis*. Fort Collins, CO: The WAC Clearinghouse / Louisville, CO: University Press of Colorado. Retrieved from https://wac.colostate.edu/books/perspectives/feminist.

CHAPTER 21.

THE UNHEARD VOICES OF DISSATISFIED CLIENTS: LISTENING TO COMMUNITY PARTNERS AS FEMINIST PRAXIS

Danielle M. Williams
Baylor University

Williams draws on her recent experience teaching first-year digital writing to examine the benefits of community-based multimodal student projects for community partners. Readers learn how the involvement of volunteer community partners as evaluators of student video projects revealed "the complex and multivalent nature of 'success' in publicly-shared community-based writing projects." Examination of their evaluation processes and narratives tell the story of how community partners brought different values to the project. By listening to these different perspectives, Williams suggests interventions that feminist teachers can make to improve future projects.

> A wheel turns because of its encounter with the surface of the road; spinning in the air gets it nowhere. Rubbing two sticks together produces heat and light; one stick alone is just a stick.
>
> —Anna Tsing, *Friction*

Initially, I was pleased with what my first-year writing students had accomplished after completing a multimodal community-based writing project in which they composed videos about the General Education Development (GED) test for members of the local Waco community. Students had learned how to compose in multiple modes; actively engaged in the composing process; demonstrated rhetorical skill and new media competencies; and connected with needs in the local community. Imagine my surprise, then, when my victory lap was interrupted by an email from another community partner: "Before I vote on the videos, I would really like to talk with you. I have some concerns. Is that OK?" When I distributed a questionnaire to all of the community partners involved in the project, I learned an uncomfortable truth: this concerned community partner was not an outlier. I made it my goal as a feminist teacher-researcher to figure out how so many different people could be involved in the same project, view the same videos, and come to such radically different conclusions about the success, or failure, of the project as a whole.

In this chapter, I foreground community partner perspectives—typically underrepresented points of view that Randy Stoecker and Elizabeth A. Tryon (2009) call the "unheard voices" of service learning (p. vii)—in order to identify points in which feminist teachers can intervene to structure community-based writing projects that benefit all stakeholders. I begin by discussing the concepts of "rhetorical listening" and "strategic contemplation" to frame the recursive process of feminist praxis. I then describe a community-based writing project in which community members provided different feedback about their understanding of the project's goals, their understanding of their roles as community partners, and their definitions of what would make a multimodal community-based writing project "successful." These points of contradiction, I argue, provide ongoing opportunities for feminist teachers to learn from these differences and, in turn, to model a process of reflexive self-critique for students. I conclude with recommendations for structuring student learning and for designing community-based writing projects that challenge, complicate, or nuance our definitions of success.

THE NEED FOR MULTIPLE PERSPECTIVES IN COMMUNITY-BASED WRITING PROJECTS

Scholars in composition and rhetoric have deepened our field's understanding of the wider potential of community-based writing initiatives by describing the benefits of student engagement (Deans, 2000; Mathieu, 2005), service learning as citizen formation (Dubinsky, 2002; Cushman, 1996), community literacies (Flower, 2008; Knochel & Selfe, 2012), and feminist approaches to community engagement (Nickoson & Blair, 2014; Sheridan & Jacobi, 2014; Bowdon, Pigg & Mansfield, 2014). The pedagogical and social benefits of community-based writing projects for students are well documented, yet less is known about the affordances of these projects for other stakeholders.

The perspective of community partners is often overlooked in the literature (see Mathieu, 2005, pp. 93–95), but truly feminist praxis requires more than just cursory inclusion or, "merely adding voices" (Sheridan & Jacobi, 2014, p. 144). We need to add these voices, to be sure, but we also need to create "new architectures of participation" (Sheridan & Jacobi, 2014, p. 144) that result in reciprocal partnerships that share the burden of assessing a project's ultimate value for the community. Formal measures of assessment in composition and rhetoric typically focus on student learning, but, as Mathieu (2005) argues, "The stakes of public work are broader than classroom concerns. As such, our means for evaluating this kind of public work should go beyond traditional markers of student achievement and evaluation" (p. 93). Instead of limiting our assessment of a community-based writing project to the students, we need to listen to formative feedback from a range of stakeholders and then turn the assessment back on ourselves—the teachers and designers of the project—so that we can adapt what we are currently doing and chart a new course for what we will do in the future.

PRACTICING RHETORICAL LISTENING AND STRATEGIC CONTEMPLATION IN COMMUNITY-BASED WRITING PROJECTS

In order to understand and honor the different perspectives at work in a campus-community partnership, we need to listen to a range of stakeholders as well as to our own evolving responses over time. Feminist community-based researchers can create these new architectures of participation by systematically collecting data from community partners and "look[ing] again and again and again at rhetorical situations and events with the deliberate intention of positioning and repositioning ourselves to notice what we may not have noticed on first, second, third or next view" (Royster & Kirsch, 2012, p. 135). Krista Ratcliffe (2005) offers "rhetorical listening" as one possibility for communicating across different perspectives. Ratcliffe defines "rhetorical listening" "as a stance of openness that a person may choose to assume in relation to any person, text, or culture; its purpose is to cultivate conscious identifications in ways that promote productive communication, especially but not solely cross-culturally" (p. 25). This approach to communication is a key element of feminist praxis. Instead of deciding who gets to speak or privileging one voice over another (e.g., among community partners, between campus-community priorities, etc.), rhetorical listening can be used in community-based writing projects as a strategy to hear multiple perspectives that might clash or contradict with each other or with our own beliefs (Iverson & James, 2014; Butin, 2014). While Ratcliffe focuses on the cultural categories of race and gender, her strategies for listening across difference are valuable for addressing the contradictions that emerge between the different community partners involved in this project.

To that end, this study aims to listen to and continue to learn from the voices of community partners in order to disrupt traditional power dynamics in campus-community partnerships (Iverson & James, 2014). No feminist teacher, no matter the sincerity of their intentions, is capable of making the final call on a community-based writing project's success or failure. Instead, as Jacqueline Jones Royster and Gesa E. Kirsch (2012) argue, we need to

> [use] robust inquiry strategies . . . to gather symphonic and polylogical data that function dialectically (referring to the gathering of multiple viewpoints); dialogically (referring to the commitment to balance multiple interpretations); reflectively (considering the intersections of internal and external effects); and reflexively (deliberately unsettling observations and conclusions in order to resist coming to conclusions too quickly). (p. 134)

Listening, after all, is not just a matter of considering differing opinions; listening is an ongoing process that creates space for silence and reflection as well as creates opportunities for others to speak. Royster and Kirsch specifically refer to this posture of openness as "strategic contemplation." Strategic contemplation "entails creating a space where we can see and hold contradictions without rushing to immediate closure, neat resolutions, or to cozy hierarchies and binaries" (Royster & Kirsch, 2012, pp. 21–22). Practicing strategic contemplation in response to community-based writing projects gives us permission to pause, to acknowledge tensions, and to continue to learn from "a recursive process of thinking, writing, thinking, writing, thinking as the research spirals toward ever more fully rendered understandings and intellectual insights" (Royster & Kirsch, 2012, p. 86). Conducting this study and hearing the various perspectives of the community partners and their assessments of the project's goals and outcomes has been a continual process of discovery for me. Rhetorical listening and strategic contemplation allow me to move inward and outward—back and forth between my experiences, the community partners' responses, and existing research—to practice a dialectical, dialogical, reflective, and reflexive form of feminist praxis.

DESCRIPTION OF THE CLASS PROJECT AND METHODS

This study offers an examination of differences and what can be learned from them by presenting the results of a case study of a campus-community partnership in a first-year digital writing class I taught at Baylor University during the fall 2013 semester.[1] The videos my students created for this community writing project were 1-2-minute multimodal arguments related to some aspect of the General Education Development (GED) test. The prompt for this project

---

1 This study has been approved by the Baylor University Institutional Review Board (#390505–6).

was designed in collaboration with a member of the community who runs a community resource website and distributes an online newsletter. She selected "community experts"—people she knew who worked with individuals at various stages in the GED process. Students then chose community experts to interview and composed videos based on what they discovered through various forms of research. The videos were posted on a central YouTube channel and community partners were asked to vote to identify a video that would be featured on the local community website. The videos were also freely available under Creative Commons licenses for any of the community partners to use for their own organizations or purposes.

After the semester ended, questionnaires were distributed and interviews were conducted to see how students, community partners, and the project's designers evaluated the success of the community video project. Of the ten community partners invited to participate in this study, five completed the online community partner questionnaire, which consisted of multiple-choice questions, open-ended questions, and Likert-type scales on their experiences working with students during the community video project. The community partner participants were affiliated with the local school district, the technical college, and a nonprofit women's organization. Of the five community partner participants, four were female and one was male. Two female community partners were selected to participate in 30-minute follow-up interviews based on the contradictions that emerged between their questionnaire responses.

GOAL-SETTING WITH THE COMMUNITY PARTNERS

During the initial planning meeting with the community partners, two broad goals were discussed: (1) to end up with videos that could be used on local websites to promote the GED, and (2) to connect the Baylor students with needs in the Waco community. These two goals are similar, but the primary difference is significant. The first goal is "product-focused": this view of the project defines the main purpose of the multimodal community-based writing project to be the creation of a quality product that will raise awareness about the GED. The second goal is "process-focused." Instead of stressing the composing process itself, this conception of the project focused on the learning process and inner transformation of the student-composers themselves. The five community partners who completed the questionnaire placed different emphases on these goals. When asked to describe their understanding of the goals of the GED Community Video Project, two community partners stressed the success of the end project while three community partners also mentioned the learning process of the students.

Table 21.1. Community partners' understanding of the goals of the GED Community Video Project

Product-Focused	Product- and Process-Focused
"I understood that the students would attempt to create videos that could be used as PSAs in the Waco community that would raise the awareness and the availability of local GED programs."	"I hoped the videos would be created an [sic] reach a new audience of individuals that would be served by the GED services available in our community. A second goal, was for the Baylor student's [sic] themselves to see possibly a different side of the Waco community and how they could serve and become more involved."
"To raise awareness for the need to get an education."	"I was hopeful to broaden the understanding of why many people take the GED and what they are able to achieve upon earning their GED."
	"I was hoping the students would hear the stories of the GED candidates and translate what they learned into a video that would inspire other GED candidates."

Table 21.1 shows the community partners' individual perspectives on what they understood to be the goals of project and what they hoped the project would ultimately achieve. While two of the community partners surveyed understood the overall objective of the project to be the final products that the students created, three of the community partner respondents were hoping that the project would benefit both the community and the students. The differences between these goals are subtle, but they underscore two different orientations towards the project.

Soliciting this feedback from the community partners about their initial expectations can be an important method of feminist intervention in community-based writing projects. By doing so, we can listen to and take stock of different interpretations at various points during the project. For instance, in response to the statement, "I left the initial planning meeting in August feeling like I could express my concerns about the GED Community Video Project," two of the community partners surveyed "strongly agreed" and three "agreed." These responses indicate that the planning meeting was perceived as a collaborative experience for the community partners. This kind of information can help us identify the points in which communication might be breaking down so that we can recalibrate our approach in future projects by checking in with community partners more frequently or using multiple methods (e.g., additional surveys, emails, one-on-one meetings, brief written reflections, etc.). As Ames Hawkins and Joan Giroux observe (Chapter 18, this collection), effective collaboration—

as a class or with community partners—requires opportunities to express dissent so that we can reexamine our goals and "move together."

A DIFFERENCE IN ROLES: THE CLIENT AND THE MENTOR

Though I did not provide concrete guidelines for how the community partners should relate to students aside from being available to participate in at least one interview, the community partners defined roles for themselves according to their own objectives and anticipated outcomes. Community partners who were more interested in the usability of the final products approached the project as "clients," whereas community partners who also stressed the learning process of the students adopted roles as "mentors." A key difference between these two orientations to the project is how each community partner ranked the most important qualities (e.g., honesty, openness, patience, listening, relevant skills, transparency, empathy, tact, and knowledge) that a student could bring to a multimodal community-based writing project.

COMMUNITY PARTNER AS CLIENT

While community partners who interpret their roles in a community-based writing project as "clients" do not devalue the students' learning process, this outcome does not take precedence over their immediate material needs. Service-learning projects differ from other kinds of client-based projects in the sense that they incorporate reflection and a deeper analysis of systemic issues (Chappell, 2005, p. 38). Even so, community partners in service-learning projects are indeed clients who share their needs with university classes with the expectation that they will end up with a final product that they can use. In this conception of the community partner role, the success or failure of the project primarily rests upon the students' ability to deliver a usable product.

Kim[2] does not explicitly tell me that she saw her role in the multimodal community-based writing project as a client, but it is clear that her disappointment with the videos stems from her expectations of what she thought the final products should have been. For Kim, the purpose of this multimodal community-based writing assignment is to create videos that would appeal to the specific demographic with which she works at the GED testing center: people who are taking the GED. What she sees, instead, are videos that reflect narrow-minded stereotypes. Kim clearly expects students to have a more sophisticated understanding of the complex reasons that cause people to drop out of high school. In

---

2   Names have been changed to protect the identities of the participants.

response to a question on the community partner survey that asked participants to rank the most important qualities that a student can bring to a community-based writing project, Kim ranks "knowledge" first (out of eight qualities). When I later ask Kim to explain this choice, she explains that students need to know what they are talking about in order to be effective.

Kim is the community partner who contacted me to express her concerns about the videos before voting. When I later meet with Kim to discuss her thoughts, she references videos that she found offensive or inappropriate because they featured single mothers or young people with drug addiction issues. She shakes her head and laughs loudly, awkwardly. She is quick to affirm that some of the videos were not "that bad," but her overall assessment is negative. In hindsight, there is no way that these videos can meet Kim's needs as a client, but my initial analysis of the data simply notes that the videos were lacking audience awareness. If these students had been hired as consultants or freelancers, people "with special skills who will provide requested services" (Chappell, 2005, p. 40), they would not be hired again.

Broadly speaking, the community partners who privilege the production of the videos are dissatisfied with the set of videos; however, they observe that some of the final products are successful. Various community partners refer to at least some of the videos as "really well thought out and well done," "a great youthful approach to media and social media messaging," and "overall, good." However, the concerns that Kim raises are legitimate. Some of the videos do not accurately represent the people who earn the GED. In fact, Kim feels so strongly about some of the videos that she says she would never show them to any of the test-takers she works with because she does not want anyone to think, "Is that what people really think of me?" And, in some cases, the answer is, unfortunately, "yes." The final products that the students create reveal this tension and overall lack of understanding.

Listening to this assumption about a community partner's role as a "client" has important implications for students and instructors. When a community partner views her role as a client, students need to prepare themselves to be treated, first, as a consultant or a freelancer and, second, as a learner-in-process. Additionally, students need to be aware of—and, to a certain extent, adopt—the "social motives" that correspond with working with a community partner that values productivity and efficiency over the individual learning processes of students (Deans, 2010, p. 457). Failing to step into the role that has been created for the student can be "trouble" when a student "holds fast to school motives, which keep the student focused on . . . individual learning rather than on the collective contribution to the community partner" (Deans, 2010, p. 459). This type of campus-community configuration also affects how feminist instructors prepare students to compose videos in response to sensitive issues.

One way that we can intervene is by designing specific assignments that prepare students to meet with community partners who view their roles as clients. While service-learning projects ought to be scaffolded with texts and discussions of readings that facilitate student knowledge and sensitivity, these community partners' expectations necessitate a higher level of engagement with these topics in order to ensure that students have mastered this knowledge prior to meeting with the community partner. In this model, the informative interview might not be not as much of a fact-finding mission as it is an opportunity to nuance or complicate what a student has already discovered through earlier forms of research. By reflecting on the needs of these community partners and making students aware of expectations beyond a facilitated learning experience, feminist teachers can better prepare students to create a high-quality product that meets their client's needs.

COMMUNITY PARTNER AS MENTOR

These community partners typically see themselves as responsible for managing the students' learning experiences in addition to seeing to their own service needs. Deans (2010) reflects that these partnerships tend to be more successful because the teacher and the community partner prioritize the same motive (i.e., student learning), viewing students as "learners-in-development rather than as miniature professionals" (p. 458). Though students may not explicitly articulate this belief, this service-learning relationship is what many students expect from community-based writing experiences. Traditional schooling leads them to believe that every learning experience will be "facilitated" by an experienced teacher (Freedman & Adam, 1996). Students carry this expectation to service-learning contexts and assume that the community partner will fill this role. While this kind of mentor-mentee relationship can tax an already-overworked staff at a service organization, some community partners naturally adopt a stance towards students that places them in the role of co-teacher, or mentor.

At the time of this study, Cassie is the Community Resource Coordinator for the local K-12 school district. Her experiences with people in the community who might need to take the GED are mostly restricted to the parents of the children in the district. Like Kim, Cassie does not consciously identify her role in the project, but she demonstrates her commitment to the "mentor" role through her thoughtful ideas about structuring student learning in future community-based writing projects and her belief that "openness" is the most important quality that students can bring to projects like this. In fact, Cassie lists "knowledge" as the least important quality that a student could bring to a community-based writing project, a position that stands in contrast to Kim's perspective. When I ask Cassie to explain why she privileges openness, she reflects that, "sometimes coming in with this preconceived notion that you already know the topic or know what's going on isn't the most important thing . . . that doesn't mean that [you're] open to putting [yourself] in that person's life." According to Cassie, students should be cognizant of their lack of knowledge and open to learning.

The community partners who prioritized student growth and transformation were satisfied with the project and feel that their goals were mostly met. Cassie, for example, notices that the students cared about the work that they completed. She notes, "You could tell that the students not only wanted to complete the assignment for credit, but were emotionally invested in the project and the outcomes. Their heart made the difference." This element, heart, is impossible to quantify and has little bearing on the quality or effectiveness of the final products. However, through her interaction with students, Cassie is able to assess that they possessed an additional element that made the project successful. Thus, for some community members, success is marked by change in the individual instead of what the individual can produce as a result of a 15-week college course.

When feminist teachers are aware of this community partner orientation towards service-learning projects, they can intervene in different ways during the assignment design stage. Since these community partners are typically more invested in the students' intellectual and emotional development over time, they are often more willing to meet with students multiple times. In fact, Cassie tells me meeting more frequently would have benefits beyond a strong partnership between individuals because the secondary outcome would likely be a stronger final product that the community partner could use. Additionally, community partners who take on a mentoring role might also have ideas for more focused readings or assignments that might complement what is being done in the classroom. To that end, knowing that a community partner saw her role as a mentor from the earliest stages of the project would likely enhance the student's learning process as well as the end product.

In sum, listening to the community partners' assumptions about their roles is a critical piece of feminist praxis. These assumptions affected how we all approached the project and have implications for how feminist teachers should design community-based writing projects that address different partner's expectations. For one, these various conceptions of community partner roles create additional roles that students must inhabit (e.g., "mentee/novice" or "consultant/freelancer") that I had not initially considered or prepared for. Second, these different understandings of their roles as community partners affect how they determine their desired outcomes and, ultimately, how they will evaluate the success of the project. Third, understanding the qualities that different community partners value affects how we ought to design assignments and prepare students for their interactions with community members. And, lastly, these questions about the value of "knowledge" and "openness" can cause us to think more deeply about the context within which each community partner is working and which factors might motivate such strong and diametrically opposite responses. This information has implications for teachers, as well. For example, what do I assume about what my students know or do not know or about what they see or do not see? And at which points in my teaching do I want students to be knowledgeable or open and malleable? The only way that we can identify different orientations to the project is by seeking feedback from individual participants, listening to their different conceptions of the project, and forestalling our assessment of which perspective is "right" or more in line with our own pedagogical goals and expectations.

"HEARING WHAT WE CANNOT SEE": THE ONGOING PROJECT OF FEMINIST PRAXIS

Practicing rhetorical listening and strategic contemplation is a crucial form of feminist praxis not only because it allows us to hear conflicting reports but also because it gives us space to return to the data again and again to "[hear] what we cannot see," (Ratcliffe, 2005, p. 29). These points of disagreement about community partner roles and the most valuable qualities that a student can bring to a community-based writing project are fertile ground for further exploration. What I would like to emphasize here, however, are the limitations in my embodied perspective as a White feminist teacher at a four-year private university, which I have come to recognize by sitting with these multiple viewpoints and resisting the urge to force them to come to a neat resolution (Royster & Kirsch, 2012, p. 141). I am hopeful that I can transform what I learned from this process to design mutually beneficial community-based writing projects and to use this reflexive experience as a model for other feminist teachers and for my future students.

Kim's response to the videos as a dissatisfied client challenged me far beyond the conclusion of the class and the decision I ultimately made not to publicize any of the videos. On some level, I knew that her disappointment with the final product was grounded in more than her expectations as a client in a community-based writing project. And though I believed at the time that I was practicing rhetorical listening, the spaces for reflective and reflexive thinking encouraged by strategic contemplation allow me to see the ways in which I had truly failed to analyze my self and my lived experience in relation to what she was telling me (Royster & Kirsch, 2012, p. 149). While Kim does not cite my students' misunderstanding of race or social status in the videos, she is clearly uncomfortable with the assumptions that some of my students are making about people who take the GED. And these assumptions reflect a deeply embedded "absent presence," an "ingrained sensibility" (Prendergast, 1998, p. 37) that reveals my own assumptions for not noticing these problems with the videos sooner.

Initially, I assume that my commitment to feminism and gender equality makes me sensitive to unfair power dynamics, to privilege, to issues of difference. I assume that I am aware of my own blind spots. I am wrong. What I discover, through the process of listening to these stakeholders and as I have continually returned to the results, is that I am all too often blind to expressions of race and class. I realize I do not always recognize some of the stereotypes of GED test-takers in my students' videos as mere stereotypes until I meet with Kim and begin to "[attend] to the complexities of embodied-ness" (Royster & Kirsch, 2012, p. 149). Furthermore, I do not always notice the lack of diversity in the students' videos because seeing "whiteness [as] the unexamined norm" (Tatum, 1997) is a problem many of my students and I unfortunately share. In fact, instead of confronting this issue directly, I had been telling myself that a different community partner, incidentally a White male, had specifically requested a video that would "scare kids straight" and steered some students in the direction of these stereotypes—particularly the stereotype of drug use. Some of the final drafts of the videos actually contain what could be considered racial microaggressions, or "the brief, commonplace, and daily verbal, behavioral, and environmental slights and indignities directed towards Black Americans, often automatically and unintentionally" (Sue, Capodilupo & Holder, 2008, p. 329), in the form of these stereotypes.

The absent presence of race in these videos is made even more palpable since one of the videos that offends Kim is a video titled "Why are These White Boys Punch Dancing? And How Does it Relate to Pie?" The reference to the boys' "whiteness" is not even an absent presence in this case, yet we did not see race in this video even as we were referencing it. Sam's video was celebrated by his peers in class and, later, during interviews months after the class ended. The primarily White class voted his video "Most Entertaining," and many of the students shared a link to his video through social media. In part, the success of Sam's video for this audience is grounded in the fact that he does not look beyond himself and his own embodied experiences. After analyzing videos on YouTube, Sam concludes that humor is an essential key to success, so he composes and stars in a video of guys "punch dancing." Punch dancing typically refers to young men dancing out their feelings, usually anger, à la the classic *Footloose*. This dance style is typically sincere and only incidentally funny.

Sam's video is effective on one level because it is memorable; however, the video ultimately prioritizes humor over sensitivity to his audience. The video begins with a young man dancing, his rubbery limbs hypnotically swaying to a laidback techno track. An overlay of alphabetic text reads "Why are these white boys dancing?" Later text reveals "These horrible dancers finally decided to get their G.E.D." and the celebratory dancing-out-of-feelings continues until the video ends. The basic message is that earning the GED is "easy as pie," and the video aims to motivate viewers to sign up to take the test because then you can also celebrate by eating pie.

Sam's video is catchy, weird, and creative. However, his video also presents a troubled perspective on race, class, and gender. While he seems to be drawing on a comedic stereotype that "white men can't [insert verb here]" by making fun of how badly he and his friends are dancing, he also frames the issue of the GED in ways that could alienate his intended audience in multiple ways. For instance, he does not analyze how his odd brand of humor might play to diverse audiences or how people outside of Baylor might perceive young White men wearing Baylor shirts dancing in front of buildings at Baylor. Moreover, Kim mentions that she does not like how Sam quips that the process of earning a GED is "as easy as pie." For many GED test-takers, earning the GED is an achievement that takes considerable effort and sacrifice. Saying that the GED is as easy as pie might be catchy, but Kim observes that this description diminishes the achievement. As a result, Sam inadvertently offends a community partner who thinks that he is making light of a serious issue.

Looking back, I can see countless points in which I could have intervened to ensure that Sam and his peers better understood the community audience and context. For one, I could have designed the project from the outset to encourage more accurate GED stories and more fair representations of diversity in the videos. The critique about a lack of diversity was brought up during a mid-process workshop in which members of the community were invited to share their feedback, but students felt that they did not have enough time to re-shoot their videos. And though students conducted secondary research on issues related to race and social status, I could have structured more opportunities for students to understand the context of the GED test-taking process by asking students to tour the facility or to meet with recent test-takers. Lastly, after the project ended, I could have listened to the cues Kim was offering that misrepresentations of race or class played a role in her assessment of the final products instead of just accepting that the top five videos—as ranked by the students, the two community partners who voted, and myself—did not accurately represent the people who actually take the GED.

Despite my inclination to critique social structures that privilege one group over another, I am stunned to realize how frequently I do not see—that I am only immediately critical when I am not the one on the "right" side of the power dynamic. This truth is hard to accept, but it is also what makes listening to other perspectives and practicing strategic contemplation so important. I wish I could go back in time and confront these issues of race and class directly, a teaching moment Beth Godbee skillfully models in her essay "Pedagogical 'Too-Muchness': A Feminist Approach to Community-Based Learning, Multi-Modal Composition, Social Justice Education, and More" (Chapter 17, this collection). Instead, I missed a significant opportunity to listen to tensions, intervene at crucial moments, and provide Kim with useful videos. And, consequently, my students missed learning an important lesson about how we need to "reflect on what we are seeing or not seeing" when we compose products for community audiences (Royster & Kirsch, 2012, p. 17). While Cassie might have recognized my students' "heart" and good intentions, their growth and development was stunted by my lack of vision about the role that our embodied experiences should have played in the research and composition of these videos.

Ratcliffe (2005) exposes similar blind spots surrounding her "(in)visible whiteness;" and I echo her questions: "What lessons am I (un)consciously sending to my students, my readers, my neighbors, my daughter, myself?" (p. 3). And in what ways did I unconsciously contribute to my students' "failures" in this multimodal community-based writing project because I first failed to see how race and class are represented in these videos? Ratcliffe proposes an alternative to feeling guilt in the form of accountability, which requires us to pay attention and listen to our daily lives (p. 7). As we lay our stories next to each other, we can begin to "expose troubled identifications with gender and whiteness . . . and to conceptualize tactics for negotiating such troubled identifications" (Ratcliffe, 2005, p. 8). Like Ratcliffe, I am committed to this project of hearing what we cannot see so that we can learn from our mistakes. We can model this reflective and reflexive process of strategic contemplation for our students; we can show them our missteps and identify what we have learned; and we can, as Jess Tess, Trixie G. Smith & Katie Manthey advocate (Chapter 19, this collection), "come out" ourselves as vulnerable individuals who do not always have the right or definitive answer. And then we can begin to structure community-based writing projects in ways that fully consider the rhetorical, ethical, and feminist implications of our work.

IMPLICATIONS AND PEDAGOGICAL RECOMMENDATIONS

Rhetorical listening and strategic contemplation are strategies of feminist praxis that can help us build important feedback into new architectures of participation for community partners in community-based writing projects. These strategies have important implications for how we interact with community partners at various stages during the project; how we design course assignments; how we prepare students to interact with and reflect on their relationships with community partners; how we analyze our embodied experiences in relation to community issues; how we assess the final products; and how we revise future projects. I conclude this essay with recommendations for teachers as we compose new methods of feminist interventions in community-based writing projects. These recommendations are intended to encourage teacher-researchers who have been reluctant to collect data from stakeholders beyond the classroom during or after community-based writing projects.

First, I urge feminist teachers to solicit feedback from community partners involved in community-based writing projects. It is not enough to assess a project's success or failure based on our own or our students' impressions of learning outcomes. In particular, we need to listen to community partner perspectives in order to understand how they interpret our collaborative goals, adopt unique roles to accomplish these goals, and assess a project's usefulness for the community. We can also gain insight into the kinds of qualities (e.g., knowledge/ openness) that students ought to bring to these projects and how our teaching styles might confirm or contradict these values. This information will assist us in designing even more agile community-based projects that respond to situated and context-specific needs.

We must also consider what we will do with conflicting or contradictory approaches to the same project. I have offered rhetorical listening and strategic contemplation as two strategies of feminist praxis that create space for us to listen across difference and resist too-neat resolution. The challenge, however, is to decide how to handle impasses that require immediate action, such as "Which video should we select to feature on this website?" We must create an environment in which public sharing is not the default *telos* of a video assignment. Risks should be evaluated, and all stakeholders should be consulted before accelerating the process of digital delivery (Adsanatham, Garrett & Matzke, 2013; Porter, 2009).

Another suggestion is to include community stakeholders at more regular intervals. Community partners should be informed prior to the initial meeting what the levels of commitment could be. They should also be invited to participate on community expert panels and give feedback as often as they are available or willing. Even if the students are only composing videos for one "client," multiple community partners from different sectors should be invited so that we enact a logic of accountability and continue to grapple with different perspectives (Ratcliffe, 2005, p. 31–32). Additionally, projects like this would be vastly improved by including the perspectives of other stakeholders in the community such as the GED test-takers themselves. Community partners should be consulted to recommend additional community members who might interested in participating in a focus group interview and/or providing feedback at later stages.

Lastly, we can design more opportunities for students to practice their own forms of rhetorical listening and strategic contemplation as they interact with and compose videos for community partners. One practical suggestion is to make the due date for the final project well in advance of the last day of class so that students have time to listen to and reflect on different responses to their videos. By creating space for discordant notes, we can demonstrate the productive potential of actually hearing each other and nuancing our understanding of what is or is not a successful video. We should also design opportunities for students to reflect on their embodied experiences and examine how these elements might affect their ability to reach their intended audiences. Furthermore, we should share with our students our own mistakes while practicing rhetorical listening and strategic contemplation so that we can serve as self-reflexive models. By implementing these strategies, we can expand our empathy, our sensitivity, and our ability to communicate across different perspectives.

Community-based writing is not without its critics, but each of the community partners who took this questionnaire made comments like this "idea is a good one" and "projects like this are great." These final assessments belie the sense that projects like this might not be worth doing. Following Mathieu (2005), I would argue that we persist in participating in community-based writing even, or perhaps especially, when we disagree because we are ever hopeful that we can and will improve (p. 19). This orientation towards revision—revision, re-seeing, and trying again—is feminist praxis that drives us onward in community-based writing projects, inspiring us to intervene so that we may create new structures in which we can all participate more equitably. Listening and being open to different responses and evolving ideas is just the first step toward creating more successful community-based writing projects that enact an ethics of hope and care for the benefit of ourselves and our communities.

REFERENCES

Adsanatham, C., Garrett, B. & Matzke, A. (2013). Re-inventing digital delivery for multimodal composing: A theory and heuristic for composition pedagogy. *Computers and Composition, 30*, 315–331. http://dx.doi.org/10.1016/j.compcom.2013.10.004.

Bowdon, M., Pigg, S. & Mansfield, L. P. (2014). Feminine and feminist ethics and service-learning site selection: The role of empathy. *Feminist Teacher, 24*(2), 57–82.

Butin, D. (2014). Series editor's preface. In S. V. Iverson & J. H. James (Eds.), *Feminist community engagement: Achieving praxis* (pp. vii–x). New York, NY: Palgrave Macmillan.

Chappell, V. (2005). Good intentions aren't enough: Insights from activity theory for linking service and learning. *Reflections, 4*(2), 34–53.

Cushman, E. (1996). The rhetorician as an agent of social change. *College Composition and Communication, 47*(1), 7–28. http://dx.doi.org/10.2307/358271.

Deans, T. (2000). *Writing partnerships: Service-learning in composition*. Urbana, IL: NCTE.

Deans, T. (2010). Shifting locations, genres, and motives: An activity theory analysis of service-learning writing pedagogies. In T. Deans, B. Roswell & A. J. Wurr (Eds.), *Writing and community engagement: A critical sourcebook* (pp. 451–464). Boston, MA: Bedford/St. Martin's.

Dubinsky, J. M. (2002). Service-Learning as a path to virtue: The ideal orator in professional communication. *Michigan Journal of Community Service Learning, 8*(2), 61–75.

Flower, L. (2008). *Community literacy and the rhetoric of public engagement*. Carbondale, IL: Southern Illinois University Press.

Freedman, A. & Adam, C. (1996). Learning to write professionally: 'Situated learning' and the transition from university to professional discourse. *Journal of Business and Technical Communication, 10*(4), 395–427.

Godbee, B. (2018). Pedagogical too-muchness: A feminist approach to community-based learning, multi-modal composition, social justice education, and more. In K. L. Blair & L. Nickoson (Eds.), *Composing feminist interventions: Activism, engagement, praxis*. Fort Collins, CO: The WAC Clearinghouse / Louisville, CO: University Press of Colorado. Retrieved from https://wac.colostate.edu/books/perspectives/feminist.

Hawkins, A. & Giroux, J. (2018). Trans/feminist practice of collaboration in the art activism classroom. In K. L. Blair & L. Nickoson (Eds.), *Composing feminist interventions: Activism, engagement, praxis*. Fort Collins, CO: The WAC Clearinghouse / Louisville, CO: University Press of Colorado. Retrieved from https://wac.colostate.edu/books/perspectives/feminist.

Iverson, S. V. & James, J. H. (2014). Feminism and community engagement: An overview. In S.V. Iverson & J. H. James (Eds.), *Feminist community engagement: Achieving praxis* (pp. 9–27). New York, NY: Palgrave Macmillan.

Knochel, A. & Selfe, D. (2012). Spaces of the hilltop: A case study of community/academic interaction. *Kairos, 16*(3), Retrieved from http://kairos.technorhetoric.net/16.3/praxis/selfe_knochel/article.html.

Mathieu, P. (2005). *Tactics of hope: The public turn in English composition*. Portsmouth, NH: Boynton/Cook.

Nickoson, L. & Blair, K. L. (2014). Intervening: The value of campus-community partnerships. *Feminist Teacher 24*(1), 49–56.

Porter, J. E. (2009). Recovering delivery for digital rhetoric. *Computers and Composition, 26*(4), 207–224.

Prendergast, C. (1998). The absent presence in composition studies. *College Composition and Communication, 50*(1), 36–53.

Ratcliffe, K. (2005). *Rhetorical listening: Identification, gender, whiteness*. Carbondale, IL: Southern Illinois University Press.

Royster, J. J. & Kirsch, G. E. (2012). *Feminist rhetorical practices: New horizons for rhetoric, composition, and literacy studies.* Carbondale, IL: Southern Illinois University Press.

Sheridan, M. P. & Jacobi, T. (2014). Critical feminist practice and campus-community partnerships: A review essay. *Feminist Teacher, 24*(2), 138–150.

Stoecker, R. & Tryon, E. A. (2009). Unheard voices: Community organizations and service learning. In R. Stoecker and E. A. Tryon (Eds.), *The unheard voices: Community organizations and service learning* (pp. 1–18). Philadelphia: Temple University Press.

Sue, D. W., Capodilupo, C. M. & Holder, A. M. B. (2008). Racial microaggressions in the life experience of Black Americans. *Professional Psychology: Research and Practice, 39*(3), 329–336.

Tatum, B. D. (1997). *"Why are all the black kids sitting together in the cafeteria?": And other conversations about race.* New York, NY: Basic.

Tess, J., Smith, T. G., and Manthey, K. (2018). Trans/feminist practice of collaboration in the art activism classroom. In K. L. Blair & L. Nickoson (Eds.), *Composing feminist interventions: Activism, engagement, praxis.* Fort Collins, CO: The WAC Clearinghouse / Louisville, CO: University Press of Colorado. Retrieved from https://wac.colostate.edu/books/perspectives/feminist.

Tsing, A. L. (2005). *Friction: An ethnography of global connection.* Princeton: Princeton, University Press.

PART 5. COURSE DESIGNS

CHAPTER 22.

"WE WRITE TO SERVE": THE INTERSECTIONS OF SERVICE LEARNING, GRANT WRITING, AND THE FEMINIST RHETORICAL AGENCY

Florence Elizabeth Bacabac
Dixie State University

Linking students with community organizations upholds mutually-beneficial relationships through service learning (SL). Theoretically, SL proponents may be viewed as feminist rhetorical agents who foster social transformation through community projects that accomplish the mission of non-profit agencies. Writing grants for community partners may introduce students to rhetoric outside the academy (Coogan, 2006), but writing personal reflections completes their civic actions since subjective positions on issues of (and plans for) social change are liberally inscribed. Without critical analyses for future action, our community service efforts are futile (Herzberg, 1994) as seen in course designs with diverse forms of critical reflections, such as the creative revision projects by Julie Barger (Chapter 23, this collection), Take Back the Night engagement reflections by Katherine Fredlund (Chapter 25, this collection), and digital storytelling by Stephanie Bower (Chapter 24, this collection). This chapter promotes SL-based grant writing as a feminist intervention technique, along with student- and community partner-reflections on SL projects aimed at changing the community and the lives of its members.

INSTITUTIONAL CONTEXT

Dixie State University (DSU) is an open enrollment institution located in St. George, Utah. In 2010, *CNN Money* ranked the city of St. George as the 80th "Best Place to Live" while *Forbes Magazine* ranked it 1st on the 2013 "Top City for Job-Seeking College Grads" (*DSU Briefing Book*, 2015). DSU is the fastest growing 4-year institution in the Utah System of Higher Education with 9,000+ students (*DSU Active Learning Active Life*, 2016) and 175 faculty members plus adjunct teachers (Alder, 2014). Its enrollment growth has led to 15 new baccalaureate degrees and several associates, certificates, academic minors, and faculty members with Ph.D. or terminal degree credentials (*DSU Briefing Book*, 2015).

Accredited by the Northwest Commission on Colleges and Universities, DSU is a public comprehensive university that promotes a culture of *learning*, *engagement*, and *opportunity* (*Dixie 2020*, 2015, emphasis added). These core themes may have overlapping outcomes but altogether help fulfill DSU's mission of enrichment in which students meet their educational goals in a supportive learning environment and extend a culture of engagement and opportunity through citizenship, inclusion, collaboration, etc. Aside from the trainings they receive in small classes, DSU students are also involved in various community service projects either on their own or as part of a coursework to advance DSU's motto, "active learning. active life." The Campus to Community service program was organized in 2001 to enhance practical applications of classroom learning (*DSU Briefing Book*, 2015). This type of service deepens students' awareness and understanding of societal issues through diverse inter/disciplinary knowledge and practical experiences (Lucas, 2009).

The university's English department promotes experiential, service learning (SL) through one of its upper-division course, English 3130 or Grant and Proposal Writing, offered every spring semester. Intended for English majors in the Professional and Technical Writing program and open to students who want to learn more about grant writing, this course examines rhetorical techniques for writing effective grant proposals, the processes that lead to successful grant and proposal writing, and strategies for effective collaboration with non-profit organizations. Students write grant documents that respond to the need statements of local non-profit organizations, including those that provide community-based housing, transportation, educational, and livelihood assistance to women and children who were victims of domestic violence, etc. To institutionalize community engagement in the department, students select community partners with 501(c)(3) status and spend approximately 96 hours of service writing grants for them, while the instructor devotes 140 hours planning and directing the grant proposal-writing process. Students then receive SL certificates in a formal ceremony hosted by DSU and submit written proposals to their respective organizations at the end of the semester.

While finding non-profit agencies willing to work with students can be a challenge, clear-cut contracts and expectations for stakeholders in the beginning of the semester foster success. This arrangement has been mutually beneficial on two accounts: organizations gain *pro bono* grant writers during the semester and students acquire new writing skills that meet course learning outcomes. Grant proposals are considered technical documents, but students also learn how to navigate around their passion and logic with compelling arguments for funding (Payne, 2011). Providing tangible opportunities to write inspires them to acquire purposeful writing skills as their personal reflections provoke a sense of feminist rhetorical agency (Hawisher, 2003). On the whole, this SL-based project advances grant writing as a feminist intervention technique that changes the community and the lives of its members.

THEORETICAL RATIONALE

In her approach to rhetorical feminism, Laura Micciche (2010) promoted the integration of feminist methods into the conception and performance of writing. I argue that her conceptual framework, if applied to service learning (SL) and technical writing courses, would expect students to develop critical analysis, non-profit collaboration, and advance planning through grant writing. Specifically, upper-division writing courses with SL-based approaches would enable students to work closely with local non-profit organizations and help bolster their mission statements through funded projects for the benefit of the community. The grant writing course discussed here mirrors feminist intervention approaches, such as reciprocal collaboration, social awareness, reflection, civic engagement, agency, and changed-based writing.

Grant writers as rhetorical agents aim to show how an organization's mission matches that of a prospective funding source's. With this same purpose comes a methodological re-assessment of rhetoric and in particular, the feminist rhetorical agency, "as an embodied social praxis" (Royster & Kirsch, 2012, p. 132). Writing grants for non-profit recipients in support of funding community projects for the citizenry becomes a social responsibility akin to disrupting problematic conventions and imitating feminist rhetorical acts that are purposeful, productive, and dynamic. Such writing/communicative performance illustrates how rhetoric(s) "work, and are at work, in the world" (Griffin & Chávez, 2012, p. 19). As an argumentative piece, a grant proposal document needs to persuade its funding sponsor that a problem can be solved (or an opportunity explored) through its project plan, budget projections, and evaluative procedures.

Because funded grants impact the community and its recipients, the power to interrogate and disrupt normalcy is inevitable. Corollary to this is the fact that feminist rhetoricians often expand foundational concepts such as "rhetorical space, argument, genre, and style" (Buchanan & Ryan, 2010, p. xviii) and grant writers exhibit "ways of *doing* feminist rhetorics . . . integrat[ing] feminist methods into the conception and performance of writing" (Micciche, 2010, p. 184). For Micciche, writing is the crux of feminist inquiry and feminist rhetorical theorists must stimulate gendered assertions on composing pedagogies (Nickoson, et al., 2012). Since grant writing follows a rhetorical approach that helps student writers use effective communication strategies to accommodate change (Johnson-Sheehan, 2008), this SL-based course forges a feminist rhetorical practice that permeates Micciche's notion of writing and engagement.

Moreover, rhetoric and writing practitioners embodying feminist tactics outside the academy affect societal transformation (Cushman, 1996). *Composing Feminist Intervention's* course design narratives portray collaborative partnership tasks that stimulate change-based agents, such as Barger's collaborative connection presentations to understand feminism from a collective standpoint, Fredlund's DIY activist rhetoric projects to address a rhetorical situation and a community partner's needs, and Bower's digital storytelling to disseminate alternative stories of the marginalized in collaboration with community groups. But when project proposals satisfy a community need through grants, these awards make possible innovative solutions and new directions for intended recipients. Composing grant proposals requires careful attention to research, strategic planning, and argumentation and treats rhetoric as a "form of action aimed at producing effects" (Adler-Kassner, Crooks & Watters, 1997, p. 9). Here, community service writing builds upon conventional writing instruction and elevates the study of rhetoric, so student writers expand their understanding of rhetorical variations with pertinent skills to navigate multiple discourse communities (Bacon, 1997). They also gain practical experience, technical facility, and confidence knowing that their proposed documents may change the lives of community members.

Finally, SL cultivates disciplinary knowledge when integrated into a course where students develop problem-solving and social responsibility (Jacoby, 2009; McDonald 2011). Community service and learning outcomes, interlaced with critical reflection and civic responsibility (Deans, 2000; Gottlieb & Robinson, 2006), sets an SL-based grant writing course apart most especially when student writers receive SL certificates after each semester to authenticate their civic action-and-reflection duties and showcase a collective sense of altruism as feminist rhetorical agents closing opportunity gaps.

CRITICAL REFLECTION

What makes this SL-based course stand out from volunteerism, internship, practicum, and charity work is the merging of both course objectives and community service to promote social change. The English department's SL grant writing course (see Appendix A) enacts DSU's core themes by instilling not only the principle of *learning* for academic advancement but also the *opportunity* for service and engagement. Our pedagogical focus on the rhetoric of grant proposals assists our student writers' persuasive and strategic planning skills and while we pursue a programmatic curriculum on SL, we are also open to revisions as reflective teaching dictates.

Despite the challenges of working with community-based organizations, three major benefits support the teaching of grant writing as a feminist intervention technique within the framework of SL:

1. Reciprocal Collaborations with Community-Based Organizations Increase Social Awareness.

Ideally, working with local non-profit agencies to forge real-world writing experiences enables not only campus-community partnerships but also social awareness. Such cognizant reciprocity embodies feminist intervention as support systems and interconnected partnerships are being strengthened. Admittedly, challenges between stakeholders might arise (e.g., conflicting schedules, misunderstood expectations, lack of mutual cooperation), but these issues can easily be avoided by enforcing a set of guidelines before the semester:

- Select partners that connect to your course topic(s). Invite to class (if applicable).
- Provide a list of potential partners.
- Create an open relationship and communicate with partners.
- Coach students on how to work with non-profit agencies.
- Confirm students have completed hours. (Fisher, 2011)

In addition, designating a student-community partner contract of agreement also helps clarify common expectations between students and non-profit organizations (see Appendix B). This contract outlines the guidelines and due dates of selected grant sections that need organizational input distinct from a waiver of liability and release for service activities required of SL courses. With mutual cooperation, the entire process recognizes community-based programs as sites of power that instill social conscience and, most importantly, change. Before writing the proposal, student writers are initially asked to do *strategic planning* in which they carefully examine a selected organization's mission, goals, characteristics, etc. and propose possible projects that capitalize on strengths (and minimize weaknesses) while enforcing its mission and objectives (see https://florenb07.wixsite.com/bacabacfemschaplinks).

2. Personal Reflections and Private Writing Enhance Civic Engagement.

Instructors using an SL-based curriculum for grant writing can generate social responsibility and promote civic engagement through constant reflections or private writing. As a feminist intervention strategy, developing community engagement from the vantage point of writing performativity illustrates Micciche's stamp of "*doing* feminist rhetorics" (2010, p. 184). Writing personal reflections is an essential process for my students to transform service activities and course objectives into genuine learning. In a sense, SL courses value private writing because they integrate academic class work and community-based experiences together (Anson, 1997). These reflexive practices help my students understand their own grant writing skills and the application of these skills outside the academy. A variety of reflection activities may be assigned (e.g., journals, analytic papers, electronic forums), but asking the right questions to ensure critical thinking might also pose difficulty. In this regard, I often use the following guidelines to formulate my reflective prompts:

- Why? Reflecting on learning goals
- What? Observing and describing experiences critically
- So What? Identifying and analyzing systemic and structural issues
- Now What? Learning inventories and action plans (Jeanfreau, 2013)

The teacher might assign reflection exercises throughout the term to gradually address these points, but the *final reflection* should ask students to tease out specific details from their grant/service experiences and future action plans. I find these prompts often reveal the gravity of the current situation and/or immediacy of the proposer's evaluation/dissemination/sustainability methods through my *student reflections*. In tandem with *community partner reflections*, these discursive practices definitely enhance a more holistic sense of civic engagement and feminist praxis.

3. Acquisition of Grant Writing Skills Engenders a Feminist Rhetorical Agency.

Through service or experiential learning, students gain real-world applications of grant writing skills that legitimize a feminist rhetorical agency. An undergraduate course such as this accelerates a rare form of feminist intervention viz. experiential learning and develops one's rhetorical agency toward changed-based grant writing. By combining community service with classroom instruction through active pedagogy (Jeavons, 1995), the instructor and non-profit organizations in this context have a shared responsibility of training student writers to tackle future advocacies. Our programmatic approach to teaching SL-based grant proposals supports the militant potential for English departments to direct SL participants to "read and write, attend to cultural studies, and entertain questions about public policy" (Schutz & Gere, 1998, p. 130). Though one of the most incessant critiques many instructors might have of an SL-based curriculum concerns assessment—and we do need additional research to evaluate various SL models and their effects on student learning, etc. (Pedersen, Meyer & Hargrave, 2015)—our student reflections may equally serve as qualitative assessment, along with their graded, cumulative assignments that build on one another. In fact, I always require my students to finish each proposal section successfully before moving to the next one, and before submitting a final document, to critique someone else's intermediate draft based on a set of *review panel criteria* from class discussions. Given these points, I believe that students who acquire not only critical thinking but also grant writing skills in service of community organizations have the capacity to act as feminist rhetorical agents and affect sustainable, social change even after they exit the course. This form of feminist intervention prepares them to critically assess problems, propose solutions, or even manage funding for non-profits to level the playing field, push for equity of opportunity, and transform society at large.

REFERENCES

Adler-Kassner, L., Crooks, R. & Watters, A. (1997). Service-learning and composition at the crossroads. In L. Adler-Kassner, R. Crooks & A. Watters (Eds.), *Writing the community: Concepts and models for service-learning in composition* (pp. 1–17). Washington, DC: American Association for Higher Education.

Alder, D. (2014). *What is Dixie State University?* Dixie State University. Retrieved from http://dixie.edu/aboutdixie/.

Anson, C. M. (1997). On reflection: The role of logs and journals in service-learning courses. In L. Adler-Kassner, R. Crooks & A. Watters (Eds.), *Writing the community: Concepts and models for service-learning in composition* (pp. 167–180). Washington, DC: American Association for Higher Education.

Bacon, N. (1997). Community service writing: Problems, challenges, questions. In L. Adler-Kassner, R. Crooks & A. Watters (Eds.), *Writing the community: Concepts and models for service-learning in composition* (pp. 39–55). Washington, DC: American Association for Higher Education.

Buchanan, L. & Ryan, K. J. (2010). *Walking and talking feminist rhetorics: Landmark essays and controversies.* West Lafayette, IN: Parlor Press.

Coogan, D. (2006). Service learning and social change: The case for materialist rhetoric. In T. Deans, B. Roswell & A.J. Wurr (Eds.), *Writing and Community Engagement: A Critical Sourcebook* (pp. 211–232). Boston, MA: Bedford/St. Martin's.

Cushman, E. (1996). The rhetorician as an agent of social change. *College Composition and Communication, 47*(1), 7–28. http://dx.doi.org/10.2307/358271.

Deans, T. (2000). *Writing Partnerships: Service learning in Composition.* Urbana, IL: NCTE.

Dixie 2020: Status to Stature 2015–2020. (2015). St. George, UT: Dixie State University.

Dixie State University: Active Learning, Active Life. (2016). St. George, UT: Dixie State University.

DSU Briefing Book 2014–2015. (2015). Unpublished manuscript, Dixie State University, St. George, UT.

Fisher, A. (2011, October). *Incorporating service learning and leadership into your course.* Paper presented at the Higher Ed Hero Webinar, St. George, UT.

Gottlieb, K. & Robinson, G. (Eds.). (2006). *A practical guide for integrating civic responsibility into the curriculum* (2nd ed.). Washington, DC: Community College Press. Retrieved from http://www.nationalservice.gov/resources/service-learning/practical-guide-integrating-civic-responsibility-curriculum.

Griffin, C. L. & Chávez, K. R. (2012). Standing at the intersections of feminism, intersectionality, and communication studies. In C. L. Griffin & K. R. Chávez (Eds.), *Standing in the intersection: Feminist voices, feminist practices in communication studies* (pp. 1–31). Albany, NY: State University of New York Press.

Hawisher, G .E. (2003). Foreword: Forewarding a feminist agenda in writing studies. In G.E. Kirsch, F. S. Maor, L. Massey, L. Nickoson-Massey, M.P . Sheridan-Rabideau (Eds.), *Feminism and composition: A critical sourcebook* (pp. xv–xx). Boston, MA: Bedford/St. Martin's.

Herzberg, B. (1994). Community service and critical teaching. *College Composition and Communication, 45*(3), 307–319. http://dx.doi.org/10.2307/358813.

Jacoby, B. (2009). Civic engagement in today's higher education: An overview. In B. Jacoby & Associates (Eds.), *Civic engagement in higher education: Concepts and practices* (pp. 5–30). San Francisco, CA: Jossey-Bass.

Jeanfreau, J. (2013, March). *Is service learning a means of overcoming or reinforcing prejudices?* Paper presented at the 64th annual convention of the Conference on College Composition and Communication, Las Vegas, NV.

Jeavons, T. H. (1995). Service-learning and liberal learning: A marriage of convenience. *Michigan Journal of Community Service Learning, 2,* 134–140. Retrieved from https://ginsberg.umich.edu/mjcsl/.

Johnson-Sheehan, R. (2008). *Writing Proposals* (2nd ed.). New York, NY: Pearson Longman.

Lucas, N. (2009). The influence of integrative and interdisciplinary learning on civic engagement. In B. Jacoby & Associates (Eds.), *Civic engagement in higher education: Concepts and practices* (pp. 99–116). San Francisco, CA: Jossey-Bass.

McDonald, T. (Ed.). (2011). *Service learning for civic engagement series: Social responsibility and sustainability: Multidisciplinary perspectives through service learning.* Sterling, VA: Stylus Publishing. Retrieved from http://www.ebrary.com.

Micciche, L. R. (2010). Writing as feminist rhetorical theory. In E. E. Schell & K. J. Rawson (Eds.), *Rhetorica in motion: Feminist rhetorical methods and methodologies* (pp. 173–188). Pittsburgh, PA: University of Pittsburgh Press.

Mikelonis, V. M., Betsinger, S. T & Kampf, C. (2004). *Grant seeking in an electronic age*. New York, NY: Pearson Longman.

Nickoson, L., Hauman, K., Hurford, E., Kastner, S., Kirchoff, J. & Spike, K. (2012). [Review of the book *Rhetoric in motion: Feminist rhetorical methods and methodologies*, by E. E. Schell & K. J. Rawson]. *Feminist Teacher, 22*(2), 160–162. http://dx.doi.org/10.1353/ftr.2012.0007.

Payne, M. A. (2011). *Grant writing demystified: Hard stuff made easy*. New York, NY: McGraw Hill.

Pedersen, P. J., Meyer, J. M. & Hargrave, M. (2015). Learn global, serve local: Student outcomes from a community-based learning pedagogy. *Journal of Experiential Education, 38*(2), 189–206. http://dx.doi.org/10.1177/1053825914531738.

Royster, J. J. & Kirsch, G. E. (2012). *Feminist rhetorical practices: New horizons for rhetoric, composition, and literacy studies*. Carbondale & Edwardsville, IL: Southern Illinois University Press.

Schutz, A. & Gere, A. R. (1998). Service learning and English studies: Rethinking "public" service. *College English, 60*(2), 129–149. http://dx.doi.org/10.2307/378323.

APPENDIX A: COURSE SYLLABUS

English 3130: Grant and Proposal Writing (3 credits)

Course Description

English 3130 is an upper-division course for English majors emphasizing in Professional and Technical Writing and open to students who want to learn about grant writing. It examines the rhetorical techniques for writing effective grant proposal documents, the processes that lead to successful grant and proposal writing, and the strategies for effective collaboration with non-profit organizations.

Prerequisite: Intermediate Writing with a grade of C or better. 3 lecture hours per week.

Course Learning Outcomes

By the end of English 3130, students will demonstrate their ability to:

- Compose a grant proposal that exhibits what the fundamental elements of each section.
- Apply critical thinking when writing the current situation, goal(s), objectives, and tasks.
- Ceneratee a solid budget and project evaluation plan.

Methods of Assessment

Formative Assessment

Preparation Checks: Periodically show completion of the grant writing process based on exercises/assignments required for the Proposal

Assignments: Submit a Grant Proposal Development Notebook with graded exercises/assignments that lead toward the Grant Proposal Document:

- Ex. 1 Strategic Planning
- Ex. 2 Current Situation/Need Statement Section
- Ex. 3 Funding Sources Assignment
- Ex. 4–7 Project Plan (with Prewriting exercises)
- Ex. 8 Evaluation, Dissemination, Sustainability
- Ex. 9 Qualifications Section
- Ex. 10 Budget
- Ex. 11 Front and Back Matter
- Ex. 12 Review Panel Evaluation
  In-class Composition: Reflection Essays

Summative Assessment
End-of-Term Portfolio: Grant Proposal Document and Grant Proposal Development Notebook
Oral Presentation: Grant Proposal Software Presentation

Value-Added Assessment
Pre/Post Test: Take a course-specific pre- and post-tests to assess the ways in which learning has increased during the semester. This will be a multiple-choice test based on relevant grant writing principles from the course textbook.

This syllabus also includes required course materials and policies on revision, writing conferences, attendance, disruptive behavior, late work, plagiarism, disability statement, title IX, and resources for writing assistance.

Calendar (This class schedule is for 3-hour sessions that meets once a week.)

Recommended textbook: Johnson-Sheehan, R. (2008). *Writing proposals* (2nd ed.). New York, NY: Pearson Longman.

Week 1

Introduction to the course. Discuss Chapter 1: Introduction to Proposals and Grants. Service Learning Contract and Student-Community Partner Agreement Contract. Possible proposal projects and nonprofit organizations. Non-profit organization guest panel.

Week 2

Pre-Test. Grant Proposal Development Notebook instructions. Service-Learning Contract and Student-Community Partner Agreement Contract. Discuss Chapter 3. Review a sample Grant Proposal Document. Share each proposal idea—

how is it related to the organization's long- and short-term goals? Introduce Ex. 1: Strategic Planning Exercise and sample. Start answering Exercise 1.

Week 3

Submit Ex.1: Strategic Planning Exercise. Share learning points from doing this exercise. Discuss Chapter 4. Introduce Ex. 2.1: Current Situation Section and sample. Start Ex. 2.1: Current Situation Section.

Week 4

Ex. 2.2: Peer review of Current Situation Section. In-class revisions.

> Revision Tip: Improve your Current Situation Section by adding verifiable facts and statistics to enhance the scope and justification of your project. Review source integration and proper documentation format.

Introduce Ex. 3: Report on Funding Sources and sample. In-class workshop: Using your Current Situation's keywords, start looking for at least two (2) different types of funding sources—government, foundation, or corporate source. Discuss Chapter 2.

Week 5

Discuss and submit Ex. 2.1 Current Situation Section materials and Ex. 3: Report on Funding Sources (2 different types). Discuss Chapter 5. Introduce Ex. 4: Objectives Worksheet, Ex. 5: Mapping and Outlining the Solution exercise, and Ex. 6: WHY Table Exercise. Insert SMARTE criteria to objectives. Start working on these prewriting exercises.

Week 6

Discuss prewriting exercises in class. Introduce Ex. 7.1: Project Plan Section and start working on it.

> Note: From hereon, be sure to keep revising each section of the Grant Proposal Document returned based on teacher feedback. ☺

Week 7

Ex. 7.2: Peer review of Project Plan Section. Discuss and work on Gantt Charts. In-class revisions.

> Revision Tip: Improve your Project Plan Section by adding a Project Timeline using a Gantt Chart. Introduce and discuss

Ex.8: Evaluation, Dissemination, and Sustainability Sections with sample based on reading assignment from Mikelonis, Betsinger & Kampf (2004). Start drafting on Evaluation, Dissemination, and Sustainability Sections. In-class Composition: Midterm Reflections. Progress report: Share working relationship with your chosen non-profit organization.

Week 8

Discuss and submit Ex. 7.1: Project Plan Section (with Project Timeline/Gantt Chart) materials and prewriting exercises 6, 5, and 4. Peer review of Evaluation, Dissemination, and Sustainability Sections. In-class revisions.

> Revision Tip: Improve your Project Plan Section by adding some steps and/or tasks derived from your Evaluation and Dissemination Sections. These items are important and have budget considerations.

Introduce Ex. 9.1: Strengths and Weaknesses Worksheet and start working on it. Discuss Chapter 6.

Week 9

Discuss and submit your Ex.8: Evaluation, Dissemination, and Sustainability Sections. Work with partners and peer-review Ex. 9.1 Strengths and Weaknesses Worksheet. Introduce Ex. 9.2: Qualifications Section and start working on it.

Week 10

Ex. 9.3: Peer review of Qualifications Section. In-class revisions. Discuss and examine the Proposal Sections → Important: Prewrite ideas for your Introduction c/o Six Moves in p. 121 and Conclusion c/o Five Moves in p. 125 sections (we will continue with this draft-in-progress next meeting). Discuss Chapter 7. Introduce Ex. 10.1: Expanded Project Plan Summary and Budget Chart, examine a sample, and start working on it.

Week 11

Discuss and submit Ex. 9.2: Qualifications Section and Ex. 9.1: Strengths and Weaknesses Worksheet materials. In-class Workshop: Grab another writing team and help each other read and interpret each sponsor's guidelines. Discuss Ex 10.1 Expanded Project Plan Summary and Budget Chart in class. Discuss Chapter 8. Introduce and discuss sample models of Ex. 10.2: Budget Section with Budget Table and Budget Narrative. Revisit Proposal Sections c/o Chapter 7; keep working on your ideas for your Introduction c/o Six Moves in p. 121 and Conclusion c/o Five Moves in p. 125.

Week 12

Peer review of Ex. 10.2 Budget Section with Budget Table and Budget Narrative. In-class revisions. Discuss Chapter 12. Review Grant Proposal Document content (see sample). Introduce Ex. 11.1: Appendices (BACK), Ex. 11.2: Transmittal letter and Executive Summary (FRONT), and Ex 11.3: Cover Page and Table of Contents (FRONT). Start working on your Front and Back Matter exercises. Discuss Chapter 11.

> Note: Insert at least three (3) graphics in your Grant Proposal Document (e.g., Gantt Chart, Budget Table, and Budget Narrative Table).

Week 13

Discuss and submit your Ex. 10.2: Budget Section with Budget Table and Budget Narrative and Ex. 10.1: Expanded Project Plan Summary and Budget Chart. In-class revisions and mini-conferences on Front and Back materials. Discuss Chapter 11.

Week 14

Discuss Ex. 10.2: Budget Section with Budget Table and Budget Narrative and Ex. 10.1: Expanded Project Plan Summary and Budget Chart. Incorporate any comments into your Grant Proposal Document. In-class revisions and mini-conferences.

Week 15 *Note Extended Office Hours for Conferences*

Submit one rough draft copy of your complete Grant Proposal Document (with Introduction and Conclusion). Introduce Exercise 12: Review Panel Evaluation.

> Note: Use the form provided to you to review one another's proposals. Take your time and do a good job. The reviewers' evaluation sheets will be collected, and you will be graded on the thoroughness and effectiveness of your review. When done, discuss your reviews with one another and turn in reviewer's evaluation sheets to your instructor.

Grant Proposal Development Notebook checklist of materials. Oral Presentation sign-up sheet. Guest panel discussion: Tips from successful grant proposal writers.

Week 16

Final Exam Prep (Narrative Self-Reflection Essay and Post-Test). Debrief. Discuss what to do if the sponsor says "Yes," and what to do if the sponsor says

"No." In-class Composition: End-of-Term Reflections. Submit one copy of your Grant Proposal Document final draft and Grant Proposal Development Notebook. Oral Presentations.

Finals Week

Final Exam with Post-Test and Narrative Self-Reflection Essay.
Note: Grant Proposal Documents and Grant Proposal Development Notebooks will be returned after the exam. Based on teacher feedback, each student will revise the grant proposal and submit the draft to his/her respective community partner to comply with the Student-Community Partner Agreement.

APPENDIX B: STUDENT—COMMUNITY PARTNER AGREEMENT

The practice of service learning relies upon communication, mutual respect, and shared learning among students, faculty, community partner staff and the broader community. This agreement is a statement of common expectations.

Student Name: _____
Phone: _____
Email: _____
Community Partner/Non-Profit Organization: _____
_____
Supervisor or Contact Person Name: _____
Phone: _____
Email: _____

Service-Learning Agreement and Commitment

Dixie State University students agree to the following:

- Maintain professional behavior and demeanor at all times.
- Maintain confidentiality of agency clients at all times.
- Maintain contact with organization supervisors as needed to request for pertinent information on selected assignments that lead to the composition of the grant proposal (cf. course content and due dates below).
- Maintain academic honesty when drafting other sections of the proposal.
- Submit a copy of the revised grant proposal document to the organization at the end of the semester.

The Supervisor or Contact Person agrees to facilitate student involvement and learning in the following ways:

- Provide an orientation of the organization's mission and goals.
- Assist students as needed by providing pertinent information on selected assignments that lead to the composition of the grant proposal (cf. course content and due dates below).
- Allow students to work on other sections of the proposal on their own to develop their grant writing skills. Note that writing the grant proposal or proposal sections for students is considered cheating and will not be tolerated.
- Understand that students are still in the process of learning how to write a grant proposal for a grade; not assisting them with pertinent organization information for selected assignments will jeopardize their learning and success on the course.

Student Signature: _____
Date: _____
Supervisor/Contact Person Signature: _____
Date: _____
Faculty Signature: _____
Date: _____

Assignments with Due Dates that Need Information from Non-Profit Organizations:

Exercise 1. Strategic Planning Exercise → ***

Exercise 9.1 Strengths and Weaknesses Worksheet (to identify strengths and weaknesses of organization and possible competitors) → ***

Exercise 9.2 Qualifications Section (to show why your organization is uniquely qualified to handle the needs of the funding source) → *rough draft and final draft* ***

Exercise 10.1 Expanded Project Plan Summary and Budget Chart → ***

Exercise 10.2 Budget <u>and</u> Budget Narrative → *rough draft and final draft* ***

Exercise 11.1 Appendices → ***

Note: All other exercises are dependent on each student's grant writing skills. Grant proposals and/or proposal sections written by community partners are not allowed. (Note added appendices at https://florenb07.wixsite.com/bacabac femschaplinks)

CHAPTER 23.
MAKING THE POLITICAL PERSONAL AGAIN: STRATEGIES FOR ADDRESSING STUDENT RESISTANCE TO FEMINIST INTERVENTION

Julie Myatt Barger
Middle Tennessee State University

The author proposes that mentoring students who resist identifying as feminists even when they agree with the movement's tenets requires strategies that promote recognition of the diversity of women's lived experiences and contemplation about what motivated their responses to the opportunities granted or denied them by the cultural practices of their time. This literature class case study draws from the work of Rhetoric, Composition, and Literacy (RCL) scholars to present a framework for introducing students to the need for feminist interventions prior to involving them in community activism.

Students often possess misconceptions about feminism and resist identifying as feminists even when they agree with the movement's tenets. Mentoring these students requires strategies that promote recognition of the diversity of women's lived experiences and contemplation about what motivated women's responses to the opportunities granted or denied them by the cultural practices of their time. The following class case study presents my decision to highlight exclusionary practices and subsequent feminist interventions to introduce the concept of activism to students for whom social action may seem irrelevant. I propose that in order to develop feminist rhetors and future activists and align feminism with community engagement beyond academic borders, feminist pedagogues must help students recognize the need for social action, the responsibility of the self to her community, and the consequences of failing to engage. This proposal is grounded in the belief that one's course design can function as an early feminist intervention, one that debunks myths surrounding feminism and encourages students to cultivate the kind of critical engagement that leads feminists to effect change, thus welcoming students into the feminist community.

ON WELCOMING STUDENTS INTO THE (FEMINIST) FOLD: A REFLECTIVE OVERVIEW

I first taught Confronting HIStory: Narratives of Female Identity and Experience, a sophomore-level special topics literature course (developed with the support of a grant from my university President's Commission on the Status of Women) in Spring 2014. I teach at a large, comprehensive doctoral-granting institution in the Southeast with a substantial population of first-generation college students, and this class is the third and final general education English course required of all students, following two first-year composition courses. Students can choose from the standard course, The Experience of Literature, or from a diverse list of special topics sections. Though students enrolling in Confronting HIStory were aware of its theme, their reasons for choosing it varied; some did so because they like history, others because of the title's reference to female identity, still others simply because the meeting time was convenient. The class consisted of twenty-one women and four men; fourteen of the students identify as European American, ten as African American, and one as Latino. Students ranged in age from twenty to thirty-three and represented fifteen different majors. Four were new transfer students, and twelve were first-generation college students.

I was particularly aware of the four males in the class; in keeping with feminist ideals, I wanted our class to attend to issues of inequality affecting all groups denied power by the patriarchal order that structures our lives: this was not just a class about women's struggles for equality. Together, we would explore racial injustice, heteronormativity, and various other issues of concern to students. I was motivated to create this course because the readings had been meaningful to me personally, because I believed that many students would benefit from exposure to a different account of feminism than they had encountered previously, and because I wanted students' reflections on their own life experiences to prompt the recognition that social change is not just part of our nation's history but remains necessary even now. My impression of today's students is that they, admittedly much like my own generation, are on the whole less civically engaged than their predecessors. I don't mean to imply that this is true of all university students, and I acknowledge that a variety of factors contribute, including the changing nature of activism thanks to Web 2.0 technologies, as well as what the Pew Research Center's (2014) report on "Millennials in Adulthood" characterizes as "the timeless confidence of youth." I suppose this trait could just as easily lead to meaningful social action as complacency, and yet, significantly, another Pew Research Center report on Millennials from 2010 characterizes Millennials' "satisfaction over the state of the nation" as a "generation gap," for though "in recent decades the young have always tended to be a bit more upbeat than their elders on this key measure . . . the gap is wider now than it has been in at least twenty years. Some 41% of Millennials say they are satisfied with the way things are going in the country, compared with just 26% of those ages 30 and older." One might wonder what accounts for this; perhaps the young people of today feel less need for revolution because of the advances made by previous generations, but worth noting is that the Pew Research Center's (2013) report on "Civic Engagement in the Digital Era" asserts that "Education and income, more so than age, influence people's political involvement," with those from less educated and less wealthy classes playing less of a role in political life online.

Those who are less learned and less well off may have neither the time nor the inclination to engage in political activism; as a result, their concerns may remain unaddressed, further marginalizing them. The university where I teach has a large population of first-generation college students, many of whom are students of color from low socio-economic backgrounds who work long hours in addition to taking classes. That was certainly the case for students in the Spring 2014 course, nearly half of whom were themselves first-generation students. Instructors at our university tend to view this sophomore-level literature course as our last chance to help students cultivate a love of literature—a worthy goal, to be sure, but because of my desire to encourage students to take part in ongoing cultural debates, I also wanted the course to present literary texts as contributions to important cultural conversations, and so I set out to design a course that would motivate students to reflect on their own experiences and consider how they, like the historical figures and fictional characters we would encounter, could use writing to interrogate and challenge existing beliefs and practices (see Appendix A for the course syllabus).

As a feminist Rhetoric, Composition, and Literacy (RCL) scholar, I considered this course design (see Table 23.1) an important opportunity to mentor students in recognizing that the political is indeed personal, influencing their lives and futures, and thus must be engaged. I recognize in this pedagogy an impetus similar to that espoused by Royster and Kirsch (2012) when they explain that the new analytical model they present in *Feminist Rhetorical Practices* is not an attempt to limit avenues of inquiry or pedagogical approaches but rather to "embrace a set of values and perspectives . . . that honors the particular traditions of the subjects of study [or, in my case, students], respects their communities, amplifies their voices, and clarifies their visions, thus bringing evidence of our rhetorical past more dynamically into the present and creating the potential, even with contemporary research subjects, for a more dialectical and reciprocal intellectual engagement" (p. 14). This course design sought to connect with students in meaningful ways by helping them recognize the value feminist principles and writing hold for their own lives, thus promoting dialogue and increased engagement.

Table 23.1. Course structure

Unit 1: Recognizing Erasures and Silences called attention to the ways women have been silenced or excluded from full participation in the societal power structures that influence their lives. Among other texts, this unit featured Butler's (1979/2003) science-fiction novel *Kindred*, in which Dana, an African American woman living in 1970s California is transported to the antebellum South and charged with saving the life of a slave owner who will become her ancestor. As she moves between these two different worlds, Dana experiences life as a slave and comes to understand history's lasting impact, a theme we discussed throughout the semester. This unit concluded with consideration of how one's subject position influences the options available to her and reflection on the difficulties associated with challenging patriarchal power structures.

Unit 2: Understanding Feminism as an Unspoken Presence began with a screening of Episode 1 of the (2013) documentary film *Makers: Women Who Make America*, a text that reveals the presence of feminist ideals even during a historical moment when women were largely relegated to the domestic realm. The film portrays the birth of second-wave feminism through the personal accounts of individual women resisting established societal practices excluding them from the professional arena. Naslund's (2003) *Four Spirits* is set in 1960s Alabama during the Civil Rights Movement; its main character, European American college student Stella Silver, is a fictional counterpart to many of the women profiled in *Makers,* as she, like her African American contemporaries who also factor prominently in the novel, must find her way in a changing and often dangerous world. Lee's (2010) documentary *4 Little Girls* further brought this tumultuous time in history to life for students. The second unit encouraged students to consider not only what is gained but also what can be lost in the struggle for equality.

Unit 3: Striving for Inclusion and Equality for Women continued to draw from *Makers* but highlighted existing threats to equality as depicted in Atwood's (1985/1999) dystopian novel *The Handmaid's Tale* as well as in recent news stories surrounding reproductive justice.

Unit 4: Disrupting and Critiquing Hegemonic Narratives found us exploring narratives that challenge the patriarchal order, such as Mullen's poetry collection *Muse & Drudge*, which confronts cultural narratives about African American women, femininity, and beauty, and Bechdel's (2006/2007) graphic novel *Fun Home: a Tragicomic*, which traces the author's relationship with her gay father and her growing self-awareness through references to her childhood diary entries. These texts explicitly address the silences and erasures that we considered initially, and they illustrate how one text can respond to others, calling accepted narratives into question while allowing for other, more nuanced, understandings of identity.

THEORIZING THE COURSE AS A FEMINIST INTERVENTION

When considering how to structure the course, I turned to Ritchie and Boardman's (1999) critical historical survey of feminism in composition. I acknowledge that using Ritchie and Boardman's exploration of feminism's presence in the discipline of composition to frame a literature course may seem odd, but as a compositionist teaching a literature course, I recognized that the course texts I had chosen functioned similarly to the publications and personal accounts Ritchie and Boardman cite, as each in its own way "sought inclusion and equality for women," illustrated feminism as a "'subterranean' unspoken presence," and resulted in "disruption and critique of hegemonic narratives" (p. 587), what has elsewhere been described as the three Rs: rescue, recovery, and (re)inscription (Royster and Kirsch, p. 132). From the beginning, I envisioned the course as much a feminist intervention as a literature course, thanks to its inquiry-based, reflective nature.

A primary course objective was to introduce students to accounts of how others have found our world wanting and have endeavored to improve it; I wanted to provide students with literary and historical examples of this so that they could begin to recognize how they can use feminist principles to intervene in their own lives. As a result, I knew I needed to be especially thoughtful about how I approached course themes, and I felt an obligation to introduce students to concepts associated with feminist rhetorical work, including the notion that writing is, as Micciche (2010) asserts, "essential to feminist projects, particularly for those that critique oppressive practices and discourses, articulate strategies for change and collective action, identify and describe how rituals of the ordinary are, in actuality, problems, and generally depict the expansive multiplicity of women's and others' realities" (p. 173). Given my audience of undergraduate students either unfamiliar with—or, perhaps more often, possessing misconceptions about—the history and purposes of feminist movements, I felt it necessary to add one additional category to our course outline: "recognizing silences and erasures" so that students would understand *why* the historical figures and fictional characters we would encounter considered social action necessary. This framework gradually introduced students to feminist principles, first through attending to the inequalities motivating women to pursue social change and then by considering what was involved in their efforts to challenge accepted practices that marginalized them and others.

ADOPTING PEDAGOGICAL PRACTICES THAT ALLOW FOR AND NEGOTIATE RESISTANCE

Early on, I identified collaboration as a crucial course component, knowing that collaboration fosters community while exposing students to different perspectives and conveying that they are both responsible for and capable of contributing to the class's shared knowledge (Daniels and Bizar, 1998, p. 11). Establishing a supportive classroom community was particularly essential given the personal nature of students' final projects, discussed in detail in the following section. For the Collaborative Connection Presentation, teams created a critical analysis or public response to a historical event, recent news story, or issue of importance to women (students either selected topics from a list I provided or proposed their own). The research students conducted for these projects educated them about injustices that persist to this day while exposing them to the work of contemporary change agents. This project allowed students to understand feminism as a collective endeavor, as they worked together to craft responses to issues of interest to them, much in the way that feminist activists do when determining how best to respond to oppressive social practices and public policies.

The most effective presentations had a clear purpose and addressed a specific audience, such as the group that set out to persuade a toy company whose products and marketing were based on gender stereotypes that this practice failed to take children's diverse interests into account and could inhibit the company's sales. Where these presentations fell flat in some cases was in connecting with an audience, often because the audience or purpose were ill defined even after the groups received feedback on their presentation proposals. The group working with the topic "reproductive rights" not only called for an end to legal abortion, they included disturbingly graphic images to support their position. This example illustrates both the challenges associated with helping students recognize the value of feminist methods of inquiry and of overcoming what is, in many cases, students' limited experience using writing to solve real-world problems by addressing authentic, context-specific audiences (rather than writing for one's teacher or for a test evaluator to meet a school requirement).

I confess that I found this presentation troubling for a variety of reasons. Even now, I remain conflicted about how I handled this situation. As a result, I believe this example warrants extended consideration here for what it illustrates about mentoring students who resist feminist principles. My discomfort with this presentation resulted in part from the concern that even after nearly an entire semester discussing feminist principles, this group's interpretation of the assignment promoted misconceptions about feminism. I was similarly frustrated by the group's apparent lack of concern for their audience's personal relationship to the topic and how viewers might react to what some would characterize as disturbing images and offensive statements. Looking back, I'm fairly certain I filled the uncomfortable silence that followed this presentation by making suggestions for what the group could have done differently. Instead, I should have given the class more time to gather their thoughts before responding; I should have allowed the community that had developed over the course of the semester to let the group see the presentation from their perspective(s). I should have embraced the silence, no matter how uncomfortable it may have been, so that I, too, could have seen this presentation through eyes other than my own.

Upon further reflection, I realize that the group's argument that abortion should be illegal could be considered a feminist interruption within my planned intervention. It made me pause and reconsider this assignment; it made me ask myself whether there is room within this classroom for students to make an argument against legal abortion; it made me wonder what characterizes the best response to this kind of resistance. It also leaves me convinced that students need more mentoring, more support, and more practice contributing to the ongoing cultural conversations that affect their lives. To that end, in the future, I would reframe this topic as "reproductive justice" and would model my own connection project for the class using this topic in an effort to help students understand the complexities of communicating with diverse audiences about divisive issues. Additionally, I would schedule more time for peer feedback throughout the composing process, including dress rehearsals, so presenters could gauge how effectively their text, images, and oral comments are connecting with the intended audience, achieving their stated purpose, and responding to the exigencies informing their project. I would allow students more practice addressing an audience of their peers, for, as this example illustrates, that is also an important part of the mentoring that students receive in the feminist classroom.

Yet another possible course revision that could make this project more meaningful, further reinforcing the idea that social change is still necessary would be designating the course an Experiential Learning section requiring a beyond-the-classroom experience. The connection project could grow out of students' work conducting primary research into the following organizations, among others:

- The June Anderson Women's Center;
- MT Lambda LGBT+ student organization;
- Great Books in Middle Tennessee Prisons program;
- Local domestic violence shelters.

This change would allow students to see firsthand how existing inequalities affect life in the local university and community context, encouraging a better understanding of how these practices are the product of systemic, not individual, problems. This sort of primary research would also help students understand that activism grows out of relationships, much as the students cited in Bower's course design do. Such a realization could make activism more meaningful for students, potentially resulting in it becoming, as it does for Bowers' students, "simply part of how they live in the world."

MAKING THE POLITICAL PERSONAL BY VALUING STUDENTS' EXPERIENCES AND INVITING CRITICAL ANALYSIS

The most successful aspect of the class came when students were given the opportunity to link class themes to their own life experiences. Through this practice, teaching as a form of feminist mentoring effectively repaired the broken relationship between the political and the personal, helping students recognize the value of political action. Ritchie and Boardman propose that "narratives of experience should be encountered not as uncontested truth but as catalysts for further analysis of the conditions that shape experience" (p. 588). The (Re)Writing Your History Creative Project (Appendix B) invited students to examine their own experiences as evidence of the need for critical intervention in today's world. Students composed narratives representative of their own experiences in the genre of their choice, along with a composer's commentary—inspired in part by Shipka's (2005) "heads-up statement"—explaining the rationale informing their genre/design choices while also making explicit the class themes and cultural beliefs, values, and practices their project addressed.

By writing about their own experiences not in isolation but in conversation with course themes and texts, students recognized experience as valuable, using it to support both their assessments of the past and their proposals for how the future could be different—and better. In a fitting and inspiring end to the semester, students shared their creative projects with the classmates who had served as their intellectual and emotional support system throughout the writing process. A number of them had written letters: to single mothers, thanking them for their sacrifices; to employers, calling attention to gender discrimination in the workplace; one even wrote to herself, promising to finish college and thus make the women who preceded her in the quest for gender equality proud. Two wrote and illustrated comic books, one on escaping an abusive relationship and another on rediscovering her self-confidence through neo-burlesque. Several composed poems: on how families reinforce societal expectations for masculinity; on the policing of female sexuality; on how being born a black male is the equivalent of two automatic strikes. One student, in an effort to protect her decision to work outside the home, created a marriage contract outlining her expectations for herself and her future partner. Yet another presented a speech modeled after Truth's (1851) "Ain't I a Woman?" in which she commented on how others' expectations for her to comply with traditional gender roles have served as obstacles to her own personal life goals.

This project confirmed the importance of having students read literary works not in isolation but by considering their relevance to their own lives. As Gallagher (2015) argues, "If we teach students to think only inside the four corners of the text, we are telling them what not to think. And when we tell students what they cannot think, oppression and hegemony occur" (51). Not only were students' presentations incredibly moving, they demonstrated that writing, as a feminist intervention, could effectively disrupt the influence of societal structures in their own lives that had hurt them or held them back. Inviting students to engage in this critical self-reflection allowed them both to reconsider their previous associations with the nature and purpose of contemporary feminism and to recognize aspects of their own lives that would benefit from revisions to current cultural beliefs, values, and/or practices. These projects confirmed that writing *can* change the world. Whether by traveling back through time to address a past injustice or by charting a course for one's future self that is more expansive than the well-traveled paths of patriarchy, these students conducted critical analyses and envisioned alternate outcomes.

By completing this creative project, they engaged in play of the sort Micciche describes as "involving performance, critical engagement with texts, considerable rhetorical skills, audience awareness, capacity to negotiate voice and tone, and an understanding of social relations—pragmatic, rhetorical knowledge, in other words." Micciche does not stop there; importantly, she continues, "In addition, though, play entails wonder, curiosity, idealism, hyperbole, and imaginative leaps—an expansive horizon that purposefully exceeds predetermined limits" (p. 182). This is some serious play. It allows students to look critically at the power structures that define, order, and limit our lives. Encouraging curiosity and leaps of imagination may not seem like radical pedagogy, but it is one very significant way feminist rhetors can mentor students and encourage future social action. Whether or not any of these students now consider themselves feminists I do not know, but I am quite certain that they possess a better understanding of feminist action, the need for social change, and the role writing can play in promoting change than they did prior to this class. In that regard, this course succeeded in meeting its objective of introducing students to accounts of what brought others to write the world they want to live in into being, so that students could recognize how to use writing and feminist principles to effect change in their own lives.

PURPOSEFULLY EXCEEDING THE LIMITS OF THE PAST BY FOREGROUNDING RHETORIC AND READING

Raymond (2008) asks, "What happens when a literature course gets delivered through writing pedagogy?" (476). The Confronting HIStory course owed much to the field of (RCL), and were I to teach the course again, I would draw even more heavily from my own RCL expertise, explicitly introducing rhetorical principles from the beginning so students would approach each text we read with questions about exigencies, audience, and purpose, questions every writer must learn to address. Inviting students to ask these questions recasts course readings as mentor texts students can model their own writings from; ultimately, they will consider how to use the knowledge they gain from course texts to make their own lives better. By promoting this kind of critical intervention in their own lives, I hope to convey to students that they, like the feminist activists we studied, possess the ability to use writing to improve the world, both now and in the future.

To that end, in future iterations of the course I would, following Fredlund's example of having students analyze activist rhetoric before creating their own, incorporate additional reading instruction so that students could more thoroughly consider the choices writers make when working toward social change. This would involve, among other practices, coupling nonfiction texts, such as suffragettes' speeches or those from the Civil Rights Era, with the directive to "read like a writer" in the way Bunn (2011) describes when he suggests "trying to figure out how the text you are reading was constructed so that you learn how to 'build' one for yourself" (p. 74). As a feminist rhetor and composition instructor, I consider the practice of introducing students to the concept of writing as social action an essential form of mentoring. Helping students recognize that our world is still in need of change is not enough; we must also provide them with a flexible rhetorical education that will allow them to address the needs of a future we cannot yet even imagine. After all, helping students recognize that our world is still in need of change will not accomplish much if we do not also help them acquire the tools needed to build a better world.

REFERENCES

Atwood, M. (1999). *The handmaid's tale*. Toronto, Canada: McClelland & Stewart. (Original work published 1985).

Bechdel, A. (2007). *Fun home: A family tragicomic*. Boston, MA: Mariner Books. (Original work published 2006).

Bunn, M. (2011). How to read like a writer. In C. Lowe & P. Zemliansky (Eds.), *Writing spaces: Readings on writing: Vol. 2* (pp. 71–86). Anderson, SC: Parlor Press.

Butler, O. (2003). *Kindred*. Boston, MA: Beacon Press. (Original work published 1979).

Daniels, H. & Bizar, M. (1998). *Methods that matter*. Portland, ME: Stenhouse.

Gallagher, K. (2015). *In the best interest of students: Staying true to what works in the ELA classroom*. Portland, ME: Stenhouse.

Goodman, B., Wagner P. M., Ephron, J. (Producers). (2013). *Makers: Women who make America* [Motion picture]. United States: Kundhardt McGee Productions, Storyville Films, and WETA Washington DC.

Lee, S. (Producer) & Lee, S. (Director). (2010). *4 little girls* [Motion picture]. United States: Home Box Office.

Micciche, L. (2010). Writing as feminist rhetorical theory." In E. Schell and K.J. Rawson (Eds.), *Rhetorica in motion: Feminist rhetorical methods & methodologies* (pp. 173–188). Pittsburgh, PA: University of Pittsburgh Press.

Mullen. H. (1995). *Muse and drudge.* San Diego, CA: Singing Horse Press.

Naslund, S. J. (2003). *Four spirits.* New York, NY: Perennial.

Pew Research Center. Civic engagement in the digital age. (2013). Retrieved from http://www.pewinternet.org/2013/04/25/civic-engagement-in-the-digital age/.

Pew Research Center. Millennials: Confident. connected. open to change. (2012). Retrieved from http://www.pewsocialtrends.org/2010/02/24/millennials-confident-connected-open-to-change/.

Pew Research Center. Millennials in adulthood: Detached from institutions, networked with friends (2014). Retrieved from http://www.pewsocialtrends.org/2014/03/07/millennials-in-adulthood/.

Raymond, R.C. (2008). When writing professors teach literature: Shaping questions, finding answers, effecting change. *College Composition and Communication, 59*(3), 473–502.

Ritchie, J. & Boardman, K. (1999). Feminism in composition: Inclusion, metonymy, and disruption. *College composition and communication, 50*(4), 585–606.

Royster, J. J. & Kirsch, G. E. (2012). *Feminist rhetorical practices: New horizons for rhetoric, composition, and literacy studies.* Carbondale, IL: Southern Illinois University Press.

Shipka, J. (2005). A multimodal task-based framework for composing. *College Composition and Communication, 57*(2), 277–306.

Truth, S. (1851). Ain't I a woman? Speech delivered at the Women's Rights Convention. Akron, Ohio. Retrieved from http://www.nps.gov/wori/learn/historyculture/sojourner-truth.htm.

APPENDIX A: ABBREVIATED COURSE SYLLABUS

English 2020: Confronting HIStory: Stories of Female Identity & Experience
Students will read a variety of texts situated in different eras and cultural settings, thus encouraging contemplation of the significance of specific moments in (and even outside of) history for female identity. By representing women of different eras, races, classes, and sexual orientations, assigned texts will promote recognition of the diversity of women's lived experiences along with contemplation about what motivates women's responses to the opportunities granted or denied them by accepted practices of their time and place. Additionally, students will encounter diverse genres, including nonfiction accounts, historical novels, and poetry collections, as well as science fiction novels, graphic novels, and films.

A course drawing from such diverse genres and perspectives has potential to engage students in considering not only the importance of history in our lives but also the value of challenging accepted practices that reify patriarchal power structures.

Required Texts:
- Atwood, Margaret. The Handmaid's Tale, 1985 (novel)
- Bechdel, Alison. Fun Home: A Family Tragicomic, 2007 (graphic memoir)
- Butler, Octavia. Kindred, 1979 (science fiction novel)
- 4 Little Girls (documentary film to be screened in class)
- Makers: Women Who Make America (documentary film to be screened in class)
- Naslund, Sena Jeter. Four Spirits, 2003 (novel)

Please note: some of the texts we read may contain content you consider explicit; though you are required to complete all assigned readings and complete informal written responses, you always have a choice in what you write about for major projects.

Overview of Student Work:

Participation—15%
Reflects written and oral participation in informal responses and class discussion, preparation for class, and completion of project drafts.

Short Analysis Essay—20%
Students will conduct a close textual analysis of one course text (3–4 pages).

Comparison Essay—25%
Students will conduct a sustained analysis of two course texts (5–6 pages).

Collaborative Connection Presentation—20%
Students will work in groups to conduct a critical analysis/public response to a historical event, recent news story, on issue of importance to women (a list of approved topics will be provided by the instructor). The presentation must draw connections between the event and course themes and/or texts.

(Re)Writing Your History Creative Project—20%
Students will compose narratives representative of their own experiences in the genre of their choice by creating their own short stories, scripts, graphic stories, poems, etc., to be submitted along with their own composer's commentary that makes explicit the class themes and cultural beliefs, values, and practices their project addresses.

APPENDIX B: (RE)WRITING YOUR HISTORY CREATIVE PROJECT

Brief Description

For this final project of the semester, you are to work individually to compose narratives representative of your own experiences pertaining to course themes. Your narrative will be composed in the genre of your choice: short story, script for a short play, graphic story, poem, etc.

Just as writers such as Harryette Mullen and Alison Bechdel employ elements of autobiography to challenge dominant cultural narratives, with this assignment you have the opportunity to use your own life experiences to speak back to cultural narratives you find troubling, restrictive, or even oppressive. In the act of writing about your personal history, you may very well revise history by calling attention to problems that exist in our society and then by envisioning how your experience could have been different. Your work also has the opportunity to affect the future by challenging dominant ideologies and practices meant to preserve patriarchy, keep women or those labeled "other" in line and out of sight, etc. Regardless of the experience and genre you choose, your project should reveal your knowledge of course themes and your ability to link them to your own life experiences.

Questions for Consideration

These are intended to help you generate topic ideas; you are not meant to answer every question in your project.

- Did a certain character's experiences resonate with you? Why? What from your life resembles something we read about?
- When was a time you were silenced or excluded from full participation in the societal power structures that influence your life?
- How does your subject position influence the options available to you?
- Have you ever tried to challenge patriarchal power structures?
- Have you ever felt as though you were losing something in your search for equality?
- What are your thoughts on cultural beliefs and practices that seem to dictate how you should perform gender, enact your sexuality, etc.?
- How do you think our understanding of what it is to be a man or woman in today's world needs to be complicated or expanded?
- How do you understand your place in the world? Do others see it the same as you do?
- What identities would you like to be available to you that may not be at present? What is preventing this from becoming a reality?

Composer's Commentary

In addition to the project itself, you will be required to complete a 1-page Composer's Commentary that introduces your project to its intended audience; explains how it addresses course themes as well as cultural beliefs, values, and practices; introduces the rationale informing your genre/design choices; and articulates your goals for the project so that reader/viewers will understand what you want them to take away from this text.

CHAPTER 24.

"BECAUSE YOUR HEART BREAKS AND IT MOVES TO ACTION": DIGITAL STORYTELLING BEYOND THE GATE

Stephanie Bower
University of Southern California

I describe an upper-division composition course my colleague John Murray and I have developed that explores new means and ends of activism. Our course opens up the gates, literally and figuratively, to create collaborations with community groups premised upon digital storytelling, a vehicle that equalizes the footing between town and gown and shifts cultural and material capital from the university to the community. Drawing upon feminist methodologies that seek to disrupt hierarchies of knowledge, we invoke a more explicitly activist framework by producing and disseminating alternative stories from groups usually stereotyped or ignored. Activism in our view takes on different possibilities when we move students into the community, the community into the campus, and ultimately the voices of the marginalized and the powerless into the public sphere.

A little more than forty years ago, Adrienne Rich characterized the university as a "hierarchy built on exploitation," "a breeding ground not of humanism but of masculine privilege." She wondered whether such a "man-centered" institution could "become a force and magnet for a 'female counter-force,'" whether "this male-created, male-dominated structure is really capable of serving the humanism and freedom it professes." And she suggested how the university might transform itself to accomplish those goals through a radical reorientation of its purpose and practice. In her ideal reckoning, even the boundaries of the university become porous, so that "instead of the familiar city on-a-hill frowning down on its neighbors, or the wrought-iron gates by which town and gown have traditionally defined their relationship," the university "would serve the needs of the human, visible community in which it sits," organizing its "resources around problems specific to the community."

Now, forty years later, those goals seem both closer at hand and as elusive as ever. Due in no small part to the institutionalization of feminism and service learning within the academy, universities increasingly offer courses and programs that have shifted focus to the communities outside their gates. Too often, however, such programs reify the hierarchies Rich sought to undo. Feminist scholars, for example, have critiqued how the discourse of civic engagement is "rooted in a neutral and universalizing language that reinscribes forms of democracy and citizenship that erase difference, conceal power, and perpetuate social injustice" (Costa & Leong, 2013, p. 171). The university's ability to do good while doing well contributes to the skepticism about the way service-learning programs have become embedded within the neo-liberal corporatization of higher education (Mathieu, 2005).

In this essay, I describe an upper-division composition course my colleague John Murray and I have developed that draws inspiration from Rich's imagined reorientation of the university's relationship with its neighbors. Our course opens up the gates, literally and figuratively, to create collaborations with community groups premised upon digital storytelling, a vehicle that equalizes the footing between town and gown and shifts cultural and material capital from the university to the community. Drawing upon feminist rhetorical practices that seek to disrupt hierarchies of knowledge, we invoke a more explicitly activist framework by producing and disseminating alternative stories from groups usually stereotyped or ignored (Royster & Kirsch, 2012). After eight years of teaching the course, we have found the results both more and less than we originally intended: less dependent on the material resources of the university with the evolution of DIY technology; and more dependent on the simple yet transformative acts of listening. Activism in our view takes on different possibilities when we move students into the community, the community into the campus, and ultimately the voices of the marginalized and the invisible into the public sphere.

Nine years ago, when we first proposed introducing a service-learning component into an upper-division composition course, we drew inspiration from scholars and teachers in composition and feminist studies who recognized that many service learning programs continued to be permeated with assumptions of unexamined privilege. With this recognition emerged a shift in focus from inside the gates to out as projects took shape from relationships formed with community groups, moving from a model of service to one of engagement and reciprocity. What matters for scholars such as Parks (2010), Goldblatt (2007), Matheiu (2005), Bickford and Reynolds (2002) and Cushman (2010) is not raised consciousness or some vague rhetoric of empowerment, but reshaping our collective notion of "common sense" and using this revised understanding to bring about action in the interests of a more just social order. Similarly, the feminist rhetorical practices delineated by Royster and Kirsch provide tools of inquiry to help us conceptualize both the processes and the products of our collaborations, particularly their definition of "critical imagination" as a "mechanism for seeing the noticed and the unnoticed, rethinking what is there and not there, and speculating about what could be there instead" (p. 20) as well as an attention to an "ethics of hope and care" (p. 145) that permeates every component of our course. Royster and Kirsch also point to the possibilities contained within "the intersection of genre, technology, and rhetorical agency" (p. 65) that can "invite democracy quite boldly into the public sphere" (p. 67) by using multimodal texts to give disenfranchised communities a voice.

Influenced by these scholars, we wondered how the tools of digital storytelling might work as a form of alternative literacy, one that would offer a more equal platform for students and community partners. The Digital Archive of Literacy Narratives provides one touchstone for this type of project, since it too uses digital media to disseminate stories that would otherwise not find an audience. Another inspiration comes from the principles of "participant produced media," and in particular, its intersection with feminist epistemologies, to realize the activist praxis that generated the course itself (McIntyre and Lykes, 2004). What distinguishes this approach is a commitment for those in the university to step out of the way, to speak "alongside" rather than "for" or "about." For feminist filmmakers and scholars committed to social justice, this model renders "relevant forms of local, subjugated knowledge that are typically discounted and drowned out by authoritative and erudite forms of knowledge" (Gubrium, Krause & Jernigan, 2014, p. 320). As Orr notes in the influential white paper, "Women's Studies as Civic Engagement: Research and Recommendations," "Women's Studies strives to tell alternate stories" through a "simultaneity of foci," wide-angle and close up, personal and institutional; so too our approach uses personal images, voices and stories to challenge the meaning-making conventions within dominant discourses.

Our course capitalizes on these points of connection by introducing a participant-produced methodology to a digital storytelling project, itself integrated into a sequence of linked written assignments. Writing 340 is a required upper-division writing course intended to build on the foundations of critical thinking, reading, and writing established in the university's first-year composition course. It is run on disciplinary lines, with sections in "Arts and Humanities," "Social Sciences," etc., designed to give students practice writing in professional, personal and academic contexts. Students typically produce 35 pages of writing, with a portfolio collected at the end of the semester. When we first started the course, almost a decade ago, we created our own section, "Writing in the Community," with the same underlying objectives as other versions, but with an additional emphasis on the way writing can be a powerful tool of social change, not the "busy work" students sometimes associate with the academic writing they've done in previous classes [see Appendix A for the course syllabus]. By partnering students with community groups and giving them real issues and real audiences, we hoped that we would reinvigorate their sense that writing matters and that these texts can make a difference beyond the confines of the classroom. Not coincidentally, our class tends to be more diverse than the typical 340 classroom, with students from the mostly low-income neighborhood surrounding our campus mixing with students from wealthier Orange County and also international students, now a large percentage of USC's student body. Most are traditional students, although because our class offers more autonomy and creativity than other offerings, we also attract returning students.

Inspired by the resurgence of storytelling in venues such as *This American Life* and *The Moth* as well as by Rich's vision of a university open to its neighbors, our course integrates a multimedia assignment where students take the tools of digital and visual literacy beyond the gate to record the stories of community partners—schools, non-profits, advocacy groups and other organizations in the neighborhood around our campus. This final assignment is supported by more traditional assignments designed both to scaffold and to complement the project: a blog giving students the chance to reflect on their experiences beyond the gate; a film review intended to train students in the visual literacy that helps them construct their own videos; a research paper that helps students investigate the broader historical and political context for the issues that emerged within these partnerships; and the final assignment, an op-ed piece that encourages students to take action on the issues explored in their videos and their research papers.

We have found that community partnerships work best when they have time to grow. Like any relationship, trust takes time. Of course, this isn't always possible—community groups often have schedules that make such sustained partnerships difficult if not impossible. But we do our best to arrange students in groups quickly, and then encourage students to reach out to their partners to begin the process together. The first task for these collaborations is to decide upon the purpose and audience of the video. Many groups want to promote the work of their agency; some want to highlight a particular issue relevant to their lives; others simply want to tell their stories to USC students. Working with their partners, students fill out a video planning document that encourages them to think about not just the components of their video (interviews, b-roll, sound) but also the overall purpose and its corresponding ethical and aesthetic challenges [see Appendix B for our video planning document].

For the digital storytelling project, we worked with Edward O'Neill, then a specialist at our campus's Center for Scholarly Technology, to take advantage of how smart phones and editing software have significantly downscaled the level of expertise and equipment needed to make videos. With digital cameras now embedded in most smart phones and iMovie available on many laptops, students already carry around the technology they need for the course. At the beginning of the semester students complete a technology survey about access to and familiarity with a sliding scale of documentary tools, from the very high end video equipment and editing software down to the minimal movie apps available on most smartphones. This information enables us to try to distribute expertise across groups, ensuring that most groups have at least one or two people who have some experience making movies.

Students tend to approach this component of the course with some degree of anxiety—what's video doing in a composition course?—so with O'Neill's guidance, we have embedded the skills needed to complete the final project within the curriculum. We have found that the skills tend to be mutually reinforcing, so the time spent teaching visual literacy and developing assessment criteria for the documentary transfers quite well and naturally to the work students do in more traditional written assignments. In fact, students often are able to understand more clearly the moves involved in writing when they are exposed to them in another genre. For example, a short workshop on creating order within documentaries through patterns of visual images perfectly encapsulates strategies for activating familiar organizational patterns to link ideas together in essays. The evaluative criteria that emerges within these discussions also transfers across genres and privileges from the beginning not just aesthetic criteria—in fact, since students don't have the technical training or equipment, we don't weigh high production values as part of our criteria—but more importantly the ethical and social justice questions that factor into every discussion [see Appendix C for our evaluative rubric]. The democratization of video-making tools has meant too that our community partners now have access to the same technologies, increasing our opportunities to better realize a participant-produced methodology.

The work of the partnerships happens mostly outside the classroom, in living rooms and schools, offices and city streets, prisons and community centers, wherever our students meet their community partners. Within the classroom, we embed video in many of our activities to enhance students' familiarity and ease with the technology, reinforce the evaluative criteria we use to assess these videos, and prepare them for the other written assignments in the class. In the first of several low-stakes multimedia assignments, we ask students to experiment with lighting and sound choices while interviewing partners and gathering ideas for video and research questions. Students practice workflow issues by capturing video, transferring it to their computers, and uploading these short clips to YouTube, and we take a class session to discuss both the ideas that emerge from these clips and the ways that technical choices (lighting, camera angle, shot composition, editing, etc.) inform our understanding of these ideas. By training students to look at their videos through the eyes of their viewers, we alert them to the importance of audience in both visual and textual mediums. Similarly, for the last multimedia assignment we ask them to remix their videos using different arrangements of visual material so that they see how the order of shots determines the meanings available, a lesson that also of course applies to organizational choices within written texts [see Appendix D for the multimedia assignments].

By building partnerships based on reciprocity rather than hierarchy, we embed a feminist methodology within even more traditional composition assignments. For example, our students disrupt the "banking" model of education that grants authority only to those with degrees by using what they learn from their community partners as the source and support for their research paper (Freire, 1970; Giroux, 1988; Webb, Cole, and Skeen, 2007). Students derive research questions from their collaborations with community partners—after school programs, non-profits that serve Latina women and children, transitional housing facilities for former prisoners, etc. By "'starting off thought' from the lives of marginalized peoples," our students begin to expose the assumptions that normalize the status quo (Harding, 1993, p. 445). What happens, for example, when we look at sexual harassment policies through the eyes of the middle-schoolers they affect? How does our understanding of domestic violence change when we hear the voices of Latinas rather than middle-class white women? What do communities think about city-wide injunctions against fast-food restaurants? Students learn to reckon with multiple perspectives on complicated issues, and navigate conflicting ideas of what's wrong and how to fix it. And they learn that the personal can never be detached from the political, that claims to "objectivity" are disingenuous at best since they pretend to an understanding somehow detached from the lives necessarily entangled within histories and ideologies. Once freed from the bogus objectivity they associate with academic discourse, their own voices emerge loud and clear (hooks, 1989).

From such methodology emerges an activist praxis also aligned with feminist pedagogy (Orr, 2011). What we have noticed is that students' understanding of activism shifts during the course of the semester. Similar to the types of student resistance Julie Barger and Katherine Fredlund identify in their course designs (this collection), our students too initially describe activism as "scary," something distant from their own lives, associated with protests and sit-ins located elsewhere, far from their own pursuits. Even the students who self-identify as activists question the value of having activism located within the classroom or within their own everyday passions and paths. As one student put it in an initial blog entry, "perhaps the radical needs to stay radical." By the end of the semester, after partnering with groups committed to the work of bettering their communities, our students have a more complex and nuanced formulation. Some of them locate activism on a continuum with volunteering, with each serving a necessary and important purpose, complementary rather than antithetical. Many describe activism in terms of relationships: spending time with the people affected by otherwise abstract issues gives a deeper understanding of these issues and offers multiple perspectives on its origins and also potential solutions. And relationships build both trust and an emotional investment that generates an intrinsic call to action (Noel, 2011). As one student puts it: "and you are not motivated to act simply on principle, but because your heart breaks, and it moves to action." Activism for many is now woven into their local spaces and activities, simply part of how they live in the world. Michael, a student who worked with a veteran's group, put it this way: "I have gone from someone who wouldn't dare stand out with those 'crazy' guys to being one of the 'crazy' guys standing out there with a sign on Sunday afternoon. They need young guys to carry on the torch of their cause. Bob thinks it should be me. I think it might be."

Towards the end of the semester we invite our community partners to campus, first to give their input on the rough cuts and later for a reception and screening of the final videos, followed by a forum where our partners speak about the videos and the issues they raise. Many of our partners—groups of immigrant women and their children, former prisoners recently released from their prison, former gang members, parent activists, volunteers—have never been inside the gates of the university even though many live within blocks of the campus. Some of the children turn the campus into their playground, skating on the paths and sliding down balustrades. At a recent screening, one of the former prisoners talked about being afraid to enter before he was invited to speak to our students. Opening up the campus to outsiders seems a simple gesture, yet it has profound if subtle implications once we recall the cultural capital symbolically and materially accrued within its gates. Walking inside opens up new possibilities for these marginalized groups, who may not have previously ever envisioned themselves on college campuses, and transforms too the experiences of those accustomed to these spaces by creating a more inclusive community that shifts our vision of who belongs and who does not.

Over the seven years we have offered the course, students have created over two dozen videos which have collectively received over 30,000 views on You-

Tube. And though it's true that for students and community partners the process is far more impactful than the product, it's also true that the videos themselves are transformative in their aesthetics and their ability to imagine and promote social change. Unlike mainstream productions, which often ignore or stereotype marginalized groups, the videos that emerge from these partnerships use a feminist ethos that interrupts and interrogates familiar scripts, calling attention to the silences and disruptions that remind us of the limits of our knowledge. Further, rather than smoothing over the differences between our students and their partners, the videos make these power differentials part of their story and use these moments of discomfort to generate new ways of imagining each other and the world we live in. With their deliberately low-tech production values and with YouTube as a platform for distribution, the videos move outside the university to open up conversations far beyond their original creation [see Appendix E for links to videos from the course and also a short interview with students about its value].

REFERENCES

Bickford, D. & Reynolds, N. (2002). Activism and service-learning: Reframing volunteerism as acts of dissent. *Pedagogy 2*(2), 229–52.

Costa, L. & Leong, K. J. (2013). Critical community engagement: Feminist pedagogy meets civic engagement. *Feminist Teacher 22*(3), 171–180.

Cushman, E. (2010). The rhetorician as an agent of social change. In T. Dean (Ed.), *Writing and community engagement: A critical sourcebook* (pp. 235–254). Boston, MA: Bedford/St. Martin's.

Freire, P. (1970). *Pedagogy of the oppressed.* New York, NY: Continuum.

Giroux, H. (1988). Border Pedagogy in the age of postmodernism. *Journal of Education, 170(3)*, 162–181.

Goldblatt, E. (2007). *Because we live here: Sponsoring literacy beyond the college curriculum.* Cresskill, NJ: Hampton Press.

Gubrium, A. C., Krause, E. L. & Jernigan, K. (2014). Strategic authenticity and voice: New ways of seeing and being seen as young mothers through digital storytelling. *Sexuality Research and Social Policy, 11*(4), 337–47.

Harding, S. (1992). Rethinking standpoint epistemology: What is "strong objectivity?" *The Centennial Review, 36*(3), 437–470. Retrieved from http://www.jstor.org.libproxy1.usc.edu/stable/23739232.

hooks, b. (1989). *Talking back: Thinking feminist, thinking black.* London, England: Sheba.

Mathieu, P. (2005). *Tactics of hope: The public turn in english composition.* Portsmouth, NH: Heinemann.

McIntyre, A. &. Lykes, M.B. (2004). Weaving words and pictures in/through feminist participatory action research. In M. Brydon-Miller, *Traveling companions: Feminist, teaching and active research* (pp. 57–77). Westport, CT: Praeger.

Noel, J. (2011). Striving for authentic community engagement: A process model from urban teacher education. *Journal of Higher Education Outreach and Engagement, 15(1)*, 31–52.

Orr, C. (2011). Women's studies as civic engagement: Research and recommendations. The Teagle Working Group on Women's Studies and Civic Engagement and the National Women's Studies Association.

Parks, S. (2010). *Gravyland: Writing beyond the curriculum in the city of brotherly love.* Syracuse, NY: Syracuse University Press.

Rich, A. (1979) Toward a woman-centered university. In *On lies, secrets, and silence* (pp. 125–157). New York, NY: W.W. Norton, 125–157.

Royster, J. J. & Kirsch, G. (2012). *Feminist Rhetorical Practices: New horizons for rhetoric, composition, and literacy studies.* Carbondale, IL: Southern Illinois University Press.

Webb, P., Cole, K. & Skeen, T. (2007). Feminist social projects: Building bridges between communities and universities. *College English, 69*(3), 238–259.

APPENDIX A: COURSE SYLLABUS

Writing 340: Writing in the Community

Course Description

This Writing 340 class builds on the foundations of critical thinking, reading, and writing established in Writing 140, polishing these skills and augmenting them with an emphasis on the professional, public, and academic aspects of majors and career fields.

This particular course places writing in a real-world context by partnering USC students with community groups to identify local problems and to use rhetorical tools for solving these problems. It is aimed for students interested in writing with and about the community surrounding USC, developing research projects based on community issues and partnering with community organizations to produce multimedia projects designed to reach a public audience.

Course Expectations

This is an alternatively structured course in terms of contexts of learning and design of assignments. Working in teams of 3–5 students, you will be partnering with community groups to develop research proposals and to produce a collaborative multimedia documentary. This will entail multiple visits to these sites over the course of the semester, as well as a considerable amount of time both in class and out learning the basic theory and practice of visual storytelling.

This class takes as its subject and goal learning across difference; this kind of learning can't be simply memorized, regurgitated and forgotten. It involves intellectual honesty and a willingness to ask difficult questions, to recognize when things aren't working, and to think creatively about solutions. We will need each student to take responsibility for the overall success of the course, to let us know if you encounter any difficulties, and to recognize that learning can take place in moments of confusion or frustration and not just in the results.

Because your active engagement is so crucial to your learning, we expect you to attend class regularly, to participate in class discussions, ask questions, share work in progress, and respond thoughtfully to the drafts of others. Note, in particular, that you will be collaborating with classmates and community partners during much of the semester. Others will be relying on you and therefore it is vital that you demonstrate motivation, respect, and accountability during the community projects.

Course Requirements

- Participation/Attendance
- Observation/Reflection Postings

Papers

- Documentary Analysis
- Research Paper
- Take Action Essay
- Final Project

Research Paper

Using input from your community partners, you will define a problem from the local community and use the tools of the academy as well as community perspectives to deepen our understanding of the problem and to map out potential solutions. This will entail: initial meetings with community groups to define relevant issues; developing research strategies to locate sources and generating an annotated bibliography; conducting interviews with community groups to get multiple perspectives on these issues; writing a 10–12 page paper reflecting your research and your conclusions. Although your community research will be conducted in groups, each student will write his or her own paper. (20%)

Take Action Essay

In this assignment you will use your expertise to get involved in a public debate on the issue. You will first identify where debate over the issue takes place (radio? Newspapers? Blogs? Editorials? Books? Public forums?), then use the tenets of good rhetoric to write a compelling argument that makes a call for social action regarding the community issue/s you have examined. (5%)

You will revise two of these essays for a final portfolio due on the last day of class. (25%)

Final Project

For the final project in this class, students will produce a five minute documentary-style multimedia presentation of a social issue relevant to their research projects. The goal here is to use innovative approaches to explore the unique perspectives and voices of community members to make the issues come alive for a broad public audience. Students will post these final projects on YouTube to invite comment from community groups. Final projects will be evaluated on three main criteria: 1) how well the design of the project incorporates community perspectives as agents rather than as subjects 2) how well the film addresses the relevant issue and 3) how the form of the film works to support the content. (20%)

These projects will be produced in teams of 4–5, working in collaboration with community groups. To give you the help, practice, tools, encouragement and advice in all the components of visual storytelling, we are integrating several multimedia assignments, workshops and labs into the class. (5%).

APPENDIX B: VIDEO PLANNING DOCUMENT

How might you plan, shoot, edit and organize your work to achieve a specific ethical and rhetorical goal?
(Created by Edward O'Neill)

Whose story are you trying to tell?	
What challenges & pitfalls reside in bringing this topic to an audience?	
What kinds of footage can you get? E.g., observation, interviews, b-roll, music?	

What formal strategies might you use? E.g., how can you weave together continuing actions, implied arguments, audiovisual patterns?	
What sound and lighting obstacles might you face? How might you adjust your shooting?	
What breakdown of labor or roles do you plan to use?	

APPENDIX C: EVALUATIVE RUBRICS

(Created by Edward O'Neill)

The course aims to enable students to move fluidly amongst three categories.

Argument Elements	Essay Parts	Documentary Elements & Parts
Provides a context, situation or problem. Makes a claim. Provides supporting evidence. Attributes all sources clearly. Presents or anticipates & refutes counter-claims. Tells relevant stories. Balances appeals by ethos, logos, pathos. Makes a call to action.	An introduction previews or hooks. A topic is clear to the reader. A body contains clear sub-topics, previews, transitions & recaps. A conclusion provides a new perspective rather than merely summarizing.	Elements: • interviews • observation • on-screen titles • b-roll Parts: • an intro & outro • segments • alternation/cross-cutting

Where am I in the process of producing a polished documentary from footage?

A progressive roadmap

Starting Out	The students have edited the interview footage down to a manageable size.
	The students have intercut different types of footage or sequenced chunks to make a larger pattern.
Intermediate	The rough cut sets up a problem, situation or context for the viewer.
	The rough cut gives the viewer relevant information to make an informed judgment.
	The filmmakers have integrated b-roll footage somewhat.
Finalizing	The filmmakers have integrated b-roll footage artfully.
	The filmmakers have adjusted the color and sound with care.

Some Evaluative Criteria: Ethical Reflection, Argumentation, Form & Style

How does the video treat its subjects?	How does the video treat the viewer?
distorts their identities and views,	provides little information, background or context
exploits for emotional or other purposes,	pushes the viewer to a single point of view,
fails to capture them as rounded human beings,	provides the viewer with the information needed to make a judgment,
represents them fully but not indulgently.	provides multiple points of view and allows the viewer to decide.

How effective is the video as an argument?	How effective is the video as form and style?
topic/argument	message
lacks a clear focus,	no message
has a topic or focus more than an argument or claim,	unclear or mixed message
makes a clear argument	simple, clear message
offers multiple viewpoints and balances them gracefully	complex message
	unity
evidence	has extraneous parts
offers some evidence,	the parts don't clearly connect
does not identify sources clearly,	forms an integrated whole
supports its claims with evidence,	style
provides rich, contextualized evidence.	not coordinated, unclear purpose
	simple but effective
appeals	polished and stylish
does not use ethos, logos and pathos,	
emphasizes one to the detriment of the others,	
uses multiple sources of appeal in a sophisticated way.	

APPENDIX D: MULTIMEDIA ASSIGNMENTS

These exercises are designed as scaffolding for the skills you'll need to create your final documentary. By building these in early, we're hoping to accomplish three goals: 1) to build up a sense of familiarity with these tools early on so you won't panic the weekend before the documentary is due 2) to use the technology to enhance the other components of the course and 3) to develop a shared sense of evaluative criteria that we'll use to assess the final documentaries you'll create.

For every assignment, we ask that you use the available technology within your group, and that you post your clips to YouTube 24 hours before our course. (Follow YouTube instructions for how to upload, then copy the link to our discussion board in Blackboard.) Most of these are group assignments, meaning that each group will post one clip. Please make time to view all the clips before class.

Remember, too, these are designed to get your hands wet with these tools so that you'll develop a sense of familiarity and expertise when you create your final documentary. The most important thing is to master all the steps, not create a masterpiece. Get them in on time and you'll have fulfilled the assignment. (5% of your grade for the class.)

1. Interview strategies. Due 2/19 (24 hours before class) on YouTube.

Goal: to experiment with different techniques for producing quality sound and image. Interview people at your site about possible research/documentary ideas by recording three short (under one minute) unedited video segments using available camera and/or audio equipment and manipulating the following variables:

- Position camera closer or farther depending on the subject's speaking voice
- If possible, experiment using a separate audio recording device rather than one inside your camera.
- Interview outside using direct sunlight
- Interview inside using florescent light

2. Short rough cuts. Due 3/12 (24 hours before class) on YouTube

Goal: to see how your footage plays for an audience so that you can learn how to internalize these responses. Post two minutes of footage from your documentary. What's interesting?

3. VERY rough cuts. Due 4/14 IN CLASS.

Goal: to get suggestions for revising your documentary to better meet your audience's expectations.

APPENDIX E: LINKS TO VIDEOS

Through Glass: https://vimeo.com/93339925

One Hundred Universes: https://www.youtube.com/watch?v=RJwgyd-VWYo&list=PLjhYGo2R1FpKXEaRTaABViVCZbqaWpdbg&index=7

Twenty Years Later: Commemorating the Gang Truce in Los Angeles: https://www.youtube.com/watch?v=Kurb6r6MamQ&list=PLC7A89FDFA05DE3E5&index=5

Is USC a College with a Conscience? https://www.youtube.com/watch?v=6BKfHRxKM2g

Students Talk about the Course: https://www.youtube.com/watch?v=hvJTl7t8RNk

CHAPTER 25.

FEMINIST ACTIVISM IN THE CORE: STUDENT ACTIVISM IN THEORY AND PRACTICE

Katherine Fredlund
University of Memphis

Fredlund writes on her experience teaching Student Activism in Theory and Practice, a senior-level, writing-intensive general education course. Enrolling 45 students from majors all over campus, Fredlund's students collaborated with their community partner to plan and organize the University's annual Take Back The Night event. In her reflection, Fredlund explains how instructors can negotiate student resistance to the terms "feminist" and "activist" while asking the same students to participate in explicitly feminist activism. She emphasizes how engaging with a community partner alleviates some of the tension inherent in requiring feminist activism in general education courses while simultaneously providing instructors an opportunity to teach students about rhetorical effectiveness and civic purposefulness.

INTRODUCING THE COURSE

Student Activism in Theory and Practice is a senior-level and writing-intensive general education course that fulfills a requirement for graduation at Indiana State University (ISU). The course enrolls 45 students and welcomes students from a variety of disciplines across campus, meeting once a week for three hours. While some students may be enrolled in our Gender Studies minor, most students enter the class with little knowledge of either activism or feminism. Despite this lack of initial knowledge, the course's culminating experience asks students to organize our University's annual Take Back The Night (TBTN) event in collaboration with our community partner (a local domestic violence shelter). The course is offered every Fall semester, and TBTN occurs once a year in November.

Immediately following the resource fair, the students hold a rally (in 2014 over 500 people attended the event) that intends to increase awareness of problems of gendered violence both on campus and in our community while also empowering survivors and their supporters. The event ends with a lengthy march throughout campus (seen in Figure 25.2) that aims to disrupt the normally quiet evenings by chanting and holding signs that remind those who did not attend the event that gendered violence continues to be an issue. Throughout the event, students sell t-shirts, collect material donations, and hope to raise money for a community partner that helped them understand the importance of this issue throughout the semester. The course aims to teach students to solve problems, evaluate the ideas of others, express themselves effectively both orally and in writing, and demonstrate the skills for effective citizenship. A full list of the course's learning outcomes can be found in the "Syllabus" section below.

Figure 25.1. The Resource Fair before Take Back The Night 2014.

CREATING AND ANALYZING ACTIVIST RHETORICS

Due to the variety of majors enrolled in the course, we begin with a brief introduction to feminism before turning to our two primary subjects of study: student activism and gendered violence. Like Julie Myatt (Chapter 23, this collection), I often find that while many students agree with the general tenets of feminism, they resist labeling themselves with the term. As a result, I introduce feminism as a conceptual term with Chimamanda Ngozi Adichie's *We Should All Be Feminists*. I have found that this book speaks to students because it is accessible, and they recognize the author's name from Beyonce's 2014 VMA performance. My community partner then helps students see feminism as an operational term by discussing their everyday work and the importance of supporting survivors of gendered violence. This combination of reading and seeing feminism helps students understand both the ideas behind feminism and the work of feminism.

Throughout the course, students are challenged to reconsider their beliefs about activism and gendered violence through readings, discussions, and guest speakers. Class periods are often discussion based. The written assignments are designed to help students build their rhetorical abilities. Just as Julie Nelson's students face a new writing genre (Wikipedia writing), my students are unfamiliar with activist rhetoric, and we, too, begin with rhetorical analysis. Their first assignment asks them to analyze a specific example of activist rhetoric. Next students are asked to create activist rhetorics of their own through two different assignments. For one assignment, they are split into eight work groups that will collaboratively organize TBTN. These groups have different tasks that range from obtaining permits to creating promotional videos to coordinating with community organizations.

The second assignment asks students to create their own project for change (DIY Activist Rhetoric). For this project, students are asked to consider our Community Partner's needs as well as the needs of Take Back The Night. In consultation with their teacher, students develop proposals for this project, and as long as the project produces activist rhetoric and supports either TBTN or our Community Partner, it will be approved. In the past, students have written and then performed Slam Poetry at the Rally, developed an awareness campaign about the services our Community Partner offers, created informational brochures at our community partner's request, developed PSAs for our Community Partner to be played on the campus radio station, and composed videos to be played during the resource fair. This project asks students to identify and then respond to a rhetorical situation while also writing for our community partner. As one student explained, "Our group had to write and perform a slam poem, which was a positive experience. When writing the poem and other parts of the program, it was important to remember who the audience was and what the intention of each part was; that sort of guided how we composed each separate part." Students can work alone or collaborate for their DIY Activist Project. All of this experience creating activist rhetorics is not enough to ensure students have "Demonstrated the skills for effective citizenship and stewardship." In order to meet that learning outcome, reflection is necessary. In Florence Bacabac's discussion of her grant writing course (Chapter 22, this collection), she notes the importance of student reflection within courses that require civic engagement. Recognizing reflection as an essential aspect of feminist intervention, the final writing assignment asks students to compose a reflection that synthesizes their experiences (organizing TBTN, working with our community partner, and composing activist rhetorics) with the course readings.

Feminist interventions seek to create change in the University and beyond. In this course, a number of different feminist interventions take place. First, I challenge my students to think beyond their preconceived (and often negative) notions about feminism and activism. Next, we work together to change the way gendered violence is discussed on campus through our production of TBTN. Additionally, we work with our community partner to create a stronger relationship between the partner and the University, increasing our partner's visibility and their ability to reach both students and community members who could benefit from their services. Finally, like Stephanie Bower's course (Chapter 24, this collection), we work to make the invisible visible—providing survivors of gendered violence with a public space where they can use their voices and (sometimes finally) be heard.

Figure 25.2. Students and other attendees march through campus after the TBTN Rally.

LEARNING ABOUT ACTIVIST WORK

Since the University where I teach is located in a conservative area, many of my students enter the course with very negative opinions about activism. In a survey distributed after the course was completed, 100% of the students who responded claimed they either didn't know anything about activism or had negative opinions about activism when the course began. In a follow-up question that asked how students felt about activism before and after the course, one student explained,

> [Activism] made me a little nervous, honestly. I was a little more critical of protests than I am now. I felt like I would never personally engage in something like a sit-in or major protest. [Now] I have a much more positive outlook. I understand more about the logistics of activism, what kind of activism best suits what types of situations, and so on . . . Now, I feel like I would definitely participate in a sit-in, given the right cause.

Our work with our community partner teaches students lessons about activism that they couldn't learn from the readings. The same student explained, "Doing the hands-on work for [our community partner] is eye-opening. It connects real people to real situations and also shows that there is more to helping others than just talking about it—it takes a lot of grunt work." The combination of readings by activists (found below in the syllabus) and working for an activist community partner helps students learn not only about the important work that activists do but also about the kind of work that happens behind the scenes. Because the organization of the event takes so much time and work, the readings are front-loaded, allowing class time to be devoted to the planning and organization of TBTN as we get closer to the event.

Through a combination of course readings, class discussions, written assignments, interactions with our community partner, and the organization of TBTN, this course aims to introduce students to feminism, activism, gendered violence, and rhetoric. I use feminist pedagogy to challenge my students to question their assumptions and beliefs. As I explain to them, I don't expect them to leave my course as activists or feminists, but I do expect that they leave the course knowing what feminism and activism are and what feminists and activists do. As Susan Jarratt (2001) explains, feminist pedagogy "is not about forcing all the students to subscribe to a particular political position but rather engaging with students on the terrain of language in the gendered world we all currently inhabit" (p. 118). Students are asked to collaborate with each other, with their community partner, with a variety of campus and community organizations, and with their teacher. They are asked to take part in feminist interventions by producing rhetoric intended to prompt change and awareness. This is an unsurprisingly messy process, but feminism, activism, and writing are all messy too. Ultimately, students leave the course knowing that they composed activist rhetorics, organized an event that reached hundreds of students and community members, connected many different campus and community organizations, raised money for our community partner, and helped raise awareness of gendered violence through their collaborative production of an activist event.

REFLECTIONS

I have found Jacqueline Jones Royster and Gesa E. Kirsch's principle of an "ethics of care and hope" as a useful way to think about how I approach this course. While they discuss this principle in terms of research, this course has taught me that it is also a useful way to think about feminist pedagogy. They explain:

> An ethics of hope and care requires a commitment to be open, flexible, welcoming, patient, introspective, and reflective. It requires looking and looking again, reading and returning to texts, learning about the contexts of those who

> use rhetorical strategies under conditions that may be very
> different from our own. It is learning to withhold judgment,
> to linger, to observe, and notice what is there and what is
> missing. It is an attitude, a stance, an inclination to discover
> new well-embodied truths and to revise old truths. (146)

Approaching the classroom with an ethics of care and hope helps me engage in conversations about gendered violence with my students with patience and empathy. It reminds me that I do not know the experiences that have led them to my classroom, and I do not have the right to judge their complicated relationships with the course content. Instead, I approach their statements and their writing as Royster and Kirsch suggest we approach a text: by "[assuming] a more patient, receptive, quiet stance . . . to think about it—slowly, rather than to make a more aggressive stance in order to 'do something to' it as a mechanism for arriving at and accrediting its meaning" (146). This ethics of care and hope gives my students the respect they deserve and creates a classroom environment where students feel safe sharing both their opinions and their experiences.

In this course, I use feminist pedagogy as intervention in order to create change in my University community and often in my students' lives. At the 2015 TBTN, 9 students from the course chose to stand on stage as stories they wrote about their experiences with sexual assault, rape, and domestic violence were read to the crowd by other classmates. After all of their stories were read, all 9 students returned to the stage, ripped off the pink tape that had been placed in an X over their mouths, threw the tape on the stage, grabbed each other's hands, and looked at the audience as they said the words "Silent No More" in unison. The host group came up with this idea, but they, like me, were shocked and excited when so many students wanted to stand in front of hundreds of people and have their stories told—often for the first time.

While I approach this course with a feminist pedagogy that intends to intervene in my University Community by creating a student-centered vision of TBTN, my students are the ones who make the lasting impact with their own feminist interventions. I carefully select the course readings and guest speakers in order to help my students see the important work feminists do in our community and elsewhere, but what they do with their newfound knowledge about feminism is what creates a lasting impact. They design the event with my guidance, and this makes the event speak to the University's students in a way that events run by faculty and staff simply cannot. Often for the first time, students from across the University hear how gendered violence impacts people they know. Both times I taught this course, students from my other classes approached me after the event to note that they had no idea that their friend had survived gendered violence and that hearing their story was both inspiring and educational. Learning about the topic from other students and friends at TBTN inspires and educates students from across the University. My own feminist intervention only ensures that student voices and ideas become the heart of the event. It is their voices and ideas that then create a lasting impact, and whether students consider themselves feminists or not doesn't seem to matter because for at least one semester they are committed to combating gendered violence through collaboration, education, and rhetorical production.

REFERENCES

Adiche, C. N. (2015). *We should all be feminists*. New York, NY: Anchor Books.
Carry That Weight. (2015). Why a mattress and a pillow? And who is Emma Sulkowicz. Retrieved from http://www.carryingtheweighttogether.com/.
Gould, J. E. (2011). A sleepy campus in crisis: Pepper spray at UC Davis sparks online uproar, calls for a chancellor's resignation. Retrieved from http://time.com.
hooks, b. (2000). *Feminism is for everybody: Passionate politics*. Brooklyn, NY: South End Press.
Jarratt, S. (2001) Feminist pedagogy. In G. Tate, A. Rupiper & K. Schick (Eds.), *A guide to composition pedagogies*. New York, NY: Oxford University Press.
Kilmartin, C. & Allison, J. (2007). *Men's violence against women: Theory, research, and activism*. Mahwah, NJ: Psychology Press.
Krakauer, J. (2015). Missoula: *Rape and the justice system in a college town*. New York, NY: Doubleday.
Lorde, A. (2007). *Sister outsider: Essays and speeches*. New York, NY: Crossing Press.
Malone, N. & Demme, A. (2015). "I'm no longer afraid": 35 women tell their stories bout being assaulted by Bill Cosby, and the culture that wouldn't listen. *New York Magazine*. Retrieved from http://nymag.com.
Maule, L. (2010) NARRATIVE WS 450: Student activism in theory and practice. Retrieved from http://www2.indstate.edu/fs/approvedCourses.htm.
Orley, E. (2010). The next chapter: MSA president Chris Armstrong works to re-define his presidency after Andrew Shirvell. *The Michigan Daily*. Retrieved from http://www.michigandaily.com/.
Pason, A. (2011). Reclaiming activism for students. In S. Kahn and J. Lee (Eds.), *Activism and rhetoric: Theories and contexts for political engagement*. (pp. 190–197). New York, NY: Routledge.
Royster, J. J. &Kirsch, G. E. (2012). *Feminist rhetorical practices: New horizons for rhetoric, composition, and literacy studies*. Carbondale, IL: Southern Illinois UP.
Take Back The Night. (2014). Retrieved from http://takebackthenight.org/.
Udwin, L. (Producer and Director). (2015). *India's Daughter* [Motion Picture]. United Kingdom: Berta Film.
Zinn, H. (2002). *You can't be neutral on a moving train: A personal history of our times*. Boston, MA: Beacon.

APPENDIX A: COURSE SYLLABUS

Course Description

We will begin the course by introducing both feminism and activism and then by discussing a variety of student activist movements—considering how activists use rhetoric both effectively and ineffectively. We will then learn about gendered violence both locally (through our community partnership) and more globally (through a variety of readings and documentaries). During the first half of the semester, we will spend a lot of time learning about activism, feminism, and gendered violence through readings, visits from our community partner, guest speakers, and class discussions. The second half of the semester will be devoted to our collaborative organization of Take Back The Night. The culminating experience of this course asks students to work with their instructor, community partner, and campus community in order to organize our University's annual Take Back the Night Rally and March. The written assignments in this course will ask you to analyze activist rhetoric, create activist rhetoric, and then reflect on your experiences as an organizer of Take Back The Night.

Learning Outcomes

- Locate, critically read, and evaluate information to solve problems
- Critically evaluate the ideas of others
- Apply knowledge and skills within and across the fundamental ways of knowing
- Demonstrate the skills for effective citizenship and stewardship
- Demonstrate an understanding of diverse cultures within and across societies
- Demonstrate an understanding of the ethical implications of decisions and actions
- Express yourself effectively, professionally, and persuasively both orally and in writing (Maule 2010)

Required Texts

Adiche, Chimamanda Ngozi. (2015). *We should all be feminists*. New York, NY: Anchor Books.

hooks, bell. (2000). *Feminism is for everybody: Passionate politics*. Brooklyn, NY: South End Press.

Krakauer, Jon. (2015). *Missoula: Rape and the justice system in a college town*. New York, NY: Doubleday.

Zinn, Howard. (2002). *You can't be neutral on a moving train: A personal history of our times*. Boston, MA: Beacon.

Assignments

Activist Analysis: In class, we will discuss a variety of instances of student activism, read a professor's autobiography about his activism with his students, and watch documentaries about student activism. In order to understand how activism works (and doesn't work), this assignment will ask you to choose ONE student activist movement or specific event and analyze the rhetorical tactics that made this event or movement successful or unsuccessful. In order to complete this assignment successfully, you will need to first summarize the event or movement. Next you will explain the variety of rhetorical tactics the event used, and finally, you will analyze how these rhetorical tactics made the event or movement effective or ineffective. This paper will be 3–4 pages and will make up 20% of your final grade.

DIY Activist Rhetoric: In this course, we will work with a community partner and put on a large campus event. As a student in the course, you will be asked to respond to one or both of those rhetorical situations. Through consultation with your instructor, you will design your own assignment. You can create a printed document or a new media project. You can work alone, or you can work with others. You will be required to get your plan approved by your instructor. In the past, students have written and then performed slam poetry at the TBTN rally; created educational pamphlets about gendered violence to be distributed at the resource fair; developed an educational exercise to be presented at the Rally; met with our community partner to learn about their needs and then created educational documents for them; and created a website for TBTN at our University. This assignment gives you the freedom to choose what you will create for this course. The only requirements are that you create a document or new media project that will be posted or distributed publicly, that the project is for TBTN or our community partner, and that you meet with your instructor to get this project approved. This project is worth 30% of your final grade.

Organization of Take Back The Night: This class will put on TBTN for the University. For TBTN, the class will be divided into eight student groups. Students will be placed in groups based on a discussion we have as a class and an individual survey that asks about your preferences when working with others. Each student group will have a different responsibility during the organization of the event. This assignment will make up 20% of your grade. 10% of that grade will be decided by the teacher. The other 10% will be decided by the members of your group. These will be anonymous and will judge your contribution to the group. The groups are as follows:

1. Hosts and Coordinators: This group will organize and host the Rally. You will make decisions about the content of the Rally and coordinate with speakers and other participants.
2. March Organizers: This group will design the March route, research and create chants for the March, and work with University Police to obtain the appropriate permits.
3. T-Shirts: This group will create multiple t-shirt designs, present those designs to the class for a vote, price options from a variety of local t-shirt makers, and work with the cheapest t-shirt maker to get the shirts made. After all of this is completed, you will sell the t-shirts the week of TBTN.
4. Materials: This group will create posters, pamphlets, programs, and other promotional materials at the request of other groups. You will need to create promotional documents that can be shared digitally and printed.
5. Video: This group will create two videos. One will be a promotional video to be shared with campus before the event. The other will be educational and played either during the resource fair or the rally.
6. Promotion: This group's main goal is to get people to our event. You should work with campus organizations and student groups (particularly sororities, fraternities, and student athletes) as well as teachers and administrators. You should develop a pitch that you can give when you go to speak with classes and student organizations.
7. Fundraising: This group will raise money to help us put on the event. We will need enough money to buy t-shirts and materials for the event, and we want to raise money that we can donate to our community partner as well. This group should begin fundraising early in the semester.
8. Resource Fair and Drive: This group will coordinate with our community partner as well as other campus and community groups in order to develop a resource fair that takes place before the Rally and March. This fair should provide attendees with information about a variety of organizations that actively seek to either support survivors of gendered violence or stop gendered violence. You will also work closely with our community partner to learn about their needs and hold a drive that collects donations of food and other resources.

TBTN Reflection: While your participation in the planning of the event will be graded, you will also be asked to critically reflect on your experiences planning and attending TBTN and working with our community partner. This reflection should consider what you learned about activism and community engagement through your participation in TBTN and your DIY Activist Rhetoric Project.

You can discuss both your successes and failures. This reflection should be a minimum of 3 pages and is worth 10% of your final grade.

Reading Quizzes: In order to ensure students are doing the reading in the course, reading quizzes will be given randomly. These readings are essential to your ability to write the larger assignments for the course. These quizzes will be worth 10% of your final grade.

Class Participation: Class Participation (speaking in class, actively engaging in the material, etc.) will be worth 10% of your final grade, as your participation in discussions on the reading and the preparation of TBTN will be essential to this course's success.

Course Schedule

The below course schedule is organized by weeks and includes readings, class activities, and due dates. All readings should be completed before class on the day they are listed. After Week 5, students are expected to be working with their groups to plan TBTN both in and outside of class. After the first week, students are invited to send me news stories or other current events that connect to our course for discussion at the beginning of each class.

Week 1: Course Introduction

- Discussion of Syllabus and Take Back The Night.
- Introduction to our Community Partner: a representative from the Organization will come to class to discuss what they do in our local community and what we can do as a class to help them.
- Read Audre Lorde's "The Transformation of Silence into Language and Action" in class. After completing the reading, students should spend 5–10 minutes responding to the following questions in writing:
  - What (not who) are you willing to die for?
  - What are you afraid of?
  - What have you been silent about?

Week 2: Introducing Activism and Feminism

- Read "Reclaiming Activism for Students" by Amy Pason.
- Read *We Should All Be Feminists* by Chimamanda Ngozi Adichie.
- Class discussion of readings.
- Guest Speaker: Hearing from an Intimate-Partner Violence Survivor.

Week 3: Student Activism

- Read *You Can't be Neutral on a Moving Train* "Introduction," Chapters 1–7.

- Read about student activism and response at UC Davis (Silent Protest), Columbia (Carry That Weight and Emma Sulkowicz), and the University of Michigan (the first openly Gay student President).
- Class discussion of readings.

Week 4: Activism and Hope

- Finish reading *You Can't be Neutral on a Moving Train*.
- Activist Analysis Assignment Discussion.
- In groups, students will investigate and analyze an activist movement or event of their choosing.
- Class discussion about collaboration and organizing TBTN.
- Students complete questionnaire about work preferences for TBTN groups.

Week 5: Gendered Violence on Campus

- Read Parts One, Two, and Three from Jon Krakauer's *Missoula: Rape and The Justice System in a College Town*.
- Class discussion of reading and sexual assault on college campuses.
- During this session, students will be placed into groups for TBTN, and each group will meet during class to begin to discuss their group's plans for their part of the organization. (From here on out, each class will devote at least 30 minutes to TBTN. Students should expect 30 minutes at the end of class to meet with their group, coordinate with other groups, and propose ideas to the entire class during this time.)

Week 6: Student Survivors

- Activist Analysis DUE.
- Finish reading *Missoula*.
- Sexual Assault Survivors and Supporters (SASS) will come to class and help us discuss Missoula and gendered violence on campus.
- Discussion of DIY Activism Assignment.

Week 7: Feminism is for Everybody

- Read selections from bell hook's *Feminism is for Everybody*.
- Read "Cosby: The Women. An Unwelcome Sisterhood."
- Visit from Community Partner: During this visit, students should plan to discuss ideas for their DIY Activism assignment with the community partner. Idea need to be approved by your instructor (via email) by noon on Monday.

Week 8: Inventing Take Back The Night

- Read "What is Take Back the Night."
- During this class period, we will look at a variety of different ways TBTN has been put on both at our University and other Universities in the past. We will look at these as examples and begin to troubleshoot as a class about the elements we want to include in our own event.
- For the second half of class, students will be in their TBTN groups working on their part of TBTN. During this time, students will meet with the instructor individually in order to discuss plans for the DIY Activism Assignment.

Week 9: Understanding Intimate Partner Violence

- Read PDF: "Understanding Gender-based Violence" By Christopher Kilmartin and Julie Allison.
- Discussion of reading and the "Cycle of Violence."
- While we have worked with our community partner throughout the semester, the first half of this class period will be devoted to helping us better understand the complexities of gender-based violence. Our Community Partner will visit class once again, so if you have more questions for our partner about TBTN or your DIY Activism project, then this is the time to present those questions.
- Watch India's Daughter.

Week 10: Organizing TBTN

- Each group should come to class prepared to present their plans for TBTN to the class. The class will provide feedback on how to improve or revise your plans. During this class period, groups that need to coordinate with one another should also do so.
- Our Community partner will visit today. All students need to bring a rough draft of your DIY Activism project.
- If you are writing for our partner, then you will meet with them to discuss your draft. If you are writing for TBTN, then the host group and instructor will meet with you to discuss your draft.
- Students will also fill out a mid-project feedback form for the rest of their group. This form is intended to help you improve your collaborations anonymously.

Week 11: Writing Workshop

- TBTN is 3 weeks away!

- All students should bring a revised draft of the DIY Activist Rhetoric project to class. We will workshop these projects in groups. The groups will be organized by the instructor and divided by project type.
- The Materials Group should bring posters, markers, etc. to class, and each member of the class will make a sign to carry at the march and Rally.

Week 12: Planning TBTN
- TBTN is only two weeks away!
- This class session will be devoted to group work, allowing students to work in their groups or on their DIY Activism projects. Group work should be put first, but if there is nothing you can do in class, then you can use the time for your DIY Activism projects.

Week 13: Dress Rehearsal
- TBTN is one week away!
- DIY Activist Rhetoric project is DUE!
- During this class period, we will finalize our arrangements for TBTN, have a dress rehearsal, and set a schedule for the following week of preparations.

Week 14: TAKE BACK THE NIGHT
- Meet in Event Room at 4 pm. All students must be present for set-up, the event, and clean-up.
- All students will work with their group and the class to put on a great event!

Week 15: Reflecting on TBTN
- During this class we will discuss how TBTN went, consider how it could have gone better, and brainstorm ways to improve TBTN as a way to combat gendered violence.
- Each student will also evaluate their peers' contributions to their group's role in TBTN using the Peer Evaluation Form provided by the instructor.
- Introduction to and discussion of Reflection Assignment.

Week 16: Celebration!
- Reflection Paper Due.
- During this period, our Community Partner will join us, and we will give them the materials we collected for them as well as announce the amount of money we raised. We will celebrate together with a potluck.

CHAPTER 26.

RHETORICAL INTERVENTIONS: A PROJECT DESIGN FOR COMPOSING AND EDITING WIKIPEDIA ARTICLES

Julie D. Nelson
North Carolina Central University

While some scholars have claimed the neutral, unbiased style of Wikipedia writing might be at odds with feminist pedagogies that support experiential knowledge and personal narrative, this project design presents Wikipedia writing to students as a rhetorical challenge. Employing Royster and Kirsch's (2012) four terms of critical engagement from Feminist Rhetorical Practices, *this project narrative describes a sequence of assignments that encourages students to 1) consider how knowledge emerges and is culturally situated; 2) analyze the rhetorical motives and limits of Wikipedia as a community; and 3) practice feminist interventions through the composing and editing of Wikipedia articles.*

When my fall 2015 ENG: 3130 Writing for Social Change class looked at the Wikipedia page for our university chancellor, my students were stunned. Debra Saunders-White, who had an impressive career ranging from IBM to the U.S. Department of Education and who was the first female chancellor at our Historically Black University, had a Wikipedia page with three sentences. Saunders-White's page was scant in comparison with the pages of chancellors and presidents at other local and similarly-sized schools. My students knew her accomplishments rivaled theirs, so why, they asked, was her page so meager? Unfortunately, it is no surprise that an African American woman's Wikipedia page is undeveloped compared to her mostly white and male colleagues' pages, given Wikipedia's well-documented gender gap and its self-acknowledged "systemic bias."

Race and gender disparities in Wikipedia coverage and authorship are disheartening, but they also offer students and teachers valuable opportunities to rectify disparities, by writing for Wikipedia. Teaching wiki writing encourages not just collaboration and complication of the writer-reader relationship (Lundin, 2008; Alexander, 2008; Cummings et al. 2008) but also reconsideration of knowledge production and revision (Cummings, 2009; Purdy, 2009, 2010). When students write and edit Wikipedia articles, they produce and revise knowledge, creating a prime opportunity for feminist intervention in Wikipedia (Vetter & Harrington, 2013; Vetter, 2013). However, some scholars suggest that Wikipedia is not conducive to feminist ways of knowing and writing. Cattapan (2012) and Gruwell (2015) argue that the methodologies valued in Wikipedia and its writing style (specifically the requirement to use a neutral point of view) prohibit students from contributing experiential, embodied, or narrative knowledge.

In this project design, I respond to these concerns and assert that when teachers present writing for Wikipedia as a rhetorical challenge, students learn to push the boundaries of acceptable Wikipedia style and content—making feminist and socially conscious interventions—in rhetorically appropriate ways (see appendices A and B for course and project descriptions). I describe a writing for Wikipedia project assigned in a course called Writing for Social Change, a writing-intensive course whose objective was to study and produce activist and socially-motivated texts. Students enrolled were mostly upper-level English and communication majors who identified as African American and female. While a lot of in-class time was dedicated to the project the first half of the semester, in the latter half, students worked independently on their articles, and class time was devoted to other readings and assignments. Through the stages of this project, students engaged in feminist inquiry and practice by questioning "truth" and who makes knowledge, looking for gaps or underrepresented perspectives, contributing their own knowledge, and writing for a public audience. Similar to Stephanie Bower's digital storytelling project (Chapter 24, this collection), writing for Wikipedia encourages students to engage in community-based research and writing in two important ways: 1) as students go into their communities to find local, valuable, and underrepresented knowledges and 2) as students produce those knowledges and stories to share with (and intervene in) the global Wikipedia community. After outlining some of the potential obstacles for feminist contributions to Wikipedia, I describe the project and its attempts to engage with and overcome these obstacles.

WIKIPEDIA AS A SITE FOR FEMINIST INTERVENTION

Wikipedia, like many encyclopedias, privileges white male, western histories and epistemologies. Sources vary, but most suggest that women make up only 8–16% of editors, and topics more interesting to female audiences are often undeveloped or absent (Wikimedia Foundation, 2011; Lam et al., 2011; Cohen, 2011). According to Lam et al. (2011), the average female editor makes half the number of edits of the average male editor, female editors tend to leave Wikipedia sooner, and articles with mostly female contributors are often more regulated and contentious. While there are no solid statistics on the race and ethnicity of editors, the dearth of articles related to marginalized histories and cultures, in addition to the demographics of the average user, suggests a serious disparity (Smith, 2015). The Wikimedia Foundation, which runs Wikipedia, acknowledges this "systemic bias" and reports that the average user is a young white educated man with internet access ("Wikipedia: Systemic Bias," 2015).

Given these biases, it is no wonder why college instructors assign writing for Wikipedia in their courses, yet some instructors suggest the assignment may work against feminist goals and pedagogies. For example, women's studies professor Alana Cattapan (2012) asked her students to contribute articles related to the women's movement in Canada. While the assignment was largely successful, she lamented, "Students cannot write in their own voices in Wikipedia, and must conform to a model of writing that might not be true to their understanding of an issue, or reflective of their perspectives" (p. 128). Wikipedia articles are required to use a neutral point of view (NPOV), "which means representing fairly, proportionately, and, as far as possible, without bias, all of the significant views that have been published by reliable sources on a topic" ("Wikipedia: Neutral point of view," 2015). This policy prevents students from writing first-person narratives, reflecting on their embodied social positions, or explicitly sharing their perspectives—common feminist values. Leigh Gruwell (2015) echoes these concerns in her study of female Wikipedia editors, suggesting that the "objective" and "encyclopedic" writing style discourages women from contributing. The results of her study suggest "the values of the male-dominated discourse community discount feminist ways of knowing, thus alienating and silencing alternative epistemologies and subjectivities" (p. 120). Many of the practices feminist teachers include in their courses conflict with Wikipedia's guidelines.

However, in addition to these practices, feminist rhetorical scholars encourage using creativity and flexibility to work around/in potentially exclusionary discourses and communities. While NPOV poses some obstacles for making feminist interventions, NPOV and one's own voice are not mutually exclusive. Beyond the inability to use first-person, there are other ways to express one's perspective, for example, through construction of a page (e.g., organization, content, images, and links) and through references (e.g., referencing sources, quotes, and statistics that express one's perspective). Although original research is not an acceptable reference in Wikipedia, finding published texts that support students' perspectives is still a valuable task. Writing in NPOV does not require disregarding or betraying one's beliefs; rather, it may just take more rhetorical work to find ways to express those beliefs. Feminist ways of knowing and writing are expressed in more than just style; publishing a page on a marginalized historical person or revising a page to express an underrepresented point of view is also a feminist intervention.

Cattapan and Gruwell are right that Wikipedia restricts feminist writers in some ways, but we should not overlook other kinds of intervention in the processes preceding publication and writing strategies that push Wikipedia's guidelines in rhetorically appropriate ways. I define feminist interventions on Wikipedia broadly, as revisions or additions of missing or underrepresented knowledge or perspectives, not necessarily written by or about females or explicitly using "feminist." While a final draft of an article may not explicitly reflect feminist views, the process of students analyzing, writing, and contributing to Wikipedia is still valuable feminist rhetorical work. I draw my understanding of this work from Royster and Kirsch's *Feminist Rhetorical Practices* (2012) which identifies four central terms of engagement in feminist rhetoric and composition: strategic contemplation, critical imagination, social circulation, and globalization. The assignments that I designed for this project urge students to engage with these particular terms and practices.

From the very first week of class, students engaged in "strategic contemplation," which Royster and Kirsch explain involves entering into a dialogue with texts, considering multiple perspectives, dealing with contradictions, and recognizing that lived, bodily experiences shape the way we research. After digesting articles and statistics about the biases and gaps on Wikipedia, students began to look for the silences and absences in the Wikipedia articles they read. I asked students to complete an analysis of controversial topic pages to identify the rhetorical strategies used to hold multiple points of view in one place (Appendix C). Through this assignment, students saw how editors inserted their perspectives in articles and identified rhetorical strategies that reflected marginalized perspectives. "Critical imagination" pushes students to find those marginalized perspectives. According to Royster and Kirsch, it is an inquiry tool that urges researchers to look for untold stories, question notions of "truth," and recover important events and stories from the past. To do this work, I took my students to our university's archives to look for potential article topics (Appendix D). This assignment physically immersed students in the research process and challenged them to find ways to share their findings, carefully and ethically. Relatedly, Royster and Kirsch's third term "social circulation" emphasizes the social nature of rhetoric, specifically how language moves, changes, and relates—and how power dynamics are reflected in those relations. To employ this term, my students analyzed the systemic biases of Wikipedia articles that were similar to the ones they were writing and then addressed those biases in their own writing (Appendix E). Finally, "globalization," Royster and Kirsch's fourth term, is at the heart of the whole project, as students contributed their own, often local and underrepresented, knowledge to a global (English-speaking) community.

OVERVIEW OF WRITING FOR WIKIPEDIA PROJECT

I assigned this project in an upper-level writing course at a mid-sized, public Historically Black University. Because of the lack of African American historical and cultural articles on Wikipedia (Smith, 2015), I encouraged students to find projects to fill the gap. The final assignment required students to write a new 500- to 700-word article or expand an existing Wikipedia article by 500–700 words. Because student success with new media projects is often tied to how central and embedded the project is in the course (Sura, 2015), I introduced the project the first week of class and spent the first half of the semester focusing much of our class time on the development of the project. The following describes its five stages, which may be expanded or condensed to meet the demands of various courses.

STAGE ONE: RECOGNIZING THE FEMINIST RHETORICAL CHALLENGE

Because writing for Wikipedia is unlike most other kinds of writing students have done, analyzing Wikipedia is useful for familiarizing students with its style and content guidelines. In some early class discussions, I asked students to identify different kinds of topics/articles (e.g., person, place, event, theory, etc.) and analyze the organization and rhetorical strategies commonly used in each kind. To introduce students to the technical aspects of Wikipedia, students completed a Wikipedia Training ("Wikipedia: Training/For students," 2015) and The Wikipedia Adventure ("Wikipedia: The Wikipedia Adventure," 2015) during this first stage. While the former introduces students generally to the purpose and policies of Wikipedia, The Wikipedia Adventure asks students to complete seven "missions," including starting an account, editing articles, and using talk pages. These interactive assignments help students who are overwhelmed by using wiki markup (the language or code used in Wikipedia) and other technical aspects of the project.

In this first stage, I presented the project as a rhetorical challenge. While I acknowledged that Wikipedia is a community that discourages certain kinds of feminist writing and points of view, I also pointed out opportunities for making meaningful contributions or revisions. This is when we began discussing NPOV and its restrictions—a conversation which I couched in a larger discussion of how dominant and feminist epistemologies manifest in encyclopedias. I asked students to analyze controversial pages on Wikipedia to identify some of the strategies they saw used to present varying, unorthodox, and radical opinions in conventionally appropriate ways (Appendix C). Some of the strategies my students identified were word choice; number of facts and statistics; amount of contextual information and content; cultural points of view included and excluded; organization; direct quotes from the subject or from parties directly involved; links to other pages (making conceptual connections to other people, events, or ideas); and visual arguments (e.g., photos, videos, tables, and graphs). I suggested students use these same rhetorical strategies in the composing of their articles, to find ways to include their critical or feminist perspectives in rhetorically acceptable ways for Wikipedia.

STAGE TWO: FINDING A GAP OR DISPARITY

The main goal in this stage is to help students find a topic. I took my class to our university archives where students looked through artifacts related to the history of our university and city. Students completed a two-part assignment (Appendix D) that asked them to immerse themselves in the archives, to seek out intriguing stories, and to find a corresponding gap on Wikipedia. As students discovered accounts of the significant events, people, and organizations that built our community, they often found stories they felt compelled to share and developed a sense of responsibility to the community to present their research ethically. The archive trip encouraged personal connections to community research yet challenged students to determine how to express that investment in Wikipedia. For students who did not find a topic in the archives, I shared the WikiProject Directory which lists groups dedicated to developing articles in particular areas, e.g., African diaspora and women's history. At the end of this stage, I asked students to write a proposal for an article, and I held one-on-one conferences with them to address their individual questions and concerns.

STAGE THREE: BECOMING THE EXPERT

During this stage, students gathered all of the sources and content for their articles and began organizing it. In class, we developed outlines, organized information, and practiced paraphrasing sources. Another useful in-class activity was expanding an undeveloped university-related page together; this allows the class to walk through the process of finding and evaluating sources according to Wikipedia's guidelines, organizing the writing based on analysis of similar pages, paraphrasing sources, and drafting, revising, and writing together. Through this process, students negotiated together how to communicate their investments and values in the campus community to the global Wikipedia community. Once the class had a working draft, I showed students how to move it into a Wikipedia

Sandbox (a test-run space in which writers experiment with wiki markup) where we could practice making section headings, adding references and footnotes, and linking to other pages. Finally, I published our contribution during class so students could see that process.

Stage Four: Reconciling Feminist and Neutral Point of Views

Through workshops and peer review, students continued to develop and revise their articles. In class, we reviewed NPOV, since adhering to it is necessary for successful publication. To think more about the purpose and limitations of NPOV, students completed an exercise about systemic bias on Wikipedia (Appendix E). Going over systemic bias at this point helps students figure out how they might respond to or counteract those biases in their own articles, making more or less explicitly feminist interventions in the Wikipedia community. Additionally, reflective assignments during this stage are valuable supplements that offer students opportunities to write about their experiences in first-person; these exercises also spur discussions about if/how some of that writing could be revised using NPOV and included in their drafts. At the end of this stage, I held a second round of one-on-one conferences with students to address their individual questions about their articles and publication.

Stage Five: Connecting Communities

Finally, students moved their articles into sandboxes so they could practice using wiki markup and adding headings, references, footnotes, links, etc. I recommend asking students to publish their articles with at least a few weeks remaining in the semester so teachers may work with students whose articles may be flagged or removed. To recognize and celebrate students' addition of locally significant stories to Wikipedia, I asked students to share their contributions in a final class period.

REFLECTIONS

The results of this project were mostly impressive: students published or expanded articles on valuable topics like notable university alumni/ae, local Civil Rights movements, African American politicians, and the effects of urban renewal on our city. However, my dual goals of wanting students to engage in feminist analysis and produce a text in wiki markup proved to be frustrating for some students. While students' work throughout the semester certainly showed critical analysis of the purpose and limits of Wikipedia, when it came to writing their own articles, students were often more concerned about meeting the guidelines for publication rather than finding ways for rhetorical feminist intervention. Some students included images, design, or quotes to put forth their perspective on a topic, but many students seemed to feel uncomfortable pushing the boundaries. I designed assignments to encourage students to question what it means to create knowledge and to work against dominant, masculine discourses, but it was hard to sustain that work when students felt the mounting pressures of choosing a topic, researching, and writing. Students' concerns about the logistics of the assignment often eclipsed my plans for critical discussions and analyses of dominant epistemologies and methodologies. This tension is somewhat unavoidable, but starting the project early in the semester allows some flexibility in the schedule to address particular concerns as they arise. This extra time is especially important for students to acclimate to the unique conventions of Wikipedia. Also, focusing more on editing existing articles and adding marginalized perspectives might help students focus their energy less on finding a topic and more on developing feminist and critical intervention in existing pages.

Despite offering many possibilities for feminist intervention, writing for Wikipedia is a challenging project for students and teachers. Both my students and I had our writing on Wikipedia changed, reverted, or flagged. Recognizing the difficulty of entering a self-regulating, internet-savvy community like this is important to take into account when assessing this project. Because students need to simultaneously use their technical, research, and writing skills, I found it constructive to include in-class and take-home assignments that strengthen these three skills in tandem. I suggest grading the project holistically based on all of the assignments and drafts leading up to publication and not weighing the results of publication too heavily. Explaining to students how the project will be assessed alleviates some of the pressure of publishing. The stakes are understandably high for students—what they spent a whole semester writing could be reverted in an hour. Still, this project provides opportunities for feminist critique of dominant discourses and openings for feminist, local interventions in the Wikipedia community. Writing for a global public audience is a challenge but also a call to contribute knowledges and perspectives that need to be shared.

REFERENCES

Alexander, J. (2008). Media convergence: Creating content, questioning relationships. *Computers and Composition, 25*, 1–8.

Cattapan, A. (2012). (Re)writing "feminism in Canada": Wikipedia in the feminist classroom. *Feminist Teacher, 22*(2), 125–36.

Cohen, N. (2011, Jan. 30). Wikipedia ponders its gender-skewed contributions. *The New York Times*. Retrieved from http://www.nytimes.com/2011/01/31/business/media/31link.html.

Cummings, R. E. (2009). *Lazy virtues: Teaching writing in the age of Wikipedia.* Nashville: Vanderbilt UP.
Cummings, R. E. & Barton, M. (Eds.). (2008). *Wiki writing: Collaborative learning in the college classroom.* Ann Arbor: University of Michigan Press.
Gruwell, L. (2015). Wikipedia's politics of exclusion: Gender, epistemology, and feminist rhetorical (in)action. *Computers and Composition, 37,* 117–31.
Lam, S., Uduwage, A., Dong, Z., Sen, S., Musicant, D., Terveen, L. & Riedl, J. (2011, Oct. 3–5). WP: Clubhouse? An exploration of Wikipedia's gender imbalance. Paper presented at WikiSym, Mountain View, CA.
Lundin, R. W. (2008). Teaching with wikis: Toward a networked pedagogy. *Computers and Composition, 25,* 432–48.
Purdy, J. P. (2009). When the tenets of composition go public: A study of writing in Wikipedia. *College Composition and Communication, 61*(2), 351–371.
Purdy, J. P. (2010). The changing space of research: Web 2.0 and the integration of research and writing environments. *Computers and Composition, 27*(1), 48–58.
Royster, J. J. & Kirsch, G.E. (2012). *Feminist rhetorical practices: new horizons for rhetoric, composition, and literacy studies.* Carbondale, IL: Southern Illinois University Press.
Smith, J. F. (2015, Feb. 19). Howard University fills in Wikipedia's gaps in black history. *The New York Times.* Retrieved from http://www.nytimes.com/2015/02/20/us/at-howard-a-historically-black-university-filling-in-wikipedias-gaps-in-color.html?_r=0.
Sura, T. (2015). Infrastructure and wiki pedagogy: A multi-case study. *Computers and Composition, 37,* 14–30.
Vetter, M. (2013). "Composing with Wikipedia: A classroom study of online writing." *Computers and Composition Online.* Retrieved from http://candcblog.org/mvetter/public_html/composingwithwikipedia/.
Vetter, M. & Harrington, S. (2013). Integrating special collections into the composition classroom: A case study of collaborative digital curriculum. *Research Library Issues, 283,* 16–20.
Wikimedia Foundation. (2011, April). Wikipedia editors study: Results from the editor survey. Retrieved from https://upload.wikimedia.org/wikipedia/commons/7/76/Editor_Survey_Report_-_April_2011.pdf.

APPENDIX A: COURSE DESCRIPTION AND SLOS

ENG 3130: Writing for Social Change

Course Description

We often think of the writing that we do in college as a means to pass a course or earn a degree, but our writing also has social and political implications. This course explores how writing and rhetoric (traditionally conceived but also including oral, visual, auditory, digital, and bodily texts and discourses) works to effect social change. One of the goals for this course is to expand the audiences for our writing beyond the classroom, to reach people in our campus community and the other communities that each of us is a part. Thus, we will begin by analyzing texts that inspire (or intend to inspire) social change to determine what kinds of rhetorical choices are available to us as we produce our own texts. Through the study of the purposes, contexts, audiences, and rhetorical choices attached to particular texts and social issues, we will develop a better understanding of how we might most effectively persuade in the development of our own projects. For the purpose of this course, writing or composing will be broadly defined. While I will ask you to produce more traditional kinds of academic writing that require scholarly analysis and research, I will also ask you to read and create a variety of texts across genre and media (e.g., personal narrative, digital texts, visual texts).

Student Learning Outcomes

- Given instruction in genre analysis strategies, students will apply the method to several documents to help them clarify the characteristic features of unfamiliar genres.
- Given instruction in rhetorical concepts (e.g., rhetorical situation, exigence, kairos, audience, purpose), students will rhetorically analyze their own and others' writing.
- In the process of composing their own civic writings, students will use the aforementioned methods to understand a given writing situation and make choices among approaches.

APPENDIX B: PROJECT SYLLABUS FOR WRITING WIKIPEDIA ARTICLES

ENG 3130: Writing for Social Change

Assignment *Description*

One of your main projects in this course will be writing or expanding a Wikipedia article. Wikipedia, while a great advancement in democratizing who produces, edits, and accesses knowledge, still largely represents those who are already predominant in world history: western white males. The presence of women and minorities on Wikipedia—as writers and subjects of articles—is seriously lacking. In this project, you will add content to Wikipedia's global, digital body of knowledge. You will write a Wikipedia article that does not yet exist on a topic you deem important or expand an existing article. We will complete a sequence of assignments that will ask you to analyze Wikipedia as a knowledge-producing community; conduct research to find a topic for your article or expansion; study

Wikipedia's style and structure rhetorically; practice writing in NPOV style; and finally draft, revise, and publish your own writing on Wikipedia.

Goals for the Project

- (Re)consider how knowledges are created, shared, valued, and culturally situated
- Analyze the rhetorical motives and limits of Wikipedia as a community
- Use wiki markup (e.g., headers, links, images, references, etc.) to structure writing in rhetorically purposeful ways
- Practice writing for social change through adding missing or underrepresented knowledge to Wikipedia

Schedule Overview: In-Class Assignments

Stage One (weeks 1–2) Recognizing the Feminist Rhetorical Challenge	Introduce the project; Analyze articles to identify different kinds of pages and common rhetorical strategies; Discuss knowledge production and feminist epistemology; Introduce NPOV; Complete Analyzing Controversial Topic Pages assignment (Appendix C)	Complete Wikipedia training for students and the Wikipedia Adventure; Read "Wikipedia is Good for You" (James Purdy), excerpt from *Writing to Change the World*, (Mary Pipher), "The Transformation of Silence into Language and Action" (Audre Lorde)
Stage Two (weeks 3–4) Finding a Gap or Disparity	Take a trip to the university archives; Look at the Wikiproject Directory; Conference one-on-one about proposals	Complete Trip to the Archives assignment (Appendix D); Write a proposal for article/ expansion
Stage Three (weeks 5–6) Becoming the Expert	Take a trip to the library to find sources; Practice expanding a university-related article as a class and publish it; Practice paraphrasing sources and referencing in wiki markup	Write outline for article/expansion, Contribute writing to the university-related article the class is expanding
Stage Four (weeks 7–9) Reconciling Feminist and Neutral Point of Views	Complete Systemic Bias assignment (Appendix E); Review NPOV; Peer review drafts; Conference one-on-one about final drafts and publishing	Write draft of article/expansion; Return peer review feedback; Watch YouTube tutorials on making a Sandbox and publishing; Revise draft

Stage Five (weeks 10–11) Connecting Communities	Troubleshoot any issues with publishing	Move drafts to a Sandbox; Publish article/expansion
Post-Project (weeks 12+) Additional 2–3 weeks built in for students whose writing has been flagged or removed	Reflect on project; Meet one-on-one as needed	Present Wikipedia contribution

APPENDIX C: ANALYZING CONTROVERSIAL TOPIC PAGES ON WIKIPEDIA ASSIGNMENT

The goal of this assignment is to identify the rhetorical strategies used to express multiple, conflicting, or radical points of view in Wikipedia pages. These same strategies may be used in the composition of your Wikipedia articles.

Choose 1) a controversial social or political issue; 2) a controversial person; and 3) a controversial event.

Find the corresponding Wikipedia pages and answer the following:

1. How do the pages represent the various sides of the controversies?
2. Are these pages organized or designed differently than pages about less controversial topics? If so, how?
3. What kinds of sources do these pages use?
4. What kinds of words are used to describe what is controversial about the topics? List at least 10 for each page.
5. Imagine that you have a radical opinion about these topics. How could you include that opinion in ways that would be acceptable for Wikipedia's guidelines?

APPENDIX D: TRIP TO THE ARCHIVES ASSIGNMENT

Today we will take a trip to our university's archives to look for potential article topics.

Goals for this assignment

- Find some artifacts that reflect an underrepresented history that you think is worth sharing with the global Wikipedia community.

- Practice reading and analyzing different kinds of texts to determine what information would be most interesting/important to contribute.
- Following research in Wikipedia, identify ways to interject that information in socially conscious ways.

Part One: Collecting Data

For the first part of this assignment, you will record the artifacts that you find in the archives.

Make a list of the various topics you encounter in the archives (e.g., people, places, monuments, ideas, theories, things, organizations, events, etc.). What stories did you find? What kinds of social issues were highlighted? What was most surprising about what you found?

Part Two: Finding the Knowledge Gaps on Wikipedia (after class)

Now that you've had a chance to sift through the archives, do some research in Wikipedia to see what and how the topics you found in the archives are represented. Write a few paragraphs describing the gaps you found and how you might fill them with the research that you did in the archives. Consider whether the sources you found in the archives would be acceptable to use on Wikipedia.

APPENDIX E: SYSTEMIC BIAS ON WIKIPEDIA ASSIGNMENT

The goal of this assignment is to identify different kinds of systemic biases in Wikipedia articles and to consider how you can counteract systemic biases in composing your own article.

According to Wikipedia's page on "Systemic Bias," the average Wikipedian is

> (1) a male, (2) technically inclined, (3) formally educated, (4) an English speaker (native or non-native), (5) aged 15–49, (6) from a majority-Christian country, (7) from a developed nation, (8) from the Northern Hemisphere, and (9) likely employed as a white-collar worker or enrolled as a student rather than being employed as a blue-collar worker.

English Wikipedia acknowledges the following systemic biases, present both in number of articles and/or in perspective:

1. Social class bias (e.g., because access to the internet requires a certain amount of privilege, topics relating to the less privileged are often neglected)
2. Reference/source bias (e.g., many of the most cited references are for-profit news corporations)

3. Perspective bias (e.g., universal topics, like "lunch," are written from the perspective of those in industrialized countries instead of developing countries)
4. Geographical bias (e.g., there are many more pages on Anglophone/European topics than Chinese or Indian, despite China and India having most of the world's population)
5. Popular culture bias (e.g., media produced in the US, UK, and Japan are more widely covered than media produced in other countries)
6. Language bias (e.g., native English speakers tend to rely on sources written in English, perhaps overlooking important texts in other languages)
7. Publication bias (e.g., because it is easier to find sources online, print or hard to find sources may be neglected)
8. Cultural impact bias (e.g., tragedies in developed countries are portrayed as more important than in developing countries)
9. Historical bias (e.g., in descriptions of historical events, some accounts are valued over others)
10. Religious bias (e.g., articles that include a "Religious Views" section often include only Christian, Islamic, or Jewish perspectives but not other religions)
11. "Controversial fringe topic" bias (e.g., controversial topics receive more attention than non-controversial ones)
12. Marketing or corporate bias (e.g., people or organizations may use articles as marketing tools)
13. Length bias (e.g., articles interesting to English-speaking audiences are longer than those written for audiences who speak other languages)
14. Name bias (e.g., a search for an article whose name has several meanings defaults to what is most popular to the average Wikipedian)
15. Timing bias (e.g., current events in English-speaking nations are covered and edited more frequently than others)
16. Hemisphere bias (e.g., more articles are written from a Northern Hemisphere perspective, which is especially significant for science-related topics)
17. Image bias (e.g., it may be harder to find images that adhere to Wikipedia's guidelines for profiles of people in developing countries)

[These examples are paraphrased from the "Systemic Bias" page in 2015.]

Responding to Systemic Biases

Look at several articles that are related to or similar to the one you will be writing/expanding and consider the following questions:

1. What kinds of biases (see list above) do you see in those articles?
2. How are these biases present (e.g., in content, style, organization, images, references, etc.)?
3. How can you respond to existing biases in your proposed article or expansion?
4. Finally, what kinds of bias do you have, given your location, experiences, beliefs, identities, etc.? How might you work against them in composing your article/expansion?

AFTERWORD

Krista Ratcliffe
Arizona State University

Composing Feminist Interventions: Activism, Engagement, Praxis asks the question: how does the positioning of teacher/researchers as feminists affect their community-based teaching and research? To answer this question, the authors in this collection offer narratives of their community-based teaching and research practices. The focus on narrative-as-method is important. As stories grounded in personal experience and scholarly conversations of community engagement (such as those forwarded by Berry et al., 2012; Deans et al., 2010; and Grabill, 2007), the narratives in each chapter function not simply as personal expressions but, rather, as crafted stories grounded in critical self-reflection and critical reciprocity. As such, the narratives afford the authors of the chapters, their community partners, and their readers the ability to identify operative categories and tactics used to frame the narrative events, first, so that writers and partners may collaborate in defining their experiences as well as their interpretations of their experiences and, second, so that readers may (when appropriate) transfer the operative categories and tactics to their own locales. In conceptualizing narrative as a dominant method in this collection, the editors Kris Blair and Lee Nickoson invoke a scholarly tradition of teacher/researchers who have employed narrative as a critical tool for understanding not just their own subjectivities but also the subjectivities of students and the cultural spaces that they all share. As a contribution to that scholarly tradition, the chapters in this collection introduce feminism(s) as a lens for conceptualizing and performing community-based activism, engagement, and practices, including pedagogy.

As a method of critical reflection for teaching and research, narrative has been championed by prominent theorists in a variety of disciplines. For example, education specialists Patricia Cranton and Edward W. Taylor (2012) argue in "Transformative Learning" that such learning is grounded in the narratives that we construct about our daily lives: "Individual experience is the practical knowledge, skill, and understanding of the wor[l]d that every adult brings into the classroom"; thus, narratives of these experiences function as "'pedagogical entry points'" for classroom activities that are potentially transformative (p. 198). Additionally, in *Time and Narrative*, philosopher Paul Ricoeur (1990) defines subjectivity in terms of narrative emplotment (pp. 52–54): "By bringing together heterogeneous factors into its syntactical order emplotment creates a 'concordant discordance,' a tensive unity which functions as a redescription of a situation in which the internal coherence of the constitutive elements endows them with an explanatory role" (Atkins). In these two representative samples, narrative emerges as an important method of pedagogical and scholarly practices, and such practices of narrative serve three important functions. First, narratives explain to ourselves and to others what events we are narrating. Second, narratives explain to ourselves and to others what we have learned about these narrated events. And third, narratives explain to ourselves and to others how we are constructing our own subjectivities (as points of view), the subjectivities of others (as characters in our own narratives), and the cultural spaces that we all share (as settings).

But how are these three expository functions of narrative complicated when storytellers are positioned as feminists?

This question invokes the problem of gender and feminism that has haunted narrative studies as well as gender studies. In "Gender and Narrative" Susan Lanser (2013) defines the problem as follows: "Whether we date the inception of narrative poetics to the ancient Greeks, the Russian Formalists, the Anglo-American New Critics or the French structuralists, we can safely say that questions of gender were not among the field's early distinctions or concerns." But late twentieth-century feminism brought such questions to the fore, identifying possibilities, limitations, and complications of narrative as a method of generating knowledge.

Examples of late-twentieth-century feminists that engaged narrative include bell hooks (1989), Judith Butler (1990), and Kimberlé Crenshaw (1991). In *Talking Back* hooks celebrates the possibilities of narrative as a tactic of resistance. Though ever mindful of white appropriation of black stories, she nonetheless advocates storytelling as one means of talking back, a tactic of resistance that allows storytellers to redefine their own, and others', subjectivities as they engage in activist projects; in this way, hooks links telling stories to writing theory (p. xi). While sympathetic to the link between storytelling and theory building, Butler (a plenary speaker at the 2017 Conference of the International Society for the Study of Narrative) nevertheless invokes Lacan in *Gender Trouble* to delineate the limits of storytelling, particularly for understanding one's own subjectivity (and, by implication, others' subjectivities as well). Butler warns:

> The constitutive identifications of an autobiographical narrative are always partially fabricated in the telling. Lacan claims that we can never tell the story of our origins, precisely because language bars the speaking subject from the repressed libidinal origins of its speech; however, the foundational

> moment in which the paternal law institutes the subject seems to function as a metahistory which we not only can but ought to tell, even though the founding moments of the subject, the institution of the law, is equally prior to the speaking subject as the unconscious itself. (p. 91)

Further complicating feminist functions of narrative and its impact on understanding subjectivities and cultural locations, Crenshaw advocated for feminists to adopt intersectionality as defined in her *Stanford Law Review* article, "Mapping the Margins: Intersectionality, Identity Politics, and Violence Against Women of Color." Though Crenshaw originally posited intersectionality to "denote the various ways that race and gender interact to shape the multiple dimensions of Black women's employment experiences" (p. 1244), the concept has since been extended to argue "that diverse aspects of identity [e.g., race, gender, class, region, age] converge to create the social positions, perceptions, limitations, and opportunities of individuals and groups" (Lanser). This extended concept of intersectionality renders feminism as only one intersecting thread of a teacher's or a researcher's identity even as it recognizes the multiplicity of feminisms.

With the aforementioned ideas of narrative, subjectivity, and intersectionality providing a discursive background for *Composing Feminist Interventions*, the authors of each chapter provide readers ways to link not just personal storytelling to composition theory but also personal storytelling to methods associated with the teaching and research associated with community outreach. In the process, the authors in this collection perform disciplinary changes in rhetoric and composition studies that have been instigated by feminism.

In *Feminist Rhetorical Practices: New Horizons for Rhetoric, Composition, and Literacy Studies* (an oft-cited book in this collection), Jaqueline Jones Royster and Gesa Kirsch (2012) identify myriad disciplinary changes in rhetoric and composition studies that have been effected by feminism. One obvious disciplinary change identified by Royster and Kirsch and performed in this collection is the construction of "a new and changed landscape for narratives in the history of rhetoric" (p. 13). This "changed landscape for narratives" emerged, in part, because of work associated with what Royster calls "the critical imagination," a method that attempts "to account for what we 'know' by gathering whatever evidence can be gathered and ordering it in a configuration that is reasonable and justifiable in accord with basic scholarly methodologies" (p. 71). Both as history writ large and as individual rhetor-theorist writ individually, this renarrating of rhetorical history makes a space for authors in this collection to tell stories their own activism and engagement at a variety of community sites. For example, in "Historical Female-run

Settlement Culture as a Blueprint for Contemporary Place-based Pedagogy," Liz Rohan (Chapter 5) broadens the map of rhetorical history by narrating events associated with "female-run settlement culture," constructing a method that interconnects archival research with narrative and critical imagination.

A second disciplinary change advocated by Royster and Kirsch and performed in this collection is an enhanced study of "social circulation," a term Royster and Kirsch define as "[s]ense making at its best . . . dynamic, with knowledge and expertise drawing from many sources that cannot always be neatly contained within traditional disciplinary boundaries" (p. 138). *Composing Feminist Interventions* embodies this change in that its focus extends into many different community sites, its methods are constructed to offer analyses of myriad social/cultural structures, and its community-based teaching and research topics vary widely—from the emergence of social media (e.g., Mary Sheridan's chapter 11 on "Digital Media Academy as Site of Graduate Student Professional Development), to the effects of technologies on collaboration in the public sphere (e.g., Douglas Walls, et al.'s "Safely Social," Chapter 20, which investigates how women who have suffered from domestic abuse may link to their online support networks without comprising their own safety), to the effects of activism on public policy (e.g., Barbara George's "Literacy, Praxis and Participation in Environmental Deliberation," Chapter 13, which analyzes the rewriting of energy production policies within three different states).

A third disciplinary change identified by Royster and Kirsch and performed in this collection is an emphasis on ethics, specifically feminist ethics. The chapter authors are concerned with identifying the feminist ethics that undergird their feminist teaching and research practices; in addition, the authors are concerned with the ethical implications of their teaching and research practices. For example, in "Post-research Engagement: An Argument for Critical Examination of Researcher Roles after Research Ends, Megan Adams (Chapter 1) calls attention to the ever-changing role of feminist researchers and the resulting need for clearly planned ethical engagements with project communities. In "Methodology and Accountability: Tracking Our Movements as Feminist Pedagogues," Emily R. Johnston (Chapter 3) defines feminist "ethical practice" as methods that challenge students to stretch the limits of their privileged comfort zones—methods that may not be feasible, desirable, appropriate, or indeed "ethical" in other settings where feminist research happens, thus calling attention to the kairotic influence on ethics. In "Listening to Research as a Feminist Ethics of Representation," Lauren Rosenberg and Emma Howe (Chapter 4) define feminist ethics in terms of "a feminist ethos of responsible, strategic practice" of ethnographic and archival research, a practice that keeps its eye on how gender influences citizens in the public sphere.

Given my own interests in rhetorical listening as well as other means for inviting listening into conversations about rhetoric, I am delighted that this collection broadens our disciplinary understanding of how listening may serve as a feminist tactic. In "Reciprocity as Feminist Intervention and Political Activism: An 'after-action review,'" Mariana Grohowski (Chapter 2) incorporates listening as a tactic for developing productive reciprocity among researchers and participants who work together to analyze case studies in order to figure out how civic engagement occurs. In "Listening to Research as a Feminist Ethics of Representation," Rosenberg intersects my rhetorical listening with Royster and Kirsch's "strategic contemplation" (pp. 21–28) in order to develop a tactic of mutual contemplation that enables her to teach "citizenship literacy" while her co-author Howe develops an accompanying tactic of archival listening. In "Ohio Farm Histories: A Feminist Approach to Collaboration, Conversation, and Engagement," Christine Denecker and Sarah Sisser (Chapter 9) offer the tactic of listening deeply as a feminist means of honoring, not appropriating, the farm stories collected as part of their project. In "Competing Definitions of Success: Rhetorical Listening in Multimodal, Community-based Writing Projects," Danielle Williams (Chapter 21) extends rhetorical listening to the digital realm, describing how rhetorical listening helps develop assessment methods that community partners may use to evaluate students' community-based multimodal projects. And in "'Because your heart breaks and it moves to action': Digital Storytelling Beyond the Gates," Stephanie Bower (Chapter 24) also extends listening into the digital realm, advocating a tactic of active listening that she claims engenders transformative learning.

And with the idea of transformative learning, I have returned to where I began.

So in conclusion, what I admire about this collection is how the narratives of feminist teaching and research merge the academic sphere and the public sphere, the classroom and the community. As such, these narratives have important implications for feminist research practices. That is, knowledge and knowledge-making are located not just within the university but also beyond its walls. The authority for knowledge-making resides in reciprocal interactions among students, community partners, and teachers, not simply in teachers' proclamations or textbooks' claims. Project assignments reflect real-world needs and purposes; project designs cross genres and media; and finished products benefit from actual participant-audience input. And everyone involved in each project reflects on the ethics of their actions (or inaction).

This last implication holds promise for feminist pedagogy. For when students study narrative as a tool of critical self-reflection and critical reciprocity, they develop as citizen-scholars who are invested in knowledge and engagement and who are possessed of a feminist literacy. As such, these students as citizen-scholars will, it is to be hoped, know the difference between facts and opinions. They will recognize how they are invested not just in their own successes but also in local and global communities. They will understand that reasonable people may disagree but that such disagreements may be performed in good faith and are best engaged not as agonistic debates that demand winners and losers but as reciprocal interactions that represent the will of the majority while respecting the rights and the dignity of the minority. And finally, they will be able to recognize the ethics undergirding the feminist teaching and research practices to which they are exposed, and, as a result, they will be able both to recognize how power dynamics haunt their daily lives and then to discern when and how to perform activism, engagement, and other needed praxes.

REFERENCES

Atkins, K. (n.d.). Paul Ricoeur. *Internet Encyclopedia of Philosophy* (A Peer Reviewed Academic Resource). Retrieved from http://www.iep.utm.edu/ricoeur/.

Berry, P., Hawisher, G. E. & Selfe, C. L. (2012). *Transnational literate lives in digital times*. Logan, UT: Utah State University Press / Computers and Composition Digital Press.

Butler, J. (1990). *Gender trouble: Feminism and the subversion of identity*. London, England: Routledge.

Cranton, P. & and Taylor, E. W. (2012). Transformative learning. In P. Jarvis & M. Watts (Eds.). *The Routledge International Handbook of Learning* (pp. 194–204). New York, NY: Routledge.

Crenshaw, K. (1991). Mapping the margins: Intersectionality, identity politics, and violence against women of color. *Stanford Law Review, 43*(6), 1241–1299.

Deans, T., Roswell, B. & Wurr, A. (2010). *Writing and community engagement: A Critical Sourcebook*. Boston, MA: Bedford/St. Martin's.

Grabill, J. (2007). *Writing community change: Designing technologies for citizen action*. Cresskill, NJ: Hampton.

hooks, b. (1989). *Talking back: thinking feminist, thinking black*. Cambridge, MA: South End Press.

Lanser, S. (15 Sept. 2013). Gender and narrative. *The living handbook of narratology*. Retrieved from http://www.lhn.uni-hamburg.de/article/gender-and-narrative #Crenshaw.

Ratcliffe, K. (2005). *Rhetorical listening: Identification, gender, whiteness*. Carbondale, IL: Southern Illinois University Press.

Ricoeur, P. (1990). *Time and narrative Vol. 1*. 1984. Chicago, IL: University of Chicago Press.

Royster, J. J. & Kirsch, G. (2012). *Feminist rhetorical practices: New horizons for rhetoric, composition, and literacy studies*. Carbondale, IL: Southern Illinois University Press.

CONTRIBUTORS

Megan Adams is Assistant Professor of Communication at The University of Findlay in Findlay, Ohio, where she serves as Co-Director of The Center for Storytelling and Participatory Media. Her work on digital storytelling has appeared in *Computers and Composition: Online* and *Kairos: A Journal of Rhetoric, Technology, and Pedagogy*. Her most recent research project centers on work with *Hollow: An Interactive Documentary*. She also serves as co-editor of *Computers and Composition Online*.

Mustari Akhi is currently a first-year medical student at the Charles E. Schmidt College of Medicine at Florida Atlantic University, hoping to graduate with her M.D. by the year 2020. Prior to this, she graduated with a Bachelor's of Science from Nova Southeastern University in 2015, majoring in biology and minoring in behavioral neuroscience. Due to the positive influence her own mentors have had on her throughout her life, Mustari is especially passionate about volunteering with socioeconomically disadvantaged and/or marginalized populations through mentorship and pipeline programs. Although free time is rare in medical school, whenever she is not in class or clinic, Mustari enjoys creating both traditional and digital forms of art and design, watching foreign shows and documentaries, and meditating in nature.

Florence Elizabeth Bacabac is Associate Professor of Professional and Technical Writing at Dixie State University (DSU) in St. George, Utah. Her articles have appeared in *Business and Professional Communication Quarterly, Journal of Business and Technical Communication,* and *Journal of Literacy and Technology*, among others. She is a recipient of the Utah Campus Compact's 2014 and 2011 Civically Engaged Scholar Awards for service learning and community involvement. Aside from teaching, she also serves as director of DSU's Women's Resource Center where access to resources, mentoring, and support are given to women across the disciplines for their academic and professional development. She was a state board representative of the Utah Women in Higher Education Network (UWHEN) for four years and currently works with the American Association of University Women (AAUW)—St. George Branch to strengthen its ties with DSU.

Kristine L. Blair is Professor of English and Dean of the College of Liberal Arts and Social Sciences at Youngstown State University. She has taught courses in digital composing and scholarly publication in the Rhetoric and Writing Doctoral Program at Bowling Green State University from 1996–2016, where she also served as English Department Chair from 2005–2014. In addition to her publications in the areas of gender and technology, online learning, electronic portfolios, and faculty development, Blair currently serves as editor of both the international print journal *Computers and Composition* and its separate companion journal *Computers and Composition Online*. She is a recipient of the CCCC Technology Innovator Award and the Computers and Composition Charles Moran Award for Distinguished Contributions to the Field. In 2017, Blair received the Lisa Ede Mentoring Award from the Coalition of Feminist Scholars in the History of Rhetoric and Composition.

Beth A. Boehm is Professor of English, Vice Provost for Academic Affairs and Dean of the School of Interdisciplinary and Graduate Studies at the University of Louisville. Her research and teaching across three different areas of English studies: Modern British literature; narrative studies; and rhetoric, composition and pedagogy. She regularly teaches first-year composition, undergraduate literary surveys and special topic courses, and graduate courses in narrative, rhetoric, contemporary British literature and teaching literature. Since she joined the provost's office and the graduate school, most of her research has focused on issues in higher education, particularly the education of graduate students.

Stephanie Bower is Associate Professor of Teaching in the Writing Program at the University of Southern California. For the last eight years she has worked with her colleague, John Murray, along with community activists and organizers such as Amalia Molina (Center for Restorative Justice Works), Rick McGregor (Fades for Grades), Jennifer Ralls (Para Los Ninos), and Sr. Teresa Groth (Francisco Homes) to bring USC students and community members together in a digital storytelling project that has generated dozens of videos and over 30,000 views on YouTube. Her work has appeared in *The Chronicle of Higher Education*, *The Los Angeles Book Review*, *Legacy: A Journal of American Women Writers*, and *Modern Fiction Studies*. She wishes to extend profound thanks to collaborator John Murray and tech impresario Edward O'Neill for their generosity in sharing their insights in this piece. Gratitude also goes out to her wise and compassionate students for giving her permission to quote their reflections.

Jenn Brandt is the Director of Women's and Gender Studies and Assistant Professor of English at High Point University. Her work focuses on identity and narrative and has appeared in *Critique: Studies in Contemporary Fiction*, *Studies in 20th and 21st Century Literature*, the *Journal of Graphic Novels and Comics*, as well as a number of edited collections of in the fields of literary and gender studies.

Kimberly Z. Lopez Clemente has been involved in the feminist movement since her first year at Nova Southeastern University. Passionate about becoming a gynecologist, she saw the value of incorporating feminism to her career goals. Kimberly has tried to be involved in the community through various organizations such as The Women of Tomorrow Program, Alpha Phi Omega, and Science Alive and quite a few more. Her main goal is to help females of all ages to become comfortable with their bodies and to feel empowered about their abilities.

Kelly Concannon is Associate Professor of Writing in the Department of Writing and Communication at Nova Southeastern University. Her research interests include community engagement, service learning, feminist theory, social justice education, and literacy studies. Her book, *Peace and Social Justice Education*, was published in 2015, and she has published in major journals including *Reflections: A Journal of Public Rhetoric, Civic Writing, and Service Learning, The Journal of Feminist Scholarship, Academic Exchange Quarterly, Enculturation, Community Literacy, Journal for Expanded Perspectives on Learning, College Literature*, and *The Journal of Advanced Composition*. She also serves as an undergraduate mentor for the Undergraduate Journal of Service Learning and Community-Based Research.

Angela Crow is Associate Professor and teaches digital literacies at James Madison University in the School of Writing, Rhetoric, and Technical Communication. She volunteers in the local community as part of the Shenandoah Valley Bicycle Coalition's education group, studies the impact of social media on local advocacy initiatives for bicycling and walking, and tries to imagine best practices for rescripting/rewriting streets to create more hospitable options for those who would prefer active transportation alternatives.

Christine Denecker is Chair and Professor of English at the University of Findlay in Findlay, Ohio, where she also serves as the University's Director of the Center for Teaching Excellence. Her work in the application of feminist rhetorical theories has appeared in *Stories That Speak to Us* and will be included in the forthcoming *Cultivating Spheres: Agriculture, Technical Communication, and the Publics*. In addition, her research into multimodal composition as well as dual enrollment composition instruction has appeared in *Twenty Writing Assignments in Context: An Instructor's Resource for the Composition Classroom, Composition Studies, Computers and Composition: Online*, and *The Writing Instructor*. She also serves on the Board of Directors for The National Alliance of Concurrent Enrollment Partnerships.

Brandy Dieterle is a doctoral candidate in the Texts & Technology Program at the University of Central Florida. Her research interests are in multimodality, digital rhetoric, and, more specifically, digital identity and gender representations in social networks. Her work on teaching multimodality in first-year composition has appeared in the *Journal of Global Literacies, Technologies, and Emerging Pedagogies* and in *Composition Forum*. She also has a co-authored publication in the journal *Computers and Composition* on the subject of developing spaces in multiliteracy centers to promote collaboration and multimodal composing. Design decisions regarding Safely Social discussed in this chapter have also been published in the conference proceedings from Special Interest Group on the Design of Communication (SIGDOC).

Katherine Fredlund is Assistant Professor of English and Director of First-Year Writing at the University of Memphis. Her research has appeared in *College English, Rhetoric Review, Peitho, Feminist Teacher*, and elsewhere. She specializes in nineteenth-century women's rhetoric, activist rhetoric, and collaboration. She previously taught at Indiana State University for four years, and her chapter discusses a course she taught there.

Barbara George is a doctoral candidate and Teaching Fellow at Kent State University. Her research interests include ecocriticism, rhetorics, literacies and critical discourse analysis surrounding environmental concerns, and community literacies. She is actively involved in several sustainability initiatives across the curriculum at Kent State University.

Joan Giroux is an interdisciplinary artist, activist and educator. An Associate Professor at Columbia College Chicago, she has received awards and grants, performed and exhibited in the US and abroad, and been invited to several international symposia on arts and the environment. Giroux received her MFA at Bard College and BFA at Parsons School of Design, and she studied with Shinkichi Tajiri at Berlin's Hochschule der Künste.

Beth Godbee is Assistant Professor of English at Marquette University. Her work addresses matters of equity in education, relational communication, and composition theory and pedagogy. Among her publications are articles in *Research in the Teaching of English, Community Literacy Journal, Feminist Teacher, Writing Center Journal, Across the Disciplines*, and *Praxis*. She has also co-authored chapters in *Writing Centers and the New Racism* (2011, Utah State UP) and *Stories of Mentoring* (2008, Parlor Press). She is currently working on projects focused on relational communication, community literacy, microaggressions, and epistemic injustice and rights.

Mariana Grohowski is editor of the *Journal of Veterans Studies*. She previously taught college writing, but now works in marketing and public relations on Lake Superior's shore..

Ames Hawkins is a writer, educator, and art activist. An Associate Professor in the Department of English at Columbia College Chicago, and a practitioner of collaboration as a radical act, Ames teaches and co-teaches courses in first year writing, cultural studies, and literature. Ames uses writing and art to explore the interstices of text and image, theorizing the power and pleasure of queer(ing) form; her most recent creative and critical work appears in *Computers and Composition Online, Slag Glass City, The Feminist Wire, Interdisciplinary Humanities*, and *Water-Stone Review*. She served as curator and co-editor of the Lambda Literary Foundations 25th Anniversary 2103 eBook Collection, *25 for*

25: An Anthology of Works by 25 Outstanding Contemporary Authors and Those They Inspired. Ames is currently working on the installation/book project, *These Are Love(d) Letters: e, l, o, r, s, t, v*, and is co-host and co-producer of *Masters of Text* (mastersoftext.com), a scholarly podcast exploring alternative alphabetic texts and creative-critical scholarship.

Emma Howes is Assistant Professor of English at Coastal Carolina University in Conway, South Carolina. Her scholarly interests include literacy studies, feminist theory and pedagogy, archival research methods and methodologies, and historical Appalachian Studies. Howes's current research explores literacy campaigns in early twentieth-century cotton mill villages that targeted female mill workers. In particular, she is looking at mills in the Carolinas. Howes is also interested in developing feminist archival methodologies, exploring approaches to historical research about populations difficult to access through traditional methods. She contributed a chapter to the collection, *Rewriting Appalachia: Literacy, Place, and Cultural Resistance*.

Emily Ronay Johnston is a postdoctoral researcher in writing pedagogy at the University of Delaware (UD). She studies student uptake of reading and writing about sexual trauma in contemporary fiction, film, medical literature, and trauma theory. While she began her teaching career working with first graders in her hometown of San Francisco, Johnston has since taught composition, creative writing, gender studies, and English as a second language courses at University of Alaska Fairbanks, University of Nevada Reno, Illinois State University, and her current institution, UD. Johnston earned her Ph.D. in English Studies from Illinois State University ('16), earned an MFA in Poetry from University of Alaska Fairbanks ('07), and is Managing Editor of SRPR (*Spoon River Poetry Review*). Johnston contributed an article on trauma theory as activist pedagogy to a special pedagogy issue of *Antipodes: A Global Journal of Australian/New Zealand Literature*, and a review of the campus sexual assault documentary, *The Hunting Ground*, to *Women's Studies in Communication*.

Cara Kozma is Assistant Director of Service Learning and Assistant Professor of English at High Point University. Her research interests include service learning, community literacy and publishing, and composition pedagogy. She works with faculty across the disciplines to integrate service learning effectively into their teaching and codirects a university-sponsored community writing center that facilitates interdisciplinary service learning classes and community publishing projects.

Katie Manthey is Assistant Professor of English and Director of the Writing Center at Salem College, a women's college in Winston Salem, NC. Her research and teaching are focused around cultural rhetorics, dress studies, and civic engagement. She is a body positive activist and moderates the website Dress

Profesh, which highlights the ways that dress codes are racist, cissexist, ageist, classist, etc. Her work has appeared in *Peitho: The Journal of the Coalition of Women Scholars in the History of Rhetoric & Composition, Jezebel,* and *The Journal of Global Literacies, Technologies, and Emerging Pedagogies.*

Keri E. Mathis is a doctoral candidate in English at the University of Louisville and the research assistant to Dean Beth Boehm in the School of Interdisciplinary and Graduate Studies. In this role, she has assisted in developing professionalization programs, including teaching, technology, and career workshops for graduate students. Her research interests in rhetoric and composition include the study of how genre and developments in technology have influenced the way people write and learn to write in historical moments marked by rapid technological innovation. While pursuing her degree at UofL, she has served as the Vice-President and active member of the Graduate Student Council and a graduate student senator for the Student Government Association.

Jennifer Roth Miller is a graduate research associate and doctoral candidate in the Texts and Technology Doctoral Program at the University of Central Florida. Jennifer's research interests seek to better understand digital citizenship by exploring the convergence of communication, technology, philanthropy, and education. Jennifer's current projects involve digital privacy and domestic violence, cancer awareness and digital activism, tragedy response, Holocaust remembrance, and social media's relationship to access and pedagogy. Jennifer is a HASTAC (Humanities, Arts, Science, and Technology Alliance and Collaboratory) Scholar. Her work has been published in *Xchanges* and *Enculturation: A Journal of Writing, Rhetoric, and Culture.*

Morgan Musgrove is a neuroscience major at Nova Southeastern University and will be graduating in May 2017. She is a STEM concentrated activist and focuses most of her efforts on female, high school students. Morgan is also a tutor at her university's writing center and has taken part in a writing internship helping high school students surpass the difficulties of academic writing. She is actively working in two labs looking at the psychophysiological and behavioral relationship between bilingualism and executive functioning of the brain. When she is not partaking in academic endeavors, she enjoys lifting weights and the company of her bloodhound.

Julie Myatt Barger is Associate Professor of English at Middle Tennessee State University, where she serves as Co-Director of General Education English and teaches undergraduate writing and literature courses and graduate courses in composition theory and pedagogy. She is currently researching the rhetorical strategies and coalition-building practices of a contemporary grassroots organization advocating on behalf of women and children. She earned her Ph.D. in Rhetoric and Composition from the University of Louisville, is a National

Writing Project fellow, and serves as Co-President of WPA Midsouth, an affiliate of the Council of Writing Program Administrators.

Julie D. Nelson is Assistant Professor at North Carolina Central University, where she teaches courses in rhetoric and composition. Her research interests include rhetorical theory, emotion studies, and archival work.

Ashley Nichols is a graduate student at Nova Southeastern University in Fort Lauderdale, Florida, where she currently studies business. Nichols maintains a passion for activism and social justice, and has completed several projects intended to assist at risk youth. She is an active mentor in the community, and her research has appeared in *Peace and Social Justice Education on Campus: Faculty and Student Perspectives*. Nichols has participated in several leadership conferences, where she argues for creative initiatives intended to address gender inequalities. She is pursuing a master's in management, with an ultimate goal of using her passion to create a non-profit which assists at risk students.

Lee Nickoson is Associate Professor of English and Director of the General Studies Writing Program at Bowling Green State University. Her teaching experiences and interests span undergraduate- and graduate-level courses and include a shared investment in collaborating with student writers in investigations of writing as a form of activism. Understanding teaching, researching, and WPA as deeply connected intellectual efforts, Nickoson engages feminist methodologies to explore methods and motivations writing researchers call upon.

Jessica Ouellette is Assistant Professor of English and Women and Gender Studies and Director of Writing Programs at the University of Southern Maine. She specializes in contemporary feminist rhetorics, digital rhetorics, and transnational studies. She has written about both the affordances and limitations of digital spaces as sites for feminist activism in the *Harlot Journal*, and she is currently working on a book project that explores the relationship between feminist rhetorical practices, affect, and digital circulation.

Kathryn Perry is Assistant Professor of English at California State University, Los Angeles. Her research focuses on community literacy as it takes place at the intersections of university and community agendas, narrative theory, and composition pedagogy. She seeks opportunities to use storytelling to facilitate serendipitous yet sustainable growth for university and community relationships surrounding literacy. Her work has appeared in the *Journal of Composition Theory* and *Kairos: A Journal of Rhetoric, Technology, and Pedagogy*.

Krista Ratcliffe is Professor and Chair of English at Arizona State University in Tempe, Arizona. She has served as the CCCC Representative and Chair of NCTE's College Forum, as President of the Coalition of Women Scholars in the History of Rhetoric and Composition, and as President of the Rhetoric Society of America. Her research focuses on the intersections of rhetoric, feminist theory, critical race theory, and pedagogy. Her publications include *Anglo-American Feminist Challenges to the Rhetorical Tradition*, *Who's Having This Baby* (with Helen Sterk, Carla Hay, Alice Kehoe, and Leona VandeVusse), *Rhetorical Listening: Identification, Gender, Whiteness* (2006 *JAC* Gary Olsen Award; 2007 CCCC Outstanding Book Award; 2007 RSA Outstanding Book Award), *Silence and Listening as Rhetorical Arts* (co-edited with Cheryl Glenn) and *Performing Feminist Administration* (co-edited with Becky Rickly). Her work has appeared in edited collections, as well as in *CCC, JAC, Rhetoric Review,* and *College English*.

Liz Rohan is Associate Professor of Composition and Rhetoric at the University of Michigan-Dearborn. With Gesa Kirsch, she is the editor of *Beyond the Archives: Research as Lived Process* (Southern Illinois Press, 2008). Her research that reflects her ongoing interests in pedagogy, feminist research methods and America's progressive era has appeared in journals such as *Rhetoric Review, Composition Studies, Pedagogy, JAEPL, Reflections, Composition Forum, Peitho,* and also in several book chapters.

Lauren Rosenberg is Associate Professor at New Mexico State University where she directs the writing program and serves as Associate Department Head. She is the author of *The Desire for Literacy: Writing in the Lives of Adult Learners* (CCCC/NCTE, 2015). Threaded through all of Rosenberg's work is a commitment to examining and advocating for equity through community engagement and public activism. Her literacy research extends from the study of adult learners in her book to a current project on the writing practices of military veterans while in service and as university students. Her writing has also appeared in *Community Literacy Journal* and *Reflections, A Journal of Public Rhetoric, Civic Writing, and Service Learning* as well as in a number of co-authored articles and book chapters, including *Feminist Rhetorical Resilience: Possibilities and Impossibilities*.

Jacqueline Schiappa is a postdoctoral writing fellow at Macalester College. Schiappa teaches in multiple disciplines including departments of Communication Studies, English, Gender Women and Sexuality Studies, Writing Studies and Environmental Studies. She has published on feminist debates about intersectionality in the "Slutwalk" phenomenon, and her current research focuses on networked counterpublics' social media strategies. For example, she has recently published work on Black Twitter's use of multimodal hashtag campaigns like #IfTheyGunnedMeDown to rebut mainstream media representations of Black victims of state violence. She remains invested in civically engaged scholarship, focusing projects on social media activism, social justice movements, and public rhetoric.

Mary P. Sheridan writes and teaches on questions relating to digital composing, community engagement, and feminist methodologies. She has written

Girls, Feminism, and Grassroots Literacies: Activism in the GirlZone and *Design Literacies: Learning and Innovation in the Digital Age* (with Jennifer Rowsell) and has co-edited *Writing Studies Research in Practice: Methods and Methodologies* as well as *Feminism and Composition: A Critical Sourcebook*. Her articles have appeared in *CCC, Computers & Composition, Kairos, JAC, Written Communication, Feminist Teacher, Composition Studies,* and *Journal of Basic Writing*. Sheridan won the 2010 Winifred Bryan Horner Outstanding Book Award from Coalition of Women Scholars in the History of Rhetoric and Composition; the 2009 Civic Scholarship/Book of the Year Award from *Reflections: A Journal of Writing, Service-Learning, and Community Literacy*; and, as part of a collaborative group, *Computers and Composition's* Michelle Kendrick Outstanding Digital Production/Scholarship Award for 2008.

Sarah Sisser is Executive Director of the Hancock Historical Museum in Findlay, Ohio. Sisser holds a BFA in Historic Preservation from the Savannah College of Art & Design (SCAD) in Savannah, Georgia. While in Savannah, Sarah served as an Assistant Preservation Planner for the Chatham County-Savannah Metropolitan Planning Commission. Sisser also holds a Master's degree in Community Planning from Auburn University. In her work at the Hancock Historical Museum, Sisser oversees the facilities, events, and programming that bring an annual attendance of more than 20,000 people, including approximately 3,500 Hancock County schoolchildren.

Trixie G. Smith is Director of the Writing Center and the Red Cedar Writing Project, as well as a member of the faculty in Writing, Rhetoric & American Cultures and the Center for Gender in Global Contexts at Michigan State University. Her teaching and research are infused with issues of gender, queerness, and activism even as they revolve around writing centers, writing across the curriculum, writing pedagogy, and teacher training. Whenever possible, these areas are intersected with her interests in pop culture, community writing, and the idea that we're just humans learning with/from other humans (with bodies, feelings, lives outside the academy).

Jessica E. Tess is Special Lecturer in the Writing and Rhetoric Department at Oakland University. She graduated with her Master's in Critical Studies in Literacy and Pedagogy from the Writing, Rhetoric, and American Cultures Department at Michigan State University in 2014 with a graduate certificate in Community Engagement. After graduating, she worked for over a year as a social media specialist for MSU Extension, where she contributed to a federally-funded national project studying community behavioral health. She has also worked as a writing consultant in two writing centers. Her research interests include community engagement, feminist pedagogies and methodologies, digital humanities/social sciences, and social media research.

Contributors

Douglas M. Walls is Assistant Professor of English at North Carolina State University, where he is a member of the faculty in the Master's of Science in Technical Communication (MSTC) and the Communication, Rhetoric, and Digital Media (CRDM) programs. His research interests are in the design of user experiences for underrepresented or traditionally marginalized groups and nonprofit organizations, especially in social media contexts. Douglas received Honorable Recognition in 2015 for the Ellen Nold Award in Computers and Composition Studies for his article "Access(ing) the Coordination of Writing Networks." His work has appeared in both traditional and new media forms in the *Journal of Business and Technical Communication, Computers and Composition*; *Kairos: A Journal of Rhetoric, Technology, and Pedagogy*; and various edited collections.

Danielle M. Williams is Interim Director of First-Year Writing and Lecturer in Professional Writing & Rhetoric in the Department of English at Baylor University. She teaches courses in first-year composition, technical and professional writing, and multimodal composition. Her research interests include digital media and composition pedagogy, service-learning and community-based writing, and digital civic engagement. Her work has appeared in *Computers and Composition*.

The Reverend Angela W. Zimmann is Vice President for Advancement and Adjunct Professor of Preaching at United Lutheran Seminary. Prior to arriving at the seminary in 2014, Zimmann served in Jerusalem, Israel/Palestine as Pastor and Special Assistant to Bishop Munib Younan, (President of the Lutheran World Federation) and co-pastor of the English congregation at Church of the Redeemer in Jerusalem. She has also served as pastor of Trinity Lutheran Church, Riga, MI and run for congress in the 5th District of Ohio She taught full-time at Bowling Green State University from 2008–2013 after receiving her doctorate from BGSU's Rhetoric and Writing Program in 2007. She has taught preaching courses at Gettysburg Seminary occasionally since 2007.

www.ingramcontent.com/pod-product-compliance
Lightning Source LLC
Chambersburg PA
CBHW070123080526
44586CB00015B/1531